BLUE GUIDE **LONDON**

D1021882

THE BLUE GUIDES

ATHENS AND ENVIRONS
AUSTRIA
BELGIUM AND LUXEMBOURG
BOSTON AND CAMBRIDGE
CATHEDRALS AND ABBEYS OF ENGLAND AND WALES
CHANNEL ISLANDS
CRETE
CYPRUS
EGYPT
ENGLAND
FLORENCE
FRANCE
GREECE
HOLLAND
IRELAND
ISTANBUL
LITERARY BRITAIN
LONDON
MALTA
MOSCOW AND LENINGRAD
MUSEUMS AND GALLERIES OF LONDON
NEW YORK
NORTHERN ITALY
OXFORD AND CAMBRIDGE
PARIS AND ENVIRONS
PORTUGAL
ROME AND ENVIRONS
SCOTLAND
SICILY
SOUTHERN ITALY
SPAIN
VENICE
WALES

BLUE GUIDE

LONDON

Ylva French

Maps and plans drawn by John Flower

A. & C. Black
London

W. W. Norton
New York

Twelfth edition 1986

Published by A. & C. Black (Publishers) Limited
35 Bedford Row, London WC1R 4JH

© A. &. C. Black (Publishers) Limited 1986

Published in the United States of America by
W. W. Norton & Company Inc.
500 Fifth Avenue, New York, N.Y. 10110

ISBN 0-7136-2786-7

ISBN 0-393-30081-1   {U.S.A.}

British Library Cataloguing in Publication Data
London — 12th ed. — (Blue Guide)
    1. London (England) — Description and travel —
    1981– — Guide-books
    I. French, Ylva
    914.21'04858   DA679

    ISBN 0-7136-2786-7

PREFACE

When I first came to London as a student in the 1960s, I soon discovered how vast and varied the capital is. The variety was and is its greatest asset but the sheer size of London inhibits visitors and Londoners from straying too far from the area they know. This book will, I hope, encourage readers to explore further afield and to learn something about London's history and how it has developed. With this knowledge it is possible to feel at home and to come to love London, as I have.

This book gives a little of London's history; there are several others which I have listed below which are more detailed and use a different approach to describe London's growth. It is sad to reflect, however, that little is learnt from history and the mistakes and successes of the past. As this book is published, the Greater London Council is in the last few months of life (due to be abolished as from April 1986). Those who fought long and hard during the 19th and 20th centuries to create a more unified and equal London where the City's influence was reduced and planning was carried out for London as a whole will be turning in their graves. I hope when a further edition of this Guide is published we will have returned to the idea of a London-wide authority to represent and plan for the people of London.

In the meantime many historic houses, parks and other buildings mentioned in the text as being run by the GLC are being transferred either to the individual London boroughs or to English Heritage, the Government's Historic Buildings and Monuments Commission. The South Bank will be run by the Arts Council, the river-piers and the Thames Barrier by the Thames Water Authority and the GLC's showpiece, Covent Garden, by Westminster City Council. There will be some time before the policies of these various bodies become clear; and the future of County Hall itself is uncertain. Certainly there is the prospect of a much better developed River Thames as a result of the Thames Water Authority's involvement with investment promised both in the piers and in river-born commuter services.

It is now the London boroughs which are responsible for most services in Greater London. It is therefore appropriate that this edition of the Blue Guide has been expanded to include more information on places of interest in Outer London. The local government reorganisation of 1965 produced a pattern of London boroughs which brought together parts of London which are still fighting hard to retain their previous identities. Those who live in Hampstead would not say they lived in the London Borough of Camden; on the fringes of Greater London anomolous postal addresses of Kent, Surrey and Middlesex survive to confuse everyone except those who live there.

London is a city of contrasts and those who explore from the centre outwards will travel through a band of neglected inner boroughs where high-rise council flat developments of the 1960s are sliding into decay. The inner boroughs struggle to maintain and improve these parts of London and on the whole provide excellent cultural and social services in a poor environment. The true London 'village' survives in a few places in Outer London such as Hampstead, Highgate and Barnes; other former towns which are now part of London have been extensively developed and it may be harder to discover their historic past, as at Kingston, Croydon, Bromley and, gradually commercialised, Richmond upon Thames.

To the East and North East what was once known as the 'East End' has been virtually obliterated through redevelopment; most East Enders now live further East and in the new towns of Essex. Pockets of gentrification are appearing, attempting to recreate something of the area's past. The imaginative development of London's docklands will certainly not restore the past—but is instead opening up an area of London previously hidden behind walls for commercial, residential and recreational use.

Something like 40 percent of visitors to London from overseas stay with Londoners as do many more who come here from other parts of Britain. Most likely there is something of interest on their doorstep. The local parish church makes a good starting point, although it may be difficult to find it open. Local museums, sometimes part of the local library, may not offer the riches of the Museum of London but the staff know a great deal about their area, and there are some surprising finds. There is almost bound to be a local manor house; it is probably used as council offices or headquarters for the local golf club but it should be possible to visit it; look out also for almshouses, windmills and tithe barns.

When this book appears it is quite likely that more than one national museum (see the National Maritime Museum) will be charging visitors or asking for a contribution. This will not in itself be a bad thing if the money received can be ploughed back into improving the museums and their collections, but it will be to everyone's disadvantage if it goes straight to the Chancellor. Readers will find less detailed coverage of the contents of museums compared with past editions; 'Blue Guide Museums and Galleries of London' now covers this subject in such detail that it was decided that this Guide should provide more of a general introduction to each institution and describe some of the highlights, as chosen by the author.

I would like to thank all my friends and colleagues who have made helpful suggestions during the updating of this edition, particularly Andrea McHarg and Peter Matthews. Also Christopher and Tony who have provided great support.

This edition has been substantially revised during 1985; I have added new material on Outer London and the Docklands, and updated the information on the West End and the City of London. However, much of the historical information is based on previous editions, the result of the work of previous editors, particularly Stuart Rossiter, who died in 1982.

Bibliography

History: 'A History of London', Robert Gray (1978); 'Everybody's Historic London', J. Keek (1985); 'The Making of Modern London', Weightman & Humphries (1984); 'Beyond our Ken—the battle for London', Forrester, Lansley, Pauley (1985).

Other reading: 'Art and Architecture of London', Ann Saunders (1984); 'Blue Guide Museums and Galleries of London', Malcolm Rogers (1986); 'London Under London', Trench and Hillman (1985); 'The Buildings of England—London 1, 2', N. Pevsner; and 'London as it Might Have Been', Barker and Hyde (1982).

CONTENTS

8   CONTENTS

CONTENTS **9**

Maps and Plans

CENTRAL LONDON	*At the end of the book*
OUTER LONDON	*At the end of the book*
LONDON UNDERGROUND	*Inside back cover*
BRITISH MUSEUM	184–5, 186
GREENWICH	*Atlas section* 24
HAMPSTEAD AND HIGHGATE	*Atlas section* 22–23
HAMPTON COURT PALACE	352–3
HOUSES OF PARLIAMENT	82–3
INNS OF COURT	204
LONDON ZOO	168–9
NATIONAL GALLERY	95
NATIONAL MARITIME MUSEUM	*Atlas section* 24
ST. PAUL'S CATHEDRAL	217
SCIENCE MUSEUM	143
TATE GALLERY	151
THEATRES	30
TOWER OF LONDON	260–1
VICTORIA AND ALBERT MUSEUM	136–7, 140–1
WALLACE COLLECTION	173
WESTMINSTER ABBEY ENVIRONS	66–7
WESTMINSTER ABBEY	69
WINDSOR CASTLE	*Atlas section* 25

EXPLANATIONS

Type. The main routes are described in large type. Smaller type is used for branch-routes and excursions, for historical and preliminary paragraphs, and (generally speaking) for descriptions of greater detail or minor importance.

Asterisks indicate points of special interest or excellence.

Plans. References in the text (Pl. 1;1) are to the colour Atlas at the back of the book, the first figure referring to the page, the second to the square. There is a generous overlap between one page and another: the reference most convenient for the direction being described has been given. Ground Plan references are given as a bracketed single figure.

Abbreviations. In addition to generally accepted and self-explanatory abbreviations, the following occur in the Guide:

AA = Automobile Association
Abp = Archbishop
Adm = Admission, Admiral
Bp = Bishop
BH = Bank Holiday
BR = British Rail
BTA = British Tourist Authority
c = circa (about)
C = century
EE = Early English
exc. = except
GLC = Greater London Council
incl. = including
LB = London Borough of ...
ITA = Independent Television Authority
LCC = London County Council
LRT = London Regional Transport
LVCB = London Visitor and Convention Bureau
m = mile(s)
MCC = Marylebone Cricket Club
NT = National Trust
O.E. = Old English
Pl. = Atlas Plan
PLA = Port of London Authority
RA = Royal Academician
RAC = Royal Automobile Club
Rest. = restaurant
Rfmts = refreshments
RHS = Royal Horticultural Society
Rte = Route
seq. = sequentia, etc. (following)
SS = Saints
St. = Saint
St = Street
YH = Youth Hostel

LONDON TODAY

London, the capital of England and of Great Britain, is situated on the River Thames about 40 miles from the coast. Greater London consists of 33 separate boroughs and covers an area of 625 square miles. The population of London has declined gradually during this century and reached 6.8m in 1983; the majority are women (3.5m) and an estimated 30 percent of Londoners were born elsewhere, including other Commonwealth countries, creating a heterogeneous mix which has done much to change London into the cosmopolitan city it is today.

London's three most important industries in terms of employment are retailing, the public sector and tourism, followed by banking and insurance, transport and communications and manufacturing.

Central London's population increases dramatically during weekdays; daily some 821,000 people travel into the City and West End by public transport and 200,000 by private transport.

In 1984 an estimated 8.5m overseas and 14m British visitors stayed at least one night in the capital, a total of 93.3m tourist nights in all (1983). There are an estimated 130,000 beds in London's 1030 hotels, and guest houses registered by the London Visitor and Convention Bureau.

London's parks and open spaces are famous; there are some 387 parks over 20 acres in Greater London as a whole; the royal parks cover an area of 6000 acres, GLC parks over 5000 acres and the London Boroughs' parks 28,000 acres. Even the City of London has 7000 acres of parkland but most of that consists of Epping Forest to the NE of the capital.

London is divided roughly into two halves by the River Thames—the southern area traditionally more residential and industrial while the commercial and entertainment worlds are mostly located on the North Bank in the City and the West End. The City, which also incorporates much of Legal London, has expanded its commercial influence westwards into Holborn and increasingly eastwards into the London Docklands, particularly the Isle of Dogs.

The West End includes the shopping areas and office districts of Victoria, Mayfair and Marylebone as well as the political world of Westminster. Bloomsbury retains its educational emphasis, with the University of London and the British Museum stamping their character on the area. Soho, in the shadow of the now popular and trendy Covent Garden, is coming out of the worst of its 'blue' period while remaining London's principal so-called red-light district.

PRACTICAL INFORMATION

I Arriving in London

Airports. London has two major international airports, Heathrow and Gatwick, and two small airports, Luton and Stansted, which principally serve the charter trade. Stansted has been designated to become London's third major airport over the next 15 years.

Heathrow is 15m W of London along the M4 motorway (Tel.: Terminal 1 01- 745 7702; Terminal 2 01-745 7115; Terminal 3 01-745 7412). Public transport connections to and from Heathrow are excellent. The Underground, Heathrow Central, is accessible from all three terminals (for Terminal 4 see below), and services, which take 40-45 minutes to Central London, operate on the Piccadilly Line 20 hours a day. Change at Hammersmith for the District Line. London Regional Transport also operates Airbus Services on three routes with pick-up points from all three terminals. These services go to Grosvenor Gardens (Victoria Station), via Cromwell Road (Forum Hotel), Paddington (Sussex Gardens), via Kensington (Hilton International), and Bayswater Road and Euston Station via Hammersmith and Bloomsbury. The trip takes 50-60 minutes, depending on the traffic.

Heathrow's Terminal 4, due to open in 1986, will be served by an extension of the Piccadilly Line. Green Line operates service 767 to and from Heathrow in 45 minutes, stopping at Victoria, Hyde Park Corner and Kensington.

Connections with Gatwick. A helicopter service operates between Heathrow and Gatwick. A Green Line Coach service (No. 747) also connects them. Once the M25 is completed, the helicopter service may be discontinued (late 1986).

Taxis. There are authorised (black-cab) taxi ranks outside each terminal. Fares are shown on the meter and the drivers must accept rides of up to 20 miles from the airport, if they are in the rank. There are additional charges for luggage, extra persons, travelling after 20.00 and at weekends; these are also displayed on the meter. (Tipping, etc., see p 48.) Do not accept approaches from drivers of unauthorised taxis (so-called mini-cabs) as they are not metered.

Car Hire. All the major car hire companies are represented at Heathrow; many others will arrange for pre-booked cars to be waiting for customers on arrival.

Car Parking. There are multi-storey car parks for each terminal to be used for up to 24 hours; for longer parking periods the long-term car parks are recommended. A shuttle coach service connects them with the terminals.

Information. The British Airports Authority has desks in each terminal providing information; announcements for missed contacts, lost children, etc., can be arranged. There are 24-hour banking facilities.

Hotel Bookings. Booking desks operate in all the terminals; the London Visitor and Convention Bureau operates a hotel booking and information service in conjunction with London Regional Transport in Heathrow Underground Station.

Gatwick is situated 28m S of London on the M23 motorway (0293 28822). It has one main terminal, a satellite terminal connected by high-level trains, and one runway. A second terminal under construction will come into operation in 1987. A high-speed train service (27-minute journey) connects Gatwick with Victoria Station in Central London. Trains depart every 15 minutes during the day and hourly after midnight. There are also direct train services to East Croydon,

Brighton, and other towns in SE England.

A Green Line Coach service (No. 747) connects Gatwick and Heathrow; another service 777 runs to Victoria Coach Station (journey time 70 minutes).

Taxis. A local taxi service is based at the airport; recommended only for short journeys. Central London is best reached by train.

Car Hire. Major car-hire companies are represented at the airport; others will arrange to meet customers.

Car Parking. There are three short-term and several long-term car parks with a shuttle service to and from the airport.

Information. The British Airports Authority has information desks in the terminal. There are 24-hour banking facilities.

Hotel Bookings. There is a reservation service based at the airport; alternatively use the service at Victoria Station; see below.

Victoria Station Terminal for Gatwick. This new terminal is situated on the W side of the station with direct access from Buckingham Palace Road (due to open in 1987). A separate taxi rank serves arrivals from Gatwick. Check-in for British Caledonian services takes place here. Hotel booking services are available, including that of the London Visitor and Convention Bureau in the Tourist Information Centre in the station forecourt; see below.

Stansted (0279 502380) is 34 miles NE of London and connected via the M11 and M25 motorways with Central London and SE England. A train service via Bishops Stortford takes 50 minutes to Liverpool Street Station. A Green Line Coach service (No. 799) runs between Stansted and Victoria Coach Station in c 2 hours.

Luton (0582 36061) is a small airport, 30 miles NE of London. Trains to Luton (35 minutes) run from St. Pancras and King's Cross; taxi or bus to the airport from Luton in about 10 minutes. Green Line Coach service No. 757 operates to Luton Airport from Victoria Coach Station (70 minutes).

Connecting Services. Regular scheduled services connect Heathrow and Gatwick with major cities in the UK and on the Continent. Quick check-in services between Heathrow and Edinburgh, Glasgow, Manchester and Belfast are provided by the British Airways shuttles.

Seaports. Major seaports with London connections are Tilbury (Fenchurch Street Station), Harwich (Liverpool Street Station), Dover and Folkestone (Victoria Station), and Southampton (Waterloo Station). There are regular train services from all these port terminals to the London mainline stations. Hovercraft land at Dover and connect with trains to Victoria Station. **Arrival by Car**. Car-ferry services operate into the major seaports (see above) as well as Newhaven, Portsmouth and Plymouth.

Major Railway Stations. London's major termini serve different sectors of Outer London and the UK. The list below gives a general indication of the areas covered:

Charing Cross (01-928 5100). SE London and parts of S England.

Euston (01-387 7070). Liverpool, Manchester, NW England, Glasgow.

Fenchurch Street (01-283 7171). Southend, Tilbury.

King's Cross (01-278 2477). Stansted, Leeds, York, NE England, Edinburgh.

Liverpool Street (01-283 7171). Harwich, Felixstowe, Ipswich, Cambridge, East Anglia.

Paddington (01-262 6767). Oxford, Bristol, SW England, Wales.

St Pancras (01-387 7070). Luton, Leicester, Sheffield.

Victoria (01-928 5100). Gatwick, Brighton, Dover, Folkestone, S and SE London.

Waterloo (01-928 5100). Southampton, S England, SW London.

Other useful British Rail services include *Motorail* to Scotland and SW England (contact Euston, 01-387 8541; King's Cross, 01-833 2805; Paddington, 01-723 7000). Seat and sleeper reservations are available on Inter-city services; book through a travel agent or at the relevant London terminus. Personal callers are welcome at the Britain Travel Centre, 4-12 Regent St, London, W1.

Coach Services. A national network of scheduled coach services (usually cheaper than rail) operates from Victoria Coach Station, Buckingham Palace Road. The Coach Station is c 400m from the Victoria Railway and Underground Stations. During peak periods a minibus shuttle service operates. The Coach Station is at times severely overcrowded. General information is available on 01-730 0202 (24 hours).

Passports, Visas. A valid national passport or alternative document must be produced on arrival in the UK. Visitors from some countries require a visa, but this is not necessary for most holiday or business visitors. At present there are no special vaccination requirements.

Quarantine. Animals and birds must be placed in quarantine on arrival in Britain (6 months for animals; 35 days for birds) as part of rabies control measures. *Attempts to circumvent the restrictions carry severe penalties.*

Customs. A red and green channel system operates at most points of entry. The green channel is for those with nothing dutiable to declare, or with only the permitted level of duty-free goods.

Foreign Exchange. The UK imposes no restrictions on the import or export of bank notes of any currency. The major London airports have 24-hour banking services with foreign-exchange facilities. Bureaux de change operate at London's major railway termini; check exchange rates and commission charges before entering into a transaction (see p 48). Most hotels also offer foreign exchange facilites.

Normal opening hours for banks are 09.30-15.30, Monday to Friday. Some suburban bank branches now open on Saturday mornings.

II   Hotels, Eating and Drinking, Shopping

London's wide range of accommodation includes everything from luxury hotels to *en famille* bed and breakfast, camp-sites to self service apartments. From Easter to October it is advisable to book in advance, although hotel rooms can be found for those who arrive without prior bookings, through LVCB's hotel accommodation service at the Tourist Information Centre, or other hotel booking agencies. However, this may not be in the area or price-range preferred.

A Book-A-Bed-Ahead Service operates between tourist information centres in major towns in England. Including London. This operates on the same day but ensures that travellers around Britain have a room when they arrive in London and vice versa.

The English Tourist Board operates a grading and classification system for hotels and other forms of accommodation throughout England · In London look for membership of the London Visitor and Convention Bureau which means that certain minimum standards have been met. The Bureau will also deal with complaints (see p 43).

'Where to Stay in London' (£1.50) lists a wide range of hotels, bed and breakfast establishments, and hostels. It is available from LVCB (see above) and bookshops. (Hotel booking agencies, see p 44.)

Hotels are concentrated in Mayfair, Bayswater, Paddington, Bloomsbury, South Kensington, Earls Court, and Victoria. There are large international hotels at Gatwick and Heathrow Airports, and smaller hotels in London's suburbs.

Self-Service apartments are available throughout London; consult BTA's 'London Apartments' booklet or LVCB's membership listing.

Camping and Caravan sites are listed in LVCB's 'Camping and Caravan Sites' leaflet; en famille accommodation bookings are handled by a number of different agencies; contact BTA or LVCB for an up-to-date list.

Hotel Charges. Hotels charge per person rates; either for a single or a twin-bedded room. VAT (at 15 per cent) should be included in the price quoted. Breakfast is usually included in the lower priced hotels. Service is mostly included in the total bill and no additional tipping is necessary except for personal services at the guest's discretion. A room reservation is a binding contract and hotels are entitled to hold on to a deposit or make a charge if a booking is cancelled at short notice and the room cannot be re-let. Prices of hotel rooms must be displayed and guests are entitled to see the room before agreeing to a reservation. Normally guests vacate their rooms before 12.00 on the day of departure. If arriving after 18.00 the hotel should be notified, or else they may release the room.

The *Youth Hostels Association* of Great Britain operates five hostels in London: Highgate (01-340 1831), Holland House (01-937 0748), Hampstead Heath (01-458 9054), Earl's Court (01-373 7083), and Carter Lane (01-236 4965). Additional accommodation is made available during the summer in student halls of residence. Book in advance by writing to the Youth Hostels Association, 36 Carter Lane, London EC4.

Membership of the Association is available for a small fee. Advance booking during peak periods is essential.

The YMCA maintains the Y-Hotel at 112 Great Russell Street, WC1 (01-637 1333) and the London City YMCA, Barbican (01-628 0697). The YWCA Central Club, 16-22 Great Russell Street, WC1 (01-636 7512) has 178 beds and leisure facilities.

Camping and Caravan information can be obtained from the Camping Club of Great Britain, 11 Lower Grosvenor Place, London SW1 (01-828 1012), and the Caravan Club, East Grinstead House, London Road, E Grinstead, Sussex (0342 26944).

Restaurants, Pubs and Winebars. Eating out and going to the pub or winebar are some of the greatest pleasures that London has to offer. The range and style of restaurants vary enormously—every month a new restaurant opens and somewhere else another closes its doors. Standards have in general improved and most first-class restaurants now offer an Anglicised version of nouvelle cuisine with emphasis on fresh vegetables and relatively small portions of meat or fish. Traditional English restaurants serving roast beef and steak and kidney pudding still survive but in the main it is the pub/restaurants and also carveries in many West End hotels, which are keeping this style of cooking alive.

But it is the variety of food which is London's greatest asset; nearly every corner of the globe is represented. Some of the best Indian and Chinese restaurants in the world can be found here.

Fast food restaurants serving pizzas, hamburgers, or fish and chips are convenient stopping places for visitors; they usually stay open all day and into the evening and fit comfortably into sightseeing schedules. Many also welcome children, and most hamburger restaurants will produce high-chairs. Children are not made to feel quite so welcome in restaurants which cater to a large business clientele at lunchtime nor in the evening; the exceptions are hotel coffee shops and Chinese and Italian restaurants with a tradition of serving families.

On the whole it is advisable to use a guide-book or recommendation when looking for a special lunch or dinner and to book in advance. A short list of a range of restaurants appears below, but the following restaurant guides are recommended: Time Out's 'Eating Out in London', 'The Good Food Guide', published by the Consumers' Association, and the 'Egon Ronay Guide'. Use the current edition.

Prices (including VAT) and menus now have to be displayed outside restaurants; increasingly service is also included in the final bill, so an extra tip is at the customer's discretion. Wine tends to be marked up approximately 100 per cent, and look for extra charges for vegetables which can increase the final bill substantially. Set price menus, common in some of the best hotel restaurants at lunchtime, offer exceptionally good value for money and often include wine. Restaurants, in general, serve lunch between 12.30 and 15.00; and dinner from 18.30 or 19.30 until 22.30 or later. Restaurants which serve after 23.00 (for after-theatre suppers) have been starred in the list below.

Something has been happening to English pubs over the past 5 years; the rather dusty, dark, comfortable Victorian pub is giving way to a gleaming, high tech themed environment with bouncers on the door and vibrating disco music inside, serving cocktails rather than beer. Fortunately this development is limited mostly to suburban pubs where the breweries are busy attracting a younger market, and the sheer number of pubs in Greater London ensures that many will survive in more traditional form. The list below includes some well-known names; in most cases they are mentioned in the text where some of their history is given.

Pub-food varies in quality but if in doubt stick to the cheese, paté and bread which (served as a traditional 'Ploughman's lunch') is a filling meal with a pint of best bitter; wine is generally available and more pubs are now serving coffee. Under present regulations children are only welcome in pubs if there is a children's room or a separate area set aside for meals. Children of 14 and over may be admitted to a bar and consume non-alcoholic drinks with an adult at the landlord's discretion. Children are welcome in the garden or terrace area of pubs (these regulations also apply to winebars).

Pubs are generally open between 11.00 and 15.00, and 17.30 and 23.00 weekdays; 12.00 to 14.00, and 19.00 to 22.30 on Sundays. These hours may be shorter in the suburbs and in the City of London most pubs close at 20.00 and stay closed at the weekend. These licensing hours also apply to winebars and restaurants, which cannot serve alcoholic drink outside these hours, unless they have a special licence. The restrictions do not apply to hotel guests staying in a licensed hotel where alchoholic drinks can be served at any time.

Fortunately it looks as though some of the anomalies of the present licensing hours will be reformed before the end of this decade!

Winebars offer a relaxing environment in which to enjoy a good selection of wine and some delicious food. As in pubs, the choice and freshness of the food is more inspiring at lunchtime. Winebars cater to a very local clientele in the same way as pubs and have their own character. A few have been mentioned below.

Most restaurants in London look after women customers just as well as men; only a few of the more traditional are likely to seat a lone woman by the door to the kitchen. Many are also getting used to women being hosts, tasting the wine and paying the bill, although a little prompting may be necessary. On the whole winebars offer a more pleasant environment for women out on their own than pubs.

Soho, traditionally a centre of good restaurants, is improving again after years of decline. Covent Garden is the up-and-coming area where many new restaurants have opened in the last few years.

The list below has been divided into geographical areas.

£ = moderate

££ = expensive

£££ = very expensive

* Open after 22.30 (and taking orders)

West End and Soho

Amalfi, 31 Old Compton Street, W1 (01-437 7284), Italian, £ (until 23.00)*

Anemos, 34 Charlotte Street, W1 (01-636 2289), Greek, £

Arirang Korean Restaurant, 32 Poland Street, W1 (01-437 6633), £ (until 23.00)*

Au Jardin des Gourmets, 5 Greek Street, W1 (01-437 1816), French, ££ (until 23.00)*

Bentley's Oyster Bar, 11-15 Swallow Street, W1 (01-734 4756), English, ££

Bertorelli Bros, 19 Charlotte Street, W1 (01-636 4174), Italian, £

Chez Gerard, 8 Charlotte Street, W1 (01-636 4975), French, ££, (until 23.30)*

Chicago Pizza Pie Factory, 17 Hanover Square, W1 (01-629 2669), American, £ (until 23.30)*

Chuen Cheng Ku, 17 Wardour Street, W1 (01-437 1398), Chinese, £, (until 23.45)*

Coconut Grove, 3-5 Barrett Street, W1 (01-486 5269), American, £ (until 23.15)*

The Dorchester Grill, Dorchester Hotel, Park Lane, W1 (01-629 8888), English, £££, (until 23.00)*

Dumpling Inn, 15A Gerrard Street, W1 (01-437 2567), Chinese, £ (until 23.30)*

L'Epicure, 28 Frith Street, W1 (01-437 2829), French, ££ (until 23.15)*

L'Escargot, 48 Greek Street, W1 (01-437 2679), French, ££ (until 23.30)*

Fahkreldine, 85 Piccadilly, W1 (01-493 3424), Arab, £££ (until 24.00)*

The Gay Hussar, 2 Greek Street, W1 (01-437 0973), Hungarian, ££

Le Gavroche, 43 Upper Brook Street, W1 (01-408 0881), French, £££ (until 23.00)*

Hard Rock Café, 150 Old Park Lane, W1 (01-629 0382), American, £ (until 24.15)*

Hostaria Romana, 70 Dean Street, W1 (01-734 2869), Italian, £ (until 23.30)*

Kettners, 29 Romilly Street, W1 (01-437 6437), Italian/American, £ (until 24.00)*

Langan's Brasserie, Stratton Street, W1 (01-493 6437), French, ££ (until 23.45)*

Olive Tree, 11 Wardour Street, W1 (01-734 0808), Vegetarian, £ (until 24.00)*

Pasta Fino, 27 Frith Street, W1 (01-439 8900), Italian, £ (until 23.30)*

Rasa Sayang, 10 Frith Street, W1 (01-734 8720), Malaysian, £ (until 23.45)*

Ritz Restaurant, Piccadilly, W1 (01-493 8181), International, £££

Soho Brasserie, 23-25 Old Compton Street, W1 (01-439 3758), French, £ (until 23.30)*

Verrey's, 233 Regent Street, W1 (01-734 4495), French, ££

Wheeler's, 19 Old Compton Street, W1 (01-437 2706), Fish, ££

Covent Garden/Leicester Square/The Strand

Bates, 11 Henrietta Street, WC2 (01-240 7600), English, ££ (until 23.30)*

Boulestin, 25 Southampton Street, WC2 (01-836 7061), French, £££ (until 23.15)*

Le Café des Amis du Vin, 11–14 Hanover Place, WC2 (01-379 3444), French, ££ (until 23.30)

Café Pacifico, 5 Langley Street, WC2 (01-379 7728), American/Mexican, £ (until 23.45)

Chez Solange, 35 Cranbourne Street, WC2 (01-836 5886), French, ££ (until 24.15)*

Food for Thought, 31 Neal Street, WC2 (01-836 0239), Vegetarian, £ (until 20.00)

Inigo Jones, 14 Garrick Street, WC2 (01-836 6456), French, £££ (until 23.30)*

Ivy Restaurant, 1-5 West Street, WC2 (01-836 4751), French/Italian, ££

Joe Allen, 13 Exeter Street, WC2 (01-836 0651), American, ££ (until 24.00)*

Joy King Lau, 3 Leicester Street, WC2 (01-437 1132), Chinese, £ (until 23.00)*

Last Days of the Raj, 22 Drury Lane, WC2 (01-836 1628), Indian, £ (until 23.30)*
Mon Plaisir, 21 Monmouth Street, WC2 (01-836 7243), French, ££ (until 23.15)*
The Neal Street Restaurant, 26 Neal Street, WC2 (01-836 8368), International, £££
Peppermint Park, 13-14 Upper St. Martin's Lane, WC2 (01-836 5234), American, £ (until 24.30)*
Poons, 4 Leicester Street, WC2 (01-437 1528), Chinese, ££ (until 23.30)*
Porters, 17 Henrietta Street, WC2 (01-836 6466), English, £
Rules, 35 Maiden Lane, WC2 (01-836 5314), English, ££ (until 23.15)*
The Savoy Grill, The Strand, WC2 (01-836 4347), English, £££ (until 23.15)*
Sheekey's, 28-32 St Martin's Court, WC2 (01-240 2565), Fish, ££ (until 23.15)*
Simpsons in the Strand, 100 The Strand, WC2 (01-836 9112), English, ££
Terraza Est, 125 Chancery Lane, WC2 (01-242 2601), Italian, ££ (until 23.30)*

Bayswater
Bombay Palace, 50 Connaught Street, W2 (01-723 8855), Indian, ££ (until 23.30)*
Kam Tung, 59-63 Queensway, W2 (01-229 6065), Chinese, £
Mandarin Kitchen, 14 Queensway, W2 (01-727 9012), Chinese, £ (until 23.30)

Knightsbridge/Chelsea
Borscht n'Cheers, 273 Kings Road, SW3 (01-352 5786), Russian, ££, (until 01.00)
Capital Hotel Restaurant, 22 Basil Street, SW3 (01-589 5171), French, £££
Drakes, 2A Pond Place, SW3 (01-584 4555), English, ££ (until 23.30)*
The English House, 3 Milner Street, SW3 (01-584 3002), English, ££
Ma Cuisine, 113 Walton Street, SW3 (01-584 7585), French, £££ (until 23.00)*
San Lorenzo, 22 Beauchamp Place, SW3 (01-584 1074), Italian, ££ (until 23.30)*
La Tante Claire, 68 Royal Hospital Road, SW3 (01-351 0227), French, £££ (until 23.00)*
Eleven Park Walk, 11 Park Walk, SW10 (01-352 3449), Italian, ££ (until 24.00)*
Hungry Horse, 196 Fulham Road, SW10 (01-352 7757), English, ££ (until 23.00)*
Parsons, 311 Fulham Road, SW10 (01-352 0651), American, £ (until 24.30)*

Belgravia/Victoria
Bumbles, 16 Buckingham Palace Road, SW1 (01-828 2903), English, ££
Ciboure, 21 Eccleston Street, SW1 (01-730 2505), French, ££ (until 23.30)*
Gavvers, 61 Lower Sloane Street, SW1 (01-730 5983), French, ££ (until 23.00)*
Ken Lo's Memories of China, 67 Ebury Street, SW1 (01-730 7734),

Chinese, ££ (until 23.00)*
Locket's, Marsham Street, SW1 (01-834 9552), English, ££ (until 23.00)*
Pomegranates, 94 Grosvenor Road, SW1 (01-828 6560), International, ££ (until 23.15)*
The Restaurant, Dolphin Square, SW1 (01-828 3207), French, ££
Tate Gallery Restaurant, Millbank, SW1 (01-834 6754), English, ££ (lunch only)

The City/Islington
Rudland and Stubb, 35-37 Greenhill Rents, Smithfield, EC1 (01-253 0148), English, Fish, (until 23.30)*
Baron of Beef, Gutter Lane, EC2 (01-606 6961), English, ££
George & Vulture, 3 Castle Street, EC3 (01-626 9710), English, ££
Sweetings, 39 Queen Victoria Street, EC4 (01-248 3062), Fish, ££ (lunch only)
Frederick's, Camden Passage, N1 (01-359 2888), French, ££ (until 23.30)*
Serendipity, The Mall, Camden Passage, N1 (01-359 1932), International, £ (until 24.00)*

More information from the Restaurant Switchboard on 01-444 0044.

A selection of **Winebars**:

The City
Chiswell Street Wine Vaults, 47 Chiswell Street, EC1 (01-588 5733) (until 20.30)
Mother Bunch's Wine House, Old Seacoal Lane, EC4 (01-236 5317) (until 20.30)

Belgravia/Victoria
Blushes, 52 Kings Road, SW3 (01-589 6640) (until 23.00)
Carriages, 43 Buckingham Palace Road, SW1 (01-834 8871) (until 23.00)
Tiles, Buckingham Palace Road, SW1 (01-834 7761) (until 23.00)

West End/Soho
Tracks, 17A Soho Square, W1 (01-439 2318) (until 23.00)
Cork and Bottle, 44-46 Cranbourn Street, WC2 (01-734 7807) (until 22.45)

Covent Garden
Brahms & Liszt, 19 Russell Street, WC2 (01-240 3661) (until 23.00)
Crusting Pipe, The Market, Covent Garden, WC2 (01-836 1415) (until 23.00)

A selection of **Pubs**

Bayswater and Notting Hill
Victoria, 10 Strathern Place, W2
Windsor Castle, 114 Campden Hill Road, W8

Bloomsbury and Holborn
The Lamb, 94 Lamb's Conduit Street, WC1
Museum Tavern, 49 Great Russell Street, WC1
Ye Olde Mitre, Ely Place, Hatton Garden, EC1

City
The Black Friar, 174 Queen Victoria Street, EC4
Cock Tavern, The Poultry Market, Central Markets, EC1

Dirty Dick's, 202 Bishopsgate, EC2
Fox and Anchor, 115 Charterhouse Street, EC1
Hand & Shears, 1 Middle Street, EC1
Railway Tavern, 15 Liverpool Street, EC2
Samuel Pepys, Brooks Wharf, Upper Thames Street, EC4
Ye Olde Dr Butler's Head, Masons Avenue, Coleman Street, EC2
Ye Olde Watling, 29 Watling Street, EC4

Covent Garden
Bedford Head, 41 Maiden Lane, WC2
Lamb & Flag, 33 Rose Street, off Garrick Street, WC2
Nag's Head, 10 James Street, WC2
Nell of Old Drury, Catherine Street, WC2
Salisbury, St. Martin's Lane, WC2

East London
Black Lion, 57 High Street, Plaistow, E13
Dickens Inn, St. Katharine's Way, E1
Grapes, 76 Narrow Street, E14
Hayfield, 158 Mile End Road, Stepney, E1
Prospect of Whitby, 57 Wapping Wall, E7

Fleet Street
Old Bell Tavern, 95 Fleet Street, EC4
Printer's Devil, 98 Fetter Lane, EC4
Seven Stars, 53 Carey Street, WC2
Ye Olde Cheshire Cheese, 145 Fleet Street, EC4
Ye Old Cock Tavern, Fleet Street, EC4

Knightsbridge and Belgravia
Duke of Wellington, 63 Eaton Terrace, SW1
Grenadier, 18 Wilton Row, SW1
Paxton's Head, 153 Knightsbridge, SW1

Mayfair and Marylebone
Audley's, 41 Mount Street, W1
Captain's Pub, 22 Portman Street, W1
Duke of York, 45 Harrowby Street, W1
Guinea, 30 Bruton Place, W1
Prince Regent, 71 Marylebone High Street, W1
Red Lion, 1 Waverton Street, W1
Shepherd's Tavern, 50 Hertford Street, W1
Thistle, 11 Vigo Street, W1
Ye Grapes, 16 Shepherd's Market, W1

North and North-West London
Albion, 10 Thornhill Road, N1
Bull & Bush, North End Way, NW3
Eagle, 2 Shepherdess Walk, N1
Flask, 77 West Hill, Highgate, N6
Jack Straw's Castle, North End Way, NW3
Prince Albert, 11 Princess Road, NW1
Spaniards Inn, Spaniards Road, NW3
Volunteer, 247 Baker Street, NW1

St. James's
Blue Posts, 6 Bennet Street, SW1
Red Lion, 23 Crown Passage, Pall Mall, SW1

Soho and Trafalgar Square
Sherlock Holmes, 10 Northumberland Street, WC2
Tom Cribb, Panton Street, WC2

South-East London
Anchor, 1 Bankside, Southwark, SE1
Angel, 101 Bermondsey Wall East, SE16
Fox & Firkin, 316 Lewisham High Street, SE13
The George, 77 Borough High Street, Southwark, SE1
Mayflower, 117 Rotherhithe Street, SE16
Prince of Orange, 118 Lower Road, SE16
Trafalgar Tavern, Park Row, SE10
Yacht, Crane Street, SE10

South-West London
Hand in Hand, Crooked Billet, Wimbledon Common, SW19
Ship, 10 Thames Bank, Riverside, SW14
Sun Inn, 11 Church Road, Barnes, SW13
Victoria, 10 West Temple, Sheen, SW14
White Horse on Parsons Green, 1 Parson Green, SW6
Ye Old Windmill Inn, Clapham Common Southside, SW4

Victoria and Westminster
Albert, Victoria Street, SW1
Orange Brewery, 37 Pimlico Road, SW1
St. Stephen's Tavern, Bridge Street, SW1
Two Chairmen, 39 Dartmouth Street, SW1

West London
Bull's Head, Strand on the Green, W4
City Barge, Strand on the Green, W4
Dove, 19 Upper Mall, W6

Shopping. The main shopping areas are Oxford Street/Regent Street/Bond Street, Knightsbridge, Kensington High Street and Covent Garden. Normal Monday to Saturday shopping hours are 09.00 to 17.30. Shops in Covent Garden Market stay open until 20.00 but open at 10.00. Oxford Street and area and Kensington High St stores and shops stay open until 19.00 on Thursdays; Knightsbridge until 19.00 on Wednesdays. Some West End stores (notably John Lewis and Peter Jones) close on Saturday afternoons. Shopping hours are extended in the period before Christmas; Christmas illuminations in Regent Street and Oxford Street are switched on in mid-November and continue until 6 January.

The proposed lifting of Sunday trading restrictions would allow shops and stores in the West End to open all week if they wished. At present it is mostly suburban do-it-yourself centres and garden centres which open on Sundays. Late-night 7-day a week supermarkets can be found at Trafalgar Square, in the Strand, in Queensway, in South Kensington, in Fulham Road and in King's Road. There are several good shopping guides to London; a small booklet is available from the BTA, 'Shopping in London'.

Shopping generally gives good value for money but certain goods are particularly worth buying if you are a visitor to Britain: antiques (Camden Passage, Bond Street, King's Road); woollens (Marks & Spencer, Scotch House); books (Foyles, Dillons, Hatchards); records, tapes (Our Price, Virgin, HMV Shop); hifi and photographic equipment (Tottenham Court Road).

Under the Retail Export Scheme operated by most major stores, visitors to Britain receive a refund on VAT paid in this country for certain goods. Information on how this is done is available in the stores which operate the scheme or from the BTA overseas offices; nationals from some countries will have to pay tax in their own country if they reclaim VAT paid in Britain.

III   Getting Around London

London Regional Transport operates the Underground and bus services throughout Central London and to most parts of the suburbs; South-East, South and South-West London are served by British Rail's suburban rail services.

London's public transport system is busy through the day and evening—most services end before or at midnight. (For night-buses see below.) The rush-hour on both Underground and suburban railway services is at its height between 07.30 and 09.00 and 16.30-18.00. Traffic congestion can occur at any time in Central London and in the suburbs but is more likely during the rush-hour period, particularly on main roads in and out of Central London and on cross-London routes.

There are several ways of saving money on travelling around London. Visitors arriving at Heathrow who buy their London Explorer ticket on arrival will have the fare from Heathrow to Central London included.

The *London Explorer* is available for 1, 3, 4 and 7 days and at a reduced price for children; it covers virtually the whole Underground network and the red London buses.

The *Travelcard*, which requires a photograph, is a weekly or monthly season ticket for specified zones on the Underground and buses. *Capitalcards* link the British Rail suburban network with the Underground and bus system, again based on a zonal system; see below. *Red Bus Rovers* allow unlimited travel on London's buses for one day.

Travel discount cards (described above) are available from tourist information centres (London Explorer and Red Rover only), London Transport travel information centres at Heathrow Central, Euston, King's Cross, Piccadilly Circus, Oxford Circus, St. James's Park and Victoria and from station ticket offices; Capitalcards are available from British Rail stations. Note also that off-peak day returns are available on British Rail suburban services after 09.30 (usually just over half the price of a full return). More information from London Transport's 24-hour telephone information service on 01-222 1234.

The *Underground* ('the tube') is the quickest and easiest way to travel around London and the network covers most of Greater London, except for the south-east and southern suburbs; there are some 250 stations in all on seven different lines now divided into a zonal fare system. The Central Zone is basically the area covered by and within the Circle Line. Tickets for individual journeys are available from ticket machines which now take a large selection of coins, or from a ticket office (usually with a queue at busy stations); keep a large selection of coins or buy a discount card (see above). Yellow tickets fit the automatic ticket barriers. Tickets are given up at the end of the journey. Return tickets are available on the Underground and are recommended for visits to Olympia and Earl's Court at exhibition time when there are usually large queues at the ticket office on return.

Disabled travellers in wheelchairs can use certain sections of the 'over-ground' Underground system where access is by stairs or lift; contact London Transport for details. Wheelchairs and push-chairs are not allowed, except if carried, on the escalators. Smoking is now banned on all Underground trains and in deep-level Underground stations. Trains operate from 05.30 to 24.15; but check details of last trains to any particular part of Outer London.

The London Underground has a good reputation for safety and most people will feel comfortable travelling at any time. On certain Outer London sections, women may feel comfortable with another person; alternatively choose a carriage near the guard, or the driver, on a train without guard, in the evening.

Interchange between different lines is simple through the colour-code system and good sign-posting. However, at some stations long walks can be involved. If in doubt, when carrying heavy luggage for example, check with LRT.

Buses. London's famous red double-decker buses provide convenient Central London services as well as a sightseeing service. Nos 11, 15 or 38 are good routes to catch for a 'tour' of London—sit on top at the front—smoking is now only allowed on the top-deck in the rear seats and may be banned altogether. (See also sightseeing tours, on p 26.) A queue system operates at bus stops, although it may easily break down if several buses arrive together; be prepared for some pushing in rush-hour; only five standing passengers are allowed inside (downstairs) and conductors are normally fierce on this point. Push-chairs and limited luggage as well as dogs are carried at the conductor's discretion.

One-person driver-only buses, often single deckers, operate on several routes in Outer London and on the Red Arrow service between mainline stations and to Oxford Street. The exact fare is usually required; carry 10p coins. A solid red sign at the bus stop indicates request stop; hail the bus as it approaches; to get off ring the bell on the platform. Short bus journeys are cheaper than the Underground and children's fares apply until 21.00. (See also special tickets, above.)

Nightbuses operate from Trafalgar Square from midnight and cover most parts of London. If travelling alone by bus at night, sit downstairs to be close to the conductor/driver; rowdiness is more likely on the top-deck.

British Rail, suburban network. South-East London (including Greenwich) is served from Charing Cross and London Bridge. South London (including Bromley, Orpington and Croydon) is served from Victoria Station. South-Western suburbs including those served by the District Line, (i.e. Wimbledon and Richmond as well as Kingston) are served from Waterloo. Services start from 06.00 and wind down from 22.30. Check last trains and weekend services carefully.

Commuter services to East Anglia (including Southend) operate from Fenchurch Street and Liverpool Street. Services to Hertfordshire (including St. Albans), operate from St. Pancras. The services to Amersham, Bucks from St. Marylebone are threatened by the proposed closure of this station. Services to Slough operate from Paddington.

Taxis. The characteristic black London cab (known as a 'Hackney' carriage at one time—they were first built in Hackney) is being replaced gradually with a new Land-Rover style of cab which will be more accessible for disabled persons. The Hackney Carriage Office of the Metropolitan Police controls the licensing of taxis and of drivers who have to pass a detailed examination of their knowledge of London. Black cabs can be hailed in the street when the yellow 'For Hire' notice is illuminated. They are also available from ranks or by telephone: Computercab 01-286 0286 or 01-286 2200; Dial A Cab 01-253 5000; Radio Taxi Cabs 01-272 5471.

Taxi-fares are generally increased once a year; there is a standard charge on the meter, to which additional charges are added for waiting time, additional passengers, luggage and after 20.00 and before 06.00 and at weekends. For long journeys (over 6 miles) to the suburbs or outside the Metropolitan area, it may be necessary to negotiate a fare (this does not apply to Heathrow—see p 12). Any dispute regarding fares should be referred to the Hackney Carriage Office of the Metropolitan Police; make a note of the cab number—inside the cab and also at the rear below the number plate—and if possible the driver's number; they wear a badge.

Mini-cabs are private cars, with untrained drivers, who operate taxi services mostly in the suburbs. They have to be adequately insured but their charges are not controlled or metered. Normally they work on mileage and a fare should be negotiated beforehand. They provide a useful alternative in the suburbs which are poorly served by black cabs except for major stations such as East Croydon. Look up mini-cabs in the 'Yellow Pages' telephone directory. They should not be hailed or used in Central London (except possibly late at night)—visitors have been overcharged in some cases. In cabs and mini-cabs, pay the fare and add a discretionary 10 per cent as a tip. It is quite acceptable to round up to the nearest pound, if appropriate.

Driving. Visitors can drive in Britain on a current International Driving Permit or on a current domestic licence subject to a maximum of 12 months. No-one under 17 may drive a car, no-one under 16 may drive a motorcycle. Full details of Britain's road regulations are in the Highway Code (available from bookshops). Visitors to London are strongly recommended to leave their cars and to sightsee in London by public transport. If hiring a car for touring Britain, contact LVCB for a list of car hire companies, located throughout London. Rates vary considerably.

Parking is controlled throughout Central London and in suburban centres. Limited off-street car parking is provided mostly by National Car Parks who can supply a useful guide to car parks. Contact a tourist information centre or National Car Parks on 01-499 7050. Meters apply on weekdays, on Saturday mornings in some areas and throughout Saturdays in others, from 08.00 to 18.30. Use 10p and 50p coins.

Parking on a single or double yellow line during weekdays, and on double yellow lines or in residents' parking zones without a permit at other times can result in a parking ticket—a fine to be paid—or in Central London, in clamping, which means that the car cannot be moved. The clamp is removed by the police once the fine has been paid at a nominated police station. Sometimes it will take several hours before the police van returns to remove the clamp. The police are using the clamp against foreign-number-plated cars with just as much vigilance as British registered cars—only Diplomatic cars are exempt.

Two national motoring organisations look after the interests of motorists and offer touring information and breakdown services. Contact the AA (Automobile Association, Fanum House, Leicester Square, London WC2) (01-891 1400), or the RAC (Royal Automobile Club, 89 Pall Mall, London SW1 (01-839 7050), for details of membership. The BTA issues a free guide on Vehicle Hire and Driving in Great Britain (available from overseas offices only, see p 43).

A good *map* is essential for touring Britain and Greater London; sign-posting except on motorways and major routes can be confusing. Follow road- numbers whenever in doubt rather than looking for the names of particular towns, or suburbs of London. Allow more time than distances on the map would suggest; most suburban roads and major and minor roads are congested, particularly through towns; major roads other than motorways may only be dual carriageway in patches and there is heavy traffic on routes to ports in particular.

Sightseeing. The ideal way to explore London is on foot; this guide is divided into routes which could take walkers up to half a day or more depending on how thoroughly each area is explored. There is a map section at the back of the book but an additional, more detailed map may be helpful. The most detailed are the A to Z or the Streetfinder; both show virtually every street in the Greater London area.

The *Silver Jubilee Walkway* is a 10-mile way-marked trail starting in Leicester Square and taking in the City, Bankside, South Bank, Westminster and back to Leicester Square. Redevelopments on Bankside (see p 290) have interrupted the trail but an alternative route can be taken. Use the Silver Jubilee Walkway Map, available from LVCB tourist information centres. Two shorter, similar trails in the City are the *Heritage Walks*. Heritage Walk No. 1 starts in Threadneedle Street by the Bank of England, and Heritage Walk No. 2 on the N side of St. Paul's Cathedral. These are also waymarked and a map and explanations can be found in the 'Visitors' Guide to the City of London' (50p) available from the City of London Information Centre.

Walking tours of London take place every day; these are organised by small groups of guides or small companies, such as Discovering London (0277 213704), London Walks (01-882 2763), Citisights (01-600 3699), and Streets of London (01-882 3414), as well as various societies. They publish their own leaflets which can be found at tourist information centres; 'Time Out', 'What's On Where to Go', 'The Times' and 'London Events and Entertainment' also carry daily listings. Tours on a theme such as 'Legal London', 'Jack the Ripper's London', the 'London of Charles Dickens' or geographical Hampstead or Mayfair usually start from a specified Underground station without pre-booking. There is a charge of between £2 and £3. Some tours end in a pub, while others are designed as pub tours (the Londoner from Temple Underground every Friday at 19.30). These tours are particularly recommended for visitors on their own or those who want to meet Londoners; many go on these tours particularly in the off-peak periods.

By Car. Registered driver-guides (look for Blue Badge) offer in-dividually designed tours for up to five people in private cars, limousines, or a black cab. Contact Prestige Tours, 3 Elystan Street, SW3 (01-584 3118), or the Driver Guide Association, 2 Bridge Street,

SW1 (01-907 6114). At first sight these may appear expensive, but when several people are sharing it is a very competitive alternative to a guided sightseeing tour with the advantage that the itinerary is flexible and caters for individual tastes. Tipping the guide, and sharing lunch would be expected on a full-day tour.

By Bus or Coach. Several companies run introductory London tours with or without commentary, covering most Central London sights without stopping and taking from 2 to 2.5 hours depending on traffic. London Regional Transport use the familiar red double-decker for their Round London Sightseeing Tour which starts from Victoria (Victoria Street), Marble Arch, Piccadilly Circus and Baker Street. Tours run frequently (every half hour) daily and every other one is usually guided (slightly more expensive); there are also commentaries in German and French (check with London Transport on 01-222 1234); Ebdon Coaches operate a similar service from Victoria (Grosvenor Gardens)—guided tours with regular departures daily using their own style of double-decker bus. Cityrama, using distinctive blue double-decker buses, offer recorded commentaries in up to 12 languages with departures from Victoria (Grosvenor Gardens), Trafalgar Square and Piccadilly Circus. Another service run by London Crusader in a white and green double-decker operates along similar lines from Trafalgar Square. The above services require no pre-booking and operate on a first come first served basis from approx 09.30-17.00 daily through the year, later in the summer. It may be necessary to let a bus go, to get an upper deck seat on the open-topped buses used during the good weather in the summer.

Extensive programmes of scheduled sightseeing services are operated by several tour operators including Evan Evans Tours Ltd, 27 Cockspur Street, Trafalgar Square, London SW1 (01-930 2377), Frames Rickards, 11 Herbrand Street, London WC1 (01-837 3111), and London Regional Transport (01-222 1234). These can be pre-booked at tourist information centres or through hotel porters in most hotels; there are usually several pick-up points for different tours and German, French and Spanish language tours are standard. The West End morning tour takes in the Changing of the Guard (if it is taking place that day), and Westminster Abbey as well as a general tour of the area; the City afternoon tour takes in the Tower of London and St. Paul's Cathedral as well as a panoramic drive through the City. The Whole Day London tour combines the two and includes lunch.

More adventurous tours combine a tour on the river with a visit to Greenwich; there are also Half Day and Whole Day tours to Windsor, Eton and Hampton Court. Tours go further afield to Oxford and Blenheim, Stratford on Avon, Cambridge, Stonehenge and Bath, Winchester and Broadlands, Leeds Castle, Arundel and Brighton. Full programmes and bookings at tourist information centres.

All these tour operators use Blue Badged, registered guides, trained and examined by the London Visitor and Convention Bureau. There are some 750 working guides in London speaking a variety of languages and offering some very special qualifications: in antiques, history, art, dealing with disabled visitors and so on. Contact the Guide Activities Department of the London Visitor and Convention Bureau (26 Grosvenor Gardens, London SW1, 01-730 3450) for information on particular guide services.

Culture Bus offers yet another way of getting around London. Modelled on American services, yellow double-deckers tour London's major attractions on a continuous basis; one ticket allows passengers to embark and disembark freely through the day. Tickets bought after 15.00 can be used the next day. The service operates 09.00 to

18.00 April to October, 09.30 to 18.00 November to March. Tickets are available on the bus or from the Culture Bus office at 21-23 Elizabeth Street, London SW1 (01-834 6732) or from selected agents.

By Coach. The excellent Green Line Coach network covers the South East. The coaches operate from Eccleston Bridge to a variety of destinations at competitive fares. Information from Green Line Coaches on 01-730 0202. A Golden Rover discount ticket which gives a day's unlimited travel is available.

By Bike or Scooter. Bicycles and scooters can be rented for the day or the week from several companies in London; the weekend is recommended as a gentle introduction to London's traffic! London drivers are not noted for their courtesy to cyclists. Try the London Bicycle Company, 41/42 Floral St, WC2 (01-836 2969), Dial a Bike, 18 Gillingham Street, London SW1 (01-828 4040), or Scootabout Ltd, 59 Albert Embankment, SE1 (01-582 0055). Serious cyclists should contact the London Cycling Campaign Centre, Tress House, Stamford St, SE1 (01- 928 2318) for a copy of 'On Your Bike'.

By Helicopter or Airship. Scheduled helicopter services no longer operate, but a helicopter sightseeing tour can be arranged by chartering a helicopter for 15 minutes to 1 hour using one of the London Heliports. Contact Battersea Heliport, Lombard Road, SW11 (01-228 3232). (Airship tours of London have been mooted for 1987!)

By River. One of the most pleasant and peaceful ways of seeing London is on a river-trip. There are departures through the year to the Tower and Greenwich from Westminster Pier and Charing Cross Pier; with round trip services to the Thames Barrier also from Westminster Pier. Services in the winter operate between 10.30 and 16.00; in the summer between 09.30 and 17.30 at regular intervals.

In the summer there are also up-river scheduled services to Kew, Richmond, and Hampton Court from Westminster Pier. These services operate at weekends from Easter and daily from May or June to September.

There are scheduled services between Kingston and Hampton Court from Easter to September; and between Greenwich and the Thames Barrier; there are also services around the Thames Barrier, from the Barrier Pier.

Check River services before departure by telephoning the London Visitor and Convention Bureau's River Service (01-730 4812).

Circular cruises during the day and evening operate from Westminster Pier, usually with a bar on board. There are lunch cruises on Wednesdays, Saturdays and Sundays (book with Catamaran Cruisers on 01-987 1185). Several operators run evening disco cruises as well as music hall and dinner-dance cruises. Contact Catamaran Cruisers (01-987 1185), Woods River Services (01-481 2711), or River Ride (01-930 0970). On most scheduled services a commentary is provided by the skipper. This is of varying quality and a tip is usually expected as passengers leave the boat.

By Canal. London's Grand Union Canal and Regent's Canal are well worth exploring. Services operate from Camden Lock to Little Venice and back on Jenny Wren Cruises, 250 Camden High Street, NW1 (01-485 4433) (April-Oct); from Little Venice to Regent's Park and Camden Town on Jason's Trip, 60 Blomfield Road, W9 (01-286 3428)

(April-Oct); from Little Venice to London Zoo with British Waterways Waterbus, Delamere Terrace, London W2 (01-262 6711/482 2550) (March to Sept); from Uxbridge Lock along the Grand Union Canal with Colne Valley Passengerboat Services, the Toll House, Bull's Bridge, Southall, Middlesex. (01-571-4420) (May to Sept).

By Rail. Britainshrinkers combine rail and coach travel to reach parts of England in one day which would take too long by coach. Their programme includes Bath and Stonehenge, Brighton and Arundel, Canterbury and Dover, Cardiff and Llandaff, Exeter, Dartmouth and Plymouth, York, Warwick and Coventry. Two day tours operate to Scotland. Details from Road n Rail Tours Ltd (01-629 2525). Or book at a travel agent or tourist information centre.

A luxury train journey on the Pullman coaches of the Venice Orient Express can be enjoyed to visit Bath and Bristol, or Leeds Castle. Champagne lunch or afternoon tea is served on board and one leg of the journey is usually by luxury coach. Bookings through a travel agent or contact Venice Orient Express, 20 Upper Ground, SE1 (01-928 5837).

IV Culture and Sport

Theatre. London's claim to be the theatre capital of the world may be hotly contested by New York but no visit to London, even by New Yorkers, would be complete without at least one visit to the theatre.

The early years of the London theatre can be explored at the Bear Gardens Museum on Bankside not far from the site of the original Globe Theatre where Shakespeare's plays were performed in his lifetime. A replica of the Globe Theatre is now being planned near the museum where Shakespeare's plays will be performed under open skies. The theatre of the past 200 years will be the subject of the Theatre Museum due to open in 1987 in Covent Garden when the fine Victoria and Albert Museum collection is unveiled in its own setting underneath the London Transport Museum in the old Flower Market.

The living theatre manifests itself nightly (except Sundays) at some 40 West End theatres and equally numerous suburban and fringe theatres. The range of productions is wide, from Shakespeare to modern drama and from musicals to light-hearted comedy.

The publicly funded theatre sector is dominated by the National Theatre on the South Bank and the Royal Shakespeare Company's Barbican Theatre in the City, although many fringe theatres also receive public money. The programmes of these two giants amongst theatre companies contain a mixture of classical and modern drama and occasional large-scale musicals. The National Theatre which opened in 1976 reveals inside its forbidding concrete exterior un-rivalled facilities with three auditoria: the Olivier, the Lyttleton and the Cottesloe. Early evening tours of the building include these as well as the workshops where all scenery and costumes are made.

The Barbican Theatre opened in 1982 in another, larger, concrete block which also houses a fine Concert Hall. The theatre is as large as the Olivier and the RSC also has a workshop theatre, the Pit. Both these buildings have superb technical as well as good public facilities including bars, snack-bars, restaurants, lavatories, disabled access and induction loops for the hard of hearing.

The commercial theatres alternately thrive or decline in London's West End according to the economic climate. Most belong to the Society of West End Theatres, which publishes the fortnightly 'London Theatre Guide' (free from information centres). Many of the older commercial theatres are attractions in their own right, some saved from demolition or redevelopment by the Theatres Trust. Of particular interest is the Theatre Royal Drury Lane; the present theatre dates from 1812—the fourth on the same site—and has its own ghost. Recently restored and reopened is the historic Old Vic theatre, whose decor now reflects its Victorian music-hall past. Other theatres worth a close look before the house-lights go out include the Theatre Royal, Haymarket, the Albery, the Palace, the Criterion, the Duke of York, Her Majesty's, the Shaftesbury, the Savoy and the famous Palladium.

In suburban centres, public money has funded a number of new theatres, mostly of little architectural distinction but serving local audiences with pre-West End and touring productions. The Greenwich Theatre and the Lyric Hammersmith both originate their own productions. The true 'fringe' as opposed to suburban theatres can be found all over London, including the West End, in pubs, halls, theatres and clubs. New and experimental plays and revues are performed nightly sometimes on Sundays, and at lunchtime, by professional actors and actresses. Pub-theatre is particularly enjoyable at the King's Head, Islington where a meal is served before the performance, and at the Bush, Theatre Royal Stratford East, the Albany, the Orange Tree, and the Tricycle—new playwrights are encouraged.

In summer theatre can be enjoyed out of doors at the Regent's Park Open Air Theatre where Shakespeare is magically performed under the trees and only the occasional aircraft on its way to Heathrow intrudes; Holland Park also has a theatre season in August, and in Covent Garden there is open-air theatre under St. Paul's portico and occasionally at St. Martin in the Fields through the summer. (The fringe theatres have their own joint box office at the Duke of York's Theatre.)

How to Book. At one time booking for the theatre was a major task but modern marketing techniques and new technology have combined to make it much easier. It is still best to go to the box office of the theatre itself (usually open from 10.00). Telephone bookings have become easier with the introduction of credit cards; these are usually taken on a separate telephone number and most international cards are accepted. Tickets are then held until they are collected—even if the performance has already started.

Ticket agents can be found at stations, around Piccadilly Circus and in hotels. Usually they add on a commission of 15 to 20 per cent, but this is no longer controlled. However, progress is being made with the introduction of computerised bookings. Ticketmaster UK and Keith Prowse have linked up to provide same-price tickets for an increasing number of theatres—through Keith Prowse outlets only. Group Box Office Sales is a useful contact if arranging tickets for 15 or more people. The Theatre Concert Rail Club offers reduced rail travel and theatre tickets for people living within comfortable travelling distance of London. Half-price tickets (plus a small commission charge) are available on the day of performance from the Half Price Ticket Booth in Leicester Square operated by the Society of West End Theatres. SWET also operates a discount scheme for pensioners at matinee performances and discounts are available for students at most theatres under the student standby scheme.

Evening performances start at 19.30 or 20.00; matinees are usually on Wednesdays, Thursdays and/or Saturdays at 15.00 or sometimes at 17.00. 'The London Standard', the 'Daily Telegraph', 'The Times' and 'Sunday Times' and 'Observer' have good theatre guides. 'What's On Where to Go', 'London Events and Entertainment' (free from tourist information centres), 'City Limits' and 'Time Out' provide a weekly listing with a description of each play. Theatre tickets cost from £5 to £15 depending on the production; fringe theatres cost from £3 to £5; opera costs from £5 to £50. Stalls and dress circles give the best view; boxes usually give a restricted view of the stage and the upper circle can be cramped and hot, especially in older theatres.

Keith Prowse, 01-741 9999.
Group Sales Box Office, 01-930 6123.
Theatre Concert Rail Club, 56 34475.
Half Price Ticket Booth, from 12.00 for matinees; from 14.30 for eve. performances.
Society of West End Theatres, 01-836 0971.
Fringe Theatre Box Office, 01-379 6002 (Duke of York's Theatre).

Music, Opera and Dance.
Four symphony orchestras, three opera companies and two major ballet companies have their home in London in addition to numerous smaller orchestras, large and small choirs, and a variety of dance groups. The Royal Festival Hall on the South Bank has nightly performances of mostly classical music with a ballet season in the summer and at Christmas. The Queen Elizabeth Hall and Purcell Room are part of the facilities here and are used for recitals and chamber music concerts. The Barbican Concert Hall is the home of the London Symphony Orchestra which plays for three six-week seasons a year. Visiting orchestras complete the programme.

The magnificent Royal Albert Hall in Kensington is used for a variety of events including wrestling. But in July, August and

September music takes over completely for the famous Henry Wood Promenade Concerts organised by the BBC; those with the stamina for standing can enjoy first class music inexpensively (seating is also available). The summer also sees outdoor concerts at Kenwood Lakeside and the Crystal Palace Concert Bowl.

The Greenwich Festival in June and the City of London Festival in July provide unique opportunities for enjoying music in unusual settings such as the Royal Naval Chapel at Greenwich and the livery halls in the City. Lunchtime and evening concerts can be enjoyed in smaller concert halls and churches; regular venues are St. John's Smith Square, the Wigmore Hall, St. Martin in the Fields and St. Bartholomew the Great (information from tourist information centres). The periods before Christmas and Easter see a number of special performances of church music and carols in cathedrals and churches, including Westminster Abbey, St. Paul's Cathedral and Westminster Cathedral, in addition to their regular services and choir concerts.

At Covent Garden's Royal Opera House ballet and opera alternate. The audience cannot fail to be impressed with the splendid environments and professional performances. Gradually the 125-year old building is being extended and improved back-stage to provide the facilities required by today's opera companies. The Coliseum in St. Martin's Lane offers opera in English and at Sadlers Wells opera, operetta and dance make up a lively programme which features many visiting companies. The London Contemporary Dance Theatre and Ballet Rambert appear regularly at Sadlers Wells, The Place and other venues.

The musical variety on offer in London also includes traditional music hall entertainment at the Players' Theatre (a club), in some pubs and on Thames evening cruises. Jazz flourishes in pubs as well as clubs: Ronnie Scott's and the 100 Club are perhaps the best known. A new Jazz Centre was due to open in Covent Garden in 1985 to provide a meeting place for jazz musicians and also an information point on jazz.

It is undoubtedly on the pop and rock scene that British artists have made their strongest international impact in recent years. Up-and-coming groups play in pubs and clubs. Established stars appear at bigger venues such as the Hammersmith Odeon, Wembley and Earls Court (information in 'Time Out' or music papers).

Concert and opera tickets can be booked as theatre tickets. Pop concert tickets are offered by post in advance and some are made available from agents, particularly Keith Prowse and Premier Box Office. Note: pop and rock concerts and some popular musicals attract ticket-touts who sell tickets outside the doors or by small-ads in some newspapers at highly inflated prices. This is not illegal but occasionally the tickets are not genuine or are double-booked; the buyer should beware and stick to normal sources wherever possible.

Keith Prowse, 01-741 9999.

Premier Box Office, 01-240 2245.

Glorious music can be heard in London's cathedrals and churches (mostly free of charge—collection at the end); the choirs of St. Paul's and Westminster Abbey can be heard most days; several City churches have regular concerts; St. Bartholomew the Great, Smithfield, St. Martin in the Fields, Trafalgar Square, and St. James's Piccadilly have lunchtime concerts and recitals. St. John's Smith Square is now a concert venue rather than a church.

Cinema. The cinema industry in London is going through a temporary boom despite the growth of home videos. Central London is particularly well served by large and small cinemas with a good selection of programmes; films are shown from early afternoon and several cinemas have late-night performances. Seats are usually bookable, at least direct from the box office, and most cinemas now ban smoking or allow it only in a limited section of the auditorium. The National Film Theatre (see p 289), with three auditoria and an interesting mix of films, welcomes temporary members. 'Time Out' and 'The London Standard' give details of film programmes; the former with a resumé of each film.

Art Exhibitions. At any one time there may be as many as 100 different art exhibitions in museums, and in major and minor galleries all over London. The big touring exhibitions are usually shown at the Hayward Gallery on the South Bank (see p 288) or at the Royal Academy of Arts (p 115). The Tate Gallery presents large scale exhibitions of individual artists' work and schools of painting in addition to its permanent exhibition. The National Gallery, the National Portrait Gallery, the British Museum and the Victoria and Albert Museum also stage art exhibitions. Items from the Queen's own collection are shown at the Queen's Gallery (see p 105). At the Serpentine Gallery, the Arts Council shows mainly modern art, and the Whitechapel Gallery, newly restored, offers an interesting programme of exhibitions including their own Open Exhibition for artists in the area.

The major open exhibition is of course the Royal Academy Summer Exhibition, held annually in May through to July. The Barbican Art Gallery has established itself as a major venue (see p 239) both for touring and its own exhibitions. Smaller galleries worth exploring are the Camden Arts Centre (see p 297), the Bankside Gallery (see p 286), the South London Art Gallery (see p 328), the Crafts Council Gallery (see p 100), the ICA Gallery (see p 100) and the Photographer's Gallery (see p 160).

A large number of private galleries display and sell paintings, prints, etchings and photographs. Many are concentrated in the area of Cork Street, N of Piccadilly.

Art auctions take place at London's major auction rooms: Christie's, 8 King Street, St. James's, London SW1 (01-839 9060), Sotheby's, 34 and 35 New Bond Street, London W1 (01-493 8080), and Philips, Son & Neale, Blenstock House, 7 Blenheim Street, London W1 (01-629 6602).

Spectator Sports. Main sports centres are at Crystal Palace, London Docklands and Wembley. Athletics, badminton, football, gymnastics, hockey, judo and swimming take place at the National Sports Centre, Crystal Palace, SE19 (details on p 324); the new Docklands Arena due to open in 1986 offers facilities for athletics and other sports (see p 279) and the Wembley Arena, Wembley, is used for show-jumping, and other sports. Football and rugby finals are held at the main Wembley Stadium.

Athletics. The Amateur Athletics Association, Francis House, Francis St, SW1 (01-828 9326) organises major athletics events and can give information on clubs and facilities.

Badminton. The All England championships take place at Wembley in March. Contact the Badminton Association, National Badminton Centre, Bradwell Road, Loughton Lodge, Milton Keynes (0908 568822).

Basketball. Championships are held at Wembley. The Harlem Globetrotters also play there once a year. English Basketball Association, Calomaz House, Lupton Avenue, Leeds (0532 496044).

Boxing. Amateur championships are held in May at Wembley and the Royal Albert Hall. Events details from the London Amateur Boxing Association, 68-69 Central Buildings, Southwark St, SE1 (01-407 2194).

Cricket. The cricket season begins in May and major matches take place at Lords and the Oval. Local cricket matches are played on Saturdays on 'greens' throughout suburban London and the South East. The Marylebone Cricket Club (MCC), the governing body, has its headquarters at Lord's, St. John's Wood Road, NW8 (01-289 1611); here test (international) matches, cup finals and Middlesex games are played. Surrey County matches are played at the Oval, Kennington Road, London SE1 (01-735 4911). First-class matches last for three days but there are now an increasing number of one day games.

Cycling. The Round Britain Milk Race (outside London) takes place in late May/June. There is a road circuit at Eastway Cycle Circuit, Lee Valley Park, Temple Mills Lane, London E15 (01-534 6085). Contact British Cycling Federation, 16 Upper Woburn Place, London WC1 (01-387 9320).

Association Football (soccer) is played from August to May. International matches and the finals of the FA (Football Association) and Milk Cup are held at Wembley. Tickets for cup finals are allocated through the clubs and sometimes sold through 'touts' at inflated prices, Beware! Local football matches take place on Saturday afternoons and some Wednesday evenings. Visitors are recommended to go in the stands with seating; any trouble at matches is more likely amongst standing spectators. London clubs are listed below:

Arsenal FC, Highbury Stadium, Avenell Rd, N5 (01-226 0304) (recorded ticket information 01-359 0131); *Brentford FC*, Griffin Park, Braemar Rd, Brentford (01-560 2021); *Chelsea FC*, Stamford Bridge, Fulham Rd, SW6 (01-381 6221); *Crystal Palace FC*, *Charlton Athletic FC*, Selhurst Park, SE25 (01-653 4462); *Fulham FC*, Craven Cottage, Stevenage Rd, SW6 (01-736 6561); *Millwall FC*, The Den, Cold Blow Lane, SE14 (01-639 3143); *Orient FC*, Brisbane Rd, E10 (01-539 2223); *Queen's Park Rangers FC*, South Africa Rd, W12 (01-743 0262); *Tottenham Hotspur FC*, 748 High Rd, N17 (01-808 1020); *West Ham United FC*, Boleyn Ground, Green St, E13 (01-470 1325); *Wimbledon FC*, 45 Durnsford Rd, SW19 (01-946 6311).

Greyhound Racing. This takes place mostly in the evening with betting as the most important part of the proceedings. Tracks are at: *Walthamstow Stadium*, Chingford Road, Harringay Stadium, Green Lanes, N4 (01-800 3474/6), *Wembley Stadium*, Empire Way, Wembley (01-902 8833), *Wimbledon Stadium*, Plough Lane, SW17 (01-946 5361), *Catford Stadium*, Adenmore Rd, SE6 (01-690 2261).

Horse Racing. The flat-racing season lasts from March to November; in winter it is mostly hurdle racing and steeplechasing. The main events are the Derby at Epsom (14m SW of London) in early June—a great occasion with a good social mix on Epsom Downs, followed by the slightly more upmarket and fashionable Ascot Week at Ascot Heath (5m SW of Windsor) to which the presence of the royal family adds glamour. Kempton Park (Sunbury on Thames), Lingfield Park (Lingfield Surrey), Sandown Park (Esher, Surrey), and Windsor, Berks, are convenient race courses for visitors staying in London. Details in the daily newspapers and from the Racing Information Bureau, Winkfield Road, Ascot, Berks (0990 25912). British Telecom operates a race-line service on 168 (London) or 01-246 8060 (from outside London).

Motor-Racing. The nearest circuit is at Brands Hatch, Fawkham, Kent (off the A20) (0474 872331). Stock-car racing takes place at Wimbledon Stadium, Plough Lane, SW17 (01-946 5361) on most Sundays.

Polo is played at Windsor Great Park; for details of matches contact the Hurlingham Polo Association (079 85 277).

Rowing. The most famous rowing event in the Calendar is the Oxford and Cambridge Boat Race, usually rowed on a Saturday before Easter between Putney and Mortlake (4.25m); good viewing points from the banks and bridges (see p 306). The Head of the River Event, the largest of its kind in the world, is held in March. Doggett's Coat and Badge Race is more of a traditional event and rowed in July (see p 300). Contact the Amateur Rowing Association, 6 Lower Mall, Hammersmith, London W6 (01-748 3632) for details of other events.

Rugby Union. Twickenham is the main venue for the amateur rugby union matches; local games take place at Blackheath, Richmond, Sunbury on Thames and Roehampton. The finals of the *Rugby League* take place at Wembley in May. The Rugby Football Union is at Whitton Road, Twickenham, Middlesex (01-892 8161).

Show Jumping. The two main events in London are the Horse of the Year Show at Wembley in October, and the Olympia International Show Jumping Championships at Olympia in December. Contact the British Show Jumping Association, British Equestrian Centre, Kenilworth, Warwickshire (0203 552511).

Tennis. The All England Lawn Tennis Championships take place at Wimbledon for two weeks towards the end of June. Tickets are allocated in advance although some (usually at inflated prices) are available from ticket agencies, and tour operators. It is possible to go on the day and pay an entrance charge to watch matches on the outside courts, non-ticketed, and in the standing areas of the main courts. Wimbledon is preceded by the Queen's Club tournament and a week before that the Kentish Times championships at Beckenham (see p 331) where some of the major competitors 'warm up' for the grass courts at Wimbledon. There are indoor tournaments at the Royal Albert Hall and Wembley. The sport is governed by the Lawn Tennis Association, Barons Court, London W14 (01-385 2366). The All England Lawn Tennis & Croquet Club is at Church Road, London SW19 (01-946 2244).

Participant Sports. Most of London's parks have sports facilities for the public (cricket, football, tennis, putting, golf, etc.). Apply for information to the Town Hall of the London Borough concerned, or the local library. Indoor sports facilities can be enjoyed by the public at the National Sports Centre, Crystal Palace, SE19 (01-778 0131) (small membership fee), and at Brixton Recreation Centre, 27 Brixton Station Road, SW9 (01-274 7774), entrance charge. The London Docklands Arena will also have indoor athletics facilities as well as catering for other sports. Contact the London Docklands Development Corporation, on 01- 515 3000.

Cycling. See p 28 for information on hiring bicycles. For touring information contact the Cyclists Touring Club, 69 Headrow Road, Godalming, Surrey, GU7 3HS (048 68 7217). The BTA also publishes a useful booklet.

Fishing. An extremely popular sport; join in by fishing along the canals, the Thames, and in Lee Valley Park. Information from the London Anglers Association, 183 Hoe Street, London E17 (01-520 7477).

Golf. Played all the year round on a number of courses; many of the best are club courses and an introduction from a member is essential. But there are also many good public courses: *Whitewebbs* (Enfield), *Ruislip* (Ickenham Road), *Haste Hill* (The Drive, Northwood), *Brent Valley* (Church Road, Greenford Ave, W7), *Beckenham Place* (Beckenham Junction); *Addington* (near Croydon); *Hainault Forest* and *Chingford*. These courses are crowded at weekends.

Ice Skating. There are now five ice rinks in the Greater London area: *Lee Valley Ice Centre*, Lea Bridge Road, Leyton E10 (01-533 3151); *Queen's Ice Skating Club*, 17 Queensway, W2 (01-229 0172); *Richmond Ice Rink*, Clevedon Rd, East Twickenham (01-892 3646); *Streatham Ice Rink*, 386 Streatham High Rd, SW16 (01-769 7861); *Sobell Sports Centre Ice Rink*, Hornsey Road, N7 (01-607 1632).

Riding. There are riding schools throughout Outer London who welcome visitors. Riding in Hyde Park can be a little more difficult to arrange as horses are booked by regulars. Contact: *Bathurst Riding Stables*, 63 Bathurst Mews, W2 (01-723 2813), *Ross Nye's Riding Establishment*, 8 Bathurst Mews, W2 (01-262 3791), *Lilo Blum's Riding School and Stables*, 32 Grosvenor Crescent Mews, SW1 (01-235 6846), *Roehampton Gate Stables*, Richmond Park (01-876 7089).

Skiing. Not a sport immediately associated with London! but there are dry ski slopes at Alexandra Park, N22, Crystal Palace, SE19 and Hounslow Heath. The major event is the International Ski Show at Olympia in November.

Squash. Private squash clubs have sprung up all over London. Contact the Squash Rackets Association, Francis Street, SW1 (01-828 3064) for details of clubs. The following welcome visitors: *The Oasis*, Endell St, WC2 (01-836 9555); *Wembley Squash Courts*, Empire Way, Wembley (01-902 9230), *Dolphin Square*, Chichester St, SW1 (01-828 1681).

Swimming. Olympic-size pools are at Crystal Palace and Brixton Recreation Centre (see above). Many of London's public baths have updated their facilities and become health centres with a range of facilities; some have wave machines and waterslides. Swimming outdoors at the Serpentine (see p 123). The following welcome visitors: Chelsea Manor St, SW3 (01-352 6985); Ironmonger Row, EC1 (01-253 4011); Kensington New Pools, Walmer Rd, W11 (01- 727 9923); Marshall St, W1 (01-439 4678); Merlin St, WC1 (01-837 1313);

Oasis, Endell St, WC2 (01-836 9555); Porchester Baths, Queensway, W2 (01-229 9950); Seymour Pl, W1 (01-723 8019).

Health and Fitness Centres. Several of London's hotels now offer facilities for guests (Grosvenor House, New Piccadilly Hotel, Holiday Inns, Kensington Close, John Howard Hotel, Selsdon Park, the Rembrandt Hotel: Aquilla) and a number of commercial centres welcome visitors. *Fitness Centre*, 11 Floral Street, WC2 (01-379 6613); *Westside Health Club*, 201-207 Kensington High Street, London W8 (01-937 5386); *Dance Centre*, 12 Floral Street, WC2 (01-836 6544); *Pineapple*, 7 Langley Street, WC2 (01-836 4004), *Pineapple West*, 60 Paddington Street, W1 (01-487 3444); *Dance Works*, 16 Balderton Street, W1 (01-629 6183).

V The Sights of London, Parks

The Sights. The table below gives opening hours of the most popular tourist attractions and indicates which have admission charges. In the text opening hours are given for all the attractions mentioned. In general, it should be noted that most national museums and galleries are closed on Sunday mornings (usually they open at 14.30); they also close on Good Friday and New Year's Day, and the first May Bank Holiday (Labour Day) (first Mon in May); commercial and all other attractions including museums and galleries close on Christmas Day; some also close on Christmas Eve and Boxing Day. Check with LVCB. Season tickets for attractions are offered under the Open To View scheme, available for overseas visitors—details from the BTA Overseas Offices and tourist information centres.

The recently created English Heritage organisation also offers a season ticket to monuments in its care; the National Trust operates a similar scheme for members.

Tours and lectures in museums and galleries are usually free of charge; special lectures are put on to coincide with special exhibitions. Pre-booking is not usually required.

Children's events are organised by all the major museums during the school holidays; details from each one or from tourist information centres.

Opening hours of cathedrals and churches vary greatly and have been entered in the text; City churches are usually closed at weekends and suburban churches are usually kept locked during the week.

HOURS OF ADMISSION

	Weekdays	Sundays	Notes
Apsley House	10.00-18.00	14.30-18.00	Closed Mon & Fri
Banqueting House	10.00-17.30	14.00-17.30	Closed Mon
Bethnal Green Museum of Childhood	10.00-18.00	14.30-18.00	Closed Fri

	Weekdays	*Sundays*	*Notes*
British Museum	10.00-17.00	14.30-18.00	Closed Christmas Eve & Boxing Day
Cabinet War Rooms	10.00-17.50	10.00-17.50	Closed Mons except Easter and Summer Bank Holiday
Carlyle's House	11.00-17.00	14.00-17.00	Closed Mon & Tues except BH Mons Closed Nov-March
Chelsea Hospital	10.00-12.00 14.00-17.00	14.00–16.00	
Chiswick House	09.30-18.30	09.30-18.30	Closed Mon & Tues Oct- March and shorter hours
Courtauld Institute	10.00-17.00	14.00-17.00	
Dickens House	10.00-17.00	Closed Sun	
Dulwich Gallery	10.00-13.00 14.00-17.00	14.00–16.00	Closed Mon
Geffrye Museum	10.00-17.00	14.00-17.00	Closed Mons—but open BH Mons 10.00-17.00
Ham House	14.00-18.00	14.00-18.00	Closed Mons (12.00-16.00 in winter)
Hampton Court	0 9.30-18.00	11.00-18.00	(Shorter hours in winter)
Hayward Gallery	Mon- Wed 10.00-20.00, Thurs-Sat 10.00-18.00	12.00-18.00	During exhibitions only
Imperial War Museum	10.00-17.50	14.00-17.50	
Dr Johnson's House	11.00-17.00		Closed Sun (closed 17.30 summer)
Keats House	10.00-13.00 14.00-18.00	14.00-17.00	
Kensington Palace	0 9.00-17.00	13.00-17.00	
Kenwood	10.00-17.00	10.00-17.00	(Longer hours in summer)
Kew Gardens	10.00-dusk	10.00-dusk	
London Zoo	0 9.00-18.00 or dusk	09.00- 19.00 or dusk	(Shorter hours in winter)
Madame Tussaud's	10.00-17.30	10.00-17.30	Open until 18.00 July/Aug
Museum of London	10.00-18.00	14.00-18.00	Closed Mon
National Army Museum	10.00-17.30	14.00-17.30	

	Weekdays	*Sundays*	*Notes*
National Gallery	10.00-18.00	14.00-18.00	Wed in summer closes 20.00
National Maritime Museum	10.00-18.00	14.00-17.30	(Shorter hours in winter)
National Portrait Gallery	10.00-17.00	14.00-18.00	Open Sat 10.00-18.00; Wed in summer closes 20.00
Natural History Museum	10.00-18.00	14.30-18.00	
Osterley House	14.00-18.00		Closed Mons Open some BH Mons (12.00-16.00 in winter)
Queen's Gallery	11.00-17.00	14.00-17.00	Closed Mons except BH
Royal Academy	10.00-18.00	10.00-18.00	
Royal Mews	14.00-16.00		Wed & Thurs only Closed Ascot Week
St. Paul's Cathedral	07.30-18.00	Services	(07.30-17.00 in winter)
Science Museum	10.00-18.00	14.30-18.00	
Soane Museum	10.00-17.00		Closed Mon and Sun
Syon House	12.00-16.15	12.00-16.15	Closed Fri-Sat Closed Oct-Easter Open Sun only in Oct
Tate Gallery	10.00-17.50	14.00-17.50	
Tower Bridge Walkway	10.00-17.45	10.00-17.45	(Until 16.00 in winter)
Tower of London	09.30-17.45 (March-Oct) 09.30-16.30 (Nov-Feb)	14.00–17.45 (March-Oct)	Closed Sun (Nov-Feb)
Victoria and Albert Museum	10.00-17.50	14.30-17.50	Closed Fridays
Wallace Collection	10.00-17.00	14.00-17.00	
Westminster Abbey	09.00-16.45 (08.00-18.00 Nave, Aisles and Precinct	Services	Sat 09.00–14.45 15.45–17.45 until 20.00 Wed
Windsor Castle	10.30–16.30 March– Oct, 10.30–14.30 Nov–Feb		Precincts open daily

Parks and gardens are a special feature of London; they stay green all the year round and the Royal Parks Department (Dept of the Environment) and the individual London Boroughs (and Greater

London Council) maintain flower displays virtually all the year round, LVCB runs a London In Bloom campaign and competition annually. The major parks are covered in the text; visitors with a horticultural interest should explore Kew Gardens, Chelsea Physic Garden, Dulwich Park, Golders Hill, Greenwich Park, Hall Place Gardens, Bexley, Ham House, Hampton Court Palace Gardens, Holland Park, Horniman Gardens, the Isabella Plantation, Richmond Park, Kenwood, Hampstead, Kensington Gardens, Kensington Roof Gardens, Queen Mary's Rose Garden, Regent's Park, and Syon Park Garden, Brentford.

Specialised Museums and Collections. Almost every interest or hobby can be studied in one of London's museums or specialist collections. The list below gives an indication.

Aircraft	RAF Museum (Hendon), Science Museum, Imperial War Museum
Art	National Gallery, Tate Gallery, Courtauld Institute Galleries, Royal Academy of Arts, Dulwich Picture Gallery, Wallace Collection, Saatchi Gallery, Hayward Gallery
Antiquities	British Museum, Victoria and Albert
Chinese Ceramics	British Museum, David Percival Foundation of Chinese Art, Victoria and Albert
Clocks	Old Royal Observatory (Greenwich), Guildhall Museum
Craft	Craft Council Gallery, Victoria and Albert, British Crafts Centre
Fashion	Victoria and Albert, Museum of London, Kensington Palace (Court Dress Collection)
Industrial Design	Science Museum, Victoria and Albert (The Boilerhouse), The Design Centre
London History	Museum of London, London Transport Museum, GLC Records Library
Manuscripts, Records, Charters	British Library, Public Record Office Museum, General Register Office, College of Arms
Maritime History	National Maritime Museum, Cutty Sark (Greenwich), Science Museum, HMS Belfast
Medicine	Science Museum (Wellcome Galleries), Hunterian Museum, Old Operating Theatre (Southwark)
Musical Instruments	Horniman Museum (Forest Hill), Ranger's House (Blackheath), Fenton House (Hampstead), Musical Museum (Brentford), Royal College of Music, Victoria and Albert
Postal History and Stamps	National Postal Museum, British Museum, Bruce Castle Museum (Tottenham)
Private houses of the famous	Apsley House (Duke of Wellington), Dr Johnson's House, Linley Sambourne House, Dickens House, Keats House (Hampstead), Kensington Palace, Carlyle's House, Soane Museum

Telephones & **Technology**	British Telecom Showcase, IBA Gallery (television), Science Museum
Theatre	Bear Gardens Museum (Southwark), Theatre Museum, Covent Garden (from 1987), Victoria and Albert
Toys	Bethnal Green Museum of Childhood, London Toy and Model Museum, Pollock's Toy Museum
Sport	Cricket Memorial Gallery, Lords, Wimbledon Tennis Museum, Wembley Stadium Tours
War	Imperial War Museum, National Army Museum, Tower of London, Cabinet War Rooms, Royal Artillery Museum & Rotunda (Woolwich), HMS Belfast, RAF Museum
Transport	London Transport Museum, Science Museum, The Heritage Collection (Cars), Syon Park

VI   Calendar of Major Events

Below are some of London's major annual events. For exact dates
check with tourist information centres. (Traditional events marked *.)

January	International Boat Show, Earls Court World Doubles Tennis Championships, Royal Albert Hall
30	*Charles I Commemoration, Trafalgar Square
February	Crufts Dog Show *Pancake Day Races, various locations
Jan/Feb	Chinese New Year, celebrations in Soho
March	Ideal Home Exhibition, Earls Court Oxford v Cambridge Boat Race Head of the River Race
Easter	*Butterworth Charity, St. Bartholomew the Great *Maundy Money (Westminster Abbey every 4th year) Easter Parade, Battersea Park *Harness Horse Parade, Regent's Park International Model Railway Exhibition, Wembley International Festival of Country Music, Wembley
April	Chelsea Antiques Fair, Chelsea Old Town Hall *St. George's Day, Shakespeare's Birthday, Southwark Cathedral London Marathon (Greenwich to Westminster) London Book Fair, Barbican Centre
May *1st Mon*	Bank Holiday; Marches; May Festival FA Cup Final, Wembley Rugby League Final, Wembley Royal Windsor Horse Show, Windsor Park Biggin Hill Air Fair, Biggin Hill
Ascension Day	*Beating the Bounds, Tower of London

	Chelsea Flower Show
	Fine Art and Antique Fair, Olympia
End	Royal Academy Summer Exhibition—until July
	Open Air Theatre, Regent's Park—until August
last Mon	Bank Holiday
29	*Oak Apple Day, Royal Hospital, Chelsea
June	*Beating the Retreat, Horse Guards
2nd Sat	*Trooping the Colour, Horse Guards Parade; Queen's Official Birthday
	The Derby, Epsom
	Ascot week, Ascot
	Greenwich Festival (two weeks)
	Stella Artois Tennis Tournament, Queen's Club
	Grosvenor House Antiques Fair
	All England Lawn Tennis Championships, Wimbledon
	Antiquarian Book Fair
	*Garter Ceremony, St. George's Chapel, Windsor
	London to Brighton Bicycle Race
July	Henley Regatta
	Royal Tournament (three weeks)
	City of London Festival (two weeks)
	Henry Wood Promenade Concerts, Royal Albert Hall—until September
	*Swan Upping; from Maidenhead
	*Doggetts Coat and Badge Race
	Metropolitan Police Horseshow, Imber Court, Surrey
	Street Entertainers Festival, Covent Garden
August	*London Riding Horse Parade, Hyde Park
	Greenwich Clipper Weeks, Greenwich
last Mon	Bank Holiday: Greater London Horse Show, Clapham Common
	Fairs, Hampstead Heath and other locations
September	Thamesday, Waterloo to Westminster Bridges
	Chelsea Antiques Fair, Chelsea Old Town Hall
	Burlington House Antiques Fair, Royal Academy
	British Craft Show, Syon Park
	*Horseman's Sunday, Church of St. John and St. Michael, W2
	*Punch and Judy Festival, Covent Garden
October	Park Lane Antiques Fair, Park Lane
	*Law Courts Open, Westminster Abbey
	London to Brighton Road Running Race
	Horse of the Year Show, Wembley
	*Pearly Kings and Queens, Harvest Service, St. Martin in the Field
21	*Trafalgar Day, Trafalgar Square
	Motorfair, Earls Court
	British Philatelic Exhibition, RHS Halls
November	*State Opening of Parliament (or late October)
	London to Brighton Veteran Car Run (Hyde Park)
5	Guy Fawkes Day, fireworks, bonfires, various locations

Sun	
nearest 11th	*Remembrance Sunday
2nd Sat	*Lord Mayor's Show
.. ..	Christmas Illuminations in West End
	World Travel Market, Olympia
December	Royal Smithfield Show, Earls Court (5 days)
	Christmas Tree illuminated, Trafalgar Square
	Olympia International Showjumping Championships,
	Olympia
25/26	Christmas Day/Boxing Day—public holidays

VII Useful Contacts

Tourist Information. Before arrival in London, information is available through the overseas offices of the **British Tourist Authority** in many countries. Make contact by telephone or post for up-to-date information. Below are listed some of BTA's offices:

Australia: BTA, Associated, Midland House, 171 Clarence St, Sydney, NSW 2000 (29-8627).

Canada: BTA, 94 Cumberland St, Suite 600, Ontario M5R 3NR (416 925-6326); or Suite 451, 409 Granville Street, Vancouver, B.C., V6C 1T2 (604 669-2414).

Netherlands: BTA, Leidseplein 23, 1017 PS Amsterdam (020 23 46 67).

New Zealand: BTA, Box 2402, Auckland.

South Africa: BTA, 7th Floor, JBS Building, 107 Commissioner Street, Johannesburg 2001; PO Box 6256, Johannesburg 2000 (29 6770).

USA: BTA, John Hancock Centre, Suite 3320, 875 N Michigan Ave, Chicago, Illinois 60611 (312 787 0490); Plaza of the Americas, 750 North Tower LB346, Dallas, Texas 75201 (214 748-2279); 612 South Flower Street, Los Angeles, California 90017 (213 623-8196); 3rd Floor, 40 West 57th Street, New York, NY 10019 (212 581-4700).

Tourist information in London is available through the services provided by the **London Visitor and Convention Bureau** (LVCB; formerly the London Tourist Board).

Tourist Information Centre, Victoria Station Forecourt, SW1. Open 09.00-20.30 7 days a week; 08.00-22.00 July and August. Services include tourist information on London and England, instant hotel bookings in London and throughout England, theatre and tour bookings, sales of tourist tickets, guidebooks and maps in extensive bookshop.

LVCB, Tourist Information Centre, West Gate, HM Tower of London, EC3. Open 10.00-18.00 daily. Summer only.

LVCB, Tourist Information Centre, Selfridges Department Store, Ground Floor, Oxford Street, W1. Open store hours.

LVCB, Tourist Information Centre, Harrods Department Store, Fourth Floor, Knightsbridge, SW7. Open store hours.

LVCB, Information Centre, Heathrow Central Underground Station, Heathrow Airport. Open 09.00-18.00, 7 days a week. Services include tourist information, hotel reservations and tour booking.

Telephone enquiries to LCVB on 01-730 3488 (Mon-Fri 09.00-17.30). Riverboat information is available on 01-730 4812. Written enquiries should be addressed to LVCB, Central Information Unit, 26 Grosvenor Gardens, London SW1W 0DU.

The City of London Information Centre is at St. Paul's Churchyard, EC4. Open 09.30-17.00 Mon to Fri, 09.30-12.00 Sat (01–606 3030).

An all-Britain Travel Centre is due to open at Lower Regent St, W1 in 1986.

Local information is available from the following centres:

Clerkenwell Heritage Centre, 33 St. John's Square, EC1 (01-250 1039); **Croydon Tourist Information Centre**, Katharine Street, Croydon (01-688 3627, ext. 45/46); **Greenwich Tourist Information Centre**, Cutty Sark Gardens, SE10 (01-858 6376); **Hillingdon Tourist Information Centre**, 22 High Street, Uxbridge, (0895 50706); **Kingston-upon-Thames Tourist Information Centre**, Heritage Centre, Fairfield West, Kingston-upon-Thames (01-546 5386); **Lewisham Tourist Information Centre**, Borough Mall, Lewisham Centre, SE13 (01-318 5421/2); **Richmond Tourist Information Centre**, Central Library, Little Green, Richmond (01-940 9125); **Tower Hamlets Tourist Information Centre**, 88 Roman Road, E2 (01-980 3749); **Twickenham Tourist Information Centre**, District Library, Garfield Road, Twickenham (01-892 0032).

Other Information Services:

London Regional Transport: 55 Broadway, SE1 (01-222 1234; 24 hrs).

British Rail: see pp 13, 14.

Airports: see p 12. **British Airports Authority**, Gatwick Airport Head Office, Gatwick, W Sussex (0293 517755).

Leisureline: recorded events informations. English on 01-246 8041, French on 01-246 8043, German on 01-246 8045.

Daily Telegraph Information Bureau: general information on 01-353 4242.

Artsline: information on access to the arts and venues for disabled people on 01-625 5666/7.

Kidsline: school holiday information for parents and children on 01-222 8070.

Metropolitan Police: 01-230 1212; use 999 for emergencies only.

Lost Property: for articles lost in taxis write to the Metropolitan Police Lost Property Office, 15 Penton Street, N1. For property lost on buses and the Underground contact the Lost Property Office, 200 Baker Street, NW1; open for callers Mon—Fri 09.30-14.00. For property lost on British Rail contact the appropriate main line station.

Childminders: 01-935 2049; Universal Aunts Ltd, 01-352 5413. Hotels may also have contacts.

Embassies, etc.: *Australia*, Australia House, Strand, WC2 (01-438 8000); *Canada*, Canada House, Trafalgar Square, SW1 (01-629 9492); *Irish Republic*, 17 Grosvenor Place, SW1 (01-235 2171); *New Zealand*, New Zealand House, Haymarket, SW1 (01-930 8422); *South Africa*, South Africa House, Trafalgar Square, SW1 (01-930 4488); *United States*, 24 Grosvenor Square, W1 (01-499 9000).

Hotel Bookings (other than LVCB): Expotel Ltd, Banda House, Cambridge Grove, W6 (01-568 8765; telex 8811951); HBI/HOTAC,

Globegate House, Pound Lane, London NW10 (01-451 2311; telex 8814032); British Hotel Reservations Centre, 10 Buckingham Palace Road, SW1 (01-828 2425; telex 916122); Concordia Ltd, 52 Grosvenor Gardens, SW1 (01-730 3467; telex 916988). Note: these are correspondence addresses only.

Arts Council of Great Britain: 105 Piccadilly, W1 (01-629 9495); information about exhibitions and activities.

Tourist Boards: *British Tourist Authority*; Thames Tower, Black's Road, Hammersmith, W6 (01-846 9000). This is the head office of the BTA and the English Tourist Board. No public tourist information services are offered but trade and media enquiries are welcome. *Scottish Tourist Board*, 19 Cockspur Street, SW1 (01-930 8661); *Wales Tourist Board*, 34 Piccadilly, W1 (01-409 0969); *Northern Ireland Tourist Board*, c/o Ulster Office, 11 Berkeley Street, W1 (01-493 0601). (All-Britain Travel Centre—see above.)

English Courses: ARELS/Felco (Association of English Language Schools/Federation of English Language Course Organisers), 125 High Holborn, WC1 (01-242 3136) provide information on English language courses in England.

English Heritage: PO Box 43, Ruislip, Middlesex HA4 0XW, provides information on monuments in the care of the Department of the Environment, and operates a season ticket scheme.

Museums Association: 34 Bloomsbury Way, WC1 (01-404 4767).

National Art Collection Fund, Granby House, 95 Southwark Street, SE1 (01- 928 0444). Membership gives access to National Art Library at the Victoria and Albert Museum.

National Trust, 36 Queen Anne's Gate, SW1 (01-222 9251). Information on events and stately homes; membership gives free admission to NT properties throughout the country.

The Victorian Society, 1 Priory Gardens, W4 (01-994 1019); lectures, walking tours and events.

British Waterways Board, Melbury House, Melbury Terrace, NW1 (01-286 6101); information on canals and cruising throughout Britain.

Civic Trust, 17 Carlton House Terrace, SW1 (01-930 0914); encourages a high standard of architecture.

Royal Institute of British Architects, Portland Place, W1 (01-580 5533); exhibitions, library and lectures.

Inland Waterways Association, 114 Regent's Park Road, NW1 (01-586 2510); organises walks along the Regent's Canal.

Royal Horticultural Society, Horticultural Hall, Vincent Sq., SW1 (01-834 4333); organises Chelsea Flower Show and other flower shows throughout the year.

Local libraries and the Yellow Pages for different parts of London are good sources of local information.

VIII General Information

Weather and The Seasons, a constant topic of conversation. English weather varies not just from day to day but sometimes from hour to hour. In general, winter temperatures rarely drop below freezing although there are occasional cold snaps with snow and deep frost. Fog on the outskirts of London and in the countryside can make driving hazardous. Spring is dominated by changeability with warm days (up to 15°C) and quite a lot of rain. The English spring with its array of blossom is probably one of the prettiest in the world— from March onwards the cherry trees blossom in London's suburbs and through Kent there are special apple blossom trails for motorists. The summer starts in May or sometimes in June and coincides with the traditional London season into which all the major events of the social calendar were once crammed. This is no longer the case but the events list (p 41) shows the many traditional events which make up the London season, from the Royal Academy Summer Exhibition to the race meetings at the Derby and Ascot and the Regatta at Henley. July and August can be hot and dry with temperatures up to 25-28°C, or they can be cold and dismal months. The autumn, another attractive season in London's parks and countryside, starts at the end of September and is usually dry and sunny with more rain towards Christmas; temperatures are in 10 to 15°C range. Rain can occur at any time and the wise sightseer carries an umbrella or fold-away raincoat.

For up-to-date news on the weather tune into London's local radio stations before setting out in the morning: LBC, London's news station, offers news, traffic and travel information and weather forecasts every quarter of an hour. Capital Radio has much the same information interspersed with music and BBC Radio London offers a third variation.

Summer Time. Between the end of March and October, Britain adopts Summer Time which means that clocks go forward one hour and then back in October to Greenwich Mean Time. Despite Britain's membership of the EEC, it does not seem to have been possible to coincide these change-overs with those which also take place on the Continent. Visitors travelling in Europe should check their watches, airline timetables, etc. carefully, particularly during March/April and September/October.

Bank Holidays and Business Hours. Bank holidays were introduced in the 19C before statutory holidays to give working people a day off; they have survived as follows: New Year's Day, Good Friday, Easter Monday, first Monday in May (instead of 1 May); last Monday in May (instead of Whitsun); last Monday in August; and Christmas Day, Boxing Day and possibly 27 December, if one of those is a Sunday. In general not much business is done between Christmas and the New Year, but there is no general closing down in London during the summer months, as on the Continent. Business hours are from 09.00 to 17.30 with lunch between 13.00 and 14.00 (banks, see below) Monday to Friday. A fair amount of business is done over lunch and several hours may be spent. Restaurants catering for the business market tend to close on Sundays.

Money. The £1 sterling is divided into 100 pence. 'Silver' coins come as 50p, 20p, 10p and 5p; with copper coins worth 2p and 1p (the ½p is no longer legal tender). The £1 coin, small and gold-coloured, is replacing the £1 note; other notes are £50, £20, £10 and £5. Banks are open Monday to Friday 09.30-15.30. In the suburbs some are open on Saturday mornings; at Heathrow and Gatwick there are 24-hour banks. Bureaux de Change with late hours and Sunday opening can be found at or near major railway stations, at Piccadilly Circus and Leicester Square, South Kensington and Bayswater. Check the rate of exchange and commission charge (which can be very high) before entering into a transaction. Some post offices also operate a Bureaux de Change service (see below).

Tipping. In general service charges are now included on bills in hotels and restaurants. If in doubt ask, and only leave an extra tip if the service has been exceptionally good. If not included, add 10 to 15 per cent. Taxi drivers expect a tip of around 10 to 15 per cent; porters a minimum of 50p; cloakroom attendants 10 to 50p and barbers and hairdressers a minimum 50p. Barmen in hotel cocktail bars will expect something left on the plate, but otherwise do not tip in bars, cinemas, theatres, etc.

Post. Stamps are sold from Post Offices which are open Monday to Friday 09.00-17.30 and Saturday 09.00-13.00 (in some cases). Stamps can also be bought from some hotel desks. European mail goes airmail but airmail stickers and extra stamps are required for the service outside Europe. The Trafalgar Square Post Office is open Monday to Saturday 08.00-20.00, Sunday and Bank Holidays 10.00-17.00. (There are stamp machines outside most post offices.)

Telephones. Britain's telephone system has been denationalised and is now operated by a public company, British Telecom. But telephoning in Britain still remains a very costly activity. There are three scales for charges: Monday to Friday 09.00-13.00 (very expensive); Monday to Friday 08.00-09.00 and 13.00-18.00 (expensive); all other times including the weekend (less expensive). Overseas calls are not subject to these time bands. Charges vary with time and distance, and calls made in hotels (other than from a public telephone booth) are charged at a higher rate which includes the hotel's costs in providing the service. It is possible to direct dial from London to most places in the world; consult the telephone directory or dial 100 for the Operator. Telephone booths in the traditional red are being replaced with more functional boxes and new telephones have been introduced which take coupons rather than coins. Coupons can be bought at bookstalls. Carry 10p and 50p for local calls. British Telecom operates an International Telephone Bureau, 1a Broadway, London SW1 (Underground, St. James's Park). For emergency calls, fire, police, and ambulance dial 999. In this book London telephone numbers have been shown with the prefix 01—this is to be used when telephoning from outside London only.

Public Lavatories. London has a better range of public lavatories than most European cities and they are usually well-signposted. Unfortunately cutbacks in public spending mean that their opening hours do not always suit demand. The introduction of coin-in-the-slot French-style public lavatories such as the one in Leicester Square, in Soho and in Victoria Street, may serve a purpose but do not add much beauty to the general environment. Stores, railway stations, restaurants, even some pubs, and good class hotels have excellent lavatory facilities.

Facilities for Disabled Visitors. Some London hotels have bedrooms generally suitable, or adapted for disabled guests. A list is available from the London Visitor and Convention Bureau. In some cases these same hotels will also have suitable public lavatory facilities, which make them a good choice for dinner or meetings when disabled access is required. The Berners Hotel, Berner Street, London W1, and the London Tara, Scarsdale Place, London W9 are particularly recommended.

British Rail is improving facilities at stations for disabled travellers with dropped kerbs, toilet facilities and assistance if required. Both Heathrow and Gatwick Airports are well geared to the requirements of the disabled traveller and produce advance information (see p 44 for addresses). Tourist attractions, restaurants, and pubs vary in their accessibility, but most museums and galleries are accessible. Some theatres have induction loops and access for wheelchairs. More information from 'Access in London', published by Nicholson, and up-to-date advice from Artsline on 01-625 5666/7.

Medical Services. Visitors to Britain are able to use the accident and emergency services of the National Health Service free of charge. In Central London casualty clinics can be found at the Middlesex Hospital, Mortimer Street, London W1, St. Thomas's Hospital, Lambeth Palace Rd, SE1, Westminster Hospital, Horseferry Rd, SW1. Boots The Chemist at Piccadilly Circus is open Mon to Fri 08.30–20.00, Sat 09.00–20.00. Bliss, 5 Marble Arch, W1 is open 09.00-24.00 every day, and John Bell and Croyden, 50 Wigmore Street, W1 is open Mon-Fri 09.00-19.00, Sat 09.00-13.00.

The National Health Service charges for non-emergency treatment of visitors to Britain unless there is a reciprocal arrangement with the country of origin. Countries which have reciprocal arrangements are EEC Countries, most other W European countries, Hong Kong, New Zealand, and the USSR.

Visitors not from these countries (e.g. USA, Canada and Australia) are recommended to take out health insurance before travelling to Britain. Private medicine is provided by a growing number of clinics and hospitals. Information from the BTA/LVCB.

People. London's population has fallen below 7m, but as many more live in the surrounding area but work within Greater London the numbers swell considerably during the week. Immigration mainly from Commonwealth countries since the Second World War (now severely curtailed) has produced a great cultural mix reflected in changes in some parts of London, the ethnic mix of restaurants, fashion and the music scene. Visitors will find people of many different national origins working in London's service industries, and a growing proportion of particularly smaller hotels owned by Asian families and companies.

Comments and Complaints. The British Tourist Authority and the London Visitor and Convention Bureau will deal with comments and complaints, in writing.

IX Chronology

AD 43	Growth of London began when invading Romans crossed the Thames close to the site of the later London Bridge. Population approx. 30,000.
60	London was severely damaged in conflict between the forces of Queen Boadicea and the occupying Romans.
200	London became a walled city in which trade flourished. Population approx. 45,000-50,000.
410	London reverted to a farming community following Roman withdrawal from Britain.
604	Thames became main artery for trade with the port of London.
836	London invaded by Vikings.
871	During the reign of Alfred the Great the office of alderman was created, in recognition of the growing dependence of the Crown on city wealth.
1014	London continued to be coveted by warring Saxon factions and was stormed for the last time by Olaf.
1052	Edward the Confessor removed his court to Thorney Island, W of the cify, having been refused monetary support. Westminster Abbey was built on this site, once a Benedictine Abbey.
1066	Norman Conquest. City beseiged. William I crowned. Charter established office of sheriff. Population approx. 14,000-18,000.
1087	William II crowned.
1097	White Tower of London completed as defensive bastion. Westminster Hall built by William II as part of the medieval palace of Westminster.
1100-1140	Henry I crowned. In return for supporting the Crown, city was allowed to raise its own taxes and elect its own governors.
1123	Saint Bartholomew's hospital built.
1135	Stephen, Count of Blois, crowned.
1154	House of Plantagenet began as Henry II was crowned.
1189	Jews banned from coronation of Richard Coeur de Lion were attacked. Population approx. 20,000-25,000.
1191	Henry FitzElywin elected first Mayor of London.
1199	King John crowned.
1215	King John as a reward for financial support recognised the authority of Lord Mayor and agreed to the election of 24 aldermen. City not satisfied and helped rebellious barons draft the Magna Carta.
1216	Henry III crowned.
1217	London Bridge rebuilt in stone and remained London's only bridge until the 18C.
1224	Westminster Hall became the chief law court of England.
1225	St. Thomas's Hospital established in Southwark.
1263	Trade guilds exercised their increasing power by wresting control of city from aldermen.
1269	New Westminster Abbey consecrated following dispute with city.
1272	Edward I crowned.

Westminster and Southwark, from Hollar's Long View (1647)

1280	Old St. Paul's Cathedral completed and displaced many inhabitants of the city.
1290	Jews expelled from England.
1301	Temple Bar gateway built to prevent sovereign from freely entering the city without Lord Mayor's permission.
1304	Recorder was elected by governors of city as spokesman. Buildings surrounding St. Paul's grew.
1307	Edward II crowned.
1326	Riots against the King result from city squalor.
1327	Edward III crowned.
1338	King made Palace of Westminster the regular meeting place of Parliament.
1348	Black Death halved the city's population to 30,000.
1377	Richard II crowned.
1381	Peasants' Revolt. Wat Tyler led army of labouring people to end feudalism and occupied London for two days. Tyler was killed by Mayor.
1394	Westminster Hall rebuilding began.
1399	City and Parliament combined to depose the autocratic Richard II. House of Lancaster began as Henry IV was crowned.
1400-1500	The increasing wealth of professional soldiers and merchants began to undermine feudalism.
1411	Construction of Guildhall in the city began.
1413	Henry V crowned.
1422	Henry VI crowned.
1430	Jack Cade led Kentishmen in protest against financial oppression and incompetence of King. Occupied London for three days.
1456	Riots against aliens.
1461	House of York took power under Edward IV, victor of the War of Roses. In return for city's support many London citizens were knighted.
1483	Child King Edward V crowned and then replaced by Richard III.
1485	Tudor period began with crowning of Henry VII.
1499	Perkin Warbeck, Pretender to the throne, hanged at Tyburn.
1500-1600	London commerce increased substantially. Financial expertise and flourishing market established London as a major trading port with the Continent.
1509	Henry VIII crowned.
1510	St. Paul's School opened to provide secondary education in the city.
1533	Closure of monasteries during the Reformation increased land available for building. Wealthy merchant families became the new gentry.
1553-1558	Period of instability under the fiercely Roman Catholic Queen Mary. Executions took place at Smithfield in the city.
1558	Queen Elizabeth I crowned.
1562	Queen forbade any new building within three miles of the city, in response to the growth of slums.
1599	Globe Theatre built by Burbage on Bankside in Southwark.

1600	New landed families began to construct mansions on estates extending into the 'West End' and beyond.
1603	City began to resent the autocratic style of the Stuart King, James I, which did not improve with the accession of Charles I.
1605	Gunpowder plot to blow up Parliament and the royal family discovered.
1613	Globe Theatre burnt down.
1625	Charles I crowned.
1630	First square in London built at Covent Garden.
1637	Hyde Park became the first public park.
1642	Civil War began. City financed Parliament. Fortifications built and manned by citizens.
1649	Charles I beheaded in Whitehall and Commonwealth declared by Oliver Cromwell. Puritanism dominated social and political life.
1650	Population approx. 350,000-400,000.
1652	First Coffee House opened in St. Michael's Alley, Cornhill, and became centre for financial transactions.
1656	Jewish families re-entered London.
1660	Reaction against the constraints of fanatical religious egalitarianism lead London to support the return of Charles II. The Royal Society was founded.
1663	Theatre opened in Drury Lane. 'King's Performers' were the only company allowed in London.
1665	The Great Plague killed up to 100,000 and caused a major exodus of wealthy families to outlying districts.
1666	The Great Fire began in Pudding Lane and destroyed the medieval City of London.
1667	Act to allow rebuilding stipulated that stone should be used. City appointed commissioners to be responsible for sewers.
1675	Christopher Wren began construction of new St. Paul's Cathedral. Royal Greenwich Observatory built to mark meridian, celebrating Britain's supremacy in navigation.
1685	Religious intolerance forced French Protestants to seek refuge in England, many settling in London. James II crowned.
1689	William and Mary crowned.
1692	Chelsea Hospital, designed by Wren, was completed.
1694	Royal Charter established Bank of England to pay for war with France.
1696	Howland Great Wet Dock constructed, first wet dock in England, became Greenland Dock, on South Bank.
1700-1750	Wren's plans for developing London as the 'Venice of the North' defeated by complex ownership of land. Skyline of City, however, profoundly altered by the spires of 51 churches designed by him. Villages to the W of London engulfed by spread of building. Poorer neighbourhoods to the S and E notorious for high gin consumption. Population approx. 600,000.
1702	Queen Anne crowned.
1711	Academy of Art opened.
1712	Handel settled in London.
1714	House of Hanover began as George I was crowned.

1720-	Many major London hospitals built; Guy's, London, St.
1760	George's, Westminster and Middlesex.
1727	George II crowned.
1732	Covent Garden Theatre opened.
1733	City commissioners no longer prepared to dredge Fleet River, so it was arched over.
1739	London's second bridge constructed at Westminster.
1743	Riots against Act to control the sale of gin.
1749	Bow Street Runners set up to prevent crime around the vicinity of legal centre of London.
1750	Population approx. 650,000.
1759	British Museum opened.
1760	George III crowned. Battersea Bridge built.
1770	First canal in London completed from River Lea to Thames.
1774	Act created an embryonic office of district surveyor. Radical Whig reformer, John Wilkes, was elected as Mayor for the self-governing City.
1780	Gordon Riots. 850 lost their lives in protest against the repeal of anti-Catholic legislation.
1785	'The Times' newspaper began, formerly known as 'Daily Universal Register'.
1788	Bank of England moved to building designed by John Soane.
1798	Demands for parliamentary reform were suppressed when members of the London Corresponding Society were arrested.
1799	During the next few decades various acts were passed to allow the construction of commercial docks. Traffic on Thames remained in private hands creating considerable confusion and hardship throughout the next century.
1801	First census records 1,117,290, most of whom lived outside the City boundaries. London continued to be a centre for reform agitation. River Police established.
1803	Surrey Canal completed from docks to Peckham, improving local trade.
1810	Riots in support of radical MP Sir Francis Burdett. John Nash began to build terraces along Regent St northwards into London heathlands.
1811	Waterloo and Southwark Bridge designed by John Rennie.
1812	Regents Canal joined the Grand Union to link London with Midland industries.
1818	George IV crowned. London still without effective local government. Act established system for voting-in parish officers.
1820	Plot to assassinate Cabinet uncovered, Cato Street conspiracy. Earth removed from new docks helped to stabilise land around Belgravia.
1822	Lambeth Bridge built.
1825	Buckingham House altered by Nash and became residence of sovereign. London Bridge rebuilt to Rennie design.
1827	Hammersmith Bridge built, an early example on the suspension principle.
1829	Metropolitan Police force established. Area of operation did not include City. First regular horse-drawn bus service

began along Marylebone Road. Construction of Trafalgar Square began.

1830 William IV crowned.

1831 Reform Riots in London. During the next 40 years Sir Thomas Wilson tried to enclose Hampstead Heath. Opposition to his schemes was based on free public access for urban families.

1832 Construction of National Gallery began.

1833 Police called to disperse reform protestors in Clerkenwell. First railway sanctioned by Parliament to run between London Bridge and Greenwich.

1834 Palace of Westminster destroyed by fire.

1835 London was exempted from Municipal Reform Act so many pressing public health problems could not be dealt with effectively. Cholera and destitution increased. City established its own police force.

1836 First railway opened between Deptford and Bermondsey. University of London established.

1837 Queen Victoria crowned. Geological Museum opened in Kensington. London Bridge Station opened.

1838 Euston Station opened.

1840 Sir Charles Barry designed new Houses of Parliament in Gothic style. First station in City opened at Fenchurch St.

1841 Younger Brunel designed Hungerford Bridge.

1843 First tunnel under the Thames from Rotherhithe to Wapping.

1844 Width of streets in the entire metropolis controlled by new act.

1848 Women students admitted to University of London.

1849 'Morning Chronicle' published Mayhew's systematic survey 'London Labour and the London Poor'. Cholera killed 14,000. Harrods opened as a small grocery store.

1850 Brunel designed Paddington Station and asked Wyatt to design decoration.

1851 Great Exhibition held in the Crystal Palace, Hyde Park.

1852 Victoria and Albert Museum began in Marlborough House. King's Cross Station opened, designed in avant-garde style by Lewis Cubbitt.

1854 Great Western Hotel built at Paddington.

1855 Board of Works set up for London under new act. Disreputable Bartholomew Fair closed.

1858 The Great Stink, outside the Houses of Parliament, resulted in a bill for creation of a sewerage system for London. During the next 15 years many public health acts undertaken. Chelsea Bridge built.

1859 Vauxhall Gardens, once elegant pleasure gardens, closed.

1860- Many refugees from Eastern Europe entered London.

1880 They tended to settle E of City; Aldgate, Whitechapel and Spitalfields.

1860 Grosvenor Bridge, first railway bridge across Thames.

1863 First underground railway opened, Metropolitan Line.

1865	Blackfriars Bridge, designed by J. Cubbitt, opened on 18C site. St. Pancras, Charing Cross and Broad St stations opened. St. Thomas's Hospital moved to Lambeth.
1866	Riots developed when police tried to break up Reform League meeting in Hyde Park. The setting-up of Speaker's Corner resulted; Hyde Park has remained one of the most popular sites for large demonstrations to the present day.
1867	Clerkenwell Prison was bombed in an attempt to free Fenians (Irish Radicals).
1868	Gothic-style hotel built at St. Pancras.
1870	First tramcar service ran from Brixton to Kennington and Whitechapel to Bow.
1871	Hampstead Heath saved for the public.
1872	Bethnal Green Museum, part of V & A collection, opened.
1873	Albert Bridge built. Natural History Museum at South Kensington opened.
1874	Liverpool Street Station opened.
1880	Norman Shaw designed Bedford Park, Chiswick which became the forerunner of the garden city.
1884	Toynbee Hall opened in the East End as the first 'university settlement'.
1886	Tower Bridge opened.
1887	Black Sunday. Social Democratic Federation meeting in Trafalgar Square broken up by police, causing casualties.
1888	Series of murders in Whitechapel associated with 'Jack the Ripper'. New Unionism began with strike of badly paid women matchmakers.
1889	First London dock strike to protest at falling wages managed to unite a traditionally competitive workforce. Major act established strong local government for London, the London County Council.
1890	Battersea Bridge rebuilt.
1893	Tate Gallery construction began on site of the old Millbank Prison.
1894	First Lyons tea shop opened in Piccadilly.
1897	Queen Victoria celebrated her Silver Jubilee as prosperity of London continued.
1899	Marylebone Station opened amidst controversy and local opposition.
1901	House of Saxe-Coburg began as Edward VII was crowned. Population of London: Inner London 4,536,267, Greater London 6,506,889 and the City only 37,709.
1903	Water supply for London controlled by new Metropolitan Water Board.
1909	Port of London Authority took over running of docks.
1910	Privately-owned powered motor vehicles began to challenge horse-drawn public transport. House of Windsor began as George V was crowned.
1911	Second London dock strike against insecurity of employment. Seige of Sidney St followed an unsuccessful robbery by Eastern European anarchists.
1912	New Waterloo Station construction began.
1914	Women operated many services in London during First World War.
1915	First Lyons Corner House opened on the Strand.

1920- **1940**	Clearance of slums allowed Modernist style estates to be built. Peckham Health Centre built as model for treatment of deprived inner-city children.
1928	Science Museum opened.
1932	Green Belt established around London to control spread of suburbs.
1933	London Transport created.
1936	British Broadcasting Corporation began television broadcasting from Alexandra Palace, N London. Battle of Cable St: East Enders and anti-fascists prevented march of Oswald Moseley's Black Shirts through mainly Jewish districts. Edward VIII abdicated 325 days after his coronation. George VI was crowned.
1939	Population of Greater London reached its peak at 8,615,050.
1940	City and East End severely damaged by bombs during the Blitz. Docks were targets for air raids.
1945	A mixture of private and public funds set a side for rebuilding of London.
1947	Legislation to protect buildings of historic and architectural importance began.
1951	Festival of Britain helps to revive the nation during post-war austerity. Battersea Park opens a funfair, a 'Dome of Discovery and Skylon Obelisk' were constructed on the South Bank and the Royal Festival Hall opened.
1952	Queen Elizabeth II was crowned.
1954	Temple of Mithras discovered as the City was rebuilt.
1956	'Pea soup' fogs of London finished after the Clean Air Act was passed.
1958	Race Riots in Notting Hill.
1960- **1968**	London becomes known as the 'Swinging City', as music and fashion develop.
1963	New Euston Station was built, destroying Victorian entrance arch.
1965	Greater London Council formed as strategic planning authority.
1967	Conservation areas identified and given statutory protection, over 300 have been established in London. East India Dock was closed in response to declining traffic and economic pressure. Old London Bridge sold and rebuilt in Arizona.
1968	Anti-Vietnam war demonstrations escalate into confrontation with police in Grosvenor Square. Ronan Point, tower block damaged by gas explosion.
1969	Greater London Development Plan proposed housing, open space and major road works in and through London.
1974	Covent Garden market moved to Nine Elms, South London. Existing buildings saved for redevelopment.
1976	Museum of London opened. National Theatre company moved from the Old Vic to new South Bank complex.
1980- **1985**	Restored Covent Garden Market reopens as shopping and entertainment centre. London Docklands Development Corporation created by government to co-ordinate use of derelict docks.
1980	Listed Firestone Building demolished.
1981	Brixton Riots. Chelsea Barracks IRA bomb.

1982	Billingsgate market moved to West India Dock. Barbican Centre opened. Thames Barrier completed to prevent flooding of London. Hyde Park bandstand IRA bomb.
1983	Population of London falls to 6,754,500. Harrods IRA bomb.
1984	Parliament announces plans to control local government spending.
1985	London Regional Transport set up without GLC control. Parliament approves legislation to abolish GLC by 1986.

X Outer London Touring Tips

Most Londoners know more about the attractions of the city centre than about those of their own area; good sources of information, apart from tourist information centres, are local libraries. These have information on local sights and facilities, and collections of literature compiled by historical and architectural societies.

Travelling between suburbs without a car can be difficult; rail and bus routes are designed largely to carry traffic into and out of London. Bus services between suburbs tend to be unreliable, where they exist at all.

Some suburban shopping centres retain early closing on one weekday (usually Wednesday or Thursday), but most purpose-built shopping centres and multiple stores are now open six full days a week. Sunday opening is less common in the suburbs than in Central London.

Due to vandalism, many churches are kept locked except when services are being held. Sometimes a sign on the door will indicate where a key-holder can be reached, or when the church is open; otherwise ask at the local library.

There are many good restaurants in Outer London—consult a reliable restaurant guide. When in doubt look for a comfortable pub or winebar. Hamburger and pizza restaurants, including international chains, can be found in almost every High Street.

London High Streets are very similar stylistically—mainly Victorian or Edwardian, and with an overlay of multiple stores and shops with exactly the same frontage whether they are in Wembley or Bromley. To appreciate the quality and character of these buildings look up at the first and second storeys where original architectural details have usually been retained.

Modern development has introduced concrete, wind-swept shopping plazas in many suburbs; except where they are very comfortable and attractive, as at Brent Cross or Ealing Broadway, shoppers seem still to prefer the traffic fumes of the local High Street.

In residential areas, sudden gaps in rows of terraced Victorian houses filled with unattractive '50s blocks are usually the result of Second World War bombing. They are common in SE and E London, and much of Docklands. These areas were extensively damaged by bombing and a rash of new housing spread as the opportunity to carry out extensive slum-clearance was taken. Some of the high-rise housing put up in the process has quickly turned to slums and boroughs such as Newham now plan to demolish tower blocks of flats.

I THE WEST AND NORTH WEST

The **West End** means different things to different people but broadly includes the areas of Mayfair, Westminster, Belgravia, Soho and Covent Garden; to some it means all the fashionable shopping areas including Knightsbridge and Kensington High Street and to others, mainly theatre and restaurant land—the area around Picadilly Circus and Leicester Square.

1 Westminster

Access: Underground, Westminster, St. James's Park.

The **City of Westminster** is the London borough covering most of the West End from its boundary with the City of London in the East, marked by heraldic dragons, to Knightsbridge and Chelsea in the West; northwards it stretches as far as Marylebone. Westminster itself refers to the political heart of London—the area around the Houses of Parliament and Whitehall. Parliament Square was created in 1926 as the first 'roundabout' in London. Whitehall and Trafalgar Square are to the N and to the SE are the dignified buildings of the *Houses of Parliament* with *Westminster Hall* in front of them. Due S are the towers of *Westminster Abbey*, beyond the picturesque *St. Margaret's Church*. The *Middlesex Crown Court* (formerly Middlesex Guildhall) and the *Royal Institute of Chartered Surveyors*, both dating from the beginning of this century, are on the W side, and on the N side along Parliament St is the flank of the huge *Government Offices Building*; just outside is a free-standing map-guide identifying the buildings of the square—part of the Silver Jubilee Walkway.

Round the lawn in the centre of the square are statues of eminent statesmen: *Field-Marshal Smuts* (1870-1950), by Epstein, *Lord Palmerston* (1784-1865), by Thos. Woolner *Lord Derby* (1799-1869), by Matthew Noble, *Disraeli* (1804-81), by Mario Raggi, and *Sir Robert Peel* (1788-1850), by Noble. In front of the Middlesex Court stands *Abraham Lincoln* (1809-65), a replica of the statue by Saint-Gaudens at Chicago, and *George Canning* (1770-1827), by Sir Richard Westmacott. Disraeli's statue is annually decorated with primroses, said to have been his favourite flower, on 19 April ('Primrose Day'; the anniversary of his death in 1881). The NE corner is occupied by Ivor Roberts-Jones' bronze of *Churchill*.

St. Margaret's Church, dating from 1485-1523, has been repeatedly altered and restored. Founded before 1189 as the parish church of Westminster, it is also (since 1621) the 'national church for the use of the House of Commons'. It is a fashionable church for weddings; Samuel Pepys was married here in 1655, Milton (for the second time) in 1656, and Winston Churchill in 1908. Sir Walter Raleigh, who was executed in 1618 in front of the Palace of Westminster, is buried in the chancel; and in the church or churchyard rest also William Caxton (1422-?91) and Wenceslaus Hollar (1607-77), the Bohemian etcher who depicted London before the Great Fire. The peaceful interior is adorned with unobtrusive Elizabethan and Jacobean wall monuments

*Westminster from the air: the Houses of Parliament by the
Thames in the centre; the three high rise blocks in the
foreground are the Departments of Transport and
Environment offices at Marsham St, SW1*

The font, in the S aisle, is by Nicholas Stone (1641). At the E end of
the S aisle is the notable tomb of Lady Dudley (d 1600), and on the
E wall, memorials to Caxton and Raleigh. Over the W door is a large
window dedicated by Americans to the memory of Raleigh (inscription
by J.R. Lowell); while that at the W end of the N aisle, with an
inscription by Whittier, commemorates Milton. The richly coloured

*The statue of Churchill in Parliament Square (Ivor
Roberts-Jones, 1973)*

*East Window, made in Holland before 1509, celebrates the betrothal (1501) of Catherine of Aragon to Prince Arthur, Henry VII's eldest son. It was bought for St. Margaret's in 1758. On the external E wall is a leaden bust of Charles I (c 1800). A blue sundial was added to the N face of the tower in 1982.

Opposite St. Margaret's in front of the Houses of Parliament is **Westminster Hall** with, outside it, a statue of Oliver Cromwell by Sir Hamo Thornycroft (1889). To the S opens OLD PALACE YARD (outside the House of Lords) where an admirable bronze equestrian statue of Richard I by Marochetti (1860) stands.

Facing the Lords, beyond a pathway anciently connecting the Abbey with the Palace of Westminster, stands a memorial to *George V*, by Sir W. Reid Dick and Sir Giles Scott (1947), backed by fine plane-trees and the chapter house. Immediately behind the attractive early-19C mansion flanking it is the low, moated **Jewel Tower** (1366), a survival of the medieval Palace of Westminster (open weekdays, 09.30-18.30 (summer) 09.30-16.00 (winter). Admission free). Built by Edward III as a royal treasure-house, it served from 1621-1864 as the Record Office of the Lords, and thereafter until 1938 as an assay office of weights and measures. It retains fine original bosses in the vaulting. The three storeys house capitals (c 1090) from Westminster Hall, finds from the moat (Saxon sword), and medieval carvings from Whitehall Palace.

The ragstone wall of 1374 (10ft high) surrounds the Abbey precincts; cross Abingdon Street Gardens (underground car park) past 'Knife Edge', a sculpture by Henry Moore (1967) and turn right into Great College Street.

To the S are quiet Georgian streets. *Barton Street* (where at No. 14 lived T.E. Lawrence) and its continuation Cowley St lead to Great Peter St, whence Lord North St goes on to *Smith Square* (1726; plaque on No. 5). Here are the headquarters of the Conservative Party (Central Office) and the former Labour Party base, Transport House (now in Walworth Road). The eccentric shape of the Baroque church of *St. John the Evangelist*, completed in 1728 by Thomas Archer, was likened by Dickens to 'a petrified monster on its back with its legs in the air'. The four angle towers are said to have been designed to ensure that the swampy foundations settled uniformly. Restored after bomb damage, it is used for concerts and lectures as St. John's, Smith Square.

Millbank follows the Thames S to the Tate Gallery (Rte 12). Fine views of the river may be had from the flanking *Victoria Tower Gardens*. Here are a bronze replica (1915) of a *Group by Rodin (erected at Calais in 1895), representing the devoted *Burghers of Calais*, who surrendered themselves to Edward III in 1340 to save their city from destruction, and memorials to *Mrs Emmeline Pankhurst* (1858-1928) and her daughter *Dame Christabel Pankhurst* (1881-1958), leaders of the women's suffrage movement.

At the end of Great College St an archway (right) leads into DEAN'S YARD, once a portion of the Abbey Gardens. On the E side are entrances to the cloisters of the Abbey and to **Westminster School**, or *St. Peter's College*, the ancient monastic school, referred to as early as 1339, refounded by Queen Elizabeth in 1560, and now one of the great public schools. The school is built round *Little Dean's Yard*, on the site of the monks' quarters, relics of which remain. Visitors are admitted on written application to the bursar. The College

Hall, with a fine hammerbeam roof, dates from the time of Edward III and was formerly the abbey refectory. The Great School Room was the monks' dormitory. *Ashburnham House* is the Library but can be visited.

Ashburnham House, Dean's Yard, SW1 (01-222 3116) is open during Easter school holidays (not Good Friday and Easter Monday) Monday to Friday 10.00-16.00. Admission charge. Access: Underground, Westminster, St. James's Park.

The red brick house dates from 1400 but was rebuilt in 1660, probably to a design by John Webb. Once the home of the Earls of Ashburnham it is now used by Westminster School. The unusual and impressive staircase (c 1665) is arranged around a spacious well; there are good ceilings and carved doorcases, portraits of Elizabeth I and former headmasters.

Westminster School now educates over 400 boys, and some girls. They enjoy certain privileges in connection with the Abbey, and shout the 'Vivats' at coronations. They attend a daily service there. On Shrove Tuesday 'tossing the pancake' takes place in the Great School Room, the boy securing the largest fragment being rewarded with a guinea. In the long list of famous pupils are the names of Ben Jonson, George Herbert, Dryden, Locke, Wren, Cowper, Charles Wesley, Lord Mansfield, Warren Hastings, Gibbon, Southey, Lord Raglan, G.A. Henty, A.A. Milne, and Sir Henry Tizard.

On the S side of Dean's Yard is *Church House*, by Sir Herbert Baker (1937-40), the headquarters of the Canterbury Houses of Convocation, the House of Laity, the National Assembly of the Church of England, and over 50 Church societies. In 1940-44 it was used on several occasions as a meeting-place for Parliament. Later, it housed the Preparatory Commission of the United Nations, and the first sessions of the Security Council were also held here. The Assembly Hall, with its fine timber roof, and the Hoare Memorial Hall are sometimes open to visitors. On the W side is the *Abbey Choir School*, whose boys share the central green with Westminster School.

A passage at the opposite corner of Dean's Yard leads to BROAD SANCTUARY in front of Westminster Abbey. The name recalls the sanctuary to the N and W of the Abbey in which refugees were protected from the civil power by the church; a privilege abolished by James I. The Westminster Column, a Gothic memorial of red granite by Sir Gilbert Scott (1861), was erected in memory of Old Westminster boys who fell in the Crimean War and the Indian Mutiny. This is the Westminster Abbey setting-down point for coach tours of the West End. Opposite is the new *Government Conference Centre*, due to open in 1986, with facilities for high-level international 'secure' meetings and also available for commercial use.

At the corner of Tothill Street rises the large domed *Central Hall* (open to visitors when not in use), built in 1912 as the headquarters of the Methodist Church and also used for concerts and public meetings. In January 1946 it became the first home of the General Assembly of the United Nations. Despite French Renaissance trappings it has a steel frame and is one of the earliest examples of this method of construction in London.

The *Imperial Collection of Crown Jewels* opened in rooms at the rear of Central Hall in 1980; entrance from Mathew Park St, SW1. Open April to Oct 10.00-18.00, Nov to March 11.00-17.00. Admission charge.

2   Westminster Abbey

Westminster Abbey, Broad Sanctuary, London SW1. Tel. 01-222 7110. Admission: the nave, aisles and precinct daily 08.00-18.00 (Wed until 20.00). Admission free.

The ambulatory, transepts and chapels Mon to Fri 09.00-16.45, Saturday 09.00-14.45, 15.45-17.45 Admission charge (Wed 18.00-20.00 admission free). Super Tours (1.5 hours) Mon to Fri 09.45, 10.15, 11.00, 14.15, 14.45, 15.30. Sat 10.00, 10.45, 12.30. Admission charge (book at desk in South Aisle—includes Jericho Parlour and Jerusalem Chamber not otherwise accessible). The Abbey is closed or with restricted entry during special services. Regular services are held.

Access: Underground, Westminster, St. James's Park.

Special services are held in the Abbey on the opening of the Law Courts in October, when judges in their robes walk in procession from the House of Lords, and every fourth year on Maundy Thursday, when the Royal Maundy money is distributed to as many poor persons as there are years in the sovereign's age. (The figures in italics after monuments refer to the plan on p 69.)

**Westminster Abbey (Pl. 18; 2), more officially the *Collegiate Church of St. Peter in Westminster*, holds a unique position in English history as both the crowning-place and the burial-place of most English sovereigns. Though built at different periods, it is, with the exception of Henry VII's magnificent Perpendicular chapel at the E end and the 18C W towers, in the Early English style, of which it constitutes one of the most beautiful and best preserved examples. Cleaning is revealing the details of external carvings and decorations.

According to tradition a church built on *Thorney Isle*, or Isle of Thorns, by Sebert, king of the East Saxons, was consecrated by Mellitus, first bishop of London in 616, but there is no authentic record of any earlier church than that of the Benedictine Abbey, founded here probably between 730 and 740, which was dedicated to St. Peter and received the name 'West Minster', or western monastery, probably from its position to the W of the city of London. Edward the Confessor (d 1066; canonised 1163) rebuilt the abbey on a larger scale, and in his Norman church, consecrated in 1065, the body of the sainted builder was placed in 1163. Within this church, or its successor, every English sovereign since Harold (except Edward V and Edward VIII) has been crowned. In 1220 a Lady Chapel was added at the E end, and in 1245 Henry III decided to honour St. Edward by rebuilding the entire church in a more magnificent style, as we now see it. The architects were Henry de Reyns (1245-53), John of Gloucester (1253-60), and Robert of Beverley (1260-84). The influence of French cathedrals such as Rheims and Amiens and of the Sainte Chapelle can be seen in the height of the nave, and the arrangement of the radiating chapels around the apse. In 1269 the new church was consecrated. From this time until the reign of George III the Abbey became the royal burial-church. About 1388 Henry Yevele began to rebuild the nave for Abp Langham, and the work was continued after 1400 by William of Colchester; the design of Henry III's time was followed with even the details little changed. The nave-vault was completed by Abbot Islip in 1504-06. The new nave was hardly finished when the Lady Chapel was pulled down to make way for the magnificent Chapel of Henry VII (1503-19), attributed to Robert Vertue.

The lower part of the W facade dates from c 1390, but was altered by Hawksmoor; the towers (225ft high) were added by the same architect about 1739. The whole of the exterior was restored by Wren and Wyatt in 1697-1720. In 1875-84 the facade of the N transept was entirely remodelled by Sir Gilbert Scott and J.L. Pearson. The light and delicately shaped walls of Henry VII's Chapel remain the most pleasing part of the solemn heavily-buttressed exterior.

Elizabeth I made the church a 'Royal peculiar' under an independent Dean

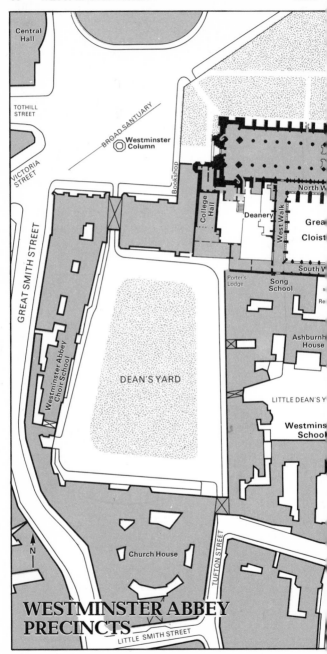

Central
Hall

TOTHILL
STREET

BROAD SANCTUARY

Westminster
Column

VICTORIA
STREET

Bookshop

College
Hall

Deanery

North W

West Walk

Grea
Cloist

South V

GREAT SMITH STREET

Porter's
Lodge

Song
School

s

Re

Westminster Abbey
Choir School

Ashburnh
House

DEAN'S YARD

LITTLE DEAN'S Y

Westmins
School

N

Church House

TUFTON STREET

WESTMINSTER ABBEY
PRECINCTS

LITTLE SMITH STREET

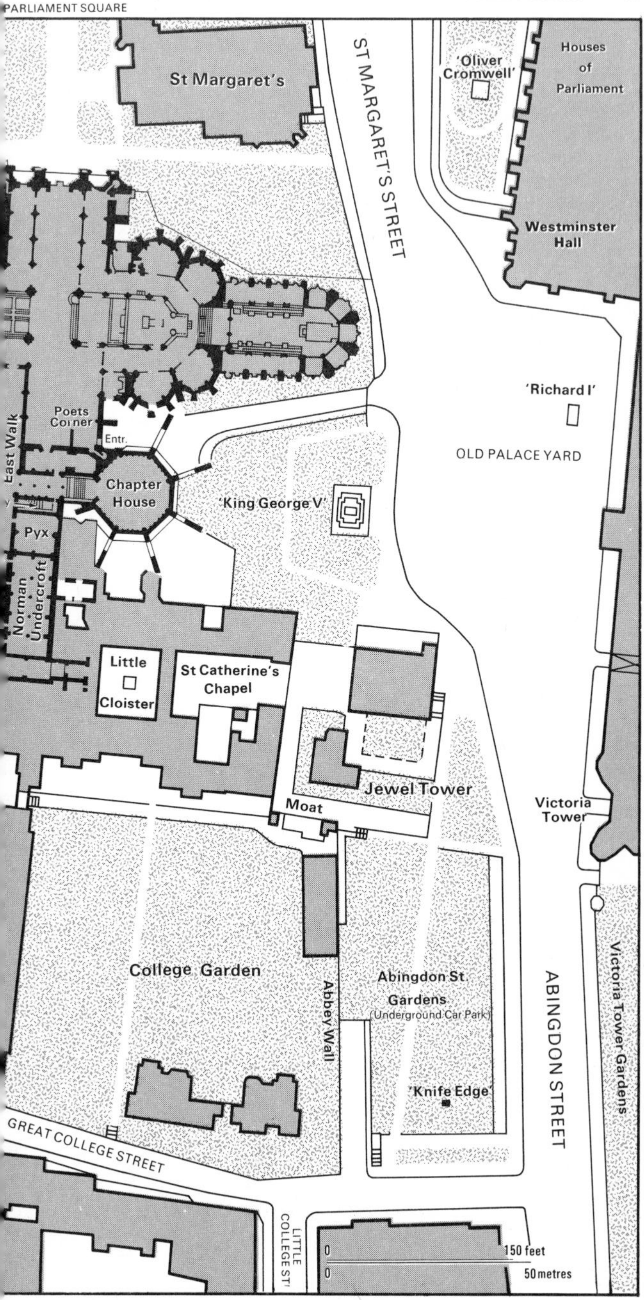
PARLIAMENT SQUARE
St Margaret's
ST MARGARET'S STREET
'Oliver Cromwell'
Houses of Parliament
Westminster Hall
'Richard I'
OLD PALACE YARD
Poets Corner
Entr.
East Walk
Chapter House
'King George V'
Pyx
Norman Undercroft
Little Cloister
St Catherine's Chapel
Jewel Tower
Moat
Victoria Tower
College Garden
Abbey Wall
Abingdon St Gardens
(Underground Car Park)
ABINGDON STREET
Victoria Tower Gardens
'Knife Edge'
GREAT COLLEGE STREET
LITTLE COLLEGE ST
0
150 feet
0
50 metres

and Chapter, whose successors rule it today. The extant monastic buildings date mainly from the 13C and 14C, but there is Norman work in the Chamber of the Pyx and the adjoining Undercroft.

Measurements. The Abbey is 513ft in length, including Henry VII's Chapel, 200ft broad across the transepts, and 75ft broad across the nave and aisles. The Chapel of Henry VII is 104.5ft long and 70ft broad.

Enter by the West Door, and pass below a gilded teak group of Christ between St. Peter and St. Edward the Confessor, by Michael Clark (1967). Visitors should allow the beautiful interior of the church to make its impact, before diverting their attention to the monuments. The architectural and sculptural details can be fully appreciated since the interior cleaning was completed in 1965. The height of the nave is at once striking; separated from the aisles by a tall arcade supported on circular columns round each of which are grouped eight slender shafts of grey Purbeck marble, it is the loftiest Gothic nave in England. Above the arches runs the double triforium with exquisite tracery and diaperwork and still higher, the tall clerestory.

Nave. Burial in the nave took place only after the Reformation. Many monuments throughout the church commemorate men who are not buried in the Abbey. A few paces from the W door in the middle of the nave a slab of green marble (1) is simply inscribed 'Remember Winston Churchill'. It was placed here 'in accordance with the wishes of the Queen and Parliament' on the 25th anniversary of the Battle of Britain. Churchill's body lies at Bladon. Immediately to the E, isolated by poppies, is the tomb of the *Unknown Warrior* (2), brought from Flanders and interred here on 11 Nov 1920, as representative of all the nameless British dead in the First World War, 'the bravely dumb that did their deed and scorned to blot it with a name'. He rests in earth brought from the battlefields. In contrast, a florid monument to *William Pitt* (1759-1806), by Westmacott crowns the W door. On the SW pier hangs a •Portrait of *Richard II* (3), the oldest contemporary portrait of any English monarch. Below is a memorial to the Earl and Countess Mountbatten (1985).

At the foot of the W piers are two fine bronze candelabra by Benno Elkan, representing the Old and the New Testaments (1940). A stone NE of the Unknown Warrior's tomb marks the spot where the remains of *George Peabody* (1795-1869), the American philanthropist, lay for a time before being removed to Massachusetts. The *Earl of Shaftesbury* (1801-85) and *Baroness Burdett Coutts* (1814-1906), likewise benefactors of London, are commemorated nearer the W door.—In the centre of the nave, farther E, are the graves of *David Livingstone* (1813-73; 4), African traveller and missionary, and of *Thomas Tompion* (1639-1713; 5), 'father of English watch-making'.

North Aisle of Nave. Across the front of the NORTH-WEST or BELFRY TOWER (containing ten bells, recast in 1971) is a bronze effigy of *Lord Salisbury* (1803-1903; 6). On the W wall are busts of *General Gordon* (1833-85), the defender of Khartoum, by Onslow Ford, and *Joseph Chamberlain* (1836-1914), by John Tweed. Among the crowded monuments is one (E side) to *Viscount Howe* (1725?-58; 7) by Scheemakers, erected by the Province of Massachusetts while it was a British colony.—Behind it, in the next bay, called by Dean Stanley the 'Whigs' Corner', is a large monument to *Charles James Fox* (1749-1806; 8). Floor-slabs commemorate *Earl Attlee* (1883-1967),

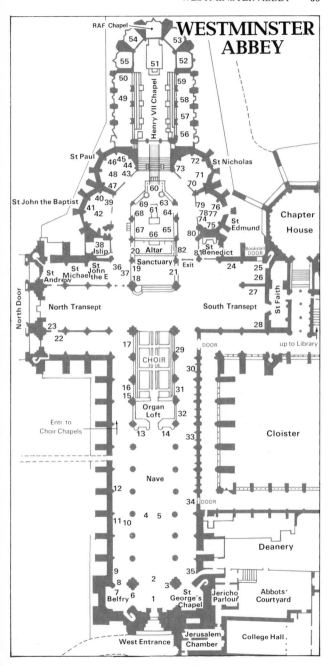

WESTMINSTER ABBEY

RAF Chapel

54 53
55 51 52
50 59
49 58
57
56

Henry VII Chapel

St Paul 46 45 44 73 72 St Nicholas
48 43 71
47 70

St John the Baptist 40 39 79 76
41 42 78 77
74
69 63 75 St Edmund
68 61 64
67 66 65 80
82 St Benedict
38 Islip 20 Altar 81
St 36 37 Sanctuary 19 Exit Bookstall DOOR
St John 18 21 24 25
Andrew Michael the E 26
27

North Door

North Transept South Transept

23 28
22

17 29 DOOR
CHOIR up to Library
30
16 31
15
Organ 32
Loft
13 14 33 Cloister

Entr to
Choir Chapels

Nave

12

34 DOOR

11 10 4 5

Deanery

9
8 2 35
7 6 1 3 St George's Jericho Abbots'
Belfry Chapel Parlour Courtyard

Jerusalem
West Entrance Chamber College Hall

Chapter House

St Faith

Ramsay MacDonald (1866-1937), *Ernest Bevin* (1881-1951), and *Sidney* and *Beatrice Webb* (1859-1947; 1858-1943). On the wall is a monument to *Campbell-Bannerman* (1836-1908; 9).—In the 3rd bay, a small stone in the pavement, inscribed 'O Rare Ben Jonson', marks the grave of the dramatist and poet *Ben Jonson* (1573?-1637; *10*); the original stone may be seen at the foot of the adjoining wall, beneath the monument to *Thomas Banks* (1735-1805; *11*), the sculptor. In the 4th bay is one of the earliest monuments in the nave, of unusual design, to *Mrs Jane Hill* (d 1631). In the 5th bay, at the foot of the window, *Spencer Perceval* (1762-1812; *12*), prime minister, who was shot by a madman in a lobby of the House of Commons; monument with a relief depicting the murder, by Westmacott.—A slab in the 7th bay marks the grave of *Sir John Herschel* (1792-1871); nearby is a memorial to *Sir William Herschel* (1738-1822; buried at Slough), like his son, an astronomer.

The choir screen (1828; re-gilded) is the work of Edward Blore. Set in to the W side are two impressive works by Rysbrack and Kent commemorating *Sir Isaac Newton* (1642-1727; *13*) and *Earl Stanhope* (1673-1721; *14*). Beside Newton's grave is that of *Lord Kelvin* 1824-1907), mathematician and physicist.

South Aisle of Nave. Several of the bays have interesting old coats of arms. To the left, in the 7th bay, *Major John André* (1751-80; *33*), hanged by Washington as a spy during the American War; on the bas-relief Washington receiving André's vain petition for a soldier's death. Floor slabs in front of the next bay (usually covered by stalls) mark the graves of *Andrew Bonar Law* (1858-1923) and *Neville Chamberlain* (1869-1944), prime ministers. The 5th bay has unusual Morland monuments with trilingual inscriptions including Hebrew, Coptic, and Greek.—Above the W cloister door is a dramatic monument by Roubiliac to *Field-Marshal George Wade* (1673-1748; *34*), who provided the Scottish Highlands with roads and bridges in 1720-30. In the last bay is a small gallery of oak called the *Abbot's Pew* (*35*), erected by Abbot Islip (16C), and below, *William Congreve* (1670-1729), the dramatist.

The South-West Tower, or Old Baptistery, is now the CHAPEL OF ST. GEORGE, dedicated to all who gave their lives in the World Wars and containing a tablet to the million British dead. In the wrought-iron screen is the trophy sent by Verdun to the Lord Mayor. Below is a tablet to *Lord Baden-Powell* (1857-1941), founder of the Scout movement. In the floor, slabs mark the graves of *Lord Plumer* (1857-1932) and *Lord Allenby* (1871-1936), and on the S wall is an oak screen in memory of *Henry Fawcett* (1833-84), the blind statesman, and his wife, *Dame Millicent Fawcett* (1847-1929). Outside on the W wall is a plaque in memory of *President Franklin Roosevelt* (1882-1945).

THE NORTH CHOIR AISLE has fine examples of early heraldry on the N wall. A series of medallions under the organ (right) commemorate famous scientists, among them *Charles Darwin* (1809-82; tomb in N nave aisle) and *Lord Lister* (1827-1912). Three matching diamonds in the pavement honour *Elgar, Vaughan Williams*, and *Stanford*. In the next bay *William Wilberforce* (1759-1833; *15*), one of the chief opponents of the slave-trade, and *Sir Stamford Raffles* (1759-1833), founder of Singapore, sit pensive in effigy above the tomb of *Henry Purcell* (1659-95; *16*), composer and organist of the Abbey. Beyond, a bust of *Orlando Gibbons* (1583-1625; buried at

Canterbury) faces the tomb of *John Blow* (d 1708) and a memorial to *Dr Burney* (1726-1814), historian of music. At the entrance to the transept (right), *William Hesketh* (d 1605; *17*), with bright Jacobean decoration.

Sanctuary. The 18C roof of the lantern destroyed by incendiary bombs in May 1941 was replaced soon afterwards. The Sanctuary, or raised space within the altar-rails, where coronations take place, has a venerable pavement of Cosmati work laid by Master Odericus in 1268 (protected by carpets). On the left are the three most beautiful architectural •Tombs in the Abbey, dating from between c 1298 and 1325. The nearest one is that of *Aveline, Countess of Lancaster* (d c 1273; *18*), first wife of Edmund Crouchback. The others commemorate *Aymer de Valence* (d 1324; *19*), and *Edmund Crouchback, Earl of Lancaster* (d 1296; *20*), second son of Henry III and founder of the house of Lancaster. On the canopies of the two later tombs are representations of the deceased on horseback, and all three are adorned with rich painting and gilding (now much faded). The statuettes around Aymer de Valence's tomb are among the most exquisite small sculptures in England (better seen from ambulatory; see below).—On the right side of the Sanctuary are sedilia dating from the time of Edward I, with paintings (1308) of Sebert, St. Peter and Ethelbert, and an ancient tapestry from Westminster School. On this is hung a Florentine triptych, by Bicci di Lorenzo (1373-1452), of the Madonna between SS. John Gualberto and Anthony of Padua (right) and SS. John the Baptist and Catherine of Alexandria; it was given to the Abbey in 1948 by Lord Lee of Fareham. Below is the tomb of *Anne of Cleves* (d 1557; *21*), fourth wife of Henry VIII. The 17C pulpit, replaced in 1935, is matched by a lectern (1949) in memory of William Carey (1761-1834), the missionary. The choir fittings were designed by Ed. Blore in 1830.

Transepts. The uniformity and proportions of the architecture have been upset by the host of monuments. In the N transept the E aisle is partially closed off, while in the S transept the E walk of the cloister accounts for the W aisle. Each transept is lit by a large rose-window (the glass in the N transept is the oldest in the Abbey, dating from 1721-22), below which are exquisitely carved censing angels, sculpted by Master John of St. Alban's c 1250; the S transept retains also two figures below the window.

The North Transept is the burial-place of several eminent statesmen. In the W aisle is a delicately carved monument to *Jonas Hanway* (1722-86; *22*), the philanthropist, and busts of *Richard Cobden* (1804-65; buried at West Lavington), the apostle of free trade, and of *Warren Hastings* (1732-1818; buried at Daylesford), Governor-General of India. On the wall behind, in the nave, is a huge monument to *William Pitt, Earl of Chatham* (1708-78; *23*), and statues of *Lord Palmerston* (1784-1865) and *Lord Castlereagh* (1769-1821). In the pavement are the graves of *Henry Grattan* (1746-1820), the Irish patriot and orator, and *C.J. Fox* (1749-1806). Towards the E wall, statues of *George Canning* (1770-1827), by Chantrey; *Benjamin Disraeli, Earl of Beaconsfield* (1804-81; buried at Hughenden), by Boehm; *William Ewart Gladstone* (1809-98), by Brock; and *Sir Robert Peel* (1788-1850; buried at Drayton), by Gibson.

The three chapels (usually locked) of ST. JOHN THE EVANGELIST, ST. MICHAEL, and ST. ANDREW occupy the E aisle of the N transept. At the entrance to the chapels is an overwhelming monument to *General Wolfe* (1727-59; buried at Greenwich), who fell at the capture of Quebec. To the left, as we enter, *Sir John Franklin* (1786-1847), lost in the search for the North-West Passage, with a fine inscription by Tennyson.—To the right, *Sir Francis Vere* (1560-1609), a distinguished soldier of Queen Elizabeth. This magnificent Renaissance tomb is modelled on that of Engelbert II of Nassau (d 1504) at Breda. *Lady Elizabeth Nightingale* (d 1731), a skilful but theatrical sculpture by Roubiliac. The large tomb in the next chapel is that of *Lord Norris* (1525?-1601) and his wife (neither buried here); the only one of their six sons who survived them may be distinguished by his attitude. On the N wall, *Sir James Young Simpson* (1811-70; buried in Edinburgh), who first used chloroform as an anaesthetic. *Mrs Siddons* (1755-1831) as the Tragic Muse, by Chantrey after Reynolds. *Sir Humphry Davy* (1778-1829; buried in Geneva), inventor of the safety lamp. *John Kemble* (1757-1823), the actor, designed by Flaxman. *Thomas Telford* (1757-1834), engineer and bridge-builder. On the right *Adm. Kempenfelt* (1718-82), who went down in the 'Royal George', by Bacon. South Transept, see below.

Choir Chapels. The choir-apse is rounded and contains the Chapel of St. Edward, so that the high altar is placed somewhat far forward, and the ritual choir extends into the nave. In the ambulatory are two fine brasses for *Abbot Estney* (1498; *36*) and *Sir John Harpedon* (1457; *37*). The three tombs in the Sanctuary are well seen here (see above).

The two-storeyed CHAPEL OF ABBOT ISLIP (lower storey not shown) contains the grave of *Adm. Sir Charles Saunders* (d 1775; *38*), who shared with Wolfe the glory of taking Quebec. On the carved screen appears the abbot's rebus: an eye with a slip of a tree or a man slipping from a branch. The upper chapel (adm. on application), with a too graphic window (1950), is now the Nurses' Memorial Chapel.

The CHAPEL OF ST. JOHN THE BAPTIST is entered through the tiny Chapel of Our Lady of the Pew. Above the entrance is a delicately carved alabaster niche from the demolished Chapel of St. Erasmus (15C). Traces of the painted vault remain from the late-14C; a statue of the Madonna by Sister Concordia was placed in the niche in 1971. To the right in the polygonal Chapel of St. John the Baptist are several 15C tombs of abbots, notably *William de Colchester* (d 1420; *39*). The huge tomb of *Lord Hunsdon* (d 1596; *40*), cousin and Lord Chamberlain to Elizabeth I, is a masterpiece of Elizabethan bombast. The plain tomb by the NE wall of *Hugh* and *Mary de Bohun* (*41*), dates from 1304-05. Behind is a monument to *Col. Popham*; the inscription was removed because of his Parliamentarian activities. In the centre is a large monument to *Thomas Cecil, earl of Exeter* (1542-1623; *42*), son of Lord Burghley, with his effigy and that of his first wife, his second wife refused to accept the less honourable position on his left hand and was buried in Winchester Cathedral.

In the ambulatory opposite the chapel, the mosaics on the tomb of Henry III are well seen. The well-lit CHAPEL OF ST. PAUL is the easternmost chapel of the North Ambulatory and contains (right) the tomb of *Lord Bourchier* (d 1431; *43*), recently repainted, which forms part of the screen. On the monument of *Lord Cottington* (d 1652; *44*) is a bust of his wife (d 1633), by Le Sueur. On the site of the altar,

Frances Sidney, countess of Sussex (d 1589; *45*), founder of Sidney Sussex College at Cambridge. The fine monument to *Dudley Carleton* (d 1632; *46*) is by Nicholas Stone. Beyond good monuments to *Sir Thomas Bromley* (1530-87) and *Sir James Fullerton* (d 1631) is one to *Sir John Puckering* (1544-96; *47*), Speaker of the House of Commons. In the centre, *Sir Giles Daubeny* (d 1508; *48*) and his lady, with fine contemporary costumes. To the right of the exit, bust of *Sir Rowland Hill* (1795-1879), champion of penny postage. In the ambulatory, opposite the exit from this chapel, note the *Grate of Queen Eleanor's tomb, an admirable specimen of English wrought-iron work by Thomas of Leighton, 1294. Beneath are traces of paintings by Walter of Durham. Above can be seen the Chantry of Henry V, forming a bridge over the ambulatory. The flight of steps leads to the Lady Chapel (Chapel of Henry VII), entered appropriately through a spacious barrel-vaulted vestibule, decorated with bright panelling.

**Chapel of Henry VII. Built in 1503-19, this chapel is the finest example in England of late-Perpendicular or Tudor Gothic. Henry ordered it to be 'painted, garnished and adorned in as goodly and rich a manner as such work requireth and as to a king's work apperteyneth'. Of its profuse decoration the culminating glory is the superb fan-tracery vaulting, hung with pendants in the nave, and stretched as a canopy to accommodate the bay windows in the aisles. The beautiful tall windows, curved in the aisles and angular in the apse, are particularly ingenious. The carving throughout is of the highest quality, and includes a series of 95 (originally 107) statues of saints popular at the time, with a frieze of angels and badges below. The chapel was begun as a shrine for Henry VI, and carved stalls of the Knights of the Bath separate the nave from the aisles, which have separate entrances at the W end.

In 1725, when George I reconstituted the most honourable Order of the Bath, this chapel became the chapel of the Order, with the Dean of Westminster as its perpetual dean. After 1812, however, no installation of knights was held until 1913, when the ceremony was revived with all its ancient pomp and the present banners placed in position.

NORTH AISLE OF HENRY VII'S CHAPEL. The tall canopied *Tomb in the centre of the aisle was erected by James I to *Elizabeth I* (1533-1603; *49*), who rests here in the same grave as her sister *Mary I* (d 1558); 'Consorts in throne and tomb, here we sisters rest, Elizabeth and Mary, in hope of the resurrection' (epitaph). The marble figure is the work of Cornelius Cure (1605-07).

  The E end of this aisle (*50*) was called 'Innocents' Corner' by Dean Stanley, for here are commemorated two infant *Children of James I* (d 1607), one represented in a cradle which is the actual tomb; and in a small sarcophagus by the E wall are some bones, reinterred as those of *Edward V* and his brother *Richard, Duke of York*, the young sons of Edward IV, who were murdered in the Tower c 1483. Edward V had been born in the Sanctuary of the Abbey.

  NAVE OF HENRY VII'S CHAPEL. The beautiful oak doors plated with bronze at the entrance date from the 16C. The heraldic devices that appear on them and recur elsewhere in the decoration of the chapel refer to Henry VII's ancestry and to his claims to the throne.

The Welsh dragon indicates his Tudor father; the daisy-plant and the portcullis refer to the names of his Lancastrian mother, Margaret Beaufort; the falcon was

the badge of Edward IV, father of Elizabeth of York, Henry's wife; the greyhound
that of the Nevilles from whom she was descended. The crown on a bush recalls
Henry's first coronation on Bosworth field; while the roses are those of Lancaster
and York united by his marriage. Other emblems are the lions of England and
the fleur-de-lis of France.

Within, on each side, are the beautiful carved stalls of the Knights of
the Bath, each with the arms of its successive holders emblazoned
on small copperplates and the banner of the current holder suspended
above. The lower seats are those of the esquires (no longer used as
such) with their coats-of-arms. Beneath the seats are a number of
grotesquely carved misericords (supports for monks when standing),
one of which (8th stall on S side) dates from the 13C. At the W end
is the naval sword of George VI, with which he conferred the accolade
of the Order. The altar (1935) is a reproduction of the original, with
a 15C altarpiece by Bart. Vivarini.

Beneath the pavement between the door and the altar reposes
George II (d 1760; the last king buried in the Abbey), with *Queen
Caroline* and numerous members of his family. Below the altar is the
grave of *Edward VI* (d 1553). Behind it is the beautiful *Tomb (51)
of *Henry VII* (d 1509) and *Elizabeth of York* (d 1503), an admirable
work by Torrigiani, completed about 1518. The noble effigies of the
king and queen repose on a black marble sarcophagus, with a carved
frieze of white marble and adorned with gilt medallions of saints.
The fine grate is the work of Thomas Ducheman. *James I* (1566-1625)
is buried in the same vault as Henry VII and his queen. The first
apse-chapel on the S is filled by Le Sueur's monument to *Ludovick
Stuart, duke of Lennox and Richmond* (1574-1624; 52) with a gilt
canopy; in the next is buried *Dean Stanley* (1815-81; 53), with a fine
effigy by Boehm. Here too lies the *Duc de Montpensier* (1775-1807),
brother of Louis-Philippe.

The E chapel is now the ROYAL AIR FORCE CHAPEL. The window
by Hugh Easton, commemorating the Battle of Britain (July-Oct
1940), incorporates in the design the badges of the 63 Fighter
Squadrons that took part. The Chapel keeps the Roll of Honour
(facsimile in adjoining chapel) of the 1497 airmen of Britain and her
allies who fell in the battle. Nearby is the grave of *Lord Dowding*
(1882-1970), who commanded the air defence of Great Britain, and
on the S side that of *Lord Trenchard* (1873-1956), 'father' of the RAF.
In this chapel were buried *Oliver Cromwell* (1599-1658; tablet), *Henry
Ireton* (1611-51), *John Bradshaw* (1602-59) and *Admiral Blake* (1599-
1657). At the Restoration all were removed from the Abbey; Blake
was reinterred in St. Margaret's churchyard, but the bodies of the
others were treated with ignominy, and their heads were struck off
at Tyburn and afterwards exposed on Westminster Hall. (See also
Red Lion Square, p 182.)

In the next chapel is a vault (usually covered with an organ) with
the graves of *Anne of Denmark* (1574-1619; 54), queen of James I,
and *Anne Mowbray*, the child wife of Richard, Duke of York, reburied
here in 1965. In the last chapel is the large tomb by Le Sueur, of
George, Duke of Buckingham (assassinated in 1628; 55), the favourite
of James I and Charles I, with statues by Nicholas Stone of his
children. The low stone screen preserved here is in keeping with the
originality of the design of the outer walls of the chapel.

SOUTH AISLE OF HENRY VII'S CHAPEL. At the end of this aisle
are memorials to *Lord Cromer* (1841-1917), *Lord Curzon* (1859-1925),

Viscount Milner (1854-1925), and *Cecil Rhodes*. In the centre, tomb of *Margaret, Countess of Lennox* (d 1578; *56*). Her son, Henry Darnley, was husband of Mary, Queen of Scots, and father of James I of England; and his figure among the effigies of her children on the sides of the tomb may be identified by the (restored) crown over his head (as Henry I of Scotland). Next, under a tall canopy, is a recumbent *Figure of *Mary, Queen of Scots* (1542-87; *57*), whose remains were removed hither from Peterborough Cathedral in 1612 by order of her son, James I. The work of Cornelius and William Cure (1605-10), this was the last royal tomb erected in the Abbey.

The next *Tomb is that of *Margaret Beaufort, Countess of Richmond* (1443-1509; *58*), mother of Henry VII, patron of Wynkyn de Worde, and foundress of Christ's and St. John's Colleges at Cambridge. The beautiful recumbent figure in gilt-bronze, the masterpiece of Pietro Torrigiani of Florence, is noted for the delicate modelling of the hands. It is surrounded by a contemporary screen. On the wall to the N is a fine bronze bust of *Sir Thomas Lovell* (d 1524), also by Torrigiani. The statue of a Roman matron beside it, by Valory, commemorates *Catherine Lady Walpole* (d 1737).

The incongruous monument to *General Monk, duke of Albemarle* (1608-70; *59*), restorer of the Stuarts, covers a vault containing the remains of *Charles II* (d 1685), *Mary II* (d 1694), her husband *William III* (d 1702), *Queen Anne* (d 1714), and her husband *Prince George of Denmark* (d 1708).

Cross a reinforced glass bridge (1971) past the tomb and beneath the CHANTRY OF HENRY V (1387-1422). His dispoiled effigy (*60*) rests on a slab of marble and was originally covered with silver-gilt plates, stolen together with the solid silver head in the reign of Henry VIII. The head was replaced in 1971 in gilt bronze by Louisa Bolt. In the chantry (no adm except for special services) *Katherine of Valois* (d 1437), Henry's 'beautiful Kate', lies beneath the altar; she was originally interred in the old Lady Chapel. On a beam still higher are a shield, saddle, and helmet, probably made for Henry's funeral.

*Chapel of St. Edward the Confessor, at once the most gorgeous as it is the most sacred part of the church. In the middle stands the mutilated *Shrine of St. Edward the Confessor* (d 1066; *61*), erected in the late 13C for Henry III by 'Peter of Rome', probably the son of Odericus (see above), and showing traces of the original mosaics. The upper part, now of wood (1557), was originally a golden shrine decorated with jewels and gold images of saints, all of which disappeared at the Dissolution. In the recesses of the base sick persons used to spend the night in hope of cure. Roman Catholic pilgrims visit the shrine on St. Edward's Day (13 Oct). On the S side of the shrine is the tomb of *Philippa of Hainault* (d 1369; *63*), wife of Edward III, with the alabaster effigy of the queen by Hennequin of Liegè, sculptor to the king of France. The elaborate tomb of *Edward III* (d 1377; *64*) has niches in which were statuettes of his fourteen children, six of which remain (seen from S ambulatory); the contemporary wooden canopy is fine. The last tomb on this side is that of *Richard II* (d 1400; *65*) and his first wife *Anne of Bohemia* (d 1394), which is in the same style as that of Edward III. It is profusely decorated with delicately engraved patterns, among which may be distinguished the broom-pods of the Plantagenets, the white hart, the rising sun, etc.; the beautiful paintings in the canopy represent the Trinity, the Coronation of the Virgin, and Anne of Bohemia's coat-of-arms. At the W end is a beautiful screen (mid-15C) with 14 scenes of the life of Edward the Confessor. In front are remains of the Cosmati pavement, and the *Coronation Chair (66)*, made in oak by Walter of Durham c 1300-01. It has left the Abbey only thrice—when Cromwell was installed as Lord Protector in Westminster Hall, and for safety during the two World Wars. It encloses the famous 'Stone of Scone', carried off from Scotland by Edward I in 1297, used for all subsequent coronations of English monarchs. Beside it are the *State Sword* (7ft long) and *Shield* of Edward III.

The *Stone of Scone*, on which the Scottish kings were crowned from time immemorial down to John Baliol, was regarded as the palladium of Scottish independence, and its character is supposed to have been vindicated when James VI of Scotland became also James I of England in 1603. A long but quite mythical history attaches to this block of reddish sandstone from central Scotland. It is traditionally identified with Jacob's pillow at Bethel, afterwards the 'Lia Fail' or 'Stone of Destiny' on the sacred hill of Tara, in Ireland. Historically, it is recorded as being used for the enthronement of Macbeth's stepson at Scone in 1057, and was certainly in use there earlier. On 24 Dec 1950, the stone was stolen by Scottish 'Nationalists' and taken to Arbroath; it was replaced on 13 April 1951.

On the N side is the plain altar-tomb, without effigy, of *Edward I* (d 1307; *67*); in 1744 his body (6ft 2in long) was found to be in good preservation, dressed in royal robes with a gilt crown. Beyond are the beautiful Gothic *Tombs of Henry III* (1207-72; *68*), and his daughter-in-law, *Eleanor of Castile* (d 1290; *69*), wife of Edward I. Henry's tomb was designed by Peter of Rome, and Eleanor's was executed by Richard Crundale with paintings by Walter of Durham; but both the beautiful bronze effigies, the earliest cast in England, are by William Torel, a goldsmith of London. The canopy over Eleanor's tomb dates from the 15C, when the old one was destroyed by the erection of Henry V's Chantry.

THE CHAPEL OF ST. NICHOLAS, off the S ambulatory, has a fine stone screen. On the right of the door, *Philippa, Duchess of York* (d 1431; *70*). In the centre is the fine tomb of *Sir George Villiers* (d 1606; *71*) and his wife (d 1630), parents of the Duke of Buckingham. The large monument on the S wall, to the *Wife* and *Daughter of Lord Burghley* (c 1588; *72*), and that on the E wall, to the *Duchess of Somerset* (d 1587; *73*), widow of the Protector, are good examples of the Renaissance period. Below this chapel is the vault of the dukes of Northumberland, the only family with right of sepulture in the Abbey. In the Ambulatory, opposite this chapel, has been placed an oaken *RETABLE, a precious example of French or English painting of c 1255, with rich decorations.

THE CHAPEL OF SS. EDMUND AND THOMAS THE MARTYR is separated from the ambulatory by an ancient oaken screen. To the right, inside *William de Valence, Earl of Pembroke* (d 1296; *74*), half-brother of Henry III. This tomb consists of an oaken coffin and effigy of the deceased, which were formerly coated with Limoges enamel, remnants of which may still be seen. *Edward Talbot, Earl of Shrewsbury* (d 1617; *75*) and his wife, a handsome Jacobean tomb, to accommodate which, however, some of the arcading was destroyed. *Sir Richard Pecksall* (1571), master of the buckhounds. *Sir Bernard Brocas* (d 1395), captain of Calais. Beyond the large monument to *Lord John Russell* (d 1584; *76*), with his infant son, is the seated figure of his daughter, *Lady Elizabeth Russell* (1576-1601), the earliest non-recumbent statue in the Abbey. In the floor, grave of *Edward Bulwer Lytton* (1803-73), the novelist. In the centre of the chapel are the tombs of *Robert Waldeby, archbishop of York* (d 1397; *77*), the companion of the Black Prince, with a brass representing him in full eucharistic vestments, and of *Eleanor de Bohun, duchess of Gloucester* (d 1399; *78*), in conventual dress, the largest and finest brass in the Abbey. Near the E wall, *Frances, Duchess of Suffolk* (d 1559), mother of Lady Jane Grey. Adjoining are the finely modelled but mutilated effigies of two children of Edward III (1340). Beside the door into the chapel, *John of Eltham* (1316-37; *79*), second son of Edward II; this tomb, with the earliest alabaster effigy in the Abbey, is especially interesting for the careful representation of the prince's armour. Opposite the entrance to this chapel we see the outer side of Edward III's tomb, with beautiful little brass *Statuettes of his children, with enamelled coats of arms.

Between this chapel and the next a small altar-tomb (*80*) covers the remains of four children of Henry III and four of Edward I. Opposite is the CHAPEL OF ST. BENEDICT (no adm.), best seen from the S transept. Beside the railing on this side is the alabaster tomb of *Simon Langham* (d 1376; *81*), abbot of Westminster and afterwards archbishop and cardinal. In the ambulatory is the so-called tomb of *Sebert* (*82*) and his wife; then a tablet to Anne Nevill (1456-85), queen of Richard III. Above is the back of the sedilia in the sanctuary, with 14C paintings of Edward the Confessor and the Annunciation (mutilated). Outside the gate (right) is a monument to *Dr Richard Busby* (1606-95), a famous headmaster of Westminster School.

The South Transept is known as **Poets' Corner**, taking its name from the tombs of Chaucer and Spenser. The tombs of the poets have overflowed into the S end of the central aisle also. On the end wall of the transept are two magnificent Wall-paintings of St. Christopher and the Incredulity of St. Thomas. Uncovered in 1936, they are ascribed to Walter of Durham (c 1280) and are outstanding examples of the Westminster school of painting.

On the left side of the E aisle is a bust of *John Dryden* (1631-1700), and on the pier opposite (right) is a bust of *William Blake* (1757-1827), by Epstein. By the next pillar (left) is a bust of *Henry Longfellow* (1807-82), placed by the English admirers of the American poet in 1884. Beneath the next window is the Gothic *Tomb of Geoffrey Chaucer* (1340?-1400; *24*), the poet of the 'Canterbury Tales', erected 155 years after his death. The space at the end of the altar-tomb is perhaps a prayer recess. Further on, *Michael Drayton* (1563-1631). Beneath the pavement in front of Chaucer's tomb is the grave of *Robert Browning* (1812-89), and memorials to *Alfred Tennyson* (1809-92), *T.S. Eliot* (1888-1965), and *Lord Byron* (1788-1824).

At the SE angle are two doorways. Outside that in the E wall is an ancient pathway going straight to the Palace of Westminster, and a tablet on the left marks the approximate site of Caxton's original printing press (1477), six years before he set up in larger premises in the Almonry. In the S wall is the entrance to the *Chapter-House Crypt* (no adm.), an eight-sided undercroft (1248) with a massive central column, once used as the royal treasury.

On the S wall, above the door to the crypt, is a medallion of *Ben Jonson* (1573?-1637; buried in the nave). Farther on, *Edmund Spenser*

(1552?-99; *25*), the poet of 'The Faerie Queene'; the present monument is a copy (1778) of the original. *John Milton* (1608-74; *26*; buried at St. Giles, Cripplegate), a memorial delayed by political feeling for over 60 years after the poet's death. Below, *Thomas Gray* (1716-71; grave at Stoke Poges). On the partition-wall, the remarkable monument to *Matthew Prior* (1664-1721), designed by Gibbs, executed by Rysbrack, with a bust by Coysevox. On the next pier, beyond a bust of Tennyson, *Adam Lindsay Gordon* (1833-70), the poet of Australia, and *Thomas Campbell* (1777-1844). In the floor a little to the N, gravestone of *Thomas Parr* (d 1635; 'Old Parr'), said to have lived 152 years and under ten sovereigns, while farther S are those of *Dr Samuel Johnson* (1709-84), with a bust by Nollekens above it, *David Garrick* (1717-79), and *Sir Henry Irving* (1838-1905). On the W side of the partition-wall. *William Wordsworth* (1770-1850; buried at Grasmere); *Samuel Taylor Coleridge* (1772-1834; buried at Highgate); and *Robert Southey* (1774-1843; buried at Crosthwaite), epitaph by Wordsworth. *William Shakespeare* (1564-1616; *27*; buried at Stratford-on-Avon). On the monument, by Scheemakers, which was erected in 1740, are inscribed some lines from 'The Tempest', and at the corners of the pedestal are carved heads representing Elizabeth I, Henry V, and Richard III. *John Keats* (1796-1821) and *P.B. Shelley*

Handel's memorial in Westminster Abbey

(1792-1822), both buried in Rome, are commemorated above. *James Thomson* (1700-48; buried at Richmond), author of 'Rule Britannia'. Above, *Robert Burns* (1759-96; buried at Dumfries). Below, the *Brontë Sisters*, with a line from Emily's 'Old Stoic': 'with courage to endure'. Above the door to the Chapel of St. Faith, *Oliver Goldsmith* (1728-74; date of birth given wrongly in the epitaph; buried in the Temple), with an epitaph by Dr Johnson.

The *Chapel of St. Faith* (c 1249 restored 1972), formerly the revestry, is used for private devotion.

To the right of the chapel, *Sir Walter Scott* (1771-1832; buried at Dryburgh), and above, *John Ruskin* (1819-1900; buried at Coniston). The monument to *John Campbell, Duke of Argyll* (1680-1743; 28) is a fine work by Roubiliac. Above on the W wall, *George Frederick Handel* (1685-1759). Below is a memorial plaque to Jenny Lind, d 1887, the 'Swedish Nightingale'. A slab in the floor marks Handel's grave, and one beside it that of *Charles Dickens* (1812-70). In the floor are a tablet commemorating *Thomas Hardy* (1840-1928) and the grave of *Rudyard Kipling* (1865-1936). By the pier, *William Makepeace Thackeray* (1811-63; buried at Kensal Green). *Jos. Addison* (1672-1719). *Lord Macaulay* (1800-59). New additions to Poets' Corner are Dylan Thomas (d 1953), D.H. Lawrence (d 1930) and Noel Coward (d 1973).

South Choir Aisle. Opposite the E door into the cloisters are two good monuments to *William Thynne* (d 1584), and to *Sir Thomas Richardon* (29), in black marble, by Le Sueur. To the left in the next bay is an inappropriate monument to *Sir Cloudesley Shovel* (1650-1707; 30) between memorials to *Admiral Blake* (1599-1657) and *Robert Clive* (1725-64). Above is a monument to *Sir Godfrey Kneller* (1646-1723; buried at Kneller Hall), the only painter commemorated in the Abbey. In the 3rd bay (right), the tomb of *Thomas Owen* (d 1598; 31), with a fine painted alabaster figure. On either side of it, are the tomb of *General Pasquale Paoli* (1725-1807), the Corsican patriot who died as a refugee in England, and a tablet to *William Tyndale* (1490-1536), translator of the Bible. Opposite, medallions to *John Wesley* (1703-91) and *Charles Wesley* (1707-88), both buried elsewhere, *H.F. Lyte* (1793-1847), author of 'Abide with me', with *Dr Isaac Watts* (1674-1748; buried in Bunhill Fields), the hymn writer, beneath. Under the organ loft is a monument to *Thomas Thynne* (1648-82; 32), with a bas-relief depicting his assassination.

Cloisters and Conventual Buildings. The earliest parts of the present CLOISTERS date from the mid-13C, the remainder from 1344-70. The cloisters are connected with the church by two doors in the S nave aisle, affording convenient entrance and exit for conventual processions. Visitors should quit the church by the one to the E, entering the cloisters at their NE angle, the earliest and finest part. The external carving on the doorway should be noticed. In the *E Walk* a tablet on the wall in the second bay bears the touching inscription 'Jane Lister, dear Childe', with the date 1688. We pass the entrances to the Chapter House and to the Chamber of the Pyx, between which is the entrance to the Library and Muniment Room. The *South Walk* (14C) was the burial-place of the abbots for nearly 200 years after the Conquest. The three effigies beneath the wall seat are of Abbots Laurence (d 1173), Gilbert Crispin (d 1117), and William de Humez (d 1222). The recesses in the wall beside the old

entrance to the Refectory served as towel-cupboards. The *W Walk*
(14C) was used as the monastery school. On the wall is a memorial,
by G. Ledward, to the members of the submarine branch of the Royal
Navy who lost their lives in the two World Wars, and to members of
the Commandos, the Airborne Forces and Special Air Service killed
in 1939-45. In the *N Walk* (14C; being restored) is buried *General
Burgoyne* (1722-92), who surrendered to General Gates at Saratoga
in 1777.

The Chapter House and the Chamber of the Pyx. Open April-September Mon
to Sat 09.30-17.00, Oct.-March Mon to Sat 10.30-16.00. Admission charge. The
vestibule of the Chapter House is being refurbished and will reopen in June
1986; at about the same time the Chamber of the Pyx will reopen with improved
displays of Abbey treasures.

The *CHAPTER HOUSE is entered from the East Walk. Over the
entrance are sculpted figures, much mutilated, of the 13C. The
vaulted vestibule has fine bosses. At the top of the stairs *James
Russell Lowell* (1819-91), the American writer, and *Walter Hines
Page* (1855-1918), American ambassador, are commemorated. Opposite, the coffin-lid, with a cross in relief, is perhaps the only extant
relic of Sebert's church; the Roman sarcophagus was buried in the
green N of the Abbey. Note the original tiled *Pavement. The
beautiful octagonal room, 56ft in diameter, was built c 1245-55 above
the crypt of the Confessor's chapter-house. On the left is the Roll of
Honour of the Royal Army Medical Corps. The lofty roof is supported
by a single central shaft, 35ft high, and it is lit by six huge windows.
These, destroyed by bombing in 1941, were reset in 1950 with some
of the original glass; they show scenes from the abbey's history and
the arms of benefactors. The tracery, like the roof, is modern, though
copied from the blank window which escaped mutilation. The
arcading on the walls is adorned with paintings (partly restored) of
the life of St. John and of the Apocalypse, with a frieze of animals
below, presented by John of Northampton (1372-1404), a Westminster
monk. The beautiful Madonna and angel above the door date from
1250-53. The Chapter House is especially memorable as the 'cradle
of representative and constitutional government throughout the
world', for here the early House of Commons, separated from the
House of Lords in the reign of Edward III, held its meetings down to
1547, when it migrated to St Stephen's Chapel. From c 1550 to 1865
it served as a State muniment room and it is still in the charge of the
government, not the Abbey authorities.

THE CHAMBER OF THE PYX (admission as above), entered from
the E walk by a Norman archway and massive doors with seven
locks, is part of the Confessor's building. Originally a chapel, it was
afterwards used as the abbots' treasury and contained many sacred
relics. It subsequently became the depository of the 'pyx', or chest
containing the Exchequer trial-plates of gold and silver used as
standards of reference at the periodical tests of the coins of the realm.
The altar here is the oldest in the Abbey.

Westminster Abbey Treasure Museum, Norman Undercroft, Westminster
Abbey, London SW1. Tel. 01-222 5152. Open daily 10.30-16.30. Access as
above. The Museum is closed for refurbishment and will reopen in October
1986. The layout may then be somewhat different, focussing on the effigies.

The E walk of the cloisters is continued to the S by the *Dark* or

Norman Cloister (11C), whence the NORMAN UNDERCROFT is entered. Here is a museum illustrating the history of the abbey, and containing effigies carried at royal funerals.

It used to be the custom to show the embalmed bodies of royal persons at their funerals; the actual bodies were later replaced by life-like effigies of wood, plaster, or, at a later period, wax. Notable among the wooden effigies or heads here are those of Edward III (perhaps the oldest in Europe) and Henry VII, both death-mask portraits. The plaster head of Mary II is less successful. Anne of Bohemia, Katherine of Valois, Elizabeth of York, and Anne of Denmark represent the queens-consort. The eleven wax figures are interesting both as portraits and for their costumes. The oldest is that of Charles II, the one of Elizabeth I having been remade in 1760; others represent Lady Frances Stuart, William III, Mary II, and Queen Anne. The figures of Nelson and Chatham are not funeral effigies, but were added to attract visitors; they are outstanding as portraits.

Also displayed here are the royal writ and seal of Edward the Confessor and William I; a letter from John of Gaunt; the lease made out to Chaucer for premises in the garden of the old Lady Chapel; and the Coronation service book. A complete medieval arrow (unique), in the case opposite, was found in the top of Henry V's Chantry, possibly having been used as a pigeon scarer. Among other objects found in the Abbey are: the sword of Henry V; the ring of Bp Courtenay of Norwich (d 1415) found in his grave in 1953; the ring said to have been given by Elizabeth I to the Earl of Essex, and to have been intercepted by the Countess of Nottingham when Essex, on his condemnation, sent it back to the Queen in hope of pardon; a trunk thought to belong to Lady Margaret Beaufort; and the frater bell of the monastery. The building accounts of the nave also survive here, and 17C-20C plate is on display.

Farther on an arched passage on the left leads to the LITTLE CLOISTER, on the site of the monks' infirmary, a retired and picturesque spot, though modernised and restored after damage in 1940-41. In the E walk survives the 14C doorway of *St. Catherine's Chapel* (1165-70; the infirmary chapel), the ruined arcades of which may be viewed through a doorway to the left. In the S walk a door leads to *College Garden* (open to visitors on Thurs 12.00-16.00 or 18.00; entrance also from Great College St). The Dark Cloister ends at the yard of Westminster School (p 64).

From the junction of the W and S walks of the great cloister a corridor leads to the W to Dean's Yard. Near its W end, on the right, is a passage admitting to the *Abbots' Courtyard*, lying between the Deanery, formerly the Abbots' Palace, on the right, and the College Hall, on the left. The steps at the end ascend to the *Jericho Parlour*, or panelled ante-room, to the **Jerusalem Chamber** (14C), the abbots' retiring room, now used as the chapter-room and shown only by special permission of the Dean. In this chamber Henry IV died in 1413, having had a stroke while praying at the shrine of the Confessor. (Only open on Super tours—see p 65.)

The *Library and Muniment Room* (adm. by special permission only), occupying part of the monks' dormitory, above the chapter-house vestibule and the Chamber of the Pyx, is entered from the E walk of the cloister by the original day-stairs. The library was founded c 1623 and contains contemporary book-presses, as well as a priceless collection of books, charters, etc. For Dean's Yard, and the precinct wall, see Rte 1.

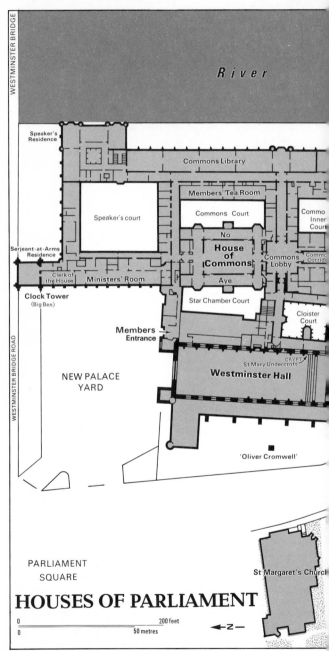

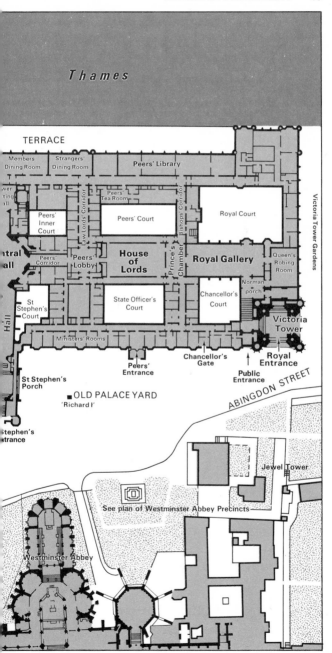

Thames

TERRACE

Members Dining Room

Strangers' Dining Room

Peers' Library

Peers' Tea Room

Peers' Court

Royal Court

Lower Waiting Hall

Peers' Inner Court

Law Lords' Corridor

Bishops Corridor

Central Hall

Peers' Corridor

Peers' Lobby

House of Lords

Prince's Chamber

Royal Gallery

Queen's Robing Room

State Officer's Court

Chancellor's Court

Norman porch

Hall

St Stephen's Court

Ministers' Rooms

Peers' Entrance

Chancellor's Gate

Public Entrance

Royal Entrance

Victoria Tower

Victoria Tower Gardens

St Stephen's Porch

■OLD PALACE YARD
'Richard I'

St Stephen's Entrance

ABINGDON STREET

See plan of Westminster Abbey Precincts

Jewel Tower

Westminster Abbey

3   The Houses of Parliament

Access: Underground, Westminster

N.B. The Houses of Parliament and Westminster Hall are no longer open to visitors, except for those attending debates or visiting in an organised party arranged by a Member of Parliament or a peer. There is public access to the Central Lobby through St. Stephen's entrance for those who wish to lobby their Member of Parliament.

Admission to debates: to obtain a ticket for the afternoon session in the House of Commons, write to your own Member of Parliament or to your Embassy in London. Prime Minister's Question Time is on Tuesdays and Thursdays at 15.15. Those without tickets should queue outside St. Stephen's entrance and the head of the queue is usually admitted from 16.15 (11.30 on Fridays) for the House of Commons and from 14.30 for the House of Lords.

The House of Commons usually meets on Monday to Thursday at 14.30 and on Fridays at 11.00. After the Speaker's procession through the Central Lobby, there are prayers (public not admitted) and then Question Time. Public business usually begins at 15.30 and continues until 22.30 or later. On Fridays, private members' bills and motions are debated and the House rises at 16.30. Visitors to the public gallery may obtain the Order Paper from the doorkeeper as well as a pass for the cafeteria. The House of Lords usually meets at 14.30 and the sittings are shorter. The Houses of Parliament have short recesses at Christmas and Easter and a long summer recess from the end of July until the middle of October. The official State Opening of the parliamentary session usually takes place in early November.

The **Houses of Parliament** (Pl. 19; 1), or *Palace of Westminster*, a stately pile in an admirable late-Gothic style, rises close to the Thames. The rich external decoration of oriels, pinnacles, and turrets is well balanced by the imposing towers; recent cleaning and restoration has revealed the intricate details and a glorious sandstone colour. The building, which incorporates the ancient Westminster Hall and the crypt and cloisters of St. Stephen's Chapel, was designed by Sir Charles Barry, and was built in 1840-50. Augustus Pugin provided many of the detail drawings. It covers 8 acres and has 11 courtyards, 100 staircases, 1100 apartments, and 2 miles of passages. Besides the Houses of Commons, in the N half, and the House of Lords, in the S half, it contains the dwellings of various parliamentary officials (including the Speaker). The W front is interrupted by Westminster Hall, which stands between New Palace Yard and Old Palace Yard; but the E, or river facade, extends unbroken for a length of 940ft, and is preceded by a terrace on the river, 700ft long. This long facade (best seen from the river) is embellished with the statues and royal arms of British sovereigns from William the Conqueror to Victoria, while figures of the earlier English kings, from the Heptarchy to the Conquest, appear on the short N front. Exterior cleaning is revealing every detail of the fine sculpture work.

Of the three towers, the tallest and the finest is the noble *Victoria Tower* (336ft high; 75ft square), at the SW angle, said to be the loftiest square tower in existence. The archway, 50ft high, below this tower, is the royal entrance to the building. The *Central Spire* (300ft) rises above the Central Hall and serves also as a ventilating shaft. The finial of the *Clock Tower* is 320ft from the ground. The clock (still wound by hand), an authoritative time-keeper, has four dials, each 23ft square; the figures are 2ft high; and the minute-hands are 14ft long. The hours are struck upon 'Big Ben', a bell weighing 13.5 tons, named after Sir Benjamin Hall, First Commissioner of Works when it was hung.—A flag on the Victoria Tower by day and a light in the Clock Tower by night indicate that Parliament is sitting. MPs usually use the entrance in New Palace Yard (adorned with catalpa trees); beacons on the gate posts warn them of a division (comp. below). During the construction of an underground car park in 1973, successive fountains (12C and 15C) were unearthed.

The Houses of Parliament occupy the site of an ancient palace, and in virtue of that fact still rank as a royal palace and are in the charge of the hereditary Lord Great Chamberlain (not to be confused with the Lord Chamberlain of the Household). This palace was the chief London residence of the sovereign from the reign of Edward the Confessor (or perhaps earlier) until Henry VIII seized Whitehall in 1529. Old Palace Yard was an inner court of the palace, and down to 1800 the House of Lords assembled in a chamber at its S end, which, in 1605, was the scene of the Gunpowder Plot. In 1512 the palace was very seriously damaged by fire, and it was never completely rebuilt. In 1547 the House of Commons transferred its sittings from the Chapter House of Westminster Abbey to St. Stephen's Chapel, and in 1800 the House of Lords removed to the old Court of Requests. In 1834 the entire palace was burned down, with the exception of Westminster Hall, the crypt of St. Stephen's Chapel, and part of the cloisters, but the rebuilding was at once begun, and the Lords removed to their new abode in 1847, the Commons to theirs in 1852. During the Second World War the buildings were damaged on more than twelve occasions. The worst attack caused the almost complete destruction of the House of Commons on 10 May 1941, besides other damage.

The INTERIOR of the building is handsomely fitted up in a style characteristic of its period, with fine ceilings, friezes, mosaic pavements, and metal work. The *Royal Staircase* leads to the NORMAN PORCH, intended to be decorated with statues and frescoes illustrating the Norman period.

Around the QUEEN'S ROBING ROOM, used as the House of Lords in 1941-50, runs a series of carved panels, by H.H. Armstead, with episodes from the Arthurian legend, while frescoes above, by W.A. Dyce, illustrate the virtues of chivalry.

The ROYAL GALLERY is a fine hall, 110ft long, through which the sovereign passes on the way to the House of Lords. Here are portraits of George III and Queen Charlotte, George VI and Queen Elizabeth, George V and Queen Mary (by Sir William Llewellyn), Queen Victoria and Prince Albert (by Winterhalter), and Edward VII and Queen Alexandra (by Luke Fildes). The two huge mural paintings by D. Maclise represent the Death of Nelson and the Meeting of Wellington and Blucher after Waterloo. The gilt statues of English Monarchs are by B. Philip. A recess at the S end forms a War Memorial to Peers and their sons, by John Tweed. The floor of Minton tiles is noteworthy.

The PRINCE'S CHAMBER, which follows, is decorated in a more sombre tone, with dark panelling. In the recess opposite the entrance is a white marble statue of Queen Victoria, enthroned between Justice and Mercy, by Gibson. On the walls are portraits of the Tudor kings and their consorts (1485-1603). Below bronze reliefs depict events of their reigns.

The **House of Lords**, a lavishly decorated and colourful Gothic hall by Pugin (90ft long, 45ft wide, and 45ft high), was used by the House of Commons from the destruction of their own chamber in 1941 until the opening of the rebuilt House of Commons in 1950. The gilded ceiling was extensively repaired in 1984. The televising of the House of Lords started on an experimental basis in 1985. At the S end, beneath an elaborate canopy, is the throne of the Sovereign. In front, separated from the throne by a gilded railing, the Woolsack, a plain cushioned ottoman stuffed with wool, is occupied by the Lord Chancellor, as presiding officer of the House of Lords. It is said to have been adopted in the reign of Edward III as a reminder of the importance to England of the wool trade. At the N end is the Bar, where the Commons, headed by their Speaker, attend at the opening of Parliament, and lawsuits on final appeal are pleaded. Above it is the *Press Gallery* with the *Strangers' Gallery* behind. The six frescoes above are by Maclise, Cope, Dyce, and Horsley.

The PEERS' LOBBY, a handsomely decorated chamber, has a fine encaustic tiled pavement and good brass gates in the S doorway. Over the N and S doors are the arms of six dynasties of English rulers (Saxon, Norman, Plantagenet, Tudor, Stuart, and Hanoverian), with the initial letter of the dynastic name below each. In the PEERS' CORRIDOR, leading N to the Central Hall, are eight paintings, by C.W. Cope (1856-66), of the Stuart and Commonwealth periods.

The CENTRAL HALL (usually called the Central Lobby), an ornate octagonal vestibule, 60ft in diameter and 75ft high, separates the precincts of the Lords from those of the Commons. On the floor is the text, in the Latin of the Vulgate: 'Except the Lord keep the house, their labour is but lost that build it'. The ceiling is inlaid, between the massive ribs of the vaulting, with Venetian glass mosaic, showing various royal badges. Over the doorways, the patron saints of Great Britain and Ireland are represented in glass mosaic by Poynter and Anning Bell. In niches around the hall are statues of English sovereigns of the Plantagenet line and their consorts; and on pedestals are statues of eminent statesmen.

The **House of Commons**, approached by the COMMONS' CORRIDOR and COMMONS' LOBBY, lies to the N of the Central Hall. The original chamber was destroyed by fire on 10 May 1941; a new chamber (130ft long, 48ft wide, and 43ft high) designed by Sir Giles Gilbert Scott in a less inspired and more sombre interpretation of the late-Gothic style, was opened in Oct 1950. The structural oak and the stonework are English; many of the furnishings were gifts of the Empire. The chamber is entered from the Commons Lobby through the CHURCHILL ARCH, built of stones battered and flaked by the fire of 1941, and flanked by statues of Churchill (1966; by Oscar Nemon) and Lloyd George.

The Speaker's chair (from Australia) is at the N end of the chamber. In front of the chair is the table of the House (from Canada), on which the mace rests during the sittings of the House. When the House is 'in Committee' the mace is placed 'under the table'. On either side are the 'front benches', the ministerial on the Speaker's right, the opposition on his left. On the floor of the House and in the side galleries are seats for 602 of the 630 members. Above the Speaker's chair is the Press Gallery, with 161 seats, and at the other end, facing the Speaker, is the gallery seating for *Distinguished and Ordinary Strangers*. The House is flanked on each side by *Division Lobbies*, into which the members file when a vote is being taken, 'Ayes to the right' (W), 'Noes to the left' (E).

To the W of the Central Hall is ST. STEPHEN'S HALL, the walls of which roughly correspond with the ground plan of St. Stephen's Chapel, founded by Edward I and completed by Edward III, 1292-1364. In this chapel, the chapel royal of the Old Palace of Westminster, the House of Commons met from 1547 until 1834. In the angles of the hall are figures of the early Norman kings, and on pedestals by the walls are statues of British statesmen. The panels beneath the windows illustrate The Building of Britain. ST. STEPHEN'S PORCH, leads to Westminster Hall. The beautiful large window on the left originally formed the S end of this hall, but was moved to its present position by Sir Charles Barry. The stained glass, by Sir N. Comper (1953), and the sculpture below, by Sir B. Mackennal (1922), are war memorials to Members and Officers of both Houses of Parliament.

The venerable and beautiful *Westminster Hall** (239.5ft long, 67.5ft wide, and 92ft high), originally built by William II in 1097, received its present form, and more especially its magnificent oaken *Roof, from Richard II in 1394-1402. Entirely bare of ornament and usually quite empty, the hall is one of the finest and largest timber-roofed buildings in Europe. The mason was Henry Yevele and the carpenter Hugh Herland. From the 13C until 1882 the chief English law courts sat at Westminster Hall, at first in the hall itself, afterwards in buildings (now pulled down) erected for the purpose on the W side. A thorough restoration of the roof was completed in 1923 and the war damage of 1941 has likewise been repaired.

Westminster Hall is perhaps specially memorable as the scene of the condemnation of Charles I in 1649. A brass tablet on the steps at the S end marks the spot where the king sat during his trial. But it has witnessed many other historic events and grave state-trials. Here Edward II abdicated in 1327, and, by the irony of fate Richard II, the builder of the hall, was here deposed in 1399, soon after its completion. A tablet on the E wall marks the position of the door through which Charles I passed in 1641 when he attempted to arrest the Five Members in their seats. Since then no sovereign entered the Commons until 1950, when George VI visited the rebuilt chamber. In 1653 Oliver Cromwell was here installed as Lord Protector. Among those who have been condemned to death in this hall are William Wallace (1305), Lord Cobham (1417), Sir Thomas More (1535), Sir Thomas Wyatt (1554), the Earl of Essex (1601), Guy Fawkes (1606), and Strafford (1641). The last public trial in the hall was that of Lord Melville for malversation in 1806. Since the 19C the hall has been used for the lying-in-state of monarchs and eminent statesmen. The Opening Session of the American Bar Association was held here in 1985.

From the SE angle of Westminster Hall a staircase descends to *ST. STEPHEN'S CRYPT, the ancient crypt of St. Stephen's Chapel, now known also as the church of *St. Mary Undercroft*. The crypt, with its finely groined vaulting retaining most of the original bosses, has been restored and richly decorated and is still occasionally used for christenings and marriages in the families of Members of Parliament.

A doorway on the E side of Westminster Hall opens upon the beautiful *St. Stephen's Cloisters* built by Henry VIII, with a fan-tracery ceiling little inferior to that of Henry VII's Chapel in Westminster Abbey. A small oratory or chapel projecting from the W walk is traditionally said to be the place where the death-warrant of Charles I was signed.

4   Whitehall

Access: Underground, Westminster and Embankment.

The brief half-mile known as **Whitehall** which separates Westminster from Charing Cross has been a thoroughfare at least since the 15C. In the 16-17C most of the region between Charing Cross and the present Westminster Bridge and between the Thames and St. James's Park was occupied by the ROYAL PALACE OF WHITEHALL, of which little now remains but the name and one building. The association of the area with government began as early as the 17C, and today it is the political centre of Great Britain, lined on the W side of the street with public offices, which range in date from 1725, at the N end, to 1919, at the S end. Recent cleaning has greatly enhanced their effect.

Whitehall Palace originated in a mansion purchased by Walter de Grey, Archbishop of York in 1240, which for nearly 300 years became the London residence, known as *York Place*, of his successors. When Card. Wolsey succeeded to the Archbishopric he embellished the Palace (sited on the river side of the thoroughfare) with characteristic extravagance, and Henry VIII seized the desirable property in 1529. He renamed the palace 'Whitehall', a name then generally applied to any centre of festivities, and acquired more land towards St. James's Park, on which he erected a tiltyard, cockpit, and tennis courts. Whitehall became the chief residence of the court in London. Anne Boleyn was brought here on the day of her marriage to Henry in 1533, and in 1536 it was the scene of his marriage to Jane Seymour. In 1547 Henry died in the Palace, and under Elizabeth the festivities of her father's reign were revived. Masques by Ben Jonson, with sets by Inigo Jones, and by James Shirley were frequently presented at court in the time of James I and Charles I. Plans for a huge and sumptuous new palace for James I drawn up by Inigo Jones and John Webb were never carried out, although the Banqueting House was rebuilt after fire in 1622. Charles I was executed in 1649 in front of this hall, and Oliver Cromwell died in the palace in 1658. Under Charles II Whitehall became the centre of revelry and intrigue described by Pepys; and hence James II fled into exile in 1688. The offering of the Crown to William and Mary provided the last great ceremonial function here. In 1698 the palace was accidentally burned to the ground, and the royal residence transferred to St. James's Palace. The government offices already established here, such as the Horse Guards (1663), the Paymaster-General's Office (1676), the Admiralty (1694), and the Treasury (1698) remain to the present day.

From Parliament Square, Parliament Street leads into Whitehall and on to Trafalgar Square. On the left (W) side are large blocks of government offices; the corner building (1907; by Brydon) is connected by a bridge over King Charles Street with the Foreign and Commonwealth Office. During the Second World War an underground network of bombproof rooms was developed for the War Cabinet underneath the western part of the building. They opened as a museum in 1984 under the care of the Imperial War Museum.

Continue up Whitehall along the W side past King Charles Street; at the end of the street steps descend past a statue of Lord Clive by John Tweed (1912) to St. James's Park and the *Cabinet War Rooms*.

Cabinet War Rooms, entrance from Horse Guards. Open: Tues to Sun 10.00-17.50. Admission charge. Tel. 01-930 6961.

Nineteen underground rooms survive as they were when the Second

World War ended. The total Cabinet War Room complex covered a huge area and was protected from bombs by a vast slab of concrete above. Among the rooms on view are the Cabinet Room, the Transatlantic Telephone Room, from which Churchill spoke to President Roosevelt in the White House, the Map Room and Churchill's bedroom. There is a shop selling postcards and wartime posters.

From here the facade of the *Foreign and Commonwealth Office* by Sir George Gilbert Scott (1832) in the style of Inigo Jones can be appreciated. The building covers 5.5 acres and will be undergoing extensive renovations over the next 15 years. A statue of Lord Mountbatten of Burma (1900-79) was unveiled by HM The Queen in 1983 (by F. Belsky). Return to Whitehall.

In the middle of Whitehall rises the **Cenotaph**, commemorating in dignified simplicity the Glorious Dead of 1914-18 and 1939-45. The monument, designed by Sir Edwin Lutyens, was first erected in plaster as a saluting point for the Allied Victory March of 1919 and was rebuilt in stone and unveiled on 11 November 1920; the later inscription was unveiled in 1946. Every November the ceremony of Remembrance Sunday takes place on the Sunday nearest to the 11th. Members of the royal family, the government and opposition, and representatives of Commonwealth countries lay 'poppy' wreaths around the Cenotaph and two minutes' silence is observed. The wreaths remain in place for two weeks afterwards.

The redevelopment of Whitehall is most evident on the right (E side) of Parliament Street and Whitehall; on the corner of Parliament Square, the Bridge Street site will be redeveloped behind the listed facade; *St. Stephen's Tavern*, popular with Members of Parliament, is due to remain and the building may become the new library of the House of Commons. The Norman Shaw South Building which fronts Bridge Street itself will be used as offices for MPs. The Norman Shaw building just to the N of the former New Scotland Yard (1891), has already been converted into MPs' offices.

Facing Whitehall are the remains of *Richmond Terrace*, a Grade II Georgian building of 1822-25 which was demolished and the facade reconstructed with a new six-storey building behind. When completed it may become the offices of the Overseas Development Administration.

On the left (W side) is the narrow DOWNING STREET, built in 1683-86 by Sir George Downing (who was the second graduate at Harvard in 1642) and famous out of all proportion to its appearance as the residence of British Prime Ministers since 1735. (Access to the street is frequently restricted for security reasons.) *No. 10 Downing Street* became the property of the Crown in 1732 and George II offered it as a gift to Sir Robert Walpole who accepted it for his office as First Lord of the Treasury. From that day it became the official residence of Prime Ministers, although many in the early years preferred to live in their own, probably grander, houses. William Kent redesigned the interior in 1732 and further alterations were made by Sir John Soane. The narrow front of the building belies its size and it contains offices as well as the Prime Minister's private apartment. *No. 11 Downing Street* became the residence of the Chancellor of the Exchequer in 1805; No. 12 was first the Judge Advocate General's official residence but is now the Government Party Whips' office.

At the beginning of the street on the right is the office of the Judicial Committee of the Privy Council, the final Court of Appeal for countries of the Commonwealth without their own Supreme Court of Appeal. It was built by Soane in 1827.

Before Downing Street became an official residence for the Prime Minister, other well-known people lived in it, including James Boswell who took lodgings here in 1762 and Tobias Smollett who set up a doctor's practice here c 1745-48.

Although it is possible to reach *Treasury Green* from Downing Street, access is often restricted; so the tall brick wall of Henry VIII's smaller tennis court of Whitehall Palace, revealed in 1961 and marked with a tablet, is best reached from Horse Guards.

The *Cabinet Office* and the *Old Treasury* front Whitehall from Downing Street northwards; it was designed by Kent, Soane and Barry and completed in 1845. During restorations in the '60s remains of Henry VIII's Whitehall Palace were uncovered (see smaller tennis court, above). The building is best seen from Horse Guards. *Dover House* (1758) is now used by the Scottish Office; Lord Melbourne (1779-1843) was born here. The delicate portico and circular hall are by Henry Holland (1787). In Whitehall is an equestrian statue of Earl Haig (1861-1928).

The massive *Ministry of Defence* building, (1935-53; by Vincent Harris) dominates the right (E) side of Whitehall as well as the river-view (see p 299). In front on the lawn facing Whitehall is a statue of Sir Walter Raleigh (1552-1618) by William McMillan (1929), and Field Marshall Montgomery in combat uniform by Nemon (1980). The main entrance of the Ministry of Defence is in Horse Guards Avenue flanked by colossal sculptures (Earth and Water; 1949-53) by Sir Charles Wheeler. In the gardens on the river side is a statue of General Gordon (1838-85) by Hamo Thornycroft; here is the surviving part of Queen Mary's Terrace, built for Mary II in 1691 with steps descending to the 17C water level.

Underneath the building is the King Henry VIII Wine Cellar, a brick vaulted undercroft of York Place. Its preservaton involved moving it bodily in 1950, 43ft to one side and 20ft downwards. It may be visited by special permission from the Department of the Environment or Ministry of Defence; increasingly more difficult to obtain.

Gwydyr House (1772), an attractive building in Whitehall on the E side, is now the Welsh Office.

Next to it is the **Banqueting House**, the main survival of Whitehall Palace. This superb example of Palladian architecture was erected in Portland stone by Inigo Jones in 1625, on the site of a banqueting hall of 1607 burned down in 1619. The weathercock at the N end of the roof is said to have been placed there in 1686 by James II to show whether the wind was favourable or not to the approach of the Prince of Orange. The hall is open to visitors.

Banqueting House, Whitehall, SW1 (01-930 4179). Open 10.00-17.30 (Tues to Sat) 14.00-17.30 (Sun). Admission charge. (Sometimes closed without prior notice.)

The lofty main hall (115ft long, 60ft wide and 55ft high) was decorated in 1635. The nine allegorical ceiling paintings were designed for Charles I in 1629-34 by Rubens, who received £3000 and a knighthood in return. The principal subject in the large central oval is the Apotheosis of James I; to the S James is enthroned between Peace and Plenty and to the N is an allegory of the birth and coronation of Charles I.

Through a window of this hall Charles I passed in 1649 to the scaffold erected in the roadway in front of it (tablet beneath the lower central window; in fact it was probably a window in a N annexe, since demolished). From 1698 to c 1890 the hall was used as a Chapel Royal, and later as the museum of the United Service Institutions. It is now used for government and other functions, including concerts, when not open to the public.

Beyond the Banqueting House on the right is a huge building by William Young (1906), formerly the War Office, now part of the Ministry of Defence. In front is a statue by Adrian Jones of the Duke of Cambridge (1819-1904), Commander in Chief of the British armies in 1856-95. The *Ministry of Agriculture and Fisheries* is next door in a building by John Murray (1910) and this is followed by *Great Scotland Yard*. Here stood the headquarters of the Metropolitan Police until 1891. The street name originates in a mansion occupied before the 15C by the kings of Scotland and their ambassadors when in London. The stables of the Metropolitan Mounted Police remain here (appointment by request); the main establishment is now at Imber Court, East Molesey (01-398 1102).

Also on the right (E) side of Whitehall is *Harrington House*, at Craig's Court, once the residence of Joseph Craig (1692); the facade is preserved.

Horse Guards on the left (W) side of Whitehall (1760, by Kent and Vardy) is a pleasant stone building with a central arch surmounted by a low clock tower, built on the site of a guard house of 1649 which stood on the old tiltyard of the Palace of Whitehall. It is now the office of the Commander in Chief of the combined forces. Two mounted troopers of the Life Guards or Royal Horse Guards (or Blues and Royals) are posted here daily from 10.00 to 16.00 and there are two dismounted sentries within the archway. The former are relieved hourly, the latter every two hours. At 11.00 (10.00 on Sundays), the guard on duty is relieved by a new guard of 12 men who troop from the Knightsbridge Barracks via the Mall.

The passage beneath the clock-tower leads to the large Parade Ground, Horse Guards' Parade and to St. James's Park. In May and June the *Parade Ground* is used for the ceremony of Beating the Retreat (public admitted, tickets from the Ticket Office, Bridge Street, SW1), when military music and parades are performed under floodlight in the early evening, and Trooping the Colour, the Queen's Official Birthday parade on the second or third Saturday in June. Tickets by ballot only: write to Household Division HQ, Horse Guards, SW1, before March 1; two tickets per application only; those unsuccessful may receive tickets for the rehearsal on the previous Saturday.

The Trooping the Colour ceremony, at 11.00, is preceded by a parade along the Mall, when the Queen and other members of the royal household ride or travel by royal coach to Horse Guards. In 1983 and 1985 there were Son-et-Lumière performances on 'Horse' Guards during August and September, recreating its history. On the N side is the large *New Admiralty*, built in 1894-95, now housing a Government department. It is connected on the N to Admiralty Arch and on the W to the Citadel (see p 100). Looking back from the Parade, the elevation of Admiralty House, the former Paymaster General's Office, is to the left; the long rusticated facade of Horse Guards (by William Kent) opposite, Dover House (1758 by James Paine) to the right, the Portland stone facade of the Old Treasury (1736 William Kent) and then the barrel vaulted Treasury Passage to Downing Street. To the right behind a statue by Tweed of Earl Kitchener (1850-1916) are the gardens of Downing Street.

In front of the Horse Guards are equestrian statues of Viscount Wolseley (1833-1913) by Goscombe John, and Earl Roberts (1832-1914) by H. Bates, and a huge mortar from Cadiz presented by the Spanish Government in 1814 encased in a carriage made in Woolwich. On the edge of St. James's Park is the *Guards' Memorial* for 1914-19 by G. Ledward and H.C. Bradshaw.

Return to Whitehall; on the left going towards Trafalgar Square is the former *Paymaster-General's Office* (1732-33 by John Lane; now the Parliamentary Counsel); the flank of *Admiralty House* (1786-88; by S.P. Cockerell) is set back behind a wall and railing. Beyond is the *Old Admiralty* (by Ripley; 1725-28) with a tall classical portico in a small courtyard masked from the street by an attractive stone screen designed by Robert Adam in 1759. This was the Admiralty of Nelson's time and here his body lay in state in 1805; it is now used by the Home civil service. Immediately behind facing on to Horse Gaurds Parade is the *New Admiralty*, and then TRAFALGAR SQUARE.

The *Whitehall Theatre* (1932) on the left gave its name to a 'trouser-dropping' style of comedy—the Whitehall farce—in the '50s and '60s but subsequently went into decline; for a time in the 1980s it was used by Paul Raymond as a Theatre of War, recreating the more gory and sentimental aspects of the Second World War and was due to become a theatre again in 1986.

5   Charing Cross and Trafalgar Square

Access: Underground, Charing Cross; Embankment.

Contrary to popular usage, *Charing Cross* is the irregular open space at the top of Whitehall just before Trafalgar Square; not the open space in front of Charing Cross Station. It was here that in 1291 Edward I erected the last of the series of thirteen crosses that marked the stages in the funeral procession of his wife Eleanor to Westminster Abbey. It was destroyed in 1647 and a replica later erected in front of Charing Cross Station. The cross gave its name to the ancient road junction which is now the site of the fine equestrian statue of Charles I by Hubert Le Sueur (1633) on a pedestal by Joshua Marshall, from a design by Wren. Those who risk their lives in the traffic to reach the small island will also note a tablet in the ground from which all mileages to and from Central London are measured.

At the entrance of Charles II to London in 1660, 600 pikemen were stationed here, and later in the same year it was the scene of the execution of Harrison and seven other regicides, witnessed by Pepys, who commented, 'Thus it was my chance to see the King beheaded at Whitehall and to see the first blood shed in revenge for the blood of the King at Charing Cross'. In 1668 Punchinello, 'ye Itallian popet player', performed here. At the pillory set up near the statue Defoe (1703) and John Middleton (1723) suffered.—On 30 January, the anniversary of the execution of Charles I, the statue is adorned with the wreaths by sympathetic adherents of the Jacobite tradition.

To the E, beyond Charing Cross Station, runs the Strand (Rte 17), leading to Fleet St and the City. To the W, Admiralty Arch gives access to the Mall and St. James's Park (Rte 6). The wide Northumberland Avenue descends past the *Royal Commonwealth Society* to the Thames Embankment. Grand Buildings on the corner is being redeveloped. On the left in Northumberland Avenue (10

Northumberland Street) is the Sherlock Holmes pub mentioned in 'The Hound of the Baskervilles', there called the Northumberland Arms Hotel. Upstairs is a perfect reconstruction of Holmes' study and in the bar are mementos and memorabilia relating to the hound and Sherlock Holmes. There is also a restaurant.

Trafalgar Square (Pl. 14; 4), laid out in 1829-c 1850 at the suggestion of Nash, is said to have been described by Sir Robert Peel as 'the finest site in Europe'. Since the reign of Edward I the area had been a royal mews. Except when disturbed by the periodic political or social demonstrations for which the square is a traditional rendezvous, pigeons crowd the area by day and starlings take refuge in the surrounding buildings at dusk. This is the location for the annual New Year's Eve celebrations, more strictly controlled after two fatalities in 1983. From early December until Christmas Eve there are Christmas carols under the Christmas tree donated by the people of Norway in gratitude for help during the Second World War.

The NELSON MONUMENT, 185ft high, by William Railton (1841), carries a colossal statue of Lord Nelson, victor at the Battle of Trafalgar in 1805, by E.H. Bailey (1840-43). The fluted granite column rises from a base guarded by four huge bronze couchant *Lions, beloved of children. These were modelled by Sir Edwin Landseer and cast by Marochetti in 1867. At the foot are four bronze reliefs cast from French cannon captured at the naval battles they depict. The monument is annually decorated on the anniversary of the Battle of Trafalgar (21 October).

In the square are two fountains, designed by Lutyens in 1939 with fine sculptures by Charles Wheeler and W. McMillan. The statue of *Sir Henry Havelock* (1795-1857) is by Behnes, and that of *Sir Charles James Napier* (1782-1853) by G.G. Adams. At the NE corner an equestrian statue of *George IV*, by Chantrey, was intended to top the Marble Arch in front of Buckingham Palace. Against the N wall are bronze busts of *Lord Cunningham* (1883-1963) by Franta Belsky, *Lord Jellicoe*, (1859-1935), by W. McMillan, and *Lord Beatty* (1871-1936) by Sir Charles Wheeler. In the centre are the former Imperial standards of length, placed here in 1876.

Around Trafalgar Square are several large buildings: to the E, *South Africa House* (1933), designed by Sir Herbert Baker; and to the W, *Canada House*, built in 1824-27 by Sir Robert Smirke. Streets lead hence to Pall Mall and the West End (Rte 7). Above the N side of the square rises the National Gallery (see below). On the grass in front are a bronze statue of James II in Roman costume by Grinling Gibbons, and a copy in bronze of Houdon's marble statue of George Washington at Richmond, Virginia.

The large church of **St. Martin in the Fields**, at the NE corner of Trafalgar Square, built in 1722-24, is perhaps the finest work of James Gibbs. The controversial combination of a steeple and classical portico has been often copied, but less successfully. In the interior, with its richly decorated ceiling by Artari and Bagutti, are a font (1689), from the previous church on this site, and a handsome 18C pulpit brought here after 1858. The side aisles, with canted walls and 'closet' pews, are particularly attractive. The *Crypt* (entered from the porch at the SW end), originally a burial vault, contains the old parish chest (1597) of elm, and whipping post (1751). In 1930-45 it served as a shelter for the homeless. Off the S side opens the *Dick Sheppard Chapel* (1954), a memorial to the vicar who in 1914-27 began the tradition of social service still carried on by the church. The gateway to the chapel commemorates the 'Old Contemptibles' of the First World War.

In this church Bacon, Hampden, and Charles II were christened and Tom Moore married; while the burials of George Heriot, Nell Gwynn, Farquhar, Roubiliac, Chippendale, and John Hunter are here recorded. The first broadcast religious service was celebrated here in 1924. A bust of Gibbs by Rysbrack is preserved in the Vestry Hall. The church provided the start for the now world-famous Academy of St. Martin in the Fields Orchestra. The musical tradition continues with regular lunch-time concerts. The church is also the regular venue for memorial services of actors, actresses and people from the entertainment world generally.   Just beyond is the 'all-night' Post Office; see p 48.

On the 'island' in St. Martin's Place is a poignant monument by Frampton (1920) to Nurse Edith Cavell, who was shot at Brussels in 1915, and across Charing Cross Road is a statue of Sir Henry Irving (1838-1905).
    On the N side of Trafalgar Square is the **National Gallery**.

National Gallery, Trafalgar Square, London WC2. Tel. 01-839 3321. Open Mon to Sat 10.00-18.00, Sun 14.00-18.00 (until 20.00 in summer). Admission free.
    Educational facilities; lectures, room talks or films Mon to Fri at 13.00 Sat at 12.00—guided lecture tours Mon to Fri 11.30. Self-service restaurant. Bookshops with catalogues, guidebook, postcards, posters and Christmas cards. Access: Underground, Charing Cross, Leicester Square.

The National Gallery is one of the greatest art galleries in the world with a representative collection of masterpieces of all schools and of the greatest European painters from the 15th to the early 20C.

The idea of a national collection of paintings was first given effect in 1824 when Parliament voted £60,000 for the purchase of 38 paintings from the collection of the financier John Julius Angerstein (1735-1823). A regular grant for purchases followed in 1855 and since that date the policy of successive directors has been to build up a representative collection of Western European art.
    The collection was first shown in Angerstein's house in Pall Mall and moved to the present building in 1838. This was constructed by William Wilkins who used some of the columns from the demolished Carlton House in the facade. Extensions were later made by E.M. Barry and further extensions to the NW were opened in 1975. Proposals for a further extension on the vacant site to the W were rejected in 1984 and the shape of the development, which will combine an extension to the gallery with offices, is uncertain.

On the E facade of the building is Flaxman's 'Minerva', originally made for Marble Arch. The Vestibule contains a series of mosaic pavements designed and executed by Boris Anrep (1952) illustrating abstract ideas, and showing eminent people in unusual settings. (A pamphlet on these mosaics is available in the bookshop.)
    It is impossible to take in the range of paintings on view in one visit. Below is a small selection of some of the most famous paintings on view (although changes in display are frequent).

British School (Rooms 35-39): Constable, 'The Haywain'—the picture which epitomises the rural landscape with a view of the River Stour near Flatford Mill in Suffolk—first exhibited in 1824 when it won a gold medal. Gainsborough, 'Mrs Siddons' (1785), an elegant portrait, and 'The Morning Walk' (1785), a poetic evocation of young love. Hogarth, 'Marriage à la Mode'—six canvases satirising the morals of high society. Lawrence, 'Queen Charlotte' (1789), Eton College is in the background.

NATIONAL GALLERY

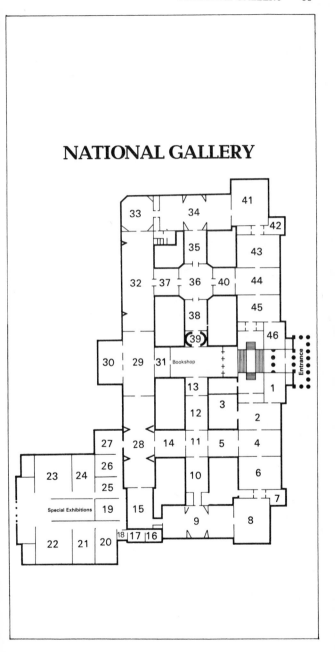

Reynolds, 'General Sir Banastre Tarleton' (1782)—in a striking pose. Stubbs 'The Melbourne and Milbanke Families' (1770s)—a glossy and formal composition. Turner, 'The Fighting Temeraire tugged to her last berth', with a characteristic Turner sunset.

Dutch School (Rooms 15-19): Avercamp, 'Winter Scene' (1609). Cuyp, 'Maas at Dordrecht in a Storm' (mid-1640s)—a rare storm scene. Hals—a good group of portraits. Hobbema, 'The Avenue, Middelharnis', (1650s), one of the most famous of all Dutch landscapes with a marvellous illusion of depth. De Hoogh, 'Woman and Maid in a Courtyard' (1660), with the old town wall of Delft behind. Rembrandt—a large, representative group of works: note 'Self-Portrait' (1640), Rembrandt aged 34 and influenced by Titian, 'A Woman Bathing in a Stream' (1655), a sensuous study of his model and mistress Hendrickje Stoffels, 'Margaretha de Geer' (1661), a second portrait of the wife of Jacob Trip; this 40 years later. Vermeer, 'Young Woman standing at a Virginal' (1670).

Flemish School, 17C (Rooms 20-2): Van Dyck, 'Equestrian Portrait of Charles I' (1630s), one of the most celebrated images of majesty—expressing his confidence as a horseman. An outstanding group of Rubens' work: note 'Rape of the Sabine Women' (late 1630s), 'The Watering Place' (1620s), which inspired Gainsborough to paint a similar painting, 'Judgement of Paris' (c 1600), painted after arrival in Italy, 'Samson and Delilah' (1610), influenced by Italy.

French School: 17C (Room 32): Claude, a superb collection of the great French classical landscape painter's work; note 'Seaport, Embarkation of the Queen of Sheba' (1648). Poussin, 'Adoration of the Golden Calf' (late 1630s), a biblical variant of the bacchanals which were a favourite theme of the artist—after a recent attack it has been restored.

French School: 19C Impressionists and Post-Impressionists (Room 40-46): Cézanne, 'Les Grandes Baigneuses' a late work (c 1904) foreshadowing Cubism. Dégas 'Helene Rouart in her Father's study', unfinished painting towards the end of Dégas' active period (1886),—'La-La at the Cirque Fernando' (1879). Gauguin, 'Flower Piece' (1896), painted in Tahiti. Manet, 'Music in the Tuileries Gardens' (1862), including Manet and some of his friends. Monet, 'Water Lily Pond' (1899)—one of ten views of the bridge and pond in the artist's garden —'Water Lilies', one of thirty of these huge canvases which Monet worked on between 1916 and his death, 'The Thames below Westminster' painted on his first visit to London (1871). Picasso, 'Fruit Dish, Bottle and Violin' (1914), the first abstract painting acquired by the National Gallery. Pisarro, 'Lower Norwood under Snow' (1870), 'The Avenue Sydenham' (1871). Redon, 'Ophelia Among the Bower', richly coloured pastels. Renoir, 'The Umbrellas' (1890s), painted in two stages, the girls and the woman (right) in an earlier style. Rousseau, 'Tropical Storm with a Tiger' (1891). Van Gogh, 'Sunflowers' (1888), one of six versions in that year .

Italian School: 13th to 15C (Rooms 1-7, 10-13): richly represented are Fra Angelico, Bellini, 'Doge Leonardo Loredan', c 1501, probably the most famous of all Venetian portraits, Botticelli, 'Venus and Mars', (1485), love triumphs over war . 'Mystic Nativity' (1500), with an inscription by the artist in Greek at the top—a personal prayer for peace. Leonardo da Vinci, 'The Virgin of the Rocks' (1483-1508).

Italian School: 16C (Rooms 8, 14, 30): Bronzino, 'An allegory with Venus and Cupid' (c 1550s), highly finished—a sophisticated defiance of naturalism. Michelangelo, 'The Entombment' (1506), unfinished, influenced by antique sculpture. Raphael, 'Pope Julius II' (1512), thought to be a copy but revealed by cleaning to be an original, very influential work, 'The Ansidei Madonna' for the family chapel in Perugia, a serene harmony. Paintings by Tintoretto and Titian.

Italian School: 18C (Room 34): Canaletto, paintings of Venice and London, 'London, Interior of the Rotunda at Ranelagh' (1754), also 'Eton College', and Tiepolo, an excellent group of small-scale works.

Early Netherlandish School (Rooms 24, 25): Van Eyck, 'The Arnolfini Marriage', signed and dated 'Jan van Eyck was here 1434'; he may be glimpsed in the mirror of this famous painting full of symbolic details. 'Man in Turban', signed and dated 21 October 1433 and inscribed with a Flemish proverb 'As I can, not as I would'.

Spanish School (Rooms 41 and 42): Goya, 'Dona Isabel de Porces' (1805), apparently painted over a male portrait, but still very beautiful. El Greco, 'Christ driving the Traders from the Temple' (c 1600), one of many versions. Murillo, 'The Two Trinities', an altarpiece painted in 1681. Velasquez, 'Toilet of Venus/The Rokeby Venus', his only known female nude, named for the Yorkshire house where it hung in the 19C; damaged by a suffragette in 1914.

Immediately N of and behind the National Gallery is the **National Portrait Gallery**.

National Portrait Gallery, St. Martin's Place, London WC2. Tel. 01-930 1552. Open Mon to Sat 10.00-17.00, Sun 14.00-18.00, (until 20.00 Wed in summer). Education facilities, public lectures, temporary exhibitions. Access: Underground, Charing Cross, Leicester Square.

The National Portrait Gallery contains a most interesting and historically valuable collection founded in 1856, of over 10,000 portraits (paintings, sculptures and drawings) of men and women of significance. The present building, in Italian Rennaissance style by Ewan Christian, was donated by William Henry Alexander, and opened in 1896. It is now a little over-crowded and only a small proportion of the collection can be shown at any one time. The collection is arranged chronologically beginning on the 2nd Floor; the rooms are decorated and lightly furnished so as to give a feeling of historical period. There are regular changes in displays; below are some of the highlights—chosen for their historical significance—to look out for. (Start on the 2nd Floor and work down.)

Room 1, *The Tudors*. 16C portraits of early kings and queens: 'Henry VII' by Michael Sittow (1505), painted for a prospective bride; 'Henry VIII' in Holbein's large cartoon (c 1536-37) in black ink and coloured washes on paper. Henry VII also appears in this drawing for a fresco in Whitehall Palace (destroyed). Nearby is another portrait of Henry VIII after Holbein. Other portraits include Henry VII's wife Elizabeth of York, and three of Henry VIII's wives: Catherine of Aragon, Anne Boleyn and Catherine Parr. Elizabeth I and her marvellous costumes are portrayed in a group of paintings including 'The Coronation Portrait' formerly at Warwick Castle, by an unknown artist (c 1575), and 'The Ditchley Portrait', by Marcus Gheeraerts the Younger, painted in commemoration of the Queen's visit to Ditchley Park near Oxford. The Queen stands on the globe of the world, her feet planted on Oxfordshire. The first picture to be acquired by the Gallery was the 'Chandos' portrait of Shakespeare, attributed to John Taylor (1610) the only known contemporary portrait.

Room 2, *The Stuarts*. The early period is dominated by James I in full length by Mytens (1621), in a spectacular frame; his queen Anne of Denmark attributed to Larkin. Charles I in a full length portrait by Mytens (1631) with his queen Henrietta Maria in a portrait influenced by Van Dyck. The Civil War is recreated by portraits of Cromwell and his collaborators.

Room 3 continues with some of the smaller 17C portraits, miniatures, medals, engravings and portraits of writers.

Rooms 4 and 5, *Restoration and Late Stuart*: Charles II in full length by Hawker (c 1680), nearby his wife Catherine of Braganza by Stoop in the Portuguese costume which aroused such comment when she first arrived in England, and a group of his mistresses, including the Duchess of Cleveland (by Wright) and Nell Gwyn with a lamb (by Lely). Note Hayls' portrait of Samuel Pepys, mentioned in the latter's diaries in 1666. Pepys hired an Indian gown to wear for the portrait. James II in portraits by Kneller and Lely. William and Mary representing the Glorious Revolution.

Rooms 6 and 7, *Early 18C Arts and Sciences, the Kit-Cat Club*. Earl of Burlington builder of Chiswick House and Burlington House, by Richardson (c 1717). Wren by Kneller (1711) and a group of Kneller's portraits of members of the Kit-Cat Club (see p 343 and p 391). The club took its names from 'kit-cats', the mutton pies served at the tavern near Temple Bar kept by Christopher Cat, where the Club met in the early days when it was run by publisher Jacob Tonson. There are 42 portraits in all and a selection is shown including Congreve, Vanbrugh, Tonson, Walpole and the Duke of Newcastle and the Earl of Lincoln.

Room 8, *Early Georgian Portraits* include the full length portrait of George II from the studio of Hudson (1744), his wife Caroline of Anspach by Amigono (1735), their favourite composer Handel, by Hudson (1756), and the king's mistress the Countess of Suffolk.

Note the self-portraits of Hogarth (1758) and Thornhill (1725). There are more portraits in Room 9, Gainsborough (c 1759), William Jones by Hogarth (1740), recently acquired, and Reynolds (c 1754). Reynolds' portraits of Dr Johnson (1756) and Boswell (1785) are also here. *The British Overseas* in Room 10 are represented by Clive in a stiff portrait by Dance, and Captain Cook in a portrait painted at the Cape of Good Hope in 1776 by John Weber.

Room 11, *The Struggle for America*: George Washington, after Stuart, and representatives of both sides, including the 'Death of Chatham' (1780-81) showing Chatham's collapse in the House of Lords after speaking against withdrawal.

In Room 12, *England at War* is illustrated with a portrait of Nelson (1800-01) by Beechey and the portrait of his mistress Lady Hamilton by Romney (c 1785). And later an unflattering portrait of Wellington by Home, painted in India. Note also the political caricatures.

Room 13, *The Romantic Movement*. Representatives from literature include Burns by Nasmyth, Scott by Landseer (c 1824), Mary Wollstonecraft and her daughter Mary Shelley (1841) and Keats by Severn, Byron in Albanian dress by Phillips (1813) and Wordsworth by Haydon (1842). Artists are also represented.

Room 14, *Science and the Industrial Revolution* with portraits of inventors including Watts by Von Breda, Brunel by Drummond (c 1836) with the Thames Tunnel in the background. Chantrey's bust of Rennie (1818).

Room 15, *The Regency*, includes a number of theatrical portraits, the most striking that of Sarah Siddons by Beechey (1793). At the far end of the room is 'The Reformed House of Commons, 1833' by Hayter and William Cobbett (1831), unknown artist, and other parliamentary reformers. Note also Elizabeth Fry, the prison reformer, after Leslie. Amongst the miniatures, is Jane Austen by her sister Cassandra (1810), the only authentic likeness of the novelist.

1st Floor, Room 16, *The Young Victoria*, with Tweed's life-size plaster of 'Queen Victoria and Prince Albert as Ancient Saxons' (1868), just outside, as well as the full length portrait of the Queen by Hayter in her coronation robes.

In Room 17, Early Victorians include a number of well-known literary portraits: Tennyson by S. Laurence (c 1840), Thackeray by Frank Stone (c 1839), Dickens, by Maclise (1839), Charlotte Brontë and Mrs Gaskell in drawings by Richmond (1850 and 1850). The Brontë Sisters (c 1834) by their brother Branwell, a primitive but compelling portrait. Emile Brontë (1833) by Branwell. Jenny Lind, the 'Swedish Nightingale', a replica of a portrait by Magnus (1846) surrounded by opera bills and more theatrical portraits.

Room 19, *The Crimea, India and the Empire*—missionaries and explorers with a special display on the Crimea including Steel's bust of Florence Nightingale (1862). Room 20 continues the theme in *Victorian Science and Technology* symbolised by Prince Albert in a full length portrait by Winterhalter (1867) and engravings of the Great Exhibition. Room 21, more *Victorian writers and artists* including the Pre-Raphaelites, with portraits of Holman Hunt, Ruskin and William Morris. *Later Victorians* follow in Room 22 with well-known politicians, Disraeli and Gladstone by Millais (1881 and 1879).

Room 24, *Edwardian Arts*—theatrical and literary portraits. Note 'Ellen Terry as Lady Macbeth' by Sargent (1889). *Edwardian Arts and Politics* follow in Room 25.

Portraits of members of the royal family are on the landing and include Lavery's gracious 'Royal Family at Buckingham Palace' (1913) showing George V, Queen Mary, the Duke of Windsor and the Princess Royal. On the mezzanine are portraits of the present royal family including Annigoni's Queen Elizabeth II (1969), Bryan Organ 'The Princess of Wales' (1981), damaged but now repaired, Duke of Edinburgh (1983), also by Organ, and others.

On the ground floor is the 20C display with photographs, drawings and paintings mounted on moving turntables. Amongst the hundreds of famous faces are Churchill, sketches by Graham Sutherland, political caricatures by Beerbohm and Low, Elizabeth Frink's bust of Sir Alec Guinness, Rodrigo Moynihan's portrait of Margaret Thatcher, and Organ's portrait of Prince Charles.

6   St. James's Park, The Mall and Buckingham Palace

Access: Underground, Charing Cross, St. James's Park.

Explore this area from Trafalgar Square, entering under *Admiralty Arch* with its striking view down the 'triumphal avenue' of the Mall with the Victoria Memorial and Buckingham Palace closing the vista. This massive triumphal arch was designed by Sir Aston Webb as part of the national memorial to Queen Victoria. On the left immediately beyond the Arch is a statue of Captain Cook (1728-79) by Brock (1914); on the right a memorial to the Royal Marines by Adrian Jones (1903). The conspicuous and grim-looking building on the left is the 'Citadel' covered in Virginia creepers. It is often confused with the Cabinet War Rooms (see p 88) but was built in 1941-42 as an extension to the Admiralty to provide bomb-proof protection for the communications room. Horse Guards Parade is beyond.

The **Mall**, the spacious avenue lined with double rows of plane trees that skirts St. James's Park on the N, is so called from having been used in Charles II's time for the game of 'pail-mail' (from the Italian 'palla', meaning ball, and 'maglio', meaning mallet; a cross between croquet and golf). Overlooking it on the right is the bright *Carlton House Terrace* designed by Nash, a monumental terrace of mansions (entered from Waterloo Place, see Rte 7), with small gardens on the projecting podium below. Here are the entrances to the *Mall Galleries* of the Federation of British Artists, and, just before Duke of York's steps, at *Nash House*, to the Institute of Contemporary Arts, with galleries, an auditorium, theatre, and restaurant (open Tues-Sun 12.00-21.00). Carlton House Terrace is interrupted by the Duke of York's Column and Waterloo Place, described on p 107. Opposite is a Royal Artillery monument (1910) in memory of the dead in South Africa 1899-1902.

*St James's Park (Pl. 14; 6; 93 acres) extends from the Horse Guards Parade, on the E, to Buckingham Palace, on the W, and is bounded on the N by the Mall, on the S by Birdcage Walk. Charmingly laid out in an aristocratic surrounding of palaces and government offices, and commanding a famous view in the direction of Westminster, this park is one of the most attractive in London. The lake in the centre (5 acres) is frequented by ornamental waterfowl, for which Duck Island at the E end is reserved as a breeding place. Among the 'great variety of fowle' described by Pepys are six pelicans (their successors best seen at feeding time, at 16.00 in summer or 15.00 in winter, near Duck Island). The flower-beds are beautifully maintained, and the trees, some dating from the Restoration, add an oriental flavour to the views over the lake.

Henry VIII laid out the land between his palaces at Whitehall and St. James's in 1532 as the first royal park in London. Under the early Stuarts it was the resort of the Court and other privileged persons, among them Milton (who lived in 1652-60 in a house in Petty France overlooking the park). In 1649 Charles I walked across it on the morning of his execution from St. James's Palace to Whitehall, and here in 1660 Pepys had his first view of Charles II on his return to London: 'Found the King in the parke. There walked. Gallantry great'. After the Restoration Le Nôtre was employed to make 'great and very noble alteracions', and the scattered ponds were united to form a 'canal'. It was then opened to the public, and remains the only large park in London which has not been enclosed by railings. It became a fashionable resort, where the king was frequently to be seen strolling unattended and feeding the waterfowl for which he established a 'volary' or aviary. The park was further altered and the form of the lake changed by Nash in 1827-29, as an appendage to Carlton House, then occupied by George IV. During the First World War the lake was emptied and its bed occupied by temporary government buildings.

From June to September a band plays in the park, daily exc. Sun 12.30-14.00, 17.30-19.00.—Since 1785 chairs have been on hire in the park.

At the end of Carlton House Terrace is a double flight of steps designed by De Soissons. At the top a statue of George VI by W. McMillan (1955) fronts Carlton Gardens (p 108). The Mall now skirts the gardens of Marlborough House (see below), beyond which Marlborough Road passes between (left) St. James's Palace and (right) the Queen's Chapel and Marlborough House. The *Queen's Chapel* (open for services Easter-Aug Sun 10.45 for 11.15) was designed by Inigo Jones in 1623.

It was built as a private chapel for the Roman Catholic Infanta Maria of Spain whom Prince Charles, later Charles I, was expected to marry, and completed for Henrietta Maria, his eventual wife. With a temple-like facade, the classical double-cube hall has a superb elliptical coffered ceiling constructed of timber. The interior retains its 17C fittings, with an altarpiece of the Holy Family, by Annibale Carracci.

The view of Whitehall from the bridge in St. James's Park

Marlborough House (Pl. 14; 6), concealed behind the chapel in a pleasant garden of 4.5 acres, and approached by an unassuming entrance at the W end of Pall Mall, was the base for the Commonwealth Secretariat. The former state apartments are open, when not in use, and there are guided tours. But the building closed in 1984 for lengthy renovation (Tel. 01-930 9249). The staircases have mural paintings by Laguerre (restored), and a ceiling by Orazio Gentileschi was moved from Greenwich (Queen's House) in the 18C and inserted in the Blenheim Saloon.

Marlborough House, a good example of Wren's red brick work, was built in 1709-11 for the great Duke of Marlborough with bricks brought back as ballast from Holland after the Duke's military campaigns there. The third storey was added by Sir William Chambers in the 18C, and the porte-cochère and entrance in 1860-63. Here, next door to 'Neighbour George', the great Duchess Sarah lived for 22 years after the death of her husband at Windsor. Later occupants were Leopold I of the Belgians (before his accession), Queen Adelaide, and (as Prince of Wales) Edward VII and George V (1903-10). The last was born here in 1865. On the death of Edward VII it became the residence of Queen Alexandra (1844-1925). In 1936 Queen Mary (1867-1953) returned to her former home.—On the garden wall in Marlborough Road is an elaborate, finely wrought memorial (1932) to Queen Alexandra by Alfred Gilbert, and (on the Mall) a plaque to Queen Mary.

St. James's Palace (Pl. 14; 5; no admission), an irregular and picturesque brick building, encloses several secluded courtyards some of which are open to the public.

The palace stands on the site of a hospital for fourteen 'maidens that were leprous' which was dedicated to St. James the Less and is mentioned at least as early as 1100. Henry VIII acquired the hospital and its grounds in 1531, and built a palace here, of which only the Gatehouse, parts of the Chapel Royal, and the Old Presence Chamber (Tapestry Room) remain. Mary I died at St. James's in 1558. Charles I, most of whose children were born in this palace, spent his last days here. Charles II employed Wren to provide state apartments overlooking the park, and the palace became the principal residence of the Duke of York (afterwards James II). After 1698, when Whitehall was burned down, St. James's Palace became the official London residence of the sovereign, where all Court functions were held; the British Court is still officially known as the Court of St. James's, and the sovereign is proclaimed from the balcony in Friary Court. Among those born in the palace are Mary II (1662), Queen Anne (1664), the Old Pretender (1688), and George IV (1762). George IV employed Nash to restore and redecorate the palace. It is now occupied by 'Grace and Favour' apartments, the Gentlemen and Yeomen-at-Arms, and the Lord Chamberlain.—Sentries guard the palace in Ambassador's Court and outside the walls (unlike those at Buckingham Palace who now stand within the forecourt).

The open *Friary Court*, on the E side of the palace, takes its name from a Capuchin friary established by Henrietta Maria and demolished to make room for Marlborough House. The most attractive feature of the exterior is the fine 16C brick *Gatehouse, to the N, facing St. James's St, with its four octagonal towers. The carving over the original doors which lead into the *Colour Court* (no adm.) shows the initials of Henry VIII and Anne Boleyn. Beyond the large restored N window of the Chapel Royal, an archway leads into the charming *Ambassador's Court* from which the Chapel is entered.

The **Chapel Royal** has been greatly altered since it was built for Henry VIII, and it was enlarged in 1837. It preserves a fine ceiling, probably designed by Holbein in 1540. The music here has always been noted for its excellence; among early organists were Orlando Gibbons and Purcell. The private choir of the sovereign is composed of 6 'Gentlemen' and 10 boys; the boys wear traditional Court costume. At Epiphany (6 Jan) an offering of gold, frankincense, and myrrh is made on behalf of the sovereign, on which occasion the service is conducted by the Bishop of London. Several royal marriages have been celebrated in this chapel, including those of Mary, the daughter of Charles I and mother of William III (1641), William III and Mary II (1677), Queen Anne (1683), George IV (1795), Queen Victoria (1840), and George V (1893).—Visitors are admitted to the services held here Sun 09.15 and 11.00; closed August.

An original passage-way leads to Colour Court, and, on the S side, picturesque passages admit to Engine Court (both private). Opposite is *York House*, now the residence of the Duke and Duchess of Kent. Lord Kitchener lived here in 1915-16. The W wing (with some fine Adam details) has been restored for use as offices of the Crown.

To the W lies *Stable Yard*; the former stables (1661) remain in the N range. Facing them is the imposing entrance portico of **Lancaster House**, a massive palace built by Benj. Wyatt in 1825-27 for the Duke of York (the S facade is well seen from the Mall). It was continued in 1827-30 for the first Duke of Sutherland, earlier Marquess of Stafford, and enlarged to Wyatt's designs by Smirke and Barry in 1833-41 for the second Duke. The third Duke entertained Garibaldi here in 1864. It is now a Government Hospitality Centre. Visitors are admitted when the building is not in use (Tel. 01-212 4784) (Easter to mid-September, Sat, Sun, BH 14.00-18.00; ring first).

Known as *Stafford House* from 1842 to 1912, it was then presented to the nation by Lord Leverhulme (d 1921) and named Lancaster House. It was decorated in the Louis-Quinze style and reopened in 1950. Notable among the gorgeous fittings are Barry's double staircase, and the ceiling paintings in the great first floor gallery (Assumption of St. Chrysogonus, by Guercino), and state anteroom (Cupid with the Graces, by Veronese).

A passageway which gives access to Green Park skirts *Warwick House* (1716; by Hawksmoor). On the E side of the Court is the *Lord Chamberlain's Office* in an attractive house with fine first floor windows.

Return to the Mall by Stable Yard Road past the bright stucco flank of *Clarence House* built in 1825 by Nash for William IV when Duke of Clarence, restored in 1949 for Princess Elizabeth (Elizabeth II) and the Duke of Edinburgh, and now the residence of the Queen Mother. A piper plays in the garden every morning at 09.00 when the Queen Mother is in residence. The S facade of St. James's Palace extends eastwards (see from the Mall), built by Wren in the late 17C.

Opposite Marlborough Rd, a path, preceded by a fine wrought iron gate, leads through St. James's Park and across the lake by a bridge (1957; fine view). *Birdcage Walk* skirts the park on the S side; the name recalls a royal aviary established here in the reign of James I. A small road across Birdcage Walk leads to *Queen Anne's Gate*, to the left, a quiet street of delightful houses, built by Charles Shales (who lived at No. 15) in 1704.

The houses have carved masks to the keystones, and elaborately carved door cases with canopied hoods, unique in London. The statue of Queen Anne in state robes is contemporary. Lord Palmerston (1784-1865) was born at No. 20, and Lord Haldane (1856-1929) lived at No. 28. William Paterson, 'founder' of the Bank of England, probably assisted Shales in building the square; he lived at No. 19 in 1705-18. At No. 40 three ornamental lead cisterns are fixed on the exterior, one dated 1745 (probably used inside the house). The SDP has its party headquarters here; and so supposedly do MI5—the British secret service. At No. 36 is the headquarters of the National Trust.

Old Queen St, further W, presents a medley of domestic architectural styles, including Nos 9-15 dating from 1698-99. No. 14, possibly designed by Adam, was occupied by Charles Townley in 1777-1805 and here he entertained Renolds and Zoffany at his renowned 'Sunday dinners'. The parallel Lewisham St is a narrow alley-way of unexpectedly tall industrial buildings. The old street lighting of the area survives.

Return to Birdcage Walk via Cockpit Steps between Queen Anne's Gate and Old Queen St, and return westwards, passing attractive houses with bay windows and balconies overlooking the park. Built in 1780, all are narrow and present pleasantly varied facades. Near the W end of Birdcage Walk are the *Wellington Barracks* (1834-59) occupied by the Grenadier Guards, the new buildings spaciously laid out around the parade ground.

The **Guard's Chapel**, or *Royal Military Chapel*, is approached by a memorial cloister (1954-56), by H.S. Goodhart-Rendel, in honour of the Household Brigade in the Second World War. The chapel itself, opened in 1838 but completely transformed within in 1875-78 by G.E. Street, was wrecked by a flying bomb on 18 June 1944, during morning service, with the loss of 121 lives. The present chapel, opened in 1963, is by George, Trew, and Dunn; its austerity sets off Street's ornate apse, which survives. At the end of the narthex opposite the memorial cloister is the *Household Brigade Cenotaph*, while the six S chapels are dedicated to the five regiments of Foot Guards and the Household Cavalry. The sculptured aluminium screens are by Geoffrey Clarke. The chapel is open free Mon-Fri 10.00-16.00, Sunday 09.30-13.00 and for services on Sun at 11.00. A statue of Earl Alexander of Tunis by James Butler was unveiled outside the chapel in 1985.

At the W end of the Mall and St. James's Park, a spacious circus with planted lawns surrounded by a stone balustrade opens before Buckingham Palace. In the centre rises the conspicuous **Queen Victoria Memorial** (1911) of white marble, crowned by a gilded bronze figure of victory with Courage and Constancy at her feet, and surrounded by water.

The monument designed by Sir Aston Webb, and well sculpted by Sir Thomas Brock, consists of the seated figure of Queen Victoria (E side), and groups typifying Truth (S), Motherhood (W), and Justice (N). Other allegorical groups in dark bronze decorate the podium, representing Peace and Progress (E), Science and Art (N), Manufactures and Agriculture (W), and Naval and Military Powers (S).—The monument provides a good viewpoint for the changing the guard and royal processions.

Buckingham Palace (Pl. 14; 7), the residence of the Queen, stands between St. James's Park and a private garden of 40 acres. When the sovereign is in residence the royal standard is flown. (The guard is changed at 11.30 in the forecourt—daily May-August, every other day September-April.)

The palace takes its name from *Buckingham House*, built on this site in 1703 by the Duke of Buckingham. George III purchased this house in 1762, and here the famous interview between him and Dr Johnson took place (1767). The building was altered and remodelled by Nash for George IV about 1825, and since that time it has been known as Buckingham Palace, although neither George IV nor his successor ever occupied it. Since the accession of Queen Victoria in 1837, however, it has been the London residence of the sovereign, and here Edward VII was born in 1841 and died in 1910. The W facade towards the garden remains largely as Nash designed it; the E wing, facing the park, was added by Blore in 1847, but in 1913 the entire E facade was replaced by a much more dignified design by Sir Aston Webb. The interior of the palace, never open to sightseers, contains many magnificent and sumptuously decorated apartments, besides a very fine gallery of paintings and other works of art. The Throne Room, 66ft long, has a marble frieze representing the Wars of the Roses. The royal apartments are in the N wing.

The palace gardens, the scene in July of royal garden parties, include a lake and one of the mulberry trees planted by James I after 1609 to encourage the silk industry. These *Mulberry Gardens* soon degenerated into a place of popular entertainment (c 1630-90), described by Pepys as 'a very silly place'.

Changing the Guard takes place at Buckingham Palace, daily May to August, every other day September to April, but not in wet weather or when other state occasions occur, and is normally carried out by the Brigade of Guards. The best vantage-point is the Queen Victoria Memorial, or near the centre gates of the palace. The ceremony involves the trooping of the Queen's colour from St. James's Palace to Buckingham Palace. At approx. 11.10 one contingent of the old guard parades in Ambassador's Court, St. James's (Pl. 14; 5), and then troops to Buckingham Palace. There they join the old Palace Guard at the left side of the centre gates at approx. 11.25.

The new Guard, accompanied by a band, march from the nearby Wellington Barracks. They form up and are inspected in their barracks before coming on duty; at Wellington Barracks they are on parade by about 10.15. They enter the palace by the normal 'out' gate, and form up facing the old guard, slow marching to the right side of the centre gates. The officers of the old and new guard advance and touch left hands, symbolising the handing over of the keys, and at this point the guard is 'changed'. Eight men now peel off from the ranks to relieve sentries guarding St. James's Palace, Clarence House, and Buckingham Palace. Meanwhile music is played in the forecourt of Buckingham Palace. The old guard complete with the sentries march out of the centre gates at approx. 12.10 accompanied by the massed bands, turning right to return to barracks. The new guard is dismissed to go on duty at Buckingham Palace, while a small detachment of drums (or pipes and drums) leaves the palace by the right-hand gate to accompany the new guard back to St. James's Palace and Clarence House.

Buckingham Gate and its extension *Buckingham Palace Road* skirt the ornamental wall in front of the S wing of the palace. Here are the entrances to the Queen's Gallery and the Royal Mews. In the **Queen's Gallery** (adm. daily exc. Mon 11.00-17.00, Sun 11.00-1700, admission charge) are mounted exhibitions, changed perhaps every two years, of * *Treasures selected from the splendid royal collections.

The private chapel, in the S wing, was the part of the palace most seriously damaged in the air raids of 1940-44. It was rebuilt in 1961-62, and the W part adapted to form the Queen's Gallery.

Beyond a conspicuous pediment (with a scene of Hercules sculpted by William Theed) added by Nash to the Riding House of 1764, is the quadrangle (1824-25) and clock tower of the **Royal Mews** (Pl. 14; 7; adm. Wed and Thurs 14.00-16.00. Admission charge. Closed Ascot week and on other ceremonial occasions). Here the Queen's horses and the royal equipages, including the magnificent state carriage designed by Sir William Chambers in 1761 and painted by Cipriani, are on view. In the old Carriage House is a charming frieze of the Coronation of William IV by R. Barret Davis (1782-1854).

On the opposite side of Buckingham Palace Road are the headquarters of the *Girl Guides Association* (No. 17) and the *Scout Association* (No. 25). Westminster Theatre in Palace St is described on p 148. In *Lower Grosvenor Place*, at the SW angle of the palace grounds, two attractive Regency shop fronts (Nos 5 and 6) remain, flanking an entrance to the paved Victoria Square. For Victoria and the area to the S, see Rte 12.

On the N side of Buckingham Palace the tree-lined *Constitution Hill* (probably so named after the 'constitutionals' taken here by Charles II) leads due W to Hyde Park Corner (see Rte 10), with a sand-track for riders skirting Green Park. Here three attempts on the life of Queen Victoria were made (in 1840, 1842, and 1849), and in 1850, Sir Robert Peel was fatally injured by a fall from his horse.

Green Park (53 acres), created in 1668 with fine expanses of grass and trees, extends N to Piccadilly. The decorative Dominion gateway opposite the Victoria Memorial, leads into a broadwalk; while the paved Queen's Walk, opened in 1730 and named after Caroline, wife of George II, skirts the E border of the park (see p 103). Ice houses were built here in 1660 by Charles II when the park was used for royal picnics. The only ornament is a small fountain near Hyde Park Corner (1954; by E.J. Clack). The Tyburn (comp. p 124), now channelled underground, still crosses the park, and can be heard near the centre. The railings along Piccadilly are hung with prints, paintings and souvenirs on Sundays—a colourful but not very aesthetic display—all for sale.

7   Pall Mall and St. James's

Access: Underground, Green Park, Piccadilly Circus

Between St. James's Park and Piccadilly lies **St. James's**—an area of London where the street layout has remained virtually as it was planned in the 1670s by Henry Jermyn, Earl of St. Albans (1604-84), founder of London's West End described by Pepys in 1660 as 'a fine civil gentleman'. And St. James's has retained its gentlemanly air—the atmosphere of its 'gentlemen's clubs' and specialist shops survives amongst encroaching publishing and advertising offices.

St. James's was established as a residential district near St. James's Palace and Court and became famous in the late 18C for its bachelor lodgings. From the reign of William III the coffee and chocolate houses of St. James's (the forerunners of today's clubs) were the rendezvous of aristocratic and learned London society. Specialist shops set up to serve them as well as the Palace.

London's clubs are traditionally the preserve of men, although some now have women members and others welcome women as guests in the evenings. Financial pressures have taken their toll on some clubs but others have adapted by offering overnight accommodation, health clubs, and in some cases merging with other clubs. There are no name plates on club front doors but the elaborate flambeaux which survive outside some of them are lit by gas on state occasions.

The HAYMARKET runs S from Coventry Street to Pall Mall, parallel to Lower Regent Street. A hay market was established here in the 16C, providing hay for London's horses. The *Design Centre* at 28 Haymarket, SW1, is the showroom for the Council of Industrial Design with changing exhibitions of British-designed goods as well as an extensive register of designers, manufacturers and designs. The shop sells well-designed souvenirs and gift items. Open Mon-Tues 10.00-18.00, Wed-Sat 10.00-20.00, Sun 13.00-18.00. Further down is the *Haymarket Theatre* which opened in 1821. It has associations with Squire Bancroft and Beerbohm Tree, who later went to Her Majesty's across the road. Here Wilde's 'An Ideal

Husband' was first played (1895). In a former theatre on this site, built a century earlier, Aaron Hill, Theophilus Cibber and Henry Fielding all appeared, and Charles Macklin and Samuel Foote produced plays. The massive brick columns of the present building, by Nash, extend over the pavement. Opposite, slightly further down, is *Her Majesty's Theatre*, elaborately decorated and crowned by a Baroque copper dome, founded by Sir Herbert Tree in 1897. The first theatre which opened in 1705 on this site was designed by Sir John Vanbrugh; it burned down in 1789 and the theatre was rebuilt three times.

In the 19C it functioned as an opera house and Bizet's 'Carmen' and Wagner's 'Ring' were both given their London premieres here. The Royal Academy of Dramatic Art was founded at the theatre in 1904. During the 1920s there were performances of Diaghilev's Russian ballet and Noel Coward's plays.

New Zealand House to the S was built on half the site occupied by a previous theatre. The 16-storey building has a roof terrace with magnificent views (New Zealand passport holders are admitted on request) and below is the Martini Terrace, used for receptions, with equally splendid views of the City and Westminster.

Adjoining it (entrance in Pall Mall) is the *Royal Opera Arcade* (1816) by Nash and G.S. Repton, lit by circular skylights and hung with lamps and flower baskets. This recollects the operatic past of Her Majesty's and was London's earliest shopping arcade; it runs through to Charles II Street.

Pall Mall (Pl. 14; 6) runs from Trafalgar Square through to St. James's Palace. The end, Cockspur Street, is still the home of shipping companies and the Norwegian State Railway; also the Hong Kong Tourist Association and Cathay Pacific Airlines. A fine statue of George III by M.C. Wyatt, 'a good horse ridden by a horseman', stands at the beginning of Pall Mall proper.

Like the Mall, Pall Mall takes its name from the game of 'pail-mail' played here in the 17C. It is famous for its clubs; the first building on the SE corner of Pall Mall and Waterloo Place is the former United Service and Royal Aero Club, now the headquarters of the *Institute of Directors*. The building by Nash (1827) incorporates the main staircase from the demolished Carlton House. It was remodelled by Decimus Burton in 1842 to match the Athenaeum opposite and the horseblocks in Waterloo Place were put in for the Duke of Wellington whose favourite club this was. The club, founded in 1815, was the earliest service club in London; it closed in 1976. The Royal Academy was established on part of this site in 1768-79.

Across Waterloo Place stands the *Athenaeum*, founded in 1823 as a club for 'scientific and literary men and artists' by Sir Humphry Davy, President of the Royal Society, Lord Aberdeen (Prime Minister 1852-55) and Sir Thomas Lawrence, President of the Royal Academy. It remains the leading club for academics and politicians. Thackeray wrote some of his works in the library.

Waterloo Place, which here intersects Pall Mall, is characterised by banks and insurance offices, and by numerous statues.

The group to the N of Pall Mall commemorates the Crimean War (1854-55). In the centre is the *Guards' Monument* by John Bell, with three guardsmen and a trophy of Russian guns. In front are statues of *Lord Herbert of Lea* (1810-61; by Foley), secretary of war during the campaign; and *Florence Nightingale* (1820-1910), by A.G. Walker. The fine street lamp dates from c 1830. S of Pall

Mall is an equestrian statue of *Edward VII* (d 1910), by Sir B. Mackennal. To the left (E), *Captain Scott* (1888-1912), the Antarctic explorer, by Lady Scott (1915); *Colin Campbell, Lord Clyde* (1792-1863), the saviour of Lucknow, by Marochetti (its base damaged by a bomb in the Second World War); and *Lord Lawrence* (1811-79), Viceroy of India, by Boehm; to the right (W) *Sir John Franklin* (1786-1847), the Arctic explorer, by Matthew Noble, and *Sir John Burgoyne* (1782-1871), the Crimean general, by Boehm. The Crafts Council has a Gallery at Waterloo Place. Crafts Council Gallery, 12 Waterloo Place, SW1. Tel. 01-930 4811. Exhibitions of crafts with information library on British craftsmen and women. Open Tues-Sat 10.00-17.00, Sun 14.00-17.00.

At the S end of Waterloo Place rises the *Duke of York's Column* in Tuscan granite, 124ft high, designed by Benj. Wyatt and erected in 1834. It bears a bronze statue, by Westmacott, of the Duke of York (d 1827), second son of George III, and Commander-in-Chief of the British Army in 1795-1827. Every officer and soldier in the Army contributed a day's pay to provide funds for the monument to 'the soldier's friend'. Beyond the column the *Waterloo* or *Duke of York's Steps*, with a fine view towards Westminster, descend to the Mall. *Carlton House Terrace*, once one of the most aristocratic places of residence in London, overlooks the Mall.

Carlton House, which stood on the site of Waterloo Place and the York Column, was built in 1709. George IV, when Prince of Wales, set up his establishment here in 1783, and here celebrated the news of his accession. Nash laid out Regent St to connect the house with Regent's Park to the N, but it was demolished in 1829. On the left of Waterloo Steps, No. 10 houses the *Commonwealth Secretariat*. No. 11, built in 1831, was Gladstone's home from 1857 to 75; it is now the headquarters of the *Foreign Press Association*. In Nash House are the offices of the *Association of Societies of Art and Design* (including the ICA; entered from the Mall, see p 100). Beyond the *Crown Estates Office* (No. 13), was *Crockford's* (No. 16), founded in 1827 (comp. p 120), London's most famous gambling club, recently removed to Mayfair. The British Council building occupies the site of Carlton Mews and Spring Gardens, formed in the reign of Elizabeth I; the new offices date from 1975.

Under a tree on the right (W side) of the York Column, the tombstone of the German ambassador's terrier (Giro; d 1934) recalls the Prussian and later German Embassy at No. 9, from 1849 until 1939. *The Royal Society*, one of the most famous scientific bodies in the world, has occupied Nos 6-9 (entrance at No. 6) since 1967. It originated from a group of eminent scholars who began to meet informally in London or in Oxford in 1645. Its formal foundation dates from 1660 and its royal charter of incorporation from 1662. It now numbers about 760 fellows (FRS), with about 70 foreign members. The rooms contain many busts and portraits of distinguished Fellows, and also some interesting relics; Newton's telescope, watch, and sundial; MS of the Principia; original model of Davy's safety lamp, etc. (Admission by appointment).

Beyond the Turf Club (No. 5; formerly the residence of Lady Cunard), No. 2 (*The Royal College of Pathologists*) was occupied in 1906-25 by Lord Curzon, a statue of whom stands opposite. The attractive S facades of clubs in Pall Mall are well seen across the gardens. In 1807 F. Albrecht Winzler erected 13 gas lamp-posts outside his house here, the earliest use of gas for lighting in London. By 1820 the whole parish of St. James's was lit by gas; the area retains some of the oldest and most closely spaced lamp-posts in the city (temp. George IV).

Further W in *Carlton Gardens*, Lord Palmerston and Lord Balfour lived at No. 4 (rebuilt in 1933 by Sir Reginald Blomfield), where a tablet marks this as General de Gaulle's Free French headquarters from 18 June 1940. An attractive small square opens behind a statue of George VI (comp. p 101), and stairs descend to the Mall. No. 3 was designed by Decimus Burton. Lord Kitchener lived at No. 2 (now the Royal Fine Art Commission) in 1914-15. No. 1 was occupied by Napoleon III (1840-41) and Lord Northcliffe (1920-22); it is now the Foreign Secretary's official residence. The well-proportioned Wool House (1967, by David Hodges) stands on the site of Nos 5 and 6.

Next to the Athenaeum in Pall Mall is the *Travellers' Club*, founded in 1819, and occupying a fine building (1829-32) by Barry, in an Italian Renaisance style. It draws many of its members from the Foreign Office. Next door is the imposing *Reform Club*, founded by Radicals and Whigs after the passage of the Reform Bill. It was established here in 1836 in a building also by Barry but on a larger scale, on the site of a house which contained the National Gallery from 1824 until 1834. Once noted for its cuisine because of the chef Alexis Soyer (1837-50) who assisted in planning the kitchens, it numbers many senior civil servants and media people among its membership. The *Royal Automobile Club*, founded in 1897, with an Egyptian swimming pool and squash courts, has a long facade of 1911.

Opposite, the *Junior Carlton Club* (1966, by Norman Royce), was established in 1864 to accommodate the 'waiting list' for the Carlton Club. Benjamin Disraeli held political meetings here in 1868-74 round a circular table still owned by the club. To the W is the new building (1963) of the *Army and Navy Club*, familiarly known as 'The Rag', a contraction for 'rag and famish', a phrase used by a dissatisfied member in 1839 to characterise his entertainment.

Behind the Junior Carlton Club lies **St. James's Square** (Pl. 14; 6), laid out by Lord St. Albans (who lived on the site of Chatham House in 1675-82). Nearly all the houses have since been rebuilt several times, and offices have displaced the former fashionable residences. In the garden of flowering trees in the centre is an equestrian statue of William III, by John Bacon, the Younger (1808), based on designs by his father, and a seat designed by John Nash (1822).

Norfolk House (No. 31; rebuilt in 1939), was owned by the dukes of Norfolk from 1722 until 1937. Frederick, Prince of Wales, leased the property in 1737-41, and George III was born here. It was General Eisenhower's Allied Force headquarters in 1942 and again in 1944 (tablet). No. 32 was from 1771 till 1919 the town residence of the bishops of London. Across Charles II St (with a good view of the Haymarket Theatre), No. 4 (rebuilt by Hawksmoor in 1726-28, with an attractive garden behind) is occupied by government offices. From 1912 until 1942 this was the residence of Lord and Lady (Nancy) Astor, and in 1943-45 it was the London headquarters of the Free French forces; later it was the home of the Arts Council. No. 7 has an entrance porch rebuilt by Lutyens in 1911. On this site was the showroom of Josiah Wedgwood from 1796 until 1830. No. 10 (linked with No. 9), *Chatham House, The Royal Institute of International Affairs*, has been occupied by three prime ministers: Chatham (1759-62), Lord Derby (1837-54), and Gladstone (1890). Cast-iron railings and lamp-holders adorn the entrance.

Beyond a facade by Robert Adam at No. 11, the *London Library*, founded in 1841 by Thomas Carlyle, occupies No. 14. One of the largest private subscription libraries in Britain (c 167,000 vols), it has served Dickens, Thackeray, George Eliot, T.S. Eliot, and E.M. Forster. No. 15 has a fine classical facade by James Stuart (1764); the original house was tenanted by the Duchess of Richmond ('La Belle Stuart') in 1678-79. The *East India (and Devonshire Sports) Club* has absorbed Nos 16 and 17. Queen Caroline lived at No. 17 during her trial in 1820, while Lord Castlereagh, then foreign secretary, lived next door (No. 18). No. 20 is a fine Robert Adam building (1771-74; the magnificent interior is well maintained by the Distillers Company). The steps and carving on the door can be enjoyed from the pavement. No. 21 which skilfully duplicates the facade of No. 20, was added in 1934-37, on the site of Winchester House.The Libyan Embassy, formerly at No. 5, was under siege in 1984; a policewoman killed in the incident is commemorated with a simple stone on the E side of the square.

Duke of York Street leads N from the square past the Red Lion, with a characteristic Victorian 'Gin Palace' interior. Across Jermyn St is

St. James's Church (Pl. 14; 3), a fine building by Wren (1676-84; rebuilt after damage in the 'blitz' of 1940-41) on a spacious site. Keystones bear the arms of Lord St. Albans (see above). This was the most fashionable church in London in the early 18C, and three of its rectors became archbishops of Canterbury. The S entrance gate and railings date from c 1800. The church has a lively lunchtime and evening programme with political lectures and concerts. In the courtyard is a market and a Brass Rubbing Centre is in the basement (this may be moving). The Wren Coffee Shop serves light, wholesome food.

The sumptuous *Interior* has galleries supported by elegant columns, and an ingeniously designed roof. The limewood altarpiece is a magnificent work by Grinling Gibbons. The marble font, at which Lord Chatham and William Blake were baptised, is attributed to Gibbons. The organ, from a chapel in Whitehall Palace, was presented to the church by Queen Mary in 1690 when John Blow and Henry Purcell supervised its installation. It was built by Renatus Harris and the splendid case is again the work of Gibbons. William Van de Velde the Elder (c 1610-93) and William Van de Velde the Younger (1633-1707), the marine painters, are buried here (plaque beneath the tower). The courtyard towards Piccadilly commemorates Londoners of 1939-45; the gates were designed by Sir Reginald Blomfield (1937). A neo-Georgian rectory was built by Austin Blomfield (1955-57). The pleasant open garden with a fountain by A. Hardiman is a memorial to Lord Southwood (1873-1946), journalist and newspaper owner.

Jermyn Street, one of the first streets to be built in the area, bears the St. Albans family name. Among fashionable shops here is a specialist cheesemonger (No. 93), survivor of many in the 18C, and a perfumier (No. 89). On the corner of Duke Street the Cavendish Hotel recalls its predecessor managed by the formidable Rosa Lewis, an establishment featured in the novels of Evelyn Waugh. In the same street Benjamin Franklin lodged in 1725 as a journeyman printer. A Jermyn Street Festival takes place in September with demonstrations in the shops and entertainment at St. James's Church.

On the S side of Pall Mall Gainsborough lived from 1774 till his death in 1788 in the W wing (No. 80) of *Schomberg House*, a 17C building of red brick with stone dressings (restored in 1956, when the rest of the house was rebuilt). No. 79 (rebuilt) was given to Nell Gwynn by Charles II, with whom, according to Evelyn, she used to talk over the garden wall. The cellars of the original house survive beneath the pavement. Opposite, Nos 48-49 are the headquarters of the *Royal British Legion*, concerned with the welfare of ex-servicemen. At No. 71 the *United Oxford and Cambridge Clubs* occupy a building by Sir Robert and Sidney Smirke (1830) refurbished in 1973. At the end of Pall Mall is the entrance to **Marlborough House** (p 102). *Cleveland Row* continues W past **St. James's Palace** (see Rte 6) to Green Park.

Three mansions (now offices) overlook the park. The Reform Bill of 1832 was drafted in *Stornoway House* (1794-96; rebuilt in 1959), which became the residence of Lord Beaverbrook in 1924 and housed his Ministry of Aircraft Production in 1940-41. Beyond the delightful bow-front of *Selwyn House* (1895), the Italianate *Bridgwater House* (1841-49) with an elaborate two-storeyed hall by Barry, occupies the site of a house presented by Charles II to Barbara Villiers, duchess of Cleveland, who lived here in 1668-77.—Access to Green Park may be gained from Stable Yard (p 103), or farther N off St. James's Place (comp. below).

St. James's Street (Pl. 14; 5) leads to Piccadilly. *Byron House* occupies the site of No. 8 where, in 1811 after the publication of the 3rd Canto of 'Childe Harold', Lord Byron 'awoke one morning to find himself famous'. Berry Bros & Rudd Ltd have traded at No. 3 since 1699; the shop-front retains a late-18C design. A passage at the side admits to the secluded *Pickering Place* (c 1733); a plaque records that a legation from the Republic of Texas was set up here in 1842-45. Beyond, *Lock & Co. Ltd*, hatters, were established here in 1759, with a delightful shop front dating, in part, from the previous century.

The shop window usually displays period headgear, including an original 'bowler' hat. This was designed for the Earl of Leicester's 'beaters'; the order was sub-contracted to Thomas Bowler & Co., who produced what later became, in a modified form, the fashionable London hat. Nelson's hat (on his wax effigy in Westminster Abbey), was made here.

On the opposite side of St. James's St is the former building of the Constitutional Club (at No. 86; with elaborate carvings), where it shared premises with the Savage Club. The *Carlton Club* (No. 69) was founded by the Duke of Wellington after the defeat of the Tories in 1831 and with the Marquess of Salisbury as its chairman was used as a centre for the Tory party organisation; it remains the leading Conservative Club. Beyond the lock and safe makers, Chubb, who patented a Detector Lock in 1818, the attractive *St. James's Place* diverges left.

At the end the incomplete N front of *Spencer House* by Vardy (1756-65; fine facade on Green Park, see below) faces a block of flats (1960) by Denys Lasdun. At No. 28 lived William Huskisson (plaque). On the site of Castlemaine House, Samuel Rogers, the wealthy banker-poet, lived from 1802 till his death in 1855, entertaining at his famous breakfasts the most eminent literary men of his day. A concealed narrow passage leads alongside No. 23 to Green Park. Here the attractive facades and gardens of the mansions skirting Queen's Walk are well seen. Among them is the striking Palladian front of Spencer House with graceful statues on the pediment, and a paved terrace raised on arches extending in to the garden.
In *King Street*, across St. James's St, pre-eminent among the art dealers and galleries in the area, is *Christie's* (No. 8), fine art auctioneers since 1766 (in King St since 1823). Sales (except in Aug and Sept) are held at 10.30, 11.00 or 14.30. Viewing (usually for 1 week before the sale) (01-839 9060). The *St. James's Theatre*, now demolished, saw the first performances of 'Lady Windermere's Fan' (1892) and 'The Importance of Being Earnest' (1895). *Duke Street*, the first street in London to have a pavement, runs N from King St to Piccadilly. In the parallel *Bury Street*, Haydn lodged at No. 1 in 1794-95, and Thos. Moore at No. 28. The 17C *Crown Passage*, linking King St with Pall Mall, retains an unexpected 'village' atmosphere.

Continue up St. James's St past the raised white plaza of the *Economist building* (1964; by Peter and Alison Smithson). The offices on arcades varying in height form a striking group, and art galleries use the light ground floor premises. In *Blue Ball Yard*, opposite, attractive black and white stables survive from 1741-42. In Park Place No. 14 houses the small Pratt's Club founded in the 1840s and the offices and club of the Royal Overseas League. *Brooks's* (No. 60) is a club founded in 1764. One of the earliest members was Charles James Fox who gambled on the faro table in the fine room overlooking St. James's St. It was the leading Whig club in the 18C and the rival of the Tory White's (see below). Other members included Burke, Gibbon, Hume, Garrick, Reynolds, and Palmerston. Opposite is *Boodle's* (No. 28), founded 1762-64, also patronised by Gibbon and Fox. The building, designed by John Crunden in the Adam manner in 1775-76, has been the home of the club since 1783. *White's*, the oldest club (1736) in London, which originated in White's Chocolate House (1693), was frequented by Swift, Steele, Gray and Pope. The building, probably designed by James Wyatt (1787-88), contains a famous bow window (1881) known as the 'shrine of fashion' by Beau Brummell and his set. The proprietary clubs, Brooks's, Boodle's, and White's, were all distinguished in the 18C for fashion and gambling. Opposite was the former Devonshire Club (No. 50), where Crockford's was opened in 1827 by a successful fish salesman. In Arlington St Robert Walpole lived at No. 5 in 1742-45, and Horace Walpole was born on the site of No. 22. St. James's St ends at the busy thoroughfare of **Piccadilly** (Rte 8).

8   Piccadilly

Access: Underground, Piccadilly Circus.

Piccadilly Circus (Pl. 14; 4) is at last undergoing the transformation that planners have dreamed of for the past thirty years. When completed during 1986, it will feature a new traffic scheme, with Eros on a 'peninsula' on the S side, traffic passing to the N of it and through Windmill Street. The buildings, such as the old Swan and Edgars, and the London Pavilion (plans yet unknown) will have been cleaned and restored but there will be no tower blocks or windswept plazas as proposed in earlier plans.

Piccadilly Circus was originally a road-junction at the bottom of Nash's Regent Street. The circular pattern of buildings around it was destroyed by the building of Shaftesbury Avenue in 1886. Eros was unveiled shortly afterwards (1893) as a memorial to the philanthropist Lord Shaftesbury. The statue and fountain, designed by Alfred Gilbert, were intended to represent the Angel of Charity but soon became known as Eros. It was the first statue to be cast in aluminium and the fountain tended to overflow, as Gilbert's instructions were not followed. The statue was condemned by the critics and Gilbert, severely in debt, left the country for Belgium. But the public took to Eros and Piccadilly Circus has become perhaps the most famous meeting-place in the world. During the rebuilding of Piccadilly Underground Station in the 1920s the statue stood in Embankment Gardens; it was removed during the Second World War and is regularly boarded up for protection when large crowds are in London for football matches and other public celebrations. In 1984 it was removed for restoration and while the layout of the traffic flow progressed it was on display in the Royal Festival Hall. It was due to return to Piccadilly Circus in early to mid-1986.

The popularity of Piccadilly Circus was further enhanced with the arrival of illuminated advertisements; the first in 1910 and more in 1923. These can still be seen on the N side. The Circus was one of the locations for the massive VE celebrations of 1945. The circular Piccadilly Underground Station is the second busiest in London (after Victoria Station).

On the S side is the *Criterion Brasserie*; this is the original Long Bar of the Criterion Restaurant built in 1874 by Thomas Verity using gemstone and goldleaf tiles. The restaurant's concert hall became the Criterion Theatre and is completely underground; it opened in 1874. The Long Bar which served as a Trusthouse Grill and Griddle, its mosaic covered by Formica, was restored and reopened in 1984 as a brasserie restaurant. The gilded ceiling and gemstone tiles are now valued at more than £1m. The future of the Criterion building itself is not yet determined.

The *London Pavilion* on the N side was a 19C music hall; the present building opened in 1885 and was first a theatre and then a cinema which closed in 1982. The original facade survives and it will be developed as part of the Trocadero complex.

The **Trocadero** (entrances in Shaftesbury Avenue and Coventry Street) opened in 1984 as a shopping, restaurant and entertainment complex; the architects Fitzroy Robinson have, behind the facades of the original Trocadero, Scott's Restaurant and Lyons Corner House buildings, constructed an entirely new building with a central three-storey atrium.

The complex takes its name from the Trocadero Palace which operated on the Shaftesbury site in the late 19C as a music hall. It continued as a popular place of entertainment throughout the '30s and became known as the Troc.

The Trocadero complex offers seven-days-a-week and late-night shopping and a selection of cafés and restaurants featuring Italian, French and English food; further restaurants are located in Rupert Street, as well as two tourist attractions: The *Guinness World of Records* and the *London Experience*. Light Fantastic, a holographic exhibition gallery, opened in late 1985.

Guinness World of Records, Trocadero, Piccadilly Circus, London W1. Open 10.00-21.00 daily. Admission charge.

The exhibition on two levels illustrates the contents of the 'Guinness Book of Records'. The fattest man, the smallest woman, the longest fingernails—they are all here in actual size, with further illustrations of record-breaking attempts on video. Sporting achievements are reproduced and records stored on accessible microcomputers. The shop sells appropriate souvenirs and copies of the book.

London Experience, Trocadero, Piccadilly Circus, London W1. Tel. 01-439 4938. Open 10.00-22.00. Admission charge.

This 40-minute multi-screen audio-visual history of London was first seen in London on this site in the 1970s but closed when the building was redeveloped. It returned in 1985 in a re-written format showing the most dramatic moments of London's history, including the London of Jack The Ripper and the Blitz (with special effects). The shop sells souvenirs and there are shows hourly.

For the visitor to London, Piccadilly Circus is a convenient starting-place for exploring the West End. Coventry St runs E to Leicester Square; the broad Shaftesbury Avenue, with its numerous theatres, leads NE through Soho to High Holborn and New Oxford St; Regent St, interrupted by the Circus, leads N to Oxford St and Regent's Park and S to Waterloo Place and Pall Mall; while Piccadilly runs SW to Hyde Park.

Piccadilly runs from the top of Haymarket to Hyde Park Corner (c 1 mile). Beyond Piccadilly Circus its initial section, to the S of which is the region of St. James's, is occupied by airline offices, banks, hotels, and some distinguished shops.

The name of Piccadilly is probably derived from 'Piccadilly Hall', the popular name of a house built c 1611 near Windmill Street by a retired tailor, Robert Baker, who had made much of his fortune by the sale of 'piccadillies', apparently a form of collar or ruff. The street was thus named by 1627-28 when building began at the E end, and the name gradually extended westwards as building progressed.

On the N side of Piccadilly, beyond the Circus, is the large *New Piccadilly Hotel*, with a bold colonnade on the upper storey. Now part of Gleneagles Hotels, it has been refurbished and features a basement health centre in a former Masonic temple and a terrace restaurant overlooking Piccadilly. Opposite, *Simpson's* was built in 1935-36 by Joseph Emberton. Beyond is the forecourt of *St. James's Church*, described in Rte 7. The attractive Midland Bank (1925) adjoining the garden was designed by Edwin Lutyens. To the W the vast plate-glass window of an airline office intrudes into the lower storey of the former home of the Royal Institute of Painters in Water Colours. The inscription and roundels remain on the facade above; the busts are of Sandby, Cozens, Girtin, Turner, D. Cox, De Wint, Barret, and W. Hunt. At No. 187 *Hatchards* (opened here in 1801) is the sole survivor of the booksellers established in the area at the end of the 18C. *Fortnum and Mason*, a luxurious department store where the assistants in the grocery department wear frock coats, was founded by Charles Fortnum, a footman in the household of George III, in c 1770. A mechanical clock (1964; by Thwaites and Red) crowns the entrance. The Soda Fountain Restaurant—a popular meeting place—serves delicious afternoon teas, and lunches. Beyond, the *Piccadilly Arcade* (1909-10) has tall glass shop-fronts. On the N side of Piccadilly is the Welsh Tourist Board's information centre—further along a secluded courtyard admits to *Albany* with an apartment block.

The house, designed by Sir William Chambers for Lord Melbourne in 1771-74, was the birthplace of the 2nd Viscount and future Prime Minister in 1779. Frederick, Duke of York and Albany took possession in 1791 in exchange for his own house in Whitehall (Dover House). Albany was converted to its present use in 1803, when Henry Holland added two rows of chambers flanking a covered passage which runs N to Burlington Gardens. Among the occupants of these exclusive apartments have been Lord Byron (1814-15), Bulwer Lytton, Macaulay (1840-56), 'Monk' Lewis, Canning, and Gladstone, in addition to the heroes of many fashionable novels, and more recently, former Prime Minister, Edward Heath.

No. 100 Piccadilly

Beyond is the imposing **Burlington House** (Pl. 14; 3), the home of the Royal Academy. Three lofty archways of a facade in a somewhat heavy Italianate style admit to a quadrangle built for various learned societies in 1869-73 by R.R. Banks and Charles Barry. In the centre is a fine statue of Joshua Reynolds by Alfred Drury (1931). On the N side stands *Old Burlington House*. Its facade of 1719 was remodelled by Sidney Smirke in 1872-74 when the top storey was added with statues of Pheidias, Leonardo, Flaxman, Raphael, Michelangelo, Titian, Reynolds, Wren, and William of Wykeham. The large block of exhibition galleries behind were added at the same time.

Burlington House, originally built in 1665, enjoyed its chief celebrity and splendour under the art-loving third Earl of Burlington (1695-1753), patron of Pope, Gay, and Arbuthnot; he redesigned the house with the aid of James Gibbs, Colen Campbell, and Kent.

Old Burlington House is now occupied by the **Royal Academy of Arts**, which here maintains its free School of Art. The annual *Summer Exhibition* shows contemporary works of painting, sculpture, architecture, and engraving which have not previously been exhibited. The private view of the Exhibition and the Academy Soirée, admission to both of which is by invitation, are fashionable functions; and still more exclusive is the Academy Dinner, held on the Wed before the opening of the Exhibition. Through the year special exhibitions of great interest are held; reduced admission charge on Sunday mornings.

Admission to the Summer Exhibition, and most other exhibitions: 10.00-18.00 daily; Admission charge. A licensed cafeteria is open during the exhibitions.
    From the entrance hall with ceiling paintings by *Angelica Kauffmann* and *Benj. West*, the main staircase decorated with the works of *Seb. Ricci* (Diana and her Nymphs, and Triumph of Galatea) ascends to the galleries used for the main Exhibition. The permanent collections (not usually on view; shown sometimes on request) consist mainly of diploma works presented by Academicians elected since 1770, an interesting illustration of British art. Also good examples of the work of the original members of the Academy, including: *Reynolds* (Self-portrait), *Gainsborough*, and *Richard Wilson*; and 15 landscape studies and Dedham Lock, or the Leaping Horse, by *Constable*. The few notable earlier foreign works include the exquisite tondo in low-relief by *Michelangelo* known as the 'Madonna Taddei' (c 1505), and a full-size copy of Leonardo da Vinci's Last Supper, at Milan, by his pupil *Marco d'Oggiono*.—The Sitters' Chair, preserved here, originally belonged to Sir Joshua Reynolds.

The Royal Academy of Arts, founded in 1768, with Sir Joshua Reynolds as its first president, had its abode first in Pall Mall, afterwards at Somerset House (1780-1838), and then at the National Gallery (1838-69). It consists of 40 Academicians (RA) and 30 Associates (ARA), and vacancies in the list are filled up by vote of the whole body of members. The distinguished honorary members included Sir Winston Churchill. The fine arts *Library* is open to scholars.

Burlington House accommodates various learned societies: in the E wing, the Linnean Society, the Chemical Society, and the Geological Society; in the W wing, the Society of Antiquaries, and the Royal Astronomical Society; the British Academy moved in 1982 to Regent's Park. Visitors are admitted by Fellow's introduction only.

The *Chemical Society*, founded in 1841, possesses one of the finest chemical libraries in the world. The *Geological Society* was founded in 1807 (and incorporated in 1825) for the purpose of 'investigating the Mineral Structure of the Earth'.

The *Society of Antiquaries of London*, founded c 1586, but not formally reconstituted until 1717, holds a charter of 1751. From 1781 to 1874 it occupied quarters in Somerset House. The rooms contain interesting paintings, MSS, etc. and a fine archaeological library. The *Royal Astronomical Society* was founded in 1820. The *Linnean Society* was founded in 1788 for 'the cultivation of the Science of Natural History in all its branches'. The Society possesses the collections of Carl Linnaeus (1707-78), the Swedish botanist who created the system of scientific nomenclature for plants and animals. Sir Joseph Banks, Sir Joseph Hooker, and Thomas Huxley have all been associated with the society, and it was here in 1858 that Charles Darwin and Alfred Russel Wallace read their first joint paper on evolution by natural selection.

The long *Burlington Arcade* (1818 by Sam. Ware; S facade of 1931; N end rebuilt 1952-54), a covered passage lined on both sides with fashionable shops, provides an 'undulation conducive to the leisurely and agreeable spending of money'. Near its N end, at No. 6 Burlington Gardens, is the Italianate building originally erected in 1866-67 by Pennethorne for London University. The Civil Service Examinations were later held here, and it now houses the *Ethnographic Department of the British Museum*, renamed in 1972 the **Museum of Mankind**, Exhibitions are changed approximately every year and the collection illustrating the tribal and village cultures of the world is particularly strong in material from W Africa, Oceania, and America. The Department issues informative handbooks and guides in conjunction with exhibitions.

Museum of Mankind, 6 Burlington Gardens, London W1. Tel. 01-437 2224, Open Mon to Sat 10.00 to 17.00, Sun 14.30-18.00. Access: Underground, Piccadilly Circus.

At the E end of Burlington Gardens is SAVILE ROW, a street synonymous with fashionable tailoring since the 1850s (neighbouring Cork Stret was already famous for its tailors in the previous century). Sheridan lived at No. 14 (tablet) and died in 1816 in the front bedroom of No. 17 (where George Basevi lived in 1794-1845). The *British Association for the Advancement of Science*, at Fortress House, stimulates public interest in science and technology and their relation to social problems and promotes the advancement of science to the benefit of the community.

Return to Piccadilly via **Bond Street** (Pl. 14; 3), the S portion of which is *Old Bond Street*, while the N portion, running to Oxford St, is known as *New Bond Street*. It was laid out by Sir Thomas Bond in 1686, and, forming the E boundary of Mayfair, is renowned for its fashionable shops and picture-dealers' galleries including Asprey's at No. 34. The fine art auctioneers, *Sotheby's* (No. 35), were founded in 1744 and went into partnership with the Parke-Bernet Galleries of New York in 1964. Sales and previews Monday to Friday 09.00-16.00. At the corner of Bruton St is the Time-Life Building, with a sculpted screen by Henry Moore (1953).

Among noted residents of Old Bond St have been Sterne (No. 41), Sir Thos. Lawrence (Nos 24 and 29), and Boswell. In New Bond St lived Dean Swift, Nelson (at No. 147), and Lady Hamilton (at No. 150).

Albemarle Street, leading (right) from Piccadilly, occupies the site of Clarendon House, sold after 1664 to George Monk, Duke of Albemarle, and pulled down about 1683. Behind a long facade of Corinthian columns at the N end of the street lies the *Royal Institution*, a society founded in 1799 for the diffusion of scientific knowledge, on the initiative of the cosmopolitan Sir Benjamin Thompson (1753-1814; Count Rumford of Munich), born in Massachusetts.

Here Campbell's lectures on Poetry were delivered in 1812 and Carlyle's on Heroes in 1840. Amongst the most popular of its lectures are those for children in the Christmas holidays. The Davy-Faraday Research Laboratory here commemorates two illustrious chemists closely connected with the work of the Royal Institution. In the basement is the *Faraday Museum*.

Faraday Museum, Royal Institution, 21 Albemarle Street, London W1. Tel. 01-409 2992. Open Tues to Thurs 13.00-16.00. Admission charge. Access: Underground, Green Park. Michael Faraday's laboratory has been converted into a museum with a reconstruction of the Magnetic Laboratory where Faraday experimented with electromagnetism. Faraday's work on the discovery of benzene, alloy steels, magnetism and light is illustrated.

Opposite the Royal Institution is Brown's Hotel, founded by Lord Byron's butler and now a Trusthouse Forte hotel. In *Grafton Street*, at the end of Albemarle St, Lord Brougham lived at No. 4 and Sir Henry Irving at No. 15A (tablet). The Hong Kong Government Offices are here at No. 6.

Across Piccadilly St. James's St descends to St. James's Palace (Rte 7). In *Dover Street*, the next street on the N, *Ely House* (No. 37) a fine mansion built in 1772 by Sir Robert Taylor, was the town house of the Bishops of Ely until 1909. No. 40 (restored) is the *Arts Club*. On the corner of Piccadilly and Dover Street is a sculpture by Elizabeth Frink, 'Horse and Rider' (1975). On the S side of Piccadilly rises the large *Ritz Hotel* with an arcade over the pavement; the Portland stone exterior clothes one of the first steel-framed buildings (1904-06) in London. Its name inspired an American epithet for luxurious living. The ballroom in the basement is now the Ritz Casino. Opposite, between Berkeley St and Stratton St, a palatial block of shops and offices occupies the site of the ducal Devonshire House, one of the great Whig mansions (pulled down in 1924). The principal gateway, designed by Inigo Jones, was moved W to the N entrance of the Broad Walk in Green Park.

Berkeley Street, with the office of Thomas Cook & Son, leads N to Berkeley Square (Rte 9). Beyond Stratton Street the next three side-streets lead from Piccadilly to Curzon St. Mayfair (p 120). In *Bolton Street* Henry James lived at No. 3 in 1875-86. *Clarges Street* was the residence of C.J. Fox (No. 46), Lord Macaulay (No. 3; on the site of the Kennel Club), Edmund Kean (No. 12), and Lady Hamilton (No. 11), the last three houses are demolished. At the end of *Half Moon Street*, where Boswell, Hazlitt, and Shelley lived, a Christian Science church (p 121) closes the vista.

Offices, clubs and luxurious hotels overlook Green Park which borders Piccadilly on the S. The *Naval and Military Club*, at No. 94, known also as the 'In-and-Out' from the instructions on the gate-posts, occupies an 18C building (damaged in the War) where Lord Palmerston lived from 1855 till his death in 1865. Beyond the *American Club* (No. 95), White Horse Street diverges right for Shepherd Market. The building on the opposite corner was the site of the Public Schools Club—now offices and apartments. No. 105 Piccadilly is the home of *The Arts Council*. The Poetry Library has the largest collection of contemporary poetry in the English language, with regular readings and public access (01-6294 495), due to move in 1986. Open Mon, Tues, Thurs 11.00-17.00, Wed & Fri 11.00-19.00. Beyond Down St, at No. 107, Blücher found a temporary home in 1804. The Park Lane Hotel was completed in 1927; it has a fine art deco ballroom. Opposite the *Cavalry and Guards Club* (No. 127), is a 'Porters' Rest' (1861), an unassuming relic of the past. Next door is the RAF Club. No. 138 was the house of the notorious Duke of Queensberry (d 1810), the 'Star of Piccadilly', familiarly known as 'Old Q'. The Hard Rock Café at No. 150, Old Park Lane, London W1, Tel. 6290 382—an American hamburger restaurant—is easily London's most popular eating place with queues at most times of the day.

The last house in Piccadilly ('No. 1, London') overlooking Hyde Park Corner, and now isolated by traffic, is **Apsley House** (Pl. 13; 6), the residence of the Duke of Wellington. Acquired by the nation in 1947, and opened in 1952 as a *Wellington Museum*, it contains relics and works of art acquired by the Iron Duke.

Wellington Museum, Apsley House, 149 Piccadilly, London W1. Tel. 01-499 5676 (managed by the Victoria and Albert Museum). Open Tues-Thurs, Sat 10.00-18.00, Sun 14.00-18.00. Closed Mon and Fri. Admission charge. Access: Underground; Hyde Park Corner.

Built of red brick between 1771 and 1778 by Robert Adam, for the second Earl Bathurst (Baron Apsley), this house was bought in 1805 by Marquess Wellesley and sold by him in 1817 to his younger brother, Arthur, the famous Duke of Wellington. In 1828-29 the mansion was faced with stone by Wyatt, who added the Corinthian portico and the Waterloo Gallery, in which the Waterloo Banquet was annually held until the Duke's death in 1852. The iron shutters put up in 1832 during the Reform agitation, when the windows were broken by the mob, were removed in 1856.

Outside, the iron railings have been repainted grey; the interior has recently been renovated. In the Entrance Hall is a copy of Lawrence's whole length portrait of the Duke of Wellington, and J.W. Glass, 'His Last Return from Duty' (1853), which shows the Duke on his horse 'The Brown Mare' leaving Whitehall for the last time as Commander-in-Chief. The monumental marble bust of Wellington is by Pistrucci (1832). To the right of the entrance door is a plaque commemorating the visit in 1810 of Simon Bolivar, the Liberator, when the house was used by the Foreign Secretary, Lord Wellesley. On the W side of the Hall is the Plate and China Room, including the Duke's orders, decorations and medals—The Garter, The Golden Fleece, the Danish Order of the Elephant are amongst them. Personal relics include the Duke's travelling canteen and dressing case.

The Inner Hall contains portraits of Wellington's contemporaries. In the Basement is an engraving showing the panorama of his funeral procession. In the Staircase vestibule is Canova's nude 'Statue of Napoleon Bonaparte' carved of one block of Carrara marble—it is 11ft 4 inches high. Napoleon did not like it and the British Government bought it in 1816. The Piccadilly Drawing Room on the left was designed by Adam with apse and barrel vaulted ceiling—the decoration of frieze, doors and chimney-piece is inspired by Piranesi. The room is now hung with fine small Dutch 17C pictures, plus two English paintings, Wilkie's 'Chelsea Pensioners reading the Waterloo Despatch', commissioned by Wellington in 1816, and John Burnet's 'The Greenwich Pensioners commemorating Trafalgar' (c 1835).

The Portico Room was originally designed by Adam but transformed by Wyatt. The pictures include four large copies after paintings by Raphael or his followers which are now in the Prado. Francis Joseph's portrait of Spencer Percival was painted from a death mask after his assassination in 1812.

The Waterloo Gallery was designed by Wyatt in 1828 to house the Duke's fine collection of paintings. It is 90ft long with a superb white and gold ceiling. The eight windows have sliding shutters faced with mirror glass. This is where the Waterloo Banquets were held and an engraving of William Slater's painting of the banquet of 1836 shows how the room was arranged. Amongst the paintings are Goya's equestrian Portrait of Wellington (1812); Steen, 'The Egg Dance', one of his most elaborate; Coreggio, 'The Agony in the Garden' (1520s), an exquisite small panel, a treasured possession of the Duke; Velasquez, 'Two Young Men eating at a Humble Table' (1618-20), one of the artist's early genre scenes, and 'The Water-Seller of Seville'.

The Yellow Drawing Room was originally by Adam. Old Master paintings include works by Giordano, Vernet, Peyron, Pannini, Teniers and Platzer. The Striped Drawing Room was created by Wyatt and hung with crimson and buff striped silk tabouret with the banquettes en suite. This room has been referred to as the Valhalla, filled with portraits of the British commanders who fought with Wellington. Over the fireplace is Lawrence's portrait of Wellington (1814) and a silk tricolour standard (lent by the Queen), one of which is presented to the sovereign at each anniversary of Waterloo. These hang in the Waterloo Chamber at Windsor Castle, where the Waterloo banquets are now held. The Dining Room now houses the oak chairs and dining-table from the Waterloo Gallery and in the centre of the table is the 26ft centrepiece of the Portuguese Service presented to the Duke in 1816. On the walls are portraits of the allied sovereigns.

In front of the house on a granite base stands Boehm's equestrian bronze statue of the Duke erected in December 1888. In Hyde Park NW of the house is Westmacott's Achilles statue which honours Wellington and his soldiers, paid for by the 'women of England'.

9   Park Lane and Mayfair

Access: Underground, Hyde Park Corner. Green Park, Marble Arch, Bond Street.

Mayfair, bounded by Bond Street to the E and Park Lane to the W, was once a fashionable residential area which took its name from a fair held annually in May from the end of the 17C to the mid-18C when it was suppressed. The area still retains an exclusive air although many residences have now gone and offices, clubs and restaurants have taken their place, and there are many American connections. Unexpected pockets of less grand houses, often in individual architectural styles, may still be found, e.g. Shepherd Market, Mount Row, Waverton Street, Bruton Place, Pitts Head Mews and Farm Street. The grand houses which once occupied Park Lane have mostly gone and luxurious hotels have taken their place.

Park Lane runs N from Hyde Park Corner with Hyde Park on the W; its view of the park was screened by a high wall until the early 19C when it was replaced by iron railings. The road was widened after the great Hyde Park demonstrations of 1866 in support of the Second Reform Bill when the railings were trampled down. Most of

the great houses had gone by the 1920s and Park Lane became a
dual carriageway in 1963. Hamilton Place and Old Park Lane run
parallel to Park Lane from Piccadilly and converge at the towering
Hilton Hotel (1961-63) where the Roof Restaurant has one of the best
views in London.

At No. 4 Hamilton Place is the *Royal Aeronautical Society*. The
houses to the S occupied by the Duke of Wellington in 1814-15 were
demolished in 1972. The Inn on the Park Hotel opened in 1970; the
Inter-Continental Hotel opened in 1975 (F. Gibberd and Partners);
its top-floor supper-club overlooks Buckingham Palace Gardens. At
No. 5 is Les Ambassadeurs Club in an impressive classical style
(rebuilt in 1881).

The narrow Old Park Lane was relieved of its traffic congestion as
Park Lane was widened; at No. 17 the only surviving Regency
building houses the Women's Royal Voluntary Service. The
Londonderry Hotel (next to the London Hilton) opened in 1967 and
stands on the site of the Old Londonderry House (Hertford Street)
designed in the 1760s by James Stuart and reconstructed by Wyatt
in the 1820s for the Marquess of Londonderry. It had a grand staircase,
magnificent ballroom and a fine collection of statues—it was
demolished in 1962. The Londonderry Hotel reopened in 1985 after
complete refurbishment.

In *Hertford Street* (right) Gen. John Burgoyne lived and died (1722-92) at No.
10, occupied by Sheridan in 1796-1802. No. 20 was the residence of Sir George
Cayley (1773-1857), 'inventor of the aeroplane'. At No. 14 (destroyed), Edward
Jenner, the champion of vaccination, made an unsuccessful attempt to establish
a practice in London. In Down St (right) *Christ Church* dates from 1865-68.

Continue N along Park Lane; past Curzon Street to the right is the
Grosvenor House Hotel which stands on the site of the Grosvenor
family's London house; the family later became the Westminsters.
The present Duke of Westminster still owns the freehold of most of
the properties in the 300-acre estate which covers Mayfair and Park
Lane, including the site of the American Embassy in Grosvenor
Square. The Grosvenor's residence was the first of the grand houses
to be demolished to make way for the hotel in 1928; the W facade is
by Lutyens. The Great Room—London's biggest hotel banqueting
venue—was used as a skating rink in 1929-34 and served as an
American officers' mess in 1943. The Grosvenor House Hotel is now
part of the Trusthouse Forte group which has its headquarters here.

The *Dorchester Hotel*, further N, opened in 1931 (designed by
William Curtis Green) on the site of Dorchester House, later Hertford
House; it served as the headquarters of General Eisenhower during
the 2nd World War. Its luxury suites are popular with film stars; the
hotel is now owned by a Kuwaiti company.

Benjamin Disraeli resided at No. 93 Park Lane from his marriage
in 1839 until the death of his wife (to whom the house belonged) in
1872. The charming row of bow-fronted houses with 'Chinese'
balconies (Nos 93-99) survive from the 19C. At No. 100, Dudley
House was remodelled by Sir Basil Spence in 1970—these properties
are now used as offices.

Curzon Street, with fine older houses on the S side, runs E from
Park Lane. At No. 19 Disraeli died in 1881. *Worcester House* (No.
30) contains the showrooms of the Worcester Royal Porcelain Company in a beautiful Adam House (177). At No. 32 Lord Reading died

in 1935. The Crockfords Casino club moved to No. 30 in 1980. The Curzon Cinema (1933), which specialises in foreign and artistic films, is almost opposite *Crewe House* (in 1985 this became the Saudi Arabian Embassy), a stucco mansion set back from the road, designed by Edward Shepherd (c 1730, altered in 1813) and occupied by the Marquess of Crewe from 1899. Two archways lead S from Curzon Street to *Shepherd Market*, established by Shepherd, retaining its 'village' atmosphere and 18C layout, with a somewhat dubious nighttime reputation. The Bunch of Grapes pub (1882) has a restaurant. 'Elizabethan' entertainment can be enjoyed in the evenings in Tiddy Dols Restaurant.

At the end of Half Moon Street is the large portico of the Third Church of Christ Scientist (1910). In Queen Street, Mayfair, lived Harriette Wilson, the courtesan whose threats prompted Wellington's famous 'publish and be damned' statement. Queen St leads to Charles Street where a curious house with a timbered upper storey survives on the corner of Waverton Street. This is said to have been built by John Phillips, who worked as a carpenter in this area. The Chesterfield Hotel is next to the *English Speaking Union* in the former house of Lord Revelstoke, built from three older houses in 1890; original 18C panelling survives in one of the meeting rooms here, which are available to members and non-members. English Speaking Union, Charles Street, London W1. Tel. 01-499 7866. There is a club room, bar and library.

Charles Street leads to **Berkeley Square**, once one of the most aristocratic of London squares, built c 1739 on part of the gardens of Berkeley House. The beautiful plane trees in the open garden in the centre (planted c 1789) dwarf the Pump House (c 1800) and a statue by A. Munro (1867).

Rebuilding in the 20C has practically destroyed its elegant character and it would be difficult to hear the nightingales above the traffic. But glamour returns once a year for the fashionable Berkeley Square Ball in June/July when champagne is served in elegant marquees erected for the occasion and dancing continues until the early morning.

In the SW angle of the square *Lansdowne House* was demolished in 1985. It incorporated part of a house begun in 1762 by Robert Adam, and sold in 1768, before it was finished, to the Earl of Shelburne, the prime minister who conceded the independence of the United States and was created Marquess of Lansdowne in 1784. The new building is due for completion in 2 years time. The few remaining houses of interest in the square are situated on its W side. No. 50 is the so-called 'haunted house'. Winston Churchill lived as a child at No. 48, and at No. 47 William Pitt resided for a time with his brother, the Earl of Chatham. No. 45 was the scene of the suicide of Lord Clive in 1774, and here Lady Dorothy Nevill received Gladstone and Disraeli and the celebrities of their day. No. 44 (now the Clermont Club, a fashionable gambling den) was designed by Kent and possesses a beautiful interior staircase.

From the NW angle of the square Mount St return due W to Park Lane. Carlos St bears right past the *Connaught Hotel*—dating to 1896 when it was known as the Coburg. It was the headquarters of General de Gaulle in the 2nd World War; the restaurant is one of the best in London. Carlos St reaches **Grosvenor Square** (Pl. 13; 2), laid out in 1725 by Sir Richard Grosvenor on the site of Oliver's Mount, an earthwork hastily thrown up by the citizens in 1643, when Charles I was approaching London after the battle of Edgehill. It is dominated on the W side by the *American Embassy* (1957-58) by Eero Saarinen. A memorial in the open 6-acre garden to Franklin Roosevelt, President of the United States in 1932-44, includes a statue by Reid Dick (1948). The monumental terraces which now surround the square to house the diplomatic and other offices of the United States as well as two hotels, have conformed to a uniform style.

At the building in the NE corner of the square (No. 9) John Adams, American ambassador and later President, lived in 1785. No. 6 was the residence of W.H. Page while American ambassador in London (1913-18). No. 1 is the Sir John A. Macdonald building of Canadian offices. No. 20 (N side) was the headquarters of General Eisenhower in 1942 and 1944. In 1968 mounted police fought with demonstrators in the square.

North Audley Street leads out of the NW corner of the square. Here Lord Ligonier lived in 1730-70 (No. 12). Beyond is the American church of *St. Mark's* (1825-28), by J.P. Gundy, with a severe Greek classical porch and vestibule. The dark interior was remodelled by Blomfield in 1878. Sydney Smith died at No. 59 Green St, opposite the church.

Brook St (where Handel lived at No. 25), and Grosvenor St, leading E to Bond St, are mostly offices.

South Audley Street leads due S from the square. Across Mount St is the pleasant exterior of the independent *Grosvenor Chapel* (1730), the burial-place of Lady Mary Wortley Montagu (d 1762), and John Wilkes (d 1797), styled 'a friend of liberty' in the epitaph by himself. The U.S. armed forces used the chapel during the 2nd World War. A gate to the left admits to the quiet public *Mount St Gardens*. In the secluded *Farm Street* the Jesuit church of the Immaculate Conception (good music) by J.J. Scoles (1844-49) has a high altar by A.W.N. Pugin.

Rejoin Charles St (comp. above) by descending the pleasant Chesterfield Hill, or return W along South Street. On the corner of South Audley St *Thos. Goode*, china and glass specialists, occupy an elaborate building of 1875-90, and, opposite, No. 71 has a fine doorway of 1736-37. No. 75 is the *Egyptian Embassy*. South St continues to Park Lane.

10 Hyde Park, Knightsbridge and Belgravia

Access: Underground, Hyde Park Corner, Marble Arch, Bayswater.

Hyde Park Corner (Pl. 13; 6), the spacious area at the W end of Piccadilly and at the SE angle of Hyde Park, abandons itself to traffic. *Wellington Arch*, the triumphal arch at the end of Constitution Hill, dominates an open green reached by a maze of pedestrian subways. Designed by Decimus Burton in 1828 and crowned by a statue of Wellington, it originally stood opposite the main entrance to Hyde Park. The present group of Peace in her quadriga, by Adrian Jones, dates from 1912. A statue of Wellington, mounted on 'Copenhagen' by Boehm (1888) faces Apsley House (p 118). To the right an heroic figure of David by Derwent Wood (d 1926) is the *Machine Gun Corps War Memorial*. Close by rises the *Royal Artillery War Memorial*, for both world wars, in white marble and bronze, finely sculpted by C.S. Jagger and Lionel Pearson.

To the W is the former *St. George's Hospital*, founded in 1719, in a building by Wilkins (1827; with later extensions). It now belongs to the Grosvenor Estate and may become an exhibition centre. A bust of John Hunter (1728-93), a surgeon at the hospital, crowns the side entrance at the beginning of Knightsbridge (see p 127). *Grosvenor Place* leads S between Belgravia (see below) and the gardens of Buckingham Palace to Victoria Station (Rte 12).

On the N side of Hyde Park Corner, a delicate screen with a triple archway by Decimus Burton (1828; reproduction of Parthenon freize by Heming) gives access to **'Hyde Park** (Pl. 13; 3). Lying between Park Lane, Knightsbridge and Bayswater Road, and merging on the W with Kensington Gardens, the park has an area of 361 acres and measures 3.5m round. Together with Kensington Gardens it forms one continuous park of over 600 acres, visually sadly reduced by tower blocks protruding above a sky-line once filled only with trees.

Stretching in a curve diagonally across the centre of both Hyde Park and Kensington Gardens is the *Serpentine*, an artificial lake of 41 acres (4.5-14ft deep), frequented by waterfowl. The portion within Kensington Gardens is known as the *Long Water*. It was in this lake that Harriet Westbrook, Shelley's first wife, drowned herself in 1816.

TRAFFIC. Private cars and taxicabs are admitted to the roads skirting the park, and to The Ring, which crosses it as the Serpentine bridge.

PARKING. N of the Serpentine bridge. An underground car park is entered from Park Lane and Marble Arch.

CHAIRS may be hired.

RESTAURANTS. Dell Café and Bar (E end of Serpentine); Serpentine Restaurant and Bar (by the bridge).

BOATS. Sailing dinghies and rowing skiffs may be hired.

BANDS at the bandstands.

SWIMMING. Mixed bathing May-Sept, daily from 10.00-19.00. Admission charge. Lido.

HISTORY. The manor of Hyde belonged to the monks of Westminster Abbey from the Conquest to the Dissolution, when Henry VIII seized it and converted it into a royal hunting-park. Under Charles I the place began to be a fashionable resort, though the deer were hunted until after the middle of the 18C and did not finally disappear until about 1840. In Charles I's reign the 'Ring', a circular drive and racecourse, was laid out, and was much frequented by fashionable carriages. Under William and Mary and Queen Anne the roads leading across the park were infested by footpads, and it became a favourite resort of duellists, but under the Georges its character improved. In 1851 the first *Great International Exhibition* was held in Hyde Park on a space of about 20 acres between Rotten Row (see below) and Knightsbridge. Sir Joseph Paxton's famous exhibition-building of glass and iron was afterwards re-erected at Sydenham as the Crystal Palace.—The park contains several 'bird sanctuaries'. Some of the fine lodges by the numerous entrance gates are by Decimus Burton.

On entering the park from Hyde Park Corner on the left the carriage-road running along the S side of the park passes the Knightsbridge Barracks (see below). Almost parallel with this is

Rotten Row, the famous sand-track for riders (mounting blocks remain near many of the gates), also known as The Mile. From Hyde Park Corner another broad road runs N to Marble Arch, forming a dual carriageway (northbound) with Park Lane (described in Rte 9). On the left is a colossal bronze figure known as the *Achilles Statue*, by Westmacott, erected in 1822 in honour of the Duke of Wellington and his companions-in-arms 'by their country-women'. The statue is a modified copy of one of the Dioscuri on the Quirinal in Rome. On the right is a statue of *Byron*, by Belt (1880). Past a delightful fountain, Broad Walk leads to *Speakers' Corner*, at the NE angle of the park, where orators hold forth in the open air (on Sundays). Speakers' Corner was established as a result of the riots of 1866. Contrary to popular belief, the law has full jurisdiction over speakers here—only the free right of assembly applies. Extremists now dominate. Beyond, the four important thoroughfares of Park Lane, Oxford St, Edgware Road, and Bayswater Road radiate from a broad open space. Here, between two elaborate, landscaped traffic islands (1961-62), rises the **Marble Arch** (Pl. 13; 1), designed by Nash more or less after the Arch of Constantine at Rome, and originally erected in 1828 in front of Buckingham Palace where it proved too narrow. It was removed in 1850-51 to its present site, where it formed an entrance to Hyde Park until 1908. The gates are finely wrought.

Marble Arch is close to the site of **Tyburn**, the famous place of execution, to which during many centuries victims were dragged through the centre of the city from the Tower or from Newgate. The first recorded execution took place here in 1196, the last in 1783. From 1571 to 1759 'Tyburn Tree', a permanent triangular gallows, stood on the spot now indicated by a stone slab on the traffic island opposite the site of the Odeon Cinema.

To the W, in Hyde Park Place, is the *Shrine of the Sacred Heart and Tyburn Martyrs* where 25 nuns say mass in memory of 'the glorious martyrs who laid down their lives in defence of the Caholic faith here on Tyburn Hill 1535-1681'. The chapel was built in 1961. Just beyond, new blocks of flats have been built on the site of a cemetery; the body of Laurence Sterne was removed from here to Coxwold. No. 2 Connaught Place, nearby, was the home of Lord Randolph Churchill in 1883-92.

The Crystal Palace in Hyde Park (1851)

At the E end of the Serpentine—the Standing Stone marks a water conduit of 1861—is the rich vegetation of the *Dell*, watered by the Westbourne, and, nearby, on the shore of the lake, a pleasant open-air café. Beyond the boating pier, a road leads N to Ranger's Lodge, offices of the Park Superintendent, and a police station. The undulating *Buck Hill*, to the N, retains a pump and water-trough used when the area was pastureland (sheep still grazed here in 1937). A bird sanctuary and sunken area of green-houses lies behind a memorial 'Rima' (by Epstein; 1925) to W.H. Hudson (1841-1922). The fine bridge over the Serpentine (built in 1828 by the brothers Rennie), the last Rennie bridge still used in London, commands an open view to the towers of Westminster, and (NW) to the thin steeple of Christ Church (p 131) amidst the wooded dells of Kensington Gardens (Rte 11A). On the S side of the lake are the Serpentine Restaurant (1963; by Patrick Gwynne) and a Lido (surrounded by pavilions in summer), and fishing area, while farther S, the *Serpentine Gallery* holds exhibitions of modern art all the year round up 'till now organised by the Arts Council. The building, formerly a tea house, is by Henry Tanner (1908). The Arch by Henry Moore (1979) stands on the E bank of the Long Water.

Follow the long sweep of Rotten Row, and turn S across the site of the 1851 Exhibition (see above) to the conspicuous *Knightsbridge Barracks*. The angular buildings by Sir Basil Spence (1970) surround a tower block (310ft) which provides accommodation for men of the Household Cavalry; their horses (c 270) are stabled in the E wing. They exercise daily 6-8 in the park, and may often be seen at drill on Rotten Row. The guard for Horse Guards in Whitehall leaves the barracks beneath the fine pedimented portico daily at approx. 10.30; the old guard returns just before midday. The carriage road continues past *Bowater House* (1958-60), with the extraordinary group 'Pan' by Jacob Epstein, his last work (1959). Leave the park by *Albert Gate*.

Knightsbridge from Hyde Park Corner to Old Brompton Road, is lined with elegant shops (for Harrods, see p 127). At Hyde Park Corner is the Pizza on the Park, popular jazz-venue, and closer to Knightsbridge Underground Station, the Spaghetti House Restaurant, site of a drawn-out seige in 1975 when a robbery went wrong and the staff held hostage. The 1882 Hyde Park Hotel has a royal reputation; Queen Mary and the former King of Sweden were regular patrons. Guests can watch the Household Cavalry pass each morning from the restaurant overlooking the Park. Afternoon tea is also served here.

Now diverge right into *Wilton Place* which leads S to **Belgravia**. This fashionable residential area was developed in 1825-35 by Lord Grosvenor and Thomas Cubitt. The monumental white stucco mansions are well set off by delightful squares, and behind the spacious streets lie charming mews and less grand Georgian terraces. Beyond the fine light yellow stone facade of the Berkeley Hotel (1972, by Brian O'Rorke) is *St. Paul's, Knightsbridge*, built in 1840, with an unexpected timbered roof. A tablet on the outside wall of the church commemorates 52 members of the Women's Transport Service who died in 1939-45. At the end, the unusual *Wilton Crescent* was built in 1827 by Seth Smith. In the mews behind are several pubs; including the Grenadier in Wilton Row, once an officers' mess for the Duke of Wellington; it claims a ghost. In Kinnerton Street carriage archways admit to tiny subsidiary mews. In the Halkin Arcade (1971) are antique shops and art galleries (one devoted to the theatre arts).

Motcomb St leads W from the Crescent past the doric columns of the Pantechnicon built in 1830 by Smith as fireproof warehouses, stables and wine vaults. It burned down in 1874.

Beyond lies **Belgrave Square** (Pl. 13; 5), built by Basevi in 1825 and now the home of many embassies which surround the beautiful sunken garden in the centre (c 10 acres). The philanthropic Earl of Shaftesbury died at No. 5 in 1885, and Seaford House (SE corner) was built by Hardwick (1842). Halkin Street leads E out of the square past the Caledonian Club and Forbes House, set back amidst gardens. At the end (right) No. 6 was the residence of Sir Henry Campbell-Bannerman (1836-1908), Prime Minister in 1906-08.

Upper Belgrave Street leads out of the SE corner of the square, with several pretty Georgian streets leading E to Grosvenor Place. At No. 12 Walter Bagehot lived (1826-77). Beyond, at the E end of Eaton Square is *St. Peter's*, the scene of many fashionable weddings. The stained glass of the life of the Saint is by John Hayward. The long *Eaton Square* (Pl. 13; 8) has fine gardens flanked by two uniform rows of white stucco terraces.

In Eaton Place, parallel to the N, No. 15 was the home of Lord Kelvin, and No. 29 that of Lord Avebury. On the doorstep of No. 36 Sir Henry Wilson was shot dead in 1922. Near the W end of the square, the animated Elizabeth Street leads S to the peaceful Chester Square, with *St. Michael's*, in a retired churchyard. Matthew Arnold lived at No. 2, and Mary Shelley, widow of the poet, died at No. 24 in 1851.

In Lyall St, N of the square, Thomas Cubitt (1788-1855) lived at No. 3 while building much of the area (comp. above). On the corner of Eaton Place here, a plaque at No. 88 records the first London recital given by Chopin (1848).

At the W end of Eaton Square, Eaton Gate and Cliveden Place lead to *Sloane Square*, with the Royal Court Theatre, at the beginning of Chelsea (Rte 13). Turn N up *Sloane Street* (Pl. 23; 7), a fashionable residential and shopping street, remarkably long and straight, bordered on the E by fine gardens. Near its S end *Holy Trinity* has an E window by Burne-Jones, and elaborate art nouveau fittings. In Sloane Terrace (right) is the First Church of Christ Scientist in London. No. 44 Cadogan Place (across the gardens) was the home of William Wilberforce, the campaigner against slavery. No. 76 Sloane St, just before the intersection with Pont St, was the home of Sir Herbert Tree and Sir Charles Dilke (plaques). Strikingly seen at the far end of the red Dutch terraces of *Pont Street* (left) is the Scottish church of *St. Columba's*, well sited on a corner with a fine helm roofed tower, by Sir Edward Maufe (1950-55). Inside is a memorial chapel to the London Scottish regiment.

The *Cadogan Hotel* at No. 75 has a blue plaque to Lily Langtry; Oscar Wilde was arrested here. At No. 55 is the Danish Embassy designed by Arne Jacobsen (1978). The Holiday Inn Chelsea is at No. 17-25—it has an indoor swimming pool. The Hyatt Carlton Tower overlooks Cadogan Place and its private gardens with statues by David Wynne.

Arnold Bennett lived for many years at No. 75 Cadogan Square, S of Pont St and to the N, in Hans Place, with its thickly planted oval gardens, lived Jane Austen (at No. 23), and Shelley (at No. 41; both houses demolished).

Beyond the delightful balconied houses of Cadogan Place is the busy intersection of **Knightsbridge** at the top of Sloane Street (see below).

11 Kensington

A. Knightsbridge and Brompton to Kensington Gardens and Holland Park

Access: Underground, Knightsbridge, South Kensington, High Street Kensington, Lancaster Gate, Queensway, Notting Hill Gate and Holland Park.

Kensington was made a royal borough at the wish of Queen Victoria in 1901, and was combined in 1965, much against its will, with Chelsea. The remarkable group of museums and educational institutions between Kensington Gardens and Cromwell Road were built on land purchased from the proceeds of the 1851 Exhibition.

The thoroughfare that continues the line of Piccadilly (Rte 8) W from Hyde Park Corner, along the S side of Hyde Park and Kensington Gardens, is known at first as *Knightsbridge* and farther on as Kensington Road and Kensington High Street. It forms the main approach to Hammersmith and the W suburbs.

From Knightsbridge Station (at the top of Sloane Street, comp. p 125) *Brompton Road* (Pl. 13; 5), a wide and bustling thoroughfare, runs SW towards the South Kensington museums. It passes the huge terracotta edifice of *Harrods* (1901), a superior department store where almost anything may be purchased.

Henry Charles Harrod started a small grocer's shop in Knightsbridge in 1849. His son expanded the business; by 1880 there were some 100 assistants in a two-storey building. This was destroyed by fire in 1883; it was rebuilt in 1884 and a depository built at Barnes in the 1890s. In 1894 Harrods claimed 'to serve the world' and the expanded store installed the first escalators in London in 1898. The terracotta emporium was completed in 1905 to the designs of Stevens and Munt. The Food Hall features tiles from Ironbridge. With a staff of 5000 it is one of the world's largest stores. There are several restaurants and afternoon tea, with unlimited cakes, is served between 15.30 and 17.00. There is a tourist information centre on the 4th floor.

Beyond, opposite a stretch of raised pavement with trees, *Beauchamp Place* diverges left, its modest regency housing brightly transformed below iron balconies into fashionable boutiques and restaurants. The area to the N of Brompton Road retains some quiet residential streets (including Cheval Place, Rutland St, and Montpellier St, with Bonham's, the auctioneers). Beyond Brompton Square built in 1820 (where Stéphane Mallarmé, the poet, lived at No. 6 in 1863), an avenue of limes leads to *Holy Trinity* (1827; the chancel added by Blomfield in 1879), the rural parish church of Brompton. Across an open green behind is the colourful Ennismore Gardens Mews and Street. The headquarters of the Independent Broadcasting Authority is in Brompton Road and a small Gallery is open to visitors.

Broadcasting Gallery, Brompton Road, London SW3 1EY. Tel. 01-584 7011. Advance booking for guided tours on weekdays at 10.00, 11.30, 14.30 and 15.30 (90 minutes). Access: Underground, Knightsbridge.
    The gallery covers the history of broadcasting and the growth of world television, Independent Television News and the control of TV advertising, teletext transmission and the development of local radio.

Brompton Oratory (Pl. 12; 8), or the *Oratory of St. Philip Neri*, is served by secular priests (housed in a building of 1853 to the W of the church) of the institute of the Oratory, founded by St. Philip Neri at Rome in 1575. The institute was introduced into England by Cardinal Newman in 1848 (his statue by Chavalliaud stands to the left of the entrance). The present church, a large and elaborate edifice in the Roman Baroque style, designed by H. Gribble, was opened in 1884, the facade and dome being completed in 1896-97. The interior, which is remarkable for the width of its nave (52ft), is heavily decorated with marble and statuary (including a series of Apostles from Siena, by Mazzuoli, c 1680). The huge Renaissance altar in the Lady Chapel (S Transept) come from Brescia.

At the end of Old Brompton Road (Access: West Brompton Underground Station) is *Brompton Cemetery* which covers 39 acres between Old Brompton Road and Fulham Road to the S.

Also known as the West London and Westminster Cemetery, this is one of the most interesting in London; it was first used in 1840. Surrounded by catacombs, it has a triumphal arch at the entrance. There are many soldiers buried here due to the proximity of Chelsea Hospital which has its own granite obelisk. Amongst others buried here are Emmeline Pankhurst (d 1928) the suffragette, Princess Violette Lobanov-Rostovsky (d 1932), Frederick Leyland (d 1892), patron of the pre-Raphaelites (his tomb is in arts and crafts funerary style), and Sir Samuel Cunard (d 1865), founder of the Cunard steam ship company.

Brompton Road branches left through an area of attractive squares and crescents (Alexander Sq, Thurloe Sq, Pelham Place and Crescent, etc.) built in 1820-40; while *Cromwell Road* (Pl. 12; 7) continues due W, named from a vanished house of Henry Cromwell, son of the Protector. Though mainly lined with monotonous terraces of hotels, it begins with the long imposing Renaissance facade in stone and red brick by Sir Aston Webb (1909) of the *Victoria and Albert Museum*, the first of the **South Kensington Museums** described in Rte 11B. Opposite stands the new Islamic Cultural Centre in pink stone and glass (it includes the Zamana Art Gallery). Beyond Exhibition Road (with an entry to South Kensington Stn), the *Natural History Museum* stands amid plane trees.

In Cromwell Rd, opposite the Natural History Museum, is the *Institut Français du Royaume Uni*, a centre of French culture in London with a lycée. In Cromwell Place, No. 7 was the home of Millais (1862-79). At the corner of Queen's Gate is *Baden-Powell House* (1959-61). This is a modern hostel for members of the scout association with a small museum devoted to Lord Robert Baden-Powell (1857-1941), founder of the international scouting movement. The displays illustrate the history of the founding of the Association with photographs and relics. Outside is Don Potter's statue of Baden-Powell.

Baden-Powell Museum, Baden-Powell House, Queen's Gate, London SW7. Tel. 01-584 7030. Admission daily 09.00-17.00.

Farther W in Cromwell Road, near Gloucester Road station, Sainsbury's has a huge superstore in the former air terminal. Cromwell Hospital is in the next block. No. 39 Harrington Gardens (parallel to the S) was built in 1881 for W.S. Gilbert; its terracotta decorations recall the Savoy operas. The E wing was restored in 1972; in the W wing were the offices of the *Society of Genealogists*, now in the City.

Exhibition Road runs N, passing (left) the *Geological Museum* and the *Science Museum* (Rte 11B) and (right) a *Mormon Chapel* (1959-61) with a tapering spire covered in gold leaf. The elaborate organ is played 12.30-13.00 on most days. Beyond, on either side of the road, are the buildings of the *Imperial College of Science and Technology*, a magnificently equipped group of associated colleges, incorporated in the University of London in 1907, for advanced training and research in science, especially in its application to industry. The open Prince's Garden (right) is surrounded by residential halls. On the left side of Exhibition Rd, unimaginative faculty buildings (1958-63) surround a huge *Campanile* by Thomas Collcutt (1887-93), preserved from the former Imperial Institute, erected as a national memorial to Queen Victoria's Jubilee and designed to exhibit and promote the resources of the Empire.

Diverge left along Prince Consort Road which skirts the Royal School of Mines to reach the *Royal College of Music*, incorporated in 1883, but occupying a building opened in 1894. It contains the Donaldson Collection of ancient musical instruments (adm. on application to the Assistant Director of Studies, October to May). Opposite, steps lead up past a bronze statue of Prince Albert, on a memorial to the Great Exhibition of 1851, to the former entrance to the Royal Albert Hall. To the left is the Union building of Imperial College, and to the W is the *Royal College of Organists*, with bright sgraffito decoration. The grim yet individual building of the *Royal College of Art* (1960-61) is the last of this remarkable group of institutions devoted to science and art. Here are held periodic exhibitions.

The **Royal Albert Hall** (Pl. 12; 5), a huge amphitheatre roofed over by a glass dome, was inspired by the Roman works of Provence and built in 1867-71. The exterior, with a terracotta frieze by Minton, was cleaned in 1969-70; it measures 273ft in length, 240ft in breadth, and 155ft in height. The interior (admission if no rehearsals are in progress) has an arena of 103ft by 68ft. It is capable of containing about 8000 persons, and is used for concerts, public meetings, balls, etc., and has a celebrated Willis organ. The famous Promenade concerts founded by Sir Henry Wood are held here from July to September.

Between Exhibition Road and Queen's Gate the houses flanking the Albert Hall are known as *Kensington Gore*, from Gore House, which stood approximately on the site of the Albert Hall, and was famous for the salon held in it by Lady Blessington (1836-49). At the beginning of the 19C it was the residence of William Wilberforce.

Kensington Road runs E to Knightsbridge (comp. p 127). On the corner of Exhibition Road, the *Royal Geographical Society* in a building by Norman Shaw (1874) is adorned with statues of Sir Ernest Shackleton and David Livingstone. Admission to the small exhibition with relics of these and other explorers, and maps, is granted by the Director. .The library is available to scholars. Across Exhibition Rd, at No. 14 Prince's Gate (now the Royal College of General Practitioners), J.F. Kennedy lived while his father was ambassador to Britain (1937-40). Earl Haig (1861-1928) died at No. 21, and No. 25 is the *Royal School of Needlework* (open first Wed of each month from 10.30 or by appointment), founded in 1872, which holds evening classes and has an embroidery shop. The Iranian Embassy at No. 27 was partly demolished in the siege of April/May 1980. In Ennismore Gardens, the Russian Orthodox church of *All Saints* (ring for verger, right of entrance), in a curious mixture of architectural styles, contains sgraffito work by Heywood Sumner (1898); and on the corner of Rutland Gardens is the Westminster Synagogue. Farther on, opposite Knightsbridge Barracks (see p 125), Knightsbridge House is fronted by a pleasant bronze group, 'The Seer', by G. Ledward. The quiet streets to the S around Trevor Square are attractive.

W of the Albert Hall, beyond the wide Queen's Gate, with its statue of Napier of Magdala (d 1890) by Boehm, is Hyde Park Gate. Here at No. 18 Epstein had his studio and died in 1959; Sir Leslie Stephen (1822-1904) lived at No. 22, and at No. 28 Winston Churchill died in 1965 (plaque). Beyond in De Vere Gardens, lived Browning (in 1887-89) and Henry James (in 1886-1901).

Facing the Albert Hall is the Gothic spire of the *Albert Memorial*, the national monument to Prince Albert of Saxe-Coburg-Gotha (1819-61), consort of Queen Victoria, designed by Sir G. Gilbert Scott (1872). The statue of the prince (with the catalogue of the Great Exhibition) is by Foley. The pedestal is decorated with admirable marble reliefs of artists and men of letters by J.B. Philip (N and W sides) and H. Armstead. At the angles are allegorical groups (Agriculture, by Calder Marshall; Manufactures, by Weekes; Commerce, by Thornycroft; and Engineering, by Lawlor). At the foot of the steps are groups representing Europe, Asia, Africa, and America. The memorial is undergoing extensive repairs.

*Kensington Gardens (Pl. 12; 5) cover 274 acres; they were once the private gardens of Kensington Palace (see below), and adjoin Hyde Park on the W. Although the Round Pond and Broad Walk were planned by George I, their present aspect is largely due to Queen Caroline, wife of George II, under whose direction they were laid out by Charles Bridgeman in 1728-31. The beautiful avenues of trees are a special feature. These gardens are a favourite resort of children and their attendants.

At the N end of the *Long Water*, as the upper reach of the Serpentine is called (comp. p 123), is an attractive paved garden with a pavilion and fountains and a statue of *Jenner* by W. Calder Marshall (1858). Nearby is the charming *Queen Anne's Alcove* (originally at the S end of the Broad Walk), probably designed by Kent. The spot on the W bank of the Water, where *Peter Pan*, the hero of Sir J.M. Barrie's fairy play, first landed his boat, is marked by a delightul statue of him by Sir G. Frampton (1912). A little to the SW, a bronze cast of a fine equestrian figure by G.F. Watts (1903) represents *Physical Energy* (a replica forms part of the memorial to Cecil Rhodes at Groote Schuur, near Cape Town). An obelisk memorial to *Speke* (1827-64), the African explorer, lies to the N. A children's playgound with an 'elphin oak' occupies the NW corner of the park. And near Victoria Gate is the Pets' Cemetery started in 1880 but now full and closed to the public.

Behind the Albert Memorial the charming *Flower Walk* leads W to the *Broad Walk* which runs N between Kensington Palace and the *Round Pond* (7 acres), noted for its model yachts in summer. In the private gardens on the S side of the palace is a statue of *William III*, presented to Edward VII in 1907 by William II of Germany; and on the E side is a statue of Queen Victoria, by Princess Louise. The approach to the palace passes between a beautiful sunk garden, surrounded on three sides by a pleached walk of lime trees, and a group of bay and thorn trees in front of the brick **Orangery*, built in 1704 by Hawksmoor and Vanbrugh, with ringed half-columns flanking the entrance. Inside (open daily 10.00-16.00, but often closed) the festoons on the elaborate entablature were carved by Grinling Gibbons. The marble crater with Roman reliefs of 2C AD was found, according to Piranesi, in Hadrian's Villa, Tivoli in 1760.

Kensington Palace was bought by William III from the 2nd Earl of Nottingham in 1689, and from that time until the death of George II (1760) it was a residence of the reigning sovereign.

Kensington Palace, Kensington Gardens, W8. Tel. 01-937 9561. Access: Underground, High Street Kensington. State Apartments open Mon-Sat 09.00-17.00, Sun 13.00-17.00. Admission charge. Court Dress Collection open as above; additional charge or combined ticket.

The old house of 1605 was altered and added to by Sir Christopher Wren, and the exterior is much as he and Hawksmoor left it, but considerable interior alterations were made by William Kent in 1722-24. Mary II, William III, Anne, and George II all died in Kensington Palace. Queen Victoria was born here on 24 May 1819, and continued to live at the palace until her accession in 1837. Queen Mary was likewise born in this palace (26 May 1867). It is still the London residence of various members of the Royal Family, including Prince Charles and Princess Diana.

The State Apartments, virtually abandoned in 1760, were first restored and opened to the public in 1899. They were renovated and rehung from the royal collections in 1975.

In QUEEN MARY'S GALLERY the Vauxhall glass overmantels with gilded surrounds by Grinling Gibbons date from 1691. The fine portraits include *Adriaen Hanneman*, William III as a young man (1669); *William Wissing*, William and Mary as prince and princess; *Lely*, Anne Hyde; *Kneller*, Peter the Great. QUEEN'S DINING ROOM: *Lely*, Queen Mary aged 10 as Diana. DRAWING ROOM: *Kneller*, William, Duke of Gloucester, and *Michael Dahl*, Prince George of Denmark, Queen Anne's son and husband; paintings by *Van Dyck* and *David Teniers*. The BEDCHAMBER contains the bed belonging to James II and Mary of Modena, in which probably the 'Old Pretender' was born. The large 17C bowl in the hearth recalls Queen Mary II as a great collector of oriental porcelain. There follow two of the three rooms rebuilt in grander fashion in 1718-21 by Colen Campbell and decorated by *William Kent*. His also is the trompe l'oeil painting of the King's Staircase. The King's Gallery preserves the wind-dial made in 1694 by Robert Morden and (?) Thos. Tompion. Among the pictures, *Van Dyck*, Cupid and Psyche. Here Queen Victoria heard of her accession.

The following suite has been restored to near its appearance when occupied by the Duchess of Kent and Princess Victoria in 1834-36 with many personal mementoes. Here was Queen Victoria's bedroom which she shared with her mother. The KING'S DRAWING ROOM is hung with 17C pictures mainly acquired by Charles I or painted for Charles II. The COUNCIL CHAMBER, arranged as a memorial of the Great Exhibition of 1851, contains the ivory throne of the Maharajah of Travancore. In the CUPOLA ROOM Queen Victoria was christened. In 1984 the Queen's Court Dress Collection opened on the ground floor, including the room in which Queen Victoria was born. The uniforms and costumes date from the 18th to the 20C.

Hyde Park and Kensington Gardens are skirted on the N by *Bayswater Road*—exhibitions of paintings on Sundays along the railings of the park—S of a residential area of monotonous white stucco terraces, with many hotels. For the region around Marble Arch, see p 124. The Broad Walk reaches Bayswater Rd just W of *Queensway*, a busy street with shops and restaurants open late at night. E, in *Lancaster Gate*, the conspicuous spire of Christ Church rises behind a memorial by Hermon Cawthra (1934) to the Earl of Meath. West of Queensway, No. 1 *Orme Square* was the residence of Sir Rowland Hill, introducer of the penny postage, in 1839-45. The next turning on the right, *St. Petersburgh Place*, lead N between the tall Eastern towers of the New West End Synagogue and the tapering spire of St. Matthew's Church to Moscow Rd and the Byzantine Greek *Cathedral of the Holy Wisdom*, with mosaics by Boris Anrep. Sir James Barrie lived at No. 100 Bayswater Rd in 1902-08. Beyond Kensington Palace Gardens (see below) and the Czechoslovak Centre and Embassy (1971, by Stramek, Bocon & Stapanski; No. 25), *Notting Hill Gate* continues W. No. 57 Palace Gardens Terrace was the birthplace of Max Beerbohm (1872-1956).

Pembridge Road runs N from Notting Hill Gate to the long *Portobello Road* (left); the name commemorates the capture of Puerto Bello in the Caribbean by Adm. Vernon in 1739. Famous for its weekday vegetable and fruit market here since c 1870, it is known locally as 'The Lane'. The popularity of the Saturday antique market in the S section of the road has lead to its expansion northwards for a mile, as far as the A40 flyover. To the W, *St. John's, Ladbroke Grove* (Pl. 10; 1) was built in 1845 on the site of a grandstand; only the shape of the housing terraces and Hippodrome Place recall the racecourse here in 1837-41. Near by, Pottery Lane survives from 'The Potteries', a once notorious area of brick-making and pig-keeping, described by Dickens in 1850 as 'a plague spot scarcely equalled for its insalubrity by any other in London'.

Holland Park Avenue continues the line of Notting Hill Gate to *Shepherd's Bush*, just W of which is Lime Grove, now synonymous with BBC Television.

On the S side of Kensington Gardens, W of the fine Palace gateway (temp. William III), Kensington Road becomes *Kensington High Street*, a busy shopping centre running through the well-to-do residential district of Kensington proper. Here *Kensington Palace Gardens* (right), dubbed 'Millionaires' Row', was planned by Pennethorne in 1843, and remains a private road lined with fine mansions in gardens, many of them now used as embassies. Among the architects were Decimus Burton and Sidney Smirke who used an entertaining variety of styles including the Eastern and the Italianate (best seen at N end). No. 8 was a primary interrogation centre for German prisoners during the 'Battle of Britain'. At the top on the left is the new Czechoslovak Embassy (see above). In *Palace Green* (S end; with an informal entrance to Kensington Palace), Thackeray died in 1863 at No. 2, a house designed by himself, and No. 1 was built by Philip Webb (1863).

The next turning on the right, at the ancient centre of Kensington, is *Kensington Church Street*, the narrow main road N to Notting Hill (see above). On the corner stands the parish church of *St. Mary Abbots* (1869-81). A large church in 13C style with a conspicuous spire, it is the result of the combined efforts of Archdeacon Sinclair and Gilbert Scott. In Holland Street (a charming street of early-18C houses built for the ladies-in-waiting at Kensington Palace), tablets mark the homes of Walter Crane (No. 13; 1845-1915), the artist, and Sir C.V. Stanford (No. 50A, 1856-1924), the musician. In Pitt St, to the N, Bullingham Mansions succeed the house where Newton died in 1727.

South of Kensington High St, *Young Street* (where Thackeray lived at No. 16 from 1846-53 and wrote 'Vanity Fair') leads to *Kensington Square*, a highly fashionable quarter in the early 18C when the Court was frequently at Kensington Palace. Here Talleyrand lived after his escape from Paris in 1792. On the S side J.R. Green lived at No. 14, Hubert Parry, the musician, at No. 17, and J.S. Mill at No. 18. In the corner is the R.C. convent of the Assumption, with a surprising facade of 1860. No. 33 (NT; no adm.) built in 1695, was the residence of Mrs Patrick Campbell (1865-1940), the actress. At No. 40 lived Sir John Simon, pioneer of public health, and next door, Burne-Jones.—The Armenian church of St. Sarkis (1922) lies to the W in Iverna Gardens.

Just off Kensington High Street in Derry Street is the entrance to the *Kensington Exhibition Centre, Rainbow Suite* and *Roof Garden*.

This was part of the Derry and Toms department store which was founded in 1862 and which opened its new six-storey emporium in 1930 featuring the Rainbow Room and Roof Garden. It closed in 1973 and for a while Biba moved in, with an all-black decor, selling high-fashion clothes. It is now an exhibition centre and banqueting suite on two floors operated by Comfort Hotels/Ladbroke Hotels. On the sixth floor is a Disco/Nightclub, the Garden; there is public access to the Roof Garden during the summer, where flamingoes wander above the traffic fumes.

Opposite is the site of the old Town Hall, demolished by the local council in the teeth of a preservation order and now being redeveloped. The new Town Hall by Sir Basil Spence is in Campden Hill Road and features contrasting assymetrical blocks. It includes the Kensington and Chelsea Public Library.

Up on the left is *Queen Elizabeth College* (domestic and social science), a brick building of 1915. In this road Sir Henry Newbolt, the poet, died at No. 29 in 1938, and Galsworthy lived at No. 78. Campden Hill runs W between the science departments of the College and Holland Park School to Holland Walk (see below). Here, at Holly Lodge, died Lord Macaulay in 1859.

Aubrey Walk W leads to **Campden Hill** which descends steeply N to Notting Hill. It has been a favourite place of residence since the 17C and was once frequented as a spa for taking the waters (the springs are still active); a few of the fine houses in spacious grounds survive, though the gardens of many were absorbed by Holland Park School. Swift, Gray, and Queen Anne (as Princess) were among its famous inhabitants. The peaceful Aubrey Walk, a colony of artists in Edwardian days, ends at the gates of Aubrey House which retains its spacious park. Formerly the residence of Evelyn Underhill, it contains the private collection of the Misses Alexander (one of whom was painted by Whistler, comp. p 155). Aubrey Road leads into the delightful *Campden Hill Square* (Pl. 10; 1) which slopes steeply to the N. Here in the gardens while staying at Hill Lodge (on the corner of Hillsleigh Road), Turner painted the sunset. At No. 9 lived John McDouall Stuart (1815-66), the first explorer to cross Australia. The Windsor Castle pub at 114 Campden Hill Road has sloping floors (even before the first drink), old beams and open fires. It dates from 1835 and has a large attractive garden.

Return towards Kensington High St down *Holland Walk*, parallel to Aubrey Road (entered down the hill left off Holland Park Avenue), a pleasant lane which skirts the park of **Holland House**, a beautiful and historic Tudor mansion, famous in the time of the third Baron Holland (1773-1840) as 'the favourite resort of wits and beauties, painters and poets, scholars, philosophers, and statesmen'. The house was badly damaged by bombs in 1941 and only the E wing remains, now forming an open quadrangle with the *King George VI Memorial Hostel* (1956-58). The gateway (with piers surmounted by griffins) was designed by Inigo Jones and executed by Nicholas Stone in 1629. Plays and concerts are performed here in the summer.

Built by John Thorpe in 1607, Holland House passed by marriage to Henry Rich, created Earl of Holland (in Lincolnshire), who was executed in 1649. The house was then occupied for a time by the parliamentary generals Fairfax and Lambert, but was later restored to Lord Holland's widow. In the reign of Charles II William Penn seems to have lodged in this house, and in 1689 William III and Mary temporarily occupied it. Addison spent the last three years of his life here (d 1719). Lord Kensington, heir of the Rich family, sold the house to Henry Fox (father of Charles James Fox), who was made Baron Holland in 1763. The brilliant literary and political (Whig) circle of which Holland House was the centre is described in Macaulay's essay on Lord Holland.

The wooded ***Holland Park** (café and restaurant; free car park on W side, approached from Abbotsbury Rd) surrounds the gardens, frequented by peacocks. Beyond the Flower Garden, the *Orangery* (the statues are free copies of the famous Classical 'Wrestlers' in Naples) is used for exhibitions and concerts. The Belvedere

Restaurant has been carefully restored after a fire. Near the car park is a children's 'Jungle'.

In *Melbury Road*, at the S end of Abbotsbury Rd, No. 2B was the residence of Sir Hamo Thornycroft (1850-1925), sculptor. To the E, *Tower House* (No. 29), an eccentric '13C' mansion, was designed by William Burges for himself in 1875. At No. 31 (by Norman Shaw) Sir Luke Fildes lived in 1878-1927, and Holman Hunt died in 1910 at No. 18. In *Holland Park Road* (S of Melbury Road). *Leighton House* (No. 12) was designed as the residence and studio of Lord Leighton (1830-96) who here spent the last thirty years of his life. Amidst the Victorian furnishings are ceramics designed by William de Morgan, and paintings by Burne-Jones and Leighton. In the charming garden is a bronze athlete by Leighton.

Leighton House Museum and Art Gallery, 12 Holland Park Road, W8. Open Monday to Saturday 11.00-17.00. Admission Free. Access: Underground, Kensington High Street. A plain redbrick exterior hides an Oriental surprise designed for Lord Leighton by George Aitchison in 1866. The Arab Hall added in 1879 features a fountain in the mosaic floor, a stained glass cupola and tiles from Egypt and Greece. It is used for exhibitions and concerts.

At the S end of the park, approached from Kensington High St, is the *Commonwealth Institute*. The ungainly copper-sheathed roof hides a superb multi-level exhibition hall built in 1960-62 by Robert Matthew, Johnson-Marshall, and Partners. The instructive and colourful exhibits are provided by each Commonwealth government, and there are also a changing exhibition, a cinema, a schools reception centre, and a cafeteria restaurant.

Commonwealth Institute, Kensington High St, W8. Tel. 01-603 4535. Open Mon-Sat 10.00-17.30, Sun 14.30-17.00. Free (except for some exhibitions). Access: Underground, Kensington High Street.

Nearby in Stafford Terrace is *Linley Sambourne House*, a charming Victorian house.

Linley Sambourne House, 18 Stafford Terrace, London, W8. Open March to October Wed 10.00-16.00, Sun 14.00-17.00. Admission charge. Access: Underground, High Street Kensington.

The Victorian interior of this house, which belonged to the Punch cartoonist, Linley Sambourne, has been perfectly preserved and is now owned and operated by the Victorian Society.

On the S side of the main road is *Earl's Terrace* where at No. 12 George du Maurier lived in 1867-70, and Walter Pater in 1866-93. Behind this long facade is the charming *Edwardes Square*, with small houses, built in the early 19C by Changier. Here Leigh Hunt lived at No. 32 in 1840-51, and G.K. Chesterton at No. 1 in 1901. To the E, set back from the High Street, is the austere church of *Our Lady of Victories*, at one time the R.C. pro-cathedral. *Earl's Court Road*, with many restaurants, leads S to *Earl's Court* and its Exhibition Halls.

Kensington High St ends about 450 yards W of Holland Park at **Olympia**.

B. The South Kensington Museums

Access: Underground, South Kensington.

The **··Victoria and Albert Museum** (Pl. 12; 8) with it spacious and
well-lighted halls, galleries, and courts, contains perhaps the largest
and finest collection of applied art in the world. The high standard
of display and explanatory labels are most helpful, but repeated visits
are necessary to do justice to its store of treasures.

The Victoria and Albert Museum, Cromwell Road, London SW7. Tel. 01-589
6371. Open Mon-Thurs, Sat 10.00-17.50, Sun 14.30-17.50. Closed Fridays.
   Lectures Tues, Wed 13.15, Thurs 18.30, Sun 15.30. Gallery talks Sat 12.00
and 15.30, Sun 15.30. Admission free, except for special exhibitions. Voluntary
donations are being introduced. Self-service restaurant. Bookshop. Craftshop.

The museum has expanded and in 1982 opened the Henry Cole Wing, in an
adjoining building with its own entrance in Exhibition Road. The Boilerhouse
Project, sponsored by the Conran Foundation, opened in the basement of the
Victoria and Albert and operates separately from the museum but with the
same opening hours. Temporary exhibitions are held in the main museum, the
Henry Cole Wing and in the Boilerhouse Project. The National Art Library
housing over 650,000 volumes occupies Rooms 77-78 and is open Mon-Thurs
10.00-17.45, Sat 10.00-13.00, 14.00-16.50. Regular users should apply for a
Reader's ticket to the Keeper.

The present museum originated in the Museum of Manufactures (later the
Museum of Ornamental Art) established by the Department of Science and Art
at Marlborough House in 1852, on the initiative of Prince Albert. It was founded
with the object of developing decorative design in British manufactures, by
providing models and samples of applied art, ancient and modern, for study by
craftsmen and others. Gifts, bequests, and Government grants rapidly extended
the museum, and the present unrivalled collection fulfils far more than its
primary utilitarian function and appeals to every lover of art. The museum
galleries have been arranged in two distinct groups: the Primary Galleries,
showing masterpieces of all the arts, brought together by style, period, or
nationality; and the Study Collections, where the scholar and student can find
the exhibits grouped within the various classes—sculpture, ceramics, painting,
etc.

Below is a selection of some of the highlights of the permanent
exhibition, mainly from the Primary Galleries.
   Early Medieval Art in Room 43 is divided into three periods each
illustrated by art objects and textiles; in the third section (the West)
is the Gloucester candlestick (c 1110) in gilt bell metal, Adoration of
the Magi, a whalebone relief (Limoges; 13C), the Elternberg
Reliquary in the form of a church, gilt copper enriched with enamel
and set with walrus ivory carvings (Rhenish; 12C), Sion Gospels, with
cover in gold cloisonné and precious stones (French or German; c
1000), and the Basilewski Situla (bucket) (Milan; c 980).
   Gothic Art in Rooms 22-29 includes a collection of stained glass,
note the Winchester College Window (c 1399). In Room 24, note the
Ramsay Abbey Censer and Incense Boat (silver-gilt; mid-14C) and
oak altarpiece probably from St. Bavon, Ghent (late 15C). In·Room
26 the Campion Cup, hammered and engraved silver-gilt (English;
1500) and in Room 27 St. Mary, Salome and Zebedee (c 1506),
woodcarvings of the highest order, Veit Stoss, the Virgins, boxwood
statuette (c 1520) and other boxwood carvings. Room 38 contains fine
Gothic tapestries, mostly Flemish, dating from before 1515, the year
in which Raphael's cartoons (see below) arrived in Brussels to be

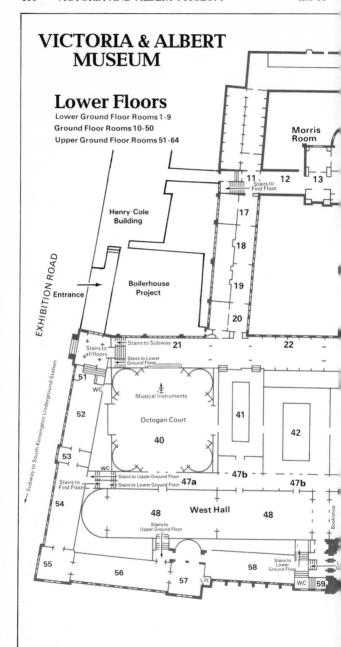

VICTORIA & ALBERT MUSEUM

Lower Floors

Lower Ground Floor Rooms 1-9
Ground Floor Rooms 10-50
Upper Ground Floor Rooms 51-64

Morris Room

Stairs to First Floor

11   12   13

Henry Cole Building

17

18

19

20

EXHIBITION ROAD

Entrance

Boilerhouse Project

Stairs to Subway   21   —   —   22

Stairs to all floors

Stairs to Lower Ground Floor

51   WC

Musical Instruments

Octogan Court

52   41

40   42

53

WC

Stairs to Upper Ground Floor

Stairs to Lower Ground Floor   47a   47b   47b

Stairs to First Floor

54

48   West Hall   48

Stairs to Upper Ground Floor

Subway to South Kensington Underground Station

55   56   57   Lift   58   Stairs to Lower Ground Floor   WC   59

Bookshop

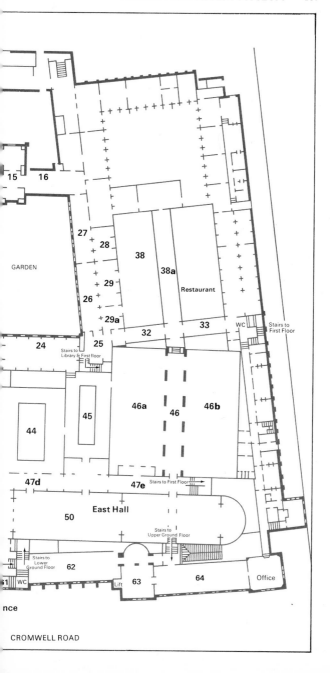

15 16

GARDEN

27
28
38
38a
29
26
Restaurant
29a
32 33 WC
Stairs to First Floor

24 25
Stairs to Library & First floor

45
46a 46 46b

44

47d 47e
Stairs to First Floor
East Hall
50
Stairs to Upper Ground Floor

Stairs to Lower Ground Floor 62
WC
Lift 63 64 Office

nce

CROMWELL ROAD

woven for the Vatican.

On the N and W sides of the main quadrangle with its attractive garden are the galleries of *Italian Renaissance Art*, with fine pieces of sculpture complemented by cases of maiolica, cassoni, etc., starting in Room 16. Off Room 13 is the *Green Dining Room* or Morris Room, decorated for the museum by William Morris and Philip Webb in 1866. The stained glass and painted panels representing the months of the year were designed by Burne Jones.

The *Gamble Room*, beyond, was designed in ornate Renaissance style by Godfrey Sykes and James Gamble, pupils of Alfred Stevens. The ceiling is in enamelled iron with a decorative freize. The Dutch Kitchen has white and blue Minton tiles representing the seasons, and stained glass windows.

Renaissance art continues in Room 17-21; the last room includes important sculpture. Danti, Leda and the Swan; Giambologna, large sketch models in red wax for the Grimaldi Chapel in San Francesco di Castelletto, Genoa (c 1579); Sansovino, Descent from the Cross, in gilt wax, and Giambologna's important group Samson slaying the Philistine (c 1565), made to adorn a fountain in the Casino of Grand Duke Francesco de'Medici in Florence, and Bernini's distinguished 'Neptune and a Triton' (c 1562), made for a villa in Rome.

Go down to Rooms 1-7 for the collection of *Continental Art* (1570-1800), arranged to convey the decorative ideas of the periods covered in a limited space, by combining furniture, textiles, sculpture, ceramics, carvings, and, in Room 2, Flemish, German and Italian ivories and silver from Italy and Spain. Room 3A also features Old Master drawings with Rembrandt and Bernini represented. Rooms 5-7 house 18C Continental Art including the Jones collection of French 18C art; furniture by Boulle is well represented.

19C Continental Art continues in Rooms 8 and 9.

English Art is on the 1st floor in Rooms 52-58 and heavily weighted in favour of furniture. Note the Great Bed of Ware (c 1580) measuring 12ft by 12ft (mentioned by Shakespeare and Ben Jonson), in Room 54.

The following rooms are of particular interest to those exploring London's history as they contain rooms from many well-known London houses, now demolished. Room 56 includes a panelled room from Clifford's Inn, London (1686-88), Room 57 incorporates a room from Henrietta Place designed by James Gibbs (c 1725) and also the Walpole Salver made for Sir Robert Walpole in 1728 with engraved decoration probably by Hogarth; note the embroidery and Spitalfields silk. Room 58 has a pine panelled room (c 1730) from Hatton Garden, Music Room from Norfolk House (1756).

On the floor above Rooms 126-118 display English Art 1750-1900, with mixed displays of furniture, textiles, china and glass, silver and paintings. In Room 125 is a chimneypiece from Winchester House, Putney (c 1750) and part of the Glass Drawing Room from Old Northumberland House, Charing Cross, designed by Adam (1773-74). Room 123 contains the Lee Priory Room from Strawberry Hill in Gothic style by James Wyatt (c 1785). In Room 122 is a bed by Chippendale (c 1775) for Garrick's villa at Hampton and also Garrick's tea and coffee service (1774-75). The Adam ceiling (c 1770) is from the great actor's drawing room at 6 Adelphi Terrace and the Adam mantelpiece from 5 Adelphi Terrace. Victorian Art continues in Rooms 120-118; note Scott's plaster model from the Albert Memorial (c 1863) in Room 120 and the furniture for the Great Exhibition. Room 119 is devoted to William Morris and his followers with wallpaper, carpet and tiles designed by Morris and furniture by members of his circle. Rooms 74 to 70 cover *British Art and Design* to the present day with work by members of the Omega Workshop, Heal and Son and sculpture by Eric Gill and Henry Moore.

Return to the ground floor and Rooms 44, 47d and 38a devoted to *Far Eastern Art* with a magnificent collection of Chinese Art from c 1550 BC to AD 1900 and a smaller section of Japanese Art.

Rooms 47C and 42 house the collection of *Islamic Art*; note particularly the carpets. The Chelsea carpet (16C) in Room 47C, often regarded as the most beautiful carpet in the world, was bought on the King's Road in the late 19C but with no earlier history. Nearby is the enormous Ardabil carpet (1539-40) perhaps the most famous carpet in the world. Room 47B contains Indian antiquities and art and in Room 41 art objects from Moghal India include a white jade cup (1657) which once belonged to the Emperor Shah Jahan and a carpet from Lahore (1630) presented to the Girdlers' Company of London.

Room 40 is the *Costume Court* with a fine collection of English and Continental fashionable costume from c 1580 to the present day arranged in tableaux with supporting illustrative material. The *Musical Instruments Gallery* is on the mezzanine floor with some outstanding harpsichords and spinets.

The famous *Raphael Cartoons* in Room 48 are seven of the celebrated series of ten drawn by Raphael (1515-16) for Pope Leo X as designs in distemper on paper for tapestries to be woven in Brussels for the decoration of the Sistine Chapel on ceremonial occasions. They are amongst the most important surviving examples of High Renaissance art, distinguished by their imaginative force, clarity of structure, fresh colour and serenity of mood. Charles I bought the cartoons in 1623 and they are on loan to the Victoria and Albert from the Queen. The tapestries are still in the Vatican. The subjects are a series of scenes from the Acts of the Apostles.

The *Henry Cole Wing*: approach by way of Room 11, Room 21 or direct via the new Exhibition Road entrance. In the entrance hall is a fine collection of sculptures by Rodin.

The Cole Building takes its name from the museum's first director, Sir Henry Cole (1808-82) and was, until ten years ago, used by Imperial College. It has been converted to make maximum use of the space available on six levels to house the Department of Paintings, Prints and Drawings and the collection of Photography as well as changing exhibitions. The Great Staircase (best seen from Level 2) was designed by Major General Henry Scott (1882-83) who also designed the Royal Albert Hall. There is a bookshop on Level 1.

British paintings in Rooms 217 and 221 include works by Thornhill, Reynolds, Gainsborough, Blake, Turner, and Watts. In Room 406 is the outstanding collection of English and Continental portrait miniatures which include Holbein's 'Anne of Cleves' and 'Elizabeth I'. Room 403 and 421 features the Ionides Bequest of European paintings. On Level 6 (good view of London) are works by John Constable.

The *Boilerhouse Project*: approach as for Henry Cole Wing, descend to basement. Permanent collection of industrial design plus temporary exhibitions on modern design.

VICTORIA & ALBERT MUSEUM

Upper Floors

First Floor Rooms 65-117
Upper First Floor Rooms 118-131
Second Floor Rooms 132-145

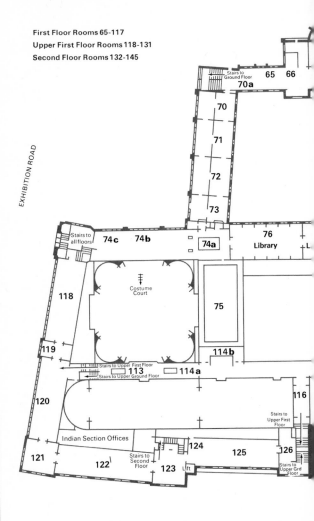

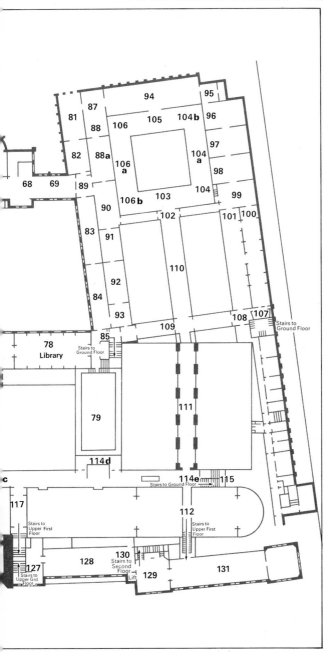

The **Natural History Museum** (Pl. 12; 7) originated in the scientific collections of Sir Hans Sloane, which were purchased for the nation in 1753 (comp. p 182). The present building, in an elaborate Romanesque style with fine terracotta detail in keeping with the function of the building, was erected in 1873-80 by Alfred Waterhouse, and the *British Museum (Natural History)*—its official title—transferred here from Bloomsbury.

The Natural History Museum, Cromwell Road, South Kensington, London SW7. Tel. 01-589 6323 (British Museum (Natural History)). Open Mon to Sat 10.00-18.00, Sun 14.30-18.00. Admission free. Lectures and film shows on some weekdays—cafeteria, bookshop with publications. Access: Underground, South Kensington.

The museum is now the national collection of fossil and living plants and animals, minerals, rocks and meteorites; it comprises five departments each with its own library and students' room—zoology, botany, mineralogy, palaeontology and entomology, with an increasing bias towards biology and man. Below are some of the highlights of the exhibition.

In the vast Central Hall on the ground floor, 170ft long, 97ft wide and 72ft high, the museum's most popular exhibits, the dinosaurs, are displayed. Note the 85ft-long plaster-cast skeleton of Diplodocus carnegii, 150 million years old and one of the largest land animals which ever lived. Nearby is the horned Triceratops prorsus and a head of Tyrannosaurus rex, Plesiosaurus and flying reptiles. In the North Hall is a temporary exhibition showing the giant panda Chi Chi who died in 1972 at London Zoo. The Bird Gallery in the West Wing contains a remarkable collection of stuffed birds, some in their Victorian display cases. The Whale Hall shows the skeletons and models of these enormous creatures including the largest, the blue whale, 91ft long, and the white whale, sperm whale and dolphins.

The Hall of Human Biology explores all aspects of man's structures and functions with emphasis on reproduction, growth and perception. Models, films, slide shows and games allow visitors to take an active part in the displays.

The Fossil Collection in the East Wing displays the remains of extinct European mammals including mastodons, mammoths, the Eirish elk, the giant sloth, and the glyptodon, a gigantic armadillo. Fossil reptiles follow and there is a small display on Mary Anning (1799-1847) of Lyme Regis who found the first complete plesiosaurus.

On the first floor (East Gallery) there is a display on Man's Place in Evolution; the Mineral Gallery shows part of the collection of 130,000 mineral specimens including a small case of items from Sloane's collection. In the Meteorite Pavilion are specimens from more than 1270 falls.

The Botanical Gallery on the 2nd floor shows plant ecology in a series of dioramas, from the British Isles to the Arizona desert.

The ****Science Museum** (Pl. 12; 7) occupies a handsome building opened in 1928. The museum, founded in 1856, is a remarkable collection of machinery and industrial plant, working models, and apparatus of every kind for scientific research and educational purposes.

The Science Museum, Exhibition Road, South Kensington, London SW7. Tel. 01-589 3456. Open Mon-Sat 10.00-18.00, Sun 14.30-18.00. Admission free.

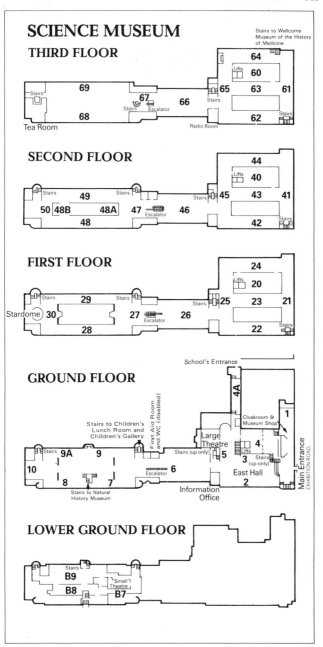

Public demonstrations daily, film shows, publications, educational facilities, cafeteria. Crowded in school term and holidays. Access: Underground, South Kensington.

The Science Museum now houses the Wellcome Museum of the History of Medicine on the top floor—see below. These are some of the highlights of the collection. Special exhibitions are held at regular intervals.

On the left of the Entrance Hall is the Foucault Pendulum for demonstrating the rotation of the earth on its own axis. Galleries 2 and 3 are devoted to steam, oil, turbine and wind engines: included are an atmospheric boiler by Francis Thompson (1791), haystack boiler (1796), Boulton and Watts pumping engine (1777), compound beam engine (c 1838), Watts beam engine (1797) and the marine triple-expansion steam engine (1903).

Gallery 6 is devoted to exploration in six areas on the fringes of present-day knowledge including spaceflight with the Apollo 10 capsule (on loan), which in May 1969 carried men around the moon, and a recreation of a moon base. To the left of the escalator stood a one million volt impulse generator which was tested several times a day with a very loud bang.

In Galleries 7 and 8 and the Centre Hall are railway locomotives and rolling stock, and relics of George Stephenson; the locomotives include Puffing Billy (1813), the oldest locomotive in the world, the Rocket Sans Pareil, and the remains of the Novelty, contenders at the Rainhill Trials of 1829. Road transport is featured in Gallery 29 with historic motorcars including the Benz three-wheeled car (1888), the first petrol car to be brought to England, the oldest Rolls Royce in existence (1904) and early examples of Daimler, Vauxhall, Wolseley and Ford.

On the lower ground floor is the Children's Gallery and small theatre with an introduction to basic scientific ideas through dioramas, working models and exhibits in which the children can participate. Also here is the Bryant and May Collection of matches. On the first floor amongst many interesting exhibits Gallery 44 is devoted to atomic physics and nuclear power with models demonstrating nuclear fission. Gallery 46 shows computing then and now with participatory displays—one of the most crowded areas in the museum. In Gallery 49 are models of merchant steamers and battleships. Gallery 60 is devoted to the history of photography with some early equipment including relics of pioneer photographer Fox Talbot (d 1877).

In Gallery 63 is the King George III Collection of instruments formerly housed at Kew Observatory and used for the scientific education of the king's children and a philosophical table by George Adams (1762) used for lectures and demonstrations for the royal pupils. Gallery 67 looks further at space exploration with the Black Arrow satellite launch vehicle (1971).

Aeronautics from hot-air balloons to Concorde, are covered in Galleries 68 to 69 where the National Aeronautical Collection is housed. Amongst the early aircraft is the Vickers-Vimy aeroplane in which Alcock and Brown made the first direct transatlantic flight (1919), the De Havilland Gipsy Moth used by Amy Johnson on her flight to Australia (1930) as well as Second World War aircraft.

The *Wellcome Museum of the History of Medicine* moved here (fourth floor) from the Wellcome Institute in 1982 (see p 180) and was considerably augmented and improved. On the lower floor is a series of 40 tableaux and dioramas entitled 'Glimpses of Medical History' which show in great detail the development of medical practice from 'Trepanning in neolithic times' to 'Intensive Care in 1980'. Note Mr Gibson's pharmacy of 1905, Lister's ward, Glasgow, in 1868, at the dentist in the 1890s, and an ironlung in the 1950s. On the upper floor the display shows the history of medicine in chronological order with the emphasis on the scientific and social background, starting with tribal societies, oriental medicine, Classical Greek and Roman medicine, medieval medicine, the scientific revolution (Renaissance) and the developments during the 18th and 19th centuries with 20C health and community medicine. Curiosities include Napoleon's silver-gilt toothbrush, Florence Nightingale's moccasins, Dr Livingstone's medicine chest, and a microscope made for Lister.

Immediately S of the Science Museum is the **Geological Museum**.

The Geological Museum, Exhibition Road, London SW7. Tel. 01-589 3444. Open Mon to Sat 10.00-18.00, Sun 14.30-18.00. Library open Mon to Sat 10.00-16.30 (closed Sat 13.00-14.00). Lectures and films on Tues, Wed, Thurs, Sat at 15.00. Educational facilities, guide leaflet, specialist publications. Admission free. Access: Underground, South Kensington.

The Geological Museum was established in 1837 in Whitehall (Craig's Court), in 1851 the collection moved to Jermyn Street and in 1935 to the present building by John H. Markham. In 1965 it became part of the Institute of Geological Sciences. Below are some of the highlights.

The central area of the main hall on the ground floor is devoted to a magnificent display of gemstones including diamonds, rubies, sapphires and emeralds in their natural state and also at various stages of cutting. Models of some of the world's most famous stones, among them the Koh-i-nor and Cullinan diamonds, are included.

The Story of the Earth, an audio-visual display, is approached through a cleft in a simulated rock face 25ft high, modelled on a cliff in the NW Highlands of Scotland. It shows the origin of the earth and evolution. The earthquake simulator is particularly effective.

The first floor shows the regional geology of England, Scotland and Wales.

On the second floor is the world's largest display of metalliferous ores, including models of large gold nuggets and useful non-metallic minerals, as well as a model of Stonehenge.

12 Victoria and Pimlico, the Tate Gallery

Access: Underground, Victoria, Westminster, St. James's Park, Pimlico.

Victoria Street connects Belgravia and Victoria with Westminster; in the last 20 years it has been completely transformed with modern clean-cut concrete and glass office blocks on either side with over-hanging colonnades to provide shelter. 19C blocks of flats survive to the S and to the N is the windswept Stag Place on the site of a former brewery. For many visitors Victoria Station is their first experience of London—not always a satisfactory first impression.

Starting from Westminster Abbey, to the S is the massive block of the Department of Trade and Industry and on the right *New Scotland*

Yard, the headquarters of the Metropolitan Police since 1967 (Chapman Taylor and Partners).

Broadway skirts New Scotland Yard and a solitary green with a memorial to women suffragettes (1970; by E. & L. Russell). In Caxton St (left) are *Caxton Hall* (1978), used for concerts, lectures (and until 1977, civil weddings), etc., under redevelopment, and the former *Blewcoat School* (1709, with attractive brickwork), the London shop of the National Trust. At the end of Broadway are the *London Regional Transport Headquarters* (1929), in an ingenious building by Adam, Holden & Pearson with a lofty tower and remarkable sculptures by Jacob Epstein, Henry Moore, and Eric Gill. In Petty France to the W, Queen Anne's Mansions, by Sir Basil Spence (1976), house the *Home Office*, its fortress appearance suggesting the potential violence of the age. Here is the *Passport Office*. For Queen Anne's Gate and the area to the N skirting St. James's Park, see Rte 6.

The streets S of Victoria St beyond Strutton Ground are described on p 149.

Further along rises the characterless *Westminster City Hall* (1965). Beyond, the rebuilding of Victoria St has been more imaginative. The new *Army and Navy Stores* has stepped upper storeys over arcaded pavements; the store was founded in 1871, and in 1891-1952 had branches in India. Two large blocks, beyond, were designed to frame a piazza opening before Westminster Cathedral. On the N side, the Albert pub, with a good Victorian interior, serves breakfast, lunch and dinner in its first floor restaurant.

*Westminster Cathedral (Pl. 18; 3), seat of the Cardinal Archbishop of Westminster, and the most important Roman Catholic church in England, was erected in 1895-1903. It was designed by J.F. Bentley (1839-1902) in an early-Christian Byzantine style, and the alternate narrow bands of red brick and grey stone of the exterior add to its exotic appearance. The church is oriented from NW to SE. The square campanile is 284ft high and commands an extensive *View (lift in the entrance vestibule; fee). The (NW) facade is richly articulated in three receding stages. In the tympanum of the main entrance is a mosaic by Anning Bell (1916): Christ, St. Peter, Edward the Confessor, Our Lady, and St. Joseph. The detail of the dark interior is hard to see, except when lit during services.

INTERIOR. The brick walls are still partly bare, but the vast size and beautiful proportions of the church are remarkably impressive, especially when viewed from the W end, from between the two great columns of red Norwegian granite (emblematic of the Precious Blood of Jesus, to which the cathedral is dedicated). The church has a basilican plan roofed with four domes. In the apse beyond the raised Sanctuary at the E end is the still higher retro-choir; the Lady Chapel lies at the end of the S aisle. When the decorative scheme is completed the walls and piers up to the height of about 30ft will be covered with coloured marble, while the upper walls and the domes will be lined with mosaics. The total length is 342ft; the height of the main arches is 90ft, while the domes are 112ft above the floor. The nave is the widest in England (60ft; or, including the aisles and side-chapels, 149ft). On the piers are Stations of the Cross, carved in stone in low relief by Eric Gill. The great rood hanging from the arch at the E end of the nave is 30ft long; it bears painted figures of Christ and (on the reverse) the Mater Dolorosa, by Christian Symons. The cosmateque pulpit was enlarged in 1934 by Cardinal Bourne (1861-1935), in commemoration of his thirty years as archbishop here.

The lateral CHAPELS are decorated with rich marbles and mosaics.

The *Baptistery*, to the right of the main entrance, is divided from the *Chapel of SS. Gregory and Augustine* by a marble screen. The chapel was designed by J.F. Bentley, and contains mosaics referring to the conversion of England. Here is the tomb of Richard Challoner (1691-1781), bishop of Debra and Vicar-Apostolic of the London district, the most prominent Roman Catholic ecclesiastic of 18C England. The *Chapel of St. Patrick and the Saints of Ireland* is a memorial to the Irishmen who fell in 1914-18. Each regiment has its own marble tablet and 'Liber Vitae'. The gilded bronze statue of the saint is by Arthur Pollen. In the pierced marble screen near the aisle appear the shamrock of St. Patrick and the oakleaves of St. Bridget. Next is the chapel, in a faithful Byzantine style by Robert Schultz Weir, dedicated to *St. Andrew and the Saints of Scotland*. Scottish marbles and stone are largely employed in the decoration, with sculpture by Stirling Lee (lights to left of grille). The fine inlaid ebony choir stalls (c 1912) are the work of Ernest Gimson. The *Chapel of St. Paul* has a mosaic floor based on a design by the Cosmati.

Cross the South Transept with an early-15C Madonna in alabaster of the Nottingham School, and (above, on the pier) a bronze panel of St. Teresa of Lisieux by Giac. Manzu. The apse of the LADY CHAPEL, beyond, contains a mosaic of the Madonna by Anning Bell. The mosaics of the walls and vault are by Gilbert Pownall, as are those in the sumptuous *Sanctuary*. Here the altar table, flanked by double arcades of coloured marble, consists of a solid block of Cornish granite, 12 tons in weight. Above it rises a white marble baldacchino, with eight monolithic columns of yellow Verona marble on pedestals of verde antico. The throne of the archbishop, to the left, is a reduced copy of the papal chair in St. John Lateran at Rome.

On the left of the Sanctuary is the *Chapel of the Blessed Sacrament*, sumptuously decorated with mosaics (1956-62), by Boris Anrep, symbolising the Trinity and the Blessed Sacrament. Immediately to the left of it is the small *Chapel of the Sacred Heart*, while opening off the North Transept is the chapel of *St. Thomas of Canterbury*, or *Vaughan Chantry*, in which is a recumbent statue of Cardinal Vaughan (1832-1903; buried at Mill Hill), archbishop during the building of the cathedral. The chapels on this side of the nave, as we return towards the exit, are those of *St. Joseph, St. George and the English Martyrs*, and the *Holy Souls*. In the first is the tomb of Cardinal Hinsley (1865-1943); in the second is the shrine of the Blessed John Southworth (1592-1654), the Jesuit martyr, while figures of St. John Fisher and St. Thomas More are seen in the altarpiece (1946) by Eric Gill. The Chapel of Holy Souls designed by J.F. Bentley, contains mosaics by Christian Symons.

The *Crypt* may be visited on request at the Sacristy (entered from the E end of the S aisle of the Lady Chapel). In the S wall of the semicircular crypt, or *Chapel of St. Peter*, are four relic-chambers, in which are preserved a mitre of St. Thomas Becket, some fragments of the True Cross, and other relics. A floor slab at the E end marks the tomb of Cardinal Griffin (1899-1956), and against the N wall is the tomb of Cardinal Godfrey (1889-1963). Off the W side of the crypt opens the *Shrine of St. Edmund*, a small chapel situated directly beneath the High Altar of the Cathedral and containing an altar under which is preserved a relic of St. Edmund (displayed on 16 Nov). In this chapel are the tombs of Cardinal Wiseman (1802-65) and Cardinal Manning (1808-92), the first two archbishops of Westminster (who were originally buried at Kensal Green).

Across Victoria St *Stag Place*, on the site of the former Stag Brewery, is a draughty and bare precinct dominated by the well-designed Portland House (1962), cigar-shaped and raised on arches, and a colossal sculptured stag. Beyond, in Palace St, is the *Westminster Theatre*, built in Welsh slate by John and Sylvia Reid in 1966. As a memorial to Peter Howard (1908-65), it is devoted to the cause of 'moral rearmament'.

Victoria Street ends in a confusing intersection. On the N side is the *Victoria Palace Theatre* built as a music-hall in 1911.

Here the original 'Me and My Girl', introducing the Lambeth Walk, ran from 1937 to '39; the Crazy Gang appeared here and the Black and White Minstrel Show started here before it became a television show. 'Annie' was a huge success recently.

On the traffic island opposite, Little Ben, a standing clock in the shape of Big Ben, was returned in 1981. The 30ft original stood near here for 70 years but was removed for street-widening. It was a traditional meeting place for the Station and the replacement clock was donated by a French oil company to mark the wedding of Prince Charles and Princess Diana.

The *Apollo Victoria Theatre* is in Wilton Road, opposite the side (E) entrance to Victoria Station; it was converted into a theatre in 1979 having started life as a cinema. It stages large shows including most recently 'Starlight Express' for which the auditorium was transformed with rollerskating tracks.

Victoria Station is an uneasy merger of two stations, one serving the London, Brighton and South Coast Railway and the other the London, Chatham and Dover Railway; a wall still runs down the middle of the station and once they had separate entrances. The station was remodelled in 1908 and the adjoining Grosvenor Hotel rebuilt. Today Victoria Station is London's second busiest railway terminal serving commuters from Kent, Surrey and Sussex, Cross-Channel travellers via Dover and Folkestone and airline passengers using Gatwick Airport. An express service links Gatwick with Victoria and British Caledonian Airways has a check-in facility at the Station. New mosaic flooring in the Eastern hall was designed by Jess Jaray and laid by Italian craftsmen in 1984-85.

London's busiest tourist information centre, operated by the London Visitor and Convention Bureau, is located in the forecourt of the station and is open seven days a week. In front of the station is a large bus terminal; the Victoria Coach Station is 400 yards away along Buckingham Palace Road; Green Line Coaches depart from Eccleston Bridge.

The bend in the river between Lambeth Bridge and Chelsea Bridge SE of Victoria Station accommodates few buildings of interest to the visitor, with the notable exception of the Tate Gallery. From Victoria, this may best be reached by underground (see p 150) or by bus along *Vauxhall Bridge Road*. This otherwise dreary street has been enhanced by an imaginative housing estate, *Lillington Gardens*, by Darborne and Dark (1969). The well landscaped slate and brick buildings set back from the road with a pub and old peoples' home surround a Gothic church, Parish Hall and school by G.E. Street (1860).

Nearby is the new *Queen Mother's Sports Centre* with swimming pools and sports facilities. In Warwick Square (No. 33) a plain neo-classical house has been converted into the Warwick Arts Trust (01-834 7856). It was built for the Victorian painter James Swinton and exhibitions are held in his studio and gallery; there are also evening recitals. The square at the bottom of Vauxhall Bridge Road is being completely transformed with new housing and office developments.

Just before *Vauxhall Bridge* (1906) which spans the river between Pimlico and Kennington, rises (right) the strangely coloured Rank Hovis McDougall House (1971, by Chapman Taylor), with a block of flats overlooking the river, and (left) a pile of cantilevered Government offices (1966), with a curious air-conditioning device in the forecourt. Turning E along *Millbank* past an attractive riverside garden, the setting for Henry Moore's 'Locking Piece' (1968), a plaque records the site of the steps down to the Thames used by prisoners from Millbank (the first national penitentiary built in 1812-21 on the site of the Tate Gallery) sentenced to deportation to Australia. The **Tate Gallery**, see below, is flanked on the W by the *Royal Army Medical College*. The former Queen Alexandra Hospital is the site for the Tate Gallery extension due to open in 1987. Just to the E rises *Millbank Tower* (1959-62), the colour of the glass reflecting the changing daylight. Return via Vauxhall Bridge Rd to Victoria, or take the more circuitous route described below on foot to Victoria St.

Millbank continues E to LAMBETH BRIDGE (1932) on the site of an ancient horse-ferry to Lambeth. *Horseferry Road* leads back to Victoria St, passing between Thames House and Imperial Chemical Industries House, and skirting the buildings of *Westminster Hospital* (founded 1719; present buildings of 1937), Smith Square (p 63) lies just to the E. The cohesion of the street has not been helped by the erection of three vast connected tower blocks to house the *Department of the Environment*. Only after a sharp bend at its W end do the buildings in the area become more interesting. Elverton St leads SW to the unexpected expanse of VINCENT SQUARE, once a bear garden, and now used as playing fields by Westminster School. To the right stands the heavy exterior of the main building (1904) of the *Royal Horticultural Society* (founded 1805). Regular flower shows are held here and in the second hall behind (1928; also used for exhibitions of stamps, model railways, etc.), with its curious barrel-vaulted roof lit with stepped skylights. In contrast is the neighbouring No. 86, with art nouveau details, and the nearby Maunsel St, a secluded terrace of early 19C cottages. Almshouses of the 19C survive off the N side of the square. At the end of Horseferry Rd in Greycoat Place are the pleasant buildings of the *Grey Coat Hospital* (1698, cupola added 1735; restored 1955), now a school for girls. From here Strutton Ground, which retains its lunchtime, Mon-Fri street market, leads back to Victoria St.

North of Victoria Station GROSVENOR GARDENS forms a double triangle of trees. The equestrian statue here of Marshal Foch (1851-1921) is by G. Malissard, a copy of one at Cassel. Between the two gardens, No. 32, formerly the *Commonwealth War Graves Commission*, was the site of Lord Birkenhead's death in 1930. Nos 42-44 are the headquarters of the *Royal National Lifeboat Institution*, the oldest organisation of its kind in the world, founded in 1824, and still an entirely voluntary service. Further N is the Riflemens' War Memorial.

Buckingham Palace Road, which skirts Victoria Station, the coach station, and the former British and Pan American Airways terminals, runs SW to Pimlico Road. *Ebury Street*, parallel to the N, is a more pleasant approach to Pimlico, crossing a series of attractive residential streets on the southern border of Belgravia (Rte 10), many connected by mews. At No. 22 is the doric portico (1830) of the former Pimlico

Literary Institute. George Moore (1852-1933) died at No. 121, and
Mozart composed his first symphony at No. 180 in 1764 at the age
of 8. Opposite, Coleshill Flats, with an outside stair and balconies
above shops, are amusing examples of 19C building.

Join *Pimlico Road*, with its attractive shops, at a small 'square' of
plane trees. Here is the well-sited church of *St. Barnabas*, built in
rusticated stone by Cundy and Butterfield in 1846. One of the earliest
'Ritualistic' churches, it was the first in London to open with all its
seats free. Continue W to Chelsea (Rte 13), or turn N into Sloane St
for Knightsbridge (Rte 10).

From Victoria Station and Victoria Street, Vauxhall Bridge Road
leads SE to Millbank and the **Tate Gallery**.

Tate Gallery, Millbank, London SW1. Tel. 01-821 1313. Open Mon to Sat
10.00-17.50, Sun 14.00-17.50. Admission free except for special exhibitions.
Educational facilities including day-time and evening lectures, room-talks and
films. Restaurant (see below) and cafeteria. Bookshop with guidebooks, publications, posters, postcards.

The Tate Gallery, in a neoclassical building by Sidney J.R. Smith,
opened in 1897 thanks to the generosity of Sir Henry Tate (1819-99),
the sugar magnate. It houses the important national collection of
British paintings and of modern British and foreign paintings and
sculpture from the Impressionists to the present day. The Gallery has
been enlarged five times; in 1979 an airconditioned extension on the
NE side increased the Gallery space by 50 per cent. In late 1986 the
Clore Gallery was due to open on the site of the old Queen Alexandra
Hospital on the E side of the Gallery to provide housing for the
Turner Bequest. This comprises 100 of his finished paintings, 182
unfinished, and over 19,000 drawings and sketches. The new Gallery,
designed by James Stirling, will have a lecture room, print room and
public reading room. The opening of the Clore Gallery will lead to
some reorganisation of the highlights described below.

The Tate Gallery Restaurant has become famous for its British style cuisine and
good wine list; it is decorated with a wonderful mural by Rex Whistler and was
refurbished in 1985. It is often used by politicians. Open for lunch only. Booking
essential although individual guests are seated together at round tables.

The Gallery owns excellent groups of works by most of the major
British artists, including Reynolds, Gainsborough, Constable, Blake
and the pre-Raphaelites. It pursues an active policy of acquisition
including purchases from the Royal Academy Summer Exhibition by
the Chantrey Bequest, a fund bequeathed by the 19C sculptor. 20C
European painting is well represented and the Gallery's special
exhibitions are renowned, sometimes spreading into the Garden.

The displays are constantly changing, but these are some of the
paintings of note.

In the Central Hall there is a changing display of representative
paintings from the collection. To the left is the Shop. The British
Collection starts in Room 1 with 16C paintings including Hilliard's
life-size portrait of Elizabeth I, Dobson's 'Endymion Porter painted
in Oxford in 1640', a group of works by Lely, and Van Dyck's 'Lady
of the Spencer Family' (1633-39), Hogarth's 'The Graham Children'

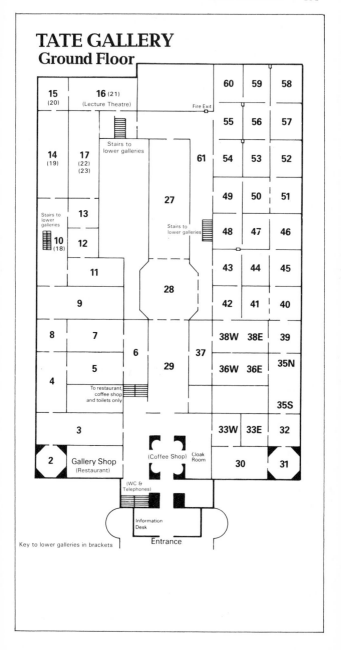

TATE GALLERY
Ground Floor

(1742), children of the wealthy apothecary of the Chelsea Hospital, and 'Thomas Herring, Archbishop of Canterbury', one of his grandest works; rivalling Van Dyck. In Room 4 among the late 18C paintings is a good group of paintings by Stubbs, including 'Mares and Foals in a Landscape' (c 1760-70), 'Horses attacked by Lion' (1769), and several important works by Gainsborough including 'Giovanna Baccelli' (c 1782), the Italian dancer, and 'Sir Benjamin Truman' (c 1773-74), the brewer.

In Room 5 paintings by Reynolds dominate including 'Three Ladies adorning a Term of Hymen' (1774), epitomising the Grand Style in late 18C British portraiture. In Room 6 dramatic paintings include: 'Titania and Bottom' (1780-90) by Fuseli, an extraordinary fantasy painted for Boydell's Shakespeare Gallery, and 'Lady Macbeth seizing the Daggers' in which the ghostly actors are Garrick and Mrs Pritchard; In Room 7 all phases of Blake, the great visionary artist, are represented. The large colour prints of 1795 with subjects from the Bible, Milton, Shakespeare and the artist's own personal mythology are Blake's first mature works and the most vigorous. The prints are finished in pen and watercolour. Among the later works are the illustrations to Dante's Divine Comedy (1824-27). Room 11 is devoted to Constable and include 'Scene on a Navigable River' (1817), Flatford Mill, reflecting Constable's nostalgic affection for the scenes of his childhood. The pre-Raphaelite collection is in Room 15 with paintings by Rossetti, Hughes, Millais, Holman Hunt, and Madox Brown. High Victorian painting in Room 16 is epitomised by 'The Lady of Shalott' by Waterhouse (1888) and more pre-Raphaelites, including Burne-Jones, 'King Cophetua and the Beggar Maid' (1884), the artist's most famous painting.

In Room 17 Whistler's views of the Thames are shown 'Nocturne in Blue and Silver: Cremorne Lights' (1872) and 'Nocturne in Blue and Gold: Old Battersea Bridge'. 'Hammersmith Bridge on Boat Race Day' is by one of his followers, Graves. The displays of the Modern Collection changes with great regularity and below are some of the paintings to look out for, in Rooms 27-48.

Degas, 'Little Dancer' (1880-81); Rodin, 'Le Baiser' (1901-04), 'The Kiss', the sculptor's most celebrated work; Matisse 'The Snail' (1953), and sculpture. Picasso's 'Clarinet and Bottle of Rum on a Mantelpiece', cubism on the brink of abstraction (1911). Munch's 'Sick Child' (1907) and again amongst the European Expressionists, Picasso's 'Seated Woman with Hat' (1923), and 'Seated Woman in a Chemise' (1923) in neo-classical style, 'The Three Dancers' (1925), showing a new emotional violence and expressionist distortion. Giacometti, 'Still Life with a Beer Mug' (1921-22), a vibrant work anticipating Op and Pop art.

Amongst the American Expressionists are Rothko's large canvases including 'Light Red over Black' (1957), and Pollock's 'Yellow Islands' (1952). Dada and Surrealism are represented by Moro, 'Metamorphosis of Narcissus' (1934); Ernst 'Celebes' (1921), and works by Chagall and Klee. American Pop and After includes Warhol, Rauschenberg, Lichtenstein. British Modern Art starts with the Bloomsbury Group and continues until today with works by Beardsley, Augustus John, Stanley Spencer, Sutherland, Lowry, Bacon, Freud, Hockney and sculptors Moore and Hepworth.

The **Turner Collection**, which will be seen in the Clore Gallery from 1986, contains paintings from every period. Those painted before his first visit to Italy in 1819 include the famous 'Snow Storm: Hannibal and his Army Crossing the Alps' (1810); Italian-inspired subjects include 'Bay of Baiae with Apollo and the Sibyl' (1823), 'Caligula's Palace and Bridge', (1831), and 'Decline of the Carthaginian Empire' (1817), where the sun sets on a great empire. Turner's later years are represented by 'Peace: Burial at Sea' (1842), a memorial to Turner's friend the painter Wilkie who died at sea in 1841 and was buried off Gibraltar, and further seascapes in Impressionistic style.

13 Chelsea

Access: Underground, Sloane Square.

Chelsea, a pleasant residential district, with interesting old mansions, and many more picturesque 18th and 19C houses, extends for about 1.5 miles along the N bank of the Thames, W of Pimlico and S of Fulham Road. From the 16C on it was the residence of many eminent people, and today, although most genuine artists have sought cheaper and quieter accommodation, Chelsea is popular with film and pop-music people, designers and others who like to be noticed; Prime Minister Margaret Thatcher had a home in Flood Street for many years.

King's Road was in the height of fashion during the 'Swinging '60s' and recovered its popularity in the later '70s and the '80s when punk fashion was not only sold in many boutiques, basement shops, etc., but also paraded each Saturday to the delight of visitors.

About 1520 Sir Thomas More settled here with his large household in a mansion afterwards known as Beaufort House, and here he was visited by Erasmus and Holbein. In 1536 Henry VIII acquired the manor of Chelsea and built a palatial new manor-house. In this new house Princess (afterwards Queen) Elizabeth seems to have spent the interval between her mother's death and her father's (1536-74), and here Anne of Cleves, Henry's fourth wife, died in 1557. After the Restoration Chelsea became a gay and fashionable resort much patronised by Charles II and his court. Sir Hans Sloane (1660-1753), the physician whose collections were the nucleus of the British Museum, bought the manor in 1712, though he did not take up his abode in Chelsea until about 1742. Thomas Carlyle (1795-1881), the 'Sage of Chelsea', lived in Cheyne Row from 1834 till his death. Turner (b 1775), the great landscape painter, died in Chelsea in 1851, but its vogue as a painters' quarter is connected with names of a later date, such as D.G. Rossetti (1828-82), J.McN. Whistler (1834-1903), J.S. Sargent (1856-1925), P. Wilson Steer (1860-1942), and Augustus John. Ellen Terry (1847-1928) occupied No. 215 King's Rd in 1904-21. Smollett lived in 1750-62 in part of a house at No. 16 Lawrence St, where the celebrated Chelsea China Factory was active from c 1740 to 1784.

The busy *Sloane Square* (Pl. 17; 1), with a fountain by Gilbert Ledward (1953) beneath plane trees, is the home of the *Royal Court Theatre*. Many of G.B. Shaw's plays had their first performance here, and John Osborne's 'Look Back in Anger' was staged here in 1956. On the opposite corner stands Peter Jones, a department store in a building of 1936, by William Crabtree. *King's Road*, a private royal way from Hampton Court to St James's until 1829, is now the haunt of young shoppers, especially on Saturdays. Some antique shops survive at its W end. It leads SW through Chelsea past the *Duke of*

York's Headquarters, built in 1801, the *Chelsea Old Town Hall*, and *Chelsea College of Science and Technology* (1964), and *School of Art* (1965).

Amongst the many restaurants along the King's Road, the most interesting is the one housed in *The Pheasantry*; the ornate facade and portico remain of the original building of 1881; earlier, pheasants were bred here. Princess Serafine Astafieva taught dance here (1916-34); among her pupils were Alicia Markova and Dame Margot Fonteyn. A club established in the basement was patronised by painters during the 1930s and '40s. It is now a bar and restaurant and the building was completely restored in 1983.

Further along on the opposite side of the road, past Chelsea Old Town Hall, are the *Chenile Galleries*; a group of antique dealers under one roof in a beautifully decorated building with its own cafeteria.

From Sloane Sq., Lower Sloane Street leads S to Chelsea Bridge Road which passes between Ranelagh Gardens and the *Chelsea Barracks* (1960-62). Just before *Chelsea Bridge* (700ft long; opened in 1858 and rebuilt in 1937), the attractive terracotta Lister Institute of Preventative Medicine has been embellished by the Wolfson wing opened in 1971.

The *Chelsea Embankment* (Pl. 17; 4), built in 1872, extends from Chelsea Bridge to Battersea Bridge, a distance of over a mile. This picturesque reach of the river is bordered on the S by Battersea Park. Just E of Chelsea Bridge the Grosvenor Canal passes under the embankment, near a Victorian Pumping Station and tall chimney. Turning W, past a memorial to the Carabiniers of the South African War, is an entrance to the *Gardens of the Chelsea Hospital* (open on weekdays; scene of the Chelsea Flower Show in May), which command a fine view of the beautiful brick buildings of the ***Royal Hospital, Chelsea** (Pl. 17; 3), built by Sir Christopher Wren in 1682-92. This refuge for old and disabled soldiers occupies the site of an unsuccesful theological college, founded about 1618. The foundation stone of the hospital was laid by Charles II; the real originator of the scheme was Sir Stephen Fox (1627-1716), and not Nell Gwynn.

The Royal Hospital, Chelsea, Royal Hospital Road, SW3. Open Mon-Sat 10.00-12.00 and 14.00-16.00, Sun, 14.00-16.00. Free. Sunday service at 11.00. Grounds Mon-Sat 10.00-dusk, Sun, 14.00-dusk.

The central portion of the building, containing the Hall and the Chapel (see below), has a Doric portico flanked by a low colonnade with coupled columns, and is surmounted by a small tower and cupola. In the projecting wings, each enclosing a court, are the pensioners' dormitories and, at the S ends, the houses of the Governor (E wing) and Lieutenant-Governor (W wing).

It was damaged several times in 1940-45, and there were a number of fatal casualties including one centenarian pensioner. The in-pensioners, about 420 in number, are boarded, lodged, clothed, nursed when ill, and receive a small weekly allowance. In summer (from 29 May, Oak Apple Day) they wear long scarlet coats, exchanged in winter for dark blue ones.

From the colonnade of the *Centre Court* enter the vestibule off which open the Chapel (E) and Hall (W), in each of which a pensioner acts as guide (gratuities). The *Chapel*, on the right, is almost as Wren left it, with elaborate oak carving. The painting of the Resurrection, in the apse, is by Seb. Ricci (restored 1948). Over the dais at the W end of the *Hall* is a huge equestrian portrait of Charles II, by Verrio.

Among the flags are some captured from the Americans in 1812-15; the portraits represent military heroes. Wellington lay in state here in 1852. In the middle of the Centre Court is a statue of Charles II, by Grinling Gibbons, which is wreathed with oak on 29 May, when the pensioners receive double rations in honour of Founder's Day. The grounds are beautifully maintained and adorned with early-18C lead flower tubs.

In the Secretary's Office Block, beyond Centre Court to the E, is the *Museum*, inaugurated in 1960. Here are photographs, prints, uniforms, medals, pewter, arms, etc., and the portrait of the pensioner William Hiseland, who served 80 years in the army and died in 1732 at the age of 112.

Immediately to the E lie the delightful *Ranelagh Gardens*, which now form part of the grounds of the Hospital and are entered from the E Walk. Nothing now remains of the spacious Rotunda which was erected here in 1742 and speedily made Ranelagh the most fashionable and frequented place of amusement in London. The gardens are home for the Chelsea Flower Show in May.

The East Walk emerges in *Royal Hospital Road* beside the graveyard (closed in 1854), where Dr Charles Burney, organist at the Hospital, is buried (d 1814). Turn left to reach the **National Army Museum**, in a modern building (1971).

National Army Museum, Royal Hospital Road, London SW3. Tel. 01-730 0717. Open Monday to Saturday 10.00-17.30, Sunday 14.00-17.30. Free. Access: Underground, Sloane Square, Bus 11, 19, 39, 137.

The collections, moved from Sandhurst and augmented by loans, cover the history of the British Army from 1485 to 1914. A vestibule with embroidered regimental colours leads up to the *Main Floor*, arranged chronologically to show phase by phase and campaign by campaign by contemporary objects the developing function of the army, together with the changing nature of command, service, and conditions. This is achieved by personal relics, accoutrements, illustrations, and captured trophies, cleverly selected to fill 93 cases, with excellent explanatory labels and maps.

Second Floor. In the *Uniform Gallery*, army dress is displayed by periods in conjunction with furniture and pictures in contemporary surroundings. On a long wall are the orders and decorations of Field Marshals (Gough, Wolseley, Kitchener, and Roberts). Beyond in the *Art Gallery* portraits and battle scenes form a representative collection of British painting in the 18-19C, including works by Wootton, Reynolds, Romney, Beechey, Raeburn, and Lawrence.

The *Reading Room* (apply in writing to the director) has 20,000 books, the archives of many famous commanders, and the Col. Crookshank collection of battle prints (from the British Museum).

Tite Street, which interesects Royal Hospital Road beyond the Museum, was the residence for 24 years of J.S. Sargent (1856-1925) who died at No. 31. No. 34 was the home of Oscar Wilde from 1884 to 1895. The wilderness opposite is the site of the White House, built for Whistler but occupied by him for a few months only in 1878-79; he lived also at No. .13 (in 1881-85) and No. 46 (in 1888). A tablet at No. 23 Tedworth Square, to the N, marks the London residence of Mark Twain (1835-1910). Margaret Thatcher lived in Flood Street which connects the Embankment with King's Road. She sold her house in 1984.

The walls of the *Chelsea Physic Garden* stretch all the way down to the Embankment. It opened to the public for the first time in 1983, other than by appointment; the entrance is in Swan Walk.

Chelsea Physic Garden, Royal Hospital Road, London SW3. Tel. 01-352 5646. Open mid April to mid October, Wed and Sun 14.00-17.00; Bank Holiday Mondays and during the Chelsea Flower Show 11.00 to 17.00. Admission charge.

Sir Hans Sloane, whose statue by Rysbrack (1733) stands in the garden, presented the site to the Apothecaries' Society in 1722 (it has been established since 1676) on condition that 2000 specimens of distinct plants grown in the garden should be sent to the Royal Society 'well dried and preserved', in annual instalments of 50, a condition which has been amply fulfilled. In 1736 Linnaeus visited the garden to collect plants and specimens and Mrs Elizabeth Blackwell illustrated her 'Curious Herb' book by drawing plants here. The display of plants and herbs grown here is mostly of interest to specialists.

Continue to the Embankment, here separated by narrow public gardens from *Cheyne Walk* (Pl. 16; 6; pron. 'chainy'), an attractive row of red-brick Georgian houses, each with its own character. Original wrought-iron railings and gates precede many of the gardens. No. 4 was occupied by George Eliot (d 1880) during the last three weeks of her life. No. 16, the *Queen's House*, erroneously connected with the name of Catherine of Braganza (d 1705), Charles II's queen, was built only in 1717. The fine railings are by Thos. Robinson. Rossetti lived here in 1862-82 and kept his menagerie in the garden. A memorial to him in the Embankment gardens by Ford Madox Brown, faces the house. In the gardens near the N end of *Albert Bridge* (1873), a statue of The Boy David by Ed. Bainbridge Copnall replaces one by Derwent Wood, stolen in 1969. A statue on the other side of the bridge is a memorial to Wood, its sculptor, placed here by members of the Chelsea Arts Club. Captain R.F. Scott, the polar explorer, lived at No. 56 Oakley St (tablet), leading N from Albert Bridge.

In the gardens on the Embankment to the W of the bridge is a fine statue of *Carlyle* (1882, by Boehm). In *Cheyne Row* (Pl. 16; 6), the quiet and unpretentious little street built in 1708 and running N from the river, behind Carlyle's statue, is the house (No. 24; formerly No. 5) in which Thomas Carlyle (1795-1881) and his wife (1801-66) lived from 1834 to the end of their lives.

Carlyle's House, 24 Cheyne Row, London SW3. Tel. 01-352 7087. Open Wed-Sat 11.00-17.00 Sun 14.00-17.00 April to October. Admission charge. No electricity.

*Carlyle's House** is preserved in the quiet and dignified simplicity impressed upon it by its famous tenants. The little rooms contain furniture used by the Carlyles; on the wall hang portraits of them and sketches and photographs of scenes and places connected with them; and in glass cases are exhibited books and MSS belonging to Carlyle and many interesting personal relics. On the top floor is the famous Attic Study with its double walls, added by Carlyle in 1853 at a cost of £169 in a vain attempt to ensure quiet. In the Kitchen in the basement (not always shown), Carlyle and Tennyson smoked together, and in the garden 'Nero', Mrs Carlyle's dog, is buried.

To the E in Cheyne Walk, Shrewsbury House flats occupy the site of a house built c 1519, and demolished in 1813. The original garden walls surround the flats. At No. 21 Carlyle Mansions Henry James died in 1916 (tablet in the church).

*Chelsea Old Church, dedicated to *All Saints*, on the Embankment, was probably founded in the middle of the 12C. Severely damaged by a landmine on 16 April 1941, it has been beautifully rebuilt by W.H. Godfrey, and was rededicated in 1958.

Chelsea Old Church, Old Church St. Open Sunday, Tues-Fri 11.00-13.00 and 14.00-17.00, Sat. 11.00-13.00.

Interior. By the first window on the right are several old *Chained Books*, given to the church by Sir Hans Sloane, including 2 vols of a fine edition of Foxe's 'Book of Martyrs' (1684). Close by is the large monument to *Lord and Lady Dacre*, erected in 1595. The *More Chapel*, almost undamaged by the mine, dates from 1325, and was restored by Sir Thomas More in 1528. In the corner, on the right, is the mutilated tomb of the *Duchess of Northumberland* (d 1555), mother of Robert Dudley, Earl of Leicester, mother-in-law of Lady Jane Grey, and grandmother of Sir Philip Sidney. The tomb, which resembles Chaucer's in Westminster Abbey, is probably not in its original position. The archway between the More Chapel and the *Chancel* dates from the 14C, but the capitals were recarved in Sir Thomas More's time, probably by French craftsmen. Near the W pillar is the finely carved pulpit (c 1679). To the right of the chancel is the *More Monument* (1532), designed by Sir Thomas More while still in royal favour, with a long epitaph composed by himself. On the left is the early 16C tomb of the *Brays*, the oldest in the church, now set into the wall under an arch. Above it is the late 16C monument of *Thomas Hungerford* and his family. To the N of the Chancel is the rebuilt *Lawrence Chapel* (1325), entered by an archway of 1563, an early example of the classic revival and a monument to *Richard Gervoise*. Henry VIII is said to have been secretly married here to Jane Seymour, some days before their public marriage. To the right is the unusual effigy of *Sara Colville* (d 1631), daughter of Sir Thomas Lawrence, and at the E end is the elaborate tomb of *Sir Robert Stanley* and two of his children (1632). To the right of this is the monument to *Sir Thomas Lawrence* and his family (1593). On the N wall of the nave *Jane Cheyne, Lady Newhaven* (1621-69), benefactress of church and neighbourhood, is commemorated in a large monument by Paolo Bernini (son of the great Gian Lorenzo).

The new tower, with clock and sundial, contains a small historical museum. In the graveyard are buried Jean Cavalier (1680-1740), leader of the Camisards in the Cévennes in 1702-04. Thomas Shadwell (1640-92), poet laureate, and Sir Hans Sloane (1660-1753).

Near the top of Old Church St is the old *Rectory* (No. 56), where Charles (1819-75) and Henry Kingsley (1830-76) spent part of their youth, when their father was rector. In *St. Luke's* (1820-24), an early example of the Gothic revival, in Sydney St, N of King's Road, Charles Dickens was married in 1836.

Outside the church is a statue of Sir Thomas More (1969; by L. Cubitt Bevis). Across Roper's Gardens (see below), with an unfinished bas-relief by Epstein on the site of his studio in 1909-14, and *Awakening*, by Gilbert Ledward, stands **Crosby Hall**. Brought from Bishopsgate in 1910 and re-erected so far as possible with the careful retention of its most beautiful features, it is now a college-hall of the British Federation of University Women. (Open 10.00–12.00,

14.15–17.00 daily. Admission free.)

Crosby Hall was the great hall of Crosby Place, a mansion built in Bishopsgate in 1466 by Sir John Crosby, a London grocer and alderman, and occupied by the Duke of Gloucester (1483), later Richard III. Sir Thomas More, whose Chelsea garden once included the site on which the hall now stands, seems to have bought the house in 1523, and his son-in-law William Roper occupied it. Roper's Gardens are now laid out on the site of Sir Thomas More's orchard. In the 16C the mansion was considered sumptuous enough to be the abode of various ambassadors. When Crosby Place was burned in the 17C the hall escaped to meet a chequered fate, finally becoming a restaurant before its purchase in 1908 by the University and City Association of London. It was used as a reception centre by the Chelsea War Refugees Committee during the First World War. The hall retains a fine oriel window and the original roof, and contains a copy of Holbein's lost group of Sir Thomas More's family, c 1527.

At 20A Danvers St died Sir Alexander Fleming (1881-1955), discoverer of penicillin; in the '30s the unrelated Peter Fleming, explorer-writer, occupied the flat above.

Battersea Bridge, an iron structure (1890) crossing the river at the end of Beaufort Street, replaces the picturesque old wooden bridge of 1771-72, which was a favourite subject with Whistler and other artists. The river, lined with warehouses, here bends S, and offers moorings for house-boats.

To the W of the bridge are several interesting old houses in *Cheyne Walk*. Mrs Gaskell (1810-65) was born at No. 93 (tablet). Whistler lived at No. 96 in 1866-78, and No. 101 was his first abode in Chelsea (1863-66). *Lindsey House* (NT), named after the Earl of Lindsey, the only 17C mansion in Chelsea, is divided into Nos 97-100; a tablet on No. 98 marks the home of the Brunels, father and son, both engineers. P. Wilson Steer died at No. 109 in 1942. At No. 118 J.M.W. Turner lived in anonymous retirement from 1846, and died here in 1851. George Meredith wrote 'The Ordeal of Richard Feverel' at No. 7 Hobury St, a little to the N, and Henry Tonks (1862-1937) died at No. 1 The Vale, farther E.

At the end of Cheyne Walk is Lots Road, with a huge London Transport power-station. Chelsea Wharf has been converted into workshops and has a restaurant. The gates in the adjoining gardens are from Cremorne Gardens. Cremorne Rd, crossing the site of the old *Cremorne Gardens* (1845-77), leads on the right to *King's Road*, the approach to Fulham.

14 Shaftesbury Avenue and Soho

Access: Underground, Piccadilly Circus, Leicester Square, Tottenham Court Road.

Shaftesbury Avenue, with several theatres and restaurants, runs from Piccadilly Circus through Cambridge Circus, and was built in 1886 as a deliberate slum-clearance move in what was then a less salubrious part of London, **Soho**. The name Soho, first recorded in 1636, probably derives from an ancient hunting cry used when the area was mostly parkland.

Soho retains its reputation of illicitness although stringent efforts are being made by Westminster City Council to control the number of sex-shops, stripclubs, clip-joints and so-called near-beer clubs—drinking clubs without alcohol licences. The area to the S of Shaftesbury Avenue has become in the last decade London's Chinatown with many settlers from the New Territories of Hong Kong opening restaurants, bakeries and supermarkets. The pedestrianisation of Gerrard Street and addition of Chinese street furniture by the Council has improved the appearance of the area which is taken over at Chinese New Year (January/February) by lion and dragon dances, Chinese pop-singers and families from all over the country.

Soho proper retains much of its cosmopolitan atmosphere with continental restaurants, patisseries and delicatessen shops amongst the sex-shops and drinking clubs. French refugees settled in Bateman Street soon after the Revocation of the Edict of Nantes in 1685. For a time it became a fashionable residential area, with great houses alongside those of French craftsmen and traders. Artists and writers began to settle here in the 18th and 19th centuries but an outbreak of cholera in the mid-19C drove the better-off residents away. The residential population has now declined considerably. The area has attracted the film, music and advertising industries and there are some attractive office developments—most of the original buildings have been destroyed or demolished.

Wardour Street has a strong association with the cinema industry. In Gerrard Street, Dryden lived from 1687 until his death in 1700 (No. 44, rebuilt; tablet on No. 43). In 1900 G.K. Chesterton and Hilaire Belloc first met in a French restaurant here.

Follow Wardour Street to *St. Anne's Soho*; only the tower of the church (1685, partly by Wren) remains, the rest was destroyed in 1940. A garden has been laid out around it. The heavy steeple (1801-03) is by S.P. Cockerell and below is the monument of William Hazlitt (1778-1830).

Old Compton Street retains a few of the delicatessens which made Soho popular and leads S to join Berwick Street, a street market popular with office workers. Fruit, vegetables, and fabrics are sold (best at lunchtime).

GOLDEN SQUARE, to the W, is now a centre of the film industry. Angelica Kauffmann lived at No. 16, Cardinal Wiseman at No. 35, and John Hunter, the surgeon, at No. 31 (all rebuilt). The statue in antique costume in the centre of the square represents George II. In Warwick St, nearby, a R.C. church survives from 1789.

Broadwick Street was the birthplace of William Blake (1757-1828) who lived at No. 74 (demolished); inscription in Marshall Street. Shelley took lodgings at No. 15 Poland Street nearby in 1811 after his expulsion from Oxford.

Walk back along Old Compton Street; *Dean Street* runs parallel with Wardour Street. Karl Marx lived at No. 28 from 1851-56 above the present Leoni's Quo Vadis Restaurant, in two cramped rooms with five children, his wife and maid. He had no regular employment and lived in great poverty. From here he walked daily to the British Museum Reading Room. The rooms may be seen on request.

In *Frith Street* is the well established Ronnie Scott's Jazz Club. Here Hazlitt died at No. 6 (1718 partly rebuilt) in 1830 and at No. 22 J.L. Baird staged his first television demonstration in 1926 (plaque in upstairs room of restaurant). Kettner's in Romilly Street is one of London's oldest surviving restaurants; it was established in 1868 and is now a brasserie with a champagne bar.

To the N lies SOHO SQUARE, laid out in 1681 (though only one 18C house survives), and now a centre of the music trade. In 1764 Mozart (then lodging at No. 20 Frith St) taught music in the house (No. 22) of Lord Mayor William Beckford, brother of Richard (see below). The statue of Charles II is by Cibber (1681). On the E side of the square, the Italianate *St. Patrick's* church (R.C.) was opened in 1793 (rebuilt, 1891-93). The French Protestant church (ring for adm. at door on right) dates from 1893.

The square was first surrounded with large mansions, including one belonging to the Duke of Monmouth, who chose 'Soho' as his password at the Battle of Sedgemoor (1685). It soon became a fashionable area, and Sir Roger de Coverley had his town quarters here. In the 18C it was a favourite residence of ambassadors. No. 32 (rebuilt), where Sir Joseph Banks came to live in 1777, was the centre in London for the scientists of the time (Cavendish, Priestley, and others) and the inaugural meeting of the Royal Institution was held there.

In the SE corner of the square the *House of St. Barnabas-in-Soho* (open Wed 14.30-16.15, Thurs 11.00-12.30; donations welcome), a mansion built in the late 1740s, has been occupied by a charity for the destitute (founded by Dr Henry Monroe in 1846) since 1862. It was the home of Richard Beckford in 1754, and he was probably responsible for the fine rococo plasterwork, wood carving, and ironwork in the interior. The chapel dates from 1862. The meeting between Dr Manette and Sidney Carton in Dickens' 'Tale of Two Cities' occurred in the rear courtyard (comp. Manette St, entered by an archway in Greek St); an old mulberry tree survives. *Greek Street* is named after a colony of Greeks from Melos whose church (founded c 1680) was in Charing Cross Road, parallel to the E.
    CHARING CROSS ROAD is divided in two by Cambridge Circus; bookshops still dominate in the northern section and theatres to the S toward Leicester Square. *Foyles*, 'the world's largest bookshop', is at No. 113-19.

It was founded in 1906 by two brothers who sold off their textbooks after failing their civil service examinations and realised they had the start of a good business. They now stock some six million books in a new five-storey building; the original building at No. 121/123 was demolished in 1966. Foyles is now run by Christina Foyle, daughter of one of the brothers.

No. 84 Charing Cross Road, home of the second-hand bookshop made famous by the American writer Helen Hanff, closed in the '70s. A play based on the book ran in the West End for three years from 1979. The Phoenix Theatre opened in 1930 with Coward's 'Private Lives'.
    The undistinguished *Cambridge Circus* may be redeveloped by Westminster City Council. The terracotta facade of the *Palace Theatre* (1888, by T.E. Colcutt) is being restored by its new owner, composer Andrew Lloyd Webber; already the gilt and marble of the interior has returned to its former appearance.

It opened as the English Opera House in 1891 with Sir Arthur Sullivan's 'Ivanhoe' and Anna Pavlova made her first London appearance here. Andrew Lloyd Webber intends to create a 'palace of music'; there are lunchtime performances.

To the S is the octagonal lantern of the Welsh Presbyterian Chapel (1887, by James Cutbitt); due to become a disco. In Great Newport Street is the Photographers' Gallery, and the small Arts Theatre, established in 1927 as a club theatre with a reputation for 'avant-garde' plays. In 1967 it became the home of the children's Unicorn Theatre—mostly daytime performances—and still stages some 'fringe' productions in the evenings.

Cranbourne Street leads W to LEICESTER SQUARE, notorious by

1700 as a scandalous centre of entertainment and well-known throughout the world from the First World War song 'It's a long way to Tiperrary'.

It was laid out in the 1670s, and named after Leicester House which stood on the N side in 1631-35. In the central garden is a statue of Shakespeare, a 19C copy of the monument by Sheemakers in Westminster Abbey. In the four corners are busts of famous local residents: Hogarth, Reynolds (painters), Hunter (doctor) and Sir Isaac Newton (scientist). The statue of Charlie Chaplin by Doubleday in the SW corner was unveiled in 1981.

Three large cinemas, the Empire (formerly a ballroom, now a disco) and the restored Hippodrome (formerly the Talk of the Town) carry on the entertainment tradition of Leicester Square, once a place for music halls. The Society of West End Theatres operate a *Half Price Theatre Ticket Booth* from a pavilion in the Square; tickets are available after 12.30 for matinees and after 14.30 for evening performances—all for same day; a charge is made.

In the 18C the area was much frequented by artists. From 1753 until his death in 1764 Hogarth had his town house at the SE corner (No. 30), Sir Joshua Reynolds lived at No. 47, on the W side, from 1760 till his death in 1792; this was the first house to acquire an official commemorative plaque (1875). Charles d'Agar lived at Nos 22 and 29, Philip Mercier at No. 40, and Michael Dahl at No. 49. Swift had rooms here in 1711. At No. 28 John Hunter built a museum for the famous Hunterian Collection, later moved to the College of Surgeons.

Here three famous 19C music halls gave place to 'super-cinemas' presenting first runs of films. First to change in 1920 was the *Empire* (rebuilt 1927) which had shown moving pictures as early as 1891. Later the *Warner* succeeded *Daly's*, where the Carl Rosa Opera had introduced 'Hansel and Gretel' to England and later musical successes included 'The Merry Widow' and 'Maid of the Mountain'. The *Odeon* occupies the site of the *Alhambra* (1854-1936), where the eclectic entertainment ranged from the 'Bing Boys' to the distinguished Diaghilev season of 1921. Outside the Leicester Square Theatre (also a cinema) a pavement of handprints of the famous was started in 1985.

In St. Martin's St, leading out of the square on the S side, the admirable *Westminster Reference Library* (free; open weekdays) replaces the house occupied by Sir Isaac Newton (1710-27) and Dr Burney (1774-94). Here Fanny Burney wrote 'Evelina'. In Leicester Place, on the N side, the French church of *Notre-Dame de France*, burned in 1940, was completely rebuilt in 1955 save for its circular wall (a relic of Burford's 'Panorama' established in 1793). In the interior is a mural by Jean Cocteau (1960), and over the altar an Aubusson tapestry.

More theatres are located in **St. Martin's Lane** (Pl. 14; 4), farther E. The *Coliseum Theatre*, with its prominent globe, became in 1968 the new home of Sadler's Wells, now the English National Opera Company. It was built (1904) as a music hall by Sir Oswald Stoll, and Ellen Terry, Lily Langtry, and Sarah Bernhardt all appeared on its elaborate stage. The *Duke of York's* (1892) saw the first performance of Barrie's 'Peter Pan'. It has been restored and is now owned by Capital Radio. A tablet on No. 6 marks the site of Chippendale's workshop from 1753; in 1764 Mozart lodged in *Cecil Court* (left) now lined with print and book shops; while *Goodwin's Court* (right) preserves some charming 18C shop-fronts.

The Albery family continues its involvement with the Albery Theatre and six other theatres in the Albery group, including the

Donmar Warehouse. St. Martin's Lane continues N as Monmouth
Street through *Seven Dials*, once a notorious thieves' quarter known
as St. Giles. A Doric pillar topped by a clock with seven faces was
erected here in 1694 at the junction of seven streets. It was taken
down in 1773 when it was falsely rumoured that a treasure was
buried beneath it. It now stands on the green in Weybridge in Surrey,
and Seven Dials is an uninteresting traffic junction (see p 199). The
Cambridge Theatre (1930) is on the S side (closed 1985).

15 Regent Street, Regent's Park, Marylebone and Paddington

Access: Underground, Piccadilly Circus, Oxford Circus, Regent's Park, Baker
Street; then Bus 74 for Regent's Park and London Zoo.

REGENT STREET, 1 mile long, a main N-S thoroughfare through the
West End, is an important shopping street. Lower Regent Street leads
from Waterloo Place to Piccadilly Circus, and continues as Regent
Street to Oxford Circus and Langham Place. It was laid out as part
of Nash's impressive West End design intended to unite the Prince
of Wales' Carlton House with Regent's Park in 1813-20, but never
completed. The curved portion above Piccadilly Circus was known
as the Quadrant; colonnades protected shoppers with, above,
balconies fronting lodging houses. The new facades designed by
Blomfield in 1925 omitted the colonnades but still retain an elegant
unity. The stores and restaurants formed an association in 1925 and
arrange for elaborate Christmas decorations each year illuminated
from the middle of November to Twelfth Night.

The Swan and Edgar store at the Piccadilly Circus end of Regent Street closed
in 1982 but many other well-known names survive, including Austin Reed,
Aquascutum, Lillywhites (Lower Regent Street), Garrard, Mapping & Webb,
Hamleys—the world's largest toy-shop which is now in a new building on six
floors—Jaeger and Dickins and Jones. Liberty, a mock-Tudor building of 1924,
stands in Great Marlborough Street. Amongst the famous restaurants are
Veeraswamy's, one of London's first Indian restaurants (No. 99), Verrey's (No.
233) established in 1848, mentioned by Sherlock Holmes, but popular with
Victorian politicians including Disraeli, and the Café Royal. This opened in
1865 and the Domino Room was used by artists and writers including Beardsley,
Oscar Wilde, Whistler, Max Beerbohm and Sickert between 1890 and 1920 (see
painting inside by Adrian Allinson, c 1916). The future Edward VIII was a
regular customer. The Café Royal was rebuilt in 1925 and the present Grill
Room became the meeting place of another generation of writers including T.S.
Eliot, J.B. Priestley and Compton Mackenzie. Today the Café Royal has five
floors of banqueting and meeting rooms, and two restaurants; the original wine
cellar is available for wine tastings and private boxing matches take place
occasionally.

Vigo Street on the left (W) side of Regent Street leads to *Savile Row*
where much of London's bespoke tailoring industry still survives;
further up on the right (E side) Beak St or Great Marlborough St lead
to Carnaby Street, now a pedestrianised gaudy relic of the swinging
'60s when this was a short-lived fashion mecca.

    West of Regent St lies *Hanover Square*, with a bronze statue of
William Pitt (1759-1806). No. 21 was occupied by Talleyrand in 1835.

St. George's, Hanover Square, to the S, was built in 1713-24, and three of the E windows contain 16C stained glass from Malines placed here c 1843. The two cast-iron dogs in the porch are said to be by Landseer. Concerts are held here, particularly during the annual Handel Festival.

The registers contain entries of the marriages of Sir William Hamilton and Emma Lyon or Hart (1791), Benjamin Disraeli and Mrs Wyndham Lewis (1839), 'George Eliot' and Mr J.W. Cross (1880), Theodore Roosevelt and Edith Carow (1886), and H.H. Asquith and Margaret Tennant (1894); also of the remarriage of Shelley and Harriet Westbrook in 1814 confirming the Scottish marriage of 1811.

Oxford Circus marks the junction of Oxford St and Regent St. On the line of a Roman road, Oxford Street, with Selfridge's and other clothing and department stores, is always crowded with shoppers (partially closed to cars during the day). In Regent St N of Oxford Circus is the *Polytechnic of Central London*, founded in 1882 for the mental, moral, and physical development of youth. The line of Regent St is prolonged to the N by the curving *Langham Place* where the tower and needle-like spire of *All Souls' Church* were built by Nash in 1823-24 and almost detached from the church in order to close the vista up Regent St. In the portico is a bust by Behnes of the architect.

Langham Place is continued northward towards the green expanse of Regent's Park by *Portland Place*, one of the broadest streets in London. At its foot (right) rises *Broadcasting House*, the headquarters of the BBC, a huge edifice by Val Myer and Watson Hart (1931), with a sculptured group of Prospero and Ariel by Eric Gill. The Corporation has spread to other buildings across the road.

The Langham, opposite, used to be one of London's grand old hotels—hard to believe for those who visit the modest BBC offices now occupying the partially reconstructed building (destroyed by a bomb in 1940). In the style of a Florentine palace, designed by Giles and Murray, it opened in 1864 and its lavish suites were frequented by the famous including exiled Napoleon III and Haile Selassie. As well as BBC offices it now houses the BBC Club.

The Adam houses in Portland Place (1776-80) are gradually yielding to larger modern structures. At No. 28 is the *Royal Institute of Public Health and Hygiene*. No. 66 is the *Royal Institute of British Architects*, in a striking building by G.G. Wornum (1934). Monuments in the roadway commemorate *Quintin Hogg* (1845-1903), founder of the Polytechnic (see above); *Sir George White* (1835-1912), defender of Ladysmith (opposite No. 47, once the house of Lord Roberts); and *Lord Lister* (1827-1912), the surgeon.

The attractive and fashionable physicians' quarter to the W of Portland Place (known generally as Harley Street) is famed for its consulting rooms of many medical and surgical specialists, oculists, and dentists. *Cavendish Square* (Pl. 6; 5; underground car park) dates from about 1717; the columned facades of two of the houses on the N side are relics of a great mansion begun in 1720 for the Duke of Chandos. The archway connecting the two wings is adorned with a Madonna by Epstein. Nelson lived at No. 5 in 1787. No. 20 is the *Cowdray Club* for nurses, formerly the house of H.H. Asquith (1852-1928), Prime Minister. Dr Brown-Sequard (1817-94; born in Mauritius), a pioneer in many fields of medicine, was also a resident in the square. In the garden is a statue of Lord George Bentinck (1802-48). In *Holles St* (S) Lord Byron (1788-1824) was born at No.

21, now the site of a department store, with a sculpture by Barbara Hepworth on the SW wall. At the end of Chandos St (NE corner of the square), the fine *Chandos House* built by Robert Adam in 1771 is part of the Royal Society of Medicine.

Wigmore Street, an attractive shopping street with restaurants and coffee shops, and Henrietta Place lead hence to the W. Chamber music recitals are held in *Wigmore Hall* (01-935 2141). At the end of Henrietta Place is the *Royal Society of Medicine*, with its famous library. Opposite *St. Peter, Vere Street*, a neat little church by Gibbs (1721-23) has unusual capitals inside. To the W of Oxford St, the attractive *Stratford Place* (1773-75) retains Stratford House, now the Oriental Club. In *Welbeck St*, leading N from Wigmore St, Anthony Trollope died at a house on the site of No. 34 in 1884. Thos. Woolner lived at No. 29 and Thos. Young at No. 48 (tablets).

Edward Gibbon published the first volumes of his great history while living at No. 7 Bentinck St (leading hence to Manchester Sq.) in 1772-83 and Sir James Mackenzie lived at No. 17 (plaques). Berlioz stayed at No. 58 Queen Anne St (on the E side of Welbeck St) in 1851 when he was a judge at the Great Exhibition competition for makers of musical instruments.

St. Christopher's Place links Wigmore Street with the busy Oxford Street to the S, just before James Street; this pedestrianised Victorian shopping street has been restored to its 19C appearance with small boutiques, hanging signs, flower baskets, outdoor cafés and restaurants. It also links with Barrett St and Giles Court.

On the N side of Wigmore St, Henry Hallam lived in 1819-40 at No. 67 *Wimpole Street*, 'the long unlovely street' of Tennyson's 'In Memoriam', written in commemoration of A. H. Hallam (1811-33). From No. 50 (rebuilt), her home since 1836, Elizabeth Barrett stole secretly in 1846 to be married to Robert Browning in Marylebone church and again a few weeks later to accompany him to Italy. Wilkie Collins, who died at No. 82 in 1889, was born in 1824 at No. 11 (demolished) New Cavendish Street which leads E to Great Portland St and W to Marylebone High St. Turner, the landscape-painter, lived for many years at No. 64 Harley St, and was also the eccentric tenant of a house in Queen Anne St (close by) from 1812-51 (house rebuilt; tablet on No. 23). No. 73 Harley St was occupied by Gladstone from 1876-82 (rebuilt). *Queen's College* (43 Harley St), founded in 1848, is the oldest college for women in England.

An unattractive area NE of Oxford Circus contains massed workshops of clothes manufacturers. In *Great Portland Street*, the main thoroughfare of this quarter with many car dealers, Boswell died at No. 122 (rebuilt). The *Central Synagogue* (left), N of New Cavendish St, was rebuilt in 1958. Margaret St runs E to *All Saints Church*, a brick building by Butterfield (1849-59), with a fine tower and spire, important to the development of Gothic revival architecture.

Mortimer Street, where (at No. 44) Nollekens, the sculptor, lived for fifty years, leads to the *Middlesex Hospital*, a noted teaching hospital founded in 1755. Here Kipling died in 1936. Behind the hospital is Foley St where lived Sir Edwin Landseer (No. 33) and Henry Fuseli (No. 37). At 82 Great Tichfield St (demolished), parallel with Gt Portland St, Samuel Morse, the American pioneer of electric telegraphy, and C.R. Leslie, the Philadelphia artist, had rooms, in 1811, before moving to No. 8 Buckingham Place, now No. 141 Cleveland St, near by. The huge new glass science building of the

London Polytechnic dominates New Cavendish St to the N. In *Charlotte Street*, the main axis of a literary and Greek quarter to the E with many publishers, Greek restaurants, and produce shops in Goodge St, No. 76 was leased by Constable in 1822 until his death in 1837, and the Rossettis lived at No. 50 in 1847 (both houses demolished).

Pollock's Toy Museum in Scala Street is based on Benjamin Pollock's shop which sold his toy-theatre sheets in Islington in Victorian times. The museum moved here in 1969 (the houses date from 1760); the collection appeals more to adults than children. A shop continues on the same premises.

Pollock's Toy Museum, 1 Scala Street, W1. Open Monday to Saturday 10.00-17.00; admission charge.

To the NE, the *British Telecom Tower*, formerly the Post Office Tower, used for television and satellite broadcasting and receiving, opened in 1964 and is 619ft high, including the 39ft-high mast. Its viewing platform and a revolving restaurant closed in 1975 after a bomb incident but may reopen to the public in the future.

The compact *Fitzroy Square* was begun (E and S sides) by the Adam brothers in 1792. Bernard Shaw lived at No. 29 in 1887-98.

Portland Place emerges in •*Park Crescent*, a fine composition (1812-22) by John Nash. Outside the International Students' House (No. 1) is a bust of President Kennedy by J. Lipchitz.

Cross Marylebone Rd (see below) and skirt Park Square Gardens to reach **Regent's Park** (Pl. 5; 4). Roughly circular in shape, the park has an area of 472 acres, and within its precincts are the Zoological Gardens.

Cars are admitted to the Inner Circle, (via Chester Road and York Bridge). Cafeteria in Queen Mary's Gardens and on Broad Walk.

An *Open Air Theatre* (with buffet) in Queen Mary's Gardens holds performances of Shakespeare plays in summer. *Bands* and puppet shows in summer.

Boats may be hired at the boat house near Hanover Gate (NE end of lake). Children's boating pond. For boats along Regent's Canal, see p 29.

Marylebone Park was claimed by Henry VIII as a royal hunting ground, and continued as such until Cromwell's day. It was laid out in its present style as an aristocratic 'garden suburb' after 1812 by Nash, and named after the Prince Regent, who contemplated building a country house here.

The park is encircled by a carriage-road known as the *Outer Circle*, the S half of which is flanked by fine monumental Regency •Terraces in the classical style, mainly by Nash. From S to N, across the E half of the park, runs the *Broad Walk* (1m) leading straight to the Zoo. In the SW portion of the park is an artificial lake of 22 acres (with many wildfowl), while to the N runs the Regent's Canal laid out by Nash in the 1820s. Near the S end of the Broad Walk are beautifully kept flower-gardens; the fine greensward covering the greater part of the park is used for cricket and other games.

From York Gate on the S a road leads to the N, to the drive known as the Inner Circle. On the left, beyond the bridge, stands the former buildings of Bedford College, a School of London University, founded in 1849 to provide for women a liberal education in secular subjects, and moved here in 1913 and to Surrey in 1985. The Holme has gone to a Middle Eastern buyer and the College buildings to Rockford

College, Illinois, a private university. The buildings were rebuilt in 1948-50 after war damage.

The circular *Queen Mary's Gardens* (18 acres; entered by elaborate gates of 1933-35), within the Inner Circle, occupied from 1840 to 1932 by the Royal Botanic Society, is now one of the prettiest little public parks in London, with a rosery, a lily-pond, the Mermaid fountain (by W. McMillan, 1950), and live open-air theatre.

St. John's Lodge, with a secluded rose-garden on the N side of the Inner Circle, was also part of Bedford College. It was enlarged by Barry in 1846-47 and altered in the '90s by Robert Weir Schulz. *Winfield House*, on the Outer Circle, was built for Barbara Hutton in 1936, and is now the residence of the American Ambassador. Residents of Nash's *Hanover Lodge* (c 1827), across the road, included Thos. Cochrane, Joseph Bonaparte, king of Naples, and Adm. Earl Beatty. Lutyens' additions were swept away in 1961-64 when the building became a hall of residence for Bedford College. *Regent's Lodge*, by Hanover Gate, houses the Islamic Cultural Centre next to the *Central Mosque* (1977). H.G. Wells (1866-1940) died at No. 13 Hanover Terrace, and Ralph Vaughan Williams (1872-1958), the composer, died at No. 11. The last home of Sir Edmund Gosse (1849-1928), the critic, was No. 17. In Sussex Place, beyond the new building of the Royal College of Obstetricians and Gynaecologists, the *London School of Business Studies* (founded in 1965; c 250

The Zoological Gardens, Regent's Park

students) occupies a pleasant new building in yellow stone (1970, by Westwood, Piet & Partners) concealed behind the fine Nash facade on the park. *St. Cyprian*, in Glentworth St to the S, has a light interior by Ninian Comper (1903). *York Terrace West* (now entered from the pleasant road to the S) has been faithfully rebuilt to Nash's design.

On the E side of the park, the monumental terraces by Nash (Chester and Cumberland Terrace, 1825-26) facing the Outer Circle have their backs to Albany Street. At the S end is the Royal College of Physicians (1962-64), a fine building by Denys Lasdun. *St. Katharine's* church at the N end, formerly the chapel of St. Katharine's Royal Foundation (see Rte 24), was built in 1823. Restored in 1950-52, it is now the church of the Danish community in London. It has fine carving on the ceiling, two wooden figures of saints (by C.G. Cibber, 1696) from the old Danish church at Limehouse, and above the windows, 39 shields of arms of the Queens of England from Matilda to Queen Mary. In Albany Street are territorial barracks, the Whitehouse and Christ Church (1837, by Pennethorne) where the Rev. William Dodsworth was the first vicar.

The **Regent's Park Zoo** (officially the *Gardens of the Zoological Society of London*) was founded by Sir Stamford Raffles and Sir Humphry Davy (1826). Situated at the N end of Regent's Park, it is bounded on the N by Prince Albert Road and on the E by Broad Walk, and intersected by Regent's Canal and by the Outer Circle. Changing attitudes towards city-based zoos have led to the transfer of many animals to the more spacious Whipsnade Zoo in Bedfordshire. Recently the Regent's Park Zoo has received some direct Government funding to upgrade facilities for both animals and visitors and a major redevelopment programme is now underway.

London Zoo, Regent's Park, London NW1. Tel. 01-722 3333. Open daily 09.00-18.00 (March to October), to 19.00 on Sundays; 10.00 to dusk (winter). Admission charge.

Access: Underground to Baker Street, Bus 74; Underground Camden Town. From April to Sept Zoo Waterbus from Little Venice. The main entrance is in the Outer Circle; car and coach park in Outer Circle Albany Road.

The Zoological Gardens opened in five acres of Regent's Park to members of the Zoological Society only, in 1825. Decimus Burton laid out and designed the enclosures; the Raven's Cage, Giraffe House, the old Camel House/Clock Tower and the East Tunnel still remain. The public was admitted in 1847 and during the Great Exhibition thousands flocked to the Zoo. Peak attendance came in 1950 and reached 3 million a year. It has since declined. The Zoo pioneered the exhibiting of exotic animals, including reptiles, insects, chimpanzees and giraffes. More recently, in 1974, the Zoo received two giant pandas (one has died).

The striking aviaries on the N side of the Zoo were designed by Lord Snowdon; they can be seen from Regent's Canal. The new Lion Terraces opened in 1976. The Charles Clore Pavilion for Mammals (1967) incorporates reversed lighting so that nocturnal animals can be watched by day. A new self-service cafeteria opened in 1984.

Institutions based here include the Wellcome Institute of Comparative Physiology, an Animal Hospital, the Nuffield Institute of Comparative Medicine, as well as the Zoological Society itself with a lecture room and library.

To the N of Regent's Park, separated from the Zoological Gardens by Prince Albert Road (where in 1855 Wagner lodged and completed 'Die Walküre'), rises *Primrose Hill*, a park of 61 acres. The top of

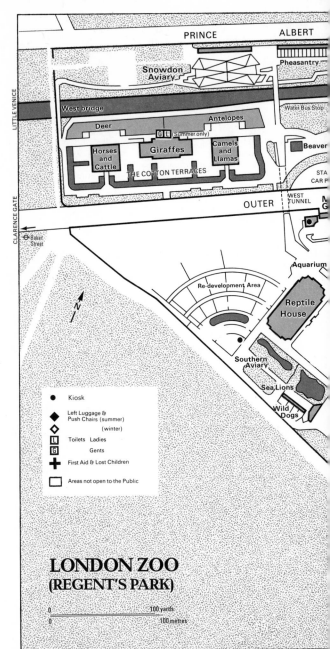

PRINCE   ALBERT

Pheasantry

Snowdon Aviary

West bridge   Water Bus Stop

Deer   Antelopes

G **L** (Summer only)

Horses
and   Giraffes   Camels
Cattle   and
Llamas   Beaver

THE COTTON TERRACES

STA
CAR P

WEST
TUNNEL

OUTER

Baker
Street

Aquarium

Re-development Area

Reptile
House

N

Southern
Aviary

Sea Lions

Wild
Dogs

LITTLE VENICE

CLARENCE GATE

- ● Kiosk

- ◆ Left Luggage &
  Push Chairs (summer)
- ◇   (winter)
- **L** **G** Toilets Ladies
           Gents
- ✚ First Aid & Lost Children

- ▢ Areas not open to the Public

LONDON ZOO
(REGENT'S PARK)

0 |————————————————| 100 yards
0 |————————————————| 100 metres

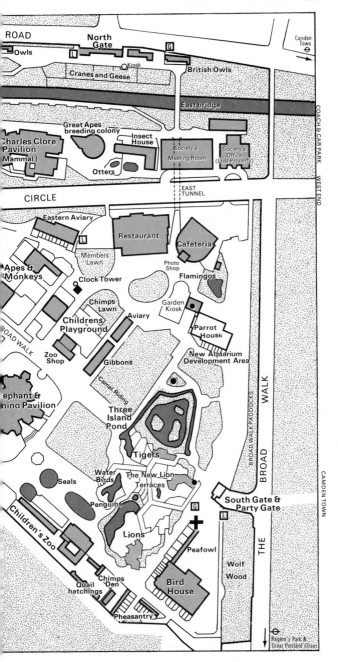

the hill (219ft) commands a fine view. To the W of it is **St. John's Wood**, a residential district extending to Maida Vale, and once a favourite quarter with artists, now a wealthy residential area. Many of its attractive villas standing in large gardens have been replaced by massive blocks of flats. Among its many distinguished residents were Sir Edwin Landseer, George Eliot, Thomas Hood, Charles Bradlaugh, Thomas Huxley, and Herbert Spencer. The *Saatchi Gallery* of modern art is at 98A Boundary Road, London NW8 (01-624 8299). At the junction of several thoroughfares quite close to Regent's Park is the church of *St. John*, in which Joanna Southcott (1750-1814) is buried (under the name of Goddard). J.S. Cotman (1782-1842), the painter, is buried in the churchyard. *Grove House*, opposite, built by Decimus Burton in 1823-24, is now the seat of the Nuffield Foundation.

Wellington Road leads NW to St. John's Wood Station and Finchley Road. To the E, the Riding School (1825) of the Royal Horse Artillery barracks (rebuilt) has been restored to use. St. John's Wood Road runs SW from the church to Maida Vale passing **Lord's Cricket Ground**, property of the Marylebone Cricket Club (the 'MCC') and headquarters of the English national game. The Cricket Memorial Gallery at Lord's Cricket Ground (open during matches only (10.30-17.00), or by appointment) houses mementoes of the game including the original urn that contained the 'Ashes' (1882-83).

In Abbey Road is the pedestrian crossing made famous by a Beatles album picturing them crossing the road from the EMI Studios on the left (W side) where many of their recordings were made in the 1960s.

To the S of the park the **Marylebone Road** (Pl. 5; 5) runs through the old borough of St. Marylebone. The name is derived from the church of 'St. Mary on the Bourne', or stream, i.e. Tyburn. Opposite York Gate is *St. Marylebone* (1813-17), by Thos. Hardwick, the church in which Robert Browning was married in 1846 (a Browning Room here contains relics of the poet). The Schulze swell organ was formerly in Charterhouse School. In a chapel in the N aisle is a painting of the Holy Family, by Benjamin West.

The site of the 18C parish church (demolished in 1949), a successor to that in which Francis Bacon was married (1606) is now laid out as a Garden of Rest in Marylebone High St (a winding relic of the old village). Lord Byron (1788) and Nelson's daughter Horatia (1801) were baptised in this church; Sheridan was here married to Miss Linley (1773). The graves of Charles and Samuel Wesley (d 1788 and 1837), James Gibbs (d 1754), John Rysbrack (1770), Allan Ramsay (1784) and George Stubbs (1806) remain in the Garden.

On the corner of Marylebone High St, to the E, a carved panel (1960, by E.J. Clack) shows Dickens and characters from six of his works written in 1839-51 when he lived in a house on this site. Opposite is the *Royal Academy of Music*, founded in 1822. To the W, are the conspicuous buildings of *Madame Tussaud's Waxworks* and the *London Planetarium*.

Madame Tussaud's, Marylebone Road, London NW1. Tel. 01-935 6861. Access: Underground, Baker Street. Open daily 10.00-17.30. Admission charge (an inclusive ticket with the London Planetarium is available, see below). Crowded in summer; go early or late.

Madame Tussaud (1761-1850) was employed at the court of Louis XVI to make wax-figures. She was imprisoned during the Revolution and took models from the heads of guillotine victims. She fled to London in 1802 with many of her original moulds; those beheaded in the French revolution can be seen in the

Chamber of Horrors. The first exhibition opened in Baker Street in 1835. The present building opened in 1884 and was restored after bomb-damage. The exhibition is continually updated with popular figures of the day from the world of politics, the arts and sports.

London Planetarium incorporating the Laserium, Marylebone Road, London NW1. Tel. 01-486 1121. Access as above. Open 11.00-16.30; Planetarium presentations at intervals; Laserium in early evening. The Planetarium was built in 1958 and features a Zeiss projector with 20,000 separate parts to create 9000 stars. Lectures are held on a variety of subjects. Laser shows with pop and classical music utilise the same equipment plus lasers.

Opposite are the huge buildings (1971, by Kinner) of the architecture and town planning departments, etc. of the London Polytechnic.

In Baker Street are the offices of the Abbey National Building Society which reputedly employs one secretary just to deal with Sherlock Holmes' post. This is the site of the fictional 221B Baker Street where Sherlock Holmes had his rooms.

BAKER STREET (Pl. 5; 5), a busy thoroughfare which runs N to S, links Marylebone Rd and Oxford St. Bulwer Lytton was born at No. 68 in 1803. No. 82 was the headquarters of the Special Operations Executive (S.O.E.) in 1940-45. Arnold Bennett died in 1931 at Chiltern Court (No. 97). In *Gloucester Place*, parallel with Baker St on the W, Wilkie Collins lived at No. 90 (now No. 65) in 1863-76 and 1883-88. George St crosses Baker St near its S end. To the right, at No. 85, Thos. Moore had his first lodgings in London, and to the left is the large R.C. church of *St. James's*, *Spanish Place* in a pure E.E. style (by Goldie, 1885-90). Spanish Place (where a tablet at No. 3 marks the house of Capt. Marryat) leads hence S to the secluded **Manchester Square**, built about 1770-88, and retaining some pleasant houses. At No. 2 lived Sir Julius Benedict, No. 3 was the home of John Hughlings Jackson, the neurologist, and No. 14 the residence of Lord Milner

The restored platforms at Baker Street Underground Station (1906)

(plaques). In Duke St, just out of the S side of the square, Simon Bolivar stayed in 1810 (No. 4).

Hertford House, once the residence of the marquesses of Hertford and afterwards that of Sir Richard Wallace (d 1890) and of Lady Wallace (d 1897), lies on the N side. The ****Wallace Collection** (Pl. 5; 7) is the most important single collection in London for the lover of art in its various manifestations; in the choiceness and variety of its contents it resembles and rivals the Château of Chantilly in France. Not its least charm is its arrangement, the beautiful furniture, porcelain, sculptures, and innumerable small works of ornamental art being admirably exhibited in the rooms containing the paintings. It is notable especially for its French paintings, furniture, and porcelain and for its European arms and armour.

The Wallace Collection, Hertford House, Manchester Square, London W1. Tel. 01-935 0687. Access: Underground, Bond Street. Open: Monday to Saturday 10.00-17.00; Sunday 14.00-17.00. Free.

All items on display are identified; a catalogue/guide is available. Below are some of the highlights. (Most of the important pieces are on the 1st Floor.)

The collection was formed mainly by the fourth Marquess of Hertford (1800-70) who resided chiefly in Paris. His father, the third Marquess, figures as Lord Steyne in Thackeray's 'Vanity Fair', and as Lord Monmouth in Disraeli's 'Coningsby'. The fourth Marquess bequeathed the collection to his natural son, Sir Richard Wallace (1818-90), who removed it to London, added to it the collection of arms and armour, besides many pictures and Renaissance works of art, and changed the name of the house to Hertford House. In 1897 the priceless collection was bequeathed to the nation by Lady Wallace. The present gallery was opened in 1900.

Entrance Hall: Family portraits of the Hertfords by Reynolds and others. Room 1: British 18th and 19C paintings, French 18C furniture. Room 2: fine Boulle furniture, Sèvres porcelain and important European paintings including Murillo, 'Virgin and Child' and Rubens, 'Christ on the Cross'. Rooms 3 and 4: Medieval and Renaissance sculpture and works of art, including an impressive Italian fireplace in marble (c 1500) flanked by two Corinthian columns veneered in malachite and topped with gilt bronze Lions of St. Mark (Russian, 19C). Limoges enamels are on display. Room 4, originally the Smoking Room, houses an important collection of Italian maiolica, from the main centres of production; note the dish signed by Maestro Giorginio Andreoli of Gubbio dated 1525, one of the most important pieces of surviving maiolica. Rooms 5-7: European armour, displayed in reverse chronological order (earliest pieces in Room 7); Oriental arms and armour in Room 8.

Room 9 was formerly the Housekeeper's Room and is now the shop, with paintings by Lawrence, 'Sally Siddons', and Landseer, 'Looking for crumbs from the rich man's table'.

Room 10 used to be the Breakfast Room, with an important group of paintings by Richard Bonington, a British artist who worked in France (1802-1828).

Room 11 is the former Billiard Room: amongst the paintings are Lemoyne, 'Time revealing the Truth'—the artist committed suicide a few hours after completing the painting. Room 12, the Dining Room, has more superb Sèvres porcelain, and a collection of 18C French gold boxes.

The white marble staircase leading to the first floor is flanked by wrought-iron and bronze balustrades made for the Palais Mazarin in

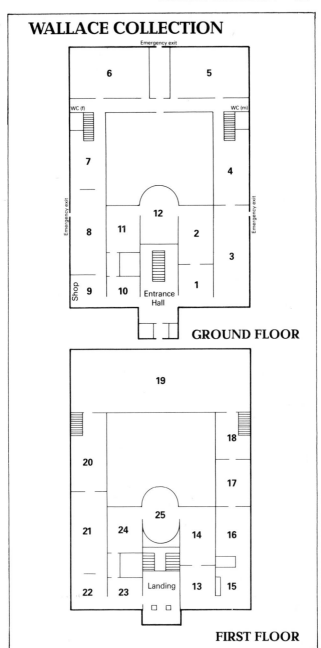

WALLACE COLLECTION

GROUND FLOOR

FIRST FLOOR

Paris. At the top of stairs canvasses by Boucher, designs for Gobelins tapestries. Room 13: paintings by Guardi and Canaletto. Room 14: more Canaletto and imitators. In the Londonderry library cabinet more Sèvres porcelain. Note the 'régulateur' clock with four dials, surmounted by figures of Time and Cupid; it belonged to Madame de Pompadour's godfather.

Room 15: three paintings by Murillo, a group of oil sketches by Rubens, and Rembrandt, 'Self-Portrait in a Cap'.

Room 16: figurative 17C Dutch paintings. Room 17: more small 17C Dutch pictures, mainly landscapes and seascapes including works by Van de Velde II and Hobbema. Room 18: mainly 17C Dutch Italianate paintings. Room 19: the largest room, 118ft long and housing the finest paintings including Murillo, 'Holy Family with St. John the Baptist', Van Dyck, 'Isabella Waerbeke', Rembrandt, 'Titus', Hals, 'The Laughing Cavalier', Rubens, 'Holy Family with Sts Elizabeth and John the Baptist', Velasquez, 'Don Baltasar Carlos in Infancy', Poussin, 'Dance to the Music of Time', and others.

Room 20: French paintings from 1820-60. Room 21: fine French 18C paintings and furniture including Watteau, Lancret, Pater and Boucher, and a rococo style chest of drawers in kingwood and mahogany made in 1739 for Louis XV's bedroom at Versailles.

Room 22: formerly Lady Wallace's bedroom. Fine paintings by Boucher. Room 23: late 18C French and English paintings.

Room 24: still life paintings. Boule furniture and clocks. Room 25: the Oval Drawing Room with later 18C French furniture, sculpture and paintings, including a roll-top desk by Riesner with marquetry. Collection of gold snuff boxes.

On the W side of Baker St lies the once sought-after area built in the 1760s round *Portman Square*. ***Home House** (No. 20) is the best surviving example of a Robert Adam town house (c 1773-76). The delightfully shaped rooms and staircase are decorated with paintings by *Zucchi*. Also here is a painting (unfinished) of the Holy Family by *Perino del Vaga*. The house belongs to the *Courtauld Institute of Art* of the University of London, founded by Samuel Courtauld in 1931, which owns the Witt Library of c 950,000 reproductions of European paintings and drawings from the Renaissance to the present day. Open by appointment (see also p 178). The Institute has spread into 21 Portman Square, a house designed by James Adam in 1772, and since 1972, the art department of the Royal Institute of British Architects. The *Heinz Gallery* contains a changing exhibition of architects' drawings, while the library consists of over 200,000 European architectural drawings (comprehensive photographic service).

Heinz Gallery, Portman Square, London W1H. Tel. 01-580 5533. This is an exhibition gallery for the Royal Institute of British Architects. Open during exhibitions Monday to Friday 11.00-17.00, Thursday 11.00-20.00, Saturday 10.00-13.00. Exhibitions are based on RIBA's collection of more than 200,000 architectural drawings; photographic exhibitions are also held here. The RIBA Library of architectural books, journals etc. is open to the public at 66 Portland Place, Mon 10.00-17.00, Tues to Thurs 10.00-20.00, Fri 10.00-19.00 and Sat 10.00-13.30.

In *Seymour Street*, to the W, a tablet at No. 30 marks the house of Edward Lear. New Quebec Street, with some pleasant shops, leads N to the attractive *Montagu Square* where Anthony Trollope lived (at No. 39) in 1873-80. In the NW corner is the Jews College (1955-57). In Robert Adam Street, NE of Portman Sq., the luxurious church of *St Paul's, Portman Square* was opened in 1970.

Portman St leads S from the square to Oxford Street which runs W to Marble Arch.

The Edgware Road (Pl. 4; 8) runs through an unattractive area N from Marble Arch in a practically straight line towards Edgware (7 miles), following ancient Roman *Watling Street*. Off Harrowby St (the sixth turning on the right), an archway leads into the narrow *Cato Street*, once notorious as the meeting-place of the 'Cato Street Conspirators' (hanged at Newgate in 1820), whose object was the wholesale murder of the ministers of the Crown at a Cabinet dinner in Grosvenor Square. To the N, in Marylebone Road, the R.C. *Church of the Holy Rosary* makes interesting use of the arch. **Paddington Station** (approached by Praed St) lies to the W. The Metropolitan Railway Company opened the first underground railway in the world in 1863 from Paddington to Farringdon. The Marylebone Flyover takes the A40 (here motorway) across Edgware Rd to forge W through an area of new building (including the Police Station, 1971). On the edge *Paddington Green* (reached by sub-way) survives around the church of *St. Mary* (1791, the successor of the church in which Hogarth was secretly married in 1729. Thomas Banks (d 1805) and Joseph Nollekens (d 1823), sculptors, and Benj. Haydon (d 1847), painter, have their tombs here. Mrs Siddons is buried at the N end of the churchyard (now a recreation ground). In 1829 the first London omnibus service pulled by three horses started from the Green on its journey to the Bank of England along the Marylebone Road.

To the NW at the REGENT'S CANAL is a tranquil green oasis (left) named **'Little Venice'** by Browning. House-boats and bright Victorian houses line the canal. In *Bloomfield Road* (No. 60) is the starting-point of Jason's canal cruises which, in summer, make trips through Regent's Park to Camden Town, and then back to Little Venice, with 'Browning's Island'. Water-buses (British Waterways Board) to the zoo depart Easter to Sept from Warwick Crescent (01-482 2550). Opposite the station (Warwick Avenue) a bas-relief by D. Thackway (1965) commemorates Browning. The tow-path from Lisson Grove (Pl. 4; 3) to Regent's Park and Camden Town has been opened for walkers.

For about a mile beyond the Regent's Canal the Edgware Road is known as MAIDA VALE, and is flanked by pleasant dwellings and large blocks of flats. The name (the pronunciation of which time and gentility have corrupted) recalls the battle of Máida, by which the British under Sir John Stuart expelled the French from Calabria in 1806. On the right extends St. John's Wood (comp. p 170).

16 Bloomsbury

A. The Squares of Bloomsbury and the districts to the North

Access: Underground, Tottenham Court Road, Holborn, Warren Street (for this walk start at Tottenham Court Road).

The beautifully-planted squares of **Bloomsbury** (Pl. 7; 3) date mainly from the 18C and early 19C. Their modest well-proportioned terraced houses have gradually disappeared as extensions to London University, hotels and offices encroach on the area. Many smaller hotels occupy houses in the formal streets. Bloomsbury is linked with the names of Virginia and Leonard Woolf, Clive and Vanessa Bell, Lytton Strachey, etc. who began here, before the First World War, an eccentric association of intellectual and artistic interests later known as 'The Bloomsbury Group'.

St Giles Circus (Pl. 6; 6), dominated by the notorious Centre Point tower block (1963-67; R. Seifert and Partners) is a busy intersection at the top of Charing Cross Road. *Tottenham Court Road*, noted for its furniture and hi-fi dealers, leads N towards Camden Town and Hampstead. On the corner of Gt Russell St (comp. below) stands the *Y Hotel* (1976), with a splendid recreation and sports club (annual membership fee) of the YMCA. Oxford Street is here continued E by *New Oxford Street.*

Before New Oxford St was constructed in 1849 through the poverty-stricken and congested region known as the 'rookery of St. Giles' the main thoroughfare E followed the shallow curve on the S (now one-way W), via St. Giles High St to High Holborn. A hospital for lepers (named for their patron saint St. Giles) was founded here in 1101 by Matilda, Queen of Henry I: Shaftesbury Ave and St. Giles High St follow the line of the walls. One of the first cases of the Great Plague in London occurred among Flemish weavers in the parish in 1664.

In High St the church of **St. Giles in the Fields**, built in 1731-33 by Flitcroft, and well restored in 1954, still preserves a rural setting. Above the W gate is an oak relief of the Resurrection carved in 1687. Inside, the Father Smith organ (1671; partly remodelled), and the pulpit (1676) survive from an earlier church. In the S aisle the upper part of a pulpit used by John and Charles Wesley in 1743-91 is preserved (formerly in West Street Chapel). In the S porch is the tombstone of Richard Penderel (d 1671), the woodman who guarded the 'royal' oak and thus secured the escape of Charles II after the Battle of Worcester. In the N aisle George Chapman (d 1634), translator of Homer, has an appropriate tomb said to have been designed by Inigo Jones, and Andrew Marvell (d 1678), the poet, is commemorated. The recumbent effigy of Lady Frances Kniveton was carved by Joshua Marshall. A memorial to Flaxman (carved by the sculptor) was placed in the porch in 1930. In the churchyard is an architectural monument to Sir John Soane. The baptism is recorded in the parish register of Milton's daughter Mary in 1648, and in 1818 of Allegra, daughter of Byron, and of Shelley's children, William and Clara.

Bloomsbury Street and Bloomsbury Way branch N from New Oxford Street. In *Bloomsbury Way* the church of *St. George's, Bloomsbury* was built by Hawksmoor in 1716-31. The Corinthian portico is impressive, and the steeple is surmounted by a statue of George I. Anthony Trollope was baptised in the church, which was the scene of the 'Bloomsbury Christening' in Dickens' 'Sketches by Boz'.

Bloomsbury Street or the parallel Museum and Coptic Streets (with bookshops and antique dealers) lead to the **British Museum** (see p 182). At the corner of Great Russell St is the home of the *Trades Union Congress* (1958). Bloomsbury St runs through the E side of BEDFORD SQUARE, built around 1776, and presenting some characteristic examples of the style of the Adam brothers.

The *Architectural Association* is housed in Nos 34-36; Lord Eldon (1751-1838), the reactionary Lord Chancellor, lived at No. 6, and Henry Cavendish, the natural philosopher, died in 1810 at No. 11.

North of the square, in Store St, are the *Department of Oriental Manuscripts and Printed Books* of the British Library and the *Building Centre* (No. 26), founded in 1930 'to provide a permanent exhibition and information service for the free use of all interested in good building' (open Mon-Fri 09.30–17.15, Sat 10.00–16.00). Across Tottenham Court Rd, the *Whitefield Memorial Church* (by E.C. Butler; 1956-58) was built on the site of the chapel erected for George Whitefield (1714-70), the famous preacher.

The severe and rectilinear *Gower Street* continues N past the *Royal*

Academy of Dramatic Art, founded by Sir H. Beerbohm Tree (d 1917), to University College (see below), and Euston Road.

At No. 2 a tablet commemorates Millicent Fawcett (1847-1929), a pioneer of women's rights. On the right, at the corner of Keppel St, is the *London School of Hygiene and Tropical Medicine*, established in 1922. At No. 69 William de Morgan (1839-1917) was born, and George Dance the Younger (1741-1825) lived and died at No. 91. No. 105 is the Royal National Institute for the Deaf. The Biological Department of London University (E side) occupies the site of a house where Charles Darwin lived in 1838-42. Giuseppe Mazzini's home was at No. 183 (N of Euston Rd) in 1837-40.

Turn E along Montague Place between the N facade of the British Museum and the Senate House of the **University of London**. Many of the administrative buildings here dominated by the central tower of the Senate House, begun in 1933, are by Charles Holden. Much of the University's work of instruction and research is carried on in institutions far removed from the administrative centre; but a number of departments and dependencies are concentrated in the area in new buildings or in the terraced houses in neighbouring squares. The fine Senate House Library is accessible to visiting scholars.

London was the last of the great European capitals to found a university. In 1836 a charter was granted constituting a University of London, with the power of granting academic degrees, without religious tests, to students of University College, King's College, and certain other affiliated institutions. In 1858 the examinations were thrown open to all students without restriction, and twenty years later (in 1878) the University of London became the first academic body in the United Kingdom to admit women as candidates for degrees on equal terms with men. Hitherto a purely examining body, it was reconstituted in 1898-1900 as a teaching university, instruction being given in existing colleges and schools. University College and King's College were incorporated as 'integral parts' of the University; these and other institutions are 'Schools of the University', each controlled by its own governing body; while others have teachers 'recognised by the University'. Students attending these colleges are known as 'internal students'; those presenting themselves for examination only are 'external students'.

Birkbeck College, founded in 1823 as a scientific and technical institute, entered its new building, facing Malet St, in 1951. The first part of the building of the *Students' Union*, adjoining on the N, was opened in 1955, while on the E side are the *School of Oriental and African Studies* (SOAS) and the *Institute of Historical Research*. Other institutes occupy temporary quarters in Russell Sq., to the SE. Between Russell Sq. and Woburn Sq. new buildings by Denys Lasdun house the *Institutes of Education and Law* and an extension to SOAS.

RUSSELL SQUARE (Pl. 7; 3) laid out in 1801, is the largest square in central London, with the exception of Lincoln's Inn Fields. On the S side of the garden is a statue of the 5th Duke of Bedford (1765-1805) by Westmacott. The *Royal Institute of Chemistry* (by Sir J.J. Burnet) is at No. 30. Over the entrance is a seated figure of Priestley. The attractive *Bedford Place* connects the square with BLOOMSBURY SQUARE (Pl. 7; 5; underground car park), one of the earliest squares in London (c 1665). The Statue of Charles James Fox (1749-1806) in its garden is by Westmacott. No. 17, occupied and refaced by Nash in 1782-83, was the home of the *Pharmaceutical Society* since 1841 now in Lambeth. At No. 2 is the College of Preceptors.

To the NW of Russell Square new buildings for the University of London intrude into *Woburn Square*. In *Christ Church* Christina

Rossetti (d 1894) is commemorated by a reredos with paintings by Burne-Jones.

On the W side of the square are the **Courtauld Institute Galleries**, a delightful collection of French Impressionist and Post-Impressionist paintings bequeathed by Samuel Courtauld (1865-1949); the collection made by Lord Lee Fareham (1868-1947) of 14-18C art, the Roger Fry Collection, the Witt Collection of Old Master Drawings and the Mark Gambier-Parry Bequest (1966) which includes many early Italian paintings. In 1978 the Count Antoine Seilern bequest of paintings and drawings by Rubens and Michelangelo amongst others was added to the Institute's collection, putting further pressure on space. The Galleries are due to move to new premises in Somerset House in the next two years.

Courtauld Institute Galleries, Woburn Square, WC2. Tel. 01-580 1015. Open Monday to Saturday 10.00-17.00, Sunday 14.00-17.00. Admission charge. Access: Underground, Russell Square, Goodge Street.

Below are some of the highlights of the collections but exhibits are changed regularly.

French Impressionist and Post-Impressionists: Cezanne, 'Card Player', 'Lake of Annecy'; Degas, 'Two Dancers on the Stage'; Gaugin, 'Nevermore'; Manet, 'Le Dejeuner sur l'Herbe' (a larger version is in the Louvre) and his last major work, 'Bar at the Folies-Bergère'; Modigliani, 'Nude'; Pissarro, 'Lordship Lane Station' (formerly mistakenly known as Penge Station); Renoir, 'La Loge'; Seurat, 'Young Woman at a Powder-table'; and Van Gogh, 'Portrait of the Artist with Bandaged Ear'.

The collection of early Italian religious works include paintings by Fra Angelico, Gaddi, and sculpture and enamels. The Seilern or Princes Gate Collection also includes French Impressionist works but is particularly well-known for the 23 drawings and 32 paintings by Rubens, 12 paintings and over 30 drawings by Tiepolo, and drawings by Michelangelo.

The Roger Fry Collection includes paintings by members of the Bloomsbury Group as well as furniture and pottery produced by the Omega Workshops founded by Fry in 1913.

The *Warburg Institute* (Woburn Square), beyond the Courtauld Galleries, faces Gordon Square; a relief panel of nine muses which decorated the original building at 1 Gordon Square has been retained in the entrance hall. The Institute, which is part of the University of London, is concerned with the study of the classics and European art and institutions. It has a large library and photographic collection. Facing the Institute is the *Church of Christ the King*, in Byng Place, a huge Gothic revival church, built in 1853 for the sect known as the Irvingites but now used by the University. At 53 Gordon Square is the unique **Percival David Foundation of Chinese Art**.

Percival David Foundation of Chinese Art, 53 Gordon Square, London WC2. Tel. 01-387 3909. Open Monday 14.00-17.00, Tuesday to Friday 10.30-17.00, Saturday 10.30-13.00. Admission free. Closed on Sat during August. Access: Underground, Euston Square.

Sir Percival David presented his collection of Chinese ceramics and his library to the University in 1951 and a further bequest was made by Mountstuart Elphinstone. The collection on three floors includes Sun, Yuan, Ming and Ch'ing porcelain (AD 960-1912) and the library may be used by scholars, on application.

At No. 46 Gordon Square Virginia Woolf lived before her marriage and the Bloomsbury Group started; Lytton Strachey and Clive Bell also lived in the Square.

Backing on to Gordon St are the buildings of **University College** (main entrance in Gower Street). It was founded in 1826 and opened in 1828, with the title of University of London, by Lord Brougham, Thomas Campbell, James Mill, and other friends of religious liberty, with the object of affording, on undenominational lines, and 'at a moderate expense the means of education in literature, science, and art'. In 1900 it became a 'school' of the University of London, with which it was incorporated in 1907. The central building with its Corinthian portico and fine dome was designed by W. Wilkins; on all sides are extensions and additions. In the hall beneath the dome is the *Flaxman Gallery*, containing original models and drawings by John Flaxman (1755-1826). In the cloisters below is the 'Marmor Homericum', with Homeric subjects in marble niello by Baron Triqueti, presented by Grote, the historian.

Flaxman Galleries, University College, Gower Street, London WC1. Tel. 01-387 7050. Open Monday to Friday 09.30-17.00. Admission free. Jeremy Bentham's embalmed body, now a clothed skeleton with a wax-head, is shown on application and during term time.

The *Petrie Museum of Egyptian Archaeology*, open Mon to Fri 10.00-12.00, 13.15-17.00, closed 4 weeks in summer, is a university teaching collection in cramped premises which includes outstanding archaeological finds from prehistoric to Coptic periods; it is looking for more space and may move.

Also at the University College in the South Wing is the Mocatta Library and Museum of the Jewish Historical Society. The Gustave Tuck Lecture Theatre is by Albert Richardson (1954).

The central *Collegiate Building*, *Union* and *Theatre* are in new buildings in Gordon Street. The *Slade School of Art*, established under the will of Felix Slade (1790-1868) the art collector, is part of the college. The *Bartlett School of Architecture* is now part of the School of Environmental Studies. In Gower Street is the *University College Hospital*, founded in 1834 but the present medical school dates from 1906. The first operation in Europe under ether was performed at the Hospital in 1846.

East of Gordon Sq. lies *Tavistock Square* (Pl. 6; 4) with a statue (1968) of Mahatma Gandhi (1869-1948). Off the NE corner of the square the *British Medical Association* stands near the site of Tavistock House, occupied by Dickens in 1850-60. Here 'Bleak House' and 'Little Dorrit' were written. Opposite is *Woburn House*, a Jewish centre.

Jewish Museum, Woburn House, Upper Woburn Place, London WC1. Tel. 01-388 4525. Access: Underground Russell Square; Open May to September, Tues to Fri 10.00-16.00, Fri and Sun 10.00-12.45, Oct to April, Tues to Thurs 10.00-16.00, Fri and Sun 10.00-12.45. Admission free.
  This collection consisting of ritual objects was founded in 1932 to show the richness of the Anglo-Jewish heritage. On display are ceramics, embroidery, manuscripts, silverwork, and an Ark in which the scrolls of the law are kept.

Tavistock Place leads E to Hunter St where the house (No. 54) in which John Ruskin (1819-1900) was born was demolished in 1969.

Endsleigh Street, with the first headquarters (1922) of the National Union of Students (No. 3), leads out of the NW corner of the square to Endsleigh Gardens. Turn left to reach the *Wellcome Institute* (entrance on Euston Rd), an important scientific foundation established in 1913 by Sir Henry Wellcome (1853-1936). The dioramas showing the history of medicine were transferred to the Science Museum in 1980, and the Wellcome Institute's Library and facilities are now available to doctors and students only, on application.

EUSTON ROAD (Pl. 6; 2), the N boundary of Bloomsbury, continues the line of Marylebone Rd E to King's Cross. It forms part of the 'New Road' laid out in 1754-56 to connect Islington with Paddington, and now bears the heavy traffic of the Inner Ring Road. *Friend's House* (1926), by H. Lidbetter, the headquarters of the Society of Friends, contains documents relating to William Penn and the foundation of Pennsylvania. To the E of *Euston Square* is **Euston Station** (restaurants), rebuilt in 1963-68, when, against considerable opposition, the old classical entrance arch was demolished. The statue in the forecourt is of Robert Stephenson who, with Philip Hardwick, designed the original station in 1836. Opposite rises the 'new' *St. Pancras Church*, built in 1819-22 by Inwood (restored in 1951-53) in a 'Grecian' style, a pastiche of various buildings in Athens. To the S, *Duke's Road* and *Woburn Walk* preserve quaint 18C shop-fronts. W.B. Yeats lived at No. 5 Woburn Walk in 1895-1919. On the N side of Euston Rd huge new office buildings (1968-70) tower above the *Elizabeth Garrett Anderson Hospital* and the *St. Pancras Library* and *Shaw Theatre* (1971).

The Shaw Theatre, Euston Road, NW1, (founded in 1971) is part of a complex which includes a library. It was named after George Bernard Shaw and is used by the National Youth Theatre, touring theatre companies and the fringe. The new British Library is being built on the former rail goods yard here.

St. Pancras Station and Chambers, a Gothic fantasy, tower above the modern **King's Cross Station**. The station, completed in 1867, was one of the wonders of Victorian engineering, a 100ft-high glass and iron structure. The adjoining *Midland Grand Hotel* was designed by George Gilbert Scott and based on his rejected plans for government offices in Whitehall. It was described as one of the most sumptuous hotels in the Empire and features an imperial staircase. It closed in 1935 and is now used as offices.

In *Pancras Road*, which leads NW, is (900 yards) *St Pancras Old Church*, of very ancient foundation, but practically rebuilt in 1848. The church is kept locked because of vandalism; the attractive interior may be seen at the services. In the old graveyard, now a public garden entered through elaborate gates, Mary Godwin is said to have first met Shelley in 1813 beside the grave of her mother, Mary Wollstonecraft (d 1797), whose remains were transferred to Bournemouth in 1851. John Flaxman (d 1826), and John Christian Bach (d 1782) are buried here, and Sir John Soane (d 1837), with his wife, in the mausoleum he designed for her in 1815. An ash tree offers protection to a curious mass of gravestones. To the E the GRAND UNION CANAL (with a nature reserve) flows behind King's Cross Station.

Pentonville Road leads towards the Angel, passing on the left the former *St. James's Churchyard* where Joseph Grimaldi (1779-1837), the famous clown, was buried. Plans are being made to create a memorial garden on the site.

A plaque at the back of the Royal Scot Hotel at 100 King's Cross Road marks a house in Percy Circus where Lenin stayed in 1905. He also lived in Holford Square in 1902 (near King's Cross); and frequented the Pindar of Wakefield pub, Gray's Inn Road, now the home of the Aba Daba Music Hall (regular evening performances).

Gray's Inn Road, a long and uninteresting commercial thoroughfare, leads S from King's Cross to Holborn, past the *Royal Free Hospital*, founded in 1828. Here also are the offices of 'The Times' (established

1785). A more pleasant route S diverges to the right opposite St. Pancras into Judd St whence Hunter St continues down to BRUNSWICK SQUARE, now overpowered by the harsh Brunswick Centre of flats and shops. At No. 40 are the headquarters of the **Thomas Coram Foundation for Children** (formerly the *Foundling Hospital*), founded in 1739 by Captain Thomas Coram (d 1751), which still cares for unfortunate children in Berkhamstead. The Foundling Hospital occupied the site of Coram's Fields (see below) from 1724-1926.

Thomas Coram Foundation, 40 Brunswick Square, London WC2. Tel. 01-278 2424. Open Monday to Friday 10.00-16.00, admission charge. (Sometimes closed at short notice.)

The present house contains many relics of the old building, including part of the oak staircase and the beautiful Court Room, re-erected here with the original woodwork, ceiling, and plaster decoration; also interesting paintings by Hogarth (*March to Finchley; Portrait of Coram), Kneller (Portrait of Handel), Gainsborough, etc.; sculptures by Rysbrack and Roubiliac; and a cartoon by Raphael. Other mementoes include a MS. score of 'Messiah' and other Handelian relics, and a number of 'tokens' formerly left with abandoned infants. Handel and Hogarth both took a great interest in the hospital and its children, and readers of 'Little Dorrit' will remember that Tattycoram was a 'Foundling'.

To the SE extend CORAM'S FIELDS, a playground with Georgian colonnades, owned by the Foundation and open to children under 18 years (9-dusk); to the N the delightful *St. George's Gardens* occupy a disused cemetery. Across the Fields at the corner of Guilford St and Doughty St stands *London House*, a hostel and centre of collegiate life for men students from overseas, by Sir Herbert Baker. In the undulating *Doughty Street*, with the vista at each end closed by trees, Sydney Smith lived at No. 14 in 1803-06. **Dickens House** (No. 48), the home of Charles Dickens in 1837-39, the period of 'Oliver Twist' and 'Nicholas Nickleby', is now a museum of great interest.

Dickens House Museum, 48 Doughty Street, London WC2. Open Monday to Saturday 10.00-17.00. Admission charge. Access: Underground, Chancery Lane; Bus, 38, 25.

Besides the most comprehensive Dickens library in the world, it contains numerous portraits, illustrations, autograph letters, and personal relics.
   The Suzannet Gift (1971) includes parts of the MSS. of 'Pickwick Papers' and 'Nicholas Nickleby', Dickens' correspondence, illustrations for the novels, etc. In the basement is a reproduction of the 'Dingley Dell' kitchen. On the first floor is Dickens' Study and recently the Drawing Room has been arranged as it would have appeared in Dickens' time. The House combines well its role of a museum while recreating the atmosphere of the home of the writer.

Lamb's Conduit Street leads S from Coram's Fields and crosses *Great Ormond Street*, which retains several attractive houses of the Queen Anne period. At its W end are the *Hospital for Sick Children* founded in 1851, and the *Royal London Homoeopathic Hospital*. No. 23 was the home of John Howard (1726-90), the philanthropist.

The Home Office Department for Alien's Registration is in Lamb's Conduit Street; in the Victorian Lamb Pub, at No. 94, Hogarth prints decorate the walls and the original snobscreens remain.
   In the retired QUEEN SQUARE, with a statue that may represent Queen Charlotte, Queen Anne, or Mary II, William Morris had his residence and workshops in 1865-81 at No. 26 (rebuilt, now the *National Hospital for Nervous Diseases*, founded in 1860). Near by is the *Italian Hospital* (1884), and the

church of *St. George the Martyr*, founded in 1706, which once provided annual Christmas dinners for 100 apprentice sweeps.

Beyond Theobald's Road (where at No. 22 Benjamin Disraeli was born in 1804) Lamb's Conduit Passage leads to RED LION SQUARE, named after the Red Lion Inn, now the Old Red Lion at 72 High Holborn, where the bodies of Cromwell, Ireton and Bradshaw were laid out in 1661 after being disinterred from Westminster Abbey; they were taken the next day to Tyburn where the bodies were desecrated and heads placed on poles at Westminster Hall. The Square was laid out in 1684 and the W side is now occupied by the former Holborn College, now part of Central London Polytechnic.

On the S side is No. 17, in which D.G. Rossetti lodged in 1851 and in which Morris and Burne-Jones lived together in 1856-59. John Harrison (1693-1776), inventor of the chronometer, and Jonas Hanway (1712-86), who has the reputation of being the first habitual user of an umbrella in London, also lived in the square. At the NE corner is *Conway Hall* (1929) the seat of the South Place Ethical Society, a pioneer of religious-humanist thought (chamber concerts on Sundays in October to April). A bronze statue of veteran international peace campaigner Lord Brockway was erected in the square in 1985.

In SOUTHAMPTON ROW, to the W, the *Central School of Art and Design* uses the theatre named in honour of Jeannetta Cohrane who taught at the school from 1914 to 1957. Many productions for children are staged here in the Jeannetta Cochrane Theatre. On the corner of Catton St, to the S, the Baptist Church House has a statue of Bunyan.

The streets leading S from the square run into **High Holborn** (comp. Rte 20).

B. The British Museum and British Library

The ****BRITISH MUSEUM** (Pl. 6; 5), unrivalled in the world for the richness and variety of its contents, is entered from Great Russell St in Bloomsbury, a few yards N of New Oxford Street, or from Montague Place, on the N. In the pediment of the colonnaded main facade (S) are allegorical sculptures by Westmacott.

The British Museum was founded in 1753, its nucleus being the Cottonian and Harleian MSS. and Sir Hans Sloane's collections. These, with subsequent additions, including the Egyptian Antiquities, the Elgin Marbles, and the King's Library (i.e. George III's), were contained until 1852 in *Montagu House*, built by Robert Hooke in 1686 on the site of the existing edifice and opened as the first public secular national museum in the world in 1759. In 1823 the main building was begun by Robert and Sydney Smirke, and in 1852 Montagu House was demolished and the present S front completed; the monumental neo-classical screen was built in the 1840s. The Reading Room (by Sydney Smirke) and Library were opened in 1857, the SE wing in 1884, and the King Edward VII Building in 1914.

In 1973, the British Library formed from the library departments of the British Museum and various other national libraries became a separate institution. Pressure on space has increased and a new building near St. Pancras Station is now under construction. The removal of the British Library will release space for the British Museum to expand which may mean further changes to its layout which has already changed considerably in the last few years. In this description, the contents of the British Museum and British Library are therefore treated separately, although for the time being they may be viewed together, and only the highlights of each collection have been mentioned. Several visits would be necessary to do justice to the enormous range and variety of items on display.

British Museum, Great Russell Street, London WC2. Tel. 01-636 1555. Open Monday to Saturday 10.00-17.00, Sun 14.30-18.00. Admission free, except for special exhibitions. Access: Underground, Holborn, Tottenham Court Road. Lectures, Mon to Sat 13.15, Gallery talks, Mon to Sat 11.30. Bookshop, guide books, new self-service restaurant.

The *collection of Greek and Roman Antiquities* is arranged in the West Wing in chronological order from the Early Bronze Age to the Roman Imperial Period, from Room 1 to Room 15. In Room 8 is the Duveen Gallery, containing the famous *Elgin Marbles*, named after Thomas Bruce, 7th earl of Elgin, Ambassador to the Porte, who in 1801-03 collected numerous sculptures which he saw being daily destroyed at Athens, and in 1816 sold them to the British Government for £35,000, i.e. half what they had cost him to remove. The collection includes other sculptures from the Erechtheion and elsewhere, and casts from marbles which were left in situ. The most important of the Elgin Marbles are the sculptures of the Parthenon or temple of Athena Parthenos (the Virgin), the patron goddess of Athens, which stood on the Acropolis, and was dedicated in 438 BC.

The sculptures were carved between 447 and 432 BC, when Pericles was leader of Athens. Pheidias, the sculptor, supervised his great building schemes, Ictinus was the principal architect of the Parthenon, and Callicrates was the second architect or perhaps the contractor. The gold and ivory (chryselephantine) statue of Athena, 40ft high, which stood in the temple, was made by Pheidias, and is believed to have been finished in 439 BC and dedicated at the Panathenaic Festival the following year. The Parthenon remained a temple of Athena for the next nine centuries, after which it became a Christian church. The E Pediment was ruined by the builders of the Byzantine apse. At the fall of Athens to the Turks it was converted into a mosque. In 1674 a draughtsman, probably Jacques Carrey of Troyes, made drawings of the architectural and sculptural remains of the Parthenon. These form an invaluable record, as in 1687, during the siege of Athens by the Venetians, the centre of the temple (then used as a powder magazine by the Turks) was destroyed through an explosion caused by a shell from the besiegers' army. The W Pediment was shattered in falling during its attempted removal by Morosini.—The South Slip Room, left of the entrance to the Duveen Gallery, contains models, drawings and photographs illustrating the structure, sculptures, and history of the Parthenon. 'Sound guide' commentaries are available.

The sculptures of the Parthenon are generally held to be the greatest ever executed. In London are preserved 15 Metopes from the S side, major fragments of both Pediments, and 247ft (rather under half) of the Frieze. What survives of the remainder is in the Acropolis Museum in Athens, that part hitherto in situ on the Parthenon itself having been removed in 1976 to prevent further deterioration.

The Central Room displays the **FRIEZE alone at eye level. It represents in low relief the Panathenaic procession up to the Acropolis, the greatest Athenian festival, which culminated in the investiture of the image of Athena in a sacred violet 'peplos' or robe. This frieze ran above the porches and around the outside of the cella wall, and must have been curiously difficult to see. Its condition varies greatly.

The W FRIEZE (right of door) shows horsemen preparing to take part in the Panathenaic procession. As the procession, which started at the SW corner, approaches the NW corner it gathers speed, and the two leading horsemen (2, 3) on the last slab are already cantering. N FRIEZE (turning left and passing

BRITISH MUSEUM

Ground Floor

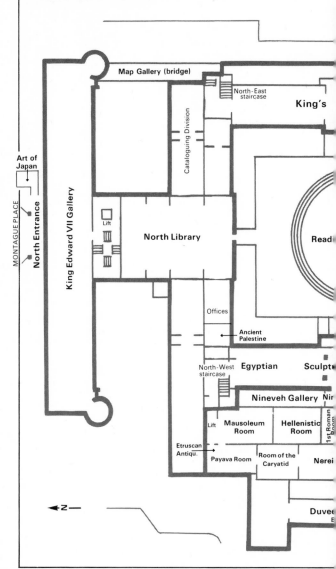

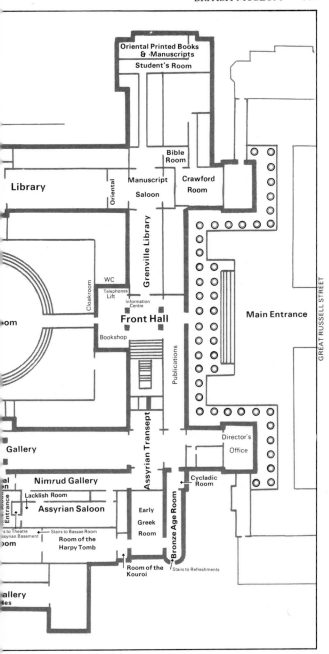

Oriental Printed Books
& Manuscripts

Student's Room

Bible
Room

Library

Oriental

Manuscript

Saloon

Crawford
Room

Grenville Library

Cloakroom

WC

Telephones
Lift

Information
Centre

Front Hall

Main Entrance

Bookshop

Publications

GREAT RUSSELL STREET

Gallery

Nimrud Gallery

Lacklish Room

Assyrian Saloon

Early
Greek
Room

Assyrian Transept

Bronze Age Room

Director's
Office

Cycladic
Room

Entrance

s to Theatre
syrian Basement

Stairs to Bassae Room

**Room of the
Harpy Tomb**

om

**Room of the
Kouroi**

Stairs to Refreshments

allery
les

the NW angle). The procession moves forward at a trot, the number of horses increases; the fine leading *Horsemen are seen on slab XXIV (NE angle). On the left of the slab is the inside of the rim of a shield and an arm holding it (belonging to chariot on opposite wall which continues the N frieze) which indicates that chariots have now joined the procession, followed by citizens and animals being led to sacrifice. E FRIEZE. Girls carrying vesels for use in the sacrifices, magistrates, and the ceremony of the sacred peplos in the presence of deities and attendants. The S FRIEZE is much more fragmentary, but the rendering of cattle and galloping horses on slabs XXXVIII and XXX (SW end of wall) is especially noteworthy (S frieze continued on SE end of opposite wall).

In the North Transept in the centre is the **EAST PEDIMENT GROUP. These sculptures are in the round and had a correspondingly projecting architectural frame. The subject represented was the birth of Athena, fabled to have sprung fully armed from the brain of Zeus.

The central group probably consisted of Zeus with Athena and Hephaistos on either side. At the left (S) end is Helios (A), the sun-god, driving his chariot out of the sea at daybreak; in front are two heads of horses from his team (B, C). Facing Helios is a male figure (D) of wonderful power and grace, seated on the skin of a lion or panther; he is thought to be Heracles, or to personify Mount Olympus, or to be Dionysos, the wine god. The head (the only remaining one in the group), though damaged, heightens the noble impression of the figure and justifies the fame of the Pheidian School. Two draped and seated female goddesses (E, F) are Demeter and her daughter Persephone. The young girl running towards them (G) is Iris or Hebe, the cup-bearer, who starts back in alarm at the miraculous event which has just taken place. The identity of the group of three figures (K, L, M) is doubtful; the Clouds, Thalassa (the sea) in the lap of Gaia (the earth), Aphrodite in the lap of her mother Dione, or the three Hesperid nymphs, are suggestions that have been made. The sculpture

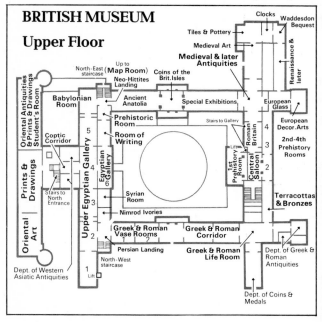

in the extreme right angle is one of the horses of Selene, goddess of the moon, descending into the waves.

On the walls are Metopes XXVI-XXXII (see below).

In the South Transept in the centre are fragments from the ****WEST PEDIMENT GROUP**, which represents the contest between Athena and Poseidon for the land of Attica.

According to the myth, Poseidon with his trident made a salt spring gush from the rock of the Acropolis; Athena caused the first olive to grow and was awarded the victory. The olive tree probably filled the centre of the pediment. Athena and Poseidon have been conducted to it by Hermes and Iris, the two torsos (H, N) to the left and right of the centre. Iris is identified by holes for the wings and by the short robe. The figure (A) in the N (left) angle of the pediment is a river god of Athens, either Kephisos or Ilissos; it has suffered less damage and is one of the most beautiful of the sculptures. The torso to the right of Iris (O) is the driver of Poseidon's chariot (as may be seen from Carrey's drawing), perhaps Amphitrite, his wife. The figure (Q) to the right may have been a sea nymph.

On the walls are ***METOPES II-IX**, square panels carved in high relief, which alternated with the triglyphs above the architrave all round the building. The fifteen originals (eight here and seven in the N Transept) together with forty-one still remaining (much decayed) in Athens and one in Paris, are all that remain of the original series of ninety-two. The metopes represent the battle of the Lapiths (a Thessalian people) and the Centaurs, one of whom tried to carry off the bride of Peirithoös, the Lapith king.

The Etruscan antiquities in Room 11 include remarkable painted wall panels, and a polychrome terracotta sarcophagus with a reclining figure.

In Room 14 is the famous *Portland Vase* (late 1C BC, or early 1C AD) of blown glass in two layers, white on cobalt blue, the white layer cut away like a cameo to leave a frieze of figures; it takes its name from the Dukes of Portland who owned it, and was deliberately shattered by a madman in 1845 but pieced together. The decoration probably shows the wooing of the sea nymph Thetis by the mortal Peleus.

The *Western Asiatic Collections* start in Room 26 nearest the main entrance but room numbering and chronology do not coincide. In the Nimrud Gallery (Room 19) are imposing reliefs from the palace at Calah (Nimrud) including a black obelisk of Shlmaneser III. Reliefs from the palace of Nineveh are in the Assyrian Saloon (Room 17A).

The *Egyptian Collections* start in Room 25 in a new display. The entrance is flanked by two black granite seated figures of Amenophis III from his mortuary temple at Thebes (c 1400 BC). On the left the famous **Rosetta Stone**, with a small accompanying display. It is named after a town near the mouth of the Nile where it was found by the French in 1797. It bears a priestly decree, inscribed twice in Egyptian (first in hieroglyphs, the writing of the priests, and secondly in ordinary, secular characters) and also in Greek translation. This triple inscription gave scholars the key to the Ancient Egyptian language and script and in turn to the whole of Ancient Egyptian culture.

Note also the so-called 'false doors' from tombs through which the spirit of the deceased passed from the burial chamber to the chapel where food offerings were presented, including the huge limestone false door from the tomb of Ptahshepses, (Middle Kingdom, XI-XII

Dynasties); a fine black granite statue of Sesostris III (c 1850 BC) (one of three), and considered to be one of the best pieces of sculpture in the gallery; the wooden figure of Ramesses I (c 1218 BC), one of the few to survive; and in the tomb-like slip-rooms on the East side smaller funerary objects are well lit and displayed.

After the Egyptian Galleries on the ground floor, it may be convenient to take in the British Library collection, as currently displayed; see below under British Library.

There are further Egyptian Galleries on the 1st floor; first the *Chinese Antiquities* (Room 34; these may also be approached directly via the North entrance to the Museum in Montague Place) are seen. These are arranged chronologically beginning with the Neolithic period. The collection of the ceramics of the Sung (960-1279), Yuan (1280-1368) and Ming (1368-1644) dynasties is unrivalled in the West and includes many world-famous pieces. The western half of the Gallery is devoted to Indian antiquities, mainly comprising sculpture and bronzes from temples in India and South East Asia.

The Egyptian Rooms on the First Floor in the North Wing of the main building contain the collection of mummies and other objects found in tombs (Rooms 60-66).

The British Museum's collection of *prints and drawings* are displayed in thematic changing exhibitions in Room 67.

Prehistoric and Romano British Antiquities begin in Room 35 with a large 4C mosaic pavement from Hinton St. Mary, Dorset. In Room 39 is the Battersea Shield, the finest example of early Celtic art in Britain (mid-1C BC). In Room 40 is the MILDENHALL TREASURE, a sumptuously decorated set of 4C Roman silver tableware, including a great dish weighing 24lbs with embossed decorations of the highest quality. At the centre is a mask of Neptune, surrounded by sea-creatures and a frieze of Bacchic revels. The set, which was discovered in 1942, is one of the finest to be found anywhere in the Roman empire and must have belonged to a high official.

In Room 41 is the SUTTON HOO TREASURE, a 7C royal ship-burial, probably that of King Redwald of the East Angles, excavated in Suffolk in 1939, and the richest and most varied burial of its kind yet found in Europe. It includes: gold and garnet strap-fittings, a sword with jewelled mounts, a magnificent helmet (restored 1971) and shield, ceremonial whetstone surmounted by a finely cast bronze stag, drinking horns and bottles with silver-gilt fittings, hanging bowls, massive bronze cauldron and iron cauldron chains. The contents of the Taplow Barrow.

Room 45 displays the ˙˙WADDESDON BEQUEST, amassed by Baron Ferdinand de Rothschild in the tradition of the Renaissance merchant-princes. Exquisite and often exotic objets d'art of the 14-17C include silver plate, cups and caskets, Limoges enamels, a Mantuan damascened shield of 1554, and a magnificent collection of gold and jewelled pendants, outstandingly the Lyte Jewel.

In the long Renaissance gallery, No. 46, note the 'magic mirror' used by Dr John Dee, the Elizabethan alchemist, the English pottery including Lambeth Delft and Fulham stoneware and the Battersea enamels. A new sculpture gallery opened in the Basement in 1985. Approach from Rooms 12, 16, and 18 on the ground floor. On view are early and later Greek sculptures previously not shown.

For the time being still housed within the Museum, the * ***British Library** is due to move out in 1991.

British Library, Great Russell Street, London WC2. Tel. 636 1555. Open as British Museum. Admission to the Reading Room and the Students' Rooms is by ticket only (apply in writing to the Director at least two days in advance; applications must be accompanied by a letter of recommendation from a person of recognised position). Tours of the Reading Room daily (weekdays) on the hour between 11.00 and 16.00. Admission free.

The British Library contains over 8,000,000 volumes. Though now surpassed in size by the Library of Congress at Washington and the Lenin State Library, it still ranks as one of the most important libraries in the world, and it is especially rich in books in foreign languages. These and older books are provided from a Treasury grant and by donation, while, by law, a copy of every book, newspaper, and so forth published in the United Kingdom must be deposited at the British Museum, where it must be accepted and preserved. The university libraries at Oxford and Cambridge and Dublin, and the national libraries of Scotland and Wales have the right to demand copies of books, etc., without the statutory duty to preserve them.

On the N side of the Main Entrance Hall is the circular **Reading Room**, tickets of admission to which are granted for purposes of research and reference which cannot be carried out elsewhere. The dome (140ft in diameter and 106ft high), is, next to that of the Pantheon in Rome (142ft), the widest in the world. The superintendent's raised desk occupies the centre, and from it a service passage leads into the library; it is ringed round with desks holding the General Catalogue, which, including the Maps and Music Catalogues, is in well over 2000 volumes. The groundfloor shelves are occupied by a large library of reference books, which may be consulted directly by readers; other books are requisitioned by filling up forms.

Newspapers are held in the collection at Colindale (see p 380).

While still at the British Museum permanent and changing exhibitions are held in the Grenville Library, Manuscript Saloon and King's Library.

The *Grenville Library*, Room 1, houses English and Continental illuminated manuscripts. In the *Manuscript Saloon* is the Library's collection of historical and literary manuscripts. Amongst the autographs are those Raleigh, Spenser, Ben Jonson, Bacon, Hobbes, Milton, Wren, Locke, Defoe, Pepys, Dr Johnson, Pope, Garrick, Sarah Siddons, Keats, Wordsworth, Byron and Shelley, Elizabeth and Robert Browning, Charlotte and Emily Brontë and Jane Austen. Note the unique manuscript of Beowulf (c 1000), and the earliest known history of England in English, the Anglo-Saxon Chronicle. Many famous continental painters and writers also have their autographs here including Luther, Goethe, Voltaire, Michelangelo, Rembrandt, and Titian. Scientific names include Galileo, Newton and Leonardo da Vinci. The most famous display is perhaps the MAGNA CARTA with two original copies, as well as the Articles of Barons sealed at Runnymede in 1215. There are royal signatures, too, including Elizabeth I, and those of prime ministers.

In the *King's Library* (Room 32) are early books including the Gutenberg Bible, and famous books including 'Das Kapital', written by Karl Marx mainly in the Reading Room here. Note also Roubiliac's life-size statue of Shakespeare (1758) which stood at Garrick's Temple at Hampton. The Tapling Collection of postage stamps of the world and other stamp collections are also on display.

17 The Strand and Covent Garden

Access: For the Strand: Underground, Charing Cross, Embankment. For Covent Garden: Underground, Covent Garden, Leicester Square.

The STRAND originally bordered on the Thames and provided the vital road-link between the City and Whitehall Palace at Westminster. The embankment of the Thames created a narrow roadway with grand houses on either side, later followed by commerce, entertainment and hotels. The music-hall song 'Let's Go Down the Strand' recalls the hustle and bustle which unfortunately has left the Strand of today, mostly lined with uninteresting office developments but with some good stamp shops, including Stanley Gibbons, enlivened somewhat by three theatres and two large hotels.

It is still occasionally used as a processional route to the City and St. Paul's Cathedral, most recently for the wedding of the Prince of Wales to Lady Diana Spencer, in 1982.

Charing Cross Station (Pl. 15; 3), near its W end, was erected in 1863 on the site of *Hungerford Market*. The town house of Walter (1st Baron) Hungerford was erected here in 1422-23, and a descendant opened the market (later destroyed by fire) in 1682. The Gothic Cross (by E.M. Barry; 1865) in the station forecourt is a memorial, but not a copy, of Eleanor's Cross. On the N side of the Strand, the facade and eccentric turrets of the Coutts's Bank building by Smirke have been 'saved'. The Nash facades have been restored; facing the Strand a large glass screen covers three floors of the building. The old Charing Cross Hospital site is being redeveloped; the hospital moved to Fulham in 1973. *Zimbabwe House*, on the corner of Agar St, was designed by Charles Holden (1908); the mutilated statues on the second floor are by Epstein.

Craven St skirts the W side of Charing Cross Station to reach the Embankment. The Charing Cross Hotel at the far side was designed by E.M. Barry (1864)—one of the first buildings to be faced with artificial stone. Benjamin Franklin lived at No. 36 (1757-62); the German poet Heinrich Heine in No. 32; Henry Flitcroft, the architect, in No. 33. Craven Passage leads under the arches of the railway station (made famous by Flanagan and Allen's song); Monday to Saturday during the day this is a specialist market selling coins, medals, books, stamps, militaria, and model cars and trains. During the night it is used as shelter by London's down-and-outs.

The Passage leads through to Villiers Street and the *Players Theatre Club*, which opened here 'underneath the arches' in 1946; the premises had been used by the Victorian music hall. After a success with 'The Boy Friend' in the '50s the Players Theatre reverted to Victorian Music Hall with performances Tuesday to Sunday night; temporary membership available (01-839 1134). On the site between Villiers St and the parallel Buckingham St, George Villiers, Duke of Buckingham, partly rebuilt (in 1624) *York House*, the birthplace in

1561 of Francis Bacon. The old *Water-Gate* survives at the end of Buckingham St; built by Nicholas Stone in 1626, it shows where the Thames reached at that time. Victoria Embankment Gardens descend to the river.

Sir Richard Steele lived in Villiers St from 1721 to 1724, and Rudyard Kipling's first London home (in 1889-91) was at No. 19 (now No. 43). Pepys occupied No. 12 Buckingham St in 1679-88; while No. 14 bears a tablet recording its tenancy, in its various transitions, by Pepys (in 1688-1700), Robert Harley, Earl of Oxford, William Etty, the painter, and Clarkson Stanfield, the marine painter. Burdett House opposite (rebuilt as the headquarters of the Royal National Pension Fund for Nurses) was occupied by Peter the Great in 1697-98. The names of David Hume, Rousseau, and Henry Fielding were also associated with this house.

John Adam Street, parallel to the Strand on the S, runs through the region known as *The Adelphi*, named after the four Scottish brothers Adam who planned a residential area on the land sloping down to the river in 1768. The ambitious scheme involved the erection of streets, houses and terraces supported on an embankment of arches and subterranean vaults. The main brick terrace overlooking the Thames was directly inspired by the Palace of Diocletian at Split. A lottery was authorised by Parliament in 1773 to rescue the enterprise from financial disaster. A few fine Adam houses survive.

Among artists and writers who came to live here were David Garrick, Rowlandson, Tom Hood, Charles Dickens (whose youthful experiences in this quarter are described in 'David Copperfield'), Bernard Shaw, Sir James Barrie, H.G. Wells, and John Galsworthy. Robert Adam himself lived at No. 10 Adam St (built in 1772; signboard).

The *Royal Society of Arts* occupies a fine Adam building at 8 John Adam Street. The Society was established in 1754 to foster art, manufacture, and trade. The hall (adm. on application; closed Sun) contains mural paintings by James Barry (1777-83), illustrating (not very perspicuously) the benefits of civilisation.

The Gilbert and Sullivan pub in John Adam St was damaged in a fire and its collection of memorabilia has been moved to the Old Bell in Wellington Street, now called the Gilbert and Sullivan. W.S. Gilbert was born in Southampton St on the N side of the Strand; Richard d'Oyly Carte lived at No. 4 Adelphi Terrace while producing the Gilbert and Sullivan comic operas at the Savoy Theatre (1881 et seq.; see below).

The *Savoy Theatre* in the Strand was built in 1881 by Richard d'Oyly Carte for Gilbert and Sullivan's operas, the first public building in London to be lit by electricity. It opened with 'Patience'. After 1893 it was used for comic operas; plays and comedies were staged. The *Savoy Hotel* adjoining the theatre opened in 1889, also financed by Richard d'Oyly Carte. This was one of the first hotels to have many private bathrooms, fitted electric lifts and electric lights. Escoffier was the first chef and his pots and pans remain at the hotel. One part of the hotel has been converted into apartments. The forecourt is the only street in London where traffic must keep to the right. Many famous people have stayed here including Henry Irving and Sarah Bernhardt.

Savoy Street leads S to the Thames Embankment past the garden of the **Chapel of the Savoy**, erected in the late-Perpendicular style in 1505, on part of the site of Savoy Palace. Entered from Savoy Hill, it is open on Tues to Fri, 11.30-15.30 (closed Aug/Sept), and for services on Sunday.

Savoy Palace, built in 1246, was given by Henry III to his wife's uncle, Peter, Earl of Savoy and Richmond (d 1268), and afterwards passed into the possession of John of Gaunt. King John of France, taken prisoner at the Battle of Poitiers (1356) died in the palace in 1364. Geoffrey Chaucer and John Wyclif here enjoyed the patronage of John of Gaunt. The palace was burned down by Wat Tyler in 1381, and the manor made over to the Crown in 1399 by Henry IV. It was rebuilt as a hospital and chapel by Henry VII in 1505. Here in 1661 took place the famous Savoy Conference for the revision of the Prayer Book.

The chapel was restored by Queen Victoria after a destructive fire in 1864. It is the Chapel of the Royal Victorian Order, and the stalls of the knights are marked by small copper plates emblazoned with the arms of the holder. A stained glass window commemorates Richard d'Oyly Carte (1844-1901; see above).

Opposite in Savoy Hill at what is now the Institute of Electrical Engineers, the BBC started the first daily radio programmes in 1922 as station 2LO. The BBC moved to the new Broadcasting House from here in 1932.

In the Strand is the traditional *Simpsons in the Strand* restaurant founded in 1848. The present building designed by T.E. Collcutt opened in 1904 and still prides itself on its roast beef; the lunchtime clientele is still male-doninated (01-836 9112). On the N side of the Strand is the *Adelphi Theatre*, opened in 1806 and rebuilt twice, famous for melodramas during the 19C (one actor was shot outside the theatre in a real drama) and musicals and comedies more recently. The *Vaudeville Theatre* dates from 1870. The undistinguished Strand Palace Hotel (1930) has a useful 'all-night' coffee shop.

The *Lyceum* in Wellington Street has a chequered history; founded as a concert and exhibition hall in 1771, it staged Madame Tussaud's first wax-work exhibition in London in 1802; it was destroyed by fire in 1830 and rebuilt a little further W in 1834 as an opera house. From 1874 it became synonymous with the brilliant actor Henry Irving who staged many Shakespeare productions here with Ellen Terry as his leading lady; the last was Coriolanus in 1901. The former LCC acquired the building in 1939 for a future road development, but since 1945 it has functioned as a dance hall. Recent plans to convert it back into a theatre have been dropped although various public campaigns continue. The Lyceum closed for refurbishment in 1985, due to reopen in 1986.

The busy *Lancaster Place*, on the right, forms the approach to Waterloo Bridge, passing the W facade of Somerset House, Beyond, Aldwych, taking the eastbound traffic, forms a wide crescent to the N (see below). Continue along the Strand, to the N facade of **Somerset House** (Pl. 15; 3), a Palladian building erected by Sir William Chambers in 1776-86. The E wing (King's College) was added by Sir R. Smirke in 1829-34, the W wing by Sir James Pennethorne in 1852-56. The chief *Facade, nearly 600ft long, fronting the Thames, stands on a terrace 50ft above the Victoria Embankment. Its basement arcade originally rose straight from the river, and the great central arch was the water-gate.

The present building occupies the site of a palace begun by the Lord Protector Somerset c 1547, but left unfinished at his execution in 1552. The palace then passed into the hands of the Crown. Elizabeth I lived here for a time during the reign of her sister Mary. Oliver Cromwell lay in state here in 1658.

Somerset House is mainly occupied by Government offices. In the W wing is the *Board of Inland Revenue*, which deals with stamps, taxes, death duties, and land values duties. The *Principal Probate Registry* (in the S wing), which formerly housed also Prerogative Court of Canterbury (PCC) wills from 1382 (transferred to the Public Record Office), now holds only wills and testaments registered in England since 1858. A copy of any will can be seen for a fee (Mon to Fri, 10.00-16.30). Other wills (pre-1858) are preserved elsewhere. The *State Rooms* in the N wing (good staircase and ceilings) are due to become the home of the Courtauld Institute Collections (see p 178).

To the E of Somerset House is the new facade (1972) of **King's College**, one of the incorporated colleges of the University of London. Following a public meeting in 1828 with the Prime Minister (the Duke of Wellington) in the Chair and the Abps of Canterbury and York in attendance, it was opened in 1831.

The names of the next series of streets leading from the Strand to the Embankment commemorate the sites of the town houses of Thomas Howard, Earl of Arundel, Surrey, and Norfolk (c 1585-1646), and of Robert Devereux, Earl of Essex (1567-1601). Off Surrey St is an alleged *Roman Bath*, fed by a rivulet (Mon to Fri 09.00-16.30 by appointment); the bricks used are small and non-porous, of an unusual kind, the Roman origin of which is by no means certain. Adjacent are the remains of an Elizabethan bath, said to date from 1588. On neighbouring sites are a hotel, and an extension to King's. During building in 1973 part of a Roman frieze from Pergamon was found, having been shipped to England in 1627 by the Earl of Arundel, and abandoned in his garden.

In the middle of the Strand stands the finely proportioned church of **St Mary-le-Strand**, with an Ionic portico and graceful steeple, built by James Gibbs in 1714, and consecrated in 1724. The barrel vault has fine plasterwork, and the pulpit is usually attributed to Gibbons. The fabric of the church is being restored. The space in front was the site of the famous Maypole where the first hackney carriage rank stood in 1634; it was removed in 1718 and bought by Sir Isaac Newton as the stand for a telescope at Wanstead House. Thomas Becket was once lay-rector of the parish and Charles Dickens's parents were married in the church in 1809.

Farther E, the church of **St. Clement Danes** forms another island in the Strand. Designed by Wren and built in 1680-82 on the site of a much earlier building, it is traditionally believed to be the burial-place of Harold Harefoot and other Danes. The tower, added by James Gibbs in 1719-20, is 115ft high and contains a famous and tuneful peal of bells ('Oranges and lemons, say the bells of St. Clement's'). In 1941 the church was gutted by fire and it has been beautifully restored as the headquarters church of the Royal Air Force.

The interior has bright white and gilt stucco decoration, and a Father Smith organ (restored). The floor is inlaid with unit and squadron badges, and Books of Remembrance line the aisles. The altarpiece is by Ruskin Spear. A fine staircase descends to the crypt which is decorated with ancient tomb slabs. William Webb Ellis, the inventor of Rugby Football in 1823, was rector here (memorial tablet). Dr Johnson was a worshipper in this church and is commemorated by a statue by Percy Fitzgerald outside the choir. A *Gladstone Memorial*, by Thomas Thornycroft (1905), stands opposite the W front of the church.

The Strand is continued by Fleet Street towards the City (see Rte 19). Turn NW into **Aldwych**, which takes its name from an old colony (ald-wych) of Danes in this vicinity before the Conquest. On the S corner is *Australia House* built in 1911-18 as the office of the Commonwealth of Australia. The groups flanking the entrance represent Exploration, and Shearing and Reaping; high above are the Horses of the Sun. Across Melbourne Place, *Bush House*, a massive pile of offices, begun in 1920 by Harvey Corbett, occupies the greater part of the area between Aldwych and the Strand. Here are located the External Services of the BBC There is a shop selling English language and BBC publications. The entrance facing Kingsway is a huge archway surmounted by a colossal group, by Malvina Hoffmann (1925; damaged by a flying bomb), symbolising the friendship of Britain and the United States. Across Aldwych, in Houghton Street, are the premises of the *London School of Economics and Political Science*. Sidney and Beatrice Webb participated in its establishment in 1895, and Harold Laski when Professor of Political Science here in 1926, instilled some of the left-wing views for which it is celebrated. In the 1968 disturbances there was a lengthy sit-in which ended in violence. *Kingsway* (Pl. 15; 1) runs N to High Holborn (comp. Rte 20). On the corner stands *St. Catherine's House*, the Office of Population Censuses and Surveys (General Register Office), the records of Births, Marriages, and Deaths in England since 1837 have been moved here from Somerset House.

Beyond Bush House, *India House* (1930) designed by Sir Herbert Baker, is the office of the High Commissioner for India. The fine interior is decorated in the Indian style and largely by Indian artists. On the last building on the island (now a bank) tablets record the site of the Gaiety Theatre, home of musical comedy in London in 1903-39, and the Broadcasting Station of Marconi's Wireless Telegraph Company from 11 May to 15 Nov 1922, when it became the first station of the BBC.

From the Aldwych turn NW into *Drury Lane* for an exploration of **Covent Garden**. This was the main S to N thoroughfare before the addition of Kingsway to the E in 1905. On the corner is the *Aldwych Theatre*, built as a pair with the Strand Theatre to the S in 1905 by W.G.R. Sprague. At the Aldwych musical comedies were followed by the famous Ben Travers farces from 1925 to 1933. From 1960 to 1982 the theatre was the London home of the Royal Shakespeare Company which has now moved to a new theatre at the Barbican Centre.

The *Theatre Royal*, Drury Lane, backs on to Drury Lane but has its entrance in the parallel Catherine Street to the W. The present theatre was designed by Benjamin Wyatt in 1811-12. The impressive portico was added ten years later and the collonade in 1830. The pillars came from Nash's quadrant in Regent Street. The auditorium which seats 2245 was remodelled in 1921 and a ghost is said to haunt the Upper Circle. The theatre has an illustrious 300-year history and is now mostly used for musicals.

The first theatre on the site was built in 1663 under a royal patent for Thomas Killigrew's 'King's company'—the first to be granted after the Restoration. Charles II was frequently in the audience and here he met and fell in love with the actress Nell Gwynne. The theatre burnt down in 1671 and was rebuilt in 1674 to a design by Wren. The theatre's stormy history includes riots and the attempted assassinations of two kings, George II and George III. During David Garrick's management from 1747 Shakespeare revivals became popular. When Sheridan took over in 1776 it became a theatre of comedies including his own 'School for Scandal'. In John Kemble's period the theatre was declared unsafe and had to be closed. It reopened in 1794 but was destroyed by fire only 15 years later. Sheridan watched the flames sipping a glass of port in a coffee-house across the road and said 'Surely a man may take a glass of wine by his own fireside'. The present theatre contains statues, busts and paintings of its famous actors, owners and managers. On the wall near the entrance there is a stone plaque commemorating August Harris, manager from 1879 to 1897.

Continue northwards along Drury Lane which is still residential in character, having once been the address of aristocratic families including Sir Thomas Drury who gave it his name. In the 18C the area deteriorated and by the end of the 19C it was one of the worst slums of London.

The Peabody Estate on the E side was one of the many estates built for the poor by the wealthy American-born philanthropist George Peabody during the 1860s and '70s in an attempt to eradicate some of the worst slum housing. This one stands on the site of original Cockpit Theatre. Further N on the E corner of Drury Lane and Great Queen Street is the huge *Freemason's Hall* (entrance in Great Queen St), the third on the site and completed in 1933 by H.V. Ashley and F. Winton Smith. It is the Headquarters of the United Grand Lodge of England. Adjoining it are the *Connaught Rooms*, which incorporate some parts of the Second Freemason's Hall including the fine banqueting hall designed by F. Cockerell, which is available for functions.

Drury Lane continues N past the New London Theatre and the Talk of London cabaret restaurant, in a new building which opened in 1973 on the site of the Winter Garden Theatre, a place of entertainment since Elizabethan times. The theatre (seating 1102) was used initially for television until the long running musical 'Cats' opened in 1980.

Turn back S along Drury Lane and then W along *Long Acre*, past the Greater London Council's new housing estate to the N, part of the renovation of the Covent Garden area. Long Acre was originally a path through the monks of Westminster's huge gardens. In the mid-17C as the area became built up coach and cabinet makers including Chippendale settled here. Today glass-blowers can be seen at work at the Glasshouse, 65 Long Acre (open 10.00-18.00 Monday to Friday, Saturday 10.00-16.00—glass-blowing twice a day at 11.00 and 15.00 or by arrangement).

Turn S into *Bow Street*, which takes its name from the shape of a bent bow. Immediately to the right is the impressive portico of the **Royal Opera House**, Covent Garden, home of the Royal Ballet and Opera companies. The present theatre, the third on the site, was designed by E.M. Barry and completed in 1860. It is dominated by the Corinthian style portico and the sculptural embellishments by Flaxman and Rossi salvaged from the previous building. The magnificent auditorium which seats 2158 is decorated in white and gold with a plaster relief by Raffaelle Monti over the proscenium. The elegant foyer and Crush Bar are equally celebrated. The cramped back-stage facilities are being improved in a ten-year programme; the first phase completed in 1982 took the building along Floral Street to James Street (to the W) in a matching design. A further extension is planned towards the Covent Garden Piazza when sufficient money has been raised.

The future of the adjoining *Floral Hall*, opened in 1860, is uncertain. It formed an extension to the Opera House and was used for balls and even iceskating. It now provides storage space and workshops. The Royal Opera House advance box office is in Floral Street opposite the Stage Entrance.

The first Royal Opera House was designed by Edward Shepherd and opened in 1732. The actor and manager John Rich had a triumphant opening with a revival of Congreve's 'The Way of the World'. There was lively rivalry with the Theatre Royal Drury Lane over the next 150 years until the Opera House became the place for Italian opera. In the 18C a disastrous fire destroyed the theatre and Handel's organ. The second theatre on the same site was modelled by Robert Smirke on the Temple of Minerva. When it opened in 1809 prices were raised, sparking off the so-called 'Old Price riots' which continued for two months until prices were reduced. Another fire followed in 1855 leaving only Flaxman's frieze undamaged.

Opposite the Royal Opera House is the Bow Street Magistrate's Court and Police Station, completed in 1880 but representing a link with law and order that dates back to the first courthouse on the site in 1740. Here the famous Fielding brothers (Henry and John) established the Bow Street Runners from 1749 to catch thieves and villains; forerunners of the Metropolitan Police which followed more than 100 years later. In the Police Station is the *Metropolitan Police Historical Museum* which recreates the history of London's police force with photographs, uniforms and set-piece reconstructions. (Open by appointment only; write to Metropolitan Police Museum, 28 Bow Street, London WC2.)

A new jazz centre was due to open at Floral Street with rehearsal rooms and an auditorium but has been indefinetely delayed due to financial problems.

Turn W into Russell Street; at No. 8 was the bookshop of Tom Davies where Boswell first met Johnson in 1763. Boswell's coffeeshop, a recent addition, marks the place today. Ahead lies the **Piazza** and **Covent Garden Central Market**.

Since the restored buildings of the Covent Garden Market opened in 1981, the area has quickly established itself as one of the liveliest in London, at the hub of theatreland, with winebars, restaurants and a variety of shops.

The area derives its name from the convent garden of the monks of Westminster Abbey. After the dissolution of the monasteries the first Earl of Bedford, John Russell, received the land from Henry VIII in 1536 and it stayed in the Bedford family until 1918. Bedford House faced the Strand to the S with gardens continuing to produce fruit and vegetables just as the monks had done. These were sold where the present piazza is today. In the 17C the fourth earl decided to take advantage of the growing demand for property. Inigo Jones, architect of the development, was influenced by Italian town-planning (notably at Leghorn), and the Piazza became one of the first and finest of its kind in London, focussed on the portico of St. Paul's Church on the W side. The N and E sides of the Piazza were made up of porticoed houses with an arcaded walk underneath—the present buildings to the N are a pale imitation. The S side was bounded by the wall and terraced walk of Bedford House gardens. The Piazza was gravelled and later a Doric column with a gilded sun-dial was added in the middle—this only remained for 100 years. Trading continued against the S wall and later as Bedford House was demolished and the gardens built over, market stalls began to appear in the centre of the Piazza creating a nuisance for the fashionable residents who began to leave the area. The 6th earl decided that the market needed a proper building and commissioned Charles Fowler to design the Central Market building.

The neo-classical *Central Market Building* transformed the open square when it was completed in 1830. The iron and glass roofs were added by Cubitts between 1875 and 1889. The Doric columns and Coade stone sculpture at the E end as well as the roofs have been magnificently restored by the Greater London Council after the

The restored Central Market at Covent Garden

vegetable market moved to Nine Elms in 1974. By then the market activities had grown to such proportions that they were causing intolerable congestion in the centre of London. The fashionable shops and restaurants now have original shop fronts and individual hanging shop signs.

The *Flower Market Building* was added in 1872 as activities at the market expanded and represents a Victorian classical design in brick and stone with some excellent glass and iron work towards the Piazza and Tavistock Street. It now houses the *London Transport Museum* (and from 1987 the Victoria and Albert Theatre Museum). A colourful mural on the transport theme adorns the outside of the building.

London Transport Museum, The Piazza, Covent Garden, London WC2. Tel. 01-379 6344. Open daily 10.00-18.00. Admission charge. Access: Underground, Covent Garden. Shop with London Transport posters, models and postcard, cafeteria.

The collection was formed in the 1920s and '30s by the London General Omnibus Company and constitutes a unique record of public transport from c 1830 to the present day. The collection moved here from Syon Park in 1980 and augmented its display with a number of additional features, including an informative display of photographs, documents and maps showing the impact on London of a growing transportation network.

The collection of London Transport posters includes the work of some of the leading British graphic artists of the 20C and special exhibitions take place regularly. Visitors may take the controls of an underground train, a bus, and a tram, and operate points and signals.

Amongst the most important exhibits are: a replica of the Shillibeer Horse Omnibus (1829-34), a Knifeboard Horse Bus (c 1850-1900), and a Garden Seat Horse Bus (c 1885-1914). The earliest motor bus on show is the Type B Bus (1910-27) and the earliest railway vehicle, a Metropolitan Railway Class A locomotive (1866).

The *Theatre Museum*. A theatre museum is due to open in the basement of the Flower Market Building in 1987. It will house the Victoria and Albert Museum's theatre collection. For further information contact the V & A.

The *Jubilee Hall* at the corner of the piazza was built at the beginning of this century to house the imported fruit market. In a compromise redevelopment scheme the original building will be retained as a sports and community hall with a market underneath; shops, offices and some parking will complete the development. In the meantime the all-week market continues, partly in the piazza with antiques on Mondays and crafts on Saturdays and Sundays; it is a general market on other days.

   St. Paul's Church on the W side of the Piazza, known as the actors' church, has its entrance in Bedford Street. The impressive Tuscan portico, well-known from 'My Fair Lady', is just a false front. During its construction the Bishop of London protested at the unorthodox location of the altar against the W wall and Inigo Jones had to move it. Although this is the highlight of Inigo Jones's Covent Garden very little money could be spent on it as heavy fees were extracted from the Bedfords by Charles I, so Jones was asked to keep costs down and promised to build 'the handsomest barn in England'. Most of the building was destroyed by fire in 1795 but reconstructed by Thomas Hardwicke to the original design. The walls are filled with memorials to the artistic—Grinling Gibbons is buried here and a carved wreath by him from St. Paul's Cathedral was added as a memorial in 1965. Others include Samuel Butler, Sir Peter Lely, William Wycherley; inside a silver casket holds the ashes of Ellen Terry. Marie Lloyd, Clement Dane, Ivor Novello and Vivien Leigh are all commemorated here.

   A plaque in the portico marks the site of the first recorded performance of a Punch and Judy show, witnessed here by Pepys in 1662; the pub opposite takes that name and there are regular Punch and Judy performances in the Piazza as well as an annual Punch and Judy Festival in the otherwise quiet churchyard. The tradition of street entertainment continues with live performances under the portico every day and music inside the Market—the only place in London where busking is legal. The market management is appointed by the GLC and they also run the Apple Market inside the Market Building where craftspeople sell their own goods on the original stalls from the Flower Market.

   During the 18 and 19C Covent Garden coffee houses attracted the writers and artists of the day. One well-known house was Bedford's Coffee House in the NE corner and others were Will's, Button's and Tom's. The tradition continued in Garrick Street (branching NW from King Street) where the *Garrick Club* has attracted actors and writers since 1831. Rose Street runs through to the Lamb and Flag pub which dates back to 1638 although the present building is 18C. Poet John Dryden was nearly assassinated here by opponents to his writings in 1679. Floral Street meets up with James Street past Covent Garden Underground station, which has some of the oldest lifts in London, and opposite is Neal Street. All along here are new shops and restaurants in former market premises. Just off Shorts Gardens is Neal's Yard, an attractive courtyard with a bakery, craft shops and a wholefood snack-bar.

Shorts Gardens leads on to *Seven Dials*; another notorious slum during the 17C. The area was rehabilitated in 1694 and the unusual scheme of seven radiating streets established with a Doric column topped by a sundial in the centre. In 1773 it was rumoured that a treasure was buried underneath and the column was taken down and plans are a foot to erect a model of the original, now established at Weybridge. This would complete the extensive redevelopment of this area which has created a new small open space, Ching Court, to the S of Seven Dials. Most of the original buildings have been restored and an oriental flavour introduced in the gateway to Sheldon Street. To the N the former Shaftesbury Hotel has been refurbished as the Mountbatten Hotel.

II THE CITY, THE NORTH EAST, EAST END AND DOCKLANDS

The **City of London**, one of the most important commercial centres in the world covers just one square mile from the Royal Courts of Justice in the Strand (Temple Bar) to Aldgate in the East and from the Thames in the South to City Road in the North. Nearly one third of this tightly built-up area was destroyed during the Second World War and has now been completely rebuilt. The surviving City churches and livery company halls, as well as the financial institutions and 'legal' London, contain much of interest for visitors, but the intimate alley-ways and courts which once characterised the City have disappeared in the shadow of huge tower blocks. The demolition of architecturally interesting buildings in the path of efficient glass and concrete office blocks has been allowed to progress further within the City, which is its own planning authority, than anywhere else in London, although the mid-1980s has seen a change of heart which has saved the City from such proposed developments as Mansion House Square—a windswept plaza surrounded by tower blocks intended to replace the existing buildings around Mansion House.

The Corporation of London has survived recent local government reforms to retain much of its independence and its own police force. It is the only part of the United Kingdom which has councillors elected by commercial interests. They form the Court of Common Council which meets at Guildhall. The Court of Aldermen forms an additional tier within the structure from which the Lord Mayor is elected. Its major function is the administration of justice. The Lord Mayor of the City of London takes up his/her appointment in November. The Lord Mayor's Show is the official procession to the Law Courts where the Lord Mayor takes the oath of office (see p 240); he or she is accompanied by Sheriffs, Sword Bearer and Common Cryer, and Aldermen. The population of the City once numbered over one million, but has declined rapidly during the 19th and 20th centuries to just 6000 people, augmented each day by hundreds of thousands (approximately 350,000) who work within the Square Mile.

The *City Information Centre*, open Monday to Friday 09.30-17.00, Saturday 09.30-12.30 (or to 16.00 in the summer) (01-606 3030), is in St. Paul's Churchyard and supplies information on the City, open days of livery halls, City churches, etc.

The City of London Festival takes place during two weeks of July with concerts at the Barbican Centre, St. Paul's Cathedral and in livery halls and churches. The extensive fringe programme includes open-air dancing and music, trails, and street-theatre.

The City of London from the air; in the foreground St. Paul's Cathedral with the towering National Westminster Bank in the background

18 The Inns of Court and Legal London

Access: Underground, Chancery Lane, Temple. Bus 11 from Victoria or Trafalgar Square.

The district between the Thames on the S and Theobald's Road on the N, bounded (roughly) on the E and W by lines running through Fetter Lane and Lincoln's Inn Fields, may be fairly described as 'Legal London', including as it does the Royal Courts of Justice, the four great Inns of Court, and the chambers of the leading solicitors and barristers.

Where the Strand and Fleet Street meet (comp. p 209) stand the **Royal Courts of Justice** (Pl. 15; 2) or **Law Courts**, an imposing Gothic pile, erected in 1874-82 for the Supreme Court of Judicature, established in 1873. The architect was G.E. Street (1825-81), who died about a year before the completion of his work, and it was finished by Sir Arthur Blomfield and A.E. Street. The main feature of the interior is the fine Central Hall, 238ft long by 38ft wide, and 80ft high, with a mosaic pavement designed by Street (admission Mon-Sat 10.30-16.30). A small exhibition of legal costume is displayed in a room off the hall. The public entrances to the courts and to the galleries of the hall are in the towers flanking the main entrance. There is a 12-storey extension to the Royal Courts proposed. These will be linked to the Thomas Moore building providing approx. 12 new Courts by 1989.

The four great **Inns of Court** (*Lincoln's Inn, Inner Temple, Middle Temple*, and *Gray's Inn*) have the exclusive right of calling persons to the English Bar. They originated in the 13C, when the clergy ceased to practise in the courts of justice, giving place to professional students of law. The members of the Inns comprise Benchers, Barristers, and Students. Barristers of the leading order are Queen's Counsel, who wear silk gowns; others wear 'stuff' gowns. Each Inn has a dining hall, library, and chapel, the Temple Church (see below) serving in the last capacity for both the Temple Inns. The Inns provide lectures for law students and examine candidates for admission to the Bar. The students may pursue their legal studies elsewere, but to become a member of an Inn they must 'keep term' or 'commons' by dining so many times in hall.

Visitors are practically always admitted freely to the quaint and quiet precincts of the Inns of Court (closed on Ascension Day), among which only Lincoln's Inn survived the Second World War without extensive damage.

From the Strand on the S side of the Law Courts turn N into Bell Yard. Across Carey Street, synonymous in England for bankruptcy proceedings which centre on the street, attractive archways admit to the dignified 17C quadrangle of *New Square*, part of **Lincoln's Inn** (Pl. 15; 2). It probably takes its name from Henry de Lacy, Earl of Lincoln (d 1311), adviser to Edward I in matters of law and a great proponent of legal education; the Inn is not on the site of his London mansion, which lay E of Barnard's Inn. A body of lawyers is known to have occupied the present site about 1292, though no formal records exist earlier than 1424. Visitors should call at the Porter's Lodge, 11A New Square, (open 08.00-19.00) or tel. 01-405 6360 for admission to the halls and chapel.

Between New Square and the *Old Buildings* to the E is the *Old Hall* (c 1492; S bay of 1624), with good exterior brickwork and fine open roof, well restored in 1926-28. It served as the Court of Chancery from 1733 to 1873, within which period falls the famous fictional case of Jarndyce v. Jarndyce (in Dickens' 'Bleak House'). The *Chapel* (open Mon-Fri 12.00-14.30), probably by John Clarke (1620-23), has been restored and enlarged; the crypt used to serve, like the Temple Church, as a rendezvous for barristers and their clients, and more recently it acted as a shelter from air raids. The side windows contain glass by Bernard van Linge (1632-34). The replica of the *Gatehouse* into Chancery Lane (comp. p 206) was originally built in 1518 by Sir Thomas Lovell (whose arms it bears). To the N are the classical range of *Stone Buildings* (1774-80) and the attractive Gardens. The imposing *New Hall and Library* (to the W) is a successful red-brick edifice in the Tudor style, by Philip and P.C. Hardwick (1843-45). The hall contains a large mural painting by G.F. Watts ('Justice—a Hemicycle of Lawgivers'; 1853-59), and many legal portraits. The brilliant heraldic glass dates from 1954. The Benchers' Rooms also contain fine paintings, including a small work by Holbein; the library is the oldest in London (1497) and contains the most complete collection of law books in England (70,000 vols), but these may be visited only with a member of the Inn.

Among the eminent names associated with Lincoln's Inn are those of Sir Thomas More, Donne, Penn, Pitt, Horace Walpole, Newman, Macaulay, Canning, Disraeli, Gladstone, Morley, Asquith, Galsworthy, and Newbolt.

An archway at the NW corner of New Square leads into **Lincoln's Inn Fields** (Pl. 15; 2; fine plane trees), the largest square in central London, the old houses surrounding which are mainly occupied as solicitors' offices. It was laid out in 1618 by Inigo Jones, who is said also to have built some houses on the W and S sides (now practically all gone). On the S side, beyond the *Land Registry Office* and *Nuffield College of Surgical Sciences*, the **Royal College of Surgeons** occupies a large building with an Ionic portico, erected in 1806-13 by G. Dance, Junior. It was modified with great skill by Sir Charles Barry (1835-37), whose library and entrance hall survive. New buildings replace Second World War damage.

The College contains the *Hunterian Collection*, the remnants of what was the greatest medical museum in the world, prepared by the celebrated surgeon John Hunter (1728-93). Many of its specimens were destroyed by enemy action in 1941.

Hunterian Museum, Royal College of Surgeons, Lincoln's Inn Field, WC2. Tel. 01-405 3473. Access: Underground, Holborn. Open Monday to Friday 10.00-17.00, by written application only. Closed during August. Children not admitted. Free.

Next door is the large new building of the *Imperial Cancer Research Fund* which extends into Portsmouth Street, where an old shop survives—perhaps the oldest shop in London—claiming to be Dickens' 'Old Curiosity Shop'; the original of the novel, however, really stood about the site of Irving's statue in Charing Cross Road. It sells memorabilia and souvenirs.

On the W side of Lincoln's Inn Fields, *Lindsey House* (Nos 59, 60) is attributed to Inigo Jones (c 1640); Nos 57-58 are imitations built in 1730, and altered by Soane. *Powis House*, at the NW corner, is a fine

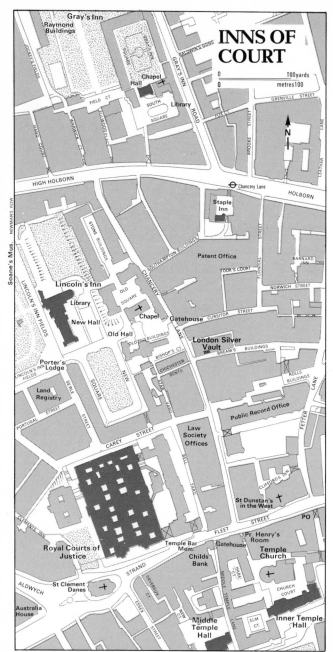

brick building of 1684-89 (restored). Among famous residents were Lord Brougham (1778-1868), Spencer Perceval (1762-1812; No. 60), John Milton, Lord Tennyson (1809-92) John Forster (1812-76; No. 58), and Nell Gwynn (1650-87).—Before their enclosure the gardens were a favourite duelling-ground and a great haunt of thieves. The pillory was often erected here. Lord William Russell was executed in Lincoln's Inn Fields in 1683. Memorials on the N side of the garden commemorate Mrs Ramsay MacDonald (d 1911), who lived at No. 3 Lincoln's Inn Fields, and Lord Hambleden (1868-1928) head of the book-distributing organisation of W.H. Smith & Son. There is a bust of Hunter (1979) in the SW corner.

The N walk of the gardens has been named *Canada Walk*, to commemorate the establishment here of the headquarters of the Royal Canadian Air Force in 1940-45 (tablet beside a memorial maple tree). In the middle of the N side of the square (where most of the fine houses have been demolished) No. 13 survives as *Sir John Soane's Museum, founded by Sir John Soane (1753-1837), architect of the Bank of England. Owing to the stipulation of the founder that his collections should be neither augmented nor disturbed, the museum has the unusual interest of retaining the character of a (admittedly somewhat eccentric) private house of the period (1813). The arrangements to make the most of the room available are exceedingly ingenious; and the effect of space is enhanced by a clever use of mirrors. The museum includes some objects that no visitor to London should miss, pre-eminently the paintings by William Hogarth and the sarcophagus of Seti I.

Sir John Soane's Museum, 13 Lincoln's Inn Fields, London WC2. Tel. 01-405 2107. Access: Underground, Holborn. Open Tuesday to Saturday 10.00-17.00. Free.

The PICTURE ROOM (shown by a custodian) on the ground floor contains two admirable series of paintings by *William Hogarth* (1697-1764), the *Rake's Progress (eight scenes; 1735) and the *Election (four scenes; 1754-57), excellent examples of his satirical humour, harmonious colouring, and able composition. Here also are The Passage Point by *Callcott*, and a Design for the Ceiling of the Queen's State Bedchamber at Hampton Court, by *Thornhill*. We descend to the SEPULCHRAL CHAMBER with the *Sarcophagus of Seti I, King of Egypt c 1370 BC and father of Ramesses the Great.—Re-ascending to the ground floor we visit the first room past the plaster casts, in which are *Turner*'s *Admiral Tromp's barge entering the Texel after his defeat of Blake in 1652, and *Canaletto*'s *View of the Grand Canal. We ascend to the FIRST FLOOR (renovated in 1970) where a connecting door admits to the adjoining house (No. 12) built by Soane for himself in 1792, and now used as a library for students. The numerous small works of art, antiquities, casts, and furniture, etc., throughout the Museum include many objects of great interest. The fine doors of mahogany and ebony deserve notice, and many of the windows are filled with old stained glass.

Leave the square by Newman's Row (at the NE corner) and emerge in High Holborn (see p 223). Turn E, cross, and turn N into Fulwood Place to reach **Gray's Inn** (Pl. 7; 6). Originally in the buildings of the manor of Portpool, it is known to have been occupied by lawyers before 1370 and takes its name from the former owners of the site, the Lords Grey de Wilton. The Inn was very seriously damaged in 1941, the Hall, the Chapel, and the Library being burned out. It has been restored in a harmonious style. Both the Chapel and Hall are open when not in use. Pass through an archway (right) to the squares either side of the *Hall* (1560), rebuilt in 1951, with a second oriel presented by the American Bar Association. It preserves its stained glass and much of the fine carved screen. Shakespeare's 'Comedy of Errors' had its first performance here in 1594, and the Court of Exchequer was held in this hall in the 18C. The *Chapel* was reconsecrated on the 19th anniversary of the fire; it preserves a stoup from the 14C manor chapel. The *Library*, in South Square, is a harmonious building by Sir Edward Maufe (1956). The *Gardens* (entered from Field Court through a gate of 1723), with their ancient catalpas, were supposed to have been laid out by Francis Bacon (whose statue stands in South Square). *Raymond Buildings* (1825) and *Verulam Buildings* (1811) skirt the gardens on the W and E in long terraces.

The great name of Gray's Inn is Francis Bacon, who became Treasurer of the Inn and retained his chambers here from 1577 till his death in 1626. Among other members were Sir William Gascoigne, the judge traditionally reported to have committed the Prince of Wales (Henry V) to prison, Sir Thomas Gresham, Thomas Cromwell, Nicholas Bacon, Burghley, Abp Laud, and Lord Birkenhead. The Council of Legal Education occupies a building in Gray's Inn Place where Sun Yat-Sen, the 'Father of the Chinese Republic', lived during his political exile from his country in the 1890s—a private plaque marks the site.

Return across High Holborn to *Chancery Lane* (Pl. 7; 6) which runs S to Fleet St.

The nine **Inns of Chancery** differed from the Inns of Court in being of minor importance and subordinate character. It was long the custom for students of law to enter first an Inn of Chancery and then graduate to an Inn of Court, but this practice had become obsolete at the beginning of the 17C. The Inns of Chancery were thenceforward abandoned to the attorneys, and by the middle of the 18C they had practically ceased to have any legal character.

Clement's Inn, *Clifford's Inn* (the oldest and most important of the Inns of Chancery), *Thavie's Inn*, and *Furnival's Inn* now exist merely as names of modern buildings. *Lyon's Inn*, *New Inn*, and *Strand Inn* have completely disappeared. The legal history of *Staple Inn* goes back to the reign of Henry V (1413-22), that of *Barnard's Inn* to the time of Henry VI (1422-61).—The two *Serjeants' Inns* were independent bodies, composed solely of serjeants-at-law ('servientes ad legem'), an order of the highest rank of barristers. The society was dissolved in 1877, but the buildings of one of their inns survived until 1941.

Chancery Lane skirts the E side of Lincoln's Inn (p 203). To the left diverges Southampton Buildings, with the entrance to the *London Silver Vaults* (Mon to Fri 09.00-17.30, Sat 09.00-12.30), storing and selling a copious stock of antique silver, etc.

Further on (right) is the *Patent Office*. The former *Patent Office Library* (318,600 vols; Mon to Fri 09.30-21.00, Sat 10.00-13.00), now Holborn Division of the British Library (British Science Library), is the finest collection of technical and scientific works in England. It is adjoined on the N by the small garden of Staple Inn.

Further S rises the **Public Record Office**, one section of the chief repository of the state archives of England (open Mon to Fri 13.00-16.00), a fortress-like building in a Tudor style (1851-66, by Pennethorne, and 1891-96, by Sir John Taylor), very reminiscent of the 19C parts of the Tower of London from which many of the archives were removed. Here are the legal and judicial records from the Conquest; 16-18C papers of Secretaries of State; and 19C census returns (see also Kew, p 344). A Reader's Ticket is necessary.

The ***Public Record Office Museum**** occupies the exact site and area of the old Rolls Chapel. Three of the monuments, erected in the old chapel, are still in their original positions on the N wall. Adjacent is the most important object in the museum, *Domesday Book* (2 vellum vols.), containing the results of the statistical survey of England made by order of William the Conqueror in 1086. The so-called *Domesday Chest*, with its triple lock, is likewise shown. The glass cases contain a remarkable series of famous and interesting historical documents and records. From 3 April to 30 September 1986 there will be a special exhibition to mark the 900th anniversary of the Domesday Book. *The museum will be closed before and after this exhibition for an unspecified period.*

Public Record Office Museum, Chancery Lane, London WC2. Tel. 01-405 0741. Access: Underground, Chancery Lane. Open Monday to Saturday 10.00-18.00, 3 April-30 Sep 1986, Admission Charge. Other times by appointment.

Almost opposite the Record Office are the massive offices of the *Law Society*, which controls the education, admission, and discipline of the solicitors' branch of the legal profession. At the foot of Chancery Lane we cross Fleet St to enter the **Temple** (Pl. 7; 8) by North's fine *Gatehouse* (1684), which opens from Fleet St near Temple Bar.

The *Temple Bar Monument* by Jones (1880) marks the boundary between the City of London and the City of Westminster. Here stood the Temple Bar (see p 209), which if it returns to London will probably be re-erected near St. Paul's. Wren's Temple Bar stood here from 1672 to 1878 when it was removed to Theobalds Park as it was an obstruction to traffic. Even today the Sovereign seeks symbolic permission to enter the City from the Lord Mayor at this point and the Lord Mayor presents the Pearl Sword.

The general name of the Temple covers two Inns of Court, the *Middle* and the *Inner Temple*, extending from Fleet St to the Thames, and named from their topographical relations to the City proper and the Outer Temple. The last, merely a piece of ground belonging to the Templars, was absorbed at an early date by private owners.

The Temple was originally the seat in England of the famous Order of Knights Templars. On the dissolution of the Order in 1312 the Temple passed to the Crown and later into the possession of the Knights Hospitallers of St. John, who leased it in the reign of Edward III (c 1338) to certain professors of the common law. The first trustworthy mention of the Temple as an Inn of Court is found in 1449. The church (see below), and the crypt and buttery of the Inner Temple Hall are the only edifices going back to the Middle Ages, the other old buildings dating mainly from the reign of Elizabeth I or just after the Great Fire of 1666. Widespread destruction in 1940-41 has been repaired, and new buildings in traditional style have been erected by *Sir Edward Maufe, Sir Hubert Worthington,* and *T.W. Sutcliffe*. Buildings belonging to the Inner Temple bear the device of the Winged Horse, those of the Middle Temple the Lamb and Flag.

Among famous members of the Inner Temple may be mentioned Granville, Hampden, Jeffreys, Lyndhurst, Thurlow, and Hallam; of the Middle Temple, Clarendon, Raleigh, Pym, Congreve, Wycherley, Sheridan, Blackstone, Fielding, Thos. Moore, De Quincey, Burke, Dickens, Blackmore, Eldon, Havelock, and Birkett.

The ***Temple Church**, or *Church of St. Mary the Virgin*, belonging to the Middle and Inner Temple in common, is the most important of the five remaining round churches in England. (Open 09.30-16.00, closed Aug, Sept.) It is a 'peculiar', i.e. exempt from episcopal jurisdiction. The round part of the church was consecrated in 1185, and is in the transition-Norman style, with handsome ornamentation. The Norman W doorway survives. The chancel ('oblong'), an admirable example of Early English, was added in 1240. The whole building was very seriously damaged in 1941, but the final touches of restoration were completed in 1961.

The chancel, entered by a new S porch, is borne by clustered piers of Purbeck marble, from the same quarry as the originals. The reredos, designed by Wren in 1682, was removed as a restoration in 1840, and so escaped damage. The stained glass of the beautiful E windows, given by the Glaziers' Company, the Middle Temple (N), and the Inner Temple (S), is by Carl Edwards. On the S is a noble effigy of a 13C ecclesiastic, and near the S door (beneath a glass slab) is the gravestone of John Selden (1584-1654), the jurist. In the round church are nine *Monuments of Associates of the Temple* of the 12-13C, with recumbent marble figures (damaged) in full armour. The two most arresting coloured *Monuments* are to Richard Martin (1618; S side) and Edmund Plowden (1585; N side).

The lawyers used to await their clients in 'the Round', just as the serjeants-at-law did in St. Paul's Cathedral. The *Master's House*, the home of the incumbent of the Temple Church, NE of the church, was re-erected after the Great Fire and totally destroyed in 1941 but has been rebuilt in its 17C form.—In the churchyard, N of the choir, is a slab (now covered) marking the whereabouts of the grave of Oliver Goldsmith (1728-74).

To the S of the church is a cloister built, by Maufe, in accordance with Wren's original design. Beyond is the **Inner Temple Hall** and *Library*, by Worthington (1952-56) replacing the 19C range destroyed in 1941. The refaced buttery at the W end and the crypt below it date from the 14C. To the E is *King's Bench Walk*, with two houses ascribed to Wren (Nos 4 and 5), popular with film companies. Towards the river lie the *Inner Temple Gardens* (no adm.); and on the other side of Middle Temple Lane are the *Middle Temple Gardens* (no adm.). In one of these, according to a well-known scene in 'Henry VI' (Pt I, ii, 4), were plucked the white and red roses, assumed as badges in the Wars of the Roses.

On the W side of the Middle Temple Lane is *Middle Temple Hall* (open Mon to Fri 10.00-12.00, 15.00-16.30. Free. Tel. 01-353 4355), a stately Elizabethan chamber of 1562-73 (100ft long, 42ft wide, 47ft high), the interior of which, heavily damaged in 1941-44, is now rebuilt and restored (inscription on the E gable). Shakespeare is said to have taken part in a performance of 'Twelfth Night' in this hall on 2 Feb 1601-02.—The *Middle Temple Library*, which lost some 65,000 volumes, is housed in Middle Temple Lane, below the hall. Middle Temple Lane is still lit manually every night (afternoon in winter) by gas.

At No. 2 Brick Court, Middle Temple Lane (destroyed), Oliver Goldsmith died. Blackstone, the celebrated jurist, occupied the rooms below Goldsmith, and complained of the noise made by his 'revelling neighbour'. Thackeray (1853-59) and Praed also had chambers in this building. Crown Office Row, where Charles Lamb was born (1775) and spent his first seven years (at No. 2), has been rebuilt. Later he lived with his sister within the Temple from 1801 to 1817, first at 16 Mitre Court Buildings and (after 1808) at 4 Inner Temple Lane (both houses pulled down). Dr Johnson occupied rooms at 1 Inner Temple Lane, replaced by Johnson's Buildings. Thackeray had rooms at 10 Crown Office Row from 1848-50. *Fountain Court*, to the N of Middle Temple Hall is indissolubly associated with Ruth Pinch's tryst with her brother Tom ('Martin Chuzzlewit'). The fountain, dating from 1681, was restored in 1919 to its original condition.

19 Fleet Street, St. Paul's, Blackfriars

A. Fleet Street to St. Paul's and Blackfriars

Access: Underground, Temple; Buses 11 or 15 from Trafalgar Square.

Where the Strand ends at the Royal Courts of Justice and meets Fleet Street the *Temple Bar Memorial* (see p 207) marks the boundary between the City of London and the City of Westminster. It was erected in 1880 on the site of old Temple Bar and has statues of Queen Victoria and Edward VII (as Prince of Wales) by Boehm. The bronze griffin is by C.B. Birch.

Temple Bar was erected by Wren in 1672, after the Great Fire, but its wooden predecessor is known to have stood here in 1501, and some kind of a bar or chain, on the boundary between Westminster and the City proper, seems to have existed as far back as the 12C. From the top of the gate projected a number of iron spikes, on which were exhibited the heads of felons and traitors (e.g. those of the rebels of 1745). The gate was removed to Plumstead Marshes in 1878, and ten years later was re-erected by Sir Henry Meux as an entrance to Theobalds Park, near Waltham Cross. Plans are periodically mooted to rescue it from its rural decay (see p 396). When the sovereign of England visits the City on state occasions, the ancient custom of obtaining permission from the Lord Mayor 'to pass Temple Bar' is still observed.

The George pub just opposite the Royal Courts of Justice was once a coffee house. The long beamed bar serves snacks and there is a restaurant upstairs (good views of the Lord Mayor's Show). Nearby is London's narrowest shop, *Twining's*, of 1787; earlier premises date to 1716. The *Wig and Pen Club* (members only but overseas visitors can apply for instant membership) just W of Temple Bar (230 Strand) occupies a quaint building of 1625 with a bar and restaurant, providing a meeting place for journalists and lawyers.

Fleet Street, the busy continuation of the Strand, leads from Temple Bar to Ludgate Circus. The 'Street of Ink' or 'Street of Shame' as it is also known remains for the time being the centre of newspaper production. Several major publishers are moving to Docklands. The name is derived from the Fleet River or Fleet Ditch (now an underground sewer) which rises amid the heights of Hampstead, flows through the Holborn Valley and joins the Thames near Blackfriars Bridge.

Newspapers are generally printed in the streets, squares, and courts on either side of Fleet Street. The neighbourhood is especially animated between 21.00 and midnight, when the daily journals go to press with their first editions, which are carried to the railway termini and airports to catch the 'newspaper trains' and increasingly flights. 'Late London editions' continue to be printed until 03.00, when the whirr of machinery subsides.

It is possible to visit most of the daily newspapers and to see the printing presses at work. Write to: The Guardian, Farringdon Road, EC4; the Daily Express, Fleet Street, EC4; The Times, Grays Inn Road, WC2.

Immediately below the Temple Bar Memorial, on the right, No. 1 Fleet St is *Child's Bank*, one of the oldest in London (founded 1671), now amalgamated with Williams and Glyn's Bank. On its books occur the names of many royal personages, of Oliver Cromwell, Marlborough, Nell Gwynn, Prince Rupert, Pepys, and Dryden. At the former *Devil Tavern*, on this site, Ben Jonson reigned supreme in the 'Apollo Club'.

Middle Temple Lane, beyond Child's Bank on the same side, leads through North Gateway to the *Temple* (Rte 18), and just beyond is another passage (Inner Temple Lane) leading to the Temple Church. No. 17 Fleet St, above this latter archway, is an interesting specimen of a timbered house of 1610, with a projecting upper storey. On the first floor is *Prince Henry's Room*, with a decorated ceiling, referring to Prince Henry, elder son of James I. Here is a collection of memorabilia of Samuel Pepys, including an original letter to Charles II.

Prince Henry's Room, 17 Fleet Street, London EC4. Tel. 01-353 7323. Free. Access: Underground, Temple. Open Monday to Friday 13.45-17.00, Sat 13.45-16.30.

The *Cock Tavern*, at No. 22, preserves some internal fittings and other interesting relics of the old tavern, which stood till 1887 on the other side of the way, and is well known from Tennyson's reference to the 'plump head-waiter at the Cock'. The original sign carved by Grinling Gibbons is preserved in the bar on the first floor.

On the N side of Fleet St, beyond a branch of the Bank of England, *Chancery Lane* (comp. p 206) runs N to Holborn. Beyond, *Clifford's Inn Passage* leads through the old gatehouse of the Inn of Chancery to a building which has appropriated the name. The octagonal church of **St. Dunstan in the West**, by John Shaw (1831-33) was well restored in 1950; it stands on the site of an earlier building. The fine tower ends in an open-work lantern. The figure of Queen Elizabeth I (1586) over the E (vestry) porch, and the statues of King Lud and his sons within it, came from the Ludgate, which stood half-way up Ludgate Hill and was pulled down in 1760. The fine clock (1671) with 'striking Jacks', from the old church, was returned from St. Dunstan's Lodge in Regent's Park in 1936.

On the S front are a bust of Lord Northcliffe (1865-1922), and a tablet to J.L. Garvin (1868-1947), journalist and editor. Inside, the chapel on the left contains a quaint brass to Henry Dacres, 'merchant taylor and alderman of the City of London', and his wife (1530). The chapel to the left of the altar is now closed by an iconostasis from Autim monastery, Bucharest, dedicated in 1966 to mark the chapel's second use by the Roumanian orthodox congregation. A stained glass window in the chapel, and a tablet to the right of the entrance porch, commemorate Izaak Walton, a vestryman of the parish. On the wall beneath are plaques to George Calvert, Lord Baltimore (1580?-1632), founder of Maryland, who was buried in 'the old church, and to Daniel Brown of Connecticut, the first Anglican clergyman to be ordained for America (1723). The communion rail was carved by Grinling Gibbons while John Donne was vicar here (1624-31). Sweeney Todd, the fictional barber who made pies out of his customers, supposedly had his shop next to the church.

Hoare's Bank, No. 37 Fleet St, on the S side, founded in 1672 by

Richard Hoare, a goldsmith and the son of a successful horse-dealer, moved to Fleet St in 1690. It is the only remaining 'private' bank in London. *El Vino's* wine bar, haunt of generations of newspaper men, is still fussy about dress and serving women. *Fetter Lane*, diverging to the N (left) beyond St. Dunstan's and leading to Holborn, derives its name either from the 'faitours' (i.e. beggars) with which it used to swarm, or from a colony of 'feutriers' (felt-makers). Swift assigned residence and property in Fetter Lane to Captain Lemuel Gulliver.

A little further on a bend in Fleet St reveals a celebrated view of St. Paul's. On the N side is a series of small courts and alleys (dating from the late 17C and probably originating as gardens), all redolent of literary and historical associations. *Crane Court* was the home of the Royal Society from 1710-80. In *Johnson's Court* Dr Johnson lived from 1765-76; in allusion to his residence here he jokingly called himself, when in Scotland, 'Johnson of that ilk'. From 1776 till his death in 1784 he lived in *Bolt Court* (both houses demolished).—Wine Office Court was another resort of Dr Johnson and the old 'Cheshire Cheese' pub and restaurant (rebuilt in 1667; entrance 145 Fleet St), in which he, Goldsmith, and Boswell are said to have foregathered (though Boswell makes no mention of it), is still extant. The authenticity of the chair here shown as Johnson's is not beyond cavil. The 14C Crypt of the Whitefriars monastery can be seen in the basement and is available for functions.—Johnson's Court and Bolt Court both lead into *Gough Square*, containing **Dr Johnson's House** (No. 17), where he lived from 1749 to 1758, engaged in the production of 'The Rambler' and of his famous 'Dictionary'. His wife died here in 1752.

Dr Johnson's House, Gough Square, London EC4. Tel. 01-353 3745. Access: Underground, Blackfriars. Open Mondays to Saturdays 11.00-1730, May to September, 11.00-17.00 October to April. Admission charge.

The house was built c 1700 and restored in 1948. Among relics of Dr Johnson are an early edition of the 'Dictionary' and autograph letters. The portraits include Dr Johnson by J. Opie, and James Boswell by Joshua Reynolds. The most notable room is the large attic in which Johnson and his six amanuenses worked at the 'Dictionary'. LBC, London's local news-radio, has its studios in Gough Square.

On the S side of Fleet St, behind No. 49, a pleasant brick quadrangle (1956) is entered by the old iron gate of *Serjeants' Inn*. Here an archway through Mitre Court Buildings admits to the Inner Temple (comp. p 207). Beyond Bouverie Street, *Whitefriars Street* perpetuates the name of the Carmelite monastery founded about 1241 and dissolved in 1538. A crypt may still be seen at No. 30 Bouverie Street; apply to the offices of the 'Sun' and the 'News of the World'. Here are the offices of the 'Observer' and nearby in Carmelite Street, the 'Daily Mail'.

The fact that the privilege of sanctuary attached to the precincts of the monastery was not abolished till 1697 apparently explains the appropriation of this quarter, under the name of *Alsatia*, by debtors, criminals, and lawless characters of all kinds (comp. 'The Fortunes of Nigel'; the name was apparently taken from the province forming a debatable ground between France and Germany). Alsatia is now predominantly a journalistic region containing the offices of 'Punch' and many other well-known papers. At the corner of Whitefriars St tablets mark the site of the home of Tompion and Graham, the clockmakers, and of the offices of the anti-Corn Law League, managed by Cobden and Bright. Hanging Sword Alley, a sordid crack opening off Whitefriars St, was the home of the rascally

Jerry Cruncher of 'Tellson's Bank'.

On the N side of Fleet St are the massive office of the 'Daily Telegraph'
and the glass house of the 'Daily Express' and the 'Standard' (1931);
and opposite is the former 'News Chronicle' office, with a bust of
T.P. O'Connor (1848-1929), journalist and parliamentarian. No. 85 (S
side) is the headquarters of Reuter's and the Press Association. Just
behind the S side of Fleet St is the church of **St. Bride** (open daily
09.00-17.00), rebuilt by Wren in 1671-75, and seriously damaged in
1940. The *Spire (1703), called by Henley 'a madrigal in stone', was
originally 234ft high, but was struck by lightning in 1764 and rebuilt
8ft shorter. It is still, however, the tallest of Wren's steeples and has
survived the damage to the rest of the church. Restoration, by Godfrey
Allen, was carried out in 1953-57, with woodwork (stalls and reredos)
in the style of Wren and Grinling Gibbons, by Alfred Banks. The
reredos is a memorial to Edward Winslow, the Pilgrim Father, a
parishioner. At the W end are statues of St. Bride and St. Paul, by D.
MacFall, while the E end has been painted by Glyn Jones, in a
trompe-l'oeil manner, to create the effect of an apsidal ending. There
are lunchtime concerts.

The old church was the burial-place of Weelkes (1623), the madrigalist, and of
Lovelace (1658), the Cavalier poet. The parish registers include entries of the
baptism of Samuel Pepys (1633; born in Salisbury Court, overlooking the
churchyard, where his father was a tailor). The Crypt of the much-rebuilt
medieval church which Wren incorporated into his own church is open to the
public. Excavations have revealed a Roman ditch (15-16ft wide) and the
pavement of a Roman building, the first recorded outside the wall of London.
Evidence of a Late Saxon cemetery was found, and remains of earlier churches
on the site (the first built in the mid-11C). The coffin of Samuel Richardson (d
1761), author of 'Clarissa Harlowe', who carried on his business as printer in
the adjacent Salisbury Square, is preserved here. A small exhibition illustrates
the development of printing in Fleet St and the church has a special connection
with newspapers and the printing industry.

Bride Lane, passing St. Bride's Church, contains (right) the *St. Bride
Institute* (1894), an educational club for printers and others. Fleet St
ends at *Ludgate Circus*, formed by its junction with Farringdon St,
Ludgate Hill, and New Bridge St. On the NW side is a tablet with a
relief portrait of Edgar Wallace (1875-1932), novelist and journalist.
  Farringdon Street, a wide thoroughfare, leads N (left) from Ludgate
Circus to Charterhouse St. On the right, beyond Seacoal Lane, is the
site of the historic *Fleet Prison*, which stood on the E side of the Fleet
River, and was used for persons committed by the Star Chamber and
for debtors. The prison was twice rebuilt, after its destruction in the
Great Fire (1666) and in the Gordon Riots (1780), and it was finally
pulled down in 1844-46. This was the prison in which Mr Pickwick
was confined. The so-called 'Fleet Marriages' arose out of the fact
that clergymen imprisoned for debt in the Fleet were not deterred
from celebrating clandestine marriages by the financial penalties
they nominally incurred. Such marriages were legal down to 1753.

Branching to the W is Shoe Lane with the *International Press Centre* where
many overseas newspapers, radio and TV stations have their London HQs. The
Cartoonist on the ground floor is a modern pub with a wonderful collection of
original cartoons.

Beyond Ludgate Circus *Ludgate Hill* (Pl. 8; 5), rises towards St. Paul's
Cathedral. To the N diverges the *Old Bailey*, which leads to Newgate

St and the Central Criminal Court (see Rte 21). Further up Ludgate Hill, to the left, is the church of *St. Martin Ludgate*, the slender spire of which shows up well against the dome of St. Paul's. This church was rebuilt by Wren in 1677-87 and has fine oaken *Woodwork, and a Father Smith organ. Captain (later Adm. Sir) William Penn, father of the founder of Pennsylvania, was married in the former church in 1643. The old church stood just within the Roman wall close to Lud Gate, the first curfew gate in London to be closed at night (comp. p 234).

At No. 3 Ludgate Hill lived William Rich (1755-1811), a pastry cook who modelled his wedding cakes on the steeple of St. Bride seen from his window, starting a fashion still followed. *Ave Maria Lane* diverges left just before St. Paul's. Here is the *Stationers' Hall*, the guildhouse of the Stationers' Company, the members of which (unlike those of most City Guilds) have some actual connection with their nominal trade.

The Hall was built soon after the first Great Fire of London in 1666, but was stone-faced in 1800, and a wing was added in 1887. It was severely damaged in 1940, but the hall has now been restored. It contains a fine screen and panelling of the late 17C, the work of Stephen Colledge.

The Stationers' Company, founded c 1402, was incorported by royal charter in 1557, and for a time it preserved the sole right of printing in England (apart from the presses at Oxford and Cambridge), while it had a monopoly of the publishing of almanacks down to 1771. Until the passing of the Copyright Act of 1911 every work published in Great Britain had to be registered for copyright at Stationers' Hall. In 1933 the company was amalgamated with that of the Newspaper Makers. A plane tree in the court behind the Hall marks the spot where seditious books used to be burnt.

Among the buildings spared by the bombing of this area is *Amen Court*, a curiously quiet little nook in the heart of London, entered from Ave Maria Lane. It contains the dwellings of the Canons Residentiary of St. Paul's, which Wren is supposed to have built.

Beyond the ugly, projecting Juxon House (1964) at the top of Ludgate Hill we reach the W facade of St. Paul's. In front stands a statue of *Queen Anne*, in whose reign the cathedral was finished; the present statue is a replica of the original by Francis Bird (1712).

New Bridge Street leads S from Ludgate Circus to Blackfriars road bridge and railway bridge, past the site of the notorious old prison, *Bridewell*.

Some kind of castle, taking its name from the holy well of St. Bride (p 212), and occasionally occupied by English sovereigns, stood here in early Norman times. Henry VIII restored it so as to form the 'stately and beautiful house' which was the residence of himself and Queen Catherine during the latter's trial. Edward VI granted it to the City of London, and in 1556 it became a prison for vagrants and immoral women. Partly destroyed in the Great Fire, it was rebuilt in 1668. New Bridewell, built in 1829, was pulled down in 1864.

To the W are the *Temple Gardens*, outside which two heraldic dragons (from the demolished Coal Exchange) mark the boundary of the 'City'. In the river are moored three ships: first the 'Wellington', serving as the livery hall of the Master Mariners' Company, then two training ships, the 'Chrysanthemum' and the 'President'. Farther on, near the bridge, the Gothic buildings of *Sion College and Library* were designed by Sir Arthur Blomfield (1886) who incorporated the original timber roof from London Wall.

Sion College (adm. on application), founded in the City in 1624, exists for the benefit of the Anglican clergy. Its chief glory is the Library (300,000 vols), which possesses many rarities, but suffered considerable war damage.—The City Livery Club is also accommodated here.

The district of **Blackfriars** was so called from the Dominicans who settled here in the 13C and erected extensive monastic buildings, of which there are now no visible vestiges. In the monastery, in 1382, an assembly condemned as heretical twenty-four Articles deduced from the teachings of Wyclif. It was here that a decree of divorce was pronounced against Queen Catherine of Aragon (1529; 'Henry VIII', ii. 4). In 1596 James Burbage established here the first covered theatre in London, in which Shakespeare (who owned a house in the district) in all probability acted. The name of *Playhouse Yard* commemorates its existence.

The next large building is the *City of London School for Boys* (to be moved to the other side of Blackfriars Bridge in 1987), opened in 1837 in Milk St, and removed hither in 1883. Lord Asquith, Sir J. R.Seeley, and Sir F. Gowland Hopkins were educated at this school.—At the curved corner of the Embankment and New Bridge St is the huge *Unilever House* (1932).

On the corner of Queen Victoria St is the distinctive *Blackfriar* pub (opposite the station) in a triangular building; the unique art nouveau interior has recently been restored; note the beaten bronze bas-reliefs of the monks at work; in the side chapel-bar there are red marble columns, an arched mosaic ceiling and decorative figures.

Queen Victoria Street (Pl. 8; 7), a wide thoroughfare about 1000 yards long, leads E, from Blackfriars Bridge (p 300) to the Mansion House. On the left beyond the railway bridge leading to Holborn Viaduct Station diverges Blackfriars Lane, in which stands the charming **Apothecaries Hall**, dating partly from 1670, partly from 1786, with portraits of James I, Charles I, John Keats (licentiate of the Hall), and others.

Also in Blackfriars Lane is the Shakespeare Tavern; a cabaret entertainment restaurant underneath the arches of the railway bridge. At Puddle Dock, S, is the *Mermaid Theatre*, established by Bernard Miles in 1956. The Mermaid Theatre reopened in 1982 after further rebuilding. Here by the river in 1963 a 2C Roman boat was uncovered. It had sunk with its cargo of building stone brought via the Medway from Maidstone to build the city walls (comp. p 234).

In nearby *Baynard House* a new Museum of Technology opened in 1982.

Telecom Technology Showcase, 135 Queen Victoria Street, London EC4. Tel. 01-248 7444. Open Mon to Fri 10.00-17.00. It illustrates the history of Britain's telecommunications and also looks to the future with many up-to-date and potential gadgets on view. The Showcase may move but not until after 1986.

During reconstruction in 1972, part of Baynard Castle was temporarily exposed. The castle was first built by William the Conqueror, and named after a follower. When the Dominicans took over the area (now Blackfriars) in 1278, a second castle was built a little to the E. A 15C successor to this castle was uncovered including the prominent towers and wall along the old line of the river (shown in Hollar's 'View of London'). The castle, which extended to the N of Upper Thames St, was destroyed in the Great Fire, and warehouses (often following the line of the old walls) were built on the site. It is hoped that the castle will be exposed permanently in the precinct of the new City of London School for Boys on the river front.

Beyond Printing House Square where 'The Times' used to be printed and where the King's Printing House was established in 1667, on the N side is *St. Andrew by the Wardrobe*, rebuilt by Wren in 1685-95, and restored in 1961 after serious war damage. It took its name from the proximity of the King's Great Wardrobe, used as an office for the keepers of the king's state apparel. At No. 146 is the now vacant building of the former *British and Foreign Bible Society*, a Grade II listed building, founded in 1804 'to encourage a wider circulation of the Holy Scriptures, without note or comment' now relocated in Swindon.—Next door is the *Faraday Building* (1933), the first building in the City allowed to go higher than the London Building Act then normally permitted, and thus the first obtrusive precursor of many into the city townscape. *Baynard House*, opposite, complements the work.

Across Goldiman St is the **College of Arms**, the seat of the official heraldic authority for England, Ireland, and the Commonwealth. The Heralds of the kings of England were first incorporated by Richard III in 1484, and in 1555 Queen Mary I gave them a new charter and the site of the present College.—The Court Room is open to the public Mon to Fri 10.00-16.00. Free. The Earl Marshal's throne is used on ceremonial occasions. The reredos is early 18C.

The original building was burnt down in the Great Fire of 1666; the present one, by Maurice Emmett (1672-88), is a good example of the period. Splendid 19C wrought iron gates, apparently made for Goodrich Court, Herefordshire, were given to the College in 1956.

The College of Arms in Queen Victoria Street (Maurice Emmett, 1671-78); the gates and railings from Goodrich Court, Herts, were added in 1956

The Officers of Arms, who are members of the Royal Household, are still appointed directly by the Crown, by letters patent under the great seal, on the advice of the Duke of Norfolk as hereditary Earl Marshal. They consist of three kings of Arms (Garter, Clarenceux, and Norroy and Ulster), six heralds (Windsor, Lancaster, Somerset, York, Chester, and Richmond), and four pursuivants (Bluemantle, Portcullis, Rouge Croix, and Rouge Dragon). The titles of the heralds are taken from Royal duchies, earldoms and castles, while those of the pursuivants are taken from national badges (Rouge Croix), royal badges (Portcullis and Rouge Dragon), and the blue mantle of the Order of the Garter. For many centuries the kings of arms have been authorised by the sovereigns to grant arms to eminent men, subject to the approval of the earl marshal.

The heraldic and genealogical records and collections are unique, and the registers of recorded pedigrees include many pedigrees of families who have settled in the Commonwealth and America.

In Bennet's Hill, to the S (footpath), is the now isolated brick church of *St. Benet* (restored after damage by arson in 1971). It was rebuilt by Wren in 1677-83, and is now used by a Welsh congregation. Henry Fielding was married here in 1748 and Inigo Jones (1573-1652) was buried in the earlier church.

On the S side of Queen Victoria St is the international headquarters (1962) of the *Salvation Army*, founded by William Booth, a Methodist, in 1865. A Christian movement organised in a quasi-military style, it is concerned with all in need. Beyond, to the N, is the church of *St. Nicholas Cole Abbey* (originally 'Cold Abbey'), rebuilt by Wren in 1671-77 and reopened in 1963 after being burnt out in 1941. A striking feature of the interior is the richly coloured glass of the E windows, by Keith New. The font and the ornamental woodwork were saved; and behind a panel on the S wall is a sculptured head from the medieval church.

St. Paul's is to the North.

B. St. Paul's Cathedral

St. Paul's Cathedral, London EC4. Tel. 01-248 2705. Access: Underground, St. Paul's, Mansion House.

Cathedral open daily April to Oct 07.30-18.00, Nov to March 07.30-17.00. Free. Ambulatory, Galleries, Crypt open Easter to Sept, Mon to Fri, 10.00-17.00, Sat 11.00-16.45, Oct to Easter closed at 16.00. Admission charge to each section.

Educational facilities and guided 'super tours' Mon to Sat at 11.00 and 14.00. Charge. Tour includes galleries, crypt, ambulatory, etc. Bookshop.

Services are on weekdays at 08.00 and 10.00, 12.30 (Wed and Fri) and 16.00. There are prayers every hour; on Sun at 08.00, 10.30, 11.30, 15.15 and 18.30. Matins and Evensong daily and the services at 12.30 on Wed and Fri and at 11.30 on Sun are choral.

'St. Paul's Cathedral (Pl. 8; 6), the largest and most famous church in the City, stands at the top of Ludgate Hill. The cathedral of the Bishop of London, it is the masterpiece of Sir Christopher Wren, a dignified edifice in a Renaissance style, dominated by the famous dome. The Portland stone of which it is built was picturesquely bleached and stained by the London climate and London smoke, until cleaning in the 1960s disclosed its golden colour and the beautiful detail of the carved stone work.

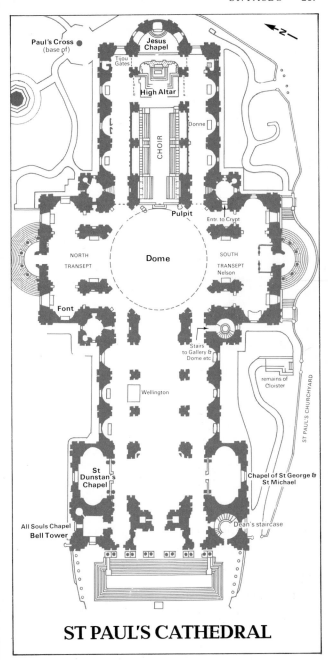

ST PAUL'S CATHEDRAL

Paul's Cross (base of)

Jesus Chapel

Tijou Gates

High Altar

Donne

CHOIR

Pulpit

Entr. to Crypt

NORTH TRANSEPT

Dome

SOUTH TRANSEPT

Nelson

Font

Stairs to Gallery & Dome etc

remains of Cloister

Wellington

ST PAUL'S CHURCHYARD

St Dunstan's Chapel

Chapel of St George & St Michael

All Souls Chapel Bell Tower

Dean's staircase

The tradition that a Roman temple dedicated to Diana stood on the commanding site now occupied by St. Paul's was repudiated by Wren, and is supported by no evidence. A Christian church, said to have been founded here in the 7C by Bp Mellitus and endowed by Ethelbert, King of Kent, was burned down in 1087 and its Norman successor was partly destroyed by fire in 1136 but immediately restored. In the 13C the steeple was rebuilt and the choir extended eastwards. This was the noble church of *Old St. Paul's*, in which John Wycliffe was tried for heresy in 1377, and Tyndale's New Testament publicly burned in 1527. It was the longest cathedral in England (600ft). The central tower was surmounted by a steeple, which, at the lowest estimate, was 460ft high, but was destroyed by lightning in 1561 and never re-erected. For a long period the church was sadly neglected, but restorations were begun under Charles I. Inigo Jones added a classical portico to the W front, one of his objects being to divert from the church the secular rabble that for over a century had used the middle aisle of the nave ('Paul's Walk') as a place of business and intrigue. In 1666 the cathedral was practically burned down in the Great Fire. Sir Christopher Wren planned an entirely new cathedral; building was begun in 1675; the first service was held in the choir in 1697; and the last stone was placed in position in 1710. (A model of Old St. Paul's and Wren's model are in the Crypt.) Between 1666 and 1723 the amount spent on the cathedral was about £748,000, most of which was raised by a tax on sea-borne coal entering London. Wren's original ground plan, designed in the form of a Greek cross, was modified at the demand of the Court party, some of whom may have looked forward to the restoration of the old religion, for the ceremonies of which a long nave and side-chapels were required. In 1941 the E end and the N transept received direct hits from high-explosive bombs; another, which did not explode, was dug out with great heroism from beneath the E end; and the building, throughout the war, was guarded from fire by the coolness and efficiency of its Night Watch.

MEASUREMENTS. The exterior length of the cathedral is 515ft; its W front, with two towers each 212.5ft high, is 180ft wide. Internally it is 479ft long and 227.5ft wide across the transepts. The nave, 125ft across (including the aisle), is 92.5 ft high. The dome is 122ft in diameter, and the total height from the pavement of the church to the top of the cross above the ball is 365ft. The area of St. Paul's is 87,400 sq. ft; that of St. Peter's in Rome 163,181 sq. ft.

The **Exterior** of St. Paul's consists throughout of two orders, the lower Corinthian, the upper Composite. On the N and S sides the upper order is merely a curtain-wall, not corresponding with the height of the aisles and concealing the flying buttresses that support the clerestory of the nave. The balustrade along the top was added against the wishes of Wren, who cynically remarked of it that 'ladies think nothing well without an edging'. The *West Front*, approached by a broad flight of steps, and flanked by towers, has a lower colonnade of twelve columns and an upper one of eight columns. In the NW tower is a peal of bells, and in the SW tower are the clock and 'Great Paul', a bell weighing nearly 17 tons (hung in 1882), which is rung daily for 5 minutes at 13.00. In the pediment of the *South Front* is a Phoenix, typifying the rise of new St. Paul's from the ashes of the old, and recalling also the incident when Wren sought a stone from the ruins to mark the centre of the new dome-space a fragment of an old tombstone was brought to him bearing the word 'Resurgam' ('I shall rise again'). The sculpture in the West Pediment and Portico and the statues above the North Pediment are by Francis Bird.—The famous *Dome* lifts its Cross 365ft above the City below. The outer dome is of wood covered with lead, and does not bear the weight of the elegant lantern on the top, which rests upon a cone of brick rising between an inner brick dome and the outer dome. The Ball and Cross date from 1721.

The **Interior**, though 'classical' in detail, has the general ground plan of a Gothic church: nave and aisles with triforium and clerestory, transepts, and choir, with, however, the great dome-space at the crossing. Against the massive piers rise Corinthian pilasters, and stone enrichments relieve the wall-spaces. Wren no doubt contemplated the use of colour in the decoration, but, though Thornhill's paintings in the dome were finished in 1720, nothing more was done until the dome and choir mosaics were added in 1863-97.

The visitor on entering St. Paul's should first walk up the centre of the NAVE to the great space beneath the dome, where the huge proportions of the church are especially impressive. The candelabra at the W end are by Henry Pegram. On the last piers are paintings by G.F. Watts; 'Time, Death, and Judgment' on the N, 'Peace and Goodwill' on the S.

The DOME, the inner cupola of which is 218ft above our heads, rests upon twelve massive supports, of which the four chief ones, at the angles, afford room in their interiors for the vestries and the library staircase. In the spandrels of the dome are mosaics executed by Salviati of Venice. Those on the W, designed by Alfred Stevens and partly executed by W.E.F. Britten, represent (from S to N) Isaiah, Jeremiah, Ezekiel, and Daniel; the others represent SS. Matthew and John (by G.F. Watts) and SS. Mark and Luke (by Britten). In the quarter-domes, at a lower level, are more recent mosaics by Sir W.B. Richmond (d 1921).—Above the arches is the Whispering Gallery, above which again are recesses with marble statues of the Fathers of the Church. The cupola, above, was decorated by Sir James Thornhill with eight scenes in monochrome from the life of St. Paul.

To inspect the monuments in the church, eloquent of the nation's history, return to the W end, and start the tour at the North-West door, leading to the NORTH NAVE AISLE. On the left is *All Souls' Chapel*, dedicated in 1925 to the memory of Field Marshal Earl Kitchener of Khartoum (d 1916) with a recumbent figure by Reid Dick and a roll of honour of the Royal Engineers. Next is the *Chapel of St. Dunstan*. The memorial under the first window is to Lord Leighton (d 1896), painter and sculptor. The great monument to the Duke of Wellington (1796–1853) is by Alfred Stevens. Above the pediments at either end are groups representing Truth plucking out the tongue of Falsehood, and Valour thrusting down Cowardice. The equestrian statue on the top was executed by Tweed in 1912 from a sketch-model by Stevens. On the opposite side is the monument to General Gordon; further down on the left is the memorial to Lord Melbourne (d 1848) with Two Angels at the Gate of Death by Marochetti. A bust by Tweed of Lord Roberts (1833–1914) is on the wall.

NORTH TRANSEPT. This transept was severely damaged by a heavy bomb in April 1941, when the transept dome and the whole of the North Porch, with the famous inscription from Wren's tomb: 'Si monumentum requiris, circumspice' ('If you would see his monument, look around you'), fell into the crypt below. Here are commemorated *Sir Arthur Sullivan* (1842-1900), the composer, *Lord Rodney* (1718-92), and *Sir Joshua Reynolds* (1723-92), the last by Flaxman. The W aisle of this transept is now the *Baptistery*. Before the entrance to the NORTH CHOIR AISLE (note the Jean Tijou gates c 1712) is the statue of Samuel Johnson (d 1784), in a Roman toga, by Bacon. The choir-screen, formed of the original altar rails, is also by Tijou. On the left is a carved wooden pulpit (1964), designed by

Lord Mottistone. The Chapel of the Modern Martyrs is at the E end of the aisle, commemorating Anglican martyrs since 1850.

The *American Chapel*, which occupies the apse of the cathedral, is the memorial to America's fallen in the Second World War, with a roll of honour containing 28,000 names of those who fell in operations based on Britain.

At the end of the S choir aisle, with fine iron gates by Jean Tijou the monument of *Dean Milman* (1791-1868), is on the left past the figure (clad in a shroud) of *Dr John Donne* (1573-1631), poet and Dean of St. Paul's. This is the only comparatively uninjured monument that survived the destruction of Old St. Paul's, and it still shows traces of fire.

SOUTH TRANSEPT: on the E wall, *Lord Hower* (1726-99), by Flaxman. On the left, farther on, *Sir Henry Lawrence* (1806-57). Opposite is the entrance to the Crypt, beyond which, at the angle of the dome-space, is a statue of *John Howard* (1726-90), the prison reformer, the first monument admitted to new St. Paul's.

On the S wall of the E transept aisle, *J.M.W. Turner* (1775-1851), the painter, and *Lord Collingwood* (1750-1810), Nelson's successor.

In the W AISLE are monuments to *Sir Ralph Abercromby* (1734-1801) and to *Sir John Moore* (1761-1809), who died at Corunna. To the left, above, is a memorial by Princess Louise to the *Colonial Troops* who fell in the South African War. On the W wall of the transept, *Monument of *Lord Nelson* (1758-1805), by Flaxman; the reliefs on the pedestal represent the Arctic Ocean, the North Sea, the Nile, and the Mediterranean.

SOUTH NAVE AISLE: on the right in the S aisle hangs 'The Light of the World', a painting by Holman Hunt. At the E end of the aisle is the ticket-office for the upper part of the church. The chapel at the W end has been since 1906 the *Chapel of the Most Distinguished Order of St. Michael and St. George*, with the banners of the Knights Grand Cross (CGMG). The order (instituted in 1818) is conferred for distinguished services in colonial or foreign affairs. The prelate's throne is a memorial of Lord Forrest (d 1918) of Bunbury, Western Australia, the first Australian peer.

On the left is the door to the Geometrical Staircase—a spiral of 92 stone steps and an iron balustrade by Tijou.

Return through the centre of the nave to the choir.

Enter the CHOIR proper. Above the High Altar is a carved and gilded baldacchino of marble and oak, by Godfrey Allen and S.E. Dykes Bower, replacing the reredos damaged in 1941 and serving as a memorial to the Commonwealth people of all creeds and races who lost their lives in the two World Wars. The tall bronze *Candlesticks* in front are copied from four now in St. Bavon's, in Ghent, which were made by Benedetto da Rovezzano for the tomb of Henry VIII at Windsor, but were sold under the Commonwealth.—The beautiful carved *Choir Stalls* and the *Organ Case* are by Grinling Gibbons. The organ was originally built in 1695 by Father Smith to John Blow's direction, and Jeremiah Clarke played for its inauguration. Although a bomb struck the E end of the choir, bringing down tons of masonry on to the Sanctuary, the priceless carvings escaped almost undamaged.

The *Mosaics* with which the vaulting of the choir is decorated were designed by Sir W.B. Richmond and were executed in 1891-1912. The stained glass windows are by the same artist. In the central panel of the great apse is Christ in majesty, seated upon the rainbow. In the shallow cupolas above the choir proper are (from W to E) the Creation of the Beasts, of the Birds, and of the Fishes.

The *CRYPT (entrance in the S transept) corresponds in size with the upper church. Here are the graves of many of those whose monuments we have already seen, as well as many additional monuments and graves. In the crypt below the S choir-aisle, at the foot of the staircase is (right) a bust of *Sir John Macdonald* (1815-91), premier of Canada. In the second bay (right) monuments to *Sir Edwin Landseer* (1802-73) and *Reginald Heber* (1783-1826), by Chantrey. In the pavement is the tomb of *Sir Lawrence Alma-Tadema* (1836-1912). In the next bay is the tombstone of *Sir Christopher Wren* (1632-1723), above which is the original tablet with its famous epitaph (see above). This bay, and the one to the N, are known as 'Painters' Corner', for here rest *Lord Leighton* (1830-96), *Benjamin West* (1738-1820), *Sir Thomas Lawrence* (1769-1830), *Landseer* (1802-73), *Millais* (1829-96), *Turner* (1775-1851), *Reynolds* (1723-92), *Opie* (1761-1807), and *Holman Hunt* (1827-1910), while on the walls are memorials to *Randolph Caldecott* (1846-86), *William Blake* (1757-1827), *Van Dyck* (1599-1641), *Constable* (1776-1837), *Wilson Steer* (1860-1942), *Lutyens* (1869-1944), and *Muirhead Bone* (1876-1953). *J.S. Sargent* (1856-1925), buried elsewhere, is commemorated by a relief-group of the Redemption, designed by himself.—The Chapel at the E end of the crypt, formerly called *St. Faith's*, was dedicated in 1960 as the Chapel of the Order of the British Empire. Farther W a wall-tablet marks the grave of *Sir Alexander Fleming* (1881-1955), discoverer of penicillin.

In the W portion of the crypt is Wellington's colossal porphyry sarcophagus and further on a memorial to *Florence Nightingale* (1820-1910). Below the centre of the dome *Lord Nelson* rests in a coffin made from the mainmast of the French ship 'L'Orient', enclosed in a sarcophagus of black and white marble originally designed for Cardinal Wolsey. In recesses to the S, *Lord Beatty* (1871-1936), *Lord Jellicoe* (1859-1935), *Lord Keyes* (1872-1945) and his son, *Lt-Col Keyes, VC* (1917-41), and *Lord Napier of Magdala* (1810-90). To the N, *Lord Wolseley* (1833-1913), *Lord Roberts* (1832-1914), and a bust of *Lawrence of Arabia* (1888-1935). A plaque commemorates 5746 men of the garrison of Kut (Iraq) who died in 1916. In the adjoining recess: *R.J. Seddon* (1845-1906) and *W.M. Hughes* (1864-1952), prime ministers of New Zealand; *Sir Stafford Cripps* (1889-1952; fine bust by Epstein). Opposite: bust of *George Washington* near a tablet to P/O William Fiske, RAF, who lost his life in the Battle of Britain, 'an American citizen who died that England might live'. Here too are memorials to *George Cruikshank* (1792-1878), the caricaturist and *W.E. Henley* (1849-1903; *Bust by Rodin), the poet and critic. In the nave: *Wilson Carlile* (1847-1942), founder of the Church Army; *R.H. Barham* (1788-1845), of the 'Ingoldsby Legends'; *Sir W. Besant* (1836-1901) and *Charles Reade* (1814-84), the novelists; and *Sir Alfred Duff Cooper* (1890-1954), the statesman.

Further W (1st bay N side) are memorials to the brothers *Sir Charles* (1782-1853) and *Sir William Napier* (1784-1860). By contrast, the next bay contains five mutilated monuments from Old St. Paul's. Next a monument to the historian *Henry Hallam* (1777-1859); opposite is one to *Lord St. Vincent* (1735-1823).

The TREASURY in the N side of the Crypt is a small museum

opened in 1981 as part of the Diocesan Treasuries Scheme of the Goldsmiths' Company. The first section shows ecclesiastical vestments, altar frontals and plate belonging to St. Paul's. In the second section ranged round St. Paul's Jubilee cope, stole and mitre designed by Beryl Dean (1977), silver on loan from the parishes of the diocese.

There is an audio visual display on the history of St. Paul's in the Crypt and near it is Wren's model of St. Paul's. The model of Old St. Paul's is on display outside the Treasury.

The **Upper Parts** of the cathedral are reached by a staircase from the S aisle (adm. see p 216). An easy ascent of 143 steps leads to the *South Triforium Gallery.*

Continue the ascent to the WHISPERING GALLERY, 112ft in diameter, within the lower dome, where words whispered near the wall on one side can be distinctly heard at the other side. This gallery is the best point from which to see Thornhill's paintings on the dome.—The STONE GALLERY, the exterior gallery round the base of the dome, commands a fine *View of London, which is still more extensive from the *Golden Gallery*, at the base of the lantern above the dome. The total ascent to the Golden Gallery involves 627 steps.

The churchyard (now a public garden) surrounding the cathedral is enclosed by massive railings. In the NE angle are the foundations of *Paul's Cross*, an open-air pulpit where sermons were regularly preached. On the S side of the church are a few fragments of the cloisters and chapter house, destroyed in 1666.

The street skirting the S side of the cathedral is likewise called *St. Paul's Churchyard*. In Dean's Court, leading S, is the *Deanery*, built by Wren c 1670; adjoining it, in Carter Lane, is the *Choir House*, with the old Choristers' School (see below; now a Youth Hostel). A tablet in Carter Lane, a few paces to the E, records Shakespeare's connection with the Bell Tavern which stood here. Further E, beyond the *City Information Centre*, extends *Old Change Court*, now flanked by modern offices. The stepped *St. Peter's Hill* reveals a view of the Thames across Queen Victoria St.

Across Cannon St the pleasant *St. Paul's Garden* is adorned with a fountain, and a statue by Georg Ehrlich. To the N the tower (and restored spire) of *St. Augustine's* has been incorporated in the new *Cathedral Choir School*, designed in 1962 by Leo de Syllas and built after his death, with four linked buildings. The church was rebuilt by Wren in 1683 and destroyed in 1941.

The area to the N of the cathedral was devastated by fire in 1940; only the *Chapter House* by Wren (re-opened in 1957) survived. New buildings with clean lines, effectively grouped but lacking individual distinction, now tower above the chapter house to form *Cathedral Place* and *Paternoster Square*. The raised piazzas (underground car park) with shops, restaurants, and pubs, afford good views of St. Paul's. The ecclesiastical character of the district survives only in some street and place-names. Panyer Alley, so named from having formerly been largely occupied by basket-makers, has been replaced by *Panyer Alley Steps* which lead down to Newgate St (N; comp. p 225). The old relief (1688) of a boy seated on a 'panier', marking the highest ground in the City, has been placed on the steps.

20 Holborn, Smithfield and Clerkenwell

Access: Holborn, Underground, Chancery Lane; Smithfield, Underground,
Farringdon; Clerkenwell, Buses 19 and 38 from Piccadilly Circus.

Holborn (Pl. 8; 5), beginning at the S end of Gray's Inn Road,
continues the line of Oxford St and High Holborn to the City. The W
limits of the City (Holborn Bars) are indicated by stone obelisks near
Chancery Lane Underground Station and opposite Staple Inn. In the
roadway stands the *War Memorial of the Royal Fusiliers* (City of
London Regiment), by Albert Toft. Holborn derives its name from the
fact that the Fleet River flowed through the valley here and was
known as the 'Hole-Bourne', or stream in the hollow.

On the right, opposite Gray's Inn Road, is ***Staple Inn**, the
picturesque gabled and timbered facade of which, dating from 1586
(last restored in 1950), is a unique survival of its kind in a London
street. The inn, which seems to have been a hostel of the wool-staplers
in the 14C, was an Inn of Chancery from the reign of Henry V until
1884. It consisted of two little quadrangles, with houses dating mainly
from the 18C, but was severely damaged in 1944, when the fine 16C
hall was demolished. This has now been rebuilt (with much of the
old material) and is occupied by the *Institute of Actuaries* and the
courtyard can be entered. Dr Johnson lived for a time in a house here
in 1759-60, and here he is said to have written 'Rasselas' in the
evenings of a single week, to pay for his mother's funeral. The second
court now contains a pleasant garden.

In Brooke St, on the left, Thomas Chatterton (1752-70) poisoned
himself at No. 39. Just beyond Brooke St rises the *Prudential
Assurance Co.*, a huge Gothic edifice of red brick (by A. Waterhouse;
1879-1906, altered in 1932). It occupies the site of *Furnival's Inn*, in
which Charles Dickens was lodging when he wrote the first part of
the 'Pickwick Papers' (memorial tablet and bust in the court). A
passage down its E flank leads to Leather Lane market.

Leather Lane market operates Monday to Saturday and is mainly a lunchtime
market geared to office and shopworkers. The name has nothing to do with
leather but probably comes from the 14C 'Lyverlane'. It is best for glassware,
plants, some clothes, fruit and vegetables. There is usually a stall selling genuine
chamois leather.

On the other (S) side of Holborn, near the corner of Fetter Lane, is
the entrance to *Barnard's Inn*. The old *Hall (late 14C), the oldest
surviving secular building in the City, has 16C panelling and good
heraldic glass. It is now School Dinners Restaurant (Tel. 01-405 5233,
to view the building).

In 1894-1959 the inn, mainly rebuilt, was occupied by the *Mercer's School*. The
school founded about 1450, had Dean Colet and Sir Thomas Gresham among
its pupils. The device of the Mercers' Company still survives above the gateway.

Beyond Fetter Lane, where the corner bank's elegant cupola
emphasises the brash, obtrusive mass of the 'Daily Mirror' building
(1958-61), Holborn reaches *Holborn Circus*. In the middle is an
equestrian statue of *Prince Albert*.

Hatton Garden, to the NW, now occupied largely by diamond merchants, takes
its name from the garden belonging to the house of Sir Christopher Hatton,

Lord Chancellor to Queen Elizabeth. A tablet with a bas-relief portrait and a device of clasped hands commemorates the residence at No. 5 of Giuseppe Mazzini, who while living in this house inspired Young Italy to struggle for freedom.

At the beginning of Charterhouse St (left) opens *Ely Place* (1772), occupying the site of the town house of the bishops of Ely, where John of Gaunt died in 1399. The garden was famous, and is mentioned in 'Richard III' (iii, 4). When forced to cede these grounds to Sir Christopher Hatton (at the picturesque yearly 'rent' of a red rose, ten loads of hay, and ten pounds), the Bishop reserved in perpetuity the right to walk in the gardens and to gather yearly twenty bushels of roses. Ye Olde Mitre Tavern in Ely Court (the quaint passageway on the left) was built in the 18C on the site of a 16C tavern. The sign probably comes from the bishop's gatehouse. Medieval tiles were exposed during roadworks in 1985. Ely Place is guarded at night by a watchman of its own. It is officially part of Cambridgeshire and the police cannot automatically enter.

The only relic of the bishop's house is the beautiful little *Ely Chapel* (*St. Etheldreda's*), a gem of 13C Gothic (1290), with an old chestnut roof. The tracery of the E and W windows and the arcaded statue-niches are superb. The notable glass and statues of English martyrs are by Charles and May Blakeman (1952-64), who also adorned the vaulted *Crypt* (1252) which stands on Roman foundations. In the entrance is a fine carved escutcheon from the time of Charles I which, until 1874, hung over the communion table. St. Etheldreda's was the first pre-Reformation church in the country to return to the Roman Catholics (purchased 1874). It is always open.

In *Saffron Hill*, parallel to the E, was Fagin's Thieves' Kitchen in 'Oliver Twist', while the name of Bleeding Heart Yard, off Greville St (left) is familiar to readers of 'Little Dorrit'.

To the right, just beyond Holborn Circus, is the church of *St. Andrew*, built by Wren in 1684-87, ruined in 1940-41, and restored in 1960-61. The interior of the medieval tower, dating from 1446 and unaltered by Wren, survives. The church is closed at week-ends.

The tomb of Captain Thomas Coram was designed by Lord Mottistone (1962); the organ was originally presented by Handel to the Foundling Hospital (p 181). In this church William Hazlitt was married to Sarah Stoddart in 1808 (Mary Lamb being bridesmaid and Charles Lamb the best man). In 1817 Benjamin Disraeli (at the age of 12) was here received into the Christian Church.

Beyond St. Andrew's is the *City Temple* (Congregational), opened in 1874, under Dr Joseph Parker, for a congregation founded in 1640. Burnt out in 1941, it was rebuilt (apart from the facade) by Seely and Paget in 1956-58. *Atlantic House* (1951), opposite, is the headquarters of *H.M. Stationery Office* and the *Central Office of Information*.

Holborn Viaduct is 1400ft long and 80ft wide, constructed at the cost of over 4000 dwellings in 1867-69, by William Haywood to carry the thoroughfare over the depression of the 'Hole-Bourne'. Beyond the bridge is *Holborn Viaduct Station*.

At the end of Holborn Viaduct, to the left, at the corner of Giltspur St (leading to Smithfield) is the church of **St. Sepulchre**, the history of which goes back to the days of the Crusaders (12C), though it was rebuilt in the 15C, altered within by Wren in 1670-77, over-restored in the 19C, and more carefully repaired in 1950. Down to 1890 the bells of St. Sepulchre were tolled on the occasion of an execution at Newgate, and before 1774 it was the custom to present a nosegay here to each condemned criminal on his way to Tyburn.

In the *Musicians' Chapel* in the N aisle windows commemorate Sir Henry Wood (d. 1943) who, at the age of 12, deputised for the organist here, Dame Nellie Melba (d. 1931), and Dr John Ireland (d. 1962). The organ (1670) is by Renatus Harris. A musical service is held on St. Cecilia's Day (22 November; admission by ticket). In the same chapel an Easter sepulchre is thought to mark the tomb of Roger Ascham (1515-68), tutor to Queen Elizabeth I. Captain John Smith (1580-1631), 'sometime Governor of Virgina and Admiral of New England' is buried in the S aisle. On a pillar near by is displayed a handbell which it was the duty of the bellman of St. Sepulchre's to ring outside the condemned cell at Newgate at midnight preceding an execution, at the same time reciting the inscribed verses. The S aisle and chapel and the garden serve as a memorial to the Royal Fusiliers.

Adjoining in Giltspur St is the rebuilt *Watch House* (1791; 1962), with a bust (1935) of Charles Lamb moved from near the site of Christ's Hospital School in Newgate St (see below), where Lamb was educated.

Opposite St. Sepulchre's, at the corner of the *Old Bailey*, rises the curved facade of the **Central Criminal Court** (1905). This occupies the site of Newgate Prison, some of the stones of which have been used in the rustic work of the lowest storey.

The *Central Criminal Court*, or *Old Bailey Court*, is the chief criminal court for Greater London, and parts of Surrey, Kent, and Essex. An extension (by McMorran and Whitby), with an impressive exterior in Old Bailey, was opened in 1970. This stood up well to a terrorist bomb in 1973. The public are admitted to trials (no children under 14): the 12 courts in the new building are entered from Old Bailey, and the 6 courts in the old building from Newgate St.

Visitors may see part of the medieval wall in *Warwick Slip* which connects Old Bailey and Warwick Lane (parallel to the E). Milton's writings justifying the execution of Charles I were burned by the common hangman in the Old Bailey in 1660.

Newgate Prison, long the the chief prison of London, was begun in 1770 and completed in 1782, after having been partly destroyed by the Gordon Rioters in 1780. It was finally demolished in 1902. Public executions, previously carried out at Tyburn, took place in front of Newgate from 1783 to 1868, and then within the prison down to 1901. Among the prisoners confined here were Anne Askew, Daniel Defoe, Jack Sheppard, Jonathan Wild, Titus Oates, William Penn, and Lord George Gordon (who died of gaol fever in 1793). Mrs Elizabeth Fry's successful efforts to improve the conditions of prison life in Newgate (1817) laid the foundation of prison reform throughout Europe.

From St. Sephulchre's church at the E end of Holborn Viaduct, Giltspur Street runs N to Smithfield, dominated by the *Smithfield Meat Market*. Plans are mooted from time to time by the City of London who operate the market that it may be moved to a less central location. In the meantime empty warehouses and other industrial buildings in the area are being restored for office use. There are some new restaurants and winebars amongst the pubs which have early morning opening hours to serve the meat market. *The Fox and Anchor*, 115 Charterhouse Street, has an Art Nouveau facade; it serves full breakfast (open 06.00-15.00). The *Smithfield Tavern*, 105 Charterhouse Street is open 06.30-09.00 and at lunchtime. NB: only market workers can buy alcohol outside normal licensing hours.

A small gilt figure of a naked boy on the corner-house of *Cock Lane*, on the left, marks *Pye Corner*, where the Great Fire of 1666, which started at Pudding Lane, near the Monument, is generally but erroneously said to have stopped.

Smithfield (Pl. 8; 3), more particularly known as West Smithfield to distinguish it from the less important East Smithfield near Tower Hill, is a place of great historic interest. Originally a spacious 'smoothfield' or grassy expanse just outside the City walls, it was the scene of various famous tournaments, and from 1150 to 1855 it was the chief horse and cattle market of London. From an early period until the reign of Henry IV it was a usual place of execution, and here Sir William Wallace, the Scottish patriot, suffered in 1305. In 1381 the rebel Wat Tyler was slain here by Sir William Walworth, the Mayor, in the presence of Richard II. Under the Tudors many persons were burned at Smithfield for their religious convictions. Anne Askew perished here in 1546. Memorials on the exterior wall of St. Bartholomew's Hospital commemorate Wallace and the Protestant martyrs of the reign of Mary I. From 1133 till 1840 Smithfield was the scene of Bartholomew Fair, held every year for several days about the Feast of St. Bartholomew (24 August), and the Royal Smithfield Show (now held at Earl's Court) had its origins at Wooton's Livery Stables here in 1799.

On the SE side of Smithfield is **St. Bartholomew's Hospital**, which, together with a priory for Augustinian canons, was founded in 1123 by Rahere, a favourite courtier of Henry I, in fulfilment of a vow made by him when lying sick at Rome. It is the oldest charitable institution in London that retains its original site. Whittington, the famous mayor, bequeathed money for its repair in 1423. At the Dissolution the hospital was spared by Henry VIII, who is regarded as its second founder. The fine gateway (1702) is by Edward Strong the Younger. The buildings in the great quadrangle were built by James Gibbs in 1730-70. Inside the gates to the left is the small octagonal church of *St. Bartholomew the Less*, rebuilt (except for the striking 15C tower) in 1823-25 and well restored in 1950. Inigo Jones (1573-1652) was baptised here. The Stairway and Hall—entrance from the Quadrangle—are open Mon to Fri 09.00-17.00.

Harvey, who discovered the circulation of the blood, was chief physician of the hospital in 1609-43; Abernethy, the famous surgeon, was a lecturer from 1791 to 1827 at its famous medical school ('Bart's').

By far the most interesting building at Smithfield is the church of **'St. Bartholomew the Great**, which belonged to the priory founded in 1123 by Rahere, and is, next to the chapel in the White Tower, the oldest church in London. It is approached from the E corner of Smithfield (to the N of the hospital), through a small gateway, once the W entrance to the S nave-aisle. Above the gateway is a house, with an Elizabethan half-timbered facade, brought to light by a Zeppelin bomb explosion in 1915 through the loosening of the tiles that long concealed it. The site of the nave, which was completed in the 13C, is now occupied by the churchyard. Enter the church by a modern porch beneath a brick tower built in 1628 to take the place of the tower over the crossing. The five bells date from 1510. The church, noted for its music, is open from 09.00-16.30; Sun services at 09.00, 11.00, and 18.30.

At the Dissolution the conventual buildings and much of the church were pulled down or alienated, and of the original priory-church there stands only the choir, built by Rahere, with the crossing and one bay of the nave, added before 1170 by his successor. The restoration of the church, begun in 1863, was resumed in 1886, with Sir Aston Webb as architect.

On Good Friday, in accordance with a custom dating from 1686, twenty-one poor widows each receive an old 'sixpence', which is laid on a flat cross tombstone in the churchyard. The sixpence is now supplemented by a hot cross bun and a share in the proceeds of the collection, mainly for children.

*St. Bartholomew the Great, founded as priory in 1123; the
tower dates to 1628*

The INTERIOR of the church, the choir of Rahere's priory-church, is most
impressive, with its heavy columns, piers, and round arches in the pure Norman
style. The clerestory was rebuilt early in the 15C, and the Norman triforium is
interrupted on the S side by *Prior Bolton's Window*, a beautiful oriel (once
communicating with the prior's house) added by Prior Bolton (1506-32), whose
rebus, a bolt and a tun, it bears. The apsidal ending of the choir, with its stilted
arches, was built in 1886 by Sir Aston Webb in place of the previous square
ending, which is supposed itself to have been an innovation of the 15C. On the
N side of the sanctuary is the *Tomb of Rahere* (d 1143), with a coloured effigy,
beneath a rich canopy (c 1400; perhaps by Yevele).—In the *South Transept*
stands the 15C font at which Hogarth was baptised in 1697. In the *South
Ambulatory* is the alabaster tomb of Sir Walter Mildmay (d. 1589), founder of
Emmanuel College, Cambridge. The *Lady Chapel*, rebuilt in 1896 and retaining
little of the original fabric of the 14C, is separated from the E end of the choir
by a beautiful modern iron screen. It was at one time used as a printing office,
and then as a fringe factory; it now serves as the chapel of the Imperial Society
of Knights Bachelor. The *North Transept* was at one time occupied by a
blacksmith's forge. The stone screen at its W end dates from the beginning of
the 15C. The screen beneath the organ has painted panels (1932) illustrating
the life of Rahere.

A Norman doorway, with the original 15C oaken doors, at the W end of the
South Ambulatory, admits to the E walk of the old *Cloister*, built c 1405 and
reconstructed in 1905-28. The arches in the wall mark the entrance to the
former chapter-house. A few ancient fragments and relics are exhibited here.

To the S of the church is *Bartholomew Close*, in which Milton sought
hiding after the Restoration in 1660. Hogarth was born here in 1697,
and here Benjamin Franklin lived while working in the printing office
in the Lady Chapel. Washington Irving also lodged here. At Nos

87-88 is *Butchers' Hall* (1959). *Cloth Fair*, skirting the N side of the church, marks the site once occupied by the booths of drapers and clothiers at Bartholomew Fair. At Nos 41 and 42 Jacobean houses (1614) here have been well preserved and restored.

The N side of the square is filled with the elaborate building of the *Central Meat Market* (built in 1867 by Sir Horace Jones); the *Poultry Market* (1963) with a vast barrel vault, lies to the W. The largest dead meat, poultry and provision market in the world, it covers 10 acres, and has a 'shop frontage' of nearly two miles. Enormous, refrigerated lorries arrive from 20.00 to unload the carcases which are then prepared by 'cutters' ready for selling at 05.00. The scene remains animated until midday when the wholesale market closes.

Charterhouse Street, skirting the N side of the market, leads E to the quiet *Charterhouse Square*. Here is the 16-18C gatehouse of the *'Charterhouse*, founded in the 14C as a monastery, but since 1611 a hostel for poor gentlemen. The buildings, dating mainly from the 16C, were badly damaged in 1941. Their restoration is now complete, much intrusive 19C work having been removed in the process. Visitors are admitted on application to the Master, usually at 14.45 on Wed in April to July. Admission charge.

In 1371 the Carthusian priory of the Salutation of the Mother of God was founded here by Sir Walter de Manny, a distinguished soldier under Edward III, on a burial-ground where 50,000 victims of the Black Death had been interred. This was the fourth English house of the Carthusians; the name Charterhouse is a corruption of the French name Chartreuse. Sir Edward North, afterwards Lord North, to whom the property was granted in 1545, built a mansion on the site of the Little Cloister. This passed later to the Duke of Northumberland who was executed in 1553 for his attempt to put Lady Jane Grey (his daughter-in-law) on the throne. The property was considerably altered by a later owner, the fourth Duke of Norfolk who was executed for complicity in a plot to put Mary, Queen of Scots, on the throne. Elizabeth I paid four visits to the mansion (then known as Howard House). James I was entertained here prior to his coronation in 1603 by Thomas Howard, later Earl of Suffolk, to whom the property had passed in 1601. In 1611 the Charterhouse was bought for £13,000 by Thomas Sutton, a shrewd Elizabethan soldier, probably also a merchant-adventurer, who here founded the 'Hospital of King James in Charterhouse', including a hospital for 80 poor brethren and a free school for 40 poor boys.

Owing to a decline in the revenues, the normal number of brethren is now 40. Pensioners must be bachelors or widowers, members of the Church of England, and over sixty years of age; and they must have been officers in the Army or Navy, clergymen, doctors, lawyers, artists, or professional men. They occupy chambers in Master's Court and Wash-House Court. The *British Records Association* also has offices here.

The *Charterhouse School* rapidly developed into one of the chief public schools of England, and in 1872 it was transferred to Godalming in Surrey. Thackeray, a former pupil, in 'The Newcomes' describes the Charterhouse under the name of 'Greyfriars'; Col. Newcome is represented as both an ex-pupil of the school and a poor brother, a coincidence that has almost never occurred in fact.—From 1875 to 1933 the site of the school, mainly around the Great Cloister, was occupied by the *Merchant Taylors' School*, founded in 1561 in Suffolk Lane, Upper Thames Street, where Spenser, Lancelot Andrewes, Clive, and Gilbert Murray were pupils. This school is now at Moor Park (see 'Blue Guide England'), and the buildings here, with large new extensions, are occupied by St. Bartholomew's medical school.

The *Chapel* was perhaps originally the chapter house of the monastery, and portions of the S and E walls belong to the 14C structure. The ante-chapel was built in 1512. The N arcade, the N aisle, the pulpit, communion table, and seats in the middle of the church date from about 1614. The elaborate tomb of Thomas

Sutton (d. 1611), with a recumbent effigy, was designed by Nicholas Stone and Bernard Jansen. Above rises a low tower containing a vaulted chamber (perhaps the monks' treasury). This is provided with a round squint affording a view of the high altar of the original church (to the S), which was demolished by Lord North to build his hall, and the site of the tomb of the founder, Sir Walter de Manny (d. 1372), was located in 1947, in front of this now vanished altar. The *Chapel Cloisters* (1613) contain memorials to famous 'Carthusians', including John Wesley. On the N side of the *Master's Court* are the *Great Hall*, and (on the first floor) the *Great Chamber*, both of the 16C, with 17C alterations, restored to something very near their original splendour by Lord Mottistone and Paul Paget (1956). To the W is the *Wash-House Court*, the best preserved part of the monastic buildings as rebuilt in the 16C, and to the N are two courts of 1826-39. The *Great Cloister*, with traces of the monks' cells, lay to the E.

From Charterhouse Street opposite the Central Meat Market, St. John Street runs N to the Angel at Islington, through **Clerkenwell**. Clerkenwell's history is based on the well, Clerk's Well, which supplied Charterhouse. The connection with water continued when Hugh Myddleton established the New River Head water supply just above Clerkenwell (see p 394) in 1613. During the 17C newcomers including French Huguenots settled here (they were not allowed in the City of London) and laid Clerkenwell's reputation as a centre of clock-makers, jewellers and opticians. The area enjoyed a period of prosperity with several fine houses built for merchants but decline followed in the 19C as slum-housing took over and in the 20C when the area was deserted by residents. It became a centre of radicalism during the 19C and Clerkenwell Green became a political meeting place and scene of Chartist marches.

The London Borough of Islington, of which Clerkenwell is now part, is engaged in a programme of revitalising the area by encouraging crafts workshops and other developments. A Heritage Centre has been established at 33 St. John's Square (01-250 1039) and there are guided tours of the area.

To the left diverges St. John's Lane, spanned by **St. John's Gate** (erected in 1504), the S gate of the once famous and wealthy priory of the Knights Hospitallers of the Order of St. John of Jerusalem, which was founded about 1130 and was suppressed by Elizabeth I.

The priory was later the residence of Edmund Tilney (d. 1610), Master of the Revels, who licensed thirty of Shakespeare's plays. In 1731-81 the gatehouse was the printing office of the 'Gentleman's Magazine', conducted by Edward Cave, to which Dr Johnson used to contribute. The premises are now occupied as the Grand Priory in the British Realm of the *Venerable Order of the Hospital of St. John of Jerusalem*, revived in 1831, which devotes itself to ambulance and hospital work. An entirely voluntary organisation 'in the service of mankind', it is supported by public donation.

The *Museum of the Order of St. John*, St. John's Lane, Clerkenwell, London EC1. Tel. 01-253 6644. Open Tues, Fri, Sat 10.00-18.00. Conducted tours of the Grand Priory Church and St. John's Gate at 11.00 and 14.30 on those days. Reference Library open by appointment. Access: Underground, Farringdon.

The collection, arranged in glass cases, relates mainly to the Order of St. John and includes the Rhodes Missal of 1504, an Annunciation by Luigi Gentile (?1648), a small oil on copper, arms and armour used by the knights, crosses displayed on the fronts of houses belonging to the Order, and some examples of the crafts and light industries of the area of Clerkenwell including clockmaking, brewery, printing and toolmaking.

In St. John's Square, across Clerkenwell Road, lies the **Priory Church of St. John** built about 1720 and incorporating the choir-walls of the ancient priory church, probably destroyed c 1381 when Wat Tyler burned the priory. The area of the original circular nave is indicated by a line in the road. In 1930 this again became the priory church of the order, and it has been sympathetically restored after its destruction in 1941. The altarpiece consists of two wings of a Flemish triptych (15C) probably removed at the Dissolution and recovered in 1932. Lion-head handles on the church doors were found in the ruins of the Muristan, the site of the original hospice of the order in Jerusalem. Below is an interesting and well-preserved *Crypt, the three W bays of which date from about 1140; the two E bays and the side-chapels were added about 1185. Monuments here include a 'memento mori' from the tomb of Sir William Weston (d 1540), last Prior of the Order, and a fine alabaster effigy (16C) of a knight of the Order, brought from Valladolid.

Among former residents in Clerkenwell were Izaak Walton (1650-61), John Wilkes (born here in 1727), Christopher Pinchbeck, inventor of the alloy that bears his name (1721), and Emanuel Swedenborg (d 1772). The old 'Clerks' Well' (on the site of 14-16 Farringdon Road, the offices of the 'New Statesman'; apply to view) mentioned as early as 1174, where the parish clerks of London used to perform miracle plays, gave name to the district.

Clerkenwell Road, its S boundary, leads from Gray's Inn Road (p 223) to Old Street, passing (left) the old *Sessions House* (1779-82), with reliefs by Nollekens, in Clerkenwell Green, with the graceful steeple of *St. James's Church* (by James Carr; 1788-91) behind. In Clerkenwell Green Nos 37 and 38, a house of 1738, contain the *Marx Memorial Library*, a pointer to the place's radical history. Open afternoons (01-253 1985). Farringdon Road, with a second-hand book market (best Mon to Sat lunchtime) of which just a few stalls remain, leads back towards Holborn.

Sadler's Wells in Rosebery Avenue (up Rosoman Street, past the Metropolitan Water Board headquarters) also recalls the area's richness in water. The first music house here, built in 1683, was a side attraction to a medicinal well on this site. Grimaldi played there in 1781-1805. During the 19C a period as a Shakespearian theatre under Samuel Phelps was followed by use as a skating rink, a boxing arena and then a pickle factory. It re-opened as a music hall in 1893 but soon closed. The present theatre dates to 1931. It was founded by Lilian Bayliss and Sir Reginald Rowe and became part of the Bayliss theatre which included the Old Vic; ballet and opera dominated but the opera company moved to the Coliseum in 1968. Sadler's Wells still stages opera, ballet and music, performed mainly by visiting companies from overseas. The original well can still be seen under a trap door. A major extension is planned to one side.

Also in Rosebery Avenue are the former offices of the Metropolitan Water Board, *New River House* (1920), now the Thames Water Authority, containing a room from the Water House of 1693. Further SE, at *Mount Pleasant*, is the largest letter and parcel sorting office in the United Kingdom, built in 1900 on the site of the Coldbath House of Correction, a prison from 1794 to 1877.

21 Newgate Street, Cheapside, the Barbican, the Museum of London

Access: Underground, St. Paul's and Barbican

Newgate Street continues the line of Holborn and leads towards the heart of the City. To the right diverges Warwick Lane, in which stands *Cutlers' Hall*, with terracotta reliefs by Benj. Creswick (1887). Opposite Warwick Lane is the first block of the Post Office, the buildings of which adjoin *Christ Church*, built by Wren in 1667-91 (steeple added in 1704) on part of the site of the great church of the Grey Friars. The church was burnt out during the 'blitz' of 1940-41 and remains a hollow shell. The steeple was re-erected in 1960 from the original stonework. Lawrence Sheriff (d 1567), founder of Rugby School, was buried in Christ Church. To the N of the church formerly stood *Christ's Hospital*, the famous 'Blue Coat School', founded by Edward VI in 1552. In 1902, however, the school was removed to the country (near Horsham in Sussex), and its site is now occupied by buildings of the Post Office and St. Bartholomew's Hospital.

A great part of the block bounded by Newgate St, Giltspur St, St. Bartholomew's Hospital, and St. Martin's-le-Grand is occupied by **The Post Office** (Pl. 8; 6). In King Edward St, on the left beyond Christ Church, is the *King Edward Building*, in which ordinary postal business is transacted. Outside is a statue of Rowland Hill. It also houses the **National Postal Museum**.

National Postal Museum, King Edward Building, King Edward Street, London EC1. Tel. 01-432 3851. Access: Underground, St. Paul's. Open Mon to Thurs 10.00-16.30, Fri 10.00-16.00. Free.

The museum was established in 1965 when Reginald M. Phillips donated to the nation his unique collection of artists' drawings, proofs, and stamps of the Queen Victoria issues of Great Britain. This collection and the comprehensive range of specimen stamps of the world, received by the Post Office through the Universal Postal Union since 1878, are displayed; temporary exhibitions of specialised material from the postal archives are mounted; and a reference library is available by appointment.

The *Post Office North*, opposite, contains the offices of Postal Headquarters including the library. An extensive network of tunnels carries the Post Office Railway from the central point below the King Edward Building in four directions, converging on Mount Pleasant sorting office. Started in 1913, it was completed after the First World War and opened in 1927. Tours by appointment: contact the Post Office Controller, King Edward Building, London EC1.

Until 1913 the General Post Office proper stood on the E side of St. Martin's-le-Grand, a street commemorating the church, college, and sanctuary of St. Martin, dissolved in 1548. The former burial-ground of Christchurch, Newgate St, has been laid out as *Postman's Park*.

On the S side of Newgate St are the new buildings in the precinct of St. Paul's, Paternoster Square (see p 216). Beyond St. Martin's-le-Grand, Newgate St is continued towards the E by *Cheapside* (Pl. 8; 6), a short and busy thoroughfare formerly known as the *Chepe* (from Old English 'ceap', a bargain). The names of the cross-streets probably indicate the position of the different classes of traders' booths at this early period. The 'prentices of Chepe were long notorious for their

turbulence. The street is lined with new buildings, the most prominent
of which is the curving neo-Georgian block of offices for the Bank
of America extending S to Watling St.

In Foster Lane stands the church of *St. Vedast* (p 233), and in Gutter Lane, the
next turning left from Cheapside, is the entrance to the new *Saddlers' Hall*
(1958). The Saddlers' Guild is thought to have its origin in Anglo-Saxon times.
On the same side, at the corner of Wood St, a plane tree grows on the site of
the church of St. Peter; it is protected by special clauses in the leases of adjoining
buildings.

In Cheapside (right), near the corner of Bread St stood the *Mermaid
Tavern*, famous for the club founded by Ben Jonson in 1603 and
frequented by Shakespeare, Raleigh, Donne, Beaumont, and
Fletcher.—John Milton (1608-74) was born in *Bread Street*, to the
right, and Sir Thomas More (1478-1535) in *Milk Street*, nearly
opposite. Milton is commemorated by a tablet (with Dryden's famous
lines) on the exterior W wall of Bow Church.

*Bow Church, or *St. Mary-le-Bow* (open 09.00-16.00, closed
weekends), in Cheapside, was begun by Wren in 1670 and completed
with the steeple in 1683, but was badly damaged 1941. It succeeds
the older church of 'St. Marie de Arcubus', 'the first in this city built
on two arches (bows) of stone'. Saxon finds indicate that a church
must have existed on this site before the crypt was built. The beautiful
*Steeple, a very fine Renaissance campanile, is 222ft high.

The restoration by Laurence King was completed in 1971. The exterior has
been restored to its original design, but the interior has been redesigned to suit
the needs of 20C worship. The beautiful E windows are the work of John
Hayward. The NE window represents the bombed City churches grouped round
Mary who holds the church of St. Mary-le-Bow in her arms. There are two
pulpits, both used in the service. Seating is provided according to need. In the
churchyard outside is a statue of Captain John Smith, founder of Virginia, a
copy of the statue in Jamestown.

The Norman *Crypt*, built about 1090, is the oldest ecclesiastical structure in
the City. Also restored, it has an etched glass entrance screen by John Hayward.
It contains the chapel of the Holy Spirit, built in the part formerly used as a
burying place, which was once the meeting-place of the ecclesiastical *Court of
Arches*.

In 1914 an ancient stone from the crypt of Bow Church was placed in Trinity
Church, New York, in reference to the fact that William III granted to the vestry
of that church the same privileges as those of St. Mary-le-Bow.

Anyone born within the sound of Bow Bells is a 'cockney', i.e. a Londoner
pure and simple. The bells that (according to the old story) called back Dick
Whittington to be three times Mayor of London, perished in the Great Fire;
their successors were destroyed in 1941, but new ones have been recast from
those salved after enemy action.

A Roman public bath (c AD 100) was found in 1955 on the other side
of Cheapside.

Beyond Bow Church *King Street* and *Queen Street* diverge to the
left and right, the former leading to the Guildhall, the latter to
Southwark Bridge. At the corner of Ironmonger Lane, just beyond
King St, stands *Mercers' Hall*, the guildhouse of the Mercers, one of
the richest of the City companies and first in order of civic precedence.
It has been rebuilt (1954-56) after wartime destruction.

In Ironmonger Lane is the tower of *St Olave's*, Old Jewry, a relic
of a Wren church demolished in 1888, now used as offices. There is
a Roman mosaic pavement beneath No. 11.

Old Jewry diverging to the left beyond Mercers' Hall was the ghetto before the expulsion of the Jews in 1290. The *Headquarters of the City Police* are at No. 26. The continuation of Cheapside is known as the *Poultry*, from its early occupation by the shops of poulterers. It is dominated by the Midland Bank headquarters by Lutyens.

From the W end of Cheapside, Foster Lane leads N past the church of *St Vedast* (open 06.00-18.00 Mon to Fri, 06.30-10.00 Sat, 07.00-14.00 Sun), rebuilt by Wren in 1670-73, and restored in 1962. Within is a richly decorated ceiling, fine carving, and a splendid sounding organ, built by Renatus Harris in 1731 and now restored. Robert Herrick was christened here. Farther on, on the corner of Gresham St, stands the *Goldsmiths' Hall*, a handsome Renaissance edifice (1835) rebuilt by Philip Hardwick, containing some interesting portraits and a fine collection of plate. The Goldsmiths' Company, which was incorporated in 1327, has the duty of assaying and stamping gold and silver plate. Its hall-mark is the leopard's head.

Across Gresham St (left) *St. Anne and St. Agnes,* a Wren church (1680), restored in 1963-68, was rehalloed for Lutheran congregations in 1966 (open for services on Sun). At the end of Noble Street a new *Plaisterers' Hall* (1971) faces London Wall.

St. Mary le Bow with the famous 'Bow Bells'. The statue is of Captain John Smith

It is slightly longer but more interesting to turn E along Gresham St, passing Staining Lane with the entrances to the *Haberdashers' Hall*, and (in Oat Lane) to the neo-Georgian *Pewterers' Hall* (1961; the original hall was built in 1496), and turn N up Wood Street. Here stands the tower of *St. Alban*, built by Wren in 1682-98, now converted into an unusual office block. Beyond the police station cross London Wall by walkway.

London Wall (Pl. 8; 6), though here realigned, still follows more or less closely the site of the old **City Wall**. Parts of the wall have been exposed in this area, especially since the clearance of bomb damage. The *London Wall Walk*, with information panels and directional signs, can be followed from the Tower to the Museum of London (or vice versa). The Walk starts just outside Tower Hill Underground Station and follows the line of the City Wall.

The **Roman Wall** around the city was 2 miles long, usually 8ft thick, and probably 20-25ft high. The best preserved section is exposed near the Tower (comp. p 257). It was built c AD 190-225 with stone shipped along the river Medway from Maidstone; one of the ships sank near Blackfriars and has been excavated. The five gates were Aldgate, Bishopsgate, Cripplegate, Newgate, and Ludgate. A sixth, Aldersgate, was added later. The fragments of wall now visible show the Roman substructure with its characteristic bands of tiles, and, above, additions made to these foundations in the succeeding centuries.

Preceding the City Wall in date was a **Roman Fort**, built AD 120-30, and discovered in 1950. Its N and W boundaries were later strengthened and incorporated into the city defensive wall. Cripplegate was on the site of the N gate of the fort. Sometime after the 13C a system of semicircular bastions was constructed outside the walls: a number of these are now visible.

Beyond lies the **Barbican** (Pl. 8; 4) where a 60-acre area, heavily bombed in the last War, has been rebuilt to provide accommodation for over 6000 people and an arts and conference centre. Designed in massive concrete in derivative styles in which medieval fortification and Le Corbusier seemingly predominate, the residential blocks are linked by raised walkways. An artificial lake, part of the air-

A reconstruction by Peter Jackson of the late Roman gateway at Aldersgate, c AD 375

conditioning system, and the residents' gardens help to alleviate the concrete harshness.

Walkways cross London Wall to podium level at the SW corner. Here the ∗∗**Museum of London**, opened by Queen Elizabeth II on 2 December 1976, presents the history, the social and domestic life, and the manners of the capital from the earliest habitation to the most recent past. It combines the former Guildhall and London Museums.

Museum of London, London Wall, London EC2. Tel. 01-600 3699. Access: Underground, St. Paul's. Open Tues to Sat 10.00-18.00. Sun 14.00-18.00. Lectures, temporary exhibitions. Cafeteria. Excellent guidebook and bookshop.

The Guildhall Museum was founded in 1826 as an adjunct to the Guildhall Library by the Corporation of the City of London. The London Museum was a national museum formed in 1911. Before 1939 it had been in Lancaster House. After 1945 both museums had temporary quarters: the Guildhall Museum in the Royal Exchange and the London Museum in Kensington Palace.

The new building, by Powell, Moya, and Partners, with interior by Higgins, Ney, and Partners, surrounds a central court and is on two levels connected by a glazed ramp.

The exhibition, on the continuous open plan, consists of chronological tableaux incorporating 'bygones' of every kind, presented as an illustrated social history of some brilliance. Later centuries are accompanied by discreetly recorded period music. Costume is particularly well represented. Exhibits come from all social levels, inevitably with some imbalance, since Tudor relics tend to survive from court and church circles, while for the 19C, equally a period of high material progress and endeavour, poverty and trivia are perhaps too preponderant, and the early 20C appears quaint rather than innovatory.

Highlights of the exhibition include the Lord Mayor's Stage Coach and a representation of the Great Fire of London. New highlights at the Museum are a pair of 17C models of English warships from Trinity Green, finely carved in white marble. Further items to look out for are detailed below.

The Museum of London's archaeological department is engaged in a number of projects around the City and new finds are incorporated in existing displays or shown separately according to space and suitability.

The arrangement is in general anti-clockwise and from the walls to the centre. Displays are numbered consecutively and well documented.

A relief model of the Thames Valley faces an imaginary section through a City cellar to demonstrate archaeological levels.

PREHISTORIC. Flint and bone tools from riverine gravel terraces (2, 5); Neolithic bowl from Heathrow (9); leaf-shaped swords of the Bronze Age (10); finds from a temple site (6C BC) found at Heathrow during airfield construction; early British coins (11); iron dagger; the Brentford Tankard (1C), of bronze-mounted oak with an ornamental handle (12).

ROMAN from AD 43 (when Claudius's soldiers crossed the Thames). Stone figure of a legionary; soldiers' accoutrements (14); imports from Italy; commercial wax letter tablet addressed Londinio (15); inscribed gravestones; tile from state tile works stamped P.P. BR. LON; head of Hadrian and other fragments of bronze statues (18).

A vantage window overlooks the remains of the 2C Roman fort; house reconstruction comprising 1C and 4C dining-rooms and kitchen grouped round a 3C tessellated pavement from Bucklersbury; cases (23, 33) contain leather

'bikini' trunks (one from a well in Queen St), probably worn by dancing girls.
    Marble sculpture (mainly 2-3C) found on the Mithraic temple site, including
*Heads of Mithras and Serapis, a colossal hand, and a 3C Bacchic group; note
also the late-Roman decorated silver box containing a strainer (43); clay jug
inscribed Londini (44); sarcophagus from Lower Clapton (39).

SAXON AND VIKING. Scramasaxes, the large knives from which the Saxons
are supposed to have taken their names (49); brooches from Saxon cemetery
at Mitcham; Celtic bell (?8C) found in the Thames at Mortlake (50); spear-heads,
axes, and other Viking weapons (53, 56); Viking grave slab (11C) with runes,
from St. Paul's churchyard (58).

MEDIEVAL. Models of William the Conqueror's White Tower (60) and Old St.
Paul's (61); 15C City chest of solid iron; chain-mail hauberk; sculptured panel
in elm (from a chest) with Chaucerian scene; huge 13C storage jar (65). Heraldic
fragments of the Cheapside Eleanor Cross (71); earliest known swinging cradle
(15C) (73); coin hoard (temp. Edward III) from Upper Norwood (79); costrels,
tallybag in leather with inscription of the Calais garrison (84). A 15C carved
door frame from the church of St. Ethelburga-within-Bishopsgate (98), flanked
by the four Civic Virtues from the medieval Guildhall (95).

TUDOR. 16C armour from Greenwich (106, 109); the *Cheapside Hoard,
probably part of the stock-in-trade of a 16C jeweller (110). In wall-cases: leather
clothing preserved from a Moorfields rubbish dump (112); *Copper plate
engraved with part of the earliest known survey of London (c 1558);
characteristic flat cap with ear-pieces; Ming bowl mounted on silver-gilt stand,
said to have belonged to Mary, Queen of Scots (115); Sir Thos. Gresham's
*Steelyard and weighing bell; fashionable *Gloves and leather hat; lace shirt;
cups and apostle spoons (116).

EARLY STUART AND COMMONWEALTH. The transition from Tudor to Stuart
is marked by scale models of Tudor London and Whitehall Palace. Relics of
Charles I (vest worn on scaffold) and Cromwell (death mask); swords from a
factory at Hounslow; *Armour made at Greenwich c 1630 and worn by John
Dymoke as hereditary King's Champion at George III's coronation. Panelled
room from Wandsworth with embroidered hangings (134); builder's sacrifice;
Mercers' Company silver flagon (135); plague relics; the 'Great Fire Experience',
an audio-visual representation of the Great Fire of 1666, with a reading from
Pepys' Diary.
    A ramp leads down to the *Lower Floor.*

LATE STUART. Pepys' chess set (154); Shop and tavern signs: Gerard the
Giant, Ape and Apple, etc. Trumpet of 1666; playing cards illustrating the
murder and other facets of the 'Popish Plot' (158); (172, 173); panelled room
from 15 Buckingham St, with a pair of virginals by James White, 1656; sedan
chair (179).

GEORGIAN. In the rotunda, enclosed by bow-fronted shop windows, printing
press (192); (194) Lambeth Delft pottery; Chelsea and Bow porcelain; Battersea
enamels; debtor's cell from Wellclose Square Lockup (visited and described by
John Howard, the penal reformer); Debtor's Door and cell from Newgate Prison.
The 'Bull and Mouth' sign (c 1810) from St. Martin's-le-Grand marks the
entrance to the:

NINETEENTH CENTURY HALL. The Woolsack from the old House of Lords;
Dickens's chair; relics from Coal Exchange and Great Exhibition (241); Hodges'
fire engine of 1862 (242).

IMPERIAL LONDON. 'Popularity', a panorama of stage artists by W.H. Lambert;
cooper's, haberdasher's, grocer's (302); chemist's, and tailor's shop interiors;
Hansom cab (305).

THE TWENTIETH CENTURY (306-338) ranges from cigarette cards to an early
broadcasting studio; Woolworth's 3d and 6d counter; lifts from Selfridge's; art
nouveau clocks; model T Ford car.

CEREMONIAL LONDON. The Lord Mayor's *State Coach, built in 1757 and
used in the annual Lord Mayor's Show; it is decorated with allegorical scenes

having a London setting, reputedly by Cipriani. Model of the last Lord Mayor's barge (1807).—In the TREASURY, opposite, reminders of the coronation ceremony.

Aldersgate Street, which skirts the Barbican on the W, takes its name from the old N City gate (pulled down in 1761). The road follows a Roman alinement; recent excavations revealed a sequence of eleven subsequent roads on its course. Nettleton Court off Aldersgate Street, next to the Museum of London, houses a John Wesley Memorial unveiled in 1981. It marks the spot of Wesley's conversion in 1783. The memorial is in the shape of the leaf of his journal and stands 15ft high. The decorative *Ironmongers' Hall*, hidden behind the new buildings, is the successor (1925) of the old hall in Fenchurch St, destroyed by enemy aircraft in 1917. *St. Botolph without Aldersgate* (open 12.00-15.00), slightly injured by the Great Fire, was entirely rebuilt in 1790.

From the museum a walkway (left) runs above London Wall to Wood St, then turns left to 'The Postern' through which a descent is made to the paved piazza around the church of **St. Giles without Cripplegate** (open Mon to Fri 10.00-14.00, Sun and summer until 16.00).

The stone tower (with a brick top storey added in 1682 by John Bridges), and the nave belong to the church built in 1390. After a fire in 1545 and alterations in the 17-18C, the edifice received a direct hit during the first enemy air attack on the City on the night of 24 August 1940, and was even more badly damaged during the great fire of 29 Dec of the same year. In 1960 it was restored; the E and W windows were renewed in 1967-68, and the fine organ (incorporating an 18C case) installed in 1969.

In this church Shakespeare attended the baptism of his nephew in 1604 while lodging near by in Silver St with Christopher Montjoy, a Huguenot and 'tire maker' whom he had known 'for the space of tenne yeres or thereaboutes'. Oliver Cromwell was married here in 1620.

In the S aisle is a monument (restored in 1971) over the burial-place of John Speed (1552-1629), topographer, and an epitaph to Thamas Stagg (1772) ending with the curt phrase 'That is all'. At the W end of this aisle a plaque records the burial here of John Milton, who died in Bunhill Row in 1674, in the same grave as his father. The bust is by John Bacon (1793). 'Paradise Lost' was sold by Milton to an Aldersgate printer; the poet occupied several houses in the region from 1643-47, and after the Restoration. A plaque to the right of the entrance door recalls other 'Men of Mark' connected with the parish, who include Sir Martin Frobisher (d 1594), seaman and explorer, John Foxe (d 1587), martyrologist, John Bunyan (d 1688), and Daniel Defoe (d 1731; the parish register records his burial in Bunhill Fields). The Great Plague was at its worst in the parish of St. Giles, and plague burials fill nearly a folio volume of the parish register (1665). The documents are now in the Guildhall Library.

Outside, tombstones have been set in to the paving, including some curious mummy-shaped tombs dating from the early 19C. A bastion built outside the City wall sometime after the 13C is prominent to the S. The *City of London School for Girls*, founded in Carmelite St in 1894, was moved here in 1964.

The Barbican's central lake is overlooked to the N by the **Barbican Centre**, which can be approached via the walkway system. Follow the signs and yellow markings.

The Barbican Arts and Conference Centre, Silk Street, London EC2. Tel. 01-638

4141. Underground, Barbican (closed on Sundays), Moorgate, St. Paul's.

The plans for rebuilding the residential area of the Barbican included a modest arts centre and premises for the Guildhall School of Music and Drama. By 1964 these plans had grown to accommodate the Royal Shakespeare Company, the London Symphony Orchestra, a library and an art gallery. At the same time the City of London Corporation aimed to give the development a commercial use by incorporating first-class conference and exhibition facilities. The complicated structure on eight levels, half of which are underground, was eventually opened by HM The Queen in March 1982; the work had taken over 25 years and the cost was £157m.

The *Concert Hall* seats 2000; it is panelled in light wood and has comfortable seating and multi-lingual interpretation facilities. The London Symphony Orchestra and others perform here in a programme scheduled around mainly daytime conference activities. The *Royal*

The Barbican with flats, the Arts Centre, and St. Giles Cripplegate (to the left)

Shakespeare Company Theatre has the highest flytower in Europe, at 110ft, and 1100 seats on four levels, none further than 65ft from the centre of the stage. The *Pit Theatre* below is used for smaller-scale works. There is a comfortable Cinema which seats 300 and also doubles as a lecture theatre.

The *Barbican Art Gallery* on two levels houses the City of London's outstanding collection of paintings which is shown at regular intervals interspersed with the changing exhibitions of modern artists. (See also foyer, below.)

Barbican Art Gallery, Level 8; details as above. Open Tues to Sat 10.00-19.00, Sun 12.00-18.00. Admission charge/free depending on exhibition.

The *Barbican Library* combines the two Libraries of the City of London with a reference section and lending library for residents.

The *Barbican Exhibition Halls* (8000 sq m) are in Golden Lane, off Beech St, and are used for special exhibitions, trade and public. Access: Underground, Barbican.

The Barbican Centre also features a Conservatory and has a carvery restaurant, a cafeteria, an outdoor cafeteria by the lake in the summer, bars and sandwich stalls in the foyers during performances. There is music on Sundays and early evenings in the foyers and an exhibition area in the foyer which stages separate exhibitions from the art gallery, as well as an outdoor sculpture court. A statue by Elizabeth Frink, 'The Running Man', stands on the terrace by the lake.

Near the Barbican Centre, in Chiswell Street, are the *Chiswell Street Vaults*, an excellent pub and restaurant in the cellars of the buildings of the Chiswell Street Brewery, part of which has been restored and opened to the public (closed at weekends). On the S side is the original brewery building, now converted to the Porter Tun Room with one of the best hammer-beam roofs in London (available for functions); below was the location for the Overlord Embroidery before it moved to Portsmouth in 1984. On the N side are stables for the 14 dray-horses which are still used each November for the Lord Mayor's Coach (see Museum of London) in the Lord Mayor's Procession and for delivering beer in the City. Beer is no longer brewed on this site, but the horses can be seen Mon to Fri 11.00-15.00. A gift shop at the stables is open Mon to Fri 09.00-17.00.

To the S in Monkwell Square is the new *Barber Surgeons' Hall*. The West Gate of the Roman Fort (comp. above) is entered from London Wall (Mon to Fri 12.30-14.00; other times by arrangement at Museum of London). On view are remains of the N guardroom, a gravelled roadway, and the central piers of the gate.

Off the E side of Wood St, in the sunken garden of *St Alphage*, another fine section of the city wall has been exposed. Above the Roman level (part of the N wall of the early fort), the additions in grey stone date from c 1350, and the red brick top was added c 1477. Near by are the remains of the N porch of *Elsing Spital*, a priory church founded in 1329 'for the sustentation of a hundred blind men'.

Cross London Wall. To the E of *Brewers' Hall*, on this site since 1420 and rebuilt in 1960 after its destruction in 1940, is the *City Business Library* (formed from the Commercial Reference Room and the Newspaper Room of the Guildhall Library). In front is a charming statue, 'The Gardener', by Karin Jonzen (1971). Here steps lead up to the Bassishaw Highwalk, with a view (left) of *Girdlers' Hall* (1961) in Basinghall Avenue. Descend a wide flight of steps past the pleasant new pavilion-like building of the *Guildhall Exhibition Hall* used for varied exhibitions relating to the City. On the W is the *Chartered Insurance Institute* (1934), with its fire-marks and fire-fighting equipment collection.

Chartered Insurance Institutes (fire engines) Museum, Aldermanbury, London EC2. Tel. 01-606 3835. Open Mon to Fri 10.00-17.00. Free. Access: Underground, Moorgate.

A small museum on the second floor of this building on the theme of fire, marine, life and accident insurance with early fire-fighting equipment including hand-drawn fire-engines, firemen's helmets, leather buckets, etc. The firemarks are particularly interesting; the fire brigades owned by the insurance companies would only fight fires in properties bearing their company's marks.

Beyond a sculptural group by K. Jonzen, a flight of steps descends right to a coloured glass fountain by Allen David.

Across *Aldermanbury* a pleasant garden surrounds the site of the Wren church of *St. Mary*, bombed in 1940 and removed in 1968 to the campus of Westminster College, Fulton, USA as a memorial to Winston Churchill (who made his famous Iron Curtain speech at the College). The memorial to the editors of Shakespeare's First Folio, Heminge and Condell, church-wardens, remains. Judge Jeffreys was buried here, having died in the Tower in 1689. The registers recording Milton's second marriage (1656) are now in the Guildhall library.

22 Guildhall, Bank of England, Mansion House and the Stock Exchange

The attractive **Guildhall**, the base of the City Corporation of London, is best approached from Gresham Street through to Guildhall Yard.

Access: Underground, Bank. Open Monday to Saturday 10.00-17.00; Sun (May to September) 14.00-17.00. Free (Crypt closed 12.00-14.00). The Court of Common Council of the City of London (see p 200) meets every third Thursday; the public is admitted.

The *Hall of the Corporation of the City of London* dates from c 1411-35, though its external appearance is substantially due to the design of George Dance, Jr (1788-89). Over the porch is the City coat-of-arms, with the motto 'Domine dirige nos'. The lower part of the great hall, the porch, and the crypt are medieval; much damage was caused by fire in 1666 and 1940; and the interior was beautifully restored by Sir Giles Scott in 1952-54.

The GREAT HALL (151.5ft long, 48ft wide, and 89ft high) was restored in 1668-71 and in 1866-70, but its 19C timber roof was destroyed in 1940 and has been replaced by stone arches with a panelled ceiling (1954). The hall (open 10.00-17.00, Sat –16.00) is now used for municipal meetings, public meetings, the election of the Lord Mayor and Sheriffs, and the state banquets of the Corporation. The most important of these last is the banquet given in November, by the new Lord Mayor and Sheriffs, to the members of the Cabinet and the Prime Minister makes an important speech. At an earlier period the hall was used also for important trials (recorded on a panel). Against the walls are a statue of *Churchill*, by Oscar

Nemon, and monuments to *Nelson* (inscription by Sheridan), *Wellington*, *Chatham* (inscription by Burke), *William Pitt* (inscription by Canning) and *Lord Mayor Beckford*; the popular wooden figures of *Gog and Magog*, by David Evans (W end), replace those burned in 1940.

The **Guildhall Library** (open 09.30-17.00; founded in 1425), is reached either by a corridor running W from the porch of the Guildhall or from an entrance in Aldermanbury. It contains about 140,000 printed volumes and pamphlets and over 30,000 MSS. It is especially rich in works on London and Middlesex, and includes several important special collections. The Commercial Reference, and Newspaper Libraries now form the City Business Library.

The *Guildhall Clock Museum* (Aldermanbury, EC2. Open Mon to Fri 09.30-17.00. Free) is one of the most important horological collections in the country, bequeathed to the Museum by the Clockmakers' Company established in 1631.

The Crypt is a very interesting survival of the building of 1411-35. The *Eastern Crypt* is borne by six clustered columns of Purbeck marble; restored in 1961.

In *Gresham Street* stands the church of *St. Lawrence Jewry*, built by Wren in 1671-77 and effectively restored by Cecil Brown (1956-57; after heavy war damage) as the official church of the City Corporation. The painting in the heavy Renaissance-style reredos is by the architect. In the N aisle is the Commonwealth Transept.

Pepys records a visit to the church 'for curiosity', and his disappointment with the sermon. Sir Thomas More delivered a series of lectures here. Among the rectors were Grocyn and Seth Ward.

To the E GRESHAM COLLEGE (now in the Barbican Centre) was founded by Sir Thomas Gresham in 1579 for the delivery of lectures in Latin and English on 'divynitye, astronomy, musicke, geometry, law, physicke, and rethoricke' by seven professors. It is now **The City University**. The lectures are now all given in English. The present building dates from 1913.

At the end of Gresham St, Prince's Street, skirting the huge wall of the Bank of England (see below) leads S to the Mansion House. Opposite the Bank a driveway admits to *Grocers' Hall*, virtually destroyed by fire in 1965. A new hall was completed in 1970, the fifth to be built on this site; it preserves part of the 17C ironwork from the second hall, and the oldest bell in the city (1458; recast since the fire). The Grocers or 'Pepperers' was first mentioned as a guild in 1180 and incorporated in 1428.

Prince's Street emerges at the Mansion House and the Bank of England.

The triangular space overlooked by the Bank, the Royal Exchange, and the Mansion House may fairly claim to be heart of the City; from it radiate eight important streets. Near by are the headquarters of all the big banks.

Access: Underground, Bank.

The **Bank of England** (Pl. 9; 5) covers about three acres between Lothbury, Bartholomew Lane, Threadneedle St, and Princes St. In 1694-1734 the bank operated in Grocers' Hall. Its first building was erected by George Sampson in 1732-34, but the bank's later aspect (one-storeyed in appearance) was due to Sir John Soane, who built the massive external wall (windowless in the interests of security) with its Corinthian columns, from 1788 onwards. The present building, facing Threadneedle St, was rebuilt by Sir Herbert Baker in 1925-39. It rises seven storeys above ground within Soane's original outer wall and has three floors below ground. The sculptures are by Charles Wheeler; in the pediment appears the 'Old Lady of Threadneedle Street'. The public are admitted by appointment.

The Bank of England was projected by William Paterson (whose connection with it was, however, brief), and incorporated in 1694 by Royal Charter, under which, and another of 1946, it now operates. The first joint stock bank in England, it had an original capital of £1,200,000, later increased to £14,553,000, which is held by the Treasury. Its affairs are managed by a Board consisting of a Governor, a Deputy Governor and 16 Directors appointed by the Crown. The Bank is the Government's banker and, on its behalf, manages the National Debt and the Note Issue of which it has the sole right in England and Wales. It is also the bankers' bank and the central bank of the country. All important overseas central banks have accounts in its books but for many years it has not undertaken new commercial banking business. After the Gordon Riots (1780) the Bank was protected nightly by a picket mounted by the Brigade of Guards until 1973.

Opposite the Bank, in the angle formed by Threadneedle Street and Cornhill, stands the **Royal Exchange**, erected by Tite in 1842-44. It is the third building of its kind on this spot; the first Exchange, erected by Sir Thomas Gresham in 1564-70, was burned down in 1666, and the second in 1838. The tympanum group above the Corinthian portico represents Commerce holding the charter of the Exchange and attended by the Lord Mayor, British merchants, and natives of various foreign nations. The campanile, 180ft high, with a peal of bells, has a statue of Gresham on its E face and a gilded vane in the form of a grasshopper (Gresham's crest).

In front of the Exchange are an equestrian statue of *Wellington*, by Chantrey (1844), and a *War Memorial* (1920), by Aston Webb and Alfred Drury. Below is the country's first public lavatory. Behind it is a seated figure of *George Peabody* (d 1869), facing a charming little fountain-group by Dalou (1878). The forecourt was recently refurbished and now features 12 Victorian style lamps—donated by 12 livery companies.

The inside of the Royal Exchange has now been taken over by the London International Financial Futures Exchange, constructed as a separate shell within the existing building. This makes it difficult to see the Turkish pavement from the first Exchange and the interior paintings, particularly the well-known wall panels painted by Lord Leighton and others and the statues of Elizabeth I by M. Watson and Charles II by John Spiller. However, LIFFE provides its own entertainment for those interested in the workings of the financial markets; there are three 'pits' in which deals are done in gold, currency and government securities—all to be completed in the future. The Visitor's Gallery is open Monday to Friday 11.30-14.00. Admission free. Leaflets are available to explain the activities. The wall paintings can be seen by appointment to LIFFE, Royal Exchange, Threadneedle Street, London EC2.

On the corner at 39 Queen Victoria Street is *Sweetings*, London's oldest fish restaurant, first established in 1830 and in the present building in 1906. Oysters, prawns and other shellfish are served from the counter and lunchtime diners queue for places at the cramped tables.

The **Mansion House**, the official residence of the Lord Mayor, faces the S corner of the Bank. It is a Renaissance edifice, with an imposing Corinthian portico, erected by George Dance the Elder in 1739-53, with a pediment sculptured by Sir Robert Taylor.

The chief feature of the interior (visitors admitted on certain Saturdays, written applications to the Secretary) is the *Egyptian Hall*, the scene of banquets, balls, and other functions, as well as numerous public meetings. Dance modelled it after the so-called Egyptian Hall of Vitruvius, which, however, bore no resemblance to Egyptian architecture. It contains some 19C sculptures. The *Long Parlour*, with a remarkable ceiling, the *Saloon*, adorned with tapestry and sculpture, the *State Drawing Room*, etc., are shown also. Visitors enter by the door in Walbrook.

The colourful *Lord Mayor's Show* is held on the second Saturday in Nov, when the new Lord Mayor is taken by coach through the streets of the City, preceded by a procession with a theme chosen by the Lord Mayor, but always traditionally including the defence services, and made especially spectacular by the presence of the Hon. Company of Men at Arms and the Household Cavalry.

In Walbrook, just behind the Mansion House, is the church of **St. Stephen**, rebuilt by Wren in 1672-79. The noble ·Interior, with its circular dome (63ft high) supported on eight arches, is one of the architect's masterpieces, and has been carefully restored since its partial destruction in 1941. The dome represents, on a small scale, Wren's original design for St. Paul's. The font is by Thomas Strong, with a fine cover by William Newman, and the rich pulpit is by Thos. Creecher. On the left wall is the 'Burial of St. Stephen', by Benjamin West. To the left a tablet commemorates Dr Nathaniel Hodges, appointed by the Lord Mayor in 1665 to combat the spread of the Plague, which had started in Mansion House Place. The fine sword rest dates from 1710, and the organ (by Hill) from 1906. A glass mosaic in the S wall commemorates John Dunstable (d 1453), 'the father of English harmony', and a tablet serves as memorial to John Lilburne (d 1657), the political agitator. In the vaults lies Sir John Vanbrugh (1664-1726), playwright and architect.

In 1964-67 the Crypt and Vestries were converted for use as the headquarters of the London Branch of the Samaritans, a world-wide organisation 'to befriend the suicidal and desperate', founded by a Rector of the church.

In Lothbury, on the N side of the Bank, is the church of *St. Margaret Lothbury*, rebuilt by Wren in 1686-90. It contains an exquisite carved font, pulpit, and canopy ascribed to Grinling Gibbons, and a fine chancel screen from All Hallows the Great, probably English work of c 1689. The elaborate sword-rests date from the late 18C. The bust of Sir Peter le Maire (d 1631), at the W end of the nave, is perhaps by H. le Sueur.—Opposite, in an alcove in the wall of the Bank, is a statue of Sir John Soane.

To the E of the Bank, beyond Bartholomew Lane, the **Stock Exchange**, the headquarters of the dealers in negotiable securities, occupies a tall tower and new buildings at its foot. The site, part of which has been occupied by the Exchange since 1802, extends to the post office where Throgmorton St and Old Broad St meet, and S to Threadneedle St. The public are admitted to the Visitors' Gallery (Mon to Fri 10.30-15.15) and to a cinema where films explaining the working of the Stock Exchange are shown.

The London Stock Exchange is operated by 'jobbers' or wholesalers who deal only with other members and only in certain types of securities. The 'brokers' act as intermediaries between the jobbers and the public. Speculators on a rise in prices are known as 'bulls'; those who speculate on a fall are known as 'bears'. There are two indices, the Stock Exchange Index and the Financial Times Index selected from a representative selection of shares, displayed prominently in the Hall. To become a member of the Stock Exchange, the broker must have worked for a member company for at least 3 years and be sponsored by two principal members as well as pass an examination. They then pay £1300 (1985) to a Nomination Fund plus £300 per annum.

In Throgmorton St, just N of the Stock Exchange, is *Drapers' Hall*, dating in part from 1667 but practically rebuilt in 1866-70 (restored 1949; entrance in Throgmorton Avenue). It contains a handsome staircase, and a famous mulberry still flourishes in the garden.—In Austin Friars, close to Drapers' Hall, stands the *Dutch Church*, by Arthur Bailey (1950-54). This lofty church (open Mon to Thurs and Sun 11.00-15.00), with its graceful fleche, replaces the 13C building—originally the nave of a priory of Augustinian friars—that was assigned by Edward VI in 1550 to Protestant refugees and was ultimately left exclusively to the Dutch. The old church was completely destroyed in 1941, and the great W window, by Max Nauta, shows Edward VI and Princess Irene of the Netherlands, who laid the foundation stone of the new church. Beneath the Communion table is the altar-stone of the priory church (1253).

Old Broad Street, diverging on the left from Threadneedle St, leads to Liverpool St Station (Broad St Station is now closed). On its E side the elegant *City of London Club*, by Philip Hardwick (1834), is near the focus of the icy swirling draughts caused by its skyscraper neighbours and only just saved from demolition to make way for the **National Westminster Tower**, the tallest office block in Europe at 600ft and 52 storeys. The original development envisaged demolishing not only the Club but also the Banking Hall which now adjoins the Tower and is used for conferences, banquets, etc. The National Westminster Tower opened in 1980 and houses the headquarters of the banking concern; there is a viewing area at the top from which the Thames Estuary, the Chilterns and the South Coast can be seen on a clear day but it is only open to guests and invited customers (try your bank manager!) of the Bank. The Tower stands between Old Broad Street and Bishopsgate; the adjoining Banking Hall at 15 Bishopsgate was designed by John Gibson (1864-65).

Farther S in Threadneedle St (No. 30) is *Merchant Taylors' Hall*, the largest of the livery company halls, incorporated in 1327, damaged by the Great Fire of 1666, gutted by fire in 1941, and reopened in 1959. A 14C crypt survives. The company, incorporated in 1327, maintains a large public school for boys. The activity of the Merchant Taylors and the needlemakers (whose hall was nearby) probably gave the name to 'Threadneedle' Street. In Threadneedle St (N side), stood the old South Sea House, built in 1711 for the South Sea Company, where Lamb was a clerk in 1789-92 and where the 'South Sea Bubble' burst in 1719. The British Linen Bank was built over part of the site in 1902. Threadneedle St ends at Bishopsgate.

From the junction of Princes St and Lothbury, near the SW corner of the Bank of England, *Moorgate* (Pl. 9; 5) runs N. On the right, in Great Swan Alley, is the *Chartered Accountants' Hall*, a Renaissance-style building by John Belcher (1890-93; extended 1930), with sculptures by Hamo Thornycroft and H. Bates. The Moorgate, built in 1415, and pulled down in 1761, stood at the junction with London Wall. To the left in London Wall stands *Armourers' Hall* (1841), founded 1453. The Barbican beyond is described in Rte 21. In its right (E) section is *Carpenters' Hall*, rebuilt 1956-60, and, farther on, the church of *All Hallows London Wall* by the younger Dance (1765-67), with a fine plaster ceiling and blue and gold decorations, well restored in 1962. The monumental pulpit is entered through steps from the vestry. Part of the medieval city wall may be seen in the churchyard.

Moorgate continues beyond London Wall; parallel to the W, *Moorfields* preserves the memory of the marshy district outside the old Moorgate, once the resort of archers, washerwomen, and (later) of booksellers. John Keats was born in 1795, the son of a livery stable keeper, on the site of No. 85 (public house; tablet). Opposite is the School of Business Studies of the City of London Polytechnic. On the right opens *Finsbury Circus* (bowling green), with Britannic House by Lutyens. In Ropemaker St (left) Daniel Defoe died in 1731. From here the line of Moorgate is continued by *Finsbury Pavement* to the unexpected expanse (reminiscent of Continental cities) of *Finsbury Square* (underground car park) laid out by George Dance the Younger. To the W runs Chiswell St, at the end of which is *Whitbread's Brewery* (see p 239).

N of the square begins the long *City Road*. Here is the entrance to the drill-ground and headquarters (*Armoury House*, 1737) of the **Honourable Artillery Company** of the City of London, the oldest military body in the country, having been incorporated by Henry VIII in 1537 under the title of the Guild or Fraternity of St. George.

It has been established at its present home since 1642, and since 1660 the captain-general has usually been the Sovereign or the Prince of Wales. Officers for the Trained Bands of London were supplied by this company, in whose ranks Milton, Wren, and Pepys served. The H.A.C. has the rare privilege of marching through the City of London with fixed bayonets.

Admission only when accompanied by member of H.A.C. or on written application. The facilities are available for functions.

Visitors should note the Long Room; and the Court Room with a fine suit of armour (Greenwich; c 1555) and a unique leading-staff of 1693.—In 1638 Robert Keayne, a member of the London company, founded the Ancient and Honourable Artillery Company of Boston, in the United States, the oldest military body in America. On 15 Sept 1784, Lunardi made a balloon ascent from the H.A.C. ground and became the first aerial traveller in the English atmosphere.

The adjoining castellated building is a Territorial Force headquarters. Immediately to the N, between the City Road and Bunhill Row (formerly Artillery Walk), lie **Bunhill Fields**, the famous cemetery of the Non-conformists, disused since 1852, the earliest burial on record being 1623. Possibly this is the site of a Saxon burial-ground which gave these two fields the name of Bon or Bone-Hill Fields. Here are the graves of *John Bunyan* (d 1688; recumbent effigy; restored 1950), in the second turning to the S from the main walk; *Daniel Defoe* (d 1731; obelisk erected in 1870 by boys and girls of England), to the N of the main walk, close by (renovated 1949); *Dr Isaac Watts*, the hymn-writer (d 1748; altar-tomb), to the E of Defoe (renovated 1951); *William Blake* (d 1828), 25 yards NW of Defoe; and *Susannah Wesley* (d 1742), mother of John Wesley (renovated 1957).

Milton wrote 'Paradise Regained' and died in 1674 at a house (No. 125; demolished) in Bunhill Row. In the *Friends' Burial Ground*, across Bunhill Row, laid out as a garden in 1952 and surrounded by new flats, is the grave of George Fox (1624-91), founder of the Society of Friends.

On the opposite side of City Road stands *Wesley's Chapel*, built in 1777, with a statue of John Wesley (1703-91), the founder of Methodism, in front of it and his grave behind. The chapel still retains Wesley's pulpit. **Wesley's House** (tablet; adjoining the chapel), where he moved in 1779, contains the simple room in which he died 12 years later. Here also are mementoes of his brother, Charles Wesley.

Wesley's House and Chapel, City Road, London EC1. Tel. 01-253 2262. Open: Chapel from 08.00-18.00, weekdays. Admission free. Sunday Service at 11.00. House, Mon to Sat 10.00-16.00. Admission charge. Access: Underground, Moorgate, Old Street.

The Foundry, near by, used by Wesley as a headquarters in 1739-78 before he built the chapel, is commemorated by a plaque in Tabernacle St (No. 21), just to the E.—A little farther on City Road crosses *Old Street* (busy roundabout) which leads right (E) to Shoreditch and left (W) to Clerkenwell, passing the partly demolished church of *St. Luke* with its obelisk steeple by Hawksmoor and John James (1727-33). Here William Caslon (1692-1766), the type-founder, is buried.

City Road continues past *Moorfields Eye Hospital* to (1m; Buses 104, 43) the *Angel*, a busy road junction named after a long-demolished but once famous coaching tavern. It was the birthplace of James Pollard (1792-1867), the artist.

23   Cannon Street, Thames Street, The Monument, Lombard Street, Leadenhall Street, Lloyds

Access: Underground, Cannon Street, Mansion House.

Cannon Street (Pl. 8; 8) runs E through an area once occupied by wax-chandlers; its name is a corruption of Candlewick Street. The *London Chamber of Commerce* (1934; left) offices are at the corner of Queen Street. In Dowgate Hill, just before Cannon St Station, are the decorative entrances to the halls of the *Tallow Chandlers* (No. 4), the *Skinners* (No. 8), and the *Dyers* (No. 10), the first two rebuilt soon after the Great Fire. The Financial Times is at *Bracken House* (1960), a striking pink building, with the FT Index prominently displayed (see p 243).

Queen Victoria St intersects Cannon St (to the W) close to Beaver House. To the N is the church of *St. Mary Aldermary*, so called, says Stow, because 'elder than any church of St. Marie in the City'. It was rebuilt by Wren after 1681 (tower 1704). The plaster fan-vaulting is especially noteworthy. Milton married his third wife, Elizabeth Minshull, in the church (1663). Beyond Queen St is the huge *Bucklersbury House* (1958) occupying most of the triangle (right) between Queen Victoria St, Cannon St, and Walbrook. In the forecourt of Temple House are the remains of a TEMPLE OF MITHRAS, unearthed in 1954 beneath the foundations of Bucklersbury House, about 80 yards to the SE, adjoining Walbrook.

Built shortly before AD 200, it is 58.5ft long and 26ft wide and has the triple W end characteristic of Mithraic temples; the bases of two rows of pillars and the walls supporting them have survived. The important sculptural finds from the site are now in the Museum of London.

In Bread St, *St. Mildred's* church (1677-83, by Wren), where Shelley and Mary Godwin were married in 1816, was destroyed in the last war. A memorial to Adm. Phillip (1738-1814), governor of the first colony of British settlers in Australia (1788), who was born in Bread St, has been moved farther N, to Gateway House in Cannon St.

Upper Thames Street runs parallel with Cannon Street to the S.

High Timber St joins Upper Thames St on its ancient line just E of the tower of *St. Mary Somerset*. The rest of the church, built by Wren in 1695, was taken down in 1871.

Although warehouses and wharves have now gone, some narrow lanes bearing historic names still run down to steps into the Thames. In a lane (right) the quaint *Samuel Pepys* pub, with views over the river, occupies a 19C warehouse. Queensbridge House and Queen's Quay have superseded *Queenhithe Dock*, once an important harbour for the City, the property of Isabella of Angoulême, and the earliest fish market in London. From the evocative cobbled lane to the E its shape and extent are still apparent. *Vintners' Hall*, near the corner of Queen St, was rebuilt in 1671, after the Great Fire, though the Court Room (1446; panelled in 1576) was preserved. The company, incorporated in 1437, owns valuable tapestries and a painting of St. Martin, by the School of Rubens (see also Swan Upping, p 300). In Vintners' Lane a statue of a Vintry Ward school boy (1840), in Coade stone, survives.

The picturesque Garlick Hill (N) once devoted to the fur trade, affords a view of the tower of St. Mary le Bow. Here the church of *St. James Garlickhithe* (open for services) is so called, according to Stow, because garlic was sold on the Thames near by. The attractive steeple, attributed to Hawksmoor, dates from 1714-17. The interior, by Wren (1676-83), with good wood-carving and ironwork, and an organ attributed to Father Smith (1697), has been pleasingly restored. Between the two lanes to the W lies the *Hall of the Painter-Stainers*, rebuilt after the Great Fire of 1666, restored after damage in 1941, and extended in 1961. A stone's throw N is *Beaver House* of the Hudson's Bay Company.

Queen St (right) forms the approach to *Southwark Bridge* (Pl. 8; 8), originally the work of John Rennie in 1813-19 but entirely rebuilt in 1913-21 (good view of the river). Beyond Queen St, on the N side of Upper Thames St, Whittington Gardens commemorate Richard ('Dick') Whittington (d 1423), three times Mayor of London, who lived in College Hill (named from a college he founded), to the N. He rebuilt and was buried in *St. Michael Paternoster Royal*, again rebuilt by Wren in 1686-94, with a steeple of 1713. It was beautifully restored (with fine windows by John Hayward) and rededicated in 1968 as the chapel and headquarters (offices in the tower) of the Missions to Seamen, a society 'ministering to the needs of seamen throughout the world'.

To the N is **Cannon Street Station** (Pl. 9; 7), rebuilt except for its decorative riverside turrets. Beneath Bush Lane House excavations in 1965 revealed traces of a Governor's Palace built c AD 80-100

beside the mouth of the Walbrook stream, overlooking the Thames.
At a lower level timber foundations suggested this was the earlier
site of a Roman fort. Opposite is the *Bank of China*, built on the site
of *St. Swithin's*, a church rebuilt by Wren and destroyed in 1940-41
(the churchyard is now a garden in Salters' Hall court). Immured in
the wall of the bank is LONDON STONE, generally believed to have
been the Milliarium of Roman London, from which the distances on
the Roman high roads were measured. This is the stone which Jack
Cade struck with his staff, exclaiming 'Now is Mortimer Lord of this
City'. In St. Swithin's Lane is *Founders' Hall* (No. 13).

In Abchurch Yard, off Abchurch Lane, the next side-street to the
left, stands *St. Mary Abchurch* (i.e. 'up' church, from its high site),
rebuilt by Wren in 1681-86 and the least altered, containing wood
carvings by Grinling Gibbons (open Mon to Fri 10.00-16.00). The
dome, with its paintings by William Snow (1708), is an architectural
tour de force; considerably damaged in Sept 1940, it has been finely
restored (1948-53). The 14C crypt is plain and vaulted. To the S, in
Laurence Pountney Hill, two houses (Nos 1 and 2) survive from 1703.

Cannon St ends at a busy crossroads where King William St
converges with Gracechurch St and *Eastcheap*, on a site believed to
have been occupied by the 'Boar's Head Tavern' where Falstaff and
Prince Hal caroused. *St. Clement Eastcheap*, to the N, was rebuilt by
Wren in 1683-87. It contains a handsome carved pulpit, possibly by
Grinling Gibbons, and font-cover, and a fine organ of 1695.

On the Thames waterfront to the S is Mondial House, the International Telephone Centre, and Angel Passage or Swan Lane lead
(right) to a terrace overlooking the Thames. Here, opposite the
graceful pinnacles of Southwark Cathedral, the moored paddle
steamer 'Princess Elizabeth', now a bar/restaurant (Mon to Fri),
affords a fine view of London Bridge. **London Bridge** (Pl. 9; 7) was
rebuilt in 1967-73 by Harold Knox King, remaining open to traffic
throughout the operation. Borne on three arches of pre-stressed
concrete faced with granite, it is 105ft wide. The former bridge,
designed by John Rennie, begun in 1825 by his sons John and George
Rennie and completed in 1832, was sold for £1,025,000. It was
dismantled into 10,000 granite slabs which were numbered and
shipped to Lake Havasu City, Arizona, where it was re-erected over
an artifical lake.

A wooden bridge across the Thames existed by the 1C AD. This probably
survived until 1176, having been repaired by the Saxons. The popular rhyme
'London Bridge is falling down' may date from this time, when it was resolved
to 'Build it up with stone so strong'. The new bridge, about 100ft W of the old,
was begun in 1176 by Peter of Colechurch, at the instance of Henry II, but it
was not completed till 1209 in the reign of King John. It stood close to the W
end of the church of St. Mary Magnus. Rows of wooden houses sprang up on
each side, and in the middle was a chapel dedicated to St. Thomas Becket. At
each end stood a fortified gate, on the spikes of which the heads of traitors
were exposed. It was notoriously difficult to navigate because of the narrow
passage between the starlings and the force of the ebb tide. After a fire in 1758
the houses were demolished and the bridge partly reconstructed and opened
in 1763. This bridge, the only bridge over the Thames until 1729, was removed
after the completion of Rennie's bridge 100ft upstream.

London Bridge divides the Thames into 'above' and 'below' bridge.
Downstream is the Port of London, the reach immediately adjacent to the bridge
being known as the *Pool*, while upstream is the *King's Reach*.

Fishmongers' Hall stands at the N end of London Bridge (entrance from the viaduct across Upper Thames St which carries King William St on to London Bridge). With a fine classical facade on the river, it was erected in 1831-34 by Henry Roberts and Gilbert Scott. It was badly damaged in September 1940, when it was the first of the City Halls to catch fire; similarly, a previous Fishmongers' Hall on this site was the first to burn during the Great Fire of 1666.

The Fishmongers' Company is one of the richest as well as one of the oldest of the twelve great livery companies. Its origin is lost in remote antiquity, but it is unquestionable that the Company existed before the reign of Henry II. The fine interior has been restored in its former style. It contains the Annigoni portrait (1955) of Queen Elizabeth II (the model for stamps and bank-notes), a painted wooden figure of Sir William Walworth, the Mayor who killed Wat Tyler in 1381, and a fine dagger he is supposed to have used; also a richly embroidered pall of the Tudor period.

On the other side of London Bridge is *Lower Thames Street*, which retains its cobbled surface and was once redolent of fish from end to end. Geoffrey Chaucer is said to have lived in this street from 1379 to 1385, during part of which period he was Comptroller of the Petty Customs in the Port of London. On the right is *St. Magnus Martyr*, rebuilt by Wren in 1671-76. The *Steeple, 185ft high, one of Wren's masterpieces, was not completed till 1705. The passage beneath the tower was from 1763 to 1832 part of the footpath of Old London Bridge. Miles Coverdale (d 1569), author of the first complete English version of the Bible (1535), was rector of St. Magnus in 1563-66 and is buried in the church.

To the N, at the top of Fish Street Hill, rises the **Monument**, a fluted Doric column, 202ft high, erected from the designs of Wren in 1671-77, to commemorate the Great Fire of London, which broke out on 2 September 1666, in Pudding Lane, at a point alleged to be exactly 202ft from the Monument. A winding staircase (of 311 steps) ascends to the upper gallery, which commands a wide and striking view. The flaming gilt urn surmounting the Monument is 42ft high.

The Monument in the foreground, City high rise in the background

The cage enclosing the gallery was added to prevent suicides. The allegorical relief by C.G. Cibber shows Charles II and the Duke of York encouraging the stricken city.

The Monument, Monument Street, EC3. Tel. 01-626 2717. Open April to Sept, Mon to Fri 09.00–18.00, Sat, Sun 14.00–18.00; Oct–March, Mon–Sat 09.00–14.00 and 15.00–16.00. Admission charge. Access: Underground, Monument.

A little further on is the former **Billingsgate Market** which moved to West India Docks in 1982. It took its name from an old gate, supposed to be called after Belin, a legendary king of the Britons and claimed to be the only market in which every variety of fish was sold—'wet, dried, and shell'.

Billingsgate Wharf, said to be the oldest on the river, was used from very early times (perhaps from the 9C) as a landing-place for fishing boats and other small vessels. The new blue glass building on the adjoining site is linked to the old building which is being converted into offices.
    The narrow Lovat Lane, opposite Billingsgate leads N to the church of St. Mary at Hill built by Wren in 1670-76. The woodwork is noteworthy, and the church is filled with box pews. The sword rests are exceptionally fine, and the organ by William Hill was rebuilt in 1971. The ceiling dates from 1849. The church is still the venue for the annual Sea Harvest Thanksgiving Festival. The Dickensian atmosphere of the neighbouring passages is being conserved. A narrow passage skirts the church on the S and emerges beneath a grim gateway surmounted by a skull and crossbones in St. Mary at Hill. Here (right) is the attractive Hall of the Watermen and Lightermen (1776-80). At the corner of St. Mary at Hill and Lower Thames St a Roman Bath was discovered in 1969 which belonged to a private house of c AD 200. Finds on the site showed the house to have been occupied until the second half of the 5C.

Beyond Billingsgate is the **Custom House**, a large classical edifice (1814-26), the fine river facade of which is well seen from London Bridge. St. Dunstan's Hill, opposite, leads up to the church of St. Dunstan in the East, rebuilt in 1671 by Wren, who added the fine square lantern tower in 1698. The body of the church was severely damaged in 1941; the shell remains and has been beautifully planted by the Worshipful Company of Gardeners as a public garden. A fig tree commemorating the coronation of George VI in 1937 survives outside the S wall. In Idol Lane (N) a wine merchant occupies a fine Georgian house. Harp Lane, a little further on, contains the Bakers' Hall (No. 9; 1963) with windows by John Piper commemorating the burning of the former halls.
    Turn W along Great Tower Street past the church of St. Margaret Pattens (restored 1956), built by Wren in 1684-87, with a fine tall spire. It is thought to be named from the pattens (shoes with iron rings attached to the soles to protect the wearer from muddy roads) once made and sold in the lane. The font and the reredos are fine works; the altarpiece is by Carlo Maratti. The two canopied pews are unique in London.

The S pew has on its ceiling the engraved monogram C.W.; possibly Christopher Wren himself occupied this pew. N of the altar is the original Beadle's pew and a punishment bench. The church is a Christian Study Centre, with conference rooms in the gallery.

Continue to the Tower (Rte 24) or head N along Rood Lane to Fenchurch Street.
    Lombard Street (Pl. 9; 5) to the W has for centuries been one of the

chief banking and financial centres of London; it is hung with decorative bank signs. It derives its name from the 'Lombard' money-lenders from Genoa and Florence, who during the 13-16C took the place of the Jews in this profession. On the right the church of **St. Mary Woolnoth** forms a monumental bastion between King William St and Lombard St. A building of great originality, it was erected by Nicholas Hawksmoor in 1716-24 and altered in 1875. It was the only City church to remain intact throughout the air raids of 1940-45. It is a guild church and used by London's German-speaking Swiss community on Sundays.

The interior contains an elaborate reredos, and ornamental woodwork. From the pulpit John Newton (1725-1807; tablet on N wall) helped to inspire William Wilberforce, Claudius Buchanan, and Hannah More to their philanthropic pursuits. On the S wall is a memorial to Edward Lloyd (p 254); and (end of the S aisle) the armour of Sir Martin Bowes (d 1566), a Lord Mayor of London, is preserved. The 'Spital Sermon' is preached here in Easter week, attended by the Lord Mayor and aldermen.

The adjacent post office occupies the site of the General Post Office from 1678 till the move to St. Martin's in 1829. Post Office Court also houses the *Bankers' Clearing House*, in which, four times daily, the mutual claims of the various banks against each other in the form of cheques and bills are compared and settled by cheques on the Bank of England. To the left is the church of *St. Edmund the King and Martyr*, completed by Wren in 1679 (steeple, 1708). In George Yard, behind, a pleasant Neptune fountain in bronze fronts the *George and Vulture*, in Castle Street, a tavern known to all readers of 'Pickwick', now a restaurant and pub, bookings on 01-626 9710. Beyond (right), is the striking grey *Lombard Bank* building, and, on the corner of Gracechurch St are the headquarters of *Barclays Bank* (1959) with sculptures by Sir Charles Wheeler.

The line of Lombard St is continued beyond *Gracechurch St* by *Fenchurch Street* (Pl. 9; 7). The *Midland Bank* (1962; right) has a sculpture by W.H. Chattaway.

Mincing Lane, named from the 'Minchens' or nuns of St. Helen's, was the headquarters of the wholesale tea trade. The *Hall of the Clothworkers*, rebuilt in 1958 on the E side after its destruction in 1941, is the sixth hall on this site since 1456. The archives and the plate, among which is a loving cup presented by Samuel Pepys, Master of the Company in 1677, were saved. A pleasant oasis of green (left) marks the churchyard of St. Gabriel Fenchurch (destroyed 1666). At the corner of *Mark Lane* (i.e. Mart Lane) is the war-memorial building of the Institute of Marine Engineers. Nearby is the 15C tower of *All Hallows Staining*, adjoining which is a 12C crypt chapel brought from a bastion of the city wall, near Cripplegate, and rebuilt here by the Clothworkers in 1872. Near the S end of the Lane is the principal seat of the grain trade, now a commodity market, with the *Corn Exchange* established here in the mid-18C; the new building was opened in 1953 (Tel. 01-480 6610 to view).

In Hart St, leading E from Mark Lane, the *Ship* has a painted stucco facade. Here is the church of ***St. Olave** (open 08.00-18.00 Mon to Sat, 10.00-18.00 Sun), one of the few churches that escaped the Great Fire of 1666. Seriously damaged in 1941, it was sensitively restored in 1951-54, when Haakon VII of Norway laid the 'King's Stone' in front of the sanctuary recalling the Norwegian birth of the patron saint, and incorporating a stone from Trondheim Cathedral. Samuel

Pepys (1633-1703) the diarist, who lived in the adjacent Seething Lane, was a regular attendant at this church (the entrance to his Navy Office Pew may be seen in the churchyard; a plaque was erected within the church in 1883). Mrs Pepys (1640-69) is commemorated with a charming bust, attributed to John Bushnell (N side of the chancel), erected by her husband. Both are buried beneath the high altar. There is an annual Pepys memorial service in June.

Below the monument to Mrs Pepys is a fine monument to the Bayning brothers (d 1610 and 1616). Over one of the pillars on the S side of the nave is a plaque to John Watts (1780), 'President of the Council of New York'. Other fine monuments include: (S aisle) Sir James Deane (d 1608); (N aisle) Peter Capponi (d 1582), a Florentine merchant who died of the plague; and Andrew Riccard (d 1672). The pulpit and altar rails are noteworthy. From the W end of the S aisle (light on left) narrow steps descend to a small Crypt (probably late 12C), with an ancient well. Here are displayed finds from the churchyard and well, and sculptural fragments of the 15-18C. The skulls over the churchyard gate in Seething Lane (Dickens's 'St. Ghastly Grim') are supposed (somewhat doubtfully) to refer to the burials during the Plague in 1665.

When Pepys was Secretary of the Admiralty the Navy Office stood in *Crutched Friars* (i.e. 'Crossed Friars', from an old monastery), the prolongation of Hart St to the E. *Crutched Friars House* (No. 42) is one of the few surviving City residences of the early 18C. It is now the residence of the Director of Toc H, the brotherhood established to perpetuate the memory and devoted spirit of the Talbot Houses of Poperinghe and Ypres. The first Toc H (i.e. T.H. in the army signaller's alphabet) opened at Poperinghe in 1915, was named in honour of Lieutenant Gilbert Talbot.

To the right, in Railway Place, is **Fenchurch Street Station** (1840), the first to be built in the City. At the corner of Fenchurch St and Lloyd's Avenue is **Lloyd's Register of Shipping**, a society (distinct from Lloyd's, see below) founded in 1760 and reconstituted in 1834. The roof is surmounted by an appropriate gilt weathervane.

Its primary object is to secure an accurate classification of merchant shipping, but it now discharges many other important functions for which 'surveyors' are maintained in the chief ports of the world. The Register Book contains full particulars of all sea-going merchant vessels of 100 tons and upwards. The highest class for steel and iron vessels is 100 A1, and for wooden vessels A1, the letter A referring to the hull and the figure 1 to the equipment.

Leadenhall St now converges with Fenchurch St, and is prolonged by *Aldgate*, a short street taking its name from one of the old City gates. A draught (draft) on *Aldgate Pump* (still standing at beginning of street) was once a cant expression for a worthless bill. Geoffrey Chaucer leased the house above the Aldgate from the City of London in 1374 (tablet). Across Mitre St is the *Sir John Cass Foundation School*, founded in 1710 by a charitable alderman (d 1718; buried in St. Botolph's) and rebuilt in 1909 (playground on the roof).

Jewry St, to the S, reminds that we are here, as the names over the shops betoken, in the great Jewish district of London, which extends eastwards to Whitechapel and Mile End. In Duke's Place, just N of Aldgate, stood the 18C GREAT SYNAGOGUE, the Jewish cathedral of London. Off Bevis Marks, in Heneage Lane, is the handsome *Spanish and Portuguese Synagogue* removed hither in 1701 from Creechurch Lane and the oldest in use in England.

Aldgate High St, continuing Aldgate, forms part of a complicated traffic system round large modern buildings, where only the *Hoop and Grapes* on the S shows the former scale—a pub with foundations dating to the 13C; the oldest in the City. The building is probably late 17C. Beyond Houndsditch is *St. Botolph Aldgate*, built by George Dance the Elder in 1741-44, and restored in 1966-71, after a fire. In the octagonal vestibule beneath the tower is a handsome font and cover. Here have been placed a memorial to Sir John Cass (1661-1718), and the monuments of Robert Dow (d 1612; with an anxious portrait bust), and Thomas Darcy and Sir Nicholas Carew, beheaded on Tower Hill in 1538. The organ, a gift from Thos. Whiting in 1676 (plaque), was built by Renatus Harris. Thomas Bray, founder of the S.P.C.K. and S.P.G., was vicar from 1708 to 1722. William Symington (1763-1831), pioneer of steam navigation, is buried here (tablet on W wall). In the S aisle is a finely carved panel of David playing the harp which, together with the lectern, dates from the early 18C. Daniel Defoe was married here in 1683, and Jeremy Bentham christened in the church in 1747. The founder of the Sir John Cass School is commemorated in February.

Houndsditch, running NW from Aldgate to Bishopsgate (see below) and forming the E boundary of this part of the City, is the headquarters of Jewish brokers and dealers. The Sunday morning activity here and in *Middlesex Street* (formerly 'Petticoat Lane'), a little E, is one of London's most popular tourist attractions.

Petticoat Lane, Aldgate, E1. Open Sunday morning (adjoining street markets operate through the week). Access: Underground, Aldgate, Aldgate East, Liverpool Street.

During the 15C this was Hog Lane which a century later started its association with cloth and clothing as traders were moved from London Bridge; particularly dealers in second-hand clothes. In 1603 a map of the area refers to it as Petticoat Lane because of its clothes stalls. Jewish immigration during the 18C gave further impetus to the market's growth. In 1870 the name was changed to Middlesex Street although the name of Petticoat Lane has continued despite efforts to end Sunday trading.

Today half the stalls in Middlesex Street and adjoining Goulston Street still sell clothing but kitchen and household goods are also available. In the side streets the market continues; each has its own character. Note particularly Cutler Street specialising in gold and jewellery.

Petticoat Lane is crowded on Sundays through the year from 09.00 to 14.00—visitors should watch their bags and wallets. Try the Jewish fare at Blooms in nearby Whitechapel High Street.

The *Minories*, running S from Aldgate to the Tower, was formerly famous for its gun-makers. Its name is derived from an old convent of Minoresses ('Sorores Minores'), or nuns of St. Clare. Off St. Clare St, within the convent precincts, was found (1964) the tomb of Anne Mowbray (d 1481), wife of Richard, Duke of York (comp. p 73).—In America Square, just W of the Minories, was the home of Nathan Meyer Rothschild (1777-1836), founder of the English branch of the family. No. 100 (rebuilt in 1969) houses the *School of Navigation* of the City of London Polytechnic (which incorporates the Sir John Cass College). The new Light Docklands Railway will operate from here, due to open in 1987.

Aldgate High Street is continued E to Whitechapel. On the corner of Whitechapel High Street and Aldgate High Street are the new glass-clad offices of the Sedgwick Group which incorporate a conference centre based on the 300-seater Chaucer Theatre (also used for recitals, concerts and ethnic plays and music).

Turn back towards Bank, along Leadenhall Street.

In *Leadenhall St*, to the right, is the church of *St. Katherine Cree* (i.e. Christchurch, from a priory founded by Maud, queen of Henry I in 1108), rebuilt in 1628-30, with a mixture of Gothic and Renaissance detail.

This church was consecrated by Laud, then bishop of London. The cover of his prayer book is kept in the vestry. The chapel in the SE commemorates both Laud and Charles and contains the tomb of Sir Nicholas Throckmorton (d 1570). The E window, with stained glass of 1630?, is in the form of a catherine-wheel. The font dates from c 1640. The organ was built by Father Smith (1686). At the SW angle a pillar of the old church projects 3ft above the floor, the level of which is said to have risen 15ft. An unverified tradition has it that Holbein (d 1543) was buried in the earlier church. The annual 'Lion Sermon' (on 16 Oct) commemorates the escape from a lion of Lord Mayor Gayer, who held office in Charles I's time. The church was restored in 1962; the Industrial Christian Fellowship has offices in the N and S aisles.

Further W, on the N side of Leadenhall St opens a spacious piazza beneath two mercantile office blocks; in contrast, at the corner of St. Mary Axe, stands the church of *St. Andrew Undershaft*, built in 1520-32. The name is derived from the ancient practice (discounted in 1517) of erecting a 'shaft' or maypole, taller than the tower, in front of the S door.

At the E end of the N aisle is the alabaster monument of *John Stow* (1526-1605); the antiquary. The pen in Stow's hand is annually renewed by the Lord Mayor in March or April. On the same wall, farther to the W, is the monument of *Sir Hugh Hamersley*, Lord Mayor in 1627, notable for the fine figures of the two attendants. In the S aisle is a tablet recording that Holbein (1497-1543) was once a resident of this parish. The font, by Nicholas Stone, dates from 1631, and the organ (restored in 1969) was built by Renatus Harris in 1696. The spandrels are adorned with 18C paintings, and the roof was restored with its 16C bosses in 1950.

In St. Mary Axe (in an area with the offices of many shipping companies) is the **Baltic Exchange**, the headquarters of a body of merchants and brokers who deal in floating cargoes, consisting of grain, timber, oil, coal, and other commodities, and now also in air charter. Visits by appointment. This institution is an amalgamation of the old Baltic (which sprang from 'The Virginia & Baltick Coffee House') and the Shipping Exchange (the modern representative of the old 'Jerusalem Coffee House'). The name 'Baltic' is now misleading.

To the S stood the palatial building of **Lloyd's of London** (Pl. 9; 6, by Sir Edwin Cooper, 1928). A larger building by Terence Heysham is on the other side of Lime St (1952-58), including the old *Under-writing Room* ('The Room').

In 1979 Lloyds received permission to demolish the 1928 building and construct a new building on the site between Leadenhall Street, Lime Street and Leadenhall Place. Designed by Richard Rogers and Partners, the new building will be occupied from Easter 1986. The unique design features the services of the building in external towers and a central interior atrium with only eight supporting columns through 12 full floors of the building. The central feature is the Underwriting Room which will move here from the Lime Street Extension. There will be a visitor's gallery on the 3rd floor providing a view of the dealings. Opening June 1986. Open Mon to Fri 10.00-16.00. (Lloyds Information Department 01-623 7100). The six external satellite towers contain lifts, staircases, lavatories and plant and the walls are of sparkling glass and transparent bands. There will be observation lifts in three of the satellite towers. A number of historic rooms from the previous building have been included such as the Committee Room, which originally came from Bowood House in Wiltshire, the old library from the 1928 building, the Special Dining Room, the Lutyen's War Memorial which will stand at the Leadenhall Market end of Green Yard and the Nelson Collection to be accommodated in a secure area.

Lloyd's Underwriting Rooms, an association of underwriters and insurance brokers transacting most kinds of insurance, arose from a gathering of merchants (1688) in Edward Lloyd's coffee-house in Tower St (later in Lombard St and in the Royal Exchange), whose original business was marine insurance. It is still the centre of shipping intelligence. Reports are sent by Lloyd's 1500 agents and sub-agents from ports throughout the world.

On the site of Lloyd's stood (till 1862) EAST INDIA HOUSE, where Charles Lamb (1792-1825), James Mill (1819-36), and John Stuart Mill (1822-58) were clerks in the service of the East India Company. The two Mills each became head of the office, but Lamb's policy of 'making up for coming late by going away early' did not lead to similar promotion.

The 28-storey block of *Commercial Union Insurance* and the 12 storey *P & O Building* are set in an open piazza off Leadenhall Street with the church of St. Helen's to the N. This attractive modern development was designed by Collins, Melvin and Ward.

To the left Whittington Avenue leads to *Leadenhall Market* (meat, game, etc.; in 1663 Pepys bought 'a leg of beef, a good one, for sixpence' here). The medieval street plan was retained when the elaborate arcaded buildings were erected in 1881 by Sir Horace

The interior of the Baltic Exchange (T.H. Smith and W. Wimble, 1900-03)

The Commercial Union Building, 387ft high, from St. Mary Axe (Gollins, Melvin, Ward & Partners, 1964-69)

Jones. The small area remains congested and lively. The buildings were built over part of a Roman Basilica and Forum erected in AD 80-100, one of the largest buildings of its kind in the whole Roman Empire. The London Metal Exchange is just off Leadenhall Market.

St. Peter's, farther on, stands on a high point of the City, occupied in Roman times by the administrative Basilica (comp. below), wrongly supposed by later tradition to have been the earliest Christian church in London. The existing structure, rebuilt by Wren in 1677-81, contains a carved wooden choir-screen, one of the only two known to be by Wren himself. The organ is by Father Smith (1681); Mendelssohn (1840 and 1842) played on the former keyboard (now in the vestry). The old bread-shelf (W wall) and the illuminated MS. of the Vulgate made for the church in 1290 are interesting, and there is a monument to the Fifth Army.

Leadenhall Street leads to *Cornhill* (Pl. 9; 5), and the Royal Exchange. Cornhill is a busy street, named from a long extinct grain-market; a Roman building for storing grain has even been discovered here. *Change Alley*, on the left, was the scene of wild speculations during the South Sea Bubble excitement in 1720. A restored pump of 1799 (left) recalls a predecessor of 1282; and drinking water still flows from a fountain of classical inspiration (1859) a few paces away. No. 39 Cornhill occupies the site of the house (burned down in 1748) in which Thomas Gray (1716-71), the poet, was born. St. Michael's Alley reveals the unexpectedly tall tower of *St. Michael's*, rebuilt by Wren and Hawksmoor in 1670-1724, and restored by Sir G.G. Scott in an incongruous Gothic style in 1857-60. At the end of the Alley a tablet on the Jamaica Wine House recalls the opening of the first London coffee house in 1657.

24 The Tower and Tower Hill/St. Katharine's Dock

Access: Underground, Tower Hill; by boat to Tower Pier from Westminster Pier or Charing Cross Pier, all the year round.

The area is dominated by the Tower of London, but the Tower Bridge Walkway, opened in 1982, All Hallows by the Tower and St. Katharine's Dock add further interest to this historic part of London. From April to September there is a tourist information centre at the Tower of London or at Tower Hill Underground Station.

A large section of the Roman and medieval wall of London (with a reproduction of a Roman funerary inscription found near by and a Roman bronze statue) can be seen in *Wakefield Gardens*, beyond the Underground station. A further, and very fine portion, with its Roman substructure, is visible in the basement of the Toc H hostel at 42 Trinity Square (adm. usually granted by courtesy, on application to the Warden's office; not Sat or Sun, or after 18.00); yet another stretch may be seen S of Midland House in *Cooper's Row* (explanatory tablet; see also London Wall Walk, p 234). It is here 30ft high; the upper part, pierced with windows and with a sentry walk along the top, was built in the 12C.

To the NE of the Tower is the building which used to house the

Royal Mint (Pl. 21; 2), built in 1810-12 by Sir R. Smirke, but since then considerably extended and damaged (1941). The Mint, first established within the Tower in 1275-85, has been moved to Llantrisant, near Cardiff.—Continue towards the Tower.

TOWER HILL is a small area just behind All Hallows by the Tower (see below); this was an important execution area from the 14C onwards with as many as 100 eminent people losing their heads here. At the execution of Lord Lovat in 1747 a public stand collapsed killing several people, and a gallows here was used during the Gordon Riots in 1780. A stone in the pavement in the *Trinity Square Gardens* on the other side of the road marks this gruesome site. Tower Hill has since been used for public gatherings, speeches and performances.

Close by is the *Mercantile Marine War Memorial*, by Lutyens (1928), extended by Maufe with sculptures by Wheeler (1955). Beyond the gardens rises a massive building by Sir Edwin Cooper (1922; until 1972 the offices of the Port of London Authority): **Trinity House**, adjacent, was erected by Samuel Wyatt in 1793-95 for the 'Guild, Fraternity or Brotherhood of the most Glorious and Undivided Trinity', the first charter of which was granted by Henry VIII in 1514.

The corporation consists of a Master (at present the Duke of Edinburgh), a Deputy Master, Wardens, Assistants, and Elder Brethren, besides a large number of Younger Brethren, and its object is the safety of navigation and the relief of poor mariners. Pepys was Master here in 1676 and 1685. The building, badly damaged in the Second World War, was restored by Sir A.E. Richardson and reopened in 1953 (adm. on Saturdays on written application to the Corporate Dept). In the main hall are statues of Captain Maples, by Jasper Latham (1683; the first lead statue known to have been made by a British sculptor), and of Capt. Sandes, by Scheemakers (1746), both formerly in the courtyards of Trinity Almshouses (p 292).

To the W is London's most visited 'parish church', **All Hallows by the Tower**.

All Hallows by the Tower, Byward Street, London EC3. Tel. 01-481 2928. Undercroft open Mon to Fri 09.00-17.30, Sat, Sun 09.00-17.30, except during services. Free except for groups. Access: Underground, Tower Hill.

Founded in the 7C, it was largely destroyed in the 2nd World War but the brick tower, from which Pepys watched the progress of the Great Fire, is the only surviving example of Cromwellian church architecture in London. The spire in the manner of Wren was added during restoration in 1958. This revealed an important Saxon arch, set now in the North wall of the new baptistery (1960). The font is of Gibraltar rock and the font-cover of limewood was carved by Grinling Gibbons (1682).

The tombs and the fine series of brasses in the sanctuary survived. In 1922 All Hallows became the guild church of Toc H (p 257); and in the sanctuary, with a 15C Antwerp painting, probably by Jan Provost, is the tomb of Alderman John Croke, with a casket containing the parent Lamp of Maintenance from which are lit all Toc H lamps around the world. In front of the sanctuary is a memorial bronze, by Cecil Thomas, to elder brethren of Toc H. In the S aisle is the *Mariners' Chapel*, with a 16C Spanish ivory crucifix. Stairs descend to the *Chapel of St. Clare*, a 17C vault, and a mid-14C crypt chapel.

The *Undercroft* is of the greatest interest. Entering from the W end note fragments of Roman remains, including some of two pavements, pottery and ashes of Roman London burned by Boudicca in AD 61, and a model of Roman London. There are also fragments of Saxon crosses, one of unusual type, later than the Danish occupation (c 1027-50). At the E end is a memorial chapel containing the ashes of members of Toc H. The plain crusading altar is from Richard I's castle at Athlit in Palestine; in front of it is the tomb in which the remains of Abp Laud rested (1645-63) before they were removed to St. John's

College, Oxford. William Penn (1644-1718), born on Tower Hill, was baptised in All Hallows; and here John Quincy Adams, sixth president of the United States, was married to Louisa Johnson in 1797.—Kitchener's Omdurman sword is preserved in the Vestry. There is a *Brass Rubbing Centre* in the crypt.

Continue downhill to the entrance to the **Tower of London** (Pl. 21; 2).

Open March to Oct, Mon to Sat 09.30-17.45, Sun 14.00-17.45; Nov to Feb, Mon to Sat 09.30-16.30; closed Sun. Admission charge. Additional charge for Crown Jewels (Crown Jewels usually closed in February for maintenance). Changing of the Guard on Tower Green 11.00 daily summer, alternate days winter. Ceremony of the Keys every night at 22.00; applications in writing to the Governor, Tower of London, London, EC3.
Long queues for admission may be experienced in summer (especially on Sundays). Yeoman Warders give frequent guided tours on fine days which begin at the Middle Tower, and include the Chapel Royal of St. Peter ad Vincula (otherwise kept locked; but the Sunday services at 09.30 and 11.00 are open to the public).

The Tower of London, a fortress of surpassing interest from its intimate connection with English history, the excellent preservation of its Norman and medieval buildings, and the many illustrious persons who have suffered within its walls, occupies a site astride the old City wall and covers an area of nearly 18 acres. The outer wall is surrounded by a deep *Moat* (drained in 1843; now beautifully planted as a public garden). Between the outer wall and the inner wall lies the narrow *Outer Ward*, and near the centre of the spacious *Inner Ward* rises the massive square *White Tower*. The entrance is near the SW corner, at the foot of Tower Hill.
A Wall Walk opened to the public in 1982 linking the towers of the Inner Wall —look for signs. Enter from Wakefield Tower and descend at Martin Tower.
The Tower, in its day a fortress, a royal residence, and a state-prison, is still maintained as an arsenal, with a garrison, and during the World Wars its former use as a prison was revived. The Constable for the Tower, always an officer of high dignity, is assisted by the Lieutenant; the duties of governor are now performed by the Major of the Tower, who is Resident Governor. Quite distinct from the garrison are the *Yeoman Warders* ('honorary members of the Queen's Bodyguard of the Yeomen of the Guard'), a body of about 40 men chosen from time-expired warrant and non-commissioned officers of the army. They wear historic costume, said to date from the time of Henry VII or Edward VI and are familiarly known as 'Beefeaters', a sobriquet probably derived from the rations anciently served to them.

History. The White Tower, the oldest part of the fortress, dates from the reign of William the Conqueror, when the Roman Wall formed the E boundary of the precinct. Of Richard I's additions only some work in the Bell Tower remains, and it was in the reign of Henry III (1216-72) that the 'small castle' was turned into a great concentric fortress. The outer curtain and the moat were added in 1275-85 by Edward I.
Built by William to overawe the citizens of London, the Tower has never been seriously assaulted, and its gloomy history is more that of a state-prison than of a fortress. Sir William Wallace (executed in 1305), King David II of Scotland (1346-57), and King John of France (1356-60) were confined here under Edward I and Edward III. James I of Scotland spent part of his long imprisonment in England (1406-24) at the Tower. In the same century the Tower witnessed the secret murders of Henry VI (1471), of the Duke of Clarence, brother of Edward IV (1478), and of Edward V and his brother, 'the little Princes in the Tower' (?1483). Henry VIII (1509-47) was here married to Catherine of Aragon and to Anne Boleyn; and here Anne Boleyn, after a trial in the Great Hall of the palace, was beheaded in 1536. Other victims in this reign were Bishop Fisher and Sir Thomas More (both beheaded 1535) and Queen Catherine Howard (beheaded 1542). Among the many prisoners of Mary's reign (1553-58) were Lady Jane Grey and her husband, Lord Guildford Dudley (both beheaded 1554), Elizabeth (afterwards queen), who was rigidly confined for two months; Cranmer and Sir

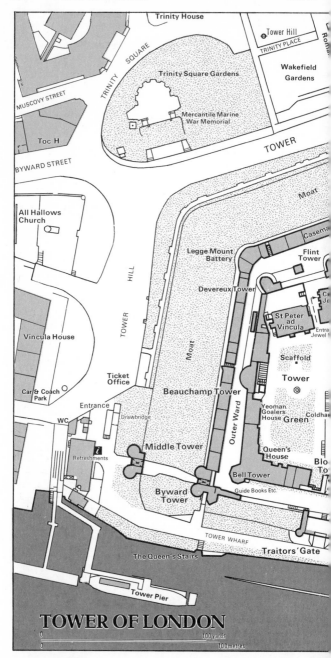

Trinity House

Tower Hill
TRINITY PLACE

TRINITY SQUARE

Trinity Square Gardens

Wakefield
Gardens

MUSCOVY STREET

Mercantile Marine
War Memorial

Toc H

TOWER

BYWARD STREET

Moat

All Hallows
Church

Casema

Legge Mount
Battery

Flint
Tower

TOWER HILL

Devereux Tower

C
Je

St Peter
ad
Vincula

Entra
Jewel

Vincula House

Moat

Scaffold

Tower

Ticket
Office

Car & Coach
Park

Beauchamp Tower

Outer Ward

Green

Yeoman
Goalers
House
Coldha

Entrance

Drawbridge

WC

Middle Tower

Queen's
House

Blo
To

Refreshments

Bell Tower

Byward
Tower

Guide Books Etc.

TOWER WHARF

Traitors' Gate

The Queen's Stairs

Tower Pier

TOWER OF LONDON

0   100 yards
0   100 metres

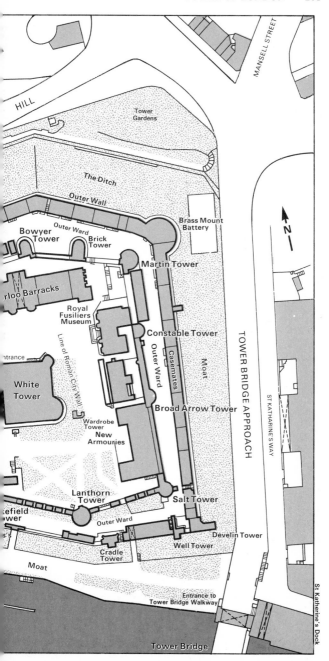

HILL

Tower
Gardens

The Ditch

Outer Wall

Brass Mount
Battery

Bowyer
Tower

Outer Ward

Brick
Tower

Martin Tower

N

rloo Barracks

Royal
Fusiliers
Museum

Constable Tower

Outer Ward

Casemates

Moat

ntrance

Line of Roman City Wall

White
Tower

TOWER BRIDGE APPROACH

ST KATHARINE'S WAY

Broad Arrow Tower

Wardrobe
Tower

New
Armouries

Lanthorn
Tower

Salt Tower

kefield
wer

Outer Ward

Develin Tower

Well Tower

Cradle
Tower

Moat

Entrance to
Tower Bridge Walkway

St Katherine's Dock

Tower Bridge

MANSELL STREET

Thomas Wyatt (beheaded 1554), by whose followers the Tower had been attacked, for the last time in its history. In Elizabeth's reign the Duke of Norfolk, who was beheaded in 1572 for intriguing in favour of Mary, Queen of Scots, and the Earl of Essex (beheaded 1601) were imprisoned here. James I (1603-25) was the last monarch who resided in the Tower. Sir Walter Raleigh was thrice confined in the Tower—1592, in 1603-16, and again in 1618, just before his execution. In 1605-06 Guy Fawkes and his companions were tortured in the dungeons of the White Tower. The Earl of Strafford and Abp Laud both passed through the Tower to the scaffold (in 1641 and 1645), followed, after the Restoration, by Viscount Stafford (1680), Lord William Russell (1683), and the Duke of Monmouth (1685). Charles II (1660-85), who here passed the night before his coronation in 1661, was the last monarch to sleep at the Tower. Lord Lovat, one of the prisoners brought to the Tower after the Jacobite risings of 1715 and 1745, was the last person beheaded in England (1747). Later prisoners in the Tower were John Wilkes (1763), Lord George Gordon (1780), Sir Francis Burdett (1810), and the Cato Street conspirators (1820). During the two World Wars several spies met their doom within its walls.

The modern entrance bridge passes over the pit of the *Drawbridge* built by Edward I. On the right is a bookshop/information centre, on the site of the former Lion Tower, where the King's menagerie was kept until 1834. Started by a gift of leopards from Frederick of Hohenstaufen to Henry III, and augmented in 1255 by an elephant from St. Louis of France, the collection finally formed the nucleus of the London Zoo. The tame ravens which haunt the inner ward are perhaps a relic of this collection. Pass through the *Middle Tower* (also built by Edward I) and cross over the *Moat* to the *Byward Tower* (late 13C; 14C additions). Opposite us rises the *Bell Tower* (late 12C), the prison of Fisher, More, and Monmouth, where curfew is still rung at sunset. Follow the *Outer Ward* or *Outer Bail* (comp. the Plan) to the E. On the right, farther on, is *St. Thomas's Tower*, above the *Traitors' Gate*, the old water-gate, through which many illustrious prisoners little deserving the name of traitor have entered the Tower. Both tower and gateway date from Edward I's reign. Opposite are the Bloody Tower and the *Wakefield Tower* (c 1225), traditionally thought to be the murdering place of Henry VI in 1471. A tablet in the floor marks the spot and flowers are laid on the anniversary of his death (21 May) by students of Eton and King's College, Cambridge. Pass under the Bloody Tower into the *Inner Ward*, dominated by the White Tower. On the right of the ascent is a portion of the medieval wall of the Inner Bailey, and part of Coldharbour Gate (1240).

The *White Tower*, the oldest part of the whole fortress, was begun about 1078 for William the Conqueror, by Gundulf, the builder also of Rochester Cathedral. It stands on a slope and rises to a height of 90ft on the S side. It measures 118ft from E to W, 107ft from N to S, and has walls 12-15ft thick. The exterior was restored by Wren, who altered all the windows but four on the S side; but the interior is still very much as it was in Norman times. Beneath an external staircase on the S side, removed during the restoration, the bones of the Little Princes were found in 1674.

Enter via the external staircase at the NE corner to the FIRST FLOOR. The interior contains a magnificent *Collection of arms and armour started by Henry VIII and first concentrated here for display by Charles II.

The first gallery shows *Hunting and Sporting Weapons* from the cross-bow to the elephant gun.—The *Tournament Gallery* contains superbly displayed and labelled exhibits which include: armour made for the Court of Emperor

Maximilian I (Innsbruck, c 1490); a suit made in Augsburg, c 1590; great wood saddle covered in rawhide (German, late 15C); half-armour made for the Elector Christian I of Saxony (1591). Most of the arms and armour for jousting was made at Greenwich (c 1610-25), and at Augsburg (16-17C). To the S the *Crypt* of St. John's Chapel houses fascinating relics of exhibitions mounted in the past; wooden heads and horses (one carved by Grinling Gibbons) used for the 'line of Kings' set up in armour in 1680; supposed trophies from the Armada; Jacobite trophies from Culloden; case of Victorian 'medieval' forgeries. Near the E end is the small cell in which Raleigh is said to have spent his final term of imprisonment.

Ascend to the BANQUETING FLOOR, and enter *St. John's Chapel, the oldest church in London and a splendid example of pure Norman architecture. Henry IV created 46 Knights here in 1399, and the institution of the Order of the Bath remains closely connected with the Chapel. The further gallery displays arms and armour from Anglo-Saxon times to the 15C. Also displayed here is a MS volume of the Making of Gunpowder and its use in the late Middle Ages (German, c 1450). At the end of the room is one of about five surviving examples of complete Gothic armour for the horse (German, c 1480). The adjoining gallery displays 16C armour, a superb array including an astonishing suit for a giant.

On the THIRD or COUNCIL FLOOR are the *Armouries, a collection from the English Royal Armour Workshop founded by Henry VIII at Greenwich, which operated from 1511 to 1642. This collection may move, possibly to Woolwich.

On the right of the entrance, Grotesque helmet presented to Henry VIII by Maximilian I (1514, Innsbruck); horse armour traditionally thought to be a present from Maximilian to Henry (1515, Flemish); armour, including magnificent horse armour, made for Henry at Greenwich (1520-35), the suits of Robert Dudley, Earl of Leicester, and of William Somerset, 3rd Earl of Worcester, both made at Greenwich (1575); and a German suit with English decoration (c 1580) made for Sir John Smythe.—The adjoining room displays infantry arms and armour of the 17C (including fabric and leather buff coats). Also, two suits probably made for Charles II (1640, and 1643, ?French); and armour belonging to James II.

From the Council Floor 114 steps descend to the DUNGEONS, where 16-19C weapons are displayed, including bronze mortars and cannon. In the Cannon Room, with a well 40ft deep, are bronze guns cast for Henry VIII, and many others, some of which are trophies of war.

The *Sub-Crypt* of St. John's Chapel is entered by a doorway traditionally regarded as the cell called 'Little Ease', where Guy Fawkes was confined, tied by his ankles and wrists to a ring in the floor.

To the N of the White-Tower is the long range of *Waterloo Barracks*, built by the Duke of Wellington (1845); in the W wing the *Crown Jewels* (separate admission charge; queues in summer) have been displayed since 1967. The ancient regalia were dispersed during the Commonwealth, and in consequence the present regalia date mostly from the Restoration when they were first publicly exhibited for a fee. The first room contains 19C banqueting *Plate*; silver gilt *Maces*; the *Great Sword of State* (1678; used at the opening of Parliament); insignia of the various *Orders of Knighthood*; silver State *Trumpets*; and the robes worn at Coronations since 1821.

Descend to the vaults protecting the Crown Jewels. The *Sword of Spiritual Justice*; *Sovereign's Sceptre with Dove*, called also the Rod of Equity and Mercy; the *Sword of Temporal Justice*.—The *Exeter*

Salt and the *Plymouth Wine Fountain* were accession gifts to Charles II.—Orbs made for Charles II and Mary II are displayed near the *Crown of Queen Elizabeth*, consort of George VI, with the famous Koh-i-Noor diamond, a spoil from the fall of Lahore presented to Queen Victoria in 1850 by the East India Company.—The *Queen Elizabeth Salt* dates from 1572-73; the font (1660) was first used for George IV's christening.—Jewelled *State Sword*, made for George IV; *St. Edward's Crown*, made for Charles II.—The *Imperial State Crown*, made for Queen Victoria's coronation, set with innumerable gems, including the large uncut ruby given to the Black Prince by Pedro the Cruel in 1367 and worn by Henry V at Agincourt, and one of the 'Stars of Africa' (317 carats), cut from the 'Cullinan' diamond, and worn by Queen Elizabeth II at her Coronation; *Sovereign's Sceptre with Cross*, containing the largest of the 'Stars of Africa' (530 carats), the largest cut diamond in the world; the *Coronation Ring* made for William IV.—The *Anointing Spoon*, of the late 12C, and the *Ampulla*, in the shape of an eagle, which dates probably from Henry IV (both restored for Charles II), are the only relics of the ancient regalia.—The *Maundy Dish* holds the Maundy money distributed by the sovereign on Thursday in Holy Week.—The display ends with the *Curtana* or point-less *Sword of Mercy*.

The *Old Waterloo Barracks*, built in 1845, also houses the Oriental Gallery and the Heralds' Museum, the latter open from April to September. The Oriental Gallery houses a striking display of arms and armour from Persia, China and Japan as well as North Africa, Turkey and the Balkans. Note the complete set of elephant armour (late 17C or early 18C) probably captured by Clive at the Battle of Plassey (1757) from the Nawab of Bengal. The Heralds' Museum illustrates the significance of heraldry in British history and society with a changing exhibition including the work of the Heralds and the College of Arms and its connection with the Orders of Chivalry.

Outside Waterloo Barracks, to the W, lies TOWER GREEN. A brass plate marks the *Site of the Scaffold*. Here suffered Anne Boleyn (1536), Catherine Howard (1542), Lady Jane Grey (1554), and the Earl of Essex (1601).—To the N is the *Chapel Royal of St. Peter ad Vincula* (adm. see above), rebuilt by 1307 and restored in 1512, and again in 1971.

Within the altar rails are buried Anne Boleyn, Catherine Howard, Lady Jane Grey, Essex, Monmouth, and other illustrious victims. In the crypt lie St. John Fisher, Sir Thomas More (bust by Raphael Maklouf, 1970), and the Jacobite lords executed in 1746; and there are many more recent memorials to distinguished soldiers. In the N aisle is the sumptuous monument of the Duke of Exeter (1447), formerly in St. Katharine's, Regent's Park.

Across Tower Green is the semicircular *Beauchamp Tower* (1281). The walls are covered with inscriptions and carvings by former prisoners, many brought here from other parts of the Tower. On the first floor are displayed some Roman tiles, etc. and medieval pottery found in the Tower. In the adjoining *Yeoman Gaoler's House* Lady Jane Grey was imprisoned; more recently Rudolf Hess was incarcerated here (May 1941). The top of the wall behind is *Princess Elizabeth's Walk*.

In the SW corner of the Green is the unpretentious Tudor *Queen's House* (no adm.), the residence of the Governor, incorporating the Bell Tower. In the council chamber of this house Guy Fawkes and his accomplices were examined in 1605. Adjacent is the *Bloody Tower* (begun probably by Henry III as a water-gate and completed by Edward I). Its portcullis is still in working order. This tower was the prison of Cranmer, Raleigh, and Laud, and of Judge Jeffreys, who died here of delirium tremens in 1689. Instruments of torture are displayed on the ground floor. The winding staircase ascends to the room in which the Little Princes are said to have been smothered by order of Sir James Tyrrell at the instigation of Richard III. Outside is *Raleigh's Walk*, where Sir Walter, during his second imprisonment, was permitted to take the air.

On the opposite side of the Inner Bailey is the *Regimental Museum of the Royal Fusiliers* (the City of London Regiment), containing uniforms, medals, equipment and relics relating to the history of the regiment from 1685 to the present. Separate admission charge.

Skirt the E side of the White Tower, passing the scanty remains of the *Wardrobe Tower* (late 12C), built against the Roman city wall, of which a fragment adjoins. Beyond, in an attractive late 17C building is the Board of Ordnance Gallery showing small arms.—Opposite, a HISTORY GALLERY opened in 1978 illustrates the history of the Tower in documents and models.

The tour of the Outer Ward towers (application should be made to the Resident Governor) starts at the *Byward Tower*, on the second floor of which an early 14C wall-painting of the Last Judgment was discovered in 1953, then proceeds to the NE part of the ward, where several German spies were shot. In the *Bowyer Tower* the Duke of Clarence is said to have been drowned in a butt of malmsey in 1478. Entering the interesting *Martin Tower*, the scene of Col. Blood's bold and nearly successful attempt to carry off the state crown (1671), the visit traverses the bailey wall along the *Constable*, *Broad Arrow*, and *Salt Towers* (the last with interesting inscriptions by prisoners), and ends at the Lanthorn Tower.

Tower Wharf (open daily), between the Tower and the Thames, with four old cannon, affords a good view of the river and its shipping. Here royal salutes are fired by the H.A.C. (see p 245) on state occasions. HMS 'Belfast' (p 286) can be reached by ferry in the summer from Tower Pier.

*Tower Bridge spans the Thames immediately below the Tower. The bridge, about 800ft long between the abutment towers, was designed by Sir Horace Jones and Sir John Wolfe Barry, and was built in 1886-94 at a cost of £800,000 (including the approaches £1,500,000). The tall towers rising from massive piers in the stream are connected with each other near the top by a lattice-work footbridge. The carriageway is formed by two bascules or drawbridges, 29.5ft above high-water, each weighing about 1000 tons and raised in 90 seconds to permit the passage of vessels through the bridge. The original steam pumping engines used to provide hydraulic power were replaced in 1975 by electric motors.

The *Tower Bridge Walkway* opened to the public in 1982 having closed in 1909 after it had become known as a haunt for prostitutes and villains.

The Tower Bridge Walkway, London EC3. Open April to Oct 10.00-17.45; Nov to March 10.00-16.00. Admission charge. Gift and Bookshop.

The entrance is in the NW tower; lift or stairs; on the 2nd floor there is an exhibition illustrating the design of the bridge. There are excellent views upstream and downstream from the two walkways which are 60ft above ground-level. In the S tower there is a display of the City's bridges and a model of Tower Bridge. Outside the S Tower there is a separate entrance to the museum in which the original steam engines which operated the bridge are on view.

St. Katharine's Dock can be reached from the Tower, from Tower Wharf on the riverside by the Tower and a subway under Tower Bridge; or from Tower Bridge by steps on the N side.

St. Katharine by the Tower is the first completed transformation of one of London's docks into a commercial and leisure centre (see Docklands, Rte 26). The St. Katharine foundation dates to 1148, established on this land near the Tower under the patronage of Queen Matilda. By the end of the 18C some 3000 people worked and lived in the precincts of the convent, which escaped dissolution thanks to Catherine of Aragon who remained its patron. Thousands more settled here, turning it into a slum. In 1825 the area was taken over for development as a dock and the inhabitants were unceremoniously evicted except for the Foundation which was found land off Regent's Park (see p 167).

St. Katharine's Dock, built by Telford, consisted of two basins and a range of

The walkways of Tower Bridge, reopened to the public in 1982

attractive warehouses by Philip Hardwick; the docks specialised in tea, rubber, marble, ivory, sugar and other valuable commodities. After considerable 2nd World War damage the docks closed in 1968 and the redevelopment plans of Taylor Woodrow Ltd were approved by the Greater London Council.

The only remaining original buildings are *Ivory House* (1854), an attractively restored warehouse, converted into self-service apartments, with shops on the ground floor, and the Beefeater cabaret restaurant located in the vaults in the basement; the *Dickens Inn* converted into a pub from a shed; the *Dockmaster's House* by Philip Hardwick, and the gates towards East Smithfield adorned with two elephants raising their trunks. Hardwick's warehouses have been destroyed by fire but the new buildings of the London World Trade Centre have been built to match the old warehouses. Next to Tower Bridge is the 900-room Tower Hotel (1973), designed by the Renton Howard Wood Partnership with good views from the Princes Room Restaurant over the Thames. There is also a coffee-shop and a carvery-style restaurant. The London World Trade Centre, in two buildings, offers facilities for new companies in London and for visiting members of the chain of World Trade Centres. There is a restaurant overlooking the yacht basin.

The *St. Katharine's Marina* provides mooring for visiting and permanent yachts and launches; Thames sailing barges moored here are available for hire. The Dickens Inn has no direct connection with Dickens except that one of his descendants, Cedric Dickens, is its patron. An extension to the existing Inn, which offers two restaurants and a public bar, was planned in 1985—this would include a shop, bar and restaurant.

Public housing by the Greater London Council and private houses by Taylor Woodrow overlook the **Historic Ships Collection** of the Maritime Trust, in the East Basin.

Historic Ships Collection, St. Katharine by the Tower, London EC3. Open 10.00–17.00 daily; later in summer. Admission charge.

The Maritime Trust was founded in 1969 and established this collection of historic ships here in 1979. The heart of the collection represents the transition from sail to steam with several coastal steam vessels including the 'Robin', sail-ships such as the 'Kathleen & May' and the Nore Light Vessel. Its most important exhibit is the RRS 'Discovery', Scott's polar research ship (1901-04), transferred here in 1980 from its Embankment mooring to undergo extensive repairs while remaining on view to the public. There was a 1-inch clearance on either side when it came through the narrow dock entrance. It is possible that it will be transferred to another location in the future.

On the N side of the area a new office block which will incorporate the cast-iron pillars from a burnt-down Hardwick warehouse will house the new London Commodity Exchange. Offices, shops and workshops and a new pier are planned on the river-front of St. Katharine's.

25 Bishopsgate and Shoreditch

Access: Underground, Bank, Liverpool Street; Bus No. 22.

Bishopsgate (Pl. 9; 5), beginning at the junction of Cornhill and
Leadenhall St, runs N to Shoreditch. To the left rises London's late
imitation of Manhattan, where the *National Westminster Bank* (600ft),
by Richard Seifert (1978) is reputedly the tallest occupied building
in Europe (see p 244). On the right is Great St. Helen's, leading to
St. Helen's (open 09.00–17.00, closed weekends, except for services),
one of the largest and most interesting of the City churches, shaded
by huge plane trees. The church is dedicated to the Empress Helena,
and legend asserts that the Emperor Constantine himself erected the
original edifice in honour of his mother.

The present church belonged to a priory for Benedictine nuns, founded c 1210.
It has two parallel naves (one the 'nuns' choir'; N), a S transept, and two chapels
added about 1374.
    The chief interest of the wide well preserved medieval Interior is in the
monuments of City worthies. N Aisle: John Robinson (d 1599) with his nine
sons and seven daughters; altar tomb of Hugh Pemberton (d 1500); (beneath
nave arches) William Kirwin (d 1594); altar tomb of Sir Thomas Gresham (d
1579); Sir Andrew Judd (d 1558), founder of Tonbridge School; and the elaborate
marble monument of Sir William Pickering (d 1574). In the N wall may be seen
the nuns' night staircase, an Easter Sepulchre and a 'squint' (peep-hole). In the
chancel are some fine 15C stalls brought from the Nuns' choir (the front stalls
are mid-17C), and a rare wooden sword-rest (1665). Beyond the tomb of Sir
John Crosby (d 1475), the Chapel of the Holy Ghost contains 15C glass. The
monument to John de Oteswich and his wife here probably dates from the early
15C.
    The fine brasses in the church (15-16C) include a Lady in a heraldic mantle
(c 1535) (brass rubbing by appointment). Among several monuments removed
from the demolished church of St. Martin Outwich is one to Richard Staper (d
1608; S wall of the nave). Beside the S entrance is the fine restored monument
of *Sir John Spencer (d 1609). The Jacobean font, pulpit, poor box, and
doorcases (W end) are noteworthy.

In St. Helen's Place, farther N, is the elaborate entrance-way to the
hall of the *Leathersellers' Company*, rebuilt 1949-59, and incorporated
in the 14C. Just beyond is the ragstone facade with an 18C turret
surmounted by a weathervane (1671) of *St. Ethelburga*, one of the
smallest and most ancient churches in London. It escaped the Great
Fire and dates in its present form from c 1400. Henry Hudson (d
1611), commemorated by three stained-glass windows, made his
Communion here before starting on his first voyage in search of the
North-West Passage. A shrine honours Blessed John Larke (1504-42),
rector of the parish, executed by Henry VIII. Above the altar is a
mural painting by Hans Feibusch (1962). The fine 17C font cover
came from St. Swithin's. The tiny garden with loggia and fountain is
charming, and has become a refuge for birds.
    The old Bishopsgate (pulled down in 1760) stood at the point where
Camomile St leads E and Wormwood St W. It is commemorated by
a bishop's mitre in the wall. Beyond, on the left, opens a garden
surrounding the pleasant church of *St. Botolph Bishopsgate* (1728).
The light interior has an unusual design. Keats was baptised here in
1795. Adjacent is the church hall (1861) with two charming statues
(1821) of charity children. The garden contains a tennis court.

Across Liverpool St is the Great Eastern Hotel and the huge **Liverpool Street Station**, a tour de force of Victorian Gothic. Constructed of cast-iron and brick, it is now being redeveloped with Broad St Station. In the booking-hall is a memorial to Captain Fryatt, master of the railway steamer 'Brussels' who was shot by the Germans at Brussels in 1916. The site was occupied by the Hospital of St. Mary of Bethlem, for centuries London's chief hospital for lunatics or 'Bedlam' (see also p 334). The hospital burial ground is now the temporary NCP Car Park next to the station. This will be part of the 10-acre Broadgate development now under way which in addition to offices will have an amphitheatre for concerts and ice skating, restaurants and shops. The first phase is due for completion at the end of 1986. Adjoining on the W was *Broad Street Station* (N London railway), now closed.

In Bishopsgate (at No. 202) is one of London's most famous pubs, *Dirty Dicks*; it takes its name from 18C recluse Nathaniel Bentley who according to the ballad closed his house on the death of his fiancée and stopped washing. The cellars of the present pub of 1870 are part of the original house and synthetic cobwebs and mice skeletons add to the atmosphere. There is a restaurant upstairs (01-283 5888). The *Bishopsgate Institute* (No. 230) was opened in 1894. The Library (open by appointment, 01-247 6844) contains a highly interesting collection of prints of old London.

At the end of Brushfield Street, past Spitalfields Market, Hawksmoor's masterpiece, **Christ Church, Spitalfields** overlooks Commercial Street. An on-going appeal has raised funds to carry out some repairs to the decayed church and the Spitalfields Festival of Music in June/July each year provides an opportunity to see the church at its best. It has a massive portico supported by Tuscan columns, and an unusual octagonal tower. The 1720 interior, including the flat coffered ceiling, has been partly restored and there are monuments by Thomas Dunn and John Flaxman. The church was supported by the Huguenot refugees who settled in this area and many of the 18C gravestones carry French names.

Spitalfields wholesale market was first established under Charles II in 1682. It is now run by the City Corporation and new market buildings opened in 1928. Trading starts at 05.00 and comes to an end in late morning.

The area of Spitalfields to the SE, once occupied by silk-weavers largely descended from Huguenot refugees, takes its name from the priory of St. Mary Spital, founded in 1197, where the 'Spital Sermon' (now delivered at St. Mary Woolnoth) was first preached. Some of the fine Georgian buildings of the prosperous 18C survive in Fournier Street and Elder Street. Many houses have been restored for private use and at 18 Folgate Street visitors can see a house of the period without electricity and with the top-floor weaving room set up as it would have been in the 18C. (Contact Dennis Sevier, 01-247 4013, to make an appointment for a tour; charge.) In the 19C the area went into decline and the 'Jack the Ripper' murders hastened the building of large blocks of artisans dwellings, most of which were occupied by the many Jewish immigrants who arrived from the 1880s onwards. Clothiers and furriers became established here; the Jewish community has now been followed by Asian immigrants mainly from Bengal and Pakistan.

Bricks were made in Brick Lane (parallel with Commercial Street to the E); here amongst the Bengali shops and workshops is the *Truman Brewery*, established in the 17C and formerly known as the Black Eagle Brewery, taking its name from Black Eagle Street. Beer is still

brewed here in an attractive adaptation of the old building by Arup
Associates (1976). Tours by appointment.

There is a market here every morning; it is particularly active on
Sundays.

Brick Lane Market (and surrounding streets), Sunday morning. Access: Underground, Liverpool Street, Buses 8, 47, 149.

The market grew up during the 18C as farmers sold some of the livestock
and produce outside the City boundary along Club Row, near Whitechapel.
(The trade in pets and small animals which continued in this section of the
market is being curtailed.) The Brick Lane market itself offers an interesting
mix of fruit and vegetables, new clothes, household goods; there are stalls
selling political literature, a reminder of the radical past and present of the East
End. Some of the side streets offer genuine antiques, second-hand clothes, and
bric-a-brac, but unsuspecting visitors to this market should be wary of buying
goods from individuals without stalls as these might be stolen.

Bishopsgate is continued N by *Norton Folgate*. Here a griffin marks
the City boundary. *High Street Shoreditch* leads N past Bethnal
Green Road through an area once famous for its boot-makers, to (½m)
a busy intersection outside **Shoreditch Church** (*St. Leonard's*). This
large church, rebuilt c 1740, was restored in 1930. James and Richard
Burbage (see below) are buried here. The stocks and whipping-post
are preserved in the churchyard.

In *Curtain Road*, parallel with High St on the W, *The Curtain
Theatre* (tablet on Nos 86-88), the first theatre in London, was erected
in 1576 by James Burbage (d 1597), father of Shakespeare's friend
Richard. In 1598, owing to a dispute about the lease, the wooden
structure was hurriedly pulled down at night by Burbage's sons, and
the materials transported to construct the Globe Theatre in
Southwark. In the vicinity stood also the *Curtain Theatre*, built in
1577.

The once densely populated district of **Hoxton** lies to the NW. West
of *Hoxton St*, with its open market now in decline, is the attractive
Waterloo church of *St. John*. In *Pitfield Street* new buildings for
Walbrook College have incorporated the facade of almshouses of
1825.

Continue N up *Kingsland Road* (to (c ¼m) the **Geffrye Museum**,
an interesting collection, well worth a visit, of woodwork, furniture,
and domestic craftsmanship.

Geffrye Museum, Kingsland Road, London E2. Tel. 01-739 8368. Access:
Underground, Liverpool Street, then Bus 22, 48, 149, 243. Open Tues to Sat
10.00-17.00, Sun 14.00-17.00. Educational facilities. Special exhibitions.
Cafeteria.

The museum occupies the old *Geffrye* or *Ironmongers' Almshouses* (1715), a
group of fourteen one-story houses ranged round a forecourt. The entrance-hall
occupies the old almshouse chapel and the whole collection is most attractively
arranged. A series of period rooms in chronological order from 1600 to the
present day provide a background not only to the history of English furniture
styles, but also to the history of England and English family life. Guides and
charts on display provide additional information. There is also a room in which
temporary art exhibitions are held.

To the N of Hoxton lie the relatively uninteresting quarters of
Haggerston, *Kingsland* and *Dalston*. Holy Trinity, Dalston contains
portraits of famous clowns and the statuette of Grimaldi formerly in
St. James's, Pentonville Rd. An annual Clowns' Service is held here
in February.

Bus No. 22 returns along Kingsland Road and Bishopsgate to the Bank (and to the West End).

Whitechapel (Access: Underground, Aldgate East, Whitechapel), immediately E of the City of London, is now part of the London Borough of Tower Hamlets.

At the end of the 19C Charles Booth described it as 'the Eldorado of the East, a gathering together of poor fortune seekers; its streets full of buying and selling, the poor living on the poor'. Waves of immigration brought Jewish settlers here through the 19C, most of whose successors have now moved on to other parts of London to make way for the Bangladeshis. Irish dock-workers, German sugar refinery workers, a lively market in hay and straw and the old clothes trade (see Petticoat Lane, p 253) added colour to the area which achieved national notoriety in 1888 with the Jack the Ripper murders of some six prostitutes. The first murder happened just off Whitechapel Road and others in alleyways in the area, including Mitre Square. The murders stopped and the villain was never caught; the London Police Commissioner resigned in disgrace.

Political confrontation came to Whitechapel in the 1930s with the Cable Street 'battle' when the Fascists led by Mosley marched through the East End; windows in Jewish shops were smashed.

Today Whitechapel is an uneasy mixture of old and new; office developments are creeping in from the City, Asian shops are opening and much of the original 'Cockney' community has moved out to new housing estates in East London and Essex. Uneasy relations between the different communities obtain throughout this area.

Whitechapel High Street continues E as Whitechapel Road and presents a mixed picture of old neglected buildings and some new developments. However, there are some buildings of interest to be explored.

At 28 Commercial St is *Toynbee Hall*, the first 'University Settlement' founded in 1884 and named after Arnold Toynbee (1852-83). *Atlee House* settlement was built by public subscription in 1971 (in memory of Earl Attlee, 1883-1967). The Curtain Theatre forms part of the community centre here. Behind, in contrast, the housing in Wentworth Street was provided by the East End Dwellings Company in 1890. Petticoat Lane extends here (see p 253).

Beyond Blooms, a popular Jewish restaurant at No. 90, is the *Whitechapel Art Gallery*.

Whitechapel Art Gallery, Whitechapel High Street, London E1. Tel. 01-377 0107. Open Tues–Sun 11.00-17.50 (Tues and Thurs until 19.50). Admission free. Access: Underground, Aldgate East. Publications, Coffee shop. Open only during exhibitions.

The gallery was founded in 1901 and the striking building, recently extensively renovated, with its art nouveau facade is by Harrison Townsend. The gallery focuses on work by living artists; the Whitechapel Open Exhibition during February/March is an opportunity for artists living in this and neighbouring boroughs to exhibit.

Adjacent is the Whitechapel Library with a decorative frieze.

On the right Adler St leads to the church of *St. Boniface* (German R.C.; 1959) with a tall concrete bell tower. Within, the florid decoration includes plants tumbling down from the choir loft. At the next right-hand turning, at 32-34 Whitechapel Road is the *Whitechapel Bell Foundry*, established in 1570. It moved here in 1738, and still occupies part of an inn building of c 1670. Here have been made the bells for Westminster Abbey since 1583, and for many churches in the City, Britain, and America. A small historical museum is housed in the front office. The foundry (partially rebuilt in 1970) may sometimes be seen by appointment.

A little farther on, across Davenant St (left) *Booth House* was built in 1968 by the Salvation Army. A quarter of a mile farther on the pavement widens and on the S rise the buildings of the *London Hospital*, founded in 1759, and one of the largest general hospitals in England. Behind is a colossal bronze statue of Queen Alexandra, by Wade. Opposite is a memorial to Edward VII, erected by the Jews of East London.

Brady Street diverges left; here is one of the four Jewish cemeteries of the area; this dates to 1761 and is closed to burials (since 1858); a peaceful oasis behind a high brick wall. Nathan Rothschild (d 1836), founder of the family bank in London, is buried here. Other prominent Jewish families are buried in the Jewish Cemetery at Alderney Road, E1 (also United Synagogue). There are two Sephardi Cemeteries in Mile End Road; the 'old' founded in 1657, is also a garden for a students' hostel; the flat marble tomb stones of the Sephardim merchants are set into the ground with Spanish or Hebrew inscriptions and skull and cross bone symbols. The 'new' cemetery was established to the E in 1733 and served the Anglo Sephardim community for over 100 years until the Golders Green cemetery was opened. Queen Mary College has built on some of the ground (some remains were moved to Brentwood) and only 19 and 20C tombstones, some with well-known names, can still be seen.

The impressive main entrance to the *Watney Mann Brewery* in Whitechapel Road dates to 1902. Further on *Cambridge Heath Road* leads N towards Victoria Park (comp. below). Immediately opposite is Sidney St, notorious for the 'siege' of 1911 of a cornered gang of anarchists against whom Winston Churchill, then Home Secretary, had called out the army. *Mile End Road* begins here 1m from the old City Wall. On the left a bronze bust commemorates William Booth (1829-1912), from whose open-air services in this neighbourhood in 1865 sprang the Salvation Army. The picturesque *Trinity Almshouses* were established in 1696 for master mariners and mates and their wives or widows. Damaged during the last war, they have been restored and now house a rehabilitation centre. The attractive chapel, known as Captain Cook's Church, is now a welfare centre. Opposite, No. 88 was the residence of Captain Cook after 1764 (plaque erected on site in 1970). Beyond Cleveland Way the ungainly upper storey of the former Empire Music Hall survives above shops; it is recalled in the cobbled Assembly Passage opposite. On the right diverges *Stepney Green*, with charming houses (c 1700) on the left. Beyond a particularly attractive house (No. 37; an ILEA Careers Centre) is the London Jewish Hospital. The Green ends at the large churchyard of •*St Dunstan's* (restored 1946-52), mostly 15C, with early 16C tombs. A Saxon •*Rood-panel* (early 11C) decorates the 13C chancel. In the wall of the S aisle is a stone with an inscription (1663) stating it to have been brought from Carthage.

On the N side of Mile End Rd, before Stepney Green Station are *Charrington's Anchor Brewery* (established in 1757) and the Mile End Municipal Baths. No. 253, formerly the Spanish and Portuguese Jews' Hospital, is now an old people's home. Behind is a small disused Jewish cemetery, granted to the Jews by Oliver Cromwell in 1656 and the oldest Jewish cemetery left in Britain. Beyond Queen Mary College is a larger Jewish cemetery opened in 1725 (see above).

The new buildings of **Queen Mary College**, a school of London University, are to the N. Beyond Bancroft Road its great hall occupies the site of the *People's Palace*, opened in 1887 and intended as a realisation of the 'Palace of Delights' in Sir Walter Besant's novel 'All Sorts and Conditions of Men' (1882). It was rebuilt after a fire in 1936 and again in 1953-56, with sculptures by Eric Gill. Just beyond is the beautifully simple University of London chapel of *St. Benedict*.

Mile End Road is prolonged by the slightly more attractive Bow Road to Bow and Stratford. **Bow**, or *Stratford-le-Bow*, noted for china in the 18C, took its name from a 12C arched bridge over the Lea. Chaucer's Prioresse probably caught her accent from Elizabeth of Hainault, who died (1375) in the Bendictine nunnery of St. Leonard's at 'Stratford-atte-Bowe'. The church of *St. Mary Stratford Bow* dates from the early 14C (tower rebuilt after 1948), and stands on an island site. To the S lies *Bromley-by-Bow* (see p 401).

Bethnal Green, East of Shoredith and North of Stepney, was during the 19th century one of London's most crowded and poorest areas. Here the Victorian social reformers built huge blocks of working-class dwellings; later efforts of slum clearance by the then London County Council created amongst others the Boundary Estate, a somewhat better environment. Now the area is a soulless mixture of old and new, with a large immigrant community.

In *Bethnal Green Road*, a general market dating back to 1853 survives (Monday to Friday). More interesting for the visitor to the area is the *Columbia Road Sunday Market*, famous for plants (best approached from Hackney Road, Bus 8, 47, or from the Brick Lane area, see p 290).

On this site was the huge Columbia Market built in 1869 by the Victorian philanthropist Baroness Burdett-Coutts to provide cheap and nourishing food for the local community. It failed and the building was finally pulled down in 1960. The plant market flourishes and garden tools, bulbs, seeds, plants, and pots are all on sale, according to season.

Club Row at the western end of Bethnal Green Road is part of the Brick Lane Market. The trade in pets here is being curtailed. At the E end of Bethnal Green Road at the junction with Cambridge Heath Road is *St. John's*, a church built by Soane (1824-28); the parish church of *St. Matthew's* is to the S and was built by George Dance (1743-6), rebuilt internally in 1859 and repaired after bomb damage, in 1961.

Opposite Bethnal Green Underground Station is the **Bethnal Green Museum of Childhood**.

Bethnal Green Museum of Childhood, Cambridge Heath Road, London E2. Tel. 01-980 2415. Open Mon to Thurs and Sat 10.00-18.00, Sun 14.30-18.00. Closed Friday. Free (part of Victoria and Albert Museum). Access: Underground, Bethnal Green. Educational facilities, art room, temporary exhibitions, lectures, bookshop.

The unusual building is based on a prefabricated structure of iron and glass similar to that of the Crystal Palace, erected in 1856 in South Kensington as the forerunner of today's Victoria and Albert Museum. It was removed here in 1872 and the brick exterior added by James Wild; the scraggito panels were executed by students of the new Royal College of Art and designed by F.W. Moody.

The interior comprises a central hall with two gallery levels and a basement; part of the museum has recently been refurbished and the displays improved.

The collection of toys includes toy trains, rocking horses, board games and a superb group of dolls' houses, among them a Nuremburg dolls' house (1673), a Dutch miniature kitchen (1709), the Tate baby house (English, c 1760), and a house of 1887 owned and furnished by Queen Mary. The collection of costumes includes children's clothes and wedding dresses from 1770 onwards. There are visual toys in the basement including puppets and a marionette theatre and marionettes, possibly for the Palazzo Carminati in Venice (early 18C).

Old Ford Road leads half a mile to **Victoria Park** (217 acres), established in 1845; some of the grounds belonged to the former Manor of Stepney. It includes a boating lake with a Chinese pagoda (1847) on an island, an open-air swimming pool, and a Gothic drinking fountain (1861). Considerable improvements have been made recently by the GLC as part of the Regent's Canal developments; the canal skirts the W edge of the park and the towpath leads N to Shoreditch and the Kingsland Basin, and S to Mile End and Limehouse.

26 London's Docklands

'The most important inner city development of the 1980s in Europe' is at present taking place in an area of London best described as London's docklands. The designated area covered by the London Docklands Development Corporation, set up in 1981, stretches from Tower Bridge in the W to well past the Thames Barrier in the E; altogether some 5000 acres of land and water-filled docks. Much of the development has yet to take shape but the description below covers the heritage of the area as well as those new projects which are completed or under way. More information from London Docklands Development Corporation, West India House, Millwall Docks, London E14. Tel. 01-515 3000.

London's prosperity during the 16th and 17th centuries depended on its growing port based on quays along the Thames, e.g. Billingsgate and Queenhithe and some deep water moorings at the Tower, Wapping and Puddle Dock. Most moorings were in the Pool of London itself, the area of water below (E of) London Bridge. Apart from two small wet docks there were no enclosed docks until the 19C when trade, and pilfering, had increased enormously. The City Corporation which operated the Pool resisted the building of docks which were developed piecemeal by private companies in the marshy land below Tower Bridge. The first to be completed was West India Dock (1802). The London Docks followed in 1805, then the East India, the Surrey Docks on the S bank, St. Katharine's in 1828 (see p 266), Royal Victoria (1855), Millwall (1868), Royal Albert (1880) and King George V (1921) in the Royal Group of Docks. Each of the docks specialised in a particular type of trade and security was tight with high walls, gates and even a drawbridge at West India Docks.

During the second half of the 19C the docks struggled in competition with the railways, rivalry with Liverpool and difficulties with labour. The formation of the Port of London Authority in 1909 removed some of the destructive competition between the various London docks but by the 1960s trade had declined to such a level that docks began to close due to the arrival of larger, container ships, served better at Tilbury and Felixstowe, labour problems, particularly restrictive practices, and slowness in modernising. Most of the London docks are now closed; the London Docks and part of Surrey Docks have been filled in, but in the main the planned redevelopment will incorporate the large expanses of water of the original docks. The high walls surrounding the old docks have come down and visitors are encouraged to come and see, for the first time, the dockland landscape, previously only visible from the river. This exploration covers Wapping and Limehouse, the Isle of Dogs, and the

The 16C Grapes pub in Limehouse

Royal Docks in Newham. For St. Katharine's Dock see p 266, and for the area from London Bridge to Rotherhithe, including Surrey Docks, see p 287.

General access: the Docklands Light Railway will operate from Tower Hill (The Minories) from July 1987 to the Isle of Dogs with intermediate stops at Wapping, Limehouse and West India Docks.

Access: Shadwell and Wapping Underground (Metropolitan Line). By car approach Wapping via Thomas More Street off East Smithfield.

Wapping High Street winds its way along the narrow river-front of **Wapping**, bounded on the N by the former, filled-in London Docks and on the river-front by tall wharves and warehouses, some restored, others in the course of redevelopment. At one time there were 36 taverns in this street serving sailors and dockworkers; in one of them Judge Jeffreys was arrested in 1688, disguised as a sailor, on his way to France.

Opposite the attractive tower of *St. John* (1760; the church was destroyed in the Second World War) is *Wapping Pierhead*. The Wapping Old Stairs of the ballad still exist (next to the Town of Ramsgate pub). Here is a modern police station for river police. Beside *Tunnel Pier* is the site of Execution Dock, where Captain Kidd (d 1701) and other notorious pirates were hanged. At *Wapping Station* a plaque commemorates the tunnel, the first for public traffic ever to be built beneath a river, designed by Marc Isambard Brunel and completed in 1843. It was used by pedestrians until 1865 when its present use as a railway tunnel for the Metropolitan Line began. (See also Rotherhithe, p 317.)

Wapping Lane leads N past (W) the development area of the former London Docks to The Highway, past the Three Swedish Crowns pub, at Wapping Lane. Once notorious as Ratcliff Highway it ran through an area of drinking dens. The Ratcliff murders took place here in 1811. Continue W along The Highway to reach *St. George in The East*, in Cannon Street Road to the N. This fine Hawksmoor church (1726) has a massive 160ft tower; gutted in 1941, it has been ingeniously restored by Arthur Bailey (1960-64). Close by in *Swedenborg Square* stood the Swedish Church in which the body of Emmanuel Swedenborg (1688-1722), mystic and philosopher, rested until it was removed to Sweden in 1908. There was a Danish Church in Welclose Square further along but this was demolished and another built to the N on Commercial Road on the corner of Yorkshire Place.

South of The Highway in Pennington Street are the new headquarters of News International, publishers of 'The Sun' and 'The Times'. Turn E again towards the Shadwell Basin; Garnet Street leads S to *Wapping Wall* and the popular *Prospect of Whitby* pub and restaurant, overlooking the river, at 57 Wapping Wall, E1 (01-481 1095). Built in 1520, its reputation was reflected in the name the Devil's Tavern because of the smugglers and thieves who drank here. The 'hanging' Judge Jeffreys was a customer as were Samuel Pepys and later Dickens and Turner. Its current name was taken from a ship in 1777. There is entertainment in the evenings in the bar.

King Edward Memorial Park (1922) further E marks the site of the old Shadwell fish market, and contains a memorial to Willoughby, Frobisher and other 16C navigators. The *Shadwell Basin* is being redeveloped, in part for housing, and offers boating facilities. A canal will link this basin with the river at Thomas More Street through the former London Dock area.

Rejoin The Highway; to the left on Shadwell Basin is *St. Paul's* church, built in 1820 by John Walters. Here Captain Cook's son James and Walter Pater were baptised. Continue E along The Highway and turn right at Butcher Row; here are the buildings of the *St. Katharine's Royal Foundation*, completed in 1925 (admission by appointment). St. Katharine's Royal Hospital was originally founded near the Tower in 1148 by Queen Matilda; in 1273 Queen Eleanor, wife of Henry III, took the wardenship into her own hands and reserved the patronage for ever for the queens of England personally. The foundation was removed to Regent's Park in 1825, when the St. Katharine's Docks were excavated; it returned in 1950. The funds are now administered for social welfare work. A cloister, with monuments from the Regent's Park chapel (comp. p 167), admits to the plain but effective *Chapel* (1952), containing *Stalls, with misericords (c 1370), and other woodwork (15C and 17C), including the Jacobean pulpit. The 18C *Warden's House* occupies the former rectory of St. James's church, which was destroyed in the Second World War.

Continue along Narrow Street to the *Grapes* pub at No. 76 (01-987 4396), set among wharves and warehouses under redevelopment; this was immortalised by Dickens as The Six Jolly Fellowship Porters in 'Our Mutual Friend'. There is a good view up and down the river from the verandah; fish is served in the restaurant. To the N is *Limehouse Basin* with new homes under construction, supported by leisure and shopping facilities. A marina is also scheduled. Limehouse Causeway, once London's notorious Chinatown, continues E to meet the West India Dock Road. Good Friends, a well-known Chinese restaurant in Salmon Lane, N of Stepney East station, carries on the tradition.

It is possible to walk by the Regent's Canal, which opened in 1820 to link the Thames with the Grand Junction Canal at Paddington. The Limehouse Basin was built to act as a trans-shipment centre, particularly for coal. The current developments at Limehouse Basin will include the Canal Walk, now best joined at Tomlins Terrace off Salmon Lane. Here Stonebridge Wharf has been landscaped as a *Canalway Park*. The walk leads N towards Mile End and Victoria Park (see p 274).

Limehouse was one of London's main shipbuilding centres during the 18 and 19C but declined as the area became more populous with labourers serving the West and East India Docks. The Chinese community established itself here in the 1890s and the area's reputation for vice and opium-dens was enhanced and romanticised by writers (including Oscar Wilde) and the press. London's Chinese community is now centred on Soho.

At Limehouse Town Hall in Commercial Road a *National Museum of Labour History* was established in 1975.

National Museum of Labour History, Limehouse Town Hall, Commercial Road, London, E14. Tel. 01-515 3229. Open Tues to Sat 09.30-17.00, Sun 14.30-17.30. Access: Underground, Stepney East. Free. Library, lectures, temporary exhibitions.

It presents the history of the labour movement from the 18C to today. Early radicals represented include Tom Paine (death mask and lock of hair) and Richard Cobden (table and chair). There are displays on the Tolpuddle Martyrs, the Peterloo Massacre, the General Strike as well as events in other countries such as the Paris Commune and Spanish Civil War.

Nearby is the church of *St. Anne* by Hawksmoor (1714-30) with the highest church clock in London. It was damaged by fire in 1850 and restored by John Morris and Philip Hardwick in 1857. They also designed the font and the pulpit. The stained glass window of the Crucifixion at the E end is by Clutterbuck. The dominating feature is the W tower with an apse as an entrance.

West India Dock Road leads S to the **Isle of Dogs**. Some way farther on, just before the railway bridge, is the unusually shaped plain brick *Danish Seamen's Church* and mission by Holger Jensen (1959). The interior, in wood and brick, with an attractive glass mosaic, contains two wooden figures (from an earlier church) of SS. Peter and Paul, by G.G. Cibber (d 1700), father of Colley Cibber. In Branch Road, opposite, begins the N approach to **Rotherhithe Tunnel**, c 1.25 miles long, which passes beneath the Thames to Rotherhithe.

Isle of Dogs, Access: Underground to Mile End then 'Dockland Clipper' bus (in Burdett Road); from 1987 Docklands Light Railway from Tower Hill.

The Isle of Dogs is the heart of the new docklands; here are the headquarters of the London Docklands Development Corporation and the Enterprise Zone which gives planning and tax incentives to developers.

The marshy peninsula of the Isle of Dogs, known as Stepney Marshes, remained relatively unpopulated until the docks were built here in the 19C bringing employment and industrialisation. The name probably comes from the royal dogs kept here for Henry VIII and other inhabitants at Placentia Palace across the river who came here on hunting trips.

The West India Docks opened in 1801 and a canal was cut across the peninsula in 1805. Millwall Docks followed. In the current redevelopment many features of the early dock period are being retained (the LDDC has produced a Heritage Trail leaflet).

Explore the area from the main dock gates in West India Dock Road. Just outside in Garford Street is a row of constables' cottages built in 1819. The Salvation Army building in a Scandinavian 'Queen Anne' style was opened in 1902 as a mission for Scandinavian seamen. The *Dockmaster's House* (1807; designed by Thomas Morris) was once the Jamaica Tavern but reverted to use as the dock manager's office. It now houses the Docklands Business Research and Information Centre.

Some of the wall topped by railing which surrounded the dock has been preserved to the W of the main entrance; there was also a ditch and a swing bridge which had to be left open at night. The *Round House* on the other side was a gunpowder magazine; a matching building (gone) on the other side was used as a lock-up for thieves caught at night.

The attractive *Ledger Building* just inside the gates was designed by George Gwilt in 1803; it now serves as offices for the LDDC. The original dock wall can be seen at the rear of the building. To the right are the *Cannon Workshops*, erected in 1825 and designed by Sir John Rennie to be used as stores, workshops and a cooperage. An original forge remains; since the docks closed in 1980 the building has been converted into offices and workshops for small businesses. Under the entrance arch a cast-iron plaque marks Trinity High Water. To the left overlooking the first dock are *Warehouses 1 and 2* (due to be developed for some kind of leisure facility). George Gwilt designed these in 1802 and John Rennie added the cast-iron columns in 1814. The red-brick road—the new road opened in 1982—now leads past *Canary Wharf*, with office developments and Limehouse Studios at the end, a commercial television production company. Further along at Blackwall Basin, Mercury has installed two satellite communication dishes.

On the other side, opposite Limehouse Studios, is the new *Billingsgate Market* which moved here in 1981. This is London's main wholesale fish market, established in the City (see p 250) from the 9C and there based on the wharf at Billingsgate. The new market building offers modern freezing and storage facilities; there is a space for a restaurant on the top-floor; tours by appointment (01-987 1118). At *Heron Quay*, which divides the second and third dock, an ambitious redevelopment will incorporate office and residential accommodation as well as retail outlets. A station on the Dockland Light Railway will be here; the railway will cross above the three West India Docks from N to S.

Continue past South Quay and along Millwall Dock; the red-brick road crosses the Dock here, but divert W along Tiller Road. Here is the location for the new Daily Telegraph building. At the end of the dock are the *Pierhead Cottages* (1860) from which the dockmaster of the Millwall Dock Company supervised the dock.

Continue along Westferry Road past the former St. Paul's Presbyterian Church (1856) now in industrial use. Further on is *Burrell's Wharf* where the 'Great Eastern' was launched. Isambard Kingdom Brunel designed the 692ft-long ironship which was built between 1853-58. Some of the original buildings survive.

In East Ferry Road is the Docklands Settlement (1905). The railway viaduct in Millwall Park was built in 1872 when a service operated to North Greenwich; it closed in 1926 and will be used for the new light railway. The *Lord Nelson* pub dates to 1859 and had a stabling block for horses. Nearby is the *Ferry House*, once the only building on the southern end of the Isle of Dogs apart from the Chapel where Chapel House Estate now stands. A new Island Gardens Pier is at the end of East Ferry Road and along Ferry Street is the entrance to the *Greenwich Foot Tunnel* at *Island Gardens*. The tunnel opened in 1902 and replaced the ferry; the walk to Greenwich under the river takes approximately five minutes and includes a ride in the Victorian lifts. There is a good view of the buildings of Greenwich from the Gardens which were laid out in 1895.

Saunderness Road leads N to the *Waterman's Arms* (1 Glenaffric Avenue), a popular pub with disco every evening. Nearby is the *Church of Christ and St. John*, designed by F. Johnstone in 1850 for William Cubitt. Stones from the old London Bridge were used in the construction. To the N is the former industrial area of CUBITT TOWN with housing built by the Cubitts for the workers in the docks, shipyards and factories. Return towards Millwall Docks along Stebondale Street and turn right across the 'Mudchute' development site, so-called from the artificial landscape created by the silted mud from the dock. An urban farm is located here and housing is being built.

The ASDA Superstore on East Ferry Road opened in 1983, considerably improving the area's shopping facilities. Where the brick road joins East Ferry Road and crosses Millwall Dock is the *Olsen Shed* which will open as the London Docklands Arena in 1986 with a 200-metre running track and seating for 5000 to 10,000 people. A 200-bedroom hotel is planned next to it with sports clinic facilities.

Return along the red-brick road to West India Dock Road, or continue N along East Ferry Road which joins Preston's Road and continues across the Blue Bridge at the entrance of West India Dock to the *Gun* pub, in Coldharbour Lane overlooking the river. Lord Nelson and Lady Hamilton are said to have met here. *Nelson House* and the northernmost houses here date from the early 19C. Nelson House was built in 1824 by Rennie who also built the *Bridge House* (1819) at the next bridge to the Blackwall Basin in Preston's Road.

The Satellite Dishes, Limehouse Studios and Billingsgate Market are over to the W (see above). Preston's Road leads to Cotton Street and East India Dock Road. East India Dock and the River Lea are still to be developed to the E. East India Dock Road leads East to Canning Town and the Royal Docks.

The **Royal Docks** in the London Borough of Newham form part of the LDDC redevelopment area and in size offer the greatest scope and potential. The Royal Group of Docks were the last to be built, between 1855 and 1921, and offered 175 acres of water and 7 miles of quay. Silvertown to the S provides a good view of the Thames

Barrier. Further E is North Woolwich and N of the Royal Albert Dock is Beckton.

Access: BR from Stratford to Custom House, Silvertown and North Woolwich.

The heritage of the area is described under Newham, see p 400. Proposed developments for the dock include a Stolport, a short take-off and landing airfield betwen King George V and the Royal Albert Docks. The Docklands Light Railway may also be extended here in a second phase.

The redundant church of *St. Mark* in Silvertown (1862) is being converted into a Church Museum by the Passmore Edwards Museum which has already opened a railway museum at North Woolwich Railway Station (see p 401). British Telecom has installed its satellite station here.

27 Southwark, Bankside, London Bridge City and Surrey Docks

Southwark, on the S side of London Bridge, has as long a history as the City of London itself; archaeological excavations have revealed Roman and pre-Roman finds, now in the Museum of London and the Cuming Museum. It was the main entry point from the S and coaching inns, such as the still extant George Inn, flourished. During the 16C it became a place of entertainment with bear-baiting, cock-fighting and eventually the theatre—all of which were banned from the City of London. Shakespeare's Globe Theatre opened here in 1599. The area was well-known for its brothels and its prisons. In 1556 it came under the jurisdiction of the City of London and was known as Bridge Ward Without to distinguish it from the Bridge Ward Within—the London Bridge and the area to the N—but it continued to enjoy its freedom from City restrictions on entertainment and other 'vices'. Wharves and warehouses were built along the Thames in the 18th and 19th centuries but with the decline in the trade on the river, Southwark was neglected. Today the London Borough of Southwark stretches as far S as Dulwich and encompasses the inner city decline of Southwark proper and the prosperity of a leafy suburb. Regeneration of the river-bank over the next decade should bring this historic part of London back to life.

Access: Underground, London Bridge (also British Rail), or approach from the N bank along London Bridge.

Thousands of commuters walk across London Bridge each day from the British Rail station to work in offices in the City, repeating the journey made by millions of Londoners and others in history over the many different bridges on this site (see p 301). To the E is London Bridge City (see below); to the W is Bankside and straight ahead is *Borough High Street*.

The High Street has from earliest times been the great highway to the SE of England and the Continent. It was the scene of countless processions and pageants in the Middle Ages, and was trodden by the feet of many pilgrims to the shrine of St. Thomas Becket at Canterbury. It abounded in hostelries, the old buildings of which, however, have almost entirely disappeared.

On the left is the approach to *London Bridge Station*, on the right is Southwark Cathedral. St. Thomas's Street skirts the S side of the station.

London Bridge Station, the first railway terminus in the capital, opened in 1837 to serve the first steam railway, to Deptford. By 1840 a proper station had replaced the wooden platform and served Croydon and Brighton. The station was completely rebuilt after extensive Second World War damage. In the vaults underneath the station is the *London Dungeon*.

London Dungeon, 28-34 Tooley Street, London SE1. Tel. 01-403 0606. Open 10.00-17.45 daily (April to Sept), 10.00-16.30 (Oct to March) Admission charge. Not suitable for children under 10.

An exhibition in the dank vaults underneath the railway arches of the horrors of the Middle Ages including the plague, torture and executions.

Continue S along Borough High Street; to the E is the *Old Operating Theatre*, St. Thomas Street, London SE1. Tel 01-407 7600. Open Mon, Wed, and Fri, 12.30-16.00.

The S wing (1842) of the original St. Thomas's Hospital which stood here from 1225 to 1865 is occupied by telephone engineers (behind post office facade). The church of *St. Thomas* (1702-03), now Southwark Chapter House, in St. Thomas's St, is another relic of the hospital. In the roof space is the Old Operating Theatre of 1821, rediscovered in 1956 and restored. In this vicinity lived Robert Harvard, the father of John Harvard (1607-38), who attended St. Olave's Grammar School, of which his father was a governor. A little farther on in St. Thomas's St stands **Guy's Hospital**, founded in 1725 by Thomas Guy, a City bookseller, who made a fortune by his speculations in South Sea stock. The hospital contains one of the largest medical schools in England. John Keats studied here in 1815-16. In the courtyard is a statue of Guy, by Scheemakers, and in an inner quadrangle is another of Lord Nuffield, by Maurice Lambert (1949).

S of the Cathedral on the W side of Borough High.Street is *Borough Market*; a street market has existed in this part of London since the 13C. It was established at its present site in 1756 and now functions as a wholesale fruit and vegetable market trading from early to mid-morning.

The pattern of yards and alleys along the E side of Borough High St survives from the Middle Ages when most contained coaching inns.

Opposite Southwark St the *King's Head* was called Pope's Head before 1540. Next door stood the White Hart, Jack Cade's headquarters in 1450 (Shakespeare, 'Henry VI', Part II, V. iv. 8: 'Hath my sword therefore broke through London Gates that you should leave me at the White Hart in Southwark?'), and where Mr Pickwick first met Sam Weller. In a courtyard beside George House is the *George Inn* (NT), the last surviving galleried inn in London. It is still a public house and restaurant, and preserves a rare 'inn-keeper's' clock inside; the facade dates from c 1676. Shakespeare plays are sometimes performed here in summer. On the site of Talbot Yard stood the most celebrated hostelry of all, the Tabard Inn, the 'Gentil hostelrye that highte the Tabard, faste by the Belle', the starting-point of Chaucer's Canterbury pilgrims. It survived (as the Talbot Inn) until 1875-76.

The *Queen's Head Inn* stood in Queen's Head Yard and was owned by the family of John Harvard. The sale of this property before his emigration to America in 1637 augmented his fortune, half of which (with his library) he left to Harvard University when he died the following year. In Newcomen Street, off the High St, the *King's Arms* (rebuilt 1890) appropriated the sign from the Great Stone Gate (1728) on London Bridge when it was demolished in 1760.

A tablet in the High Street recalls the original old prison of the **Marshalsea**, first mentioned in 1377 and abandoned in 1813, when the name was transferred to the New Marshalsea (see below). Here Ben Jonson was imprisoned for sedition in 1597. Adjoining the Marshalsea on the S stood the old **King's Bench**, the prison to which Judge Gascoigne is said to have committed Prince Henry (afterwards Henry V). Tobias Smollett was imprisoned here in 1739 for libel. In 1758 this prison was superseded by the new King's Bench, at the corner of Newington Causeway. Here John Wilkes was held for libel in 1768-70, and many debtors were imprisoned, though they were often allowed to live in lodgings near by, 'within the rules of King's Bench' (comp. Dickens's 'Nicholas Nickleby'). Mr Micawber found a 'temporary haven of domestic tranquility and peace of mind' at the King's Bench. The prison was partially burned in the Gordon Riots (1780; see Dickens's 'Barnaby Rudge'), disused in 1860, when imprisonment for debt was abolished, and finally pulled down.

At 207 Borough High St a small part of the walls survive of the *White Lion* or *Borough Gaol*, a 16C prison; to a later building on this site the name of the Marshalsea was transferred. Here Dickens's father was confined in 1824, and Little Dorrit, 'the child of the Marshalsea' was born and brought up. In *St. George's* church (first mentioned in 1122, rebuilt in 1734-36 by John Price, and since restored) Little Dorrit was christened and married. Marshalsea Road, running W from the church, leads to *Mint Street*, in which was St. George's Workhouse, usually accepted as the workhouse in which Oliver Twist asked for more (though that was not in London). The workhouse copper is preserved in the Cuming Museum. In *Lant Street*, the next turning on the right out of the High St, Charles Dickens lodged as a boy, while his father was in the Marshalsea and he himself worked at Hungerford Market. Here, too, lodged Bob Sawyer, the medical student in 'Pickwick'. *Horsemonger Lane Gaol*, in which Leigh Hunt was confined for two years for libelling the Prince Regent as a 'fat Adonis of 50' (1812), stood in Union Road, off the Borough High Street.

Great Dover Street branches left from the High Street to join the Old Kent Road (p 329). At No. 75 lived C.H. Spurgeon (see below) in 1854-56. Here is the *Pilgrim Fathers Memorial Church* (1956), the second successor to the oldest Congregational church in London (1616). In the area, Dickens Square, Merrick Square, and Trinity Church Square date from the early 19C; in the last, opposite the Henry Wood Memorial Hall, once Holy Trinity Church, is a statue of King Alfred, said to come from Westminster Hall.

The Borough High Street is continued to the S by Newington Causeway, in which is *London Sessions House*. Beyond is the **Elephant and Castle** (Pl. 20; 6), a busy traffic centre (named after a former tavern) redesigned in 1957-64 as two roundabouts linked by Newington Butts, with an uninspired shopping precinct. Facing this are the London College of Printing and the Baptists' *Metropolitan Tabernacle* (rebuilt with a modified facade 1959), the successor of the tabernacle (burned down in 1898) in which C.H. Spurgeon preached from 1861 until his death in 1892, living at No. 217 New

Kent Road.

Return to London Bridge and turn W towards **Southwark Cathedral**. Redevelopments in this area have exposed the Cathedral towards the river although it is still hemmed in by the railway and the Market.

Southwark Cathedral, Borough High Street, SE1. Tel. 01-407 3708. Services: Mon to Fri 12.30 Matins; 12.45 Holy Communion, 17.30 Evensong; Sun 09.00 Holy Communion; 11.00 Eucharist; 15.00 Evensong; Sat 11.30 Matins; 12.00 Holy Communion; 16.00 Evensong. A refectory is under construction, due to open in 1986/87.

Officially the *Cathedral and Collegiate Church of St. Saviour and St. Mary Overie, Southwark*, it has been the seat of a bishop since 1905. Often rebuilt and repaired it remains the finest Gothic building in London after Westminster Abbey.

According to legend, a nunnery was founded on this site by a ferryman's daughter called Mary, whence is derived the former title of the church, St. Mary Overy, which is explained as 'St. Mary of the Ferry' or 'St. Mary over the Ie' (water). In 852-862 this nunnery was changed by St. Swithin, Bp of Winchester, into a house for canons regular of the Augustinian order. In 1106 a church was erected, of which few traces survive. The present choir and retro-choir were built by Peter des Roches, Bp of Winchester, in 1207; the transepts were remodelled in the 15C. The nave, which had collapsed about 1838 and been replaced by a temporary erection, was entirely rebuilt by Sir Arthur Blomfield in 1890-96. Over the crossing rises a noble 15C tower, 164ft high.

Interior (open all day). NAVE. In the SW corner is a portion of 13C arcading; in the NW corner a case of splendid bosses from the 15C roof. The stained glass, mostly destroyed in 1941, is modern. Under the 6th window is the *Tomb of John Gower* (1330-1408), the friend of Chaucer. Behind the door into the Vestry may be seen the jambs of a Norman door and an ancient holy-water stoup.

TRANSEPTS. In the North Transept has been placed a dresser given to the church in 1588. The monuments here include one to John Lockyer (d. 1672), pill-maker, with an amusing hyperbolical inscription. To the E of this transept is the *Harvard Chapel*, restored and decorated in 1907 in memory of John Harvard, founder of Harvard University, Mass., who was born in the parish and baptised in this church (1607). During the restoration a Norman shaft (left of the altar) was disclosed. The stained-glass window (restored 1948) was presented in 1905 by Joseph H. Choate (d 1917). On the right a tablet commemorates the playwright and lyricist, Oscar Hammerstein (1895-1960).

CHOIR. This and the retro-choir represent perhaps the earliest Gothic work in London. The *Altar-screen, erected by Bp Fox in 1520, is a magnificent piece of work, though much mutilated and restored. The statues in the niches date from 1912. The fine tombs in the choir aisles include: (N Aisle) two handsome Jacobite monuments to John Trehearne (d. 1618), gentleman-porter to James I, and Richard Humble (d 1616), Alderman, and the wooden effigy of a Knight (1280-1300; restored); S Aisle: fine tomb of Lancelot Andrewes (1555-1626).

The beautiful aisled *RETRO CHOIR is now used as the parish church. The Lady Chapel, which extended to the E, was pulled down in 1830. Here Gardiner and Bonner held the consistorial courts in the reign of Queen Mary, and condemned Hooper, Rogers, Bradford, Saunders, Ferrar, and Taylor to the stake. Bishop Bonner later died for his own beliefs at Marshalsea (see above) in 1569.

The SOUTH TRANSEPT was rebuilt in the 15C by Cardinal

Beaufort, whose niece, Joan Beaufort, was married to James I of
Scotland in this church (1423). On the W wall is a monument in
miniature to William Emerson (d 1575), a supposed ancestor of Ralph
Waldo Emerson. Above, John Bingham (d 1625), saddler to Queen
Elizabeth and King James. Near by is a touching inscription to
Mistress Margaret Maynard (d 1653, aged 13 years). In the S aisle of
the nave, beneath a memorial window to Shakespeare (by C. Webb,
1954), is a recumbent alabaster figure of the playwright (1911).

John Fletcher and Philip Massinger, the playwrights, Edmund
Shakespeare (d 1607), the younger brother of the poet, and Henry
Sacheverell (chaplain in 1705-09), are buried in St. Saviour's, but
their graves are unidentified.

Around the Cathedral is an area of Bankside undergoing some
redevelopment. The future of *St. Mary Overie Dock* is uncertain but
it dates from the time of Winchester Palace; two plaques on the wall
(right) record the rights of local people to use the dock free of charge.
The road winds round towards Clink Street; the plaque here commemorates the Palace prison which came to give its name to prisons
in general—'the clink'. On the left are the remains of the 14C great
hall including a rose window of Winchester Palace which has now
been incorporated in a warehouse wall.

Winchester House, built in the 12C, was the town residence of the
bishops of Winchester down to 1626; it is recalled in the names of
the streets to the S. It was burned down in 1814. *Clink Street* was
named after the manor or park of 70 acres attached to Winchester
House and known as the *'Liberty of the Clink'*, where a pleasure-
quarter sprang up outside the jurisdiction of the City. In the undercroft
of the service block, the *Clink Prison* was used by the bishops as a
place of detention for heretics. It was housed across the street in the
17C, and burned in the Gordon Riots of 1780.

Clink Street continues under Cannon Street railway bridge. On the
other side is the *Anchor Inn*. Of 15C origin, the present building
dates to the 18C and has recently been restored. There are bars, a
restaurant, a minstrel's gallery and old oak beams. It once belonged
to Henry Thrale, friend of Dr Johnson. There is a good view of St.
Paul's and a model of the Globe Theatre which stood nearby.

Bank End leads into **Bankside** (Pl. 20; 2) which skirts the river
almost to Blackfriars Bridge. To the W it runs through a district of
great interest as the site of the early theatres where Shakespeare's
genius found expression. Here, too, in the Liberty of the Clink, were
the 'stews', largely inhabited by Dutch or Flemish women, and
numerous bear-gardens, used also for prize-fights. A huge electric
power-station now dominates the landscape. Bankside commands a
view of St. Paul's, especially fine at sunset, seen over a foreground
of wharves; an inscription on a 17C house (being restored) on
Cardinal's Wharf marks the house whence Wren used to watch the
building of his cathedral. Across the narrow Cardinal Cap Alley,
dating from the 17C with a secluded garden, the Cathedral Provost's
Lodgings have occupied a building of 1712 (restored) since 1958. In
Bear Gardens is the *Bear Gardens Museum*.

Bear Gardens Museum, Bankside, SE1. Tel. 01-928 6342. Open Tues to Sat
10.00-17.30, Sun 14.00-18.00. (check as opening times are frequently changed).
Educational facilities. Access: Underground, London Bridge.

The museum occupies a 19C warehouse which retains its old machine driving gear. It is devoted to the Elizabethan and Jacobean theatre; exhibits include a full-size working replica of the Cockpit Theatre (1616) (used for workshop productions), models of the first and second Globe Theatres and the Swan, a recreation of a frost fair which used to take place on the Thames at Southwark and early maps and engravings of the area.

This was the site of the *Hope Theatre* (1614-56) where Ben Jonson's 'Bartholmew Fair' was first performed. Bear-baiting began on the site before 1550 and continued in the theatre. Performances in Davies' Amphitheatre here from 1662 to 1682 were visited by Evelyn and Pepys ('After dinner, with my wife and Mercer to the Bear Garden where ... I saw some good sport of the bull's tossing of the dogs, one into the very boxes. But it is a rude and nasty pleasure', Diary, 14 Aug, 1666).

A plaque on the wall marks the approximate site of the famous GLOBE THEATRE, erected by the Burbages in 1599. Shakespeare was a shareholder and acted here for many years. Fifteen of his plays were produced at the theatre, which was a small but lofty circular building ('this wooden O'). It burned in 1613, and the second theatre was demolished in 1644. Rose Alley recalls the *Rose Theatre* put up by Philip Henslowe in 1587. The plays of Shakespeare, Marlowe, and Kyd were performed here until 1603, and Edward Alleyn was a leading actor.

Almhouses in Hopton Street, Southwark

The Globe Playhouse Trust plans to build a third Globe Theatre, modelled closely on the second theatre (see above). Sam Wannamaker, the American film producer, has received initial planning permission for this scheme.

The *Power Station* built in 1963 by Sir Giles Gilbert Scott stands on the site of Great Pike Gardens which supplied fish to ecclesiastic houses in the area in the 14C. Hopton Street (with the attractive almshouses of Hopton's Charity; 1759) leads inland to Southwark St.

At 48 Hopton Street is the new *Bankside Gallery* (01-928 7251). This is the home of the Royal Society of Painters in Watercolours and the Royal Society of Painter-etchers and Engravers. As well as open exhibitions for the two societies there are changing exhibitions, mostly of prints. The gallery was designed by Fitzroy, Robinson and Partners.

Open during exhibitions Tues to Sat 10.00-17.00, Sun 14.00-18.00. Admission charge. Access: Underground, Blackfriars, cross Blackfriars Bridge.

Nearby on the Thames in a modern housing/office development is the Founders Arms, a new pub, built on the site of a bell foundry where the bells of St. Paul's were cast. From the terrace, bar and restaurant there are good views of St. Paul's.

In Blackfriars Road is *Christ Church* (1960), the industrial mission centre of Marshall's Charity (founded 1627); replacing a predecesor ruined in 1941, it occupies the site of the manor house of Robert de Paris (temp. Richard II). As Paris Garden, the manor was in the 16-17C one of the amusement centres of London, patronised by society and even by the Court. Farther S in Blackfriars Road is Orbit House with the *India Office Library* (over 300,000 vols; MSS. and letters).

Across Blackfriars Road is Stamford Street where the portico (1823) of the demolished Unitarian Chapel forms a ceremonial entrance to the parade-ground of the *London Nautical College*. In Upper Ground, parallel to the N is part of the Coin Street development (see p 290).

Stretching E from London Bridge to Tower Bridge is the **London Bridge City** redevelopment—part of the rejuvenation of London's docklands (see Rte 26).

The first phase, due to be completed in 1986, includes office blocks, a private hospital, and the Hay's Galleria, created from Hay's Wharf, filled in, stripped of its exterior cladding to reveal the 19C brick-work, and spanned by an iron and glass roof structure. Here there will be shops, restaurants and bars. A riverside walk will lead from London Bridge through the development to a park next to Tower Bridge.

Tooley Street runs behind the new development. After a disastrous fire here in 1861 in which James Braidwood, first chief of the 'London Fire Engine Establishment' lost his life, the service was reorganised as the Metropolitan Fire Brigade, now the London Fire Brigade. The London Dungeon is on the right (see above); further along, on the left, Vine Lane leads through the new development to '*HMS Belfast*', a Southampton-class cruiser (1936-38) saved from the scrapyard and opened as a museum in 1971 by the Imperial War Museum.

HMS Belfast, Vine Lane, London SE1. Tel. 01-407 6434. Open 11.00-17.50, summer, 11.00-16.30, winter, daily. Access: Underground, London Bridge, Tower Hill. Ferry from Tower Pier, daily in summer, weekends in winter. Admission charge. Educational facilities.
  Boarding by gangway to the Quarterdeck; tour the ship following the arrows

(some confined spaces and steep ladders). The highlights are the main gun turrets, the navigation bridge, the cruiser exhibition detailing the ship's fighting history (Battle of North Cape, Normandy D-Day, Korea), the mess decks, bakery and machine shop. Special exhibitions are held regularly.

On the E side of Tower Bridge there is more new building at the former Courage Brewery site opposite the Tower Hotel and the adjoining Butler's Wharf; this complex site will be redeveloped with offices, workshops, shops and housing. The Conran Roche proposal for part of Butler's Wharf includes a design museum on the lines of Conran's Boilerhouse Project at the Victoria and Albert Museum.

Tooley Street leads E to Jamaica Road and the area of **Bermondsey**. *St. Saviour's Dock*, to the E of which lay Jacob's Island, scene of Bill Sykes' death in 'Oliver Twist', is part of the new development. New Concordia Wharf, attractive workshops and flats, has already been completed on this site.

Tower Bridge Road leads S from Tower Bridge underneath the great brick arches of London's earliest railway station (Bermondsey; 1836), passing the 19C buildings of the former *St. Olave's Grammar School* (founded in 1560), and the *New Caledonian Market* at Bermondsey Square, SE1. (Access: Underground, Borough; Buses 1, 42, 78 and 189). Open Friday 04.00-10.00.

The New Caledonian Market opened in here in 1949, moved from its pre-war site at Copenhagen Fields in Islington (see p 296). There are some 200 pitches and the standard of antiques is generally high. Dealings start unofficially before dawn and the public is welcome from 07.00. By mid-morning the serious traders have gone. The market spills over in the surrounding streets; the so-called Bermondsey Antique Market is under cover in Long Lane.

The church of *St. Mary Magdalen* here (rebuilt in 1680) has original woodwork and preserves some 12C capitals from Bermondsey Abbey, a large and powerful house founded in 1087, in which the widows of Henry V and Edward IV died. Remains of a gatehouse can be seen at 7 Grange Walk, nearby. The name, Tanner Street, recalls the area's past as the site of London's leather and tanning industry.

Jamaica Road continues towards Rotherhithe (see p 317) and (S) to the *Surrey Commercial Docks*. These were the only enclosed docks to be built on the S side of the river; the first were linked to various canal schemes— the Croydon Canal and the Grand Surrey Canal — the first proper dock with a new lock was completed in 1860. The Greenland Dock covering 22 acres was operational from 1904 handling whale cargo and then softwood from Scandinavia. The 300-acre Surrey Docks were badly damaged in the Second World War and closed in 1970. Developments proposed and under way include housing, industry, recreational and shopping facilities.

28   The South Bank, Waterloo and Lambeth

Access: for the South Bank: Underground, Embankment and Hungerford footbridge; or Waterloo; for the Imperial War Museum: Lambeth North; for Lambeth Palace and the Museum of Garden History, Bus No. 507 from Victoria or Waterloo.

The **South Bank**, representing the cultural institutions S of the Thames, has acquired identity in the last ten years, tilting the cultural balance of London slightly more towards the S of the capital, traditionally seen as a cultural wasteland from the heights of Hampstead. Developments here started with the Festival of Britain in 1951; a large exhibition was laid out on derelict ground in the area between Westminster Bridge and Waterloo Bridge with the Royal Festival Hall as its focus. Improvements extended to Battersea Park (see p 327). The area now includes three concert halls, an art gallery, the National Film Theatre and three theatres within the National Theatre. Concerted efforts were made by the Greater London Council during 1983-85 to brighten up and counteract some of the sterility created by the 1950s and '60s concrete 'bunker' style of architecture.

The South Bank is best reached over Hungerford footbridge from the Embankment; the **Royal Festival Hall** is immediately to the left of the bridge.

Royal Festival Hall, Belvedere Road, London SE1. Tel. 01-928 3641.

The main concert hall seats 3000 in this complex designed by Sir R.H. Matthew and J.L. Martin (1949-51) and completed by Sir Hubert Bennett (1962-65). There is a small recital room and the main stage will hold a choir of 250. The large ballroom/foyer is used for exhibitions and there are several eating areas including a self-service cafeteria and a winebar, with free lunch-time music. The nearby *Queen Elizabeth Hall* opened in 1967 and seats 1100. The *Purcell Room*, used for recitals, seats 330. Both were designed by G. Horsfall.

The **Hayward Gallery** just behind was designed by Ove Arup and

The Hayward Gallery, South Bank (GLC Architects Dept, 1965-68)

Partners and opened in 1968; it was until recently run by the Arts
Council and stages major temporary exhibitions.

Hayward Gallery, Belvedere Road, London SE1. Tel. 01-928 3144 Open during
exhibitions: Mon to Wed 10.00-20.00; Thurs to Sat 10.00-18.00, Sun 12.00-18.00,
admission charge. Access: Underground, Waterloo.

The **National Film Theatre** (01-928 3232) was established in 1953
and moved to its present site under Waterloo Bridge in 1958; there
are four auditoria, a restaurant and bar, as well as library facilities.
The London Film Festival is organised by the British Film Institute
and centres on the National Film Theatre in November each year.
Temporary weekly membership is available to visitors.

A small second-hand bookmarket has been set up under the bridge
just outside the National Film Theatre.

To the E is the **National Theatre**, opened in 1976, and containing
three auditoria: the open-staged *Olivier* seating 1160, the *Lyttelton*
(seating 890) with a proscenium stage, and the rectangular *Cottesloe*
with adjustable seating (up to 400), used for experimental productions.

National Theatre, South Bank, SE1. Tel. 01-928 2252. There are self-service
cafeterias and bars, as well as a full-scale restaurant; exhibitions and music
take place in the foyers which also have bookstalls. In the summer the terraces
provide a fine view over the Thames.

The idea of a National Theatre for Britain was first put forward in 1848, but not
pursued seriously until 1904 when a National Theatre Scheme and Estimate
were prepared by several leading actors and playwrights led by H. Granville
Barker; appeals raised enough funds to purchase a site in Cromwell Gardens
in 1930. The Second World War intervened and in 1944 the London County
Council made a site on the South Bank available to the Shakespeare Memorial
National Committee; Sir Laurence Olivier and Norman Marshall were appointed
joint Chairmen and Denys Lasden architect. In 1951 the foundation stone was
laid. The National Theatre Company under Sir Laurence Olivier was set up in
1962 and took over the Old Vic as a temporary home, opening with Peter
O'Toole in 'Hamlet'. In 1969 building finally started and Sir Peter Hall was
appointed artistic director for the opening in 1976. The National Theatre is
financed partly by the Greater London Council, which owns the building, and
the Arts Council, as well as its own commercial receipts. It hit financial
difficulties in 1985.

Beyond are the headquarters of London Weekend Television and
IBM (see p 286).

Waterloo Road continues S across a roundabout. The church of *St.
John* by Francis Bedford (1823-35) was restored in 1950 to serve the
Festival of Britain. It had been badly damaged in the Second World
War and only the walls, portico, steeple and 18C Italian marble font
survive of the original church.

Opposite is **Waterloo Station** (Southern Region, rebuilt in 1912-22),
London's busiest mainline terminal, handling an average of 2000
trains a day and servicing the S coast as well as the commuter belt
of Surrey and Hampshire. The station opened in 1848; in 1899 the
direct 'tube' link with the City (to Bank Station) opened and still
operates, popularly known as 'the Drain'.

The Cut Street Market, just outside the station, which also spreads
into Lower Marsh, has declined since its heyday in the 1870s when
it was a popular S London meeting place. Since much of the residential
character of this area has been lost, the market functions now mostly
as a lunch-time shopping area for office workers.

Further on in the Cut is the *Old Vic Theatre*, beautifully restored in 1984 by Canadian millionaire Ed Mirvish, and now operating as a repertory theatre for touring companies.

It was built in 1817 as the Royal Coburg Theatre; rebuilt in 1833, it changed its name to the Royal Victoria and reopened in 1871 as the New Victoria, later becoming a temperance music-hall for the working class. Lilian Baylis arrived in 1900 and took over the management in 1912, raising the standard of productions, particularly of Shakespeare, and making it one of London's leading theatres. It was damaged in 1941 but reopened in 1950; in 1963 it became the temporary home of the National Theatre (see above). After it left for its new home on the South Bank the Old Vic went through a difficult period until dramatically rescued by Ed Mirvish who has invested £1m in returning the building to its Victorian splendour.

The *Young Vic* in the Cut occupies an octagonal building (1970) seating 450 and has a small studio seating 100. It has its own independent board of management and aims to provide good theatre for young people at reasonable prices.

A large part of the South Bank between Stamford Street and Upper Ground has been derelict for years while a planning battle between local community groups and property developers was waged. Known as the Coin Street site, it includes some river frontage between Kent House and King's Reach. The property developers withdrew their scheme in 1984 and it now looks as though the area will be developed for housing and workshops financed by the Greater London Council; the local landmark, the *Oxo Tower* (Ali Moore; 1928), threatened with demolition will be retained within the redevelopment. There will be a continuation of the South Bank Riverside Walk.

Waterloo Road ends at the Royal Eye Hospital and *St. George's Circus* (Pl. 20; 5), the bold focal point of George Dance's development plan of 1769, where six roads converge.

Here Blackfriars Rd leads N to Blackfriars Bridge (p 300), passing the site of the Surrey Theatre, owned in its days as the 'Royal Circus' by Charles Dibdin, author of 'Tom Bowling'; and further on that of the old round Surrey Chapel, famous under the Rev. Rowland Hill (1744-1833). Westminster Bridge Road runs W from St. George's Circus past *Morley College*, founded in 1885 (noted for the high standard of its courses). *Christ Church*, at the corner of Kennington Road, has been rebuilt into an office block. The tower of 1876, which survived wartime bombing and on which appear the Stars and Stripes, was erected by subscription from Americans as a memorial to President Lincoln.

Return along Westminster Bridge Road to County Hall. To the right is Belvedere Road. Hereabouts was the factory for artificial stoneware started by Eleanor Coade (1733-1821) in 1759. The factory closed in 1840 and the secret of manufacture was lost. A lion, sculptured in the stone (1837), which formerly adorned the Lion Brewery, demolished in 1950, stood outside Waterloo Station in 1951-66 before being moved to its present site outside County Hall. On the left rise the two massive blocks of the *Shell Centre* (1957-62) linked by a tunnel, and one of the largest office blocks in Europe (7.5 acres).

Beyond the *Jubilee Gardens*, laid out for the Queen's Silver Jubilee in 1977, rises **County Hall**, begun as the headquarters of the London County Council in 1912 and now that of the Greater London Council. This huge Renaissance edifice, by Ralph Knott and W.E. Riley, has a river-facade (1932) 750ft long. The sculptures on the exterior are by Ernest Cole and A.F. Hardiman.

The meetings of the Council (every 4th Tuesday at 14.30) are open to the public; visitors are welcome at any time (until 1 April 1986—see Preface, p 5). The Library is open to visitors by appointment. (The GLC Records Office is in Clerkenwell.) A striking extension to the County Hall has been built on the 'island' at the end of Westminster Bridge.

The **Greater London Council** was constituted in 1964 when some 70 local authorities were combined into 32 new boroughs, and the boundaries of the County of London extended deep into Essex and Surrey and incorporated Middlesex. It is the ruling authority for the County of London (saving the jurisdiction within the City of the City of London Corporation) in such matters as main drainage, ambulance and fire services, overall planning, major roads, etc. Local administration of libraries, parks, personal health and welfare services, is in the hands of the 32 *Borough Councils* and the City of London. Responsibility for education falls on the Inner London Education Authority and the Outer London boroughs. See also p 5.

The E end of *Westminster Bridge* (Pl. 15; 7) has been guarded since 1966 by a colossal Lion (comp. above). The riverside is continued by the *Albert Embankment*, 1 mile long, completed in 1869, and adorned with delightful dolphin lamp posts. Here, opposite the Houses of Parliament, is the new *St. Thomas's Hospital*, begun in 1960. The hospital, founded in 1213, was removed there from Southwark (comp. p 281) in 1868 and built on the 'pavilion' plan devised by Florence Nightingale, who had established the first English school of nursing at St. Thomas's in 1860. The pavilions were demolished after being damaged in the Second World War.

Following the Embankment past St. Thomas's Medical School we reach ***Lambeth Palace**, the London residence for seven centuries of the archbishops of Canterbury. The building was begun by Abp Langton (1207-29), but few of his successors failed to add to or alter it; the residential part was built in 1829-38. The palace was damaged

The statue of Queen Boudicca (Boadicea) at Westminster Bridge (Thomas Thornycroft, 1850s)

in 1941. Erasmus, Thomas More, and Cranmer (who here wrote the English Prayer Book) are known to have visited the Palace. (Small parties by arrangement only.)

The entrance is by *Morton's Tower*, a noble red-brick gatehouse erected c 1490. In the courtyard is a memorial to Abp Lord Davidson (1848-1930). The *Great Hall*, rebuilt in medieval style by Abp Juxon in 1663, has a roof, 70ft in height, resembling that of Westminster Hall. It now houses the *Library*, the nucleus of which was bequeathed to the see by Abp Bancroft in 1610. It is thought to be the oldest free public library in the country. It is open to readers by appointment only (exhibitions), and contains nearly 1500 MSS., many finely illuminated, letters of Francis Bacon, Gladstone's diaries, six Caxtons, Edward VI's Latin grammar and Elizabeth I's prayer book. The *Guard Chamber*, with a 14C roof (reconstructed), contains a fine series of portraits of the archbishops since 1503, by Holbein, Van Dyck, Hogarth, Reynolds, Romney, Lawrence, and others. The beautiful *Crypt* beneath the chapel is the oldest part of the building, dating posibly from c 1200. The small *Chapel* (c 1230), rededicated in 1955, preserves stalls and other fittings provided by Abp Laud (1634). From 1273 down to the present day many English bishops have been consecrated in this chapel, and in 1787 Bp White of Pennsylvania and Bp Provost of New York were consecrated here by Abp Moore. The chapel was the scene of the second trial of Wyclif in 1378. The picturesque *Lollards' Tower* (1434-45) derives its name from the belief that the Lollards, followers of Wyclif, were imprisoned in it. In the stair-turret is the 'Lollards' Prison'.

Archbishop's Park, a portion of the palace grounds opened to the public in 1900, extends to the NE and provides a good view of the Palace (entrance in Lambeth Road).

At the gate of the palace is the church of *St. Mary Lambeth*, now a museum devoted to gardening, based on the connection with the Tradescants, father and son, both of whom are buried in the churchyard (John Tradescant d 1638)—as is Admiral Bligh (d 1817) of the 'Bounty' who lived at 100 Lambeth Road. The churchyard has been converted into a delightful botanical garden.

Museum of Garden History, St. Mary at Lambeth, Lambeth Palace Road, London SE1. Tel. 01-373 4030. Open Mon to Fri 11.00-15.00, Sun 10.30-17.00. Closed December to March. Bookshop, souvenirs. Access: Underground, Westminster; Bus, 77, 159, 170, or 507 from Victoria.

The church retains its 14C tower but was rebuilt in 1851 and is now owned by the Tradescant Trust (set up in 1977). The Tradescants were gardeners to Charles I and introduced many rare plants to Britain. The church features displays on them and their work and other aspects of garden history. Temporary exhibitions and fund-raising events are held regularly.

The well-restored church includes at the E end of the S aisle the Pedlar's Window, commemorating the bequest to the parish of the Pedlar's Acre, a piece of ground originally worth 2s 8d but sold to the LCC as the site for County Hall for £81,000. The existing window is a replacement of 1956.

From Lambeth Bridge Lambeth Road runs E to St. George's Circus passing (right) *Lambeth Walk*, popularised by the '30s musical 'Me and My Girl'. At No. 124 is Morton Place, where a tablet on No. 6 marks the residence of Miss Cons and Miss Baylis (see above).

In Hercules Rd (left) the *Central Office of Information* building has a huge mosaic mural of the Labours of Hercules. Cross Kennington Road where Charles Chaplin lived as a boy (at Nos 261 and 287 and at No. 3 Pownall Terrace; in one of these he may have been born in 1889). Beyond is the building occupied from 1815 to 1930 by Bethlem Hospital ('Bedlam'; now near Croydon; see p 334). The central portion of the old hospital (by Lewis, 1812; dome by Smirke, 1846, restored after fire) now houses the ***Imperial War Museum** (Pl. 19; 4). Opened in 1920 at the Crystal Palace, it was housed in 1924-36 in the Imperial Institute. It is concerned with all aspects of the two World Wars and with other British military operations since 1914.

The Imperial War Museum, Lambeth Road, London SE1. Tel. 01-735 8922. Open Mon to Sat 10.00-17.50, Sun 14.00-17.50. Access: Underground, Lambeth North. Educational facilities, Library and Photographic Records Dept by appointment Mon to Fri 10.00-17.00. Film shows. Bookshop with guidebooks, souvenirs, etc.
   The museum launched an appeal during 1985 to extend and improve facilities, including the addition of an in-fill building in the centre of the structure. Considerable changes in layout can therefore be expected over the next few years.

On the lawn in front of the museum are the last two surviving 15-inch British naval guns from the battleships 'Ramillies' and 'Resolution', cast in 1915 and 1916. The obelisk of 1771 in the grounds used to stand at St. George's Circus and was removed here in 1907. The grounds surrounding the museum were acquired by Lord Rothermere in 1926 and named the *Geraldine Mary Harmsworth Park* in memory of his mother. Below is a description of some of the highlights of the museum.

Gallery 1 is devoted to those who have been recognised for valour and self-sacrifice and received the Victoria and George Crosses. Amongst the documents in Gallery 2 are one of four copies of Hitler's testament dictated in his bunker on 28 April 1945, and the Munich Declaration of September 1938.
   The museum's important art collection is displayed on a rotating basis in Galleries 3 to 6, and includes Epstein's bust of Churchill. Gallery 12 illustrates trench warfare and Gallery 13 armoured fighting vehicles. In Gallery 15 are the caravans which served as Montgomery's headquarters in the Western Desert, Normandy and in Germany. The displays in Gallery 17 cover the Far East campaign including the building of the Burma railway. There are also sections of Second World War fighter aircraft. Gallery 20 looks at the origins of modern war, including the Vietnam War.

29 Islington and Camden Town

Islington, within easy reach of the City of London, was heavily developed for housing during the 19C; thousands of clerks would walk from here to their offices in the City. Much of this terraced housing is now being restored after a period of decline during the early part of the century as Islington is gentrified. The high street—Upper Street—has a radical tone with the Sisterwright Feminist Bookshop and the offices of 'City Limits'.

Access: Underground to the Angel; by road from the City via City Road.

The Regent's Canal passes unnoticed through Islington; from the City Road Basin just to the S of the Angel, where the Islington Boat Club is now established, the canal enters the longest tunnel on its route—960 yards—opened in 1816.

There is no tow path and the towing horses were led along Chapel Street (a market then—see below) while the bargees propelled their boats lying on their backs and pushing against the wall with their feet; a steam tug was introduced in 1826 and used until the 1930s. The canal emerges again at Muriel Street (where the gardens of the Barnsbury Estate made an attractive backdrop) and continues to Camden Town, Regent's Park and Paddington (see p 28 for canal tours).

Islington High Street which leads due N from the Angel soon splits into the long, still drab *Liverpool Road* and *Upper Street*. Liverpool Rd runs NW past Chapel Market (see below) to Holloway. To the W among interesting terraces and squares is Cloudesley Square with *Holy Trinity Church* in the centre, built by Barry in 1826 and inspired by King's College Chapel, Cambridge. To the N is the collegiate-style Lonsdale Square by R.C. Carpenter (c 1842-45). Parallel to Upper Street, where Kate Greenaway lived between c 1851 and c 1884, is Camden Passage (see below). Further E are the attractive Colebrooke Row and Duncan Terrace. Charles Lamb came to live at No. 64 Duncan Terrace in 1823 'never having had a house before'. It was on leaving this house that his friend George Dyer walked into the New River and nearly drowned. The New River (comp. above) is now covered at this point; its course is indicated by the garden in front of Duncan Terrace. It is carried across Regent's Canal (also underground).

Chapel Market, N1 (White Conduit Street, Grant Street, Baron Street); Tues to Sun (mornings only Thurs and Sun); Access: Underground, Angel. There has been a street market here at least since the middle of the 19C and probably longer; it is now busiest at the weekends and offers fruit, vegetables, general household goods and

The gentrification of Islington; this is Tibberton Square

clothes, and reflects the tastes of the working-class population of Islington, rather than the newcomers.

*The **Royal Agricultural Hall** (1862) in Liverpool Rd was used for cattle shows, World Fairs, circuses and the Royal Tournament. It closed in 1976 and is due to become an industrial exhibition centre in 1986—the London Business Design Centre.

In Upper Street is the *King's Head* theatre and pub (115 Upper Street, London N1; 01-226 1916). The theatre is at the back and dinner is served at narrow tables before the play, review or cabaret starts; there is live music in the bar.

Camden Passage has grown to include not only the Passage with its shops and stalls, the latter trading on Wednesday, Thursday and Saturday, but also two indoor markets. It is London's foremost antique and bric-a-brac market for individual buyers (Bermondsey is geared more to the trader) and developed during the early 1960s. There are good restaurants, such as Fredericks, but the famous Carrier's restaurant closed in 1984.

At *Islington Green* Essex Road diverges NE. On the Green is a statue of Sir Hugh Myddelton (d 1631) who projected the New River scheme for supplying London with water (comp. above). We continue N along Upper St passing (right) *St. Mary's Church* with a tall tower and spire which remains from the previous church begun in 1754. The church was restored in 1962 and contains striking mural paintings. Behind the church, with entrance from Dagmar Passage off Cross St, is the *Little Angel Theatre*, one of only two permanent puppet theatres in England.

Beyond the Town Hall Canonbury Lane diverges right into the fashionable district of **Canonbury**, with the charming Canonbury Square, begun in 1790. Further on, fronting Canonbury Place (with stuccoed houses of c 1770) is **Canonbury Tower**, a red-brick tower 66ft high and 17ft square, the chief relic of a 16C house of the priors of St. Bartholomew's. On the W side are two old three-storeyed buildings, in the first of which are the beautiful oak-panelled Spencer Room and Compton Room. The house came into the possession of Sir John Spencer, Lord Mayor of London, in 1594-95, and in 1616-25 Sir Francis Bacon was the lessee of 'Canbury House'. In the 18C the buildings were let out in lodgings and among the noted people who stayed here was Oliver Goldsmith (in the Compton Room). The tower commands an extensive view, and behind it is a pleasant garden. The buildings (with the modern hall adjoining) are occupied by the Tower Theatre; visitors are admitted to the panelled rooms on application to the Secretary. The old octagonal garden-houses that marked the SE and SW corners of the garden of the 16C house are still to be seen in Alwyne Villas (1824) and Alwyne Place (mostly late Georgian), to the S. From Alwyne Road the pleasant New River Walk leads to St. Paul's Road.

Continue along Upper St past handsome Compton Terrace with the incongruous Victorian *Union Chapel* (it contains a piece of the rock upon which the Pilgrim Fathers landed from the 'Mayflower'), to **Highbury**. In Highbury Place (with fine terraces of c 1774-79), on the SE side of Highbury Fields, Sickert had a studio at No. 1 and No. 25 was the frequent lodging of Wesley and was the residence of Joseph Chamberlain in 1845-54 (tablet). The attractive Highbury Terrace (1789) skirts the N side of the Fields. Off Highbury Hill is the *Arsenal Football Ground*, removed here in 1913 from Woolwich, where it had been founded at the Royal Arsenal Factory in 1884 (whence the sobriquet, 'the gunners').

From *Highbury and Islington Station* the wide Holloway Road leads to the NW through *Holloway*, with a well-known women's prison. It was built in 1852 by James Bunning as a House of Correction for the City. The 20ft-high perimeter walls were demolished in 1971. To the W, in Caledonian Road, is *Pentonville Prison* built in 1840. Within this prison Roger Casement was hanged for high treason on 3 August 1916, the first person hanged in England for this offence since the execution of the Cato Street Conspirators in 1820. On the opposite side of the road is the former site of a cattle market transferred here from Smithfield in 1855, and occupying 50 acres in what was formerly Copenhagen Fields. It became the famous Caledonian Market in 1924; this in turn was transferred to Bermondsey after the 2nd World War and a housing estate built here—the market taverns and clock tower remain.

Buses 172 and 271 run along the Holloway Road to Highgate (Rte 40).

North of Islington is **Tufnell Park**, an undistinguished Victorian suburb, where in 1968 a brave attempt was made by the actor George Murcell to create a Shakespearean Theatre with true 16C atmosphere, in a converted church. *St. George's Theatre*, 49 Tufnell Park Road, N7, occupies a church dating to 1866, modelled on a 15C crusaders' church. The theatre finally opened in 1976 with a series of Shakespeare plays and has faced continual financial problems.

To the W is **Kentish Town** with a mixed residential population; council housing and substantial private houses. Karl Marx and his family came to live at No. 9 Grafton Terrace, Fitzroy Road (now No. 46 Grafton Terrace) in 1856 from their cramped rooms in Soho. Later they moved to 1 Maitland Park Road nearby (the house was demolished in the 2nd World War) and a block of flats now occupies the site. In 1875 they moved to 41 Maitland Park Road (also gone) where Karl Marx died in 1881.

Camden Town is to the S. The London Borough of Camden is very diverse, stretching from Hampstead in the N to St. Pancras and Bloomsbury in the S. Somewhere in the middle, just NE of Regent's Park, is Camden Town, a mixed residential area with well-cared-for houses and blocks of flats towards Primrose Hill and Regent's Park.

The once rural aspect of Camden was changed dramatically by the building of the Regent's Canal and the wharves established at Camden Lock in the 1820s. The growing residential population suffered further upheavals with the building of the London, Birmingham and Midlands railways. Today Camden takes full advantage of its position on the Canal and an attractive market/craft workshop area with restaurants has been established at Camden Lock since the '60s.

From Camden Town Underground Station Camden High Street leads N and joins with Chalk Farm Road. Before Camden Lock Market and just past the bridge over the Regent's Canal there is a smaller market mostly trading in very fashionable clothes and bric-a-brac.

Camden Lock Market, Chalk Farm Road, London NW1. Access: Underground, Camden Town; BR, Camden Road. Market trades on Saturday and Sunday.

Camden Lock Market itself is located around Dingwalls, formerly an old timber warehouse at Camden Lock, which now offers pop and rock music and food. Workshops and showrooms of the craftspeople who work here through the week are in the buildings to the back of the market; on Saturdays and Sundays traders set up their stalls, some under cover, selling fashion, arts and crafts, and home-made sweets and other foods. There are two restaurants within the complex and, of course, the Canal at one end.

The 'Fair Lady' cruising restaurant on a traditional canal barge departs from here daily for lunch and dinner cruises (booking essential on 01-485 4433); during the summer (April to October) the 'Jenny Wren' operates cruises from here along the Canal to Little Venice and back.

The new offices of TV AM (the breakfast TV station) are to the E, adorned by giant egg-cups.

A little further along the Canal towards Regent's Park another restaurant barge, the Gallery Boat Chinese Restaurant, is moored (15 Prince Albert Rd, NW1; 01-485 8137). There are guided walks along the Regent's Canal organised by the Inland Waterways Association between May and December starting at Camden Lock or Little Venice (01-586 2510).
   The London Borough of Camden organises a festival in March each year which is based on the many different venues within the borough and also on the ethnic mix which includes Irish, West Indian, Greek, Cypriot; the jazz festival has become particularly well established. It is based at the Camden Arts Centre, Arkwright Road.

Camden Palace in Camden High Street, formerly a cinema, has been transformed into one of the most exciting pop venues/night clubs in London.
   The *Round House* in Chalk Farm Road (nearest Underground Chalk Farm) is a former engine shed of the London and Birmingham Railway, built in 1847. Later it became a warehouse and factory and in 1967 a theatre; in 1984 it was saved from demolition by the GLC who have made it a Centre for Black Ethnic Arts.

III THE RIVER THAMES

The **Thames**, once a busy highway, still provides a superb view of the capital and an insight into its history from the many sightseeing boats which operate from Westminster Pier, Charing Cross Pier, Festival Pier (summer only) and Tower Pier—downstream as far as Greenwich and the Thames Barrier, all the year round. Upstream services from Westminster Pier to Kew, Richmond, Kingston and Hampton Court operate during the summer. Full details of services on p 29.

The Roman armies founded Londinium on the N bank where a spur of gravel provided the necessary foundation for a river-crossing; Caesar called the river Tamesis and a wooden bridge was built between Southwark on the S bank and the new settlement. Londinium became an important port and London Bridge in various forms remained the only permanent crossing (other than Kingston Bridge and Putney Bridge; see p 339) until Westminster Bridge was built in 1750.

Although the Thames was a royal river—royal barges proceeded regularly between Whitehall Palace, the Placentia at Richmond, and Greenwich, and Hampton Court—the City of London retained effective control of the port and river as far W as Staines and E to the mouth of the Medway until the 19C. The first Thames Conservancy Act established the Thames Commissioners and the Port of London Authority was set up in 1909 with control of 135 miles of tidal river from Teddington to the sea. The Thames Water Authority, established in 1974 to take charge of water supply, drainage, recreation and sewerage, took over the Thames Conservancy function in 1983, while the Port of London retained its navigational role.

At times during the 18C and 19C the river would freeze and Frost Fairs were held on the ice above London Bridge—the last in 1814. The removal of the old London Bridge which acted as a dam accelerated the flow of the river and this effect was intensified by the building of the embankments. It is unlikely that the river will freeze again. However, as SE England is sinking at a rate of about 12 inches every 100 years, the river has become more liable to flood its banks. In 1928 14 people died when Central London flooded and in 1953 300 people died along the E Coast and the Thames Estuary. The Thames Flood Barrier, completed in 1983, is intended to prevent this happening again (see below).

30 Westminster to the Tower; to Greenwich and the Thames Barrier

(This is a brief description of places of interest; for full details see under the relevant area description.)

Westminster Pier adjoins Westminster Bridge on the N bank; there are plans to redevelop it in the near future as the structure is no longer sound.

Westminster Bridge, the second bridge to be built across the Thames in Central London (London Bridge was the first), was completed in 1750. When the old London Bridge was removed in 1831 the foundations of Westminster Bridge were undermined by the increased waterflow and a new bridge (designed by Thomas Page) replaced the old one in 1862. At the head of the bridge on the N side is a statue of Boadicea and on the S side a White Lion, made of Coade stone in 1837. Opposite Westminster Pier is **County Hall**, headquarters of the Greater London Council (see p 5), and above the bridge, the **Houses of Parliament** on the N bank, with *St. Thomas's Hospital* opposite.

Heading downstream, the *Victoria Embankment* is on the N side; this was completed in 1870 to a design by Bazalgette and incorporated the District Line Underground service as well as a new sewerage system. The *RAF Memorial* was erected in 1923; beyond are the buildings of the former Scotland Yard, now the *Norman Shaw Building* with offices for MPs, the plain white square of the *Ministry of Defence* built on the site of old Whitehall Palace, and the ornate Renaissance buildings of *Whitehall Court*, the *National Liberal Club* and the *Royal Horseguards Hotel*. Moored along the Embankment is the 'Tattershall Castle', a Clyde paddle-steamer, now a pub, and the 'Hispaniola', a restaurant.

On the S bank between County Hall and Hungerford Bridge are the *Jubilee Gardens*, laid out in the Queen's Jubilee Year of 1977 and the start of the 10-mile waymarked *Jubilee Walkway*.

Hungerford Bridge carries railway traffic to Charing Cross Station and also pedestrians to and from the S Bank. The original suspension bridge on this site was designed by Brunel but demolished in 1864. Just beyond on the N bank is *Charing Cross Pier*.

The **Royal Festival Hall** on the S side is part of the **South Bank Arts Complex**, opened in 1951 and designed by Robert Matthew and Leonard Martin, for the Festival of Britain celebrations that year. It seats 3400 and has restaurants, bars and changing art exhibitions. The *Festival Pier* in front of it opened in 1983. The *Queen Elizabeth Hall* and the *Purcell Room* are part of the South Bank Complex, as is the *Hayward Gallery*, just beyond.

The Victoria Embankment continues along the N bank with decorative dolphin lamp posts and moorings of lion heads with rings along the river front. **Cleopatra's Needle**, a pink obelisk, is one of a pair presented to Britain by Mohammed Ali and erected here in 1878. It stood at Heliopolis originally and dates to 1500 BC. Beyond are the *Victoria Embankment Gardens*, with summertime music and a statue of Burns. The old watergate of York House indicates that the river used to be twice as wide at this point.

The clock on *Shellmex House* is the largest in London and dates to 1932. The *Savoy Hotel* founded by Richard d'Oyly opened in 1889 on the site of the old Savoy Palace.

Waterloo Bridge provides an excellent view-point as it is located on the turn of the river. This concrete bridge was designed by Sir Giles Gilbert Scott and opened in 1942. John Rennies' original Waterloo Bridge which opened in 1817 started to sink in 1923.

Below Waterloo Bridge on the N side is the floating *Thames Police Station* and on the S side the *National Film Theatre* (with an outdoor restaurant).

Somerset House on the N side just past Waterloo Bridge was built in 1776 with its own river entrance. The E wing is *King's College*, part of the University of London, with the new Howard Hotel next to it. The area called the TEMPLE takes its name from the Order of Knights Templar. It is now used by the Inner and Middle Temple, two of the four Inns of Court. The heraldic dragons mark the boundary between the City of London and Westminster. Ships moored along here are the 'Wellington', the livery hall of the Master Mariners, and the Royal Navy training ships 'Chrysanthemum' and 'President'. The 'Discovery' has moved to St. Katharine's Dock and its mooring is used by a Thames Barge, 'Wilfred', a winebar. Near the bridge are the Gothic buildings of *Sion College* and the *City of London School for Boys* (due to move, see below).

On the S bank, the **National Theatre**, concrete and stark on the outside, is open through the day and evening with comfortable bars, buffets and a restaurant. There are three theatres: the *Olivier*, the *Lyttelton* and the *Cottesloe*. Next to it are the buildings of London Weekend Television and IBM. The *Old Barge House* stairs can still be seen with *King's Reach Tower* beyond. These watermen's steps are a reminder of the days when passengers were carried across the river by ferrymen. The *Oxo Tower* has been preserved in the Coin Street redevelopment; *Seacontainers House*, now offices, was supposed to become a hotel in 1974.

Next to Blackfriars Bridge, the modern *Doggetts Coat and Badge* pub takes its name from the red coat worn by the Thames Watermen who compete in the Doggetts Coat and Badge Race, established by Thomas Doggett, a comedian and manager of Theatre Royal Drury Lane in 1715. The 5-mile race from London Bridge to Cadogan Pier, Chelsea, takes place each year at the end of July.

The Fleet River, now in a pipeway, enters the Thames on the N side just above **Blackfriars Bridge**, named after the Dominican Priory which stood here. The original bridge opened in 1769 and the new bridge, designed by Joseph Cubitt, was opened by Queen Victoria in 1869. The Blackfriars Railway Bridge beyond leads to Blackfriars and Holborn Viaduct Stations and incorporates stones from the old Westminster Bridge. The adjoining disused railway bridge was demolished in 1985.

Along the N bank between Blackfriars and Southwark bridges is the *Mermaid Theatre* at the former *Puddle Dock*; it opened in a converted warehouse in 1959 and was rebuilt in 1981. The new *City of London School* is being built here and the *Samuel Pepys* pub is in a converted warehouse.

Vintners' Hall dates from 1671 and is the Livery Hall of the Vintners' Company, one of two companies entitled to own swans on the Thames in addition to the Queen (the other is the Dyers'). Once a year during Swan Upping, usually in July, swans are counted and marked; two nicks in the beak for Vintners' swans and one for Dyers'—the Queen's swans are unmarked. This event now takes place up-river beyond Maidenhead. On the S side along Bankside new developments have brought offices to an ancient area of London (see Rte 27). In Cardinal Cap Alley, No. 49 Cardinal's Wharf survives; Wren is said to have watched the rebuilding of St. Paul's from here.

The massive **Bankside Power Station** of 1935 was designed by Sir Gilbert Scott, who also designed Battersea Power Station. The *Founders Arms* pub is part of a new development of flats and offices and has a riverside terrace looking out on the river and St. Paul's Cathedral opposite. BANKSIDE was a traditional place of entertainment and it is planned to rebuild Shakespeare's Globe Theatre on its former site near the Bear Gardens Theatre Museum.

Southwark Bridge dates to 1921; first built by John Rennie in cast-iron in 1819. On the N bank is the *Riverside Inn* and on the S side the *Anchor*, a 300-year-old tavern in an 18C building. It has recently been restored and has a restaurant.

The massive decorative turrets of **Cannon Street Station** remain at the N side of the *Cannon Street Railway Bridge* (opened in 1866), while the station itself has been rebuilt further inland.

Past the railway bridge on the N side is the modern *Mondial House*, the international headquarters of British Telecom, and further along *Fishmongers' Hall*, a classical building completed in 1832. The fishmongers administer the Doggett and Badge Race, see above.

The 'Princess Elizabeth', a 1927 paddlesteamer, is moored at the old *Swan Pier* as a restaurant and bar.

On the S bank is the site of Winchester Palace and the old Clink Prison; a sign under the bridge tells the story. The gaol was built in the 16C in a street called Clink Street, so prison became 'the clink'. *St. Mary Overie Dock* is part of the redevelopment scheme in this area which has already opened up the front of Southwark Cathedral so that it can be seen from the river. The open space incorporates stones from the old London Bridge.

The first **London Bridge** was built by the Romans sometime after AD 43; remains have been uncovered on the N side. The wooden structure was renewed several times and a stone bridge was begun in 1176; it featured 20 arches and stone piers with a drawbridge. It took 30 years to complete and buildings were incorporated to pay for the bridge's upkeep. One of the pointed stone arches has been uncovered on the N bank. London Bridge, one of the wonders of the medieval world with its houses and shops, could not cope with increasing traffic in the early 19C. A new bridge designed by John Rennie opened in 1825 and this was widened in 1902. It was sold to Lake Havasu City, Arizona, for £1m in 1970 when a larger bridge was needed. This opened in 1973. The nursery rhyme 'London Bridge is falling down' probably refers to the earlier wooden bridges; one was apparently washed away in a flood and another was torn down by invading Vikings led by Olaf the Norseman in 1014.

Between London Bridge and Tower Bridge on the S bank, the new LONDON BRIDGE CITY is being built with Kuwaiti money; it includes office blocks, a private hospital and a park. *Hay's Wharf*, once used by giant tea clippers, has been filled in and a shopping 'Galleria' created with restaurants and cafeteria.

On the N bank there is more redevelopment next to **Billingsgate Market** which closed in 1981 when the fish market moved to West India Docks. Archaeological excavations on the adjoining lorry and car park have revealed more information about London's Roman and Saxon past. A glass encased office block now stands on the site. Horace Jones's Billingsgate opened in 1877 on the site of an ancient market of 870. The free fish market was established in 1699 and the porters wore 'bobbing hats', round, hard-topped leather hats for carrying loads of fish. The old building has a preservation order and is being developed for office use. **Custom House** next to it was designed by Laing and opened in 1817. Adjoining it is *Tate and Lyle's Sugar Quay*.

Tower Pier is just before the Tower of London, separated from the river by its own walkway leading to Tower Bridge and underneath it to St. Katharine's Dock.

'HMS Belfast' is moored on the S bank. This Royal Navy cruiser saw action in the Second World War and has been converted into a floating museum. There is a ferry from Tower Pier in summer but the ship is open all the year round; access from Tooley Street (see p 286). Visiting naval ships often moor alongside 'HMS Belfast'.

Tower Bridge, widely recognised as a symbol of London, with its two Gothic towers, is often mistakenly referred to as London Bridge. It opened in 1894 as the only moveable bridge on the river, designed by Sir Horace Jones and built by Sir John Wolfe Barry to blend with the Tower of London. The bascules, each weighing over 1000 tons, were originally raised by hydraulic power. The walkways were incorporated to allow pedestrian traffic to flow uninterrupted as the bridge was frequently opened. They became a haven for unsavoury characters and closed ten years after the bridge opened. The *Tower Bridge Walkway* reopened as a tourist attraction in 1982 (see p 265).

Along the river from the Tower to Greenwich and on to the Thames Barrier the largest redevelopment scheme in Western Europe is now under way under the direction of the London Docklands Development Corporation (see Rte 26). This means that the scene is changing fast, but the following would be seen on a river-trip (in 1985).

On the N side next to Tower Bridge is **St. Katharine's Dock**, already successfully redeveloped for business and tourism with the *World Trade Centre*, the *Tower Hotel*, the restored *Ivory House* and *Dickens Inn*, plus modern council housing and the *Historic Ships Collection*. Further plans include the London Commodity Exchange and an extension of the Dickens Inn, more shops, offices and a new pier.

Opposite is the former *Courage Brewery*, *Butler's Wharf*, *St. Saviour's Dock* and *New Concordia Wharf* (undergoing redevelopment); the last already completed with flats and workshops.

Also on the S bank is the *Cherry Garden Pier* where visiting ships sound a signal if they wish Tower Bridge to be raised—this now happens only two or three times a month. The *Angel Pub* is a fine 16C building with good views of the river.

Opposite is **Wapping** with the *Town of Ramsgate*, a 17C pub next to *Wapping Old Stairs*. Pirates tried by Judge Jeffreys were tied to the piles at low tide and suffered three tides before being untied. Judge Jeffreys is said to have watched from the Angel opposite. The headquarters of the Thames Division of the Metropolitan Police is here. Beyond Tunnel Pier is *Execution Dock* where Captain Kidd (died 1701) and other pirates were hanged. Brunel's first Thames tunnel was built from Rotherhithe to Wapping and is now used as part of the Metropolitan Underground. *Brunel's Engine House* at *Rotherhithe* has an exhibition telling the story of the building of this tunnel, the first in the world under a river.

At Rotherhithe is the *Mayflower* pub; 18C and renamed to commemorate the Pilgrim Fathers who sailed from the Thames near here; there is a restaurant and balcony with good views. The captain of the 'Mayflower' is buried in nearby St. Mary's churchyard.

Opposite is the popular *Prospect of Whitby* pub which dates from 1520 and has a restaurant.

The *Rotherhithe Road Tunnel* connects Rotherhithe and Stepney; the circular air vents can be seen on either side of the river. It opened in 1908. The *Surrey Commercial Docks* on the S side are closed and being redeveloped. At *Shadwell* on the N side *King Edward Memorial Park* marks the place of the old Shadwell fish market and includes a memorial to Willoughby, Frobisher and other 16C navigators.

At *Limehouse* another redevelopment of flats and houses is underway along the Regent's Canal and Limehouse Basin. In the 19C this was London's notorious Chinese quarter and there are still some Chinese restaurants in West India Dock Road. The *Grape's* pub overlooks the river and was frequented by Dickens and Whistler. As the river turns S the point on the S bank known as *Cuckold's Point* is said to take its name from a Mr Cuckold who ducked his unfaithful wife here; others followed suit.

The river now describes a loop around the **Isle Of Dogs**, part of the Docklands Redevelopment Scheme. Already a superstore, offices and a sports centre have been built here (see Rte 26). It was originally marshland and used as a hunting ground by Henry VIII when at Greenwich. The *West India Docks* opened in 1802 and *Millwall Docks* in 1864—now closed, it is planned to retain them as open water.

The site of the dockyard where Brunel's 'Great Eastern', a ship combining sail and steam, was built is marked on the N bank.

On the S bank, the *Royal Naval Victualling Yard* at **Deptford** is now part of a housing estate. The depot was founded in 1513 and it was here Queen Elizabeth I knighted Sir Francis Drake aboard his ship, the 'Golden Hind', kept in dry-dock. At Deptford Creek, the Ravensbourne river enters the Thames.

At the tip of the Isle of Dogs are *Island Gardens*, a small park opened in 1895 to provide a good viewing point of the buildings of Greenwich. The small domed buildings on either side of the river are the entrances to the Greenwich pedestrian tunnel (opened 1902).

On the S side are the historic buildings of **Greenwich**; on the waterfront, the 'Cutty Sark' in its dry-dock; above on the hill the **Old Royal Observatory** in *Greenwich Park*. The red time ball still drops at 13.00 each day; a signal since 1833 for ships passing on the river. Past *Greenwich Pier* is the **Royal Naval College** and the **National Maritime Museum** with the Palladian **Queen's House**.

The *Trafalgar Tavern* has a ship-style bar and a restaurant overlooking the river; the small balcony of the *Yacht* pub is just beyond. The route from Greenwich to the Thames Barrier is largely industrial. Past the Trafalgar Tavern and *Greenwich Power Station* is the *Cutty Sark*—a Georgian pub with a nautical theme. Opposite on the N bank is the *Waterman's Arms*, a popular East End pub, with entertainment. There is another entrance to the West India Dock here.

On the S side is the *Victoria Deep Water Container Terminal*, one of the few flourishing parts of the Port of London above Tilbury.

The *East Greenwich Gasworks*, founded in 1881, is now used as a natural gas distribution centre. The *Blackwall Tunnel* crosses Blackwall Reach from East Greenwich to Poplar. *Brunswick Power Station* is on the S side. From this site the Company of Merchant Venturers departed to found the State of Virginia in three ships, 'Godspeed', 'Discovery' and 'Susan Constant', commemorated by a stone cairn on the river front.

Bow Creek joins the River Lea to the Thames and to the N are the large *Royal Docks*, now closed and the site for a short-haul airport. The **Thames Barrier**, completed in 1983 and officially opened the following year by HM The Queen, was designed to save London from flooding. There is a Visitor Centre and river tours (see p 318).

Beyond the Barrier is **Woolwich** with the *Woolwich Free Ferry* established in 1889.

31   Westminster to Kew, Richmond, Kingston and Hampton Court

Upstream services from Westminster Pier to Kew, Richmond, Kingston and Hampton Court operate daily in the summer and at weekends in spring and autumn; check in advance as they are liable to change at short notice.

Travelling times: Westminster Pier to Kew 1hr 30 minutes; to Richmond 2hr 30 minutes; to Hampton Court 3hr 45 minutes (actual times depend on tides). It is possible to walk along the towpaths from Putney to Hampton Court. See p 308 for practical information.

Westminster Pier, at the N end of Westminster Bridge, is due to be rebuilt in the near future as its structure is unsound; river services may be transferred while work is being undertaken.

Opposite Westminster Pier is *County Hall*; *Westminster Bridge*, only the second bridge to be built across the Thames in central London, was designed by Thomas Page in 1862 when it replaced a stone bridge of 1750. On the N bank is the terrace of the *Houses of Parliament* where MPs and their guests enjoy tea during the summer

Battersea Power Station, now closed (Sir Giles Scott, 1937)

months. On the S bank is *St. Thomas's Hospital* with several new buildings. Adjacent to it are the walls of **Lambeth Palace**, the London residence of the Archbishop of Canterbury, and *St. Mary's Church*, Lambeth, which is now a museum of garden history.

On the N bank are *Victoria Tower Gardens*, with Westminster Abbey beyond. The *Lambeth Bridge* which replaced an ancient horse-ferry in 1862 was in use until 1929 when the present structure was built. The HQ of the London Fire Brigade is on the S side with two or more fire-boats moored outside; on the N bank there are office blocks. Note the Henry Moore statue outside Riverwalk House just before *Vauxhall Bridge*. The first Vauxhall Bridge was built in 1811-16, the earliest iron bridge to carry trams across the Thames. A new bridge replaced it in 1906; the bronze figures alongside it represent Agriculture, Architecture, Engineering, Learning, the Fine Arts and Astronomy—each holding an appropriate symbol. There are redevelopments on both sides of the bridge; those on the S bank have come to a halt after the rejection of several controversial schemes, notably the so-called 'Green Giant', a huge green-tinted office block. Further along the S bank is the *Nine Elms Cold Store*, now closed, and the *New Covent Garden Market* which moved here from Covent Garden in 1974. This is London's main wholesale fruit and vegetable market.

On the N bank are the Dolphin Square Apartments. Villa dei Cesari, a Roman-style restaurant is located in a converted riverside warehouse just in front of the the large apartment complex.

Battersea Power Station on the S bank is now closed and due to become a leisure and entertainment centre.

The *Grosvenor Bridge* was the first railway bridge to cross the Thames; the first train crossed to Victoria Station in 1860. The bridge, rebuilt in 1967, has an attractive Victorian pumping station next to it on the N bank.

Chelsea Suspension Bridge, designed by Thomas Page, opened in 1858 and was replaced by another suspension bridge in 1937. (Other suspension bridges over the Thames are Albert Bridge and Hammersmith Bridge.)

Battersea Park is on the S side of the river; part of the pier has been removed to build the Festival Pier outside the Festival Hall. The Japanese pagoda was presented to the GLC in 1985 by a Buddhist sect.

On the N bank are the grounds of the **Chelsea Royal Hospital**, where the Chelsea Flower Show is staged annually in May, and the walled *Chelsea Physic Garden*. The attractive red-brick buildings of Cheyne Walk start here and continue towards World's End. *Cadogan Pier*, just before the Albert Bridge, is the finishing point of the Doggetts Coat and Badge Race. The attractive *Albert Bridge* was designed by Roland Mason Ordish in 1873 as a cantilevered structure; it was modified as a suspension bridge by Joseph Bazalgette. After strengthening it was reopened in July 1973 but still has a weight limit and 'troops must break step' before crossing the bridge, according to a notice. The toll booths also remain and the bridge is beautifully illuminated at night.

On the N bank in *Cheyne Walk* is the King's Head and Eight Bells, a 400-year-old pub. *Chelsea Old Church* in dour brick has been completely rebuilt after Second World War damage. A new statue of Sir Thomas More stands outside. Next to it is Crosby Hall, moved here from Bishopsgate in 1910 and now used by students.

The first *Battersea Bridge* was a wooden structure completed in 1772; it was portrayed by both Whistler and Turner. The replacement was designed by Bazalgette and opened in 1890. Houseboats are moored in front of Cheyne Walk before it swings away from the Thames beyond the tower blocks of the World's End Estate. *Chelsea Wharf* has been converted into workshops and a restaurant; next to it Lots Road Power Station, built in 1904 to provide power for the Underground, is still in use. Rubbish is loaded on to barges here for transportation downstream.

On the S side is the attractive church of *St. Mary Battersea* from where Turner painted Thames sunsets. The Old Swan is a modern riverside pub, and new housing has been built in thie area. Just before the Westland Heliport at Battersea the river is crossed by the Battersea Railway Bridge. This part of the riverbank is mostly industrial, with the site of Fulham Power Station (demolished for redevelopment) on the N bank.

Wandsworth Bridge opened in 1873 and was rebuilt in 1938. The River Wandle enters the Thames here through a redeveloped industrial area. On the N bank the grounds of 18C *Hurlingham House* provide a refreshing green space; it is now home of the Hurlingham Club. Wandsworth Park is further along the S bank.

The *Fulham/Putney Railway Bridge* opened in 1899. The first *Putney Bridge*, also known as Fulham Bridge, was made of wood and opened in 1729. Bazalgette designed the replacement granite bridge in 1884; this incorporates an aqueduct. The old Putney Bridge was the first Thames bridge W of London Bridge, except Kingston Bridge, until Westminster Bridge was completed in 1750. It now carries more vehicle traffic than any other bridge over the Thames. The parish churches of Fulham and Putney are on either side of the bridge, which also marks the start of the Oxford and Cambridge Boat Race, first rowed in 1829 and now held annually in March/April. The start is marked by the Universities' Stone on the S bank near the Star and Garter pub. Putney Pier is nearby.

On the N bank is *Fulham Palace*, hidden by trees. Bishops Park skirts the river for half a mile, ending at *Craven Cottage*, Fulham's soccer ground.

On the S bank, past the attractive setting of Putney, is Barn Elms Park and sports centre; further along in the great curve of the river are the Barn Elms Reservoirs.

Some of the wharves on the N bank have been restored as offices and workshops; they include the *Riverside Studios*, a theatre and arts centre located in a former BBC studio.

Hammersmith Bridge opened in 1827; the suspension bridge designed by Bazalgette replaced it in 1887. It has twice been strengthened, most recently in 1984 after great cracks opened up. The Lower Mall, Hammersmith, along the N bank, has some fine 18C houses as well as the Rutland and Blue Anchor pubs. In Upper Mall is *Kelmscott House*, where William Morris lived, just past the 17C Dove Inn. The Old Ship, an 18C pub, also overlooks the Thames. A small island, *Chiswick Eyot*, along the N bank, provides a sanctuary for birds.

On the S bank is *St. Paul's Boys School* which moved here from the City in 1968; famous former pupils include Milton, Pepys and Field Marshal Lord Montgomery.

Hammersmith Mall is continued on the N bank as Chiswick Mall, with attractive 18C mansions. The church of *St. Nicholas* dates from the 15C; nearby is the modern *Fullers Brewery*.

On the S bank before *Barnes Railway Bridge* (opened 1849) is the large Bull's Head pub, well-known for jazz. Duke's Meadow on the N bank remains undeveloped. A wooden post marks the finishing point of the University Boat Race just before *Chiswick Bridge*, with Watney's Brewery and and the Ship Inn conveniently sited on the S bank. Chiswick Bridge was one of three opened in one day in 1933 by Edward VIII (then Prince of Wales; the others were Twickenham and Hampton Court Bridges). The boathouse on the N bank is used by the Oxford and Cambridge teams after the Boat Race.

Industrial and then residential developments now occupy both banks. Just before *Kew Railway Bridge* is the large modern *Public Records Office*. Beyond the bridge on the N bank is the picturesque Strand on the Green, with two well-known pubs, the City Barge, with a charter granted by Elizabeth I and named after the Lord Mayor's official barge which was moored here, and the Bull's Head. The small island here is *Oliver's Ait*, supposedly named after Oliver Cromwell.

From the Toll House on the S bank the Port of London Authority controls the upper part of the Thames as far as Teddington. Kew Pier is just before *Kew Bridge*, opened in 1903 by Edward VII and originally named after him. It succeeded the original timber bridge of 1758 and a granite bridge of 1789, opened with a procession led by George III.

On the N bank is *Kew Bridge Pumping Station*, open to the public at weekends as the Living Steam Museum and containing the original beam engines. In the church of *St George* is the British Musical Museum, open from April to September (and looking for new premises).

Brentford Ait, another islet, is to the N; **Kew Gardens** on the S bank here cover 288 acres (open all year). Behind Brentford Ait the riverbank is being developed with flats and a marina; here the *Waterman's Art Centre* opened in 1984. The River Brent and the Grand Union Canal enter the Thames here at the site of an ancient ford used by both Romans and Vikings. The once-busy Brentford Dock is being redeveloped with housing.

The riverbank to the N along Syon Reach is largely undeveloped until **Syon Park** with *Syon House* set back from the river, still occupied by the Duke of Northumberland (open to the public). In the grounds are the Butterfly House and the Heritage Car Collection.

Further along the N bank, opposite *Old Deer Park* with the Kew Observatory, is *Isleworth*, with the river dividing around Isleworth Ait. The village has some fine 17C and 18C houses and a modern church, *All Saints*, retaining a 400-year-old tower. Here is the London Apprentice, a 15C pub and restaurant with an Elizabethan interior. Isleworth itself is largely industrial.

The River Crane joins the Thames just past Isleworth Ait; further along is *Richmond Lock*, footbridge and sluices, the first on the up-river journey. At high tide the lock is not used but at other times sluices control the water level. The lock was opened in 1894.

Twickenham Bridge opened in 1933; it features parapets, lamps and railings in bronze. Just beyond is *Richmond Railway Bridge*. Past the houses on the S bank—including Asgill House of 1760—is

Richmond Green. The White Cross pub overlooks the river and the
Waterman's Arms is in a side street. *Richmond Ait* is just beyond the
picturesque *Richmond Bridge*; this is the oldest Thames bridge still
in use in Greater London. Built by James Paine in 1774, when it was
widened in 1937-39 the original stones were carefully replaced on
the outside. The Richmond Landing Stage is just beyond the bridge;
developments of shops and offices are being planned for this area.

The view of the Thames from Richmond Hill, by the Star and Garter
Home opened in 1924, is one of the loveliest along the river.

Petersham Village is on the S bank just beyond Glover Island; on
the opposite side are **Marble Hill Park and House**, an 18C Palladian
mansion (open to the public). Nearby is the remnant of *Orleans
House*, the Octagon Room, now used as an art gallery.

During the summer a ferry operates across the river to *Ham
Common* and *Ham House*, a fine Jacobean mansion (1610) which
now belongs to the National Trust and is open to the public.

Eel Pie Island divides the river; here are private houses and a
former hotel where British rock music was played in the 1960s.

Just before the island, on the N bank is the White Swan pub;
further on is *York House* in the centre of Twickenham, set in an
exotic garden and used as council offices. Pope's Grotto pub on the
N bank along Cross Deep takes its name from Alexander Pope's
famous Grotto in the garden of his house at Strawberry Hill, now a
school.

The turbulent waters of *Teddington Lock and Weir* lie ahead. Built
in 1811, the lock marks the dividing line between the tidal and
non-tidal waters of the Thames and an obelisk just before the lock
marks the boundary between the Thames Water Authority, which
has jurisdiction over the upper river, and the Port of London Authority.
Just beyond the weir on the N bank are the studios of Thames
Television; the Angels pub is conveniently nearby.

The Thames flows between Kingston on the S bank and Teddington
to the N past two islands, Trowlock Island and Steven's Eyot, before
reaching *Kingston Railway Bridge*, dominated by the two chimneys
of Kingston Power Station, and Kingston town centre. There was a
permanent bridge here by the end of the 12C, the second (London
Bridge was the first) bridge over the Thames. The present bridge is
the third on the site and opened in 1828; its size was doubled in
1924. The remains of the medieval bridge and of the equally ancient
Clattern Bridge over the Hogsmill tributary which enters the Thames
here can still be seen.

From Turks Boatyard there are services to Hampton Court during
the summer; Kingston Pier is just beyond the bridge. The next island
is *Raven's Ait*, with ferry access from the S bank to Hampton Court
Park. Before reaching Hampton Court the river winds round *Thames
Ditton Island* which has some houses and is linked by a suspension
bridge to the S bank.

The Hampton Court Landing Stage is just before *Hampton Court
Bridge*, designed by Lutyens in 1933 to harmonise with the palace.
It is the fourth bridge on the site. **Hampton Court Palace**, begun in
1514, is on the N bank while the village of *Hampton* is further along
the river.

Notes for Walkers: It is possible, and very pleasant, to walk along
the banks of the Thames more or less continuously from Hampton
Court to Putney. From Hampton Court use the towpath on the N side

to Kingston Bridge with small diversions (3 miles). Cross to the S bank at Kingston Bridge and follow the towpath from the power station to Richmond, past Ham and Petersham (4.5 miles); Teddington is reached by using the footbridge at Teddington Lock and Marble Hill Park is reached via the ferry (in summer). From Richmond to Chiswick Bridge follow the S bank, past Kew on the S and past Hammersmith on the N to Putney Bridge (8 miles). From here there is no continuous towpath so use a detailed street-map. Putney Bridge to Westminster Bridge is 5.5 miles.

32 Greenwich, Deptford, Rotherhithe, Woolwich, Bexley, Eltham

Greenwich on the S bank of the Thames, 4.5 miles from Central London, was once a quiet fishing village whose location on the Roman Watling Street and by the Thames brought it to royal attention in the 15C, when Humphrey, Duke of Gloucester, built himself a mansion and enclosed the park as a hunting ground. Today the magnificent buildings—the Old Royal Observatory, the Queen's House, the National Maritime Museum and the Royal Naval College—contrast strongly with the working-class housing estates which followed in the 18th and 19th centuries but still provide one of London's most impressive views from the N bank at Island Gardens (cross via the pedestrian tunnel) and from the top of Greenwich Park by the statue of General Wolfe. The revitalisation of London's dockland includes plans for a light railway from Tower Hill to Island Gardens to be completed in 1987 which will considerably improve access.

Access: BR (Charing Cross) to Greenwich or Maze Hill Stations; by river from Westminster, Charing Cross or Tower Piers to Greenwich Pier.

The Royal Naval College—formerly the Greenwich Hospital—is in King William Walk on the site of Henry VII's Palace of Placentia, developed from Bella Court, Duke Humphrey's mansion built in 1426-34. It became a favourite residence of the Tudor sovereigns; Henry VIII and his daughters, Mary and Elizabeth, were all born at the Placentia and Edward VI died here. The palace also saw Henry VIII's weddings to both Katharine of Aragon and Anne of Cleves. Here he started the liaison with Anne Boleyn which led eventually to the breach with Rome. During the reign of the Stuarts the Placentia went into decline and was demolished by Charles II.

Royal Naval College, King William Walk, London SE10. Tel. 01-858 2154. Open weekdays 14.30-17.00 (not Thursdays), Sun 14.30-17.00; check hours; closed at short notice or without warning.

The remains of the 15C Palace were found beneath the lawn of the Royal Naval College during excavations in 1970-71. The present buildings were begun for Charles II by John Webb (NW block) as part of a new royal palace. When William and Mary came to the throne Sir Christopher Wren was instructed to turn the buildings into a hospital for the benefit of seamen and Greenwich's royal connections effectively came to an end. The new buildings, mostly by Wren and Hawksmoor, were opened in 1704 with further additions in 1750. In 1869 the sick seamen were moved to more modest surroundings at the Dreadnought Seaman's Hospital (1763; threatene with closure) in nearby Romney Road and the Royal Naval College moved here from Portsmouth.

Today visitors can admire Wren's twin domes which carefully frame the Queen's House just beyond without obstructing its view from or of the river. The Painted Hall and Chapel are open to visitors. The *Painted Hall*, still used daily by the officers as a dining room and also available for functions, was decorated by Sir James Thornhill between 1707 and 1722. He and his assistants were paid £3 per square yard for the ceiling and £1 for the walls and created one of the most impressive halls in England. At the focal point of the ceiling are William and Mary, waited upon by the Four Virtues. On the far wall Thornhill himself can be seen to the right of the family of George I. Nelson's body lay in state in this Hall after his death at Trafalgar in 1805 and thousands of Londoners came to pay their respects. Opposite the Painted Hall is the *Chapel*, its delicate Wedgwood blue and white in vivid contrast to the brown and gold of the Hall. The Chapel was rebuilt after a fire in 1779 to a new classical design by James 'Athenian' Stuart. The altarpiece is by Sir Benjamin West as are the statues in the vestibule of Faith, Hope, Charity and Humility, executed in Coade stone.

There are public services on Sundays and concerts during the Greenwich Festival in June and at other times. The statue of George II in the Grand Square of the four buildings is by Rysbrack.

On the other side of Romney Road, forming part of the Royal Naval College architecturally, are the buildings of the **National Maritime Museum**, including the **Queen's House**.

Queen's House, Romney Road, London SE10. Tel. 01-858 4422. Opening hours as for National Maritime Museum, see below, but closed for repairs for two years from October 1984.

Queen's House, the first Palladian-style villa built in England, was designed by Inigo Jones and enlarged by Webb in 1662. It was built for James I's wife Queen Anne of Denmark (1616-35), begun in 1616 and completed in 1635, and

The Royal Naval College at Greenwich

faced the Placentia on one side and the park on the other; the main Dover Road went through the building. The Queen died before it was completed and it became the home of Henrietta Maria, Charles I's French wife, in 1635. After the Civil War, Charles II commissioned John Webb to enlarge the house; the road was diverted and the additions carefully matched Inigo Jones's original design. It was later used as a school and fully restored in the 1950s after wartime use by the Admiralty. It is now part of the National Maritime Museum and houses some of its finest exhibits.

The main hall, the *Cube Room*, had a beautifully decorated ceiling, since removed, with matching floor by Nicholas Stone. From one corner rises the spiral Tulip Staircase, the first of its kind in England, taking its name from the tulip motifs in the iron baluster. On the ground floor there are paintings by the De Veldes, father and son, invited to London from the Netherlands to record the great sea battles of Charles II and James II. There are paintings of Greenwich and a set of 17C navigational instruments made in ivory, the Barberini collection and 17C wall maps. Models of 17C ships are also on display. The first floor state rooms reflect the period of Henrietta Maria with a replica of her bed in the Queen's bedroom and a portrait of her by Van Dyck.

National Maritime Museum, Romney Road, London SE10. Tel. 01-858 4422. Open Monday to Saturday 10.00-17.00, Sunday 14.00-17.00; (winter) 10.00-18.00, 14.00-17.30 (summer); admission charge includes Old Royal Observatory. Car park. Cafeteria.

The two museum buildings on either side of the Queen's House provide an unrivalled collection illustrating Britain's naval history. The East and West Wings were built after Trafalgar to the design of Daniel Alexander with flanking colonnades linking them to the Queen's House, then a school for seamen's children. In 1933 the school moved and the National Maritime Museum was established. The new Neptune Hall, a Victorian extension to the West Wing, was reopened in 1972 to illustrate the development of boat building. The main entrance is in the West Wing and here there is an information counter and shop. (There is another entrance to the East Wing from Park Vista.) The *West Wing* is on three floors; from the top of the great staircase *Galleries 3, 4 and 5* deal with naval history from the first half of the 18C in paintings, documents and models. Dioramas of the main dockyards of the period (Devonport, Chatham, Portsmouth and Sheerness) are at the end of Gallery 5. Stairs descend to the *James Cook Gallery*, illustrating his explorations of the Pacific Ocean. The settlement of the United States follows in the next gallery which leads to the *Nelson Galleries* with paintings, silver and relics. The most famous is the Vice-Admiral's undress uniform coat which he was wearing on 21 October 1805, showing the bullet hole in the left shoulder. The new *Harrison Gallery* features Harrison's first chronometer and his other instruments. The *Navigation Room* is being redesigned.

The *Print Study Room* above the Navigation Gallery is open by appointment. The *Special Exhibition Gallery* with a changing series of exhibitions is next to the Picture Department.

At the entrance to the new *Neptune Hall* is a display of 19C merchant shipping artefacts and figureheads. Exhibits change regularly, but the hall contains the largest single collection of industrial maritime history including the complete fabric of the riveted steel steampaddle tug 'Reliant' built at South Shields in 1907; visitors can see the machinery in motion and walk through the stoke-hold, crew's forecastle and the master's cabin. This display on the mezzanine floor ends with the steam launch 'Donola', built in

1893. On the ground floor another steam launch, 'Waterlily', and various engines complete the exhibits on steam. As a contrast to the cabins on the 'Reliant' visitors c..n enter a first-class cabin of a 1960s Atlantic liner.

Around the sides of the Hall there is a continuous display of the development of wooden boats from prehistoric times. Royal barges in the *Barge House* opened in 1978 include Prince Frederick's 18C barge. Under the 'Reliant' is *Gallery 11* devoted to the development of iron and steel shipbuilding.

From the Neptune Hall visitors walk through the House for the royal barges into the ground floor galleries of the West Wing. *Gallery A* covers the period of shipbuilding in the 15C; *Gallery B* shows archaeological techniques, with displays illustrating the Sutton Hoo Ship found in Suffolk, and others. The *National Museum of Yachting* follows, covering aspects of the sport from the royal yachts of the 17C to the plastic yachts of today. *Gallery F* is devoted to the 74-gun ship 'Cornwallis' (slide shows).

The East Wing is devoted to the 19th and early 20th centuries. The great migration across the Atlantic is the subject of the first gallery (No. 12), showing how migrants travelled in sailing ships. The next gallery (No. 13), looks at the cargo trade along British shores; larger cargo vessels follow in *Gallery 14*, 'From Sail to Steam: the Crucial Years'. The passenger liner and its development between 1840 and the 1980s follows (Gallery 15) with models of the 'Great Britain' of 1843 and the 'Windsor Castle'. Downstairs, the *Arctic Gallery* (17) tells the story of the exploration of the North-West Passage. Two galleries, 18 and 19 upstairs, contain marine paintings from the 19C, and adjoining galleries (Nos 22 and 23) show the developments of the Navy in the 19C to the Second World War. The East Wing also contains a children's educational centre and a lecture theatre with seating for up to 120.

The National Maritime Museum stands at the edge of **Greenwich Park** which stretches up to the top of the hill and the Old Royal Observatory and beyond to Blackheath. This royal park was first enclosed by Humphrey, Duke of Gloucester, as a hunting ground in 1433. Today the park with its steep topography offers superb views of the Thames and is favoured by skateboarders and in winter by tobogganers. During the last part of the 19C the Park was the location for the increasingly notorious Greenwich Fairs, finally banned in 1870. There is a formal flower and water garden towards Blackheath and a 'wilderness' inhabited by a herd of 30 deer (not open to the public). Through the main gates on the Blackheath side thousands pour each May at the start of the London Marathon. Refreshments are available during the summer and at weekends. The Park was laid out by Sir William Boreman to a plan by André le Notre, commissioned by Charles II. The Versailles influence only remains in the southern section where an impressive chestnut avenue leads from Blackheath Gate to General Wolfe's statue by Tait Mackenzie (presented by the Canadian nation in 1930). The trunk of an oak survives where Henry VIII is said to have danced with Anne Boleyn, and where Queen Elizabeth picnicked as a child (250 yards SW of Maze Hill Gate). Near Queen Elizabeth's Bower (200 yards S of Maze Hill Gate) are the remains of a Roman Villa (Maze Hill Gate). On the side of the Park near Ranger's House are Ranger's Field, used for cricket matches, and the remains of Queen Caroline's Baths (W of

Blackheath Gate). The statue of King William IV in the NW corner of the park came from King William Street in the City. There is a Moore bronze sculpture, 'Standing Figure and Knife Edge' behind the tennis courts, NW corner.

The six buildings of the **Old Royal Observatory** are now part of the National Maritime Museum. The Royal Observatory moved to Herstmonceux Castle in Sussex in 1948 to benefit from less polluted and darker skies than those metropolitan London could provide. The attractive outline of *Flamsteed House* with its Red Time Ball crowns the hill. The Red Time Ball was installed in 1833 to give a visual indication of the time to ships on the river; it still drops at 13.00 local time every day. The 24-hour clock by the gate is 120 years old and shows Greenwich Mean Time.

Old Royal Observatory, Greenwich Park, London SE10. Tel. 01-858 1167. Opening hours as for National Maritime Museum. Admission charge (also for main Museum). Bookshop. Cafeteria in main Museum.

Wren built Flamsteed House with 'a little pompe' for the first royal astronomer, Rev. John Flamsteed, appointed by Charles II in 1675; Astronomers Royal lived here until 1948. The rooms have now been restored to their appearance at the time of Flamsteed.

The *Octagon Room* was for general astronomical use, the *Sextant House* and *Meridian Building* were added in the mid 18C. They became the location for the most important work carried out here in the development of nautical astronomy. The Prime Meridian of the World established in 1884 traverses the Meridian Building.

Enter Flamsteed House across the courtyard, crossing the Meridian marked in the ground. The displays in the Octagon Room and adjoining galleries show the history of the nautical almanac and the measuring of longitude by observation of the moon, methods of finding time by the sun, moon and stars, and the history of the first instruments of navigation.

Flamsteed's living quarters have been authentically restored in their simplicity. The Meridian Building contains original instruments and replicas. The astrolabe collection in the Halley Gallery is one of the most important in the world; the Airy Transit Circle which defines the Prime Meridian of the World and Bradley's 12.5ft Zenith Sector with which he discovered the aberration of light and the mutation of the earth's axis are also on view. There is a bookshop.

The *South Building*, a planetarium, is used by school parties and there are public lectures during the school holidays. The striking onion dome of the Victorian *Great Equatorial Building* has been restored. This and the Altazimuth Pavilion are not open to the public.

On the E side of the Park in Maze Hill is *Vanbrugh Castle*, built in 1726 by Sir John Vanbrugh for himself, as Surveyor to the Royal Hospital, in a medieval style—now privately occupied. *Woodlands*, nearby at 90 Mycenae Road, was built in 1774 as a country house for John Julius Angerstein whose collection of paintings formed the basis for the National Gallery (buried in 1823 in St. Alfege Church). Woodlands (01-858 4631) is now a local history centre and art gallery, open 10.00-19.30 weekdays, 10.00-18.00 Saturday, 14.00-18.00 Sunday, closed Wed. Free.

Ranger's House in Chesterfield Walk on the W side of the Park houses the magnificent Suffolk Collection of family portraits by William Larkin and others, famous for the details on costumes and furnishings, and musical instruments from the Dolmetsch Collection on the 1st Floor (from 1985). Recitals take place during the Greenwich Festival and in late summer and autumn. Ranger's House was built in the 1680s and later extended by the Earl of Chesterfield; it became the residence of the Ranger of Greenwich Park in 1814. In 1974 it was opened as an art gallery by the Greater London Council.

Ranger's House, Chesterfield Walk, London SE10. Tel. 01-853 0035. Open daily 10.00-17.00 (Nov. to Jan. 10.00-16.00). Free.

Nearby in Croom's Hill is *Macartney House*, home of General Wolfe's parents, and some attractive 17 and 18C buildings along this winding road which leads down into central Greenwich.

The *Greenwich Theatre* (1969), Greenwich Church Street, has a good buffet restaurant and bar. It was built on the site of an old music hall and stands opposite a car park scheduled for redevelopment. This is the location of the Greenwich Antique Market, held on Saturday mornings through the year and also Sunday mornings in the summer. Bric-a-brac, genuine antiques and second-hand books are some of the items on sale from early morning.

St. Alfege Church in the centre of Greenwich marks the spot where Alphege, Archbishop of Canterbury, was murdered by invading Danish Vikings in 1012. Henry VIII was baptised in the medieval church and Thomas Tallis, founder of English church music, was buried in the old church. The keyboard from the 16C organ is preserved in the nave of the new church designed by Hawksmoor and completed in 1714. It was restored after heavy war damage and is used for concerts during the Greenwich Festival as well as for regular services, although much work still remains to be done.

Greenwich has a traditional covered market across the busy one-way road-system and through a narrow lane. A craft market operates here on Sat and Sun. Along Greenwich High Road are the Queen Elizabeth's Almshouses, the first to be founded after the Reformation in 1576. The present buildings around an attractive courtyard were completed in 1819.

On the river-front, now known as *Cutty Sark Gardens*, the majestic 'Cutty Sark' rests in its own drydock. One of the last sailing clippers to make the voyage from China carrying tea, it was built in 1869 on the Clyde. The opening of the Suez Canal and the arrival of steam spelt the end for the sailing ships. The ship was rescued, restored and opened to the public in 1954. It now houses a fine collection of figureheads, and full-scale replicas of cabins of the period. Special exhibitions are held in the hold.

'Cutty Sark', Cutty Sark Gardens, London SE10. Tel. 01-858 3445. Open Monday to Saturday 10.30-18.00 (17.00 in winter), Sunday 14.30-18.00 (17.00 in winter). Admission charge. Nearest BR station Maze Hill.

Cutty Sark Gardens also house 'Gipsy Moth IV', the yacht in which Sir Francis Chichester circumnavigated the world single-handed in 1968. It is open the same hours as the 'Cutty Sark'; admission charge.

The Gardens are used for open-air performances and art and crafts markets during the Greenwich Festival in June and the Greenwich Clipper Weeks in August. A Bookboat is moored below the council estate to the W. The tourist information centre next to the entrance of the pedestrian subway is open all week in summer and at weekends in the winter. Tel. 01-858 6376. (This is due to be enlarged and improved.)

The pedestrian tunnel completed in 1902 is 1200ft long with attractive domed entrances and solid Victorian lifts. The riverside walk past the pier towards the E provides good views of the Royal Naval College and the Park. From here the Court saluted Willoughby and Chancellor as they set off in search of the North-East Passage in 1553; Raleigh put down his cloak for Elizabeth I and was later arrested on his return from Guiana; and George I landed here from Holland on his way to claim the crown of the United Kingdom. Recently Prince Charles welcomed members of the Transglobe Expedition here (1983).

The *Trafalgar Tavern* (built 1837) has iron balconies resembling the inside of a man-of-war. It became famous for its whitebait dinners for the Government of Queen Victoria's reign; other famous customers include Dickens, Thackeray and George Cruickshank. It closed in 1915 and reopened, restored, in 1965.

A regular river service by steamboat between Greenwich and Central London started in 1855; the railway link through Deptford was even earlier, making Greenwich as popular for Sunday outings amongst London's workers as it is with tourists today.

Blackheath, S of Greenwich, is an attractive residential suburb with claims of being S London's 'Hampstead'. The Roman Watling Street crossed Blackheath and both Roman and Saxon remains have been found. During the Peasant's Revolt in 1381 Wat Tyler assembled his supporters on the heath before proceeding towards London. It was the scene of royal celebrations such as the welcome for Charles II in 1660, and revivalist meetings in the 18C. The *Royal Blackheath Golf Club* was the first in the country (founded 1608); the *Blackheath Rugby Club* is also the oldest. But the heath had a bad reputation for highway robberies until the late 18C.

Blackheath Village developed in the mid-19C with the arrival of the railway. Blackheath's intellectual reputation is based on educational institutions founded during the Victorian period; these include a conservatoire of music and an art school.

Morden College, St. German's Place, SE3, was built in 1695 by Wren with a colonnaded courtyard to house 'decayed Turkey Merchants who had fallen on hard times'. Sir John Morden, its benefactor, was himself a 'Turkey merchant'. It continues today as a home for elderly people. Nearby is *The Paragon*, a crescent of 14 semi-detached villas linked by a single-storey colonnade, built by John Cator and designed by Michael Searles who also designed Paragon House and Colonnade House; the first tenants moved in around 1800 and it was not until earlier this century that the buildings started to deteriorate as tenants added out-buildings. They were restored to their original appearance after the Second World War.

Today the Heath is the venue for Bank Holiday fairs, football, kite-flying and the start of the annual London Marathon in April or May. The *Hare and Billet* (7A Elliot Cottages, SE3; formerly the Harrow and Crooked Billet) is a 100-year-old village pub on the heath.

Deptford, W of Greenwich, a working-class suburb based on the docks and industries of the 19C, now in decline, started as a small fishing village which rose to national importance when Henry VIII founded the Royal Naval Dockyard here in 1573. The dockyard closed in 1869 and became a foreign cattle market which survived until

1913. Sir Francis Drake moored the 'Golden Hind' at the Dockyard in 1581 and received his knighthood from Queen Elizabeth. Pepys recorded regular visits in his diaries.

Adjoining it was the *Royal Victoria Victualling Yard*, established in 1742 and closed in 1961, now the site of the Pepys Housing Estate. A colonnaded terrace and two handsome 18C rum warehouses with arcaded ground floors have been restored for the *Pepys Library* and *Deptford Sailing Centre*. At *Sayes Court* (now a small park) nothing remains of the residence of John Evelyn (1620-1706) where Pepys and Wren were entertained to dinner and where Wren was introduced to Grinling Gibbons, a local craftsman. Peter the Great was Evelyn's guest in 1698 when working in the Royal Dock.

St. Nicholas, the old parish church of Deptford, stands just beyond the busy High Street. The 15C ragstone tower is surrounded by a red-brick building added in 1697 and restored after Second World War damage. Grinling Gibbons' work can be viewed inside. Christopher Marlowe, the playwright, killed in a local tavern brawl in 1593, is buried here. *St. Paul's Church*, E of Deptford High Street, is a perfect baroque building by Thomas Archer (1730), described by Sir John Betjeman as 'a pearl in the heart of Deptford'. It has giant Corinthian columns and a rich plaster ceiling, and houses a memorial to Dr Charles Burney, brother of Fanny Burney and a rector of Deptford. In Albury Street, the local authority has restored some 18C sea-captains' houses.

Deptford Market on Fridays and Saturdays (Douglas Way and the High Street) is a lively South London event with some 250 stalls selling greengrocery, household goods, clothes and bric-a-brac.

The first London railway ran on arches between Deptford and Bermondsey in 1836 (extended to London Bridge in 1837). The Greenwich section added in 1838 involved building a bridge over the busy Deptford Creek (outlet of the Ravensbourne) with a drawbridge which it took eight men to operate.

The *Albany Theatre*, Douglas Way, Deptford, SE8, is a multi-purpose arts centre and theatre in a new building opened by the Princess of Wales in 1982.

Rotherhithe, formerly *Redriffe*, was badly affected by the closure in 1970 of the Surrey Docks, but several Thames-side wharves and warehouses have been imaginatively restored for housing and workshops and further developments are under way (see Rte 26). Rotherhithe is on the Metropolitan Underground line.

Brunel's Engine House in Tunnel Road was built by Marc Brunel as part of the Thames Tunnel (1825-43), the first underwater tunnel in the world, which linked Rotherhithe with Wapping. The newly restored 1885 Rennie engine takes pride of place inside the small brick building which also houses an exhibition on the construction of the tunnelling which cost many lives. However, Brunel's tunnelling shields had lasting impact on tunnel building in Britain and overseas. Brunel's Engine House is open April to September 10.00-16.00 Sundays only; admission charge.

Brunel's *Thames Tunnel* was at first a foot tunnel but now forms part of the Metropolitan Underground line.

Nearby is *St. Mary's Parish Church* where the captain of the 'Mayflower', Christopher Jones, is buried. The church dates back to 1714; there are mast-like pillars inside and an organ by Byfield installed in 1764. Opposite is *Peter Hills School* (1797) with two attractively carved figures of pupils at the first floor level. The *Mayflower* pub, Rotherhithe Street, overlooks the river and takes its name from the ship which sailed from the Thames to Portsmouth and to the Americas in 1620. There is a river-jetty and the pub is licensed to sell American and British postage stamps.

The *Hope Sufferance Wharf* by the river has been converted into craft workshops and houses a picture research library. In the area are the *Finnish Seamen's Church*, the *Swedish Mission* and the Norwegian church of *St. Olaf* which served the sailors of the past and today's long distance lorry-drivers (the A2 is nearby). The *Prince of Orange* pub in Lower Road next to the Swedish mission is a traditional jazz pub. The *Angel on the River* (Bermondsey Wall East, SE16) is a 16C pub with a balcony over the river where Samuel Pepys paused on his journeys to and from the Dockyard at Deptford.

Woolwich, E of Greenwich (access: BR, Woolwich), is still dominated by its naval and military past and famous for its football team, Arsenal (which moved to Highbury, N London in 1913 in search of more space), and the Woolwich Building Society founded after the Second World War on the savings of the munition workers. Henry VIII established the Dockyard here in 1513 (as at Deptford) to build the 'Great Harry', the fleet's flagship, and later the 'Sovereign of the Seas', designed by Phineas Pett and his son Peter in 1637 (both buried at Deptford). The Dockyard closed in 1869; subsequently part of it was used by the Royal Arsenal Co-operative Society, and for housing. Two of the drydocks have become swimming pools. The **Woolwich Arsenal** dates from 1716; after an explosion at Moorfields an out-of-London site was essential. 40,000 workers were employed here during the Second World War; the Arsenal closed from 1963. The Main Entrance by Sir John Vanbrugh is in Beresford Square and the 1829 gateway survives. The Brass Foundry (1717) is now used by the National Maritime Museum and the Grand Store (built 1806-13) is used by the British Library. Plans are being made for redevelopment.

Woolwich Market received its first Royal Charter in the 13C; today it thrives in Beresford Square, in the shadow of the Arsenal gates (Monday to Saturday), having abandoned Market Hill in the middle of the 19C. Greengrocery, fresh fish and household goods are on sale with cheap clothes in the nearby, rather dingy covered market in Plumstead Road. Woolwich was the home of Britain's first McDonald's restaurant in Powis Street in 1974. Nearby the former Granada cinema, now a bingo club, has a Venetian Gothic interior of 1937. The *Tram Shed* (1908) at 51 Woolwich New Road was an electricity sub-station for London's electric tramways and has been used as a theatre and music venue since 1973.

The **Thames Barrier** off Woolwich Road, crossing the Thames, was completed in 1983 and officially opened by HM The Queen in May 1984. It is the largest moving flood barrier in the world with eight gigantic piers which allow shipping to pass unhindered up and down the river. The floodgates lie on the river-bed and take from one to three hours to rise 65ft to protect London from flooding during a high winter tide. In the *Barrier Centre*, a dramatic audiovisual presentation and working models illustrate the history of the river and the threat of flooding. There is a cafeteria and buffet restaurant. A walkway along the river gives good views of the spectacular barrier and there are boat tours from the Barrier Pier.

The Thames Barrier, opened by HM The Queen in 1984

Thames Barrier, Unity Way, off Woolwich Road, London SE18. Tel. 01-854 1373
Open 10.30-17.00 daily, later in the summer. Access: BR to Charlton or Woolwich
Dockyard, then bus. Or by river from Westminster Pier direct or via Greenwich.
Shuttlebus from Cutty Sark Gardens, Greenwich in summer.

The *Woolwich Free Ferry*, 1 mile further downstream (continue E
along Woolwich Rd and Woolwich Church St to the A205 roundabout;
the ferry pier is to the left), linking the S and N banks of the Thames,
was probably established as a ferry crossing in the 15C. The present
ferry service dates from 1889. A plan to link Woolwich and Newham
by a bridge at this point is being discussed.
   The *Royal Military Academy* was founded in Woolwich Arsenal in
1721 but moved S to Woolwich Common in 1808. There are two
museums of artillery, both worth exploring, the *Royal Artillery
Museum* and the *Rotunda Museum of Artillery*.

The Royal Artillery Museum, Royal Military Academy, Woolwich Common,
Academy Road, London SE18. Tel. 01-856 5533. Open Monday to Friday
10.00-12.00, and 14.00-16.00. Free. Access: BR, Woolwich Arsenal.

The striking yellow brick Royal Military Academy was designed by James
Wyatt; the central block was inspired by the White Tower. The Royal Military
College at Sandhurst and the Academy were amalgamated in 1945. The
Museum tells the history of the regiment of the Royal Artillery, with paintings
by war artists and personal relics.

On the N side of the Common stands another impressive building,
the *Royal Artillery Barracks* (not open to the public) completed in

1802 and featuring a triumphal arch and a frontage of 1000ft with a vast parade ground. Nearby is the *Rotunda Museum of Artillery* in Repository Road, SE18. Tel. 01-856 5533. Open weekdays 12.00-17.00, Sat, Sun 13.00-17.00 (winter until 16.00). Free. Access: BR, New Cross; Bus 53.

The Rotunda started its days as a pavilion in St. James's Park in 1814 and was removed here in 1819. Nash converted it into a permanent building with a striking concave copper roof. It contains the Royal Artillery's collection of guns. In the courtyard there are large tanks and armoured vehicles.—The Armouries Museum is planning to move from the Tower of London to Woolwich, possibly to the Arsenal.

Charlton House in the village of *Charlton* between Woolwich and Blackheath (1.5m SW of Woolwich Town Centre) is a Jacobean mansion completed in 1612 and now used as a community centre and library (open Mon-Fri 09.00-17.00; Tel. 01-856 3951 for other times; BR, Charlton). In red brick, with white stone balustrades, it is beautifully set against well-used grounds. In the village the *Bugle Inn* is at least as old and *St. Luke's* church dates back to 1630. It contains a bust by Chantrey of Spencer Perceval, the Prime Minister assassinated in 1812.

Plumstead Museum in Plumstead Library, 232 Plumstead High Street, London SE18, contains local archaeological finds and sections on local history. The area is dominated by modest terraced housing of the late 19C and early 20C designed to meet the needs of the industrial and dock workers of the area.

Towards Belvedere, 3 miles E of Woolwich, the ruins of *Lesnes Abbey* are set into the hillside off Abbey Road with Abbey Woods beyond, overlooking the river and the huge new town of *Thamesmead*. The founder of the Abbey, Richard de Luci, dedicated it to Our Lady and St. Thomas Becket in 1178; the monastery was suppressed and dissolved in 1525. For a time the site was administered by Christ's Hospital but the old London County Council took it over in 1930 and excavations were carried out in 1951. The walls of the building with its refectory, cloisters and chapel are well preserved and include a doorway and some windows—all remain in the open air.

Basic refreshments are available in the attractively laid out park and Abbey Woods beyond is famous for its display of daffodils in spring.

Bexley is 6 miles SE of Blackheath along the A2. Its mainly rural environs were sprinkled with a few mansions before suburban development got under way in the early part of this century. Current developments include an impressive new shopping centre with indoor marbled malls at Bexleyheath Broadway, and Crook Logs Sports Centre in Brampton Road, Bexleyheath.

Just a stone's throw from a huge roundabout and flyover system (1.5 miles SE of Bexleyheath Town Centre) carrying local traffic, above the busy A2 stands 16C **Hall Place**. (Approach along the A220 from Bexleyheath.)

Hall Place, Bourne Road, Bexley. Tel. 01-303 7777. Open Monday to Saturday 10.00-17.00 (or dusk if earlier), Sunday 14.00-18.00 (March-October). Free. Refreshments near car park.

The building is in two parts, local flint stone and red brick, and now belongs to the London Borough of Bexley. It is used for local exhibitions and the rooms have been restored. The garden features the traditional topiary work of the period, depicting coats of arms; there is a herb garden and cottage garden and formal rose plantation. A river meanders through the park. Hall Place was the family home of Sir John Champneys, Lord Mayor of London in 1534. Stone from local monasteries was used to build it. The Great Hall features a minstrel gallery, and the organ from nearby Danson Park is now housed here.

In Bexley High Street (half a mile S along the A223, Bourne Rd) is 13C *St. Mary the Virgin*—the local parish church which retains its typical Kentish shingled spire. Inside, monuments commemorate local families including the Champneys of Hall Place, William Camden, Henry Castilayn, and Thomas Sparrow, alias Lamendby (died 1513). John Styleman of Danson (died 1734), who endowed the almshouses still in the High St, is remembered by a large pyramid memorial. The 18C lych gate is in the SE corner of the churchyard.
   Bexley Village retains many old buildings.

2 miles SW of Bexleyheath, *St. Paulinus* at **Crayford** is noted for its 12C Perpendicular style and important monuments. Amongst them are two life-sized alabaster figures of William Draper (died 1650) and his wife Mary (died 1652), surrounded by their children. This is an industrial area and David Evans, silk-printers, welcomes visitors to its silk printing plant and small museum (Crayford 57526).

In **Bexleyheath** (half a mile SW of town centre) the **Red House** in Red House Lane (off Upton Road) reveals further aspects of William Morris, who also lived in Waltham Forest and Hammersmith. Here in 1860 he had built a Gothic L-shaped two-storey house which created a sensation with its medieval steep tiled roof and use of red bricks both outside and inside. Morris lived here for only five years but the original decorations have been retained by subsequent owners. Write to the Red House, Red House Lane, Bexleyheath, Kent, enclosing a stamped, addressed envelope to arrange a visit on the first weekend of each month. Admission charge.
   Danson Park (1762) (1 mile W along the A207 from Bexleyheath town centre) stands on a hilltop in grounds laid out by Capability Brown and now a public park; access from the A207 into Danson Road. This elegant villa has stood empty for more than ten years in the care of the London Borough of Bexley.
   At *Avery Hill Park* (BR, Eltham Park) (3 miles SE of Blackheath and 1 mile E of Eltham) there is an outstanding collection of tropical and temperate plants in the Winter Garden conservatory, a collection second only to that of Kew. The Winter Gardens are open Monday to Friday 13.00-16.00, weekends 10.00-16.00 (18.00 in summer); free. A teacher training college occupies part of the grounds.

Eltham (2 miles SE of Blackheath and on the A210), a busy suburb, has retained some interesting buildings at the W end of the High Street including *Cliefden House* (18C) with stable block and orangery, and the Greyhound pub with fireplaces removed from Eltham Palace. The *Bob Hope Theatre*, Wythfield Road, Eltham, London SE9, was inaugurated by the 'local boy' himself in 1982. Court Yard just off the High St leads to **Eltham Palace**; although only open two days a week this medieval palace adds an interesting dimension to England's history. A 15C stone bridge leads over a moat to the courtyard and the Great Hall, the only remaining complete building. It is 100ft long and features a restored minstrel's gallery and oriel windows decorated with coats of arms. The magnificent hammer-beam roof is the third largest in England. The Palace and surrounding grounds are leased by the Crown to the army and the great Hall is frequently used for important banquets.

Eltham Palace, Court Yard, London SE9. Tel. 01-859 2112. Check opening hours; closed without warning at short notice. Open 11.00-16.00 (winter), 11.00-19.00 (summer) Thursdays and Sundays. Access: BR, Eltham Well Hall. Free.

Eltham Palace's royal history dates back to 1300 when it was presented to Edward II by the Bishop of Durham. Edward III received the captive John II here and established the Order of the Garter during a tournament. Geoffrey Chaucer was Clerk of Works under Richard II. The Great Hall was rebuilt in 1479 and Henry VI added further buildings to create an outer and inner courtyard; some of the half-timbered houses of the former still survive outside the gate. The Palace was not used after Cromwell and the Great Hall became a barn until it was restored in 1933 by Samuel Courtauld. Excavations now under way in the grounds have already exposed the W wall of the Palace.

Well Hall Road leads N from Eltham High St half a mile to *Well Hall Pleasaunce*, a small local park, formerly the grounds of Well Hall mansion (demolished 1931). (Access: BR, Eltham, Well Hall). The *Tudor Barn* survives as an art gallery and restaurant. Well Hall was the home of William Roper who married Sir Thomas More's daughter Margaret in 1521. The Barn, built c 1550, has a small stained-glass window featuring Margaret Roper.

33   Dulwich, Forest Hill, Sydenham, Norwood, Streatham, Wandsworth, Battersea, Brixton, Kennington, Camberwell, Peckham, Lewisham

Dulwich Village (nearest BR station West Dulwich) has a recorded history going back to 967 when King Edgar granted the manor to one of his followers; later it belonged to Bermondsey Abbey before the land was purchased by Edward Alleyn, the actor manager, in 1605. Alleyn founded **Dulwich College** (c 400 yards E from West Dulwich Station along the A205) partly as a school for the poor and partly as almshouses which are still in use. The *Old College Building* (North) in College Road is now the offices of the trust which administers Dulwich College, Alleyn's School and James Allen's Girls School. The new Dulwich College (S of A205 in College Road), designed by Charles Barry (son of the architect of the Houses of Parliament) in an ornate Italian style in 1842 with extensions in 1870, includes a *Chapel* in which Alleyn is buried; 800 pupils give thanks to him here daily. The College collects the toll from cars using the privately-owned College Road alongside—the only toll-road remaining in the London area.

The **Dulwich College Picture Gallery** is next to the Old College Building in College Rd. The collection of outstanding Dutch Masters was bequeathed to the college at the beginning of the 19C. They belonged to Noel Desenfans, a French picture dealer who left them to his friend Sir Francis Bourgeois, who in turn left them to the College. Sir John Soane was commissioned to design the gallery, the first public art gallery in Britain, which also contains a mausoleum for its founders; it opened in 1817. Recent restoration work highlights the symmetry and beauty of this simple dome-topped building. The collection has been in the news as a result of several break-ins and most recently (in 1983) thieves removed Rembrandt's 'Jacob III de Gheyn'.

Dulwich Picture Gallery, College Road, SE21. Tel. 01-693 5254. Open Tues to Sat 10.00-13.00, 14.00-17.00, Sun 14.00-17.00, closed Mondays. Admission charge. Access: BR, West Dulwich.

Three hundred paintings are on view; particularly well represented is the 17C, with superb works by Claude, Cuyp, Hobbema, Murillo, Rembrandt, Reni, Rubens and Van Dyck. Highlights include: in Room I Gainsborough's portraits of the Linley family. In Room II Van Dyck's 'Madonna and Child'; 'Samson and Delilah' attributed to Rubens. In Room III Van Dyck's 'Lady Digby on her deathbed', painted two days after her death; Murillo's 'Flower Girl'. In Room IV, the two Veroneses, one a fragment of an altarpiece. In Room VI a notable group of works by Cuyp; in the centre the Mausoleum has the tombs of Bourgeois (centre), Desenfans (right) and Mrs Desenfans (left) with busts. In Room VIII works by Rubens. Room IX, mainly 18C British portraits, followed by 17C portraits in Room X. In Room XI 17C Dutch pictures include 'Jacob's Dream', attributed to Rembrandt until 1914 but actually by De Gelder; Rembrandt's 'Girl leaning on a window-sill'. Room XII, Poussin's 'Return of the Holy Family from Egypt'.

Dulwich Park opposite the Picture Gallery covers 72 acres and is particularly noted for its fine displays of azaleas and rhododendrons in the spring. Charles I hunted in Dulwich Woods and Common, the remains of which are on the other side of the South Circular Road. Highway robberies and duels were common in the 18C. Dulwich Wells on the corner of Dulwich Common and Lordship Lane was a spa for a short time; only the Grove Tavern now marks the spot.

Dulwich Village has attractive cottages dating back to the 18C and a fine Victorian pub, *The Crown and Greyhound*; in its predecessor Dickens used to drink as a member of the Dulwich Club.

There is a local art gallery and community centre at Belair, Gallery Road, London SE21, a fine early 18C villa by Richard Shaw.

Forest Hill (1.5 miles E of Dulwich Village) attracted many German exiles in the 19C and there is a new German church (1959), *Dietrich Banhoeffer Church* in Dacres Road, off Perry Vale, half a mile S of Forest Hill Station. The *Horniman Museum and Library* is at 100 London Road, London SE23 (01-699 1872). Access: BR, Forest Hill. Open Monday to Saturday 10.30-18.00, Sunday 14.00-18.00. Free.

The striking art nouveau museum with a tall clock tower on the crown of the hill was designed by Harrison Townsend and opened in 1901. The mosaic on the facade is by Anning Bell. The park beyond features a sunken garden, rose and water gardens and has animal and bird enclosures as well as a wonderful view towards Central London. A carved totem pole was erected in the gardens in 1985.

The collection was started by Frederick John Horniman, the tea merchant, and opened to the public at first in his own home, Surrey House, Forest Hill. He financed the building of the museum and gave it in trust to the benefit of Londoners; it is administered by the Inner London Education Authority. The museum features natural history including many stuffed birds, an ethnographic collection and a small section on the history of stimulants; a collection of 5000

musical instruments was presented to the museum in 1947 (some are now in
Ranger's House, Blackheath). The education department arranges special
programmes for children and there is a cafeteria.

The once quiet village of **Sydenham** was a spa—the health-giving
water now flows in pools and streams in Sydenham Wells Park—but
came to national attention when the Crystal Palace was moved to
Sydenham Hill in 1854 after the Great Exhibition of 1851. Thousands
of Londoners travelled to Crystal Palace's huge newly built railway
station to visit the new 'entertainment' centre. Many settled in big
houses in the area of Sydenham and Norwood. By the time the
Crystal Palace was destroyed by fire on 30 November 1936 it was
already in decline and the surrounding area became a tightly built-up
middle and working class suburb.

Crystal Palace Park and National Sports Stadium, Thicket Road,
London SE20. Tel. 01-778 7148 (Park), 01-778 0131 (Sports Centre).
Access: BR, Crystal Palace. Car park, cafeteria (March to October).
Adjoining the car park the foundations of the Crystal Palace still
remain. The huge glass and iron building designed by Sir Joseph
Paxton was 1600ft long with aisles and two transepts. The 282ft-high
water towers at either end survived the fire but were removed in
1940.

The 100-acre Crystal Palace Park is managed by the GLC and includes a
boating lake and, on a series of artificial islands, models of huge prehistoric
monsters designed by Waterhouse Hawkins in 1854; a black gorilla was added
in 1961. A television transmitting mast crowns the hill; below is the National
Sports Centre built between 1956 and '64 and featuring an Olympic-size indoor
swimming pool, a sports stadium with athletic track and a ski-training slope.
Squash, badminton and other sports are also played here (membership fee).
The concert bowl in the grounds is used for pop and symphony concerts during
the summer.

Norwood, to the S, once the haunt of highwaymen, including Dick
Turpin, is now a closely built-up suburban area where the peace is
more likely to be broken by football fans attending Crystal Palace
Football Club home matches; the ground is at Selhurst Park,
Whitehorse Lane, South Norwood (access: BR, South Norwood).

The area enjoyed a period of fame in the 19C first as a spa based
on the springs at Beulah Hill (the spa opened in 1831) and later with
the arrival of Crystal Palace as a fashionable residential area; inns
and hotels followed. Well-known residents included Madame
Tussaud and (for a short time) Camille Pissarro who painted the
Palace and South Norwood Station. Sir Arthur Conan Doyle lived
and wrote some Sherlock Holmes stories at 12 Tennison Road, South
Norwood, SE25, from 1891-94. Norwood today is a slightly neglected
area overshadowed by the thriving commercial centre of Croydon to
to the S.

In Norwood High Street, opposite the Greek Revival church of *St.
Luke's*, are the impressive iron gates of *Norwood* or the *South
Metropolitan Cemetery*, next to Highgate and Kensal Rise the most
famous and still the most interesting in London. Founded in 1837,
the main buildings were designed by Sir William Tite, but have now
been mostly lost. However, the monuments survive despite neglect
and vandalism and include granite plinths, Gothic mausoleums and
particularly in the Greek part an outstanding number of monuments.
There is a large German section too based on the German community
at Forest Hill, see above. The cemetery is now in the care of the

London Borough of Lambeth and in urgent need of attention. Amongst those buried here are a number of architects and engineers including Sir Horace Jones (d 1887), Sir William Cubitt (d 1861) and builders Thomas Cubitt (d 1855) and William Colls (d 1893), as well as Mrs Isabelle Beeton (d 1865), household and cook-book author.

Streatham, 2.5 miles W of Crystal Palace, also enjoyed short-lived prosperity at the end of the 18C as a spa, based on a spring on Streatham Common. But its growth depended more on its convenient location on the main road between Central London and Croydon; City merchants built villas here in the 18th and 19th centuries. At Streatham Park overlooking Tooting Bec Common, the Thrales acquired a large estate; between 1766 and 82 Dr Samuel Johnson spent much time with them writing in the summer house, which is now at Kenwood. Other regular guests included Burke, Garrick, Fanny Burney and Joshua Reynolds. The house was demolished in 1863 and the grounds are now covered by a housing estate.

Streatham is now a busy suburb with good entertainment facilities, including *Streatham Ice Rink*, 386 Streatham High Road, London SW16 (01-769 7861; access: BR, Streatham, Streatham Common). The *Leigham Arms*, Wellfield Road, Streatham, has 16C origins and a cobbled cellar.

Tooting, 1 mile S of Streatham, has two adjacent commons, *Tooting Bec* (150 acres) and the smaller *Tooting Graveney* (half a mile W in Upper Tooting) in a residential suburban setting. St. George's Hospital moved to Blackshaw Rd, Tooting, SW17 from Hyde Park Corner in 1980. *Tooting Bec Lido* at Tooting Bec Road, SW16 (01-871 7198) is London's largest open-air swimming pool (access: Underground, Tooting Bec).

Thomas Hardy lived at 172 Trinity Road, SW17 (1878-81) and the Scottish music hall star Sir Harry Lauder lived at 46 Longley Road, SW17 from 1903-11. Daniel Defoe's supposed residence in the area (see Wandsworth) is commemorated in the *Defoe Chapel* in Tooting High Street (1766), now a betting shop.

Wandsworth, 2 miles NW of Tooting, was London's first industrial area. It was based on the Wandle river and boosted in the 18C by the arrival of Huguenot refugees when the Wandle supported some 65 watermills between Wandsworth and Merton to the S. Local industries included bleaching and dyeing, iron and copperware and brewing which still continues at the large Young's brewery. Wealthy industrialists built large villas around Wandsworth Common. Today this is mainly a residential suburb with some recent landscaping by the council of the industrial wasteland.

King George V Park is the setting for the annual Wandsworth weekend in July. At *Book House*, 45 East Hill, SW18 (01-870 9055), the National Book League holds regular exhibitions and runs a reference library. Oscar Wilde was a prisoner for six months in *Wandsworth Prison* in Heathfield Road, SW18, which dates to 1851 as 'a house of correction'. Ronald Biggs, the train robber, staged a spectacular escape from the prison in 1965.

Daniel Defoe, Thackeray and Voltaire all lived in Wandsworth for a time as did John Wesley. David Lloyd George settled at 3 Routh Road, SW18 from 1904, when he first came to London, to 1908.

Clapham. **Clapham Common** (2 miles E of Wandsworth, 1 mile S of Battersea) (access: Underground, Clapham Common) covers 220 acres; around its perimeter are some of the most attractive private houses in London dating back to the late 18th and early 19th centuries when Clapham was 'a pretty suburb', according to Thackeray.

Samuel Pepys lived until his death in 1703 at the North Side of the Common in a mansion demolished in 1754. On the site now stands *The Elms*, where Charles Barry lived and died in 1860, and *Gilmore House*, built in 1760 with busts of Shakespeare and Milton in niches on its facade. The Clapham Sect met here in the 19C. William Wilberforce lived in Broomwood which stood at the corner of Broomwood Road, and Henry Cavendish, philosopher, lived in Cavendish House, on the corner of Cavendish Road. Captain Cook is said to have lived at No. 22 North Side for a time and used the balcony on the third floor.

Clapham developed rapidly in the late 19C with terraced housing built to meet the demands for cheaper accommodation. Recently, Clapham Common has once again become a fashionable residential area. On Clapham Common there are fairs and a horse show on August Bank Holiday Weekend. The London Borough of Lambeth established a Speaker's Corner on Clapham Common in 1985, near the popular, rambling Windmill Pub and the duckpond.

At 80b The Chase, SW4, a Soseki Museum established in a private house where Japanese novelist Soseki Natsume lived is open Wed and Sat 10.00-12.00 and 14.00-17.00, Sun 14.00-17.00. Free. (Access: Underground, Clapham Common.)

Clapham Junction, once the busiest railway junction in the world with 2500 trains a day, is still important. Nearby in St. John's Hill, SW11 is *Clapham Junction Market* (access: BR, Clapham Junction) on Fridays and Saturdays with new clothes and household goods. At Northcote Road, SW11, another popular market concentrates on fruit and vegetables in a road with many ethnic grocers reflecting the cosmopolitan mix of this part of London.

Battersea (1 mile N of Clapham Common, half a mile S of Battersea Bridge), on the Thames, is an ancient settlement as indicated by the recovery in 1857 of the Iron-Age Battersea Shield now in the British Museum; today its famous landmarks *Battersea Power Station* and *Battersea Park* overshadow the suburban area beyond.

In Old Battersea on the river stands *St. Mary's Church* in Battersea Church Road, SE11, built in 1777, on the foundations of an 11C church, in dark red brick with classical details. The East window is 17C heraldic glass and there are monuments from the earlier church and church bells from the 17C. J.M.W. Turner was inspired to paint his Thames sunset by the view from the church window and the poet William Blake married the daughter of a local market gardener here in 1792. The first *Battersea Bridge* was built in the 18C; the present bridge was built by Bazalgette in 1890 and replaced the wooden structure depicted in many paintings.

Before becoming an industrial area based on the Nine Elms railway yard, Battersea served as a market garden for London. The local manor house stood next to the church and is now demolished. But *Old Battersea House* in Vicarage Crescent, SW11, 200 yards from the church, built in the style of Wren, survives and houses the William de Morgan collection of paintings and ceramics. The house is open by arrangement; write to the De Morgan Trust, 21 St. Margaret's

Crescent, London SW15 6HL. It has been renovated by the London Borough of Wandsworth. The *Vicarage* and *Devonshire House* are also attractive 18C houses.

Battersea Arts Centre in Lavender Hill, a popular local arts and community centre, opened in 1981 in the former Town Hall; it includes a modern purpose-built dance studio. Half a mile to the N along Latchmere Rd is the *Latchmere Leisure Centre* with a swimming pool, wave machine and indoor sports hall (01-871 7470).

Battersea Park, Battersea Park Road, SW11 (access: BR, Battersea Park or Underground to Sloane Square then bus 19 or 137) was laid out and opened in 1853 on the once notorious Battersea Fields where the Duke of Wellington fought a duel with Lord Winchilsea in 1829 and where the rough-necks of London used to go for illicit trading, shooting and entertainment, travelling by boat from London. The park lake was excavated in 1864 and the park was further improved as part of the Festival of Britain in 1951 with the addition of sports and entertainment facilities including a funfair which closed in 1975 when it became unsafe. There is a *Children's Zoo* (summer), an annual Easter Parade and many other events. It is owned by the GLC who erected a Japanese Peace Pagoda here in 1985.

Battersea Power Station, now a well-loved and listed monument, opened in 1933 to general public disapproval because of the fears of pollution as well as its gigantic size. Dubbed 'A Temple of Power', it was designed by Sir Giles Scott, architect of Liverpool's Anglican Cathedral, and phased out in the '70s. The four fluted chimneys are 335ft high and the interior could hold a 22-storey building. It is destined to become a leisure and entertainment centre by 1987, retaining many of its art deco interior features.

At the former railway yard at *Nine Elms*, Battersea, is the new *Covent Garden Market* which moved here from Central London in 1974. This is a wholesale fruit and vegetable market and visits are by appointment only (01-720 2211). The *Dogs' Home*, Battersea, moved to Battersea Park Road, SW18 in 1871. It takes in both stray dogs and cats and finds new homes for them.

Brixton, to the N of Streatham, shares its decline from fashionable residential area in the 19C to inner city problem area a century later with suburbs such as Hackney. Large villas along Brixton Hill and in Angell Town were built for City merchants in the late 18C but the arrival of the railway brought cheaper housing in densely built terraces. These proved ideal cheap rented accommodation for the large influx of Commonwealth immigrants in the 1950s and '60s. In between Brixton had established itself as an important shopping centre for S London; Electric Avenue was one of the first city streets with electricity when it opened in 1888. Entertainment thrived; the Ritzy cinema built in 1910 still survives. Large housing estates have now replaced some of the older housing and the area's character is set by the large West Indian community, many now second and third generation families.

Brixton Market (Monday to Saturday) in Electric Avenue, Pope's Road, and Brixton Station Road, SW9 (access: BR, Brixton, Underground, Brixton) started in the 1880s and now sells clothes, fruit, vegetables, fish, household goods and bric-a-brac—to the sound of reggae music.

Brixton Windmill in Blenheim Gardens, off Brixton Road, was built in 1816 and was in use until 1934 as a flour-mill. It has been restored by the council and surrounded by a small park. It is open from 09.00 to dusk every day.

Next to Brixton Station is the *Brixton Recreation Centre*, a new and impressive complex opened in 1985. It has a swimming pool and other facilities. *Brixton Prison* (1820) is in Jebb Avenue, SW2. It once housed a treadmill. Van Gogh stayed in Brixton in 1872 at the age of 19.

Kennington. *Kennington Common* saw the assembly of the Chartists in 1848, quietly dispersed by the police as directed by the Duke of Wellington, then Prime Minister. Now a small public park, it was used as a fairground but was also Surrey's execution ground. *St. Mark's Church* stands on the site of the gallows; the last execution was in the early 19C. The park lodge on the N side of the park is the Prince Consort's model house designed for the Great Exhibition by Henry Roberts and transferred here in 1852.

At 278 Kennington Road Charlie Chaplin was born in 1889. Attractive terraced houses of the 18th and early 19th centuries survive in Kennington Park Road, Cleaver Square and Kennington Road. The Surrey Cricket Club was established at *The Oval Cricket Ground* (nearest Underground The Oval) in 1845. It is surrounded by council flats.

The *General Cab Company Museum* is at 1, 3 Brixton Road, SW9 (01-735 7777). Open Monday to Friday 09.00-17.00, Saturday 09.00-12.00. Admission free (nearest Underground The Oval). It houses a small collection of cabs from the turn of the century to the present day.

Camberwell. *Camberwell Green* was once the site of fairs which rivalled the popular events at Greenwich but these were stopped in 1855. Today it is a mere traffic island in a busy but neglected part of London. Some impression of Camberwell's more fashionable past can be glimpsed in *Camberwell Grove* where Joseph Chamberlain was born (at No. 188) in one of the pleasant Georgian houses in 1836. Robert Browning was born at nearby No. 179 Southampton Way in 1812. In Meeting House Lane, running N from Peckham High Street, stood the Meeting House used by William Penn before his imprisonment in the Tower in 1668. The parish church of *St. Giles* in Church St was built in 1844 by George Gilbert Scott on the site of an older church destroyed by fire. The E window glass was designed by John Ruskin who lived nearby at Herne Hill.

Camberwell School of Arts and Crafts was established in 1896 and still enjoys a high reputation. It is next to the *South London Art Gallery* opened in 1891 with funds from Passmore Edwards.

South London Art Gallery, Peckham Road, London SE3 (01-703 6120). Open during exhibitions Tues to Sat 10.00-18.00, Sun 15.00-18.00. Free. Access: Underground, Elephant and Castle, then bus 12, 36.

The gallery presents temporary exhibitions including those of the students as well as displays from the permanent collection of 19th and 20th century British art.

At **Walworth** to the NE is the *Cuming Museum* on the first floor of the *Newington District Library*, Walworth Road, London SE17 (01-703 3324). Open Mon to Fri 10.00-17.30, Sat 10.00-17.00. Free. The museum has a collection of archaeological finds from Southwark and an interesting display on London superstitions. The Tudor-style red-brick building is matched by the adjoining *Town Hall* in Gothick style—both of Victorian origin. The headquarters of the British Labour Party is also in Walworth Road.

St. Peter's Church in Liverpool Grove, SE17 (a turning E of Walworth Road), was designed in 1825 by Sir John Soane; a few terraces of older houses survive here in a sea of modern council housing. The great attraction of Walworth is *East Street*, a large 100-year-old market, with 250 stalls from Walworth Rd to Flint St. (Access: Underground, Elephant & Castle, walk or bus down Walworth Rd.) The market is open on Tuesdays to Saturdays for greengrocery, clothes, and household goods and on Sunday mornings for plants. This is South London's answer to Petticoat Lane with a good, friendly atmosphere.

South of Albany Street, stretching from the Walworth Rd to the Old Kent Rd is *Burgess Park*, an imaginative development undertaken by the GLC in a heavily built-up area to create a park and leisure facilities for local residents. Already there is a lake (with fishing), football pitches and a nature centre. The park will eventually cover 135 acres, most of it reclaimed from industrial use but also from run-down housing.

In *Denmark Hill* (running S from Camberwell Green) are *King's College Hospital* (1913) and the *Maudsley Hospital* (1915) as well as the *William Booth Memorial Training College*, designed by Sir Giles Gilbert Scott in 1932 with statues of the salvation Army's founders General and Mrs Booth, outside. John Ruskin lived at 28 Herne Hill, the continuation of Denmark Hill, and at 163 Denmark Hill; both houses have gone but he is remembered in *Ruskin Park*. Part of British Rail's *Denmark Hill Station* was recently converted into a pub in the 'Firkin' brew-pub chain.

Peckham. The many thousands who rush down the A2 in cars to and from Dover hardly notice their historic surroundings as they pass along the now rather dingy Old Kent Road, formerly the Roman Watling Street. This is the route taken by Chaucer's Canterbury Pilgrims who halted at 'St. Thomas a Watering', now a Victorian pub, the *Thomas a Becket*, at 320 Old Kent Road, SE1, with a boxing theme and museum housing some 1000 exhibits (access: Underground, Elephant and Castle; 01-703 2644). Further along is the Henry Cooper pub. At the junction with Peckham Park Road stands the *North Peckham Civic Centre* with a library and theatre. The exterior mural by Polish artist Adam Kossowski attempts to capture the history of the Old Kent Road from Roman times to its recent past when costermongers sold their wares along the road.

The *Livesey Museum* is at 682 Old Kent Road, London SE15 (01-639 5604), originally a library. It stages temporary exhibitions mainly on London themes for the benefit of the local community and schools.

Peckham itself is to the S of the Old Kent Road; once an area of market gardens it also had some grand houses. *Peckham Rye Common* was saved from encroaching developments in 1868 and now adjoins a park with sporting facilities. Some 19C houses survive in Peckham Rye where Elizabeth Cadbury, Quaker and wife of the chocolate manufacturer, was born.

Tilling's first omnibus service ran from Peckham to the City in 1851 and the railway arrived in 1862. At *Nunhead*, the *Old Nun's Head* at 15 Nunhead Gardens, SE15, stands on the site of a nunnery; the Abbess's head was set on a stake on the Green, hence the name.

Nunhead also has an interesting Victorian *cemetery*, founded in Linden Grove near the Old Nun Head Tavern in 1840, with catacombs set on a hilltop wooded site. Between the wars it was completely neglected and the London Borough of Southwark took it over in 1975 to try to salvage at least a part. Amongst those buried here are Thomas Tilling (d 1893) who pioneered the horsedrawn bus, Robert Abel, cricketer (d 1936); the *Martyrs' Memorial*, an obelisk erected in 1851, commemorates five Scottish nationalists transported to Australia.

Lewisham is a busy shopping centre with a modern covered complex opened in 1975 and a lively street market in the High Street (Monday to Saturday). The *Clock Tower* at the junction of Lewisham High Street and Lee High Road was built to commemorate Queen Victoria's 1897 Jubilee. At the corner of the High Street and Ladywell Road stands Lewisham's oldest building, *The Vicarage*, built in 1692. The coping stones of the holy well at Ladywell can be seen outside *Ladywell Sports Centre*.

The *Fox and Firkin* at 316 Lewisham High Street, SE13, was the first in a series of independent brewery pubs opened in the '70s. It has a stuffed fox and home-brewed ale.

To the N, at **Lee**, is the *Manor House and Library Gardens*, Old Road, SE13, with an 18C Adam ceiling, now housing a library and the borough archives. The ruined tower of the old *St. Margaret's Church* in Lee Terrace stands in the churchyard on the other side of the road; here the astronomer royal, Edmund Halley (cf Halley's comet) is buried. In the High Street are the *Merchant Taylor Almshouses*, built in 1876 on the site of older Boone's almshouses; the old chapel (1638) remains.

Lewisham Concert Hall and Theatre is to the S at *Rushey Green*, Catford, opened in 1932 with adjoining civic buildings and a shopping precinct.

Catford has a greyhound stadium. Going S towards Bromley is the large *Downham Estate* built by the London County Council in the 1920s to provide cottage-style living for thousands of poor Inner Londoners. On the way at *Southend* (crossroad leading to Beckenham) is *Peter Pan's Pool*, a visible sign of the Ravensbourne River which flows through this area on its way to the Thames, and which once powered numerous watermills supporting local industries. Sainsbury's has built a large Homebase store overlooking the pond in the likeness of the old Crystal Palace.

Penge and Beckenham. Penge, just to the S of Crystal Palace, enjoyed a brief popularity before becoming a modest working-class suburb. In Penge High Street are the striking *Free Watermen's and Lightermen's Almshouses*, designed by George Porter in Tudor style (1841), with an impressive gatehouse and quadrangle—still in use. Nearby in St. John's Road are *Queen Adelaide's Cottages*, designed by Philip Hardwick also in Tudor style (1847) for the benefit of naval widows.

In *Beckenham Place Park* (approach from Southend Road, nearest BR station Beckenham Junction) stands a manor house built in 1774 for John Cator and now used by players on the 18-hole public golf course. There is also a nature centre and the first floor is due to become the home of the Mander and Mitchenson Theatrical Collection. The house and park are managed by the London Borough of Lewisham.

In Bromley Road, just off Beckenham High Street, are three 17C *Rawlins almshouses*, built in 1649, next to Victorian *St. George's* parish church, which has a 13C lych gate, said to be the oldest in the country. The *George Inn*, further down in the main part of the High Street, dates back to 1662 when it was a coaching inn. In Foxgrove Road, the annual Beckenham Tennis Championships take place in June, attracting international players heading for Wimbledon.

In common with Beckenham, **Bromley** is a prosperous commuting suburb which has recently developed its own commercial and shopping centre. H.G. Wells was born here in 1866 and a blue plaque on Allders department store marks the site of the family home. The parish church of *St. Peter and St. Paul* nearby in Church Road was consecrated in 1957, replacing a 13C church destroyed by bombs in the Second World War. Dr Johnson's wife, Elizabeth (d 1752), is buried in the churchyard.

Bromley College in London Road was founded by Bishop Warner for poor widows in 1666; the design is attributed to Wren and is similar to Morden College, Blackheath, incorporating pillars from Gresham's Royal Exchange destroyed in the Great Fire.

Plaistow Lodge in London Lane was built for Peter Thellusson, an eccentric Huguenot millionaire, at the end of the 18C; it is now Quernmore secondary school (due to close). *Sundridge Park* houses a management centre. The house and grounds were designed by John Nash and Humphrey Repton and Samuel Wyatt for corn merchant Claude Scott in 1801. In the grounds where the first 'bred' pheasants were shot by, amongst others, the Prince of Wales, there is now a golf course.

Bromley Palace belonged to Bishop of Rochester; the current building in Rochester Road, Bromley dates back to 1775 and used to be Stockwell College. It is now Bromley's *Civic Centre and Town Hall*. *St. Blaise's Well* in the grounds was reputed to have medicinal properties.

Amongst the new office blocks in the busy High Street is *The Churchill Theatre* and new *Library* designed by Aneurin John and completed in 1975. The theatre restaurant overlooks *Library Gardens* (access: BR, Bromley South).

In nearby **Chislehurst** (to the W) a large *Common* creates a rural atmosphere in a wealthy suburban setting (access: BR, Chislehurst, bus 227 from Bromley). *Camden Place* on the NW side of the Common was the home of Napoleon III in exile after 1871. For a time after his death his body was buried in the Catholic church of *St. Mary's* in Hawkeswood Lane, in a specially erected mortuary chapel. Later his widow, Empress Eugenie, moved to Farnborough (Hants) and his body was reburied there.

In **Petts Wood** (between Bromley and Chislehurst; BR, Petts Wood; near Orpington Rd, Chislehurst) a memorial in the form of a stone pillar was erected in 1927 to William Willett (d 1915) who conceived the idea of summer time (introduced as daylight saving in the First World War). Petts Wood is a 70-acre National Trust area in the middle of an attractive suburb.

Near Chislehurst station are the gigantic *Chislehurst caves* (100 yards from station) which run for miles in the chalk hills; they are remains of chalk mines from Roman times and were used by thousands of Londoners as shelters during the Second World War.

Chislehurst Caves, Chislehurst (01-467 3264). Access: BR, Chislehurst, bus 227 from Bromley, turn into Old Hill from A222, 300 yards further on left. Open daily 11.00-17.00 summer; winter, Sat and Sun only. Admission charge.

In **Hayes** (SE of Bromley) William Pitt and William Pitt the Younger lived at Hayes Place, demolished in 1934. Sir Everard Hambro, the banker, was a later resident and benefactor to the growing village, now a residential suburb.

To the S of Bromley, at **Farnborough**, another privately owned 19C estate has become a public golf course and park. *High Elms* was the home of Sir John Lubbock, the first Lord Avebury, astronomer and mathematician (d 1865). He planted the grounds with an unusual collection of trees; there is a nature centre and a trail through the park. Lord Avebury is best known for the introduction of Bank Holidays in 1871. The manor house burnt down in 1967. Nearby is the village of *Downe* with its attractive flint cottages and the family home of Charles Darwin.

Down House, Luxted Road, Downe, Orpington, Kent (66 59119 or 0689 59119). Access: BR, Bromley South, bus No. 146 to Downe. Open 13.00-17.30, closed Monday (except Bank Holidays), Friday and February.
   Down House became Charles Darwin's home in 1842 and he lived there until his death in 1882. In 1927 it became a museum run by the Royal College of Surgeons. Part of the house recreates the period with Darwin's study and his chair as the centre-piece. Exhibits show the developments of his theory of natural selection. In the garden visitors can trace Darwin's footsteps along the Sandy Walk. Plants, fossils and scientific instruments are also on display.

Further E, at **Keston** (3 miles S of Bromley) there is a hill-fort and windmill dating back to 1717 on the Common. The parish church in Westerham Road is in Norman style with Roman foundations. *Caesar's Well* on the Common is the origin of the River Ravensbourne.

West Wickham, towards Bromley and Beckenham, retains its castle-style manor house, *Wickham Court* (1480), now a college.

Biggin Hill, 5 miles S of Bromley, annually in May remembers the crucial role its airfield played in the Battle of Britain (1940-41) with a two-day airshow, on what is now mainly a busy civil airport under the authority of the London Borough of Bromley. A permanent memorial in the form of Spitfire and Hurricane aircraft can be seen outside the Memorial Chapel along the main road which becomes the very long Biggin Hill High Street.

The Priory at **Orpington** (3 miles SE of Bromley) is an excellent example of a pre-Reformation Rectory House, dating back in part to 1270. It was the home of rectors of St. Mary's Church until 1600 and has been restored as a local meeting place with a small museum.

Bromley Museum, The Priory, Church Hill, Orpington, Kent (66 31551). Access: BR, Orpington. Open Mon to Wed, Fri 09.00-18.00, Sat 09.00-17.00. Archaeological exhibits, Stone Age, Roman and Saxon, are on show with some Victorian relics.

The Walnuts Sports Centre adjoining the new shopping centre in the High Street offers swimming, squash and other sports.

34   Croydon, Carshalton, Cheam, Sutton, Wimbledon, Merton, Kingston

Croydon now has the largest concentration of office space in Britain outside Central London but its origin lies in the church. The Archbishop of Canterbury took over the local manor house in the 14C to create a convenient staging post between Lambeth Palace and Canterbury. Today the *Archbishop's Palace* (or *Old Palace*), now a girls' school, is overshadowed by office blocks, the result of a massive expansion of the town centre since 1954. At the heart is the *Whitgift shopping centre*—an unattractive '60s complex in plain concrete—which takes its name from Archbishop Whitgift, who founded the Grammar School, and almshouses.

The Old Palace, Old Palace Road, Croydon, is open to visitors during the school holidays (access: BR, East Croydon). Approach via Church Street, a turning off the High St, opposite George St (400 yards). It retains a 12C undercroft and the Great Hall dates back to 1390, rebuilt with a Spanish chestnut wood roof in 1452. Queen Elizabeth stayed here and her bedchamber is on view as is the original Chapel. Earl Rothesay, later James I of Scotland, spent six years in captivity in the Palace before becoming King.

The parish church of *St. John the Baptist*, in Church St next to the Old Palace, retains its medieval porch but was rebuilt after a fire in 1867 by Sir Gilbert Scott. Many of the original memorials and brasses were saved as was Archbishop Whitgift's tomb and those of five other archbishops. In the High Street on the corner with George Street are the *Whitgift Almshouses* which still provide accommodation for the poor and elderly. They date back to 1599 and some of the original furniture can be seen in the Audience Chamber. Whitgift's portrait hangs in the Chapel and there is a 16C clock in the quadrangle. (For details of access to these historic buildings contact Croydon Tourist Information Centre, Central Library, Katharine Street, Croydon. Tel. 01-688 3627.)

The first public railway in the world opened in 1803 between Croydon and Wandsworth—the wagons were drawn on rails by horses. *West Croydon* railway station opened in 1839 and *East Croydon* in 1841, signalling the start of the area's rapid growth as a commercial and residential centre.

Croydon was also in the forefront of aviation. The original *Croydon Aerodrome* building, 2.5 miles S of town centre along Purley Way, the A23, may be converted into a museum. A housing estate covers the airfield, which closed in the 1950s. Military flights started in 1915; George VI gained his wings as Prince Albert in 1919. It became London's first airport officially in 1928 and until 1959 it was used for civil and military flights; it was the base of Imperial Airways. Pioneering flights from here include Amy Johnson's record breaking flight to Australia in 1930.

In Central Croydon there is a daily street market in Surrey Street going back 700 years, now selling mostly seasonal greengrocery.

Fairfield Halls were completed in the 1960s and include a 2000-seat concert hall, 800-seat theatre, the Ashcroft, an art gallery and restaurant. Nearby is a new Holiday Inn hotel. Notable amongst the many office blocks is the octagonal, 23-storey high *NLA House* designed by Richard Seifert and completed in 1970.

Between Shirley and Beckenham, 3 miles E of Croydon in Monks Orchard Rd, is the *Bethlem Royal Hospital*. This, the oldest hospital in the world for the treatment of the mentally ill, was founded in Bishopsgate in 1247. It moved to Moorgate in 1675 where it became known as Bedlam, attracting visitors who watched the inmates from the gallery. In 1815 a specially designed building at Lambeth, now the Imperial War Museum, became the Bethlem and it moved from there to Shirley in 1926.

The archbishops of Canterbury left Croydon for *Addington Palace* in 1808, taking over a manor house in Coombe Road, until 1897 when Canterbury and Lambeth became the only two residences of the

The NLA Tower in Croydon (Richard Seifert, 1970)

archbishops. The Palace was reconstructed by Norman Shaw for private use; in 1951 it became the home of the Royal School of Church Music. The grounds are the Addington Palace Golf Course. (Access: BR, East Croydon, then bus; 3 miles SE of Croydon.)

At *Selsdon Park*, 3 miles SE of the centre of Croydon, another golf course occupies the grounds of the former Selsdon Court, now *Selsdon Park Hotel* which incorporates some medieval parts of the original building with 19C additions. It overlooks the grounds, the golf course, and Selsdon Wood, National Trust land.

In this area several nature trails and reserves reveal some of the original Surrey countryside; details from the London Borough of Croydon, Central Library, Katharine St, Croydon. Tel. 01-688 3627.

Sanderstead (3m S), Purley (2m S), Kenley (4m S) and Coulsdon (5m SW of Croydon) are attractive residental suburbs developed mainly in the early and middle part of this century.

At *Beddington*, 2 miles to the W of Croydon (in the London Borough of Sutton) excavations (in 1871) revealed the bath-house of a Roman Villa at Beddington Park. Approach via Beddington Lane S from Mitcham Rd (A236), turn left into Bath House Rd, 1 mile S of BR Beddington Lane. The manor house, Carew Manor, has been largely rebuilt but in the Great Hall, an impressive hammer-beam roof dating back to the early 15C remains. It is now a school next to *St. Mary's*, the local parish church in Church Road, off Croydon Road (A232). This is of pre-Norman origin; it contains a fine organ-case designed and painted in the William Morris workshop at Merton Abbey, decorated with flowers, leaves and angels.

In the centre of **Carlshalton** (3.5 miles W of Croydon. Access: BR, Carlshalton) is the source of the Wandle river, surrounded by attractive houses, some weatherboarded, in what is now a conservation area. From here the river flows through Sutton, Merton, Croydon and Wandsworth; the Wandle valley provided an early start for industrialisation (at the beginning of the 19C) with more than 80 mills (in 1831) along its banks providing power for a variety of industries (see also Wandsworth). Mill-wheels and mill-stones can be seen in *The Grove* public gardens, where the former manor house, *Stonecourt*, is now council offices.

Carlshalton House, Pound Street, was build in 1714 and is now a convent school. *Carlshalton Park* has a brick grotto and a dry canal; the house intended for the grounds was never built. At *Little Holland House*, 40 Beeches Avenue (01-647 5168) the hard work of one Frank Dickinson (d 1961) self-taught craftsman, can be admired. He took nearly 60 years to make every part of the house, begun in 1904. Open: 1 March-31 Oct; 1st Sun in each month and BHs, 12.00-18.00. Free (BR, Carlshalton Beeches).

At **Cheam**, *Nonsuch Park* (1.5 miles N of Sutton) serves as a reminder of Henry VIII's last palace, Nonsuch, built in 1538 and demolished in 1688. Three pillars mark the site of the palace, unearthed in 1959. Archaeological finds including stone, gilded slate, glass and pottery from the site are now in the Museum of London and at Bourne Hall Museum in Ewell.

Nonsuch Palace was a Tudor extravaganza, a two-storey building around open courtyards in the Rennaissance style, decorated by Italian craftsmen, with two towers topped by onion-shaped cupolas. Stone from Merton Priory, dissolved by Henry VIII, was used in the construction. In 1556 it passed to the Earl of

Arundel who entertained Queen Elizabeth here frequently. By 1603 it was again in royal possession, used as a hunting centre by James I and then Charles I. During Charles II's reign it was sold to Lord Berkeley who demolished it. A 17C mansion house stands in the Park.

Nonsuch Park is between London Road and Ewell Road, Cheam; approach along The Avenue. Nearest BR station Cheam. A Roman road, Stone Street, runs along the W side of the Park.

On the corner of Park Lane and Malden Road, just off Cheam High Street, stands **Whitehall**, a weatherboarded house typical of the area, which has been restored and is open to visitors.

Whitehall, 1 Malden Road, Cheam, Sutton, Surrey. Tel. 01-643 1236. Access: BR, Cheam; bus 213A. Open Nov-March, Wed, Thurs, and Sun 14.00-17.30, Sat 10.00-17.30, April-Oct, Tues-Fri and Sun 14.00-17.30, Sat 10.00-17.30.

The house dates back to c 1500 and is one of the earliest surviving two-storey buildings in England. The weatherboarding was added in the 18C to cover the gaps between the original timbers as the mixture of straw and plaster dried out. It was once Cheam School (now in Berkshire) whose famous pupils have included the Duke of Edinburgh and Prince Charles. The London Borough of Sutton organises exhibitions and concerts here.

Set back from Malden Road in Church Road is the Victorian Gothic parish church of *St. Dunstan*. The Lumley Chapel in the churchyard dates from the 13C and was turned into a memorial to Lord Lumley and his wife Jane Fitzalan in 1592 (non-royal occupants of Nonsuch Palace). Her alabaster tomb includes the children portrayed against a background of a room in the Palace. Lord Lumley's memorial depicts him as a scholar; his second wife, Elizabeth Darcy, is also included.

Cheam became a busy suburb only in the 1920s and '30s with a Tudor-style shopping centre and remains of the Old Village in the centre.

Whitehall, Cheam

Sutton (4.5 miles W of Croydon) is the commercial centre of the area; a residential suburb developed here with the arrival of the London to Epsom railway in 1847. Further house building followed in the early 20C and more recently a library, civic centre and art college were built in the centre. *St. Nicholas*, the parish church, has Saxon origins but the present building was designed by Edwin Nach in 1864. There is a lively street market on Tuesdays and Saturdays in West Street (fashion, leather and jewellery).

Wimbledon (access: BR, Wimbledon; Underground, Wimbledon, Southfields, Wimbledon Park). The remains of a pre-Roman fort known as Caesar's Camp can still be seen on what is now the Royal Wimbledon Golf Club, part of Wimbledon Common. But it was not until the 16C that Wimbledon Village came to prominence when the Earl of Exeter built Wimbledon House—later demolished.

Wimbledon Common covers, with Putney Lower Common, 1100 acres; special features include Rushmere and King's Mere ponds, the golf course and the windmill. *Wimbledon Windmill* was built in 1817 and is believed to be the only remaining hollow-post flour mill in this country. It has been restored and a small museum is open to the public on Saturdays, Sundays and Bank Holidays, 14.00-17.00 (April to October); admission charge. Approach along Parkside and turn into Windmill Road (nearest Underground Southfields).

Southside House, Wimbledon Common, SW19 (01-946 7643), is a 16C farm building with a Dutch brick facade added in 1687, now the Headquarters of the School Teachers Cultural Foundation. It is the former home of the Pennington Mellor family and contains many treasures of the family as well as of the Swedish philanthropist Axel Munthe, whose wife, Hilda Pennington Mellor Munthe, and children lived here. After war damage the LCC assisted with its restoration on condition that it remained accessible to the public. In the Music Room is a portrait of Emma Hamilton who often visited from her nearby home in Merton. Visits on guided tours only from 1 October to 31 March, Tues, Thurs and Fri 10.00–17.00 or by appointment to the Administrator, Pennington-Mellor Charity Trust, Southside House, Wimbledon Common, SW19.

Cannizaro House, West Side, Wimbledon Common, was substantially rebuilt in 1901 and is being converted into a country house hotel.

Wimbledon Common has a history of duels, the first recorded in 1652. In 1798 the Prime Minister, William Pitt fought George Tierney, MP, and in 1809 Lord Castlereagh and George Canning duelled here. The last duel was in 1840 when Lord Cardigan wounded Captain Harvey Tuckett. The Common's fictional inhabitants, the Wombles, are known to millions of children.

The *Fox and Grapes* pub in Camp Road, off the Common, has one bar named after Caesar's Camp; the 300-year-old pub is in a mock-Tudor style.

Wimbledon Village, now a large and thriving suburb, enjoys a hilltop location and some attractive buildings survive, including *Eagle House* with its distinctive gables (1613) and *Claremont*, a late 17C building. The *Rose and Crown*, also in the High Street, is 17C; the poet Swinburne drank here.

In Wimbledon Broadway stands the *Wimbledon Theatre* (1910) with a green cupola restored in 1968, showing pre-West End productions and Christmas pantomimes. Nearby is the *Polka Theatre* with a programme of children's plays and a large collection of puppets. *Wimbledon Stadium* in Plough Lane is used for dog-racing, speedway and stock-car racing. There is a local history museum run by the Wimbledon Society in The Ridgway, Wimbledon.

Wimbledon's international fame is founded on the annual tennis championships at the *All England Club* in Wimbledon Park, Church Rd, held in June, since 1877.

Access: Wimbledon (BR and Underground), special buses during the championship along the High St into Church Rd (1.5 miles).

There are 16 outside courts and two under-cover courts including the Centre Court which seats 14,000 (all grass—there are no clay courts). The *Wimbledon Lawn Tennis Museum*, Church Road, Wimbledon, SW19, overlooks the Centre Court. Open Tuesday to Saturday 11.00-17.00, Sunday 14.00-17.00 and during the championships (to those attending matches). Admission charge. Tel. 01-946 6131. Parking. The museum has a large collection of ladies tennis fashion through the last 100 years, life-size models of well-known players, a reconstruction of a racquet-maker's workshop and men's dressing-room, tennis bric-a-brac and a library.

One mile SE of Wimbledon lies **Merton** which has given its name to the London borough. It was a pioneer amongst garden suburbs but its history dates back to the 12C when Merton's Augustinian priory was founded. Students included Thomas Becket and Walter of Merton, who later founded Merton College at Oxford. Stone from the demolished priory after its dissolution was used to build Nonsuch Palace (see above). Some remains can still be seen in Station Road. Lord Nelson lived at Merton Place with Sir William and Lady Hamilton from 1801 to 1805 but the house has been demolished. His pew is preserved in the parish church of *St. Mary the Virgin,* Merton Park. The Wandle flows through Merton and provided power for early industries including Liberty's fabric-printing workshops which remained here until 1972. William Morris established a workshop here in 1887 to manufacture textiles, tiles and furniture. It was destroyed in the Second World War.

John Innes, another household name, established his Horticultural Institute at Merton Park in 1909; he first bought the estate in 1867 and transformed the farmhouse into a manor house and the surrounding grounds, now a public park, with avenues of trees and holly hedges. *John Innes Park* is at Water Lane, SW19 (nearest BR station is Wimbledon Chase—approach along Kingston Road).

In *Morden Hall Park*, along the Wandle, 1.5 miles S of Wimbledon, is a weatherboarded *snuff-mill* (early 19C) in the grounds of *Morden Hall*, owned by the National Trust. There is also a nature reserve. Morden Hall is a 17C building now used by the Council (nearest Underground Morden). The parish church of *St. Lawrence* in London Road was built in 1636 on 11C foundations; nearby is the 300-year-old *George Inn*. Beyond is *Morden Park*, with a Georgian mansion also used by the local council. The Underground railway was extended to Morden in 1926; this spurred extensive housing developments.

Mitcham, 1 mile to the E of Morden, claims the second oldest village cricket green in the country (cricket was played here before 1720). A Saxon cemetery was excavated at *Ravensbury Park* (half a mile S of town centre, off London Road, A217) earlier this century and the finds (including weapons and brooches) can be seen in the Museum of London. **Mitcham Common** cover 460 acres and joins with

Beddington (see p 335). Two pubs remain from Mitcham's turnpike days, the *White Hart* and *Burn Bullock* (formerly the King's Head) from the 18C. The council owns three mansions, *Eagle House* (1705), *Park Place* (1780) and *The Canons*; the last built in 1680 and now a centre for recreation, indoor and outdoor sports, antique fairs and other events.

Canons Leisure Centre, Madeira Road, Mitcham, Surrey (01-640 8544).

Kingston upon Thames is 10m SW of Central London; on the Thames opposite Hampton Wick (BR, Kingston). This is one of only two royal boroughs in London (the other is Kensington and Chelsea). Today it is a busy shopping centre with some office development and a complicated one-way system. It was the coronation place for seven Anglo-Saxon rulers from Edward the Elder in 900 to Ethelred the Unready in 979; seven silver pennies are set into the base of the original coronation stone outside the *Guildhall* (1935), High Street. After the Norman Conquest Kingston's economy changed as Westminster became the royal base; Kingston Bridge, completed by the end of the 12C and only the second bridge over the Thames after London Bridge, ensured growth as a market town. The present bridge dates to 1828 and was doubled in size in 1914. The remains of the medieval bridge can be seen at the end of Bridge Street. Nearby is *Turks Boatyard*, more than 200 years old, still building boats and providing a local passenger boat service.

A tributary of the Thames, the Hogsmill flows through the borough; the ancient arches of the *Clattern Bridge* (1175) can be seen next to the Guildhall (a gate leads down to the water-level; High Street/Market Square).

The *Ancient Market* dates to the 13C or even earlier; fresh food is sold here, Monday to Saturday. The Royal Charter granted in 1628 prevents any other markets from opening within seven miles; this restriction has been eased to allow markets at Sutton and Putney. Near the Market Place is the *Apple Market* with a smaller range of stalls. Kingston's biggest market is now at Fairfield West (half a mile E of town centre) on Mondays (until 13.00) with bric-a-brac, household goods, clothes, etc., offering some competition to the established stores, including Bentalls, Chiesman's in the central Market Place (with a listed Jacobean staircase) and Boots (with a Tudor facade dating to the 16C). Also in the Market Place is the *Market House* (1840), formerly the Town Hall. A statue of Queen Anne survives from an earlier building and there are two historic inns, the *Griffin* and the *Druid's Head*.

At the *Kingston Museum and Heritage Centre*, Fairfield West, Kingston (half a mile E of town centre; open Monday to Saturday 10.00-17.00), local history is displayed, including archaeological finds and Martinware pottery.

Eadweard Muybridge, founder of modern cinematography, was born in Kingston in 1830 and made his career in the United States. He bequeathed his collection of apparatus and photographs to Kingston in 1904 and it is now on view in the Museum which is also a tourist information centre (01-546 5386).

The *Kingfisher* in Fairfield Road, Kingston (01-546 1042) is a new leisure centre with swimming and sporting facilities.

The restored *All Saints' Church* in the Market Place has four arches supporting the 13C tower. The original church dates to before the Conquest and was the location of the Saxon coronations (as illustrated in the windows of the N aisles of the present church). Another 13C building, *King John's Palace*, stood at the site of the present police station. Near the Kingston Museum in London Road is a row of almshouses founded by William Cleave in 1669 and still in use. Kingston's grammar school uses the Lovekyn chapel founded in 1309.

The thriving residential surroundings of Kingston continue 3 miles S to **Surbiton**, a Victorian suburb established after the arrival of the railway in 1838, which at first by-passed Kingston.

Three miles to the S is **Chessington**, best known for its zoo, but with a medieval village church, *St. Mary the Virgin* (Garrison Road, off Leatherhead Road), which holds the smallest silver chalice in England, 3.5 inches high and hallmarked 1568.

Chessington Zoo, Leatherhead Road, Chessington (Epsom 27227). Open daily from 10.00-16.00 (winter) and 10.00-17.00 (summer). Access: Bus 65 or 71 from Kingston; BR, Kingston; or direct by Green Line. Admission charge.

The zoo has a large collection of animals in new and improved enclosures which aim to provide a natural setting. The educational Bird World area was designed by naturalist David Bellamy. A funfair and circus without animals are additional attractions. *Burnside Manor*, in the grounds, is used for 'Elizabethan' banquets and other functions.

Just to the NE of Kingston town centre is *Coombe* where John Galsworthy (1867-1933) was brought up and which he referred to as 'Robin Hill' in The Forsyte Saga.

35 Richmond, Putney, Barnes, Mortlake, Kew, Ham and Petersham, Teddington, Twickenham, the Hamptons and Hampton Court Palace

Richmond upon Thames, a flourishing suburb and growing commercial centre, has a delightul riverside location and a royal past which can still be traced at Richmond Green and in Richmond Park.

Access: BR or Underground to Richmond; by river from Westminster Pier (Easter to September only).

Edward III built Sheen Palace here in the 14C but as early as 1125 Henry I had stayed here. Sheen Palace was destroyed by fire in 1499; Henry VII had it rebuilt and renamed Richmond Palace after his Yorkshire earldom. It became one of the favourite palaces of the Tudor monarchs. Henry VII and Elizabeth I died here. After the execution of Charles I the main buildings were demolished. Royalty returned to Richmond in 1720 when George, Prince of Wales, the future George II, took over Richmond Lodge in Old Deer Park. George III also used the lodge but preferred Kew Palace.

The remains of **Richmond Palace** are in Old Palace Yard off Richmond Green and include the *Gate House*, with Henry VII's coat of arms, and the *Wardrobe*, reconstructed from the original Tudor building. At *Trumpeter's House* in Old Palace Yard, built c 1710, Metternich once stayed and was visited by Disraeli in 1849.

The four well-proportioned houses in *Maids of Honour Row* fronting the Green nearby were built in 1724 for the Ladies in Waiting of the then Princess of Wales. Old Palace Lane leads down to the Thames past the imposing *Asgill House* on the site of the watergate of Richmond Palace. This fine mansion was designed by Sir Robert Taylor for Sir Charles Asgill, Lord Mayor of London, in 1760. It is privately owned but can be viewed by appointment. A tiny public house, the Swan, is on the way. On two sides of the Green and in adjoining alleyways are attractive 17C and 18C houses including in Greenside, *Oak House* (1760), *Old Palace Place* (1700) and *Old Friars* (1687), on land which was once the monastery of Observant Friars. This architectural heritage makes Richmond Green one of the most unspoilt and attractive 'squares' in Greater London. On the Green there was jousting in Tudor times, and two centuries later cricket—the *Cricketer's Inn* is on the E side of the Green. Antique and gift shops, and boutiques now fill the alleyways which lead through to George Street and the Quadrant, the main shopping area.

On the Little Green to the E is the *Richmond Theatre*, built by Frank Matcham in 1899, its gaudy Victorian terracotta facade and green cupola somewhat out of keeping with the restrained 17C and 18C architecture. There was a Theatre Royal, known as the Theatre on the Green, on the other side from 1765 to 1884. The present theatre maintains this long theatrical tradition with pre-West End productions and Christmas pantomimes; there is fringe and cabaret at the nearby *Orange Tree Pub Theatre*. The Richmond Festival is centred on the Green and its theatres in June or July. The local tourist information centre is in the Library next to the theatre.

Richmond Bridge (turn right off Hill Street from the town centre—A305 to St. Margarets) is the oldest bridge still standing over the Thames in the Greater London area and was built between 1774 and 1777 by James Paine. Its five arches and graceful curve make it one of the most attractive as well, and it is popular with artists. Two pubs overlook the Thames here but the river frontage is liable to flooding. A major redevelopment including shops and offices is now going ahead to the E of the bridge. The local parish church, *St. Mary Magdalen*, in the centre of the town, has a 15C flint and stone tower. It is set back in Church Walk.

The view from *Richmond Hill* is famous and is best reached from the town centre via Paradise Road, Mount Ararat Road, and the Vineyard. In Paradise Road is *Hogarth House* (1748), the home of Leonard and Virginia Woolf from 1915 to 1924, where they founded the Hogarth Press. In the Vineyard are three groups of almshouses, *Michel's* (1811), *Bishop Dippa's* (1667, rebuilt in 1850) and *Queen Elizabeth's* (1767, founded in 1600), and in Ormond Road, just off Hill Rise, attractive 18C houses.

Below Richmond Hill are the *Terrace Gardens*, laid out as a public park in 1887 with the famous view of the Thames winding S and W, Petersham Meadows and Ham Common on one side and Marble Hill House and Park on the other. The *Richmond Gate Hotel* occupies several 18 and 19C buildings and its restaurant enjoys the same view. The *Star and Garter Home* for disabled seamen was built in 1924 in bright red brick and stands on the site of the famous inn connected with Charles Dickens and Thackeray. The nearby pub is the Lass of Richmond Hill. Attractive houses along Richmond Hill include *The Wick*, built in 1775 by Robert Mylne, and *Wick House*, built a few years earlier for Sir Joshua Reynolds by Sir William Chambers.

Here is the entrance to **Richmond Park**, although the 2500-acre park can be approached from several different directions.

This was a royal hunting ground enclosed in 1637 by Charles I. Some oak trees date back to the Middle Ages and there are about 600 red and fallow deer which now roam freely in this natural parkland. In the centre are the man-made *Pen Ponds* and the beautiful *Isabella Plantation and Woodland Gardens*, most impressive from mid-April to the end of May when hundreds of azaleas and rhododendrons bloom. Several buildings stand within the Park although nothing remains of the royal Richmond Lodge in Old Deer Park (on the other side of Twickenham Road and fronting the river) except the *King's Observatory*, built by Sir William Chambers and now used by the Meteorological Office. (Approach Old Deer Park along the Twickenham Road through Richmond's town centre.)

In Richmond Park is the *White Lodge* (three-quarters of a mile NW of the Robin Hood Gate in Roehampton Vale), built in 1727 as a hunting lodge for George I, influenced by Chiswick House across the river. Queen Mary, George V's consort, grew up here and her eldest son, later Edward VIII, was born here. It was the first married home of Queen Elizabeth, the Queen Mother. It is now the Royal Ballet Junior School, and is open to the public in August only, daily 14.00-18.00.

Pembroke Lodge (half a mile S of Richmond Gate—Richmond Hill) was the home of Lord John Russell and the childhood home of his grandson, the philosopher Bertrand Russell; it is now a restaurant and cafeteria. (01-940 8207; open January to October daily, November to December, weekends only.

Thatched House Lodge (1.5 miles S from Richmond Gate) was built by Sir Robert Walpole and is now the home of Princess Alexandra. It stands on the mound of a former icehouse.

Near Pembroke Lodge a prehistoric barrow provides the high ground from which it is said that Henry VIII watched for the rocket announcing Anne Boleyn's execution—St. Paul's Cathedral can be seen from here amongst high-rise office blocks.

There is access nowadays for cars (except commercial vehicles) through the park from 07.00 in March to November and from 07.30 from December to February until 30 minutes before lighting-up time. There are gates at East Sheen, Roehampton, Kingston Hill, Kingston and Ham in addition to Richmond Gate.

Richmond Ice Rink is on the other side of the river, in Clevedon Road, Twickenham (01-892 3646). There are walking tours of Richmond in the summer; contact Richmond Tourist Information Centre on 01-940 9125.

Putney, **Barnes** and **Mortlake**, to the NW of Richmond and on the S bank of the Thames, are attractive residential suburbs in the news once a year during the Oxford and Cambridge boat race in March, rowed from Putney to Mortlake. Near the start of the race at Putney is the *Duke's Head* (Lower Richmond Road) with attractive Victorian engraved glass. Nearby is the jazz-pub, the Half Moon. **Putney** itself is a growing commercial centre with a large heath to the S adjoining Wimbledon Common; this is the setting for the annual Putney Show in June. *St. Mary's Church* by Putney Bridge is being restored after a fire in 1977; the 15C tower and fan-vaulted chantry chapel survive but the brasses are lost. The first *Putney Bridge*, a wooden structure erected in 1729, was only the third bridge over the Thames (after London Bridge and Kingston), preceding Westminster Bridge built in 1750. The present bridge was built by Bazalgette in 1886.

Along Kingston Road, on the opposite site to Richmond Park, is the *Putney Vale Cemetery*, established in 1887 and one of the more fashionable in London with some interesting monuments erected before restrictions were introduced. Amongst those buried here are Jacob Epstein, sculptor (d 1959), Sir George Reid, Australian politician (d 1918), and William Routledge, the explorer (d 1939).

The village atmosphere survives in **Barnes** with an attractive green and duck-pond. *St. Mary's Church*, Church Road, SW13, damaged by fire in 1978, is being rebuilt—a Norman wall was exposed by the fire and the 15C brick tower survives. In *St. Mary Magdalene's*, North Walpole Way, the explorer, traveller, and translator of 'The Arabian Nights', Sir Richard Burton lies buried in an exotic tomb shaped like an Arabian tent.

The estate of *Barn Elms* in Rooks Lane, the former manor of Barnes, was leased to Sir Francis Walsingham in 1579 by the Crown; Elizabeth I stayed here. In 1884 it became the base for the fashionable Ranelagh Club (closed in 1939). Another house in the grounds was occupied by Jacob Tonson, the publisher, who hosted the meetings of the Kit-Cat Club from 1700-20 and also built a gallery for Sir Godfrey Kneller's portraits of its illustrious members (see National Portrait Gallery). Nothing remains of the houses but the grounds were used by William Cobbett in 1827-31 for a variety of farming experiments including the growing of maize. It is now *Barn Elms Park*, and school playing fields.

In Castelnau Road, Barnes, there are some imposing Victorian villas, and in the 18C Barnes Terrace the writer Henry Fielding lived at Millbourne House in 1750; later the actor Tom Sheridan lived in the same house. The composer Gustav Holst lived at No. 10 from 1908 to 1913. Actors and television personalities are the local residents of today and Barnes sports one of London's best-known jazz-pubs, the *Bull's Head*, in Lonsdale Road, SW13.

At **Mortlake** James I established a tapestry workshop in 1619 staffed by Flemish weavers; the workshop went into decline after the Civil War and by 1703 Queen Anne closed it down. Mortlake tapestry can be seen at Ham House, Hampton Court, and in the back of the priest's chair at *St. Mary's*, the parish church in the High Street, where there is also some local pottery on view. The church (1543) was rebuilt to a design by Sir Arthur Blomfield in 1905. There are monuments to Viscount Sidmouth, Prime Minister, 1908-04, and to his wife. John Dee (d 1608), a local resident and Elizabethan astrologer, was buried in the chancel of the old church. From the garden of *The Limes*, Mortlake High Street, Turner painted two views of the Thames. The house, now used as offices, was built in 1720 for Countess Stafford. The *Ship* in Ship Lane, SW14, is a 16C terraced pub, at the end of the Boat Race.

Watney's Brewery by the river occupies land previously the grounds of Mortlake Manor, once a residence of the Archbishops of Canterbury. The Earl Spencer, father of the Princess of Wales, is the present Lord of the Manor and keeper of the Court Rolls. Tours of the brewery can be arranged (01-876 3434).

East Sheen on the higher ground to the W has attractive houses in Christ Church Road; only the old stables and clock tower survive of *Sheen House*, built in 1786 and occupied by Lord Grey in 1830.

Kew (1.5 miles NE of Richmond by road, and on the Thames) owes both its botanic garden and attractive village setting at Kew Green to the existence of nearby royal Richmond Palace. The large Georgian houses around the Green were built for members of the King's Court in the reign of George III. The parish church of *St. Anne's* dates to 1714 and features a distinctive octagonal cupola. Thomas Gainsborough (d 1788), the painter, is buried here, and so are John Kirby, the architect, and Jeremiah Meyer, miniature painter to Queen Charlotte, Francis Bauer, George III's botanical artist (d 1840) and John Zoffany, painter (d 1810).

The *Herbarium* of the Royal Botanic Gardens on the Green houses the largest collection of dried plants in the world and is open by appointment to students. Near Kew Bridge is the new **Public Records Office**, Ruskin Avenue, Kew—the national repository of central government records (open 09.30-17.00. Tel. 01-876 3444).

Royal Botanic Gardens, Kew, Richmond, Surrey. Tel. 01-940 1171. Open daily 10.00 to dusk; museums 10.00-16.50, Sun 10.00-17.50; glasshouses 11.00-16.50, Sun 11.00-17.50 (earlier in winter). Admission charge. Access: Underground, Kew; BR, Kew Bridge. Car and coach parking.

Kew Gardens started as a small botanic garden in 1759 when Princess Augusta, mother of George III, was living on the Kew Estate in the White House (later renamed Kew Palace). Sir William Aiton was her head gardener and Sir William Chambers was employed to design several of the distinctive buildings which survive in the grounds today, including the Great Pagoda, the Orangery and three temples. The 9-acre site was considerably enlarged by George III who combined it with the Richmond Lodge estate. He and Queen Charlotte frequently stayed at Kew Palace (Richmond Lodge was then demolished); this was in turn demolished in 1802 and its position marked by the sundial in front of the present Kew Palace (formerly the Dutch House). In 1841 the now extensive Kew Gardens were handed to the nation and expanded to 300 acres. Sir Joseph Banks, who accompanied Captain Cook on his first round-the-world voyage, was the gardener from 1772 to 1819 when plants were collected from South Africa, Australia, and the Pacific. William Cobbett was a gardener here about 1775.

Sir William Hooker became the Director of the new National Botanic Institute and the Royal Botanic Gardens in 1841. Among its historic achievements are the introduction of the bread-fruit tree to the West Indies in 1791 (the purpose of the 'Bounty' voyage), quinine to India in 1860 and rubber-trees to Malaysia in 1875; in the late 19C Kew played an important part in restoring the European wine growing industry with imported American rootstock after it was wiped out by phylloxera.

Buildings of interest in Kew Gardens.

The red-brick **Kew Palace**, formerly the Dutch House, is close to the main gates. It was built in 1631 by a London merchant of Flemish descent, Samuel Fortrey. From 1727 it was leased by the Crown and became England's smallest royal residence. It is open to the public and furnished in the style of the period of George III and Queen Charlotte, who died here in 1818. Among the splendid paintings and furniture is a small collection of royal toys of the past. A formal garden in the 17C style lies behind the palace; the herb garden is most attractive.

The **Orangery**, built in 1761 to Sir William Chamber's design and one of the finest buildings at Kew, has windows only to one side. It was converted into an exhibition centre in the 1960s and provides a useful history of Kew Gardens as well as space for temporary exhibitions.

Museum No. 1, opposite the Palm House, opened in 1857. It contains information on commercially important plants such as rubber, and medicinal plants. Wood and wood products can be seen at *Cambridge Cottage*. A most remarkable display of paintings of plants can be seen in the *Marianne North Gallery*. The small red-brick building was designed in 1882 by James Ferguson to hold the collection of 832 oil paintings presented to Kew by the artist. Marianne North (d 1890) was an intrepid Victorian travelling painter and the colourful and intricate paintings overwhelm the visitor.

Kew Gardens' greenhouses are world-famous; the oldest remaining structure is the *Aroid House*, designed by John Nash in 1825 and moved here from Buckingham Palace in 1836; it houses tropical plants.

The *Palm House,* the most beautiful of all, covers 2248 square metres (24,000 sq. ft), larger than the demolished palm house at Chatsworth but only half the size of the Temperate House. It was completed in 1848 to a Decimus Burton design, and closed in 1984 to undergo major repairs and refurbishments; it is due to reopen in 1987.—The *Waterlily House* at the N end of the Palm House was built in 1852.

The *Temperate House* (recently renovated) was designed by Decimus Burton. Building started in 1860 and was not completed until 1899. It covers 5209 square metres (48,392 sq. ft). New boilers, ventilators and clean glass have greatly improved the growing conditions since it re-opened in 1982. It contains some 3000 species. The collection of greenhouses known as the T-ranges and the Ferneries is now the site for the building of a third large greenhouse, the *New Tropical Conservatory,* which will be partly underground.

The Palm House at Kew Gardens (Decimus Burton/Richard Turner, 1844-48)

This is due to be completed in 1985 and opened in 1986.

Other historic buildings include *Queen Charlotte's Cottage*, built in the 1770s as a summerhouse for the royal family and containing an exhibition of contemporary engravings.

South of Richmond lie two attractive river-side villages, **Ham** (2 miles S) and **Petersham** (1 mile S). The manor of Ham was royal land from the 12C and was included with the estate of Petersham, which belonged to Chertsey Abbey, in the dowry of Elizabeth Woodville who married Edward IV. Later the two estates passed to the Dysart family who retained possession until 1948. In 1610 Thomas Vavasour was granted permission to build Ham House within the Petersham boundary. In addition to Ham House (see below) there are attractive 17 and 18C houses in Petersham Road and River Lane. John Gay, author of 'The Beggar's Opera', lived at Douglas House from 1720 and Dickens first rented Elm Lodge in the summer of 1839. *Sudbrooke Park* in Sudbrooke Lane was completed in 1728 for the Duke of Argyll by James Gibbs. Now used by the Richmond Golf Club, it has a fine 30ft cube room and portico of Corinthian pillars. Captain George Vancouver, explorer of the Pacific coast of North America, lived in River Lane and is buried in the parish church of *St. Peter*. His death in 1798 is commemorated with an annual service in May. The church has a 13C chancel, a red-brick nave of the 16C with many later additions.

Petersham Meadows and *Ham Common* (125 acres) form part of the famous river view from Richmond Hill. Ham Common and its pond are surrounded by fine houses and charming cottages and the area is now a popular residential suburb with much 20C detached and semi-detached housing.

During the summer there is a ferry across the river from the bank near **Ham House** to Orleans House and Marble Hill House on the opposite bank.

Ham House, Ham Street, Petersham, Richmond. Tel. 01-940 1950. Open April to September, daily 14.00-18.00, October to March 12.00-16.00 (closed Mondays). Owned by the National Trust, managed by the Victoria and Albert Museum. Admission charge. Cafeteria. Access: Underground to Richmond; BR, Richmond; Bus 65 or 71 to Ham House. Car park.

Ham House was built in 1610 by Sir Thomas Vavasour, Knight Marshal to James I; successive owners altered the H-shaped building but it has been restored to its 17C appearance with original furnishings. In 1637 it became the property of Earl Dysart and passed on his death to Elizabeth, who married the Duke of Lauderdale in 1672. They enlarged and furnished the house so ostentatiously it became famous throughout the country.

Ham House is approached through a terraced garden; the doorway, surrounded by Corinthian pillars, leads into the Great Hall. The figures of Mars and Minerva on the fireplace are believed to represent the first Earl of Dysart and his wife. This floor contained the private apartments of the Lauderdales—the first floor was used for state occasions and approached via the Great Staircase from the Inner Hall. The elaborately carved staircase dates to 1637; baskets of fruit top the newel posts and the ceiling above in the Italian style is by Joseph Kinsman.

In the first floor rooms there are displays of costumes, textiles and miniature paintings, including Hilliard's portrait of Queen Elizabeth and David des Granges' of Charles II. In the Round Gallery there are portraits of Elizabeth Dysart by Lely, one as a young lady and another as the Duchess of Lauderdale. In the North Drawing Room local tapestries from Mortlake adorn the walls; the plaster ceiling and frieze are by Kinsman. The dolphin-carved chairs retain their original silk covers. There are Lely portraits in the Long Gallery. The Queen's Bedchamber was prepared for Catherine of Braganza, Charles II's consort—later it became a drawing room with fine tapestries by Bradshaw. The ceiling in the Queen's Closet is by Verrio and the landscapes by Thomas Wyck.

In the Duchess's Bedchamber on the ground floor there are four sea-paintings by Willem van de Velde and a painted ceiling by Verrio—others are in the White Closet and Private Closet. In the Withdrawing Room the furniture is covered in Spitalfields silk. The Chapel retains its original altar cloth; the furniture is carved by Henry Harlow. Paintings at Ham House in other rooms are by Cornelius Johnson, John Michael Wright, Sir Godfrey Kneller, Sir Joshua Reynolds and John Constable. The gardens are in the 17C style are most attractive and there is a pleasant cafeteria in the Orangery.

Twickenham is on the N bank of the Thames but SW of Richmond, as the river twists and turns S and W from this point. Like neighbouring Teddington it was once part of County of Middlesex and a known Saxon settlement in 704. Today it is a flourishing residential suburb, well-known for its rugby ground and some attractive historic houses of the 18C. Access: BR, Twickenham.

York House in York Street is a late 17C building now used as council offices by the London Borough of Richmond Upon Thames. It was once the property of Lord Clarendon (until 1689) and former illustrious residents include Anne Damer (from 1817), the sculptress, the Comte de Paris (from 1864) and the Indian merchant, Sir Ratan Tata who designed the gardens (1906-13) in the Italian style. The gardens are in two parts with a nymph fountain and a stone bridge across Riverside Road to a Grotto and a fine Italian sculpture group. Sion Road contains a fine terrace of 1720s houses.

St. Mary's Church in Church Street has a medieval tower and an 18C galleried interior. Alexander Pope (d 1744) is buried here; his monument reads 'to one who would not be buried in Westminster Abbey'. Further epitaphs by him and by Dryden to others commemorated in the church include one to Mary Beach, Pope's nurse and servant, Kitty Clive, the actress, and Thomas Twining of the tea family. From the embankment it is possible to cross to *Eel Pie Island*, mentioned in Dickens' 'Nicholas Nickleby'; in the 1960s rock and roll artists such as the Rolling Stones and the Who made the now closed hotel famous.

Follow Whitton Road, N from the town centre, past Chertsey Road to Rugby Road and *Twickenham Rugby Ground*—headquarters of the Rugby Football Union and the site of England's home internationals since 1910. Further along in Kneller Road is *Kneller Hall* built for Sir Godfrey Kneller, the royal portrait painter, in 1709-11; the house was remodelled by George Mair in 1848 and imposing turrets and pillars in the neo-Jacobean style added. It is now used by the Royal Military School of Music and there are open air concerts here on Wednesday evenings from May to August. (In a cost-cutting exercise it is proposed to move the School to Chatham.) *Twickenham Tourist Information Centre* in the *District Library*, Garfield Road

(01-892 0032), can provide more information. Church Street in the centre of Twickenham is now partially pedestrianised and there is a variety of speciality shops and boutiques. The Church Street Fair is held here during Twickenham Week in May.

To reach the site of Alexander Pope's villa head S from Twickenham towards Strawberry Hill along Crossdeep (about half a mile). A girls' school, *St. Catherine's Convent*, occupies the present building of 1842. Pope lived here from 1719 to 1744 and the fantastic garden became famous, designed to match the Gothic splendour of the house. *Pope's Grotto* survives and can be visited by prior application on Saturday mornings (01-892 5633).

Further along Crossdeep is *Radnor Gardens*, now a bowling green, and then **Strawberry Hill**, Horace Walpole's famous house. This is now *St. Mary's Training College* (Waldegrave Road, Twickenham) but the 'Gothick' interior has been carefully preserved. The house can be visited by prior application on Wednesdays and Saturdays (01-892 0051). It took Horace Walpole 30 years from 1747 to turn this simple 'plaything' house into a magnificent castle with details copied from famous buildings throughout Britain, including Old St. Paul's, Canterbury Cathedral and Westminster Abbey. Walpole wrote 'The Castle of Otranto' while living here (1754-76).

Marble Hill House is in Richmond Road, Twickenham, three-quarters of a mile to the N of the town centre (01-892 5115). It is open February to October, daily 10.00-17.00 and November to January 10.00-16.00, closed Fridays. Access: Underground to Richmond, BR, St. Margarets. Buses. Car park.

Marble Hill House and its 66-acre park are owned by the Greater London Council; there is a cafeteria in the stable block (open April to September).

The house was built in the Palladian style in 1729 for Henrietta Howard, Countess of Suffolk and mistress of George II. The final design was by the Earl of Pembroke; the builder was Roger Morris. The ground floor rooms are now used for exhibitions and the first floor has been furnished in the style of the period. An impressive mahogany staircase leads from the hall to the Great Hall on the first floor with carvings by James Richards. Small arcades and columns divide the rooms. Lady Suffolk received John Gay and her neighbours Alexander Pope and Horace Walpole here. Pope helped to plan the garden.

Lord Tennyson lived in nearby 18C *Chapel House*, Montpelier Row, in 1851-52, and *South End House*, Montpelier Row was the home of Walter de la Mare in 1950-56.

The remnant of *Orleans House*, the *Octagon Room*, is in Lebanon Park Road and houses the *Orleans House Gallery*, open from April to September, Tuesday to Saturday, 13.00-17.30, Sundays and Bank Holidays 14.00-17.30, October to March 13.00-16.30, and Sundays and Bank Holidays 14.00-16.30. Admission free. Access as for Marble Hill House.

On view is the Ionides Collection of 400 topographical works of Richmond and Twickenham as well as temporary exhibitions which sometimes take over the complete gallery. Orleans House was built in 1710 by John James and the Octagon added in 1720 by James Gibbs for James Johnston, Secretary of State for Scotland. The elaborately decorated stucco walls and ceilings were carved by Guiseppe Artaria and Giovanne Bagutti. From 1814 to 1817 Louis Philippe, Duc d'Orleans (King of France in 1830-48) lived here. A woodland garden surrounds the octagon which is all that remains of the house.

From the riverside there is a ferry service in summer (weather permitting) to Ham House opposite.

Teddington, 1.5 miles SW of Twickenham (access: BR, Teddington), was a fashionable residential area in the 19C with large houses whose grounds stretched down to the Thames. Most of these are now gone and have been replaced by substantial suburban houses. Thames Television has large studios in Broom Road by the river and other film and video companies are established nearby. The Anglers pub is a popular venue for the television community.

There is a footbridge from Ferry Road to Ham with a good view of Teddington Lock and Weir, the highest tidal point of the Thames.

Teddington has two parish churches: *St. Albans* at the Twickenham Road/Ferry Road junction, was begun in 1887 to a grandiose design by W. Niven but left half finished. It overshadows the old *St. Mary's,* opposite, of 16C origin. The actress Margaret Woffington (d 1760) is buried in the church and has given her name to a row of 18C cottages nearby. Sir Orlando Bridgeman, Charles II's Lord Keeper of the Great Seal is also buried in the church and the author of Lorna Doone, R.D. Blackmore (d 1900) who lived in Teddington, is buried in the nearby Victorian cemetery.

All Hallows church, in Chertsey Road towards Twickenham, is a modern building completed in 1940 but with an ancient tower moved stone by stone from All Hallows, Lombard Street in the City, when the 17C Wren church was demolished (1938-39). Memorials and furnishings also moved to the new church include a carved pulpit from which John Wesley preached his first sermon (in 1735), and the 18C organ.

Bushy Park, half a mile S of Teddington, can be reached from the town centre via Park Road, or from Hampton Court (BR, Hampton Court). It covers 1000 acres and opened to the public in 1838. The former home of the park ranger, *Bushy House* at the Teddington end, is now the *National Physical Laboratory.* The one-mile-long Chestnut Avenue which leads from Teddington to Hampton Court is edged by 274 horse chestnut trees. The Diana Fountain near Hampton Court was designed by Francesco Fanelli and placed here by Wren in 1714. To the W of Chestnut Avenue are the *Waterhouse Woodland Gardens,* Lime Avenue, and the artificial Longford River. Further W towards Hampton is *Garrick's Villa*; David Garrick lived here from 1754. On Garrick's Lawn, approached from Hogarth Way, a turning off Hampton Court Road, is *Garrick's Temple to Shakespeare* (1755) an Ionic Temple which housed the Roubiliac statue of Shakespeare now in the British Library. It is open Wednesday 14.00-16.00 during summer or by appointment (01-940 8351; see also p 355).

The Hamptons. ˙˙**Hampton Court**, 13m W of Central London, stands on the site of an early Saxon settlement. The manor established here at the time of the Domesday Book (1086) was vested in Walter de St. Valery and acquired by the Knights Hospitaller of St. John of Jerusalem in 1236. They sold the lease to Thomas Wolsey in 1514. A small village developed around the manor but 1m further W the village of Hampton became established, while 1m downstream to the E, Hampton Wick formed its own parish. During the 19C Hampton developed northwards towards Twickenham and the area here (just 1m W of Teddington) became known as New Hampton and later Hampton Hill. Today Hampton Court refers just to the area around the Palace, and the Hamptons have developed into separate suburbs. As late as 1980 former market gardens to the NW of Hampton were developed for housing.

HAMPTON COURT PALACE.

Access: BR, Hampton Court; Green Line, 716, 718 and 726; river services during
summer from Westminster Pier and Kingston. Tel. 01-977 8441. Open April to
Sept daily 09.30-18.00, Sunday 11.00-18.00, Oct to March 09.30-17,00, Sunday
14.00-17.00 (Palace); 07.00 to dusk (Park); March to Oct 10.00-18.00 (the Maze).
Admission charge. Car and Coach park. Free daily guided tours May to Sept
(except Sunday) at 11.15 and 14.15. Restaurant and Cafeteria in the grounds.

Hampton Court Palace is one of the most attractive historic buildings
in Greater London, with delightful gardens, a large park, and riverside
walk (administered by the Department of the Environment).

The Palace was begun in 1514 by Cardinal Wolsey, who intended a building
surpassing in splendour every other private residence. In 1529, as the Cardinal
fell from favour, he was obliged to surrender his Palace to Henry VIII, who
added the Great Hall and the Chapel. From that time for two centuries Hampton
Court was a favourite royal residence conveniently located on the Thames.
Edward VI was born here in 1537 and William III, who died in 1702 after a fall
from his horse in the Home Park, employed Sir Christopher Wren to substitute
the present East and South Wings for three of Wolsey's courtyards. After the
death of George II the Palace was no longer a royal residence but state functions
still take place here occasionally. The 'Grace and Favour' apartments surrounding the smaller courts are still the residences of pensioners of the Crown and
others. A Son-et-Lumiere production was held here most recently in 1984 over
two months in the summer, recreating the history of the Palace.

In the mellow red brick front of the Palace stands the *Great Gatehouse*
with oriel windows from Wolsey's time, terracotta medallions of
Roman emperors attributed to Giovanni da Maiano, and the arms of
Henry VIII. The moat in front is crossed by a fine bridge, added by
Henry VIII and guarded by the 'King's Beasts'. The *Base Court*
beyond the Gatehouse is the largest court and survives from the

The entrance to Hampton Court Palace

original Palace. To the left are several smaller courts, recreating the atmosphere of Tudor domestic architecture. Anne Boleyn's Gateway leads to the *Clock Court*, named from the curious astronomical clock made for Henry VIII. The graceful colonnade on the right was added by Wren. The entrance to the State Apartments is at the end; before it is a small exhibition on the history of the Palace in one of the former 'Grace and Favour' apartments.

The **State Apartments** in the East and South Wings contain some 500 paintings, among which the Italian School is best represented, and much of the original furniture and decorations.

Enter via the *King's Staircase*, with walls and ceilings by Verrio, to the *Guard Chamber* which contains more than 3000 pieces of arms. Opening off this are the panelled *Wolsey Rooms*, used by members of his household, with a charming view of the Knot and Pond Gardens and fine ceilings. The portraits here include: William Scrots, *Edward VI*; Gheeraerts, *Portrait of a Lady*, and Mytens, *Charles I and Henrietta Maria*. The *First Presence Chamber* contains a portrait of William III by Kneller. In the *Second Presence Chamber* are paintings by Tintoretto, Bordone and Bassano. In the *Audience Chamber*, with a view of the Privy Gardens, are: Tintoretto, *Knights of Malta*, *Nine Muses* and *Portrait of a Man*, and Lotto, *Andrea Odoni*. In the *King's Drawing Room*: Lotto, *Portrait of a Man*; Titian, *Portrait of a Man*, and Tintoretto, *Venetian Senator*. In *William III's Bedroom*, with a ceiling by Verrio, are the King's Bed and a clock by Quare which goes for a year without winding. The *King's Dressing Room* contains works by Holbein. The *King's Writing Room* contains; Pontormo, *Madonna and Child*; Parmigianino, *Portrait of a Boy*, and Andrea del Sarto, *Holy Family*.

Enter the Queen's Rooms, starting at *Queen Mary's Closet*. Paintings include: Pieter Brueghel the Elder, *Massacre of the Innocents*. The *Queen's Gallery*, completed for Queen Anne, has Brussels tapestries depicting the story of Alexander the Great and a mantelpiece by Nost. In the *Queen's Bedroom* is the State Bed in crimson silk; the ceiling is by Thornhill. The walls and ceiling of the *Drawing Room* were painted by Verrio—the windows command a fine view of the gardens. In the *Queen's Audience Chamber* there are Dutch and Flemish portraits. The *Public Dining Room*, decorated by William Kent, contains paintings by Sebastiano, and Mytens, *Charles II and the Dwarf*.

The three small rooms to the N form a suite once occupied by Prince Frederick, son of George II. The *Prince of Wales Presence Chamber* contains fine Italian paintings. The *Prince of Wales Drawing Room* has a portrait by Gheeraerts, *Louis Frederick*. The *Prince of Wales Bedroom* contains Queen Charlotte's bed, designed by Robert Adam, and some of Kneller's Hampton Court Beauties.

Cross the *Prince of Wales Staircase* with its elaborate balustrade and Mortlake tapestries depicting the Battle of Solebay (1672), and enter a lobby with a charming portrait of Henry, Prince of Wales with the Earl of Essex (1605). Beyond the Queen's Presence Chamber, enter the *Queen's Private Chapel* where the paintings include *St. Jerome* by Georges de la Tour. In the *Private Dining Room* is Van Eden's *Landscape with Waterfall*. The *Queen's Private Chamber* has works by Jan Brueghel the Elder.

A series of small rooms leads to the *Cartoon Gallery*, designed by Wren for the Raphael Cartoons now in the Victoria and Albert

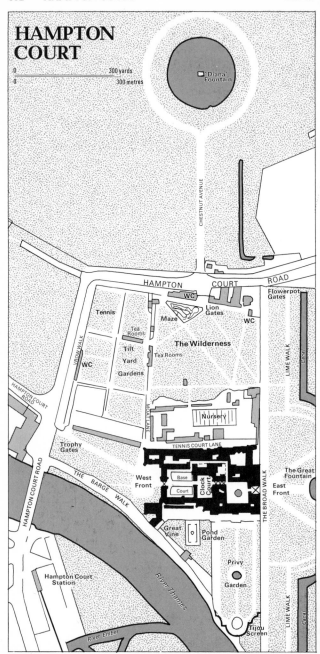

HAMPTON COURT

0   300 yards
0   300 metres

Diana Fountain

CHESTNUT AVENUE

HAMPTON   COURT   ROAD

WC

Tennis

Maze

Lion Gates

Flowerpot Gates

WC

Tea Rooms

The Wilderness

LIME WALK

Canal

Tilt Yard Gardens

Tea Rooms

VROW WALK

WC

Nursery

HAMPTON COURT ROAD

TENNIS COURT LANE

Trophy Gates

THE BARGE WALK

West Front

Base

Court

Clock Court

THE BROAD WALK

The Great Fountain

East Front

HAMPTON COURT ROAD

Great Vine

Pond Garden

Privy Garden

Hampton Court Station

River Thames

LIME WALK

Canal

River Ember

Tijou Screen

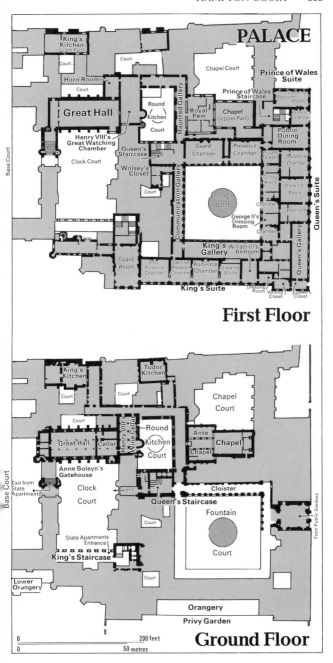

PALACE

First Floor

King's Kitchen (upper Part)
Court
Court
Chapel Court
Prince of Wales Suite
Horn Room
Court
Prince of Wales Staircase
Bedroom Room
Presence Chamber
Great Hall
Round Kitchen Court
Royal Pew
Chapel (upper Part)
Henry VIII's Great Watching Chamber
Queen's Staircase
Guard Chamber
Presence Chamber
Public Dining Room
Clock Court
Wolsey's Closet
Private Chapel
Audience Chamber
Court
Dining Room
Drawing Room
Base Court
Communication Gallery
Haunted Gallery
Fountain Court
Chamber
Bedroom
George II's Dressing Room
Chamber
Queen's Suite
Queen's Gallery
Guard Room
King's Gallery
William III's Bedroom
First Presence Chamber
Second Presence Chamber
Audience Chamber
Drawing Room
King's Suite
Dressing Room
Writing Closet
Queen's Closet

Ground Floor

King's Kitchen
Tudor Kitchen
Court
Court
Chapel Court
Great Hall
Cellar
Henry VIII's Wine Cellar
Round Kitchen Court
Ante Chapel
Chapel
Anne Boleyn's Gatehouse
Exit from State Apartments
Clock Court
exit
Queen's Staircase
Cloister
Base Court
Court
Fountain Court
From Public Gardens
State Apartments Entrance
King's Staircase
Court
Lower Orangery
Orangery
Privy Garden

0 _____ 200 feet
0 _____ 50 metres

Museum. It contains 17C Brussels tapestries copied from the cartoons, below which are paintings illustrating the life of Henry VIII. The *Communications Gallery* contains the *Windsor Beauties* by Sir Peter Lely, portraits of the ladies of Charles II's court.

The gallery leads to three small rooms including *Wolsey's Closet*, the only remaining room of his personal apartment with good linen-scroll panelling and vivid painted decorations. The *Cumberland Suite* was designed by William Kent in 1732.

Cross the upper landing of the Queen's Staircase with fine ironwork by Tijou and a brilliant allegorical painting by Honthorst of Charles I and his Queen as Apollo and Diana. Enter the *Haunted Gallery*, built by Wolsey, where the ghost of Catherine Howard is said to walk. The tapestries probably belonged to Elizabeth I.

Off it opens the *Holy Day Closet*, leading to the upper part of the *Royal Chapel*, built by Wolsey in 1505, with a fine ceiling and woodwork.

From the end of the Haunted Gallery enter Henry VIII's *Great Watching Chamber*, hung with Flemish tapestries which once belonged to Wolsey, then pass through the Horn Room to enter the **Great Hall** (106ft long by 40ft wide and 60ft high), built by Henry VIII in 1531-36 with one of the finest hammerbeam roofs in existence. The walls are hung with beautiful Brussels tapestries.

From its furthest end a flight of steps descends to Anne Boleyn's Gateway: turn right into *Base Court*.

In the right-hand corner of the Base Court is the entrance to the King's Beer Cellar and Henry VIII's New Wine Cellar; on leaving the wine cellars, turn left then right to reach the *Serving Place* and the *Tudor Kitchens* with huge fireplaces and ancient utensils. From the Serving Place dark corridors lead to *Fountain Court*, designed by Wren who occupied rooms off the W side of the walk. To the N is the entrance to the Royal Chapel (open for services on Sunday at 11.00 and 15.30).

The **Gardens**, entered from the E walk of the cloister, were laid out in their present formal style under William III. At right-angles to the Broad Walk which skirts the E front of the Palace is the Long Water which bisects the Home Park. To the left is the entrance to the old *Tennis Court* (open April to Sept), rebuilt by William III on the site of the court built by Henry VIII in 1529. Real tennis is played here occasionally. On the S side of the Palace are the *Privy Gardens*, at the end of which near the river is a fine iron gate by Jean Tijou, the *Elizabethan Knot Garden* of aromatic herbs, the *Pond Garden*, a sunken garden laid by Henry VIII and a later *Sunk Garden* in formal 17C style. Beyond is the *Great Vine*, planted in 1768 and still producing a crop of finest Black Hamburgh grapes each year.

To the right is the *Orangery* with an exhibition of horsedrawn vehicles from the Royal Mews; further on is the *Lower Orangery* with the famous series of tempera paintings, the *Triumph of Julius Caesar*, painted by Mantegna (1485-94) for the Duke of Mantua and bought by Charles I in 1629 for £10,500; they have now been restored. Opposite, overlooking the river is *William III's Banqueting House* (c 1700), decorated by Verrio (open April to September).

On the N side of the Palace is the *Wilderness*, laid out by William III with the famous *Maze*, planted in the reign of Queen Anne.

There is a restaurant and cafeteria in the Tiltyard Gardens.

On *Hampton Green*, W of the Palace-approach, are the *Old Court*

House, where Sir Christopher Wren died in 1723, and *Faraday House*, where Michael Faraday died in 1867. The *Royal Mews* and the 16C *Barn* are still in use. *Hampton Court House* on the side of the Green was built in 1757; the concert room added in the late 19C by the Twinings is now the *Hampton Court Theatre*. Along Hampton Court Road to the W is *Garrick's Villa*, given a new facade by Robert Adam when the actor came to live here in the middle of the 18C. Across the main road by the Thames Garrick had built a small temple dedicated to Shakespeare (see p 349).

St. Mary's parish church is 14C but rebuilt in the 19C, with a chancel by Sir Arthur Blomfield. Antonio Verrio, who decorated the walls and ceilings of Hampton Court Palace, is buried here.

36   Hammersmith, Brentford, Hounslow, Uxbridge, Ealing, Acton and Southall

Hammersmith (access: Underground, Hammersmith) is a busy commercial and residential suburb by the Thames in the throes of yet another redevelopment scheme at Hammersmith Broadway. Once an agricultural community supplying the City of London with vegetables, Hammersmith grew into a suburb with the arrival of the railway in the 19C. Today it supports two theatres, many historic houses and several attractive riverside pubs.

The *Lyric Theatre*, Hammersmith is in King Street, W6 (01-741 2311), in a new and otherwise undistinguished shopping centre; the interior is that of the 1895 theatre which stood in Broadmore Grove. Its greatest director was Nigel Playfair (1918-33) whose most successful production, 'The Beggar's Opera', ran for three years from 1920. The theatre closed in 1966 and was demolished in 1974. The plasterwork interior by Frank Matcham was saved and included in the main auditorium of the new theatre, designed by Derek Wool, which opened in 1979. There is a smaller theatre for experimental works, a bar and buffet.

The *Riverside Studios*, Crisp Road, W6, Hammersmith's second theatre, is located in former television studios. (Approach along Queen Caroline St from town centre.) The modest facilities are used effectively for dance, theatre and music, against a constant struggle for funding.

The *Hammersmith Odeon* in Queen Caroline Street (01-748 4081) is used for pop-concerts and the *Hammersmith Palais* for dancing (Shepherds Bush Road, Hammersmith, W6. Tel. 01-748 2812). The local parish church of *St. Paul's* in Queen Caroline Street dates to 1883; its Gothic structure is just visible above the Hammersmith flyover carrying the Great West Road. The font comes from an older church on the same site and the carved pulpit from Wren's All Hallows, Thames Street. There are memorials to William Tierney Clark, who built the first Hammersmith Bridge in 1827—London's first suspension bridge—and to Charles II, erected by royalist and adventurer Nicholas Crisp (d 1665).

Opposite is *Bradmore House* (1739), now part of the bus station designed by Thomas Archer; some of the panelling from the house is in the Geffrye Museum. Queen Caroline, wife of George IV, died in this house in 1821. Lucien Pissarro, son of Camille Pissarro and also a painter, lived at 27 Stamford Brook Road, Hammersmith, W6 (1900-44); his house became a meeting place for artists of the day, including Sickert, William Rothenstein, Charles Ricketts and Charles Shannon. The last two shared the studios at Landsdowne House, Landsdowne Rd, W11, with Glyn Philpot (d 1937).

From the present **Hammersmith Bridge**, designed by Sir Joseph Bazalgette (1887) and now closed to heavy traffic, Lower and Upper Mall stretch to the W, forming a delightful 2-mile-long river-walk towards Chiswick. Amongst the interesting houses are (from Hammersmith Bridge), the headquarters of the Amateur Rowing Association with a distinctive blue balcony, the *Blue Anchor* pub next door, and *Westcott Lodge*, an 18C house owned by the Borough Council. At *Furnivall Gardens*, attractive flower beds provide a breathing space between the river and the constant traffic on the Great West Road. The gardens are named after Dr F.J. Furnivall, the social reformer (1825-1910), whose sculling club was based at Hammersmith Pier and Creek. Privately owned boats moored here are the only reminders of the busy Creek where Stamford Brook joined the Thames; commercial river-traffic was heavy until 1921 when the Creek was filled in.

The *Dove Inn* is one of London's most famous pubs; it dates from 1750 and half of the building was used for the Doves Press. Charles II and Nell Gwynn are supposed to have met here; names of other famous customers are displayed above the great fireplace. There is a good view of the river and the boat race from the balcony. William Morris lived at *Kelmscott House*, Upper Mall, from 1878 to 1896; he named the house after his country home in Oxfordshire. Earlier it was the home of Sir Francis Ronalds, inventor of the telegraph, who laid cables in the garden in 1816 as part of his experiments. Part of his original telegraph can now be seen in the Science Museum. Morris set up the Kelmscott Press in nearby Sussex House. Plans were made in 1985 to turn Kelmscott House into a William Morris museum but it was sold into private ownership.

House-owners along the Upper Mall have secluded gardens along the river, some of which are open to the public on certain days under the National Gardens Scheme. At Rivercourt Road two large bastions mark the site of the house of Catherine of Braganza; she lived here after the death of her husband Charles II. The Old Ship Inn and the Black Lion stand on either side of the *West Middlesex Pumping Station* (1806) designed by Tierney Clark. Past famous residents of Hammersmith Terrace which follows include the artist Philip de Loutherbourg (d 1812), Sir Emery Walker, the antiquary (1903-33 at this house) and Sir Alan P. Herbert.

Chiswick. Hammersmith Terrace leads into *Chiswick Mall*, one of the most attractive groups of 18C houses in London, including Lingard House, Thames View, Strawberry House, Morton House, Eynham House, Bedford House, Red Lion House, the home of Nigel Playfair, and Woodroffe House. *Walpole House* was the home of Barbara Villiers, Duchess of Cleveland, Charles II's mistress, who died here in 1709. It is a fine example of the Restoration period. At the *Fox and Hound* pub, Alexander Pope lived with his parents until he moved to Strawberry Hill in 1719.

Past Fuller's Brewery, with its cobbled yard, 200 yards into Church

Street is the parish church of *St. Nicholas*. All that remains of the old church is the 15C tower, the rest was rebuilt in 1884. William Hogarth's grave is marked by a pedestal and urn with an epitaph by Garrick; nearby is the tomb of the artist James Whistler (d 1903). Others buried here and in the adjoining cemetery include Philip de Loutherbourg, the artist (1740-1812); William Kent (d 1748) and Colen Campbell, architects to Lord Burlington are also buried here, as is the Duchess of Cleveland (1641-1709).

Church Street leads to the busy Hogarth Roundabout—well-known from London traffic reports. Chiswick Square, with *Boston House* (1740), is nearby (left off roundabout).

Strand-on-the-Green, another stretch of fine riverside houses, is best approached from Kew Bridge (access: BR, Kew Bridge) eastwards towards Chiswick. Among famous residents of the 18C houses were the artist John Zoffany at No. 65 (1790-1810), Nancy Mitford, the writer, at Rose Cottage, Dylan Thomas at Ship House Cottage and Lord Cudlipp, newspaper owner, at No. 14. The *City Barge* at No. 27 has a 15C charter—the Lord Mayor's barge used to be moored nearby, hence the name—and the *Bull's Head* at No. 15 is 350 years old, as the exposed, blackened beams indicate.

Of great historic interest is **Chiswick House**.

Chiswick House, Burlington Lane, Chiswick, London W4. Tel. 01-994 3299. Open 16 Oct to 14 March, 09.30-16.00 (closed Mondays and Tuesdays); 15 March to 15 Oct, daily 09.30-18.30 (closed 13.00-14.00).

Main entrance from Great Chertsey Road. Access: Underground, Turnham Green; BR, Chiswick. Car park in grounds from Great West Road. Modest cafeteria in park (summer and weekends). Admission charge. Grounds open daily.

Chiswick House was built by the 3rd Earl of Burlington in the grounds of his then principal residence. As one of the greatest patrons of the arts of his day, he planned the house as 'a temple to the arts', influenced by two visits to Italy. The design was based on Palladio's Villa Capra near Vicenza but is not a copy. The summer parlour was built first and completed in 1729. William Kent was responsible for the interior and the garden. The old Jacobean mansion to which the villa was attached when completed was demolished in 1788 and the Duke of Devonshire (his mother was Burlington's only child) enlarged the house with wings designed by James Wyatt. In 1892 the Duke removed his treasures to Chatsworth and the house became a private lunatic asylum until it was purchased by Middlesex County Council in 1928. During restoration work after the Second World War the wings were removed and the house returned to its original design in 1958. It is now owned and run by the Department of the Environment.

Burlington's villa was a sensation when it was completed and influenced the architecture of private mansions throughout Britain. Artists and writers of the day were regular visitors, including Alexander Pope who lived nearby. Joseph Paxton, designer of Crystal Palace, worked when a boy in the gardens. Charles James Fox died here in 1806 and King Edward VII spent time here as the Prince of Wales in 1866-79, guest of the Duke of Devonshire.

The striking exterior design is best appreciated from the courtyard. Double staircases flanked by statues of Palladio and Inigo Jones by Rysbrack (c 1730) lead to the first floor entrance of the two-storey square, dome-topped building. Six Corinthian pillars adorn the portico, below which is the public entrance. The ground floor was Lord Burlington's private apartments and the layout radiates from an octagonal hall directly underneath the dome. The *Library* (left) contains an exhibition on the history of the building of the house and its restoration. There is a wine cellar below the hall and a corridor leads to the *Summer Parlour*, the link building with the now demolished house.

A concealed spiral staircase leads to the first floor; the *Dome Saloon* now houses the paintings which were removed to Chatsworth; *Charles I and family* (probably a copy of the Van Dyck in the Royal Collection); the *Moroccan Ambassador* by Kneller, *Louis XIII and Anne of Austria*, both by Ferdinand Elee, plus four allegorical and classical paintings by Guido Reni, Anthonie Schoonjans and Danielo da Volterra. The dome has been restored to its original colour and the busts are all replacement copies.

On the left is the *Red Velvet Room*, originally covered in velvet. The richly carved chimney pieces date to 1729 with paintings by Sebastiano Ricci.

The *Blue Velvet Room* has an elaborate marble chimney piece and a richly decorated ceiling by Kent. The Red Closet beyond also has an elaborate panelled ceiling. The *Gallery* runs the full length of the house overlooking the gardens. Despite its relatively small dimensions, it has been carefully proportioned with two arches to increase its grandeur. Statues of Mercury, Venus, Apollo and a muse adorn the central section. The central ceiling panel is probably a copy by Ricci of a work by Veronese. The *Green Velvet Room* has fine chimney pieces and a restored Venetian window. Above the doorways in the bedchamber are portraits of the Earl of Cumberland, Lady Burlington and Lady Thanet.

The *Gardens*, laid out by William Kent, marked a departure in garden design, away from the formal layout inspired by Le Notre towards an Italian style based on radiating paths, each revealing a different vista.

To the S a temple and a bridge by James Wyatt over a cascade are being restored. A tall obelisk incorporates a Roman tombstone. Most striking is the small-scale turfed amphitheatre with a pond in its centre and a small Ionic temple. N of the Summer Parlour stands the Inigo Jones gateway brought from Beaufort House, Chelsea, to Chiswick in 1736 as the stone tablets record. The path leads towards the Orangery, cafeteria and conservatory with formally planted Victorian-style flower beds in front.

Return to the Hogarth Roundabout to explore **Hogarth's House** on the Great West Road. The house survives behind a new office block.

Hogarth's House, Hogarth Lane, Great West Road, Chiswick, London W4. Tel. 01-994 6757. Open April to Sept, Monday to Saturday 11.00-18.00, Oct to March 11.00-16.00, Sundays 14.00-18.00 (16.00 in winter) (closed Tuesdays first two weeks of Sept and last three weeks of Dec). Admission free. Car park in W-bound layby of Great West Road. Access: Underground, Turnham Green; BR, Chiswick.

William Hogarth, the 18C cartoonist, painter and illustrator, used Hogarth House as his summer residence from 1749 until his death in 1764, and referred to it as 'the little country box by the Thames'.
  Following a period of neglect, a public appeal to buy the house in 1900 failed. Local benefactor Lt. Col. Robert Shipway stepped in, and restored and opened it to the public in 1902 as a Hogarth Museum. He presented it to Middlesex County Council seven years later. It was seriously damaged by bombs in 1940 and reopened after restoration in 1951. It is now run by the London Borough of Hounslow.

Hogarth House contains a selection of Hogarth prints and 18C furniture, revealing interesting glimpses of London life as well as reflecting Hogarth's strong social and moral conscience. In the Kitchen, now a gallery, three of the well-known moral series are shown: 'A Harlot's Progress', 'An Election' and 'Marriage á la Mode'. In the Dining Room hang the contrasting 'Beer Street' and 'Gin Lane' extolling the virtues of beer as opposed to gin. Hogarth's contempt for the papacy can be seen in 'O, the Roast Beef of Old England' or 'Calais Gate'. In the Best Parlour with its triple bay window, the rural view of the 1750s as shown in 'Mr Ranby's House' (Room 3) can be compared with the view of today. Hogarth's portrait is over the mantelpiece and the prints 'Industry and Idleness' show interesting glimpses of the Lord Mayor's show and an execution at Tyburn.

In the garden a mulberry tree planted by the artist still flourishes.

Brentford (1 mile W of Kew Bridge and 3 miles W from the Hogarth Roundabout), as the name suggests, was an important river-crossing and inhabited well before London itself. Julius Caesar is said to have first crossed the Thames at this point and archaeological finds from the riverbed collected by Thomas Layton (1882-1964), local archaeologist, are in the Museum of London.

The Battle of Brentford between Charles I and the Parliamentary forces in 1642 ended at Turnham Green with the royalists turning back from London. Today Brentford is recovering from its industrial growth in the late 19C which later left large areas derelict as heavy industry moved elsewhere. E.M. Forster, the novelist, lived at Arlington Park Mansions, Turnham Green (1939-70) and described the bombing of London's docks from his top-floor flat.

As part of the regeneration of the riverside, the London Borough of Hounslow and commercial interests have built housing, and in 1984 the *Waterman's Art Centre* opened. Purpose-built on the site of the old gasworks in Brentford High Street, the Centre overlooks the river and includes a 240-seat theatre, a cinema, art gallery, bar and restaurant with open air terraces. Waterman's Arts Centre is at 40 High Street, Brentford. Tel. 01-586 3312. *Waterman's Park* has been laid out on derelict ground nearby. (Access: Underground, Gunnersbury; BR, Kew Bridge.)

The *West London Pumping Station* which dominates the area visually was converted into a *Living Steam Museum* by enthusiasts who in 1975 formed the Kew Bridge Engines Trust.

Living Steam Museum, Kew Bridge Pumping Station, Green Dragon Lane, Brentford. Tel. 01-568 4757. Open Saturday, Sunday and Bank Holidays, 11.00-17.00. Admission charge. Car park. Access: Underground, Gunnersbury; BR, Kew Bridge.

The West London Pumping Station supplied London with fresh water from 1852 to the 1960s. On view are the Cornish beam engines dating from 1845 and 1869; the main beams are over 30ft long, and they are 'steamed' on public days. Electric pumps took over in 1944.

The *Musical Museum* in the former St. George's Church at 368 High Street, Brentford, Middlesex (01-560 8108), is looking for a new location. It is now (1985) open from April to October, Saturday and Sunday, 14.00-17.00. Admission charge. Car park in North Road. Access: Underground, Gunnersbury; BR, Kew Bridge. The Musical Museum contains Frank Holland's life-long collection of automatic musical instruments. There are ten reproducing piano systems and three reproducing pipe organs, including a giant Wurlitzer, as well

as 30,000 music rolls. Frank Holland will demonstrate the instruments—allow one hour for a nostalgic session of early 20C popular
and classical music.

In the centre of Brentford stands the parish church of *St. Paul's* (St.
Paul's Road), built in 1867 with a noteworthy painting of the Last
Supper by Zoffany. The older parish church, *St. Lawrence*, at the
western end of the High Street, was closed in 1976. The Butts, just
off Halfacre, was the site of parliamentary elections but is now a car
park. There are some fine early 18C houses here, including *Beaufort
House*.

The *Grand Union Canal* opened between Brentford and Uxbridge
in 1794 and Brentford, as an important trans-shipment point for goods
from the N, laid the foundations for its early industrial development.
The Canal can be explored by walking along the tow-path. Access
from Brentford High Street into Dock Road with a view over Thames
tidal lock. Several pubs survive along the canal. At *Hanwell* there is
a flight of six locks raising the canal 50ft in a third of a mile.

NW of Brentford is *Boston Manor Park* with a fine mansion house,
Boston Manor House, Boston Manor Lane, Brentford.

Open Monday to Friday 09.00-12.00, Saturdays (summer) 14.00-18.00. Tel.
01-570 7728. Admission charge. Access: Underground, Boston Manor.
   The attractive manor house was built in 1622, on the 14C estate and passed
to the Clitheroe family in 1670. They owned it until 1924 when Brentford
Council took it over and restored it. The red-brick house is well furnished; the
beautiful ceiling in the first floor drawing room which depicts the senses and
the elements is particularly noteworthy. The grounds, with 17C cedars, are a
public park.

1 mile N of Brentford is *Gunnersbury Park* with the *Gunnersbury
Park Museum* covering the history of the area.

Gunnersbury Park Museum, Pope's Lane, London W5. Tel. 01-992 1612. Open
March to October, Monday to Friday 13.00-17.00, Saturday, Sunday 14.00-18.00,
November to February, Monday to Friday 13.00-16.00, Saturday, Sunday
14.00-16.00. Park open daily. Admission free. Cafeteria (summer and weekends).
   The museum consists of two 19C villas which were the property of the
Rothschild family. It became a museum in 1925 and contains a collection of flint
instruments, other archaeological finds, exhibits on transport, domestic life,
costumes and local views. The Victorian kitchens are being restored.

The centre of the former village of **Isleworth**, 1.5 miles SW of
Brentford (access: BR, Isleworth) is by the river off Twickenham
Road. The modern church of *All Saints* by Michael Blee opened in
1969 with the 14C tower from the old church, which burnt down,
incorporated. Part of the 18C aisle walls have been preserved in the
open courtyard; a fountain has been added, and there are views of
the Thames from inside the vaulted church. There has been a church
on the site since 695. Nearby is the *London Apprentice* (1741), Church
Street, Old Isleworth, a famous river pub with original Hogarth prints
on display, named after the apprentices who rowed upstream from
the City on their day off. Across the river is *Old Deer Park*.

   Isleworth became fashionable in the 18C when large residential
properties were built along the river. But industry spread from
Brentford; Pears Soap had a factory here until 1962. Council housing
followed. At Mill Platt (off Twickenham Rd) there are 17C almshouses
founded by Lord Ingason next to the West Middlesex Hospital which
was based on the former workhouse (1837).

There are two important houses in the area open to the public: Syon House and Osterley House. **Syon House and Park**, including the Heritage Motor Museum and Butterfly House, are in Park Road, Brentford.

Access: Underground, Gunnersbury; Bus 237, 267. Car park. Syon House, Tel. 01-560 0881. Open Good Friday to end September 12.00-16.15 (closed Friday and Saturday) and Sunday in Oct. Park open all year round, summer 10.00-18.00, winter 13.00 to dusk. Admission charge. Cafeteria and Camellia Restaurant, tel. 01-568 0778.

Syon House, the property of the Duke of Northumberland who still lives here, was remodelled for the family in the mid-18C by Robert Adam. The exterior retains the simplicity of the original Tudor building constructed for the Protector Somerset after the Dissolution when he took over the Brigettine convent founded on the site in 1415. Queen Elizabeth granted the estate to the Percy family, Dukes of Northumberland.

Dramatic events from the past of Syon House include Queen Katherine Howard being confined here before her execution in 1542. Lady Jane Grey accepted the crown in 1554 and lived here for 9 days before her violent demise. Today's visitors can admire some of the best work of Robert Adam created at the height of his power.

The public entrance leads to the hall in pale colours with a diamond patterned ceiling by Joseph Rose. A large bronze, 'The Dying Gaul', a copy of an antique statue, is by the stairs which lead to the Anteroom, perhaps the finest room in the house, converted into a square by the addition of a screen of columns. The vivid colours are offset by the scagliola floor and rich gilding on the ceiling and on the capitals of the columns. The dining room is white with liberal gilding; the rich ceiling features arabesques, fans and flower motifs. The Three Graces in marble are in a panel above the fireplace. Red Spitalfields silk still covers the walls in the Red Drawing Room with paintings by Lely of Charles I and Duke of York. The deep-coved ceiling is decorated in Renaissance style with octagons and squares containing medallions of classical scenes by Cipriani in gold, yellow, pink and green. These colours, repeated in the Thomas Moore carpet, add lustre to the room. Two sideboard tables display mosaics from the Baths of Titus in Rome. In the gallery, designed to provide 'variety and amusement' for the ladies, Adam created a wide space with the use of geometric ceiling features. Authentic Adam furniture includes the marquetry tables. The Oak Passage leading to the exit is lined with 17C carved oak panels, paintings and a pictorial map of the Hundred of Isleworth, painted in 1653 by Moses Glover.

The gardens, laid out by Capability Brown in 1762 at the same time as Adam worked on the house, feature the (artificial) Long Lake, Flora's Lawn against a Doric column and mulberry trees planted during the Protector Somerset's residence here in the 16C. The *Great Conservatory* was added in 1827, designed by Charles Fowler. Paxton is said to have used it as a model for his conservatory at Chatsworth and later for the Crystal Palace. There is an aviary, aquarium and a Garden Centre selling house and garden plants but also including an exhibition of toys.

In the grounds of Syon Park are the *British Heritage Motor Museum*, in the stable block, and the *Butterfly House*.

British Heritage Motor Museum, Syon Park, Brentford. Tel. 01-560 1378. Open daily 10.00-17.30 Admission charge. Access as for Syon House.

This is the world's largest collection of historic British cars, showing production cars from 1895 to the present day including prototypes, rally and racing cars. Rides in historic cars can be arranged.

Butterfly House, Syon Park, Brentford. Tel. 01-560 7272. Open daily 10.00-17.00 (16.00 in winter). Admission charge.

A large number of different species of butterfly fly freely in a 'natural' indoor setting. During the winter months the display is limited. Good bookshop with specialist literature.

3 miles W along the Great West Road (turn right into Syon Lane, then Osterley Lane) is **Osterley House**, also of Adam design but overshadowed by its illustrious neighbour, Syon House.

Osterley House, Osterley Lane, Osterley, Middlesex. Tel. 01-560 3918. House open October to March daily 12.00-16.00; April to September daily 14.00-18.00, closed Mondays except Bank Holidays. Park open 10.00 to dusk. Admission charge. National Trust. Car Park. Access: Underground, Osterley. Cafeteria in stable block.

Sir Thomas Gresham, city gentleman, built the house in 1576 and received Queen Elizabeth I here. It became the property of the Child family of bankers in 1711 and they remodelled it between 1750 and 1780. First Sir William Chambers then Robert Adam took up the commission. The lavish interior which has survived intact is mostly the work of Adam. The Earls of Jersey left Osterley to the nation in 1923 and it is now owned by the National Trust and managed by the Victoria and Albert Museum.

The Elizabethan exterior of the building features prominent corner towers round a raised courtyard. Adam added the entrance with a six-column portico. The public rooms are on the ground floor with the private apartments above. The hall is decorated with low-relief wall panels portraying trophies of war. The gallery was probably designed by Chambers and Adam's contribution consists of the mirrored candle brackets. The original paintings have been removed and replaced by the Victoria and Albert Museum. The Eating Room is formally arranged with lyre-backed chairs along the walls. The rococo ceiling has a Bacchic theme, decorated with grapes and vines. The staircase is guarded by columns and designed as a frame for the ceiling, 'The apotheosis of a Hero' by Rubens, removed and since lost in a fire. The Library ceiling has been restored to its original bright colours; wall paintings are by Zucchi and Cipriano and the furniture is by John Linnel. The plain Breakfast Room has a rococo ceiling. The drawing room, described by Walpole as 'worthy of Eve before the Fall', features a great sunflower in the centre of the ceiling with radiating panels in green and gold; the sunflower theme is repeated in the carpet by Thomas Moore. The walls have been restored in 'pea-green silk damask'. There are two portraits by Reynolds. The tapestries commissioned for the house from the Gobelins factory to the designs by Boucher are in the Tapestry Room. In the State Bedchamber the four-poster bed designed by Adam has a small dome and a bedhead decorated with small boys riding dolphins. In the well-known Etruscan Room Adam introduced a design reminiscent of Greek vases.

The park, one of the largest estate parks still surviving in London, is cut in two by the M4; there is a Doric temple by John James (c 1720) with interior by Chambers and a lake. The Elizabethan stables and two summer houses are private residences.

Hounslow. Brentford High Street, now a backwater in Brentford, became a notorious bottleneck in the 19C as the main artery to the W. The *Great West Road* was built in 1925 to relieve this congestion and, with Western Avenue completed further to the N in 1921 (now the A40), this part of London became a major industrial growth area in the 1920s and '30s based on the large-scale use of electricity as a source of power. Along the 'Golden Mile' of the Great West Road between Hammersmith and Osterley some of the great factories of this era still survive. Wallis, Gilbert and Partners designed the art deco facades of the *Pyrene* building (1929), the *Hoover* building (1932) in Western Avenue, Perivale and the even more striking *Firestone* factory (1928), demolished in the teeth of a preservation order in 1980.

Striking London Transport architecture of the period pioneered by Charles Holden can be seen at *Osterley Station* (1934) with its curving walls and elongated 'Star Wars' pinnacle. After a period of decline, the 'high tech' industries are moving into glassfronted new buildings (Honeywell, Mowlem and Wang), although the Gillette Factory of 1936 survives.

Hounslow centre is split in two by its lengthy High Street which once carried travellers on their way to Bath. Today it is dominated by the Indian and Pakistani communities which settled here in the 1950s and '60s with specialist shops, temples, mosques and cinemas.

The parish church of *Holy Trinity* in the High Street was destroyed by fire in 1943; the new church was designed by Lt. Col. W.E. Cross. Beyond lies *Hounslow Heath*, once covering 4000 acres, but now a small park; it was notorious for highwaymen. Along the Crane river there were gunpowder and sawmills. For a short time after the First World War London's first air terminal was established on the Heath and the world's first regular commercial passenger flight took off on 25 August 1919 followed by the first regular airmail service on 11 November 1919—both to Paris. Croydon took over in 1920.

At *Heston*, 2 miles NW of Hounslow, *Heston Aerodrome* was used for private flying from 1929 to 1939. In the 19C *St. Leonard's* church, Heston, there is an Adam monument to Robert Child of Osterley Park; the tower is 15C and the lych gate a reconstruction from 15C material.

Heathrow, 15m to the W of Central London—5 miles from Hounslow—one of the three London airports operated by the British Airports Authority, was established in 1929 as a test flight base, and was used in the Battle of Britain (1941). It opened to international traffic in 1946. In 1953 it handled one million passengers and in 1984 25 million, making it the world's busiest international airport. There are three terminals (a fourth is due to open in 1986) and two runways. The Underground was extended to Heathrow in 1977 and a spur will connect the Fourth Terminal.

The *Queen's Building Roof Gardens* give good views over the airport. Open daily 10.00 to dusk. Admission charge. Tel. 01-759 4321. Access: Underground, Heathrow Central.

2.5 miles S of Hounslow at **Hanworth** the remains of Henry VIII's hunting lodge and the residence of Katherine Parr can be seen in the entrance of *Tudor Court* (Castle Way), a block of flats overlooking Hanworth Park. *Hanworth Park House* dates to 1820 and stands on part of the former manor, now a public park. *Hanworth Airport* was operational between 1929 and 1946 when it closed as Heathrow grew. *St. George's* church has medieval origins but was rebuilt in

1812; 16C stained glass survives in the N chapel.

1 mile to the NW is **Feltham**; the *Feltham Arena* is used for sporting events. At *Belfont Green* 1.5 miles further NW, almost on top of the airport, *St. Mary's* church retains its Norman doorway in a 19C building; restoration work has revealed wall-paintings of c 1250. The 'king' of the gypsies, John Stanley, was buried here in 1766.

Cranford, 2 miles further N towards the M4, has a village 'lock-up' in the High Street, the Round House, built in the 19C to detain prisoners before their appearance at the local court. *St. Dunstan's* church (15-18C), on the Feltham exit of the M4, stands in the former grounds of Cranford House, now *Cranford Park*, somewhat over-shadowed by the motorway.

Harmondsworth and **Harlington** are within half a mile of each other just to the N of Heathrow and W of Cranford, between the A4 and M4 and within the London Borough of Hillingdon in a virtual no man's land created by the airport. The church of *St. Peter and St. Paul* in Harlington is separated from its parish of Harlington by the motorway. The chancel is 12C and there is a notable carved Norman door. In Harmondsworth there are several listed cottages, a 17C pub, the *Five Bells*, and *St. Mary's* church (12-16C). Richard Cox, famous for the Orange Pippin apple, is buried here. Behind the church is a huge tithe barn, 190ft long and 36ft wide, built in the 14C on a disused farm, and in poor condition, said to be one of the finest in Europe.

West Drayton, 1 mile further N, has a traditional village green. The gateway of a mansion which belonged to Sir William Paget, secretary to Henry VIII, remains at *Drayton Hall*. The mansion, pulled down in 1750, was rebuilt by the de Burgh family in 1786. Napoleon III was entertained here in 1871. The house is now used as council offices. The family monuments are in the 15C flintstone church of *St. Martin*. Brunel tested his Great Western Railway between West Drayton and Langley, in 1837. It opened the following year, and the technical college named after him, founded in 1957, now *Brunel University*, moved to Uxbridge in 1968.

In **Hayes**, 2 miles N of Harlington, another village centre has been preserved although the area is now mainly industrial with new factories such as the Heinz building. The local manor house in the High Street is used as council offices. (Access: BR, Hayes & Harlington.) Opposite stands the church of *St. Mary's*, restored by Sir George Gilbert Scott in 1873 but retaining many of its original features and some Middlesex brasses. There is a life-size sculpture of Sir Edward Fenner, a judge, in his legal robes.

The Beck Theatre, the lively local arts centre, is in Grange Road, Hayes (01-561 7506); it provides entertainment, films, theatre and facilities for the local community. At Christmas there is traditional pantomime.

From Hayes it is possible to walk along the Grand Union Canal to Uxbridge (5m). Access in Station Road next to the Old Crown pub. It passes the *West Drayton Pumping Station* (1890) and the *Packet Boat Inn* where passengers used to depart for Paddington on barges drawn by horses.

Hillingdon, 3 miles NW of Hayes, has given its name to the whole borough. In common with nearby Uxbridge it now has a large Asian community, many of whom work at the airport. This has influenced the style of shops and restaurants in the area. The church of *St. John* *the Baptist* is cut off from the town centre by the busy Uxbridge Road at Royal Lane. The 13C church was rebuilt in 1848 by Sir George Gilbert Scott. Brasses include a magnificent one commemorating Lord and Lady Estrange (d 1479). Lady Estrange was the aunt of the little princes who died in the Tower. In Vine Lane on the other side of the main road is *The Cedars*, a 16C house which belonged to Samuel Reynardson, the botanist—he planted the cedar tree by the house in 1683. *Hillingdon Court* is a Roman Catholic convent and *Hillingdon House*, built in 1840 for the Cox family, is now owned by the RAF.

Uxbridge 1 mile to the W, once an important market town and coaching post, is now a busy commercial and industrial centre. The London Borough of Hillingdon has built new offices here. The *Civic Centre*, completed in 1977, has 700 windows set into its red-brick walls and striking sloping roofs topped by a cupola. Modern works of art inside include a stained glass window depicting Hillingdon's links with its twin towns. The meeting facilities in the Civil Centre are available for use by the public. Access: Underground, Uxbridge.

In a small conservation area in the High Street the *Market House* of 1788 has a fine hammerbeam roof dating back to the 14C. The *Treaty House* to the W was owned by Sir Edward Carr in the 17C when it was used for (unsuccessful) negotiations between Royalists and Parliamentarians in 1645. The panelling was sold to the Empire State Building in 1929 but returned as a gift to the Queen in 1955 and installed in the house which is now a pub. There is a market in the High Street on Fridays and Saturdays.

Brunel University was moved to the outskirts of Uxbridge from Ealing in 1968.

Uxbridge lies at the foot of the Colne Valley which is traversed by the *Grand Union Canal*. Villages developed into prosperous suburbs on the Buckinghamshire side and on the former Middlesex side, now the London Borough of Hillingdon. **Ickenham**, 2 miles to the NE of Uxbridge, is a good example of this growth, retaining its village centre, green, pond and an old inn in an increasingly modern environment. The local manor house, *Swakeleys*, is half a mile from the town centre (Long Lane, turn into Swakeleys Road). It was the headquarters of a sports club, but has been taken over by local residents who plan to open it to the public. The gardens are accessible. Swakeleys is a 17C building designed for a Lord Mayor of London, Sir Edmund Wright. Another Lord Mayor, Sir Robert Vyner, lived here at the time of the Great Fire of London when Pepys visited him. A mile S from the parish church of *St. Giles*, part of which is 14C, at the corner of Swakeleys Rd and Long Lane, is a 15C moated *Manor Farm* (in private ownership).

The manor of **Ruislip**, 3 miles NE of Uxbridge, was established in the 11C. Ruislip is now a residential suburb with large areas of open land to the N. Old village buildings remain: *Manor Farm House* is now council offices with one of the ancient timber barns used as the local library in the High Street. The *Great Barn* is 13C, as is part of the parish church of *St. Martin*. The wall-paintings are from the 15C. The *Swan* is a 16C coaching inn.

At *Ruislip Common*, N of the town centre, a *Lido* has been created on the side of a 40 acre stretch of water—a feeder of the Grand Union Canal. There are sandy beaches, a play area, a miniature railway and a water-ski club.

Eastcote Village, 2 miles NE of Ruislip (access: Underground, Eastcote), has some good examples of 18C and 19C building in the High Road. *Eastcote House* (demolished) belonged to the Hatreys who also owned Chequers, now the Prime Minister's official residence; a park survives.

Northwood, 2 miles to the N, is a pleasant suburb with mainly 20C housing, several old farm houses and the former manor, the *Grange*, now public offices. *Mount Vernon Hospital* has an art nouveau church of 1905, designed by F.H. Wheeler.

At **Harefield**, 3 miles NW of Ruislip, *St. Mary's* church retains its 12C walls. It is rich in monuments, including those to the local Newdigate family. Grinling Gibbons carved the marble statue of Mary Newdigate. Alice, Countess of Derby, rests in her monument on a four-poster bed, sculpted by Maximilian Colt in 1637. She is surrounded by her three daughters. Countess Alice built the nearby almshouses in the early 17C when she lived at the local manor house. Queen Elizabeth I visited her at the manor. In the rural churchyard there is an *Australian Memorial Cemetery* to 110 soldiers who died at the temporary hospital during the First World War; a special service is held on Anzac Day (25 April). At Park Lodge Farm, Harvil Road, Harefield, the GLC has established an educational centre where city children can learn about farming.

Harefield Chest Hospital is based on the former Belhamonds Mansion. Another war memorial stands near *Northolt Aerodrome* (RAF) on the busy A40, 2m S of Ruislip at Northolt. This is the *Polish War Memorial*, dedicated to the memory of 546 Polish pilots killed in action with the RAF in 1939-45. It was at Northolt Aerodrome that Chamberlain landed in 1938 after negotiating the Munich Agreement and promised 'peace in our time'. **Northolt** itself is a busy suburb which has expanded rapidly since the 1920s. There was a pony race track here in the 1930s but it has been built over. The 14C *St. Mary the Virgin* church overlooks the Green, off Mandeville Road.

Ealing, 7 miles W of Central London, was part of the Bishop of London's manor of Fulham, and was mainly farmland with residential development from the 18C. In the 1880s it was dubbed 'Queen of Suburbs' as the arrival of the railway and a tram-connection made it a popular residential area for city-workers. The Great Western Railway traversed Ealing in 1838 and the *Wharncliffe Viaduct*, Brunel's masterpiece, still spans the Brent river at the southern tip of *Brent River Park*. Industrial expansion followed with the building of Western Avenue. Some of the old coaching inns survive, including the *Old Hatte*, the *Bell*, and the *Green Man*. Today there is an attactive modern shopping centre at Ealing Broadway, opened in 1985 and designed in consultation with local residents, blending with the Victorian solidity of the Town Hall with its tower, spire and archway. (Access: Underground, BR, Ealing Broadway.)

St. Mary's church in St. Mary's Road has 12C origins but was rebuilt in 1740 and remodelled in 1866. Amongst the older monuments is one to the assassinated Prime Minister, Spencer Perceval, who lived at Elm Grove until his death in 1812. At *Ealing Green*, S from the High St, some Georgian cottages survive and in nearby *Walpole Park*, *Pitshanger Manor* was until recently used as a library (and may open to the public). The manor was built in 1770 and remodelled by Sir John Soane in 1801-02. He lived here himself until he moved to

Lincoln's Inn Fields in 1811. Later Spencer Perceval's daughters lived here and the Borough took it over in 1900. *Rochester House* at Little Ealing Lane, South Ealing, now a conference centre, belonged to the Bishop of Rochester, Zachary Pearce, and was built in 1712. *Ealing Park*, another attractive 18C house, was the home of Lord Warwick but is now a convent school. *Ealing Abbey* (Charlbury Grove off Castlebar Rd, SW6) the Catholic church, was begun in 1897 by Frederick Waters; damaged in the Second World War it was restored and reopened in 1965 with a new chapel of St. Boniface funded by the West German government.

Ealing Studios on The Green, Ealing, are now used by the BBC but were the location for the many famous Ealing comedy films of the 1950s and '60s. Ealing's *Questors Theatre* in Mattock Lane was founded in 1921 and has a 400-seat playhouse opened in 1964 for amateur productions.

Acton, 2 miles E of Ealing towards Central London, has a long history. The manor of Acton was created in the 13C and at one time belonged to the Earl of Bedford. The manor house of Berrymead was renamed the *Priory* in 1802 and is now used as borough council offices (Salisbury Street). The Tudor-style building retains some of its 16C interior features.

Turnham Green, which once joined Acton Green, was the location of a battle in 1642 during the Civil War when Charles I's forces caught up with the Parliametarians after the Battle of Brentford (see p 359). It is in S Acton toward Chiswick. Acton became a spa in the 18C and has three medicinal wells. It was soon abandoned for more

The new Ealing shopping centre (1985), designed by local architects in conjunction with the community

fashionable resorts and the assembly rooms turned into tenements.
Spurred on by the building of the Grand Union Canal, Acton
developed rapidly in the 19C with industrial and residential building.
Bedford Park, the first planned garden suburb, was built from 1876,
under the supervision of the architect Norman Shaw, in Queen Anne
style. It is now a conservation area.

On the N side of the 25-acre *Acton Park* (with sports facilities) are
the *Goldsmiths' Almshouses*, built in 1811 by the Goldsmiths' Company and distinguished by their coat of arms and clock. They still
provide a home for 20 families and widows. *St. Aidan*, the local
Roman Catholic church, was designed in 1961 by A.J. Newton;
paintings include a Crucifixion by Graham Sutherland and 'Christ
preaching to the People' by Carel Weight.

In **Shepherds Bush**, 1.5 miles E of Acton and 5 miles from Central
London, is the former *White City Stadium* (Wood Lane, W12), closed
in 1984 for redevelopment after an illustrious history. It was the venue
for the 4th Olympic Games in 1908 and in the same year it was used
for the Franco-British exhibition which attracted a million visitors.
Greyhound racing was introduced in 1927 but the Stadium continued
to be used for athletics and was also the home ground of Queen's
Park Rangers football club. The club is now based at Loftus Road,
London W12.

The main *BBC TV Studios* are in Wood Lane, W12 (nearest
Underground Shepherds Bush).

Between Shepherds Bush and East Acton along Du Cane Road is
Wormwood Scrubs, the largest prison in Britain, housing 1200
prisoners. It was built by prisoners between 1874 and 1890 to a
design by Sir Edmund Du Cane. George Blake, the spy, escaped
from here in 1966. Next to it is *Hammersmith Hospital*. *Wormwood
Scrubs Common* is used for fairs on Bank Holidays.

Southall (BR, Southall), 3 miles W of Ealing, is dominated today by
its Asian community which settled here from the early 1950s. Asian
shops, restaurants and Sikh and Hindu temples and mosques line
the High Street; local cinemas show Indian films.

Southall was granted a market charter in the 17C and still supports
a thriving market on Wednesdays, Fridays and Saturdays. The historic
cattle market is now a weekly cattle and horse market on Wednesdays,
the only one remaining in London (Southall Horse Market, Southall
High Street, Southall. Tel. 01-574 1611). There is also a Sunday
morning market, Western International, in Hayes Road, Southall,
specialising in clothes and household goods.

Southall Manor on the Green is in Tudor style with 17C interior
panelling; it is now used by the Chamber of Commerce. Southall's
parish church of *St. Mary's* at Norwood Green has Norman origins
but was rebuilt in the 15C. The altar tomb is dedicated to the family
of Edward Cheseman, of Norwood Manor.

The Martin brothers were born in Southall and moved their pottery
here from Fulham in 1877, creating the distinctive Martinware at
their workshop until 1923. There is a collection of Martinware on
view at the *Southall Public Library*, Osterley Park Road (off the
Green), Southall (access: BR, Southall).

At *Southall Railway Centre*, Merrick Road, Southall (01-574 1529)
a former railway engine shed houses a collection of steam and diesel
locomotives and rolling stock. Open Saturday and Sunday 11.00–
18.00. Admission charge.

Norwood, 1 mile S of Southall, was well-known for its brick fields which can still be seen. The bricks for the building of Buckingham Palace came from Norwood.

At **Greenford**, 1.5 miles NE of Southall, the old church stands next to a new church of the *Holy Cross*. The old church is 14C and features some excellent glass including the coat of arms of Henry VIII and Katherine of Aragon in the E window as well as the arms of Eton and King's colleges. In common with St. Mary's at Perivale, the oldest church in the borough, it has a weatherboarded tower. **Perivale**, 2 miles NE of Greenford, is an industrial suburb of the 1920s and '30s characterised by the gleaming white *Hoover* building and the *Sanderson* factory, amongst many others.

37 Windsor and Eton

WINDSOR, 21 miles W from Central London, is not within the Greater London area, but its inclusion in this book is justified by the fact that it is the most popular day-trip from London for visitors.

Access: by road, M4, junction 6; BR, from Waterloo or Paddington (change at Slough); Green Line Coach, 700 (May–Oct), 702, 704, 718 (all year) from Eccleston Bridge, Victoria; guided tours (see below).

Tourist Information Centre at Windsor and Eton Central Station (Windsor (66) 52010). Shops close early Monday and Wednesday.

English kings and queens have lived at Windsor for 900 years; Saxon kings first settled at Old Windsor but their palace of Kingsbury was allowed to crumble after William I built a wooden fortress at New Windsor in 1066. In 1276 the borough received its royal charter and in 1974 it became the Royal Borough of Windsor and Maidenhead. It is sited on the S bank of the Thames, and connected by footbridge to Eton.

Thames Street ascends from the river and car park; on the corner is a memorial to George V by Lutyens (1937). Here also is a modern shopping precinct. The High Street climbs between the Castle Bastions and 18C houses, now shops. The statue of Queen Victoria at Castle Hill is by Sir Edgar Boehm and was erected to celebrate her Diamond Jubilee—it was unveiled by the Queen in 1887. Castle Hill leads to the entrance to **Windsor Castle**.

Windsor Castle: precincts open daily except Garter Day; the Castle is open March to Oct 10.30–16.30, Nov to Feb 10.30–14.30. State Apartments, open as for Castle but closed when royal family is in residence; check on Windsor 68286. Dolls House and Exhibition of Drawings, open as State Apartments. St. George's Chapel open in winter 10.45–15.45 (Sundays 14.00–15.45) and in summer 10.45–16.00 (Sundays 14.00–16.00). Admission charge.
    The ceremony of the Changing of the Guard takes place daily (except Sunday) at 11.00 by the Castle entrance. The Garter Service is held in St. George's Chapel in June (tickets for the precinct: write to the Lord Chamberlain's Office, St. James's Palace, London SW1).

Windsor Castle is built on a chalk cliff rising abruptly above the Thames. It was rebuilt in stone by Henry II and then improved and extended by Henry III and Edward III, preserving, however, the original plan of two baileys and a mote-hill. Henry I's marriage to Adeliza of Louvain (1121) was the first royal wedding to be celebrated here; Edward III was born in the castle in 1312 and Henry IV in 1421. Three kings, David II of Scotland, John of France, and James I of Scotland, have been imprisoned within its walls; from his cell window James first saw his future wife, Jane Beaufort. Edward III's queen, Philippa of Hainault, died here in 1369. The present appearance of the building dates from the extensive restorations undertaken by Wyatville under George IV.

Enter the *Lower Ward* from *Henry VIII's Gateway*; in front is the entrance to the *Horseshoe Cloisters*, built during Edward IV's reign, at the NW angle of which stands the *Curfew Tower* with a 13C interior. The tower houses eight chapel bells and an unusual clock of 1689 which chimes every 3 hours. On the right are the houses of the Military Knights of Windsor, an order founded by Edward III as the 'Poor Knights of Windsor' at the same time as the Order of the Garter. It was given its present name by William IV in 1833. The central tower (1359) bears the arms of Philip and Mary.

St. George's Chapel is a superb Perpendicular building, begun in 1478 by Henry Janyns for Edward IV and continued in 1503-11 by William Vertue. As one of the most perfect specimens of 15-16C Gothic work, it ranks with King's College Chapel, Cambridge and Henry VII's Chapel at Westminster.

Enter by the S door and walk through the choir and the nave. The *Nave* has a fine lierne vault with carved bosses. At the SW corner is the *Beaufort Chapel* where the tomb of the Earl of Worcester (d 1526) has a Flemish bronze grating, unusual in Britain. The great West Window contains fine glass of 1503-09. In the NW corner is the tomb of George VI (d 1936) by Lutyens and Reid Dick, and of Queen Mary (d 1953), with the theatrical tomb of Princess Charlotte (d 1817) in the Urswick Chapel behind.

The *Choir* is separated from the nave by a Gothic screen (c 1785) by Henry Emlyn. The organ, originally centrally placed (as in King's College Chapel), was rebuilt in flanking sections to give a better view of the fan vaulting. In the *North Choir Aisle* is (left) the *Rutland Chapel* (1481) with effigies of George Manners (d 1513) and his wife. To the right is the *Chantry Chapel of William, Lord Hastings* with contemporary paintings of his execution in 1483; to the left is the memorial chapel of George VI (1969). To the N of the High Altar a superb pair of gates (1482) fronts the tomb of Edward IV. Above is the Royal Pew, a splendid wooden oriel provided by Henry VIII for Catherine of Aragon. In the centre of the floor is a vault containing the remains of Henry VIII, Jane Seymour and Charles I. The Stalls, in three tiers, are surmounted by the helmets, crests and banners of the 26 Knights of the Garter, whose installations have taken place at Windsor since 1348. The reverse stalls are those of the royal family, the Sovereign's Stall marked by the Royal Standard.

Past the Screen turn left; the Bray Chapel contains the cenotaph of the Prince Imperial, son of Napoleon III, killed in S Africa in 1879. In the *South Choir Aisle* the *Chantry of John Oxenbridge*, with paintings of 1522, is on the left; it also contains the great sword of Edward III and the simple slab marking the tomb of Henry VI. On the S side of the altar is the tomb of Edward VII and Queen Alexandra (by Mackennal). The SE Chapel, with the tomb of the Earl of Lincoln (d 1585), is called the *Lincoln Chapel* or *John Schorne's Tower*, from the relics of Sir John Schorne (d 1314) brought here in 1478 from North Marston in Bucks.

The E wall of the ambulatory once formed the W front of Henry III's Chapel (1240-48) and retains its original doors. Beyond the floor slab of Sir Jeffry Wyatville the NE Door leads through a slype, or passage, to the *Dean's Cloister*, preserving arcading of Henry III's chapel and a piece of fresco. To the N is the picturesque *Canon's Cloister* of 1353-56.

The **Albert Memorial Chapel** was rebuilt by Henry VII as a burial place for Henry VI but later later completed by Wolsey—his tomb was never used and was broken up during the Civil War. Queen Victoria had the chapel converted into a splendid memorial to Prince Albert (d 1861) who is buried at Frogmore. The cenotaph of Prince Albert is by Baron Triqueti. The chapel also contains the tombs of the Duke of Clarence (d 1892), the elder son of Edward VII, by Alfred Gilbert, and of the Duke of Albany (d. 1884), Queen Victoria's youngest son. Beneath the chapel George III, Queen Charlotte, and six of their sons (including George IV and William IV) are buried.

To the left of the entrance to the North Terrace is the *Winchester Tower*, where Chaucer may have lived in 1390 when Master of the Works at Windsor. From the North Terrace there is a view of the Home Park, Eton, and Stoke Poges church.

Below is St. George's School, the choir school in the building (1802) of Travers College, founded in 1795 from a bequest of Samuel Travers (d 1725) for 'Naval Knights', an order corresponding to the Military Knights (see above) but disbanded in 1892.

From the N Terrace enter the *****State Apartments**, which occupy the N wing of the Upper Ward. These are used mainly for royal functions and contain many notable paintings from the royal collections, superb furniture, and other treasures.

From the China Gallery ascend the *Grand Staircase*, with a statue of George IV by Chantrey, and armour made for Henry VIII and the sons of James I. *Charles II's Dining Room* has a ceiling by Verrio and carvings by Grinling Gibbons. In the *King's Drawing Room*, or *Rubens Room*, is a series of noble works by Rubens (Holy Family, etc.) and a St. Martin by Van Dyck. The *State Bedchamber* contains a fine Louis Seize bed; in the adjoining *Dressing Room*, or *Lesser Bedroom*, are a painting by Van Dyck (Charles I, from three points of view, for use in the execution of a bust), and many of the smaller paintings: portraits by Clouet, Memling, Dürer, and And. del Sarto; by Rubens (of himself and of Van Dyck), and by Holbein. In the *King's Closet* are Venetian views by Canaletto and portraits of David Garrick by Hogarth and Reynolds. The *Queen's Drawing Room* contains an unequalled array of portraits by Van Dyck; Charles I, Henrietta Maria, their children, and members of the court; also James II as Duke of York (Dobson); 17C French and English furniture.

Continue into an older wing (renewed by Charles II), where the *Queen's Ballroom* has more characteristic views by Canaletto. The *Queen's Audience Chamber* has Gobelins tapestries, and portraits of the Princes of Orange (by Honthorst) in frames carved by Grinling Gibbons; the *Queen's Presence Chamber* continues the series of tapestries. Both these rooms have ceilings by Verrio glorifying Queen Catherine of Braganza. Here also is a bust of Handel by Roubiliac. The *Queen's Guard Chamber* displays a fine suit of armour (1585) made for Sir Christopher Hatton, and busts (Philip II, Charles V) by Leone Leoni. Above busts of Marlborough and Wellington hang the replica standards that constitute the annual rent for Woodstock and Stratfield Saye. A bust of Churchill was commissioned from Oscar Nemon (1953). The noble *St. George's Hall*, 185ft long, in which the festivities of the Order of the Garter are held, bears on the ceiling and walls the coats-of-arms of the knights since 1348. The portraits of English sovereigns from James I to George IV are by Van Dyck, Kneller, etc. Among the parallel range of busts (by Nollekens, Chantrey, etc.) that by Roubiliac represents George II (*not* I). The *Grand Reception Room* has fine Gobelins tapestries, the *Throne Room* or *Garter Room* contains portraits of sovereigns in their Garter robes. The large *****Waterloo Chamber*, constructed in 1830 inside a 12C court, contains portraits, mostly by Lawrence, of people who were instrumental in the downfall of Napoleon. From the *Grand Vestibule* beyond, with relics of Napoleon and the Japanese surrender sword (early 15C) of 1945, descend by King John's Tower to the Quadrangle.

In a room to the left of the entrance is *Queen Mary's Dolls House* and the *Exhibition of Old Master Drawings* from the royal collection. The Dolls House was given to the nation by Queen Mary in 1923; it was designed by Lutyens and measures 8ft by 5ft. Details include books and paintings by contemporary authors and artists, working plumbing and electric lighting. The exhibition of drawings displays changing selections from the Queen's priceless collection, including works by Leonardo da Vinci and Holbein.

The **Round Tower** or *Keep* provides a magnificent view (220 steps); elliptical in plan, its lower half of 1170 was heightened by Wyatville.—The *Private Apartments of the Queen* are on the E side of the Upper Ward (no admission). The passage between the Round Tower and the Upper Ward leads through St. George's Gateway to Castle Hill, near the entrance to the *Royal Stables*.

To the N and E of the Castle is the *Home Park*; in the S part are *Frogmore House* and *Mausoleum*. The latter contains the remains of the Prince Consort and Queen Victoria. Also buried here is the Duke of Windsor, King Edward VIII (1894-1972). It is usually open on the first Wednesday and Thursday in May, 10.00-dusk, and on the Wednesday nearest to 24 May (Queen Victoria's birthday).

Windsor *Guildhall* off Castle Hill was a museum and local assembly centre but it is now closed. It was designed by Sir Thomas Fitch in 1687 and finished by Sir Christopher Wren in 1707. Wren completed the Market House and the Guildhall Chamber, supported on Portland stone pillars. It is adorned with statues of Queen Anne and Prince George of Denmark and contains royal portraits and collections of Windsor's silver plate.

The parish church of *St. John the Baptist* in the High Street was rebuilt in 1822; it contains a Last Supper ascribed to Franz de Cleyn (1588-1658) and carvings by Grinling Gibbons and others. There is a large brass-rubbing centre (open daily, Easter to November) with reproduction brasses from all over S England. Market Street and Church Street are both cobbled and have attractive houses.

In the *Royal Mews*, St. Albans Street, visitors can see the Queen's horses and carriages, including the Scottish State Coach, used at the 1981 royal wedding. Also on display is a selection of gifts presented to the Queen for her Silver Jubilee in 1977. The Royal Mews is open Monday to Saturday all the year round (as State Apartments), and Sundays 13.30-16.30.

Opposite Castle Hill is *Windsor and Eton Central Station*, half of which has been converted into *Madame Tussaud's Royalty and Railways Exhibition* (open daily 09.30-17.30. Admission charge).

The original Royal Waiting Room and large Jubilee Glass Canopy built for the present station by the Great Western Railway Company to celebrate Queen Victoria's Diamond Jubilee have been restored. Madame Tussaud's have added life-like figures of all the personalities involved; they have restored railway carriages and built a full-size replica of the Queen-class locomotive, one of the most powerful engines of the time, which pulled the train in which the foreign royal guests arrived to be received by Queen Victoria.

In Thames Street is the *Theatre Royal, Windsor*, founded in 1792; George III was its royal patron. The present building dates from 1815. The theatre is the centre of the Windsor Festival, held annually in September with concerts in St. George's Chapel and Eton College.

The *Household Cavalry Museum*, Combermere Barracks, is in St.

Leonards Road, just S of central Windsor on the way to Windsor Safari Park. The museum is open Monday to Friday all year, and on Sundays from Easter to September. It contains one of the country's most comprehensive collections of arms, saddlery, standards and uniforms

S of Windsor is **Windsor Great Park** (nearly 2000 acres), traversed by the road to Ascot and the Long Walk. The latter, planted with elms by Charles II and replanted after 1945 with horse chestnut amd plane trees, stretches straight from the Castle to *Snow Hill* (2.75 miles) which bears a huge statue of George III ('The Copper Horse') by Westmacott. Still within the park, best approached via Old Windsor village, along winding Crimp Lane (where Shelley had a cottage in 1816) is (4.5 miles) the *Savill Garden*. Open 10.00-18.00 in summer, 10.00-dusk in winter. The garden comprises 20 acres of lovely woodland named after a former park ranger.

The *Windsor Safari Park* (open daily 10.00-dusk, admission charge) includes a drive-round section (bus tours available) where wild animals such as lions, cheetahs, baboons and camels wander freely. There is a children's zoo, picnic areas and a dolphinarium, as well as restaurants.

Tours of Windsor: during the summer there are guided walking tours from the Central Station's tourist information centre, open-top bus tours from Castle Hill, and river trips from the Promenade.

Across Windsor Bridge (access from Thames Avenue; no cars) is **Eton**, a town with several attractive antique shops and **Eton College**, founded by Henry VI in 1440 and perhaps the best-known of all English schools. Famous Etonians include Fielding, the elder and younger Pitt, the Walpole brothers, Gray, Shelley, Wellington, Canning and Gladstone.

Eton College is open 14.00-17.00 during school terms, daily 10.30-17.00 during holidays (April to October, closed in winter). For guided tours contact Eton College Tourist Manager (Windsor 63593).

The main block of fine mellow brick includes two courts or quadrangles. The larger—School Yard—contains a statue of Henry VI (1719). A frieze commemorates 1157 Etonians who fell in the First World War and 748 killed in the Second. Above is the *Upper School* (1689-94) with busts of eminent Etonians, damaged in 1941 but restored; the panelled walls and staircases are covered with names of boys going on to King's (earliest 1577), with wooden pillars of c 1625. The *Chapel, a Perpendicular structure begun in 1441 and completed in 1483, has a fan vault added in 1958 by Sir William Holford. A superb series of wall-paintings (1479-88) of British workmanship was discovered in 1847 and has been restored; the stained-glass E window is by Evie Hone (1952) and the clerestory windows are by John Piper. A museum opened in 1985.

A fine gatehouse of c 1517 erected by Provost Lupton leads to the second court or *Cloisters*, with the Collegers' *Dining Hall* (1450) and the *College Library* (1725-29) above it.—In the playing fields beyond is the 'wall' which gives its name to the 'wall-game', a style of football peculiar to Eton.

Between Windsor and Staines is *Runnymede*, where King John signed the Magna Carta, the great charter of English liberties, on 15 June 1215. Runnymede was given to the nation in 1921; Sir Edwin

Lutyens designed the commemorative pillars and flanking lodges which were unveiled by the Prince of Wales, later Edward VIII, in 1932. Further memorials include the Magna Carta Memorial (1957), the John F. Kennedy Memorial (1965) and the Commonwealth Air Force Memorial (1953).

38   Wembley, Willesden, Brent Cross, Harrow, Pinner, Stanmore

Wembley, in many ways a typical suburb of the 1920s and '30s, is best known for *Wembley Stadium*, built in 1923 for the British Empire Exhibition which opened in 1924, attracting some 27 million visitors in two years. It holds up to 100,000 spectators and is the venue for the annual Football Association Cup Final (in May), other sports events and pop concerts.

Tours of the stadium (01-903 4864) include a visit to the changing rooms, a walk through the Players' Tunnel with sound effects of cheering crowds, and a visit to the Royal Box. Tours are on Monday to Wednesday and Friday to Sunday except when the stadium is being used. Admission charge.

The Palaces of Industry and Arts built as part of the British Empire Exhibition are now used as industrial warehouses in the area N of the *Empire Pool*, now known as *Wembley Arena* (1934). The arena has a spectacular 240ft-high roof; it is used for show-jumping, ice-shows and concerts. The *Wembley Conference Centre*, added to the complex in 1976, seats 2700. New owners took over in 1985 and major redevelopments are planned over the next five years.

Wembley Stadium car park is the location for a popular Sunday market; mainly new goods on sale.

The *Grange Museum* is in Neasden Lane, **Willesden**, NW10, 2 miles E of Wembley. The museum, in an early 18C stableblock, has a collection of local Brent artefacts and documents, a Victorian parlour, a 1930s sitting room, drawings and maps, and temporary exhibitions.

Open Monday to Friday 12.00-17.00 (Wednesday 12.00-20.00), Saturday 10.00-17.00. Tel. 01-452 8311. Acess: Underground, Neasden.

In *Gladstone Park*, Dollis Hill Lane, NW2 (half a mile further E) stands Dollis Hill House (not open to the public), built in 1823 and the former home of Lord Aberdeen; here Mark Twain and Gladstone were among guests. In 1941 the War Cabinet met here and an underground control centre was planned but never built (cf. Cabinet War Rooms in Horse Guards). The park has an attractive walled garden; a recent addition is a sculpted memorial (by Fred Kormis) to those who suffered in prisoner-of-war camps.

Willesden's parish church, *St. Mary*, stands high above the surrounding area on the corner of Neasden Lane and the High Road, half a mile S of Neasden. It dates to the 13C with a 14C tracery door, a Norman font, and an Elizabethan communion table. The novelist Charles Reade (d 1884) is buried in the churchyard.

S of Willesden along the industrial wasteland created by the Grand Union Canal and railway lines is the **Kensal Green Cemetery**, probably the best-known in London and with some of the most interesting monuments still standing in a London cemetery. (Access: Harrow Road; Underground, BR, Kensal Green.)

The cemetery was founded in 1832. It has chapels in a classical style and its main gateway is a triumphal arch. Towering Gothic monuments, obelisks, mausoleums and modest statues abound, and the neglect of the past may finally have been halted with the formation of a preservation society. Among the illustrious burials here are Marc Brunel (d 1849) and his son Isambard (d 1859), engineers; Princess Sophia (d 1848), daughter of George III; William Thackeray (d 1863), and Anthony Trollope (d 1882), novelists; Mary Hogarth (d 1837), Dickens' sister-in-law, and Emile Blondin (d 1897) who crossed Niagara Falls on a tightrope.

The cemetery is bounded to the S by the Grand Union Canal, Paddington Arm, which used to allow direct access by barge. Today it is possible to walk along the towpath from Warwick Avenue, Little Venice (see p 175) to Willesden Junction, passing the cemetery on the N bank and, further along to the S, Wormwood Scrubs Common, used by pioneers of flying in the early part of this century but now better-known for the prison.

St. Augustine's Church in Kilburn Park Road (off Kilburn High Road), 2 miles SE of Willesden, is one of London's largest Victorian churches, designed by J.L. Pearson and completed in 1898. The 250ft tower is an architectural triumph.

Within the London Borough of **Brent** there are recreational facilities at *Roundwood Park* to the S and the *Welsh Harp Reservoir* to the N. The latter takes its name from an old pub, demolished to make way for the main road, and not from its shape. There is a nature centre

At the junction of the North Circular Road and the start of the M1 is the *Brent Cross Shopping Centre* which opened in 1976 on a 52-acre site. (Access: Underground, Brent Cross; Bus, 16.) The centre includes two department stores, shops and a supermarket under cover in a landscaped setting with car parking.

Edgware Road follows the line of the Roman Watling Street which leads to St. Albans. The tower of the red-brick church of *St. Margaret's*, on the corner of Watling Street and Station Road, Edgware, is 14C. There are almshouses of the 1680s further along Watling Street, and timber-framed buildings survive along the W side of the High Street, including a 17C coaching inn, the White Hart.

Harrow, Hampstead and Highgate all occupy high ground to the N of central London. **Harrow** and the surrounding area were important Saxon settlements, as is shown by the earthworks at Grims Dyke. Harrow was a residence of the Abp of Canterbury and the hunting grounds attracted poachers as well as his guests. Headstone became the local manor in the 14C.

Today Harrow on the Hill is still dominated by the 16C *Harrow School*, established by a charter from Elizabeth I to a John Lyon (a yeoman of Preston, Middlesex) in 1572. There are tours of the school (01-422 2196). The school, built in 1615, was expanded in the 18C but the Fourth Form Room in the Old Schools retains oak panels scored with the names of former pupils. Across Church Hill are the Chapel and the War Memorial Building added in neo-Jacobean style in 1926 (Herbert Baker). It incorporates 16C panelling from Brooke House, Hackney, in the Fitch Room, and other historic relics. The dramatist Sheridan, a former pupil, returned to live just behind the church in 1781—'Sheridan's stables' have been incorporated in the new Leaf Schools building. The Vaughan Library and the Chapel were designed by Sir Gilbert Scott. The Speech Room in the High Street, built in 1874, has a statue of Elizabeth I in a niche over the street. The Old Speech Room, with Tudor-style windows, is now an art gallery and museum of the school.

Harrow can count seven prime ministers among former pupils including Spencer Perceval, Sir Robert Peel, Palmerston, Baldwin and Churchill. Other famous pupils include Byron, Cardinal Manning, the Earl of Shaftesbury, Trollope, Galsworthy, G.M. Trevelyan, Pandit Nehru, and Kings Faisall II of Iraq and Hussein of Jordan.

The parish church of *St. Mary* at the crown of the hill is 400ft above sea level and 200ft above the surrounding area. The view from the terrace is associated with Byron who used to sit on the flat tombstone of John Peachey 'for hours and hours'. The Harrow School song recalls 'Byron lay lazily lay, Hid from lesson and game away, Dreaming poetry all alone, Up-a-top of the Peachey stone'. The church was founded by Lanfranc, Abp of Canterbury, and consecrated by Anselm in 1094, probably on Saxon foundations. The structure is 12 and 13C and was restored by Sir Gilbert Scott in the 19C. Fittings include a 12C font and fine brasses, including one to John Lyon (d 1592), founder of the school, shown with his wife Joan. A memorial to John Lyon by Flaxman was added in the 19C. Byron's daughter Allegra lies in an unmarked grave beneath the church porch.

In the High Street is the King's Head, a 16C pub.—Modern Harrow lies 1 mile to the N and has a new shopping centre and Civic Centre. An arts complex is planned.

The Kodak company established itself in this part of London in 1887 with a factory in Headstone Drive, Wealdstone. The Kodak Museum located here closed in 1984 and the collection is now housed in the National Photographic Museum, Bradford. HMSO has printing works in Wealdstone. The stone of Wealdstone is outside the Red Lion Hotel, Harrow Weald, 2 miles N of Harrow on the Hill. It is one of several stones in the area which probably marked parish boundaries.

Pinner, NW of Harrow, was once a chalk-mining area but is now a prosperous suburb built largely in the 1930s. The Pinner Fair, granted its charter in 1336, continues once a year on the Wednesday following the Spring Bank Holiday. It is held in the High Street, where some half-timbered 16C houses survive, including the Queen's Head and Victory Hotel. The 15C church of *St. John the Baptist* in the High Street was consecrated in 1321 and restored in 1880.

In Moss Lane, Pinner, stands the oldest surviving timber-framed house in the old county of Middlesex, 15C *East End Farm Cottage*. Nearby is Tudor Cottage, a half-timbered 16C farmhouse. Moated *Headstone Manor* in Headstone Lane (1 mile NE of Pinner, nearest Underground Headstone Lane) dates to the 14C and was a residence of the Abp of Canterbury from 1344. It is well preserved but not open to the public. The Tithe Barn is 150ft long, 30ft wide, and dates from 1533-55. It was restored in 1973 and is used for meetings and entertainment (owned by the local council).

Stanmore, 3.5 miles NE of Harrow on the Hill, now a busy commercial and shopping centre with a large residential population, lies at the N end of the Bakerloo Line. Its ancient history is commemorated by an obelisk now in the grounds of the Royal National Orthopaedic Hospital and originally erected in 1750 to mark a battle between the Celts and Romans. The pond on Stanmore Common is popularly known as 'Caesar's Pond'. Two churches, both dedicated to St. John, stand in the churchyard of Great Stanmore. The medieval church was rebuilt and consecrated by William Laud, later Abp of Canterbury, in 1632; it was declared unsafe in the 19C and left as a ruin overgrown with ivy. The new church, completed in 1850, incorporates some of the monuments from the old church and includes a Nicholas Stone font with the Wolstenholme crest and arms. Sir John Wolstenholme, the church's benefactor, is also represented in life-size effigy. Outside, a white marble angel marks the grave of Sir William Gilbert.

On *Stanmore Common*, Common Road, stands *Bentley Priory*, established in the 12C and dedicated to St. Mary Magdalene.

In the 18C the manor house built on the site was pulled down and Sir John Soane designed a new mansion for the Marquess of Abercorn. In this celebrated house he entertained political and literary figures of the time. Queen Adelaide, William IV's widow, died here in 1849. The house was sold to the Air Ministry in 1925 and it was from here that the RAF staff, under Sir Hugh Dowding, controlled the British forces in the Battle of Britain in 1941.

Stanmore Hall in Wood Lane was built in 1843 and has some fine Morris interiors. It was badly damaged by fire in 1979 and is being restored.

Off Old Redding, Harrow Weald, another mansion, *Grims Dyke*, has become a hotel. The house was built in 1872 for Frederick Good, a painter, designed by Norman Shaw in Tudor style with gables, half-timbering and tall chimneys.

W.S. Gilbert lived here from 1890 until his death in 1911 (most of his work with Arthur Sullivan dates from before this period). In the Iolanthe Room a 15ft-high pink alabaster fireplace remains of the original fittings. The hotel holds regular Gilbert and Sullivan evenings in this room.

The *Grims Dyke earthworks* are 5 miles long; they are probably of Saxon origin, and designed to defend London. They can best be seen at the junction of Oxhey Lane and Old Redding.

The *George V Memorial Gardens* in Whitchurch Lane, Stanmore, are all that remains of Canon Park. A mansion stood here from 1725, built for the Duke of Chandos. The family ran out of money and the estate was broken up in the mid-18C; parts of the house were sold all over the country. Some were used for a modest country house on the site, now the North London Collegiate School for Girls, established in Camden Town in 1850 by Frances Mary Buss, a pioneer of education for women. The parish church of *St. Lawrence*, Whitchurch, has survived. The Chandos monument includes representations of two of the duke's three wives and is adorned with grisaille paintings, as are the walls and the vaulted roof, by Louis Laguerre. Bellucci was responsible for the altar paintings and the small organ was played by Handel who was the duke's private choirmaster and composed the Chandos Anthem for him in 1718.

39 Hendon, Mill Hill, Barnet, Finchley

Hendon, 7 miles NW of central London, well-known from its early aviation connections, has a history dating back to a Benedictine settlement in the Middle Ages; its woods are said to have provided the oak for the construction of Westminster Abbey. Amongst the

pleasant suburban housing of this century there are older buildings
at the Burroughs, including 18C cottages and, beyond, *Burroughs
House*, owned by All Souls College, Oxford. The centre of the old
village is in Church End Road where *St. Mary's Church* stands on
medieval foundations. It has an 11C tower, a fine square, arcaded
Norman font, and brasses and tombs including that of Sir Stamford
Raffles (1781-1826), founder of Singapore and of London Zoo.

The oldest house in the area (near the Greyhound pub) is *Church
Farm House* which belonged to the Kempe family. The main part of
the building dates from the mid-17C but there is some 16C panelling
inside. The house opened as a local museum in 1955; temporary,
local exhibitions are held on the first floor. The ground floor is
furnished in period style; the central chimney stack has a passage
through it and the large kitchen is set up as it would have been at
the end of the 18C with a mechanical spit and large kettles.

Church Farm House Museum, Greyhound Hill, Hendon, NW4. Tel. 01-203
0130. Open Monday, Wednesday to Saturday 10.00-13.00, 14.00-17.30, Tuesday
10.00-13.00, Sunday 14.00-17.30. Admission free. Access: Underground,
Hendon Central.

All that remains of Church End Farm opposite is part of a model
dairy added in the 19C.

Hendon's fame as an aviation centre started with the opening of
the London Aerodrome factory and flying field in 1910 by Claude
Grahame-White. From here Pierre Prier made the first non-stop
London-Paris flight (3 hours 56 minutes) in 1911, and from here the
first official mail flight, to Windsor, took off on 9 September 1911.
The aerodrome was commandeered in 1914 by the Royal Naval Air
Services and became the Royal Air Force Station Hendon in 1918.
From 1920-37 annual air displays in aid of RAF charities attracted
many thousands of spectators.

Most of the aerodrome land has been redeveloped as a housing estate by the
GLC; this has been named after the aerodrome's founder as the Grahame Park
Estate.

Two of the remaining hangars form the main building of the *RAF
Museum* which opened in 1972 and which has since expanded into
the separate *Battle of Britain Museum* (1978) and the *Bomber
Command Museum* (1983).

RAF Museum, Battle of Britain Museum, Bomber Command Museum, Grahame
Park Way, Hendon, NW9. Tel. 01-205 2266. Access: Underground, Colindale.
Car park. Open Monday to Saturday 10.00-18.00, Sunday 14.00-18.00. RAF
Museum free, admission charge for others. The Roundel Buffet serves drinks
and snacks.

The RAF Museum tells the story of the RAF and its forerunners and
illustrates the development of its aircraft, armaments and equipment
to the present day. The collection includes some 40 historic aircraft.

From the entrance hall explore the galleries on the first floor. On the right is
the Art Gallery with a changing display of works relating to aviation by 20C
artists, as well as commemorative and decorative RAF silver. Gallery 2 shows
a detailed reconstruction of a Royal Flying Corps and Royal Naval Air Services
workshop with the fuselage of a De Havilland BE2a of 1911 as its centrepiece.
There is a viewing platform here on to the Aircraft Gallery below. Gallery 3
features a reconstruction of a workshop in a Bessoneau hangar in France. A
case contains relics of the celebrated German ace, Baron von Richtofen,

including his flying helmet and lucky dog mascot. Gallery 4 is devoted to Lord Trenchard (1873-1956), first Marshal of the RAF, appointed Chief of Air Staff in 1918. Other RAF personalities are commemorated in Gallery 5. Gallery 6 has a display of Victoria Cross and George Cross medals. Inter-war aircraft components are shown in Gallery 7—a diorama shows a Hendon Air Display (see above). Gallery 8 has changing displays illustrating the early part of the Second World War; Gallery 9 is also devoted to this war and includes escape aids used by prisoners-of-war. Gallery 10 includes a tribute to Sir Frank Whittle, inventor of the jet engine. Gallery 11 shows sophisticated equipment of the 1980s.

Enter the Aircraft Hall via the entrance hall; here is a display of 30 historic aircraft, regularly rearranged but likely to feature the Blériot XI, Vickers Gunbus, Sopwith Triplane, Vickers Vimy, Sopwith Camel and the Hawker Sea Fury. At the far end of the hall is the Dermot Boyle Wing housing temporary exhibitions. Aviation records and the Library are on the second floor (visits by appointment).

The Battle of Britain Museum (admission charge; details above) was opened by the Queen Mother in 1978. It commemorates the battle fought over SE England during the summer of 1940 in which 640 British and Allied fighter planes and their pilots ('the Few'), overcame 2400 bombers and fighters of the German Luftwaffe.

By the entrance in the Ground Floor Gallery is the wreckage of a crashed Hawker Hurricane; nearby is a tableau of a bombed street. The collection of aircraft includes two British fighters, the Vickers Supermarine Spitfire and Hawker Hurricane, and German and Italian aircraft including the Heinkel III, two Junkers, two Messerschmitts and a Fiat Falcon. In the Eastern Aircraft Hall there is a Westland Lysander, a Supermarine Seagull, a Gloster Gladiator and a Sunderland flying boat of 1944, the only one of its kind to survive. From the First Floor Gallery there is a good view of the aircraft below as well as a collection of newspaper cuttings from the period May to October 1940, and a recreation of an Underground station used as a shelter. The reconstruction of the Group Operations Room at RAF Uxbridge shows the battle situation at the height of the conflict.

The Bomber Command Museum (admission charge; details above) opened in 1983. It is dedicated to the memory of the thousands of aircrew who died in the Second World War.

Displays illustrate the history of Bomber Command, formed in 1936. The collection of historic aircraft includes the sole surviving De Havilland 9a, a Hawker Hart (1930), Vickers Wellington (1944), Handley Page Halifax (1942), De Havilland Mosquito (1946), and Vickers Valiant (1956).

The original Tudor building of *Hendon Hall* was demolished and rebuilt in the 17C and is now the Hendon Hall Hotel, at the junction of Ashley Lane and Parsons Street, half a mile N of Hendon Central. David Garrick lived here (1756-79) and erected an obelisk in the grounds dedicated to Shakespeare; another was put up to Garrick after his death, marked now by the small Garrick Park. Many additions have been made to Hendon Hall but a special feature is the painted ceiling by Tiepolo rediscovered in 1954. The portico and Corinthian capitals are said to come from the Canons and were added by Samuel Ware, the architect and builder, in the 19C.

In *Colindale* on the other side of the Grahame Park Estate is the *British Library Newspaper Collection*.

British Library Newspaper Collection, Colindale Avenue, NW9. Tel. 01-200 5515. Open Monday to Saturday 10.00-17.00. Free. Access: Underground, Colindale.

Originally housed in the British Museum, the collection had filled all the available space by 1897; the Colindale Repository was completed in 1903. Its 20 miles of shelving hold daily and weekly newspapers from 1801, with English, provincial, Scottish and Irish newspapers from 1700, plus a large collection of Commonwealth and foreign newspapers. A bomb demolished the original building in 1940 and part of the collection was destroyed. The library is geared for research. (The Burney Collection of Newspapers is still at the British Library in Bloomsbury.)

The old village of **Mill Hill** is separated from the modern suburb by the A1 from Mill Hill Broadway, squeezed in next to the M1. The old village to the E is centred on The Ridgeway (nearest Underground Mill Hill East). It has associations with Sir Stamford Raffles and William Wilberforce. *Highwood House* in Highwood Hill, now a residential home, has a plaque marking Raffles' residence here; before that it was the home of Sir William Russell, one of the Bedfords. He was captured trying to escape through a circular window (still a feature) and executed for his part in the Rye House Plot aimed at Charles II.

William Wilberforce, a contemporary of Raffles, lived at *Hendon Hall*, also in Highwood Hill. He designed and built *St. Paul's Church* in The Ridgeway with support from Raffles. It was completed in 1836; the work of the painter Charles Muss can be seen in the glass of the E window.

Holcombe House in Holcombe Hill, now a convent school, was the home of Sir John Anderson, a Lord Mayor of London. Cardinal Vaughan stayed here while planning St. Joseph's College (see below). Some Georgian features survive, the fine portico and fanlight, and the staircase and murals by Angelica Kauffman.

St. Joseph's in Lawrence Street (reached from Mill Hill Circus) is still a missionary college, founded in 1866 by Cardinal Vaughan. An impressive campanile is topped by a statue of St. Joseph, 100ft above ground. In the High Street, possibly the shortest in London, a weather-boarded Quaker meeting-house, Rosebank, survives; it was in use from 1678 to 1719.

The best-known educational establishment in the area is *Mill Hill School* in The Ridgeway, built in the grounds of a house which belonged to the botanist Peter Collinson; some of the trees and a gate from the old garden remain.

The school was founded in 1807 as a Nonconformist institution; the classical building was designed by Sir William Tite in 1825. Among famous pupils have been the broadcaster Richard Dimbleby, fashion designer Norman Hartnell, and the architect Martin Shaw Briggs who is responsible for some of the new buildings.

At Angel Pond Green the 17C Nicol Almshouses contrast with the modern cottages designed by Richard Seifert in the 1960s. Seifert himself, architect of many London tower blocks including Centrepoint, lives in a 1930s house in Milespit Hill, Mill Hill.

3 miles N of Mill Hill is **Barnet**, which has given its name to the London Borough. High, or Chipping Barnet, set on high ground, is a thriving suburb with a small street market in St. Albans Road. The principal market for which a charter was granted in the 12C was held next to the church of *St. John the Baptist*. This has a distinctive chequer-work tower rebuilt in 1875 by Butterfield. The nave and N aisle are from the 15C. Memorials to the Ravenscroft family include

an alabaster statue and the tomb of Thomas Ravenscroft (d 1630). The red-brick *Tudor Hall* (1577) nearby in Wood Street was once part of the Queen Elizabeth Grammar School, granted a charter in 1573; the building is now used by Barnet College. Also in Wood Street is *Barnet Museum*.

Barnet Museum, 31 Wood Street, Barnet. Tel. 01-449 0321. Open Tuesday and Thursday 14.30-16.30 (16.00 in winter), Saturday 10.00-12.00, 14.00-16.00. Free. Access: Underground, High Barnet.
  The museum contains relics of the Battle of Barnet fought on nearby Hadley Common in 1471. Horseshoes, local photographs, household implements, clothes and other artefacts from the area form the rest of the collection. Part of the panelling from Tudor Hall (see above) has been preserved here.

An obelisk commemorating the Battle of Barnet stands at *Hadley High Stone*, 1.5 miles from High Barnet (Underground) past Hadley Green. It was erected in 1740 by Sir Jeremy Sandbrook to mark the last battle of the Wars of the Roses, in which Edward IV defeated the Lancastrians and the Earl of Warwick died. At *Hadley Green* the explorer David Livingstone lived in 1857 in one of the attractive Georgian houses. The nearby *Wilbraham Almshouses* date to 1612; Sir Roger Wilbraham's good deeds are commemorated in the Monken Hadley parish church of *St. Mary the Virgin* on a monument by Nicholas Stone. The 15C church is distinguished by a flint and ironstone tower topped by a beacon.

High Barnet's situation on the N route from London stimulated local trade and many coaching inns were located along the main road; one, the Red Lion at the foot of Barnet Hill, was established in the 16C. The former cattle market survives as the September Fair. The coming of the railway led to Barnet's development as a suburb, but it also killed off much of the trade engendered by the road.

Friern Barnet, 3.5 miles SE of High Barnet, was mainly woodland—Elizabeth I hunted here—until the mid 19C when it developed with the railway. *East Barnet*, 2 miles SE of High Barnet, developed in a similar way from an arable past. It has an 11C church, St. Mary the Virgin.
  Totteridge between High Barnet and Friern Barnet is a small suburban village surrounded by parkland and a golf course. Outside the parish church, *St. Andrew's*, at the E end of the attractive Totteridge Lane, stands a 1000-year-old yew tree. The church, rebuilt in brick in 1790, retains the weather-boarded bell turret of the older structure. Members of the Pepys family are buried in the churchyard.

Finchley, in two distinct parts—Church End and East Finchley—straddles the North Circular Road 6 miles from central London. *Finchley Manor House* at East End Road was built in 1723 by Thomas Allen. It is now used as a synagogue (there is a large Jewish community in this part of London) and as the HQ of the Reformed Synagogues of Great Britain.
  The local borough council recently restored and opened to the public the grounds of *Avenue House* in East End Road (01-346 4841; access: Underground, Finchley Central) which contain a fine collection of rare trees.

The house (open by appointment) was built on land originally owned by the Knights Templar. In 1874 Henry Charles Stephens, son of the inventor of modern ink and also known as 'Inky' Stephens, came to live here and established a laboratory (restored) on the first floor. He later became an MP for Finchley (now Margaret Thatcher's constituency) and made various improvements to the house including the addition of a stable block in a French Gothic style which houses the mayoral car.

Also at Church End is the parish church of *St. Mary*, much altered after bomb damage but with a surviving 12C font. In Hendon Lane is *Christ's College* with a distinctive green copper roof and pepper-pot towers.
 At the junction of the North Circular Road and Regent's Park Road to the S there is a statue by Emile Guillaume, La Deliverance, a woman holding a sword, donated to the borough to commemorate the Battle of the Marne.

40 Highgate, Hampstead, Golders Green

There is so much to see in Highgate and Hampstead that the first part of this section has been arranged as a route from Archway Underground to Hampstead Underground to be explored on foot, or possibly using the local buses or a car.

Hampstead and Highgate, separated by Hampstead Heath, are two of London's most attractive suburbs, still retaining much of their village charm.

Highgate (Underground, Archway; bus C11 to South Grove, or walk) takes its name from a tollgate sited along the Old North Road, its site marked today by the Gate House pub. Sir William Cornwallis became Lord of the Manor in the 1580s, succeeding the Bp of London, and many famous people passed through the growing village along the road to the N, including Richard Whittington, three times Lord Mayor of London.
 At the start of Highgate Hill, where the traffic whirls around a busy one-way system, head N along Archway Road. The Whittington Stone (W side of road) marks the spot where he is said to have stood and listened to the bells of Bow Church summoning him back to London. His famous cat is sculpted on top of the stone which was erected in 1821—the cat was added in 1964. Whittington bequeathed money for almshouses which stood here until 1970 when they were removed to Surrey; a pub and a hospital here have taken his name.
 Highgate Hill became such a busy thoroughfare that a cable tramway was introduced in 1884—Europe's first. Trams followed but now there are only buses and much of the traffic has been diverted along Archway to the NE. The viaduct above Archway Road dates to 1897 and replaced the Nash original. From it there is a good view of London and of the tortuous trafffic system which has been the subject of a lengthy, inconclusive planning enquiry.
 Along Highgate Hill, heading N towards the village centre, there are several attractive 17 and 18C houses. On the W side is *Waterlow Park* with the white stucco *Lauderdale House*, dating from the mid 17C and open to the public.

Lauderdale House, Waterlow Park, N6. Tel. 01-348 8716. Open daily 11.00-16.00, closed Mon.
 Lauderdale House was built for the Duke of Lauderdale in 1645; Nell Gwynn

is said to have stayed here. It later became a boarding-house and John Wesley stayed in it. In 1871 the philanthropist Sir Sidney Waterlow bought it; he opened the grounds to the public and later presented it to the London County Council. The London Borough of Camden now owns the building which is run as a community arts centre with musical and theatrical events and exhibitions (cafeteria).

Waterlow Park is open daily from 07.30. Its 27 acres are laid out as 'a garden for gardeners'; there are ponds with wildlife and an aviary.

On the E side of the hill is *Cromwell House*, an attractive Dutch-style red-brick building of the 17C. It is now used by a missionary society. (The house has no connection with Oliver Cromwell.) *St. Joseph's Church*, below, with two distinctive onion-shaped copper domes, has a monastery adjoining. Sir Francis Bacon is said to have stayed in a house in Highgate Hill in 1626 when he conducted his famous experiment in refrigeration by stuffing chickens with snow; the consequent chill killed him.

Highgate Hill becomes Highgate High Street which leads to South Grove and Pond Square. S.T. Coleridge lived at No. 3 The Grove from 1816 until his death in 1834 and he is very much associated with the area. At the Highgate Literary and Scientific Institute (01-340 3343; founded 1839) in South Grove there is an annual Coleridge festival in July. The Institute stages occasional local exhibitions and also houses the royal coat of arms from the former Fox and Crown pub in West Hill, and many important documents relating to the area. Coleridge is buried in the church of *St. Michael* in South Grove. Its conspicuous spire towers high above London—inside, a line on the vestibule wall shows that the church is level with the top of St. Paul's Cathedral. Coleridge's body was originally interred in the chapel of Highgate School, and was moved here in 1961.

Highgate School in North Road was founded in 1565; it declined

Memorial in the Western Cemetery, Highgate

in the 17C when most of its funds were spent on its chapel, but
revived in the 19C and continues to thrive. Well-known former pupils
include Sir John Betjeman, who lived in West Hill as a child. Another
poet, Roger Fry, was born at No. 6 The Grove in 1866.

The ponds of Pond Square were in-filled in 1864; the Flask pub in
Highgate West Hill (not to be confused with the Flask in Hampstead)
is one of the highway taverns at which travellers would stop to fill
their flasks. Turpin is said to have hidden in the cellar. Another
coaching inn survives in the High Street, the Duke's Head, of 16C
origin with village prints on its walls. Charles I is said to have used
the Rose and Crown in the High Street when visiting Nell Gwynn at
Lauderdale House (see above).

From South Grove Swains Lane descends to the S, past a tall radio
mast, to **Highgate Cemetery**, founded in 1838 and originally run for
profit. It is in two parts; the Western Cemetery is no longer in use
and is maintained by the 'Friends of Highgate'. Only guided tours
(every day, 10.00–16.00) are permitted in order to maintain the unique
character of the place (Tel. 01-340 1834). Amongst the overgrown
vegetation there are huge ornate tombs and catacombs, and fascinating marble and stone statues including a horse, a lion and a dog.

Those buried here include the inventor Michael Faraday (d 1867), the novelist
Mrs Henry Wood (d 1887), the poet Christina Rossetti (d 1894), Elizabeth Siddal,
wife of D.G. Rossetti, and the scientist Jacob Bronowski (d 1974).

In the public Eastern Cemetery is the famous grave of Karl Marx (d
1883)—a place of pilgrimage for visitors from all over the world. The
inscription on the stone reads 'Workers of the World Unite' and the
large bust by Laurence Bradshaw, which dominates the cemetery
here, was added in 1956. Also buried here are Herbert Spencer (d
1903), George Eliot (as Mary Ann Cross; d 1880) and many other
illustrious literary figures.

At the Wrestlers Tavern in Swains Lane the tradition of 'the Swearing of the
Horns' has been revived. Visitors are invited to take an 'oath of merriment'. In
the 18C visitors were required to 'swear the horn' at Highgate's 20 local taverns
before drinking and 'merrymaking'. Various animal horns were used.

Parliament Hill, 270 acres of open land, is just W of Highgate Road
and may have taken its name from the Gunpowder Plotters who were
to meet here to watch Parliament go up in flames. The excellent view
of London remains, as does, of course, Parliament. Highgate Ponds
are popular with anglers.

Off West Hill is Millfield Lane, leading towards the Heath and Hampstead.
Here the famous first meeting took place between Keats and Coleridge.

Between Swains Lane and Highgate West Hill is the Holly Lodge
Estate, once the suburban home of one of the 19C's wealthiest
women, Angela Burdett Coutts, heiress to the banking fortune. The
house was demolished to make way for a planned housing development, Holly Village, conceived by her as a 'rustic fantasy for the
working class'.

Hampstead is reached along Hampstead Lane from Highgate (bus
210). From central London access is via Haverstock Hill
(Underground, Hampstead).

Kenwood House on Hampstead Heath lies half a mile from Highgate along Hampstead Lane. It takes its name from the Caen river, an old tributary of the Fleet. It is open to the public and houses the *Iveagh Bequest.*

Kenwood House, Hampstead Lane, NW3. Tel. 01-348 1286. Open daily 10.00-19.00 (-17.00 October, February, March, -16.00 November, December, January). Admission free. Park open daily 08.00-dusk. Tea rooms in Coach House. Access: Underground, Golders Green; bus, 210).

Kenwood House, once the seat of the Argylls, passed to the Earl of Mansfield in 1754, who was then Lord Chief Justice to George III. He commissioned Robert Adam to remodel the house; he added a further storey and a library, encased it in stucco and added ornamental details such as the Ionic portico. The flanking wings were added later by George Saunders. The grounds were laid out in 1797 by Humphry Repton; they include the lake, now the setting for summer evening concerts; spring concerts take place in the Adam Orangery. Also in the grounds is Dr Johnson's thatched summerhouse, brought here in 1968 from Thrale Place in Streatham (see p 325).
   During the First World War the Grand Duke Michael of Russia lived at Kenwood. The contents were sold in 1922 and the land was marked up as building plots when Edward Guinness, Earl of Iveagh, bought the house and created his famous collection of paintings. As the Iveagh Bequest all of this was left to the nation (in the guise of the London County Council) on his death in 1927.

Kenwood is an attractive house with an important collection of paintings in an enviable setting. The Entrance Hall has an Adam ceiling representing Bacchus and Ceres; the painting was thought to be by Biagio Rebecca but has now been identified as the work of Antonio Zucchi, husband of Angelica Kauffman, whose work is also to be seen here. Note, among the paintings Reynolds, 'Venus Chiding Cupid', a portrait of the first Earl of Iveagh, and a bust of Lord Mansfield. By the main staircase in a display case is the Titus Clock, made for George III. The Marble Hall was added by Saunders and leads to the Dining Room, where the most important pictures hang: Rembrandt, 'Portrait of the Artist', Bols, 'Portrait of a Woman', discovered to have a false Rembrandt signature when cleaned in 1951; over the fireplace is Rubens' 'Madonna and Child and St. Joseph'. In the Vestibule there are paintings by Angelica Kauffmann; from here a door leads to the extremely attractive Library, one of Adam's finest interiors. Plasterwork decorations are by Joseph Rose and the paintings are by Zucchi. It is said that he met his future wife, Angelica Kauffmann, while both were working here.
   In Lord Mansfield's Dressing Room there are works by Reynolds, and Gainsborough's 'Going to Market'. In the Parlour is an early Turner sea-picture, 'Fishermen upon a Lee Shore', and a Van Dyck, 'James Stuart, Duke of Richmond, and Lennox'. In Lady Mansfield's Dressing Room there is a display of Adam's designs for Kenwood. Fine paintings in the Orangery include Van Dyck, 'Henrietta of Lorraine' and Gainsborough, 'Lady Howe'. The sofas were designed by Adam. In the Lobby Romney's 'Lady Hamilton at Prayer' and two Reynolds portraits are noteworthy as is the elaborate John Sandforth clock (late 18C). In the Music Room there are fine portraits by Reynolds, and in the West Hall two paintings by Landseer.

The shop stocks postcards and books. Temporary exhibitions are held on the first floor.

From the grounds of Kenwood (Pope particularly enjoyed the avenue of limes),it is possible to walk across the Heath to Hampstead Village.

Hampstead Lane leads into Spaniards Road; the road narrows where an old tollgate stood. Here is *Spaniards Inn*, a 16C tavern, once owned by the Spanish ambassador to James II. In this tavern the Gordon rioters (1780) were plied with drink by the landlord on their way to burn Kenwood—a successful diversion. Other who have enjoyed drinking here include Keats, Shelley and Byron, as well as Dickens. Dick Turpin's guns are displayed; he used the inn as a hide-out.

At the cross-roads at Whitestone Pond a flagpole marks the summit

Lakeside concert at Kenwood

of Hampstead Heath, 443ft above sea-level. Children still sail boats in the pond as Shelley did at the end of the 18C. Craft products and paintings are displayed and sold here on summer weekends.

Jack Straw's Castle has medieval origins; its name comes from one of Wat Tyler's accomplices who was executed after the 1381 rebellion. The white weather-boarding and castellation were added in the 1960s. The banker Samuel Hoare lived at nearby Heath House.

Hampstead Heath (825 acres), managed by the GLC, could easily have disappeared during the 19C, only being saved by fervent local preservationists.

The village of Hampstead began to develop in the 18C when the quality of its spring water was recognised. Well Walk and Flask Walk recall Hampstead's relatively short period as a spa with its own Assembly Rooms, now demolished. Hampstead's popularity inspired the lord of the manor, Sir Thomas Maryon Wilson, to develop the heathland beyond the village. The local community was in uproar and the struggle to prevent development continued from 1829 until Wilson's death in 1869 when his son gave in and sold 240 acres to the Metropolitan Board of Works. Further areas, including Parliament Hill Fields, were added over the next century. The sandy, wild heath was a popular excursion for 19C city-dwellers crowded into Islington and the City. Karl Marx took his family and friends for regular Sunday picnics on the Heath which even then offered donkey rides. Notable among painters of the Heath is Constable.

Activities on the Heath today include fishing, boating, dry- skiing, horse-riding, and swimming in three ponds—Hampstead Pond (mixed), Highgate Pond (men), Kenwood Pond (women).

From the cross-roads at Jack Straw's Castle North End Way leads N to Golders Green (see below) and S into Heath Street and the old village. To the E is the *Vale of Health* with attractive 19C houses; while living at South Villa in 1816 Leigh Hunt was visited by Keats, Byron, Coleridge, Shellley and Lamb. D.H. Lawrence, Edgar Wallace and Compton Mackenzie later lived here for short periods. The area's name may be an attempt by the developers to counteract the associations of its origin as a drained swamp. Willows now surround a small pond, all that remains of the swamp. The nearby fairground on the Heath expands into the car park for a fair three times a year on Bank Holidays.

East Heath Road continues along the E side of the Heath to Downshire Hill; here Michael Hopkins won a RIBA award in 1977 for his house of glass added unobtrusively in an 18C setting.

On the corner of Keats Grove and Downshire Hill is *St. John's Church* (1818) with old box pews and Georgian galleries. Keats Grove was known as Wentworth Place when John Keats came to live here in 1818. **Keats House** was originally two semi-detached houses; one was occupied by Mrs Brawne and her three children, the other by Keats's friend Charles Armitage Brown. Keats fell in love with Fanny Brawne and they became engaged in 1819; in 1820 illness forced him to travel to Italy where he died. He spent two of his most creative years at the house which is now a place of pilgrimage for his admirers. Keats House was saved from demolition in 1925 after a public appeal; it is now owned by the London Borough of Camden.

Keats House, Keats Grove, NW3. Tel. 01-435 2062. Open Moday to Saturday 10.00-13.00, 14.00-18.00, Sunday 14.00-17.00. Free. Access: Underground, Hampstead.

The Regency house contains memorabilia of the poet's life. From the entrance hall enter the Brawne Room where Keats first met Fanny in October 1818. The room is furnished in period style, with a painting of 'Keats Listening to the Nightingale on Hampstead Heath' by John Severn (1845) and a marble bust of Keats by the American sculptor Anne Whitney (1873; exhibited here since 1933; see also St. John's Church, below). In a glass case is a lock of Fanny's hair and other relics. Brown's Sitting Room, on the other side of the hall, contains the sofa on which Keats lay during his illness, and a set of Hogarth's Rake's Progress prints. In Keats' Sitting Room are his books and another portrait. A display case here contains letters and a lock of his hair. There are more letters and MSS in the Chester Room, added to the house later.

On the first floor is Keats' Bedroom, with a Regency-style tent-bed similar to the one he may have slept in when he first realised he had contracted consumption. The Keats Memorial Library is open by appointment.

In the basement are two kitchens and a wine cellar. The small garden features an ancient mulberry tree and a recent replacement of the plum tree under which Keats wrote 'Ode to a Nightingale'. The adjoining public library has a large collection of Keats's works and books relating to his life.

Keats House is now the HQ of the Keats-Shelley Memorial Association; occasional poetry readings are held here.

Downshire Hill leads W into Rosslyn Hill and Hampstead High Street. Old Hampstead may be explored from Hampstead Underground

Station in the centre of the village.

Hampstead retains its reputation acquired over the last two centuries as a centre for artists, writers and intellectuals, bolstered by actors, journalists and broadcasters, and a sprinkling of foreign diplomats and other expatriates. The topography of the village on its steep hill and strong local interests have ensured the preservation of many attractive houses and restricted new developments though there are blots, such as the massive Royal Free Hospital in Pond Street; it moved here from Grays Inn Road in 1974. Fashion boutiques have replaced some of the useful shops of the past and restaurants tend to reflect trends; hamburger places are notably absent.

Hampstead Underground Station opened in 1907 on the Northern Line; at 181ft its lift-shaft is the deepest in London. From here Heath Street climbs N to the Heath and S to Church Row (turning to the W). Church Row has attractive brown-brick Georgian houses with iron railings. The parish church, *St. John's*, on the corner of Frognal Way, has a distinctive spire; the decorative iron gates came from the Canons in Stanmore. The church (begun 1744) has a barrel vault; monuments include a bust of Keats by Anne Whitney (a replica of the original in Keats House), presented by American admirers in 1894, and memorials to Constable, Norman Shaw and George du Maurier.

Nearby in Holly Place (up Holly Walk) stands *St. Mary's Catholic Church*, at the centre of what was a community of refugees from the French Revolution. The church was built in 1816, one of the first new Catholic churches in London since the Reformation.

Frognal, parallel with and W of Holly Walk, leads to Arkwright Road and the *Camden Arts Centre*. To the E Fitzjohn's Avenue continues S to Swiss Cottage. In *Maresfield Gardens*, parallel with it, was the home of Sigmund Freud who died here in 1939. It was here that Salvador Dali sketched Freud.

In Frognal are the buildings of *University College School* (1907); the school moved here from Gower Street, Bloomsbury. Founded in 1830, famous former pupils include Lord Morley, Lord Leighton and Joseph Chamberlain. Upper Frognal Lodge was the last home of Ramsay MacDonald.

Turn back towards Heath Street along Mount Vernon where the house of a former governor of the Tower of London is hidden behind a high wall. In Holly Hill is the striking facade of the *National Institute for Medical Research* and, opposite, the much-altered house built by the painter George Romney in 1796. Later the house became lecture rooms; Constable and Faraday were among the speakers here. Steps lead down Holly Mount back into Heath Street past the picturesque Holly Bush pub (1796). Continue N along Hampstead Grove; the cottages at Nos 4-14 have medieval foundations. Opposite is 17C **Fenton House**, open to the public.

Open 11.00–17.00 daily, closed Thurs, Fri. Tel. 01-435 3471. Admission charge. Access: Underground, Hampstead.

The William-and-Mary style red-brick house was built in 1695 and became known as Fenton House in the early 19C when a merchant family of that name owned it. In 1936-52 it was the home of Lady Binning who bequeathed the house and its contents to the National Trust; on view is a collection of European and Oriental ceramics and the important Benton Fletcher Collection of musical instruments, left to the Trust in 1937. Music students are invited to play these, and this adds greatly to the atmosphere of the house.

The original entrance from Holly Hill is graced by decorative iron gates by

Jean Tijou. The present entrance is in the E front through a Regency loggia. In the entrance hall (original panelling) are 17C needlework pictures—the Dining Room contains a number of Regency pieces and a Burkat Shudi harpsichord of 1770. The Porcelain Room contains fine English and continental porcelain, and a pair of Sheraton armchairs. Sung and Ming dynasty china is displayed in the Oriental Room; Chinese snuff bottles (17-20C) are in a hanging cabinet. There are Staffordshire figures on the first floor landing and others in the Rockingham Room, where there is more needlework. Chinese blue-and-white porcelain is shown in the Blue Porcelain Room which also contains a two-manual harpsichord by J. and A. Kirckmann (1777).

In the Drawing Room Worcester porcelain is displayed in the alcoves by the fireplace. An early, grotesque Meissen teapot and cover and a pair of parrots are in the display cabinet on the N side of the room. The walnut-veneered spinet in the Pink Room is early 18C and was made in London. The service staircase leads to the Attic Floor with several musical instruments including a Dolmetsch clavichord, a painted Italian harpsichord, the earliest existing English grand piano (made by Bakers in Jermyn Street; 1763-78), and a Robert Hatley virginals (1664) with traditional flower and fruit decoration, a rare survivor of the Great Fire of London.

Concerts are given in the main dining room on the harpsichord (see above), the largest ever made in England. A harpsichord of 1612 on which Handel is said to have played is also used occasionally. The high-walled garden is attractively laid out.

George du Maurier lived further along Hampstead Grove in New Grove House, attached to Old Grove House, an impressive Georgian mansion. Opposite the Mount, Admiral's House is distinguished by the bridge-like balcony added by Admiral Matthew Barton (d 1795). Later the Victorian architect Sir George Gilbert Scott lived here. At Grove Lodge a blue plaque marks the home of John Galsworthy (d 1933) who completed the Forsyte Saga here. None of the windmills remains on Windmill Hill, nor are there judges in Judges Walk. The latter takes its name from the High Court judges who held court sessions here when the plague was prevalent in the City. Judges Walk leads back to the Heath; at the little cottage called Capo di Monte the actress Sarah Siddons stayed and is remembered by an S over the door. From this vantage point at the top of Heath Street Constable painted several views of Hampstead.

Heath Street leads back down the hill past the Quaker Meeting House of 1907. To the E is New End with council flats and *Burgh House*, a local community centre run by the Burgh House Trust.

Burgh House, New End Square, NW3. Tel. 01-431 0144. Open Wednesday to Sunday 12.00-17.00, Bank Holidays 14.00-17.00. Free. Cafeteria. Access: Underground, Hampstead.

The house, built in Queen Anne style in 1703, belonged to Dr Gibbons, physician of the wells. It takes its name from a later owner, the Rev. Allotson de Burgh, the musicologist. It was recently restored by the London Borough of Camden and opened to the public in 1979. Fine internal features include a carved staircase, fireplaces and some original plasterwork. The Exhibition Room is used for changing exhibitions of local artists' work. On the first floor is the Hampstead Museum of Local History. Rooms are used for lectures, concerts and private functions.

That this is the former spa area is reflected in the names of Well Walk and Flask Walk; the Victorian fountain in Well Walk marked 'not drinking water' is opposite the site of the original Pump House and Assembly Rooms. Keats lived at 30 Well Walk in 1816 before moving to Keats Grove; Constable lived at No. 40 in 1826-37.

Flask Walk leads back to Heath Street past the *Flask Tavern* where

The Flask in Flask Walk

the Kit-Cat Club (1700-20) met during the summer; members included Walpole, Vanbrugh, Congreve and Kneller (see also p 98). More of 20C Hampstead is found along the High Street and down Rosslyn Hill with its healthfood restaurants, bookshops and boutiques.

N of the cross-roads at Whitestone Pond, North End Way leads to Golders Green and Hampstead Garden Suburb. Not far along the road is the *Old Bull and Bush* pub, made famous by the music-hall song. The pub's 17C building was once the country home of William Hogarth. Opposite is *Golders Hill Park* with an attractive walled garden, a deer enclosure, and a children's zoo. A turning to the E leads to a preserved working farm, *Wyldes Farm*, often used in films. In North End Avenue, another turning to the E, is *Byron Cottage*, once the home of Lady Houston, who progressed from chorus girl to possession of three aristocratic husbands, and used her fortune for the benefit of women's suffrage as well as for the development of the Spitfire and Hurricane fighter planes. *Pitt House* marks the site of a house demolished in 1952. Here in 1766-67 the Earl of Chatham, then prime minister, lay ill for 18 months, refusing to see anyone, while George III and his ministers alienated the American colonies by the imposition of unfair taxes.

Sir Nikolaus Pevsner, cataloguer of England's architectural heritage, lived at North End from 1935 until his death in 1984. Further along North End Road towards Golders Green is *Ivy House*, where the ballerina Anna Pavlova lived (1912-31). There is now a small museum here (open Saturday 14.00-18.00. Admission charge). The museum, set in the studio which overlooks the gardens and lake in which she kept tame swans, contains photographs, programmes, furniture, books, and other personal effects. The main building is used as a speech and drama college.

2 miles E of North End Road is the large and well-planned **Ḥampstead Garden Suburb**. It was conceived by Dame Henrietta Barnett, inspired by the poverty and slums of London's East End, where she was the wife of the vicar of St. Jude's. She purchased 20 acres of land and construction started in 1907 under the guidance of the architects Barry Parker and Raymond Unwin. Sir Edwin Lutyens designed the Central Square, including the parish church, St. Jude's, in brick with a steeply pitched roof.

The mixed architecture of the area, now mostly middle class in character rather than socially mixed as Dame Henrietta intended, is best appreciated by walking from Wyldes Farm off the North End Road, through the Heath extension, emerging at the junction of Finchley Road and Hampstead Way. A Town Trail leaflet of the area is available from the London Borough of Barnet Library Department.

Golders Green developed rapidly this century following the arrival of the Northern Line Underground. It is now a wealthy residential suburb with a strong Jewish community. The Golders Green Hippodrome opened as a music hall in 1913 but is now used as studios by the BBC. Anna Pavlova gave her final performance here. The *Golders Green Crematorium* opened in 1902 and is one of the biggest in London with 12 acres and landscaped gardens behind the Romanesque-style buildings. Among those cremated here and commemorated by a plaque or casket are Sigmund Freud (d 1939), Kathleen Ferrier (d 1953), Ivor Novello (d 1951), Anna Pavlova (d 1931), Marie Stopes (d 1958), and R. Vaughan Williams (d 1958).

41 Wood Green, Tottenham, Stoke Newington, Enfield, Lea Valley, Epping Forest, Walthamstow

Wood Green, in the heart of the London Borough of Haringey, has the heights of Hampstead and Muswell Hill to the W and the valley of the River Lea to the E. Haringey is said to be the Saxon name, and this later became Hornsey, just to the S. *Alexandra Park*, on high ground in the centre of Wood Green, has good views over central London. (Access: BR, Alexandra Park; shuttle bus during exhibitions.)

The 480-acre park was laid out in 1863; 10 years later Alexandra Palace was built to match the Crystal Palace at Sydenham. It burnt down almost immediately, and though it was rebuilt with a circus and a racecourse in the grounds it never quite matched the glamour of Crystal Palace. In 1936 it became a household name when the first scheduled live television transmissions were made from here by the BBC. The park passed to the GLC in 1956 when the BBC moved most of its TV activities to the new Television Centre at Shepherd's Bush. It was used as an exhibition centre until again gutted by fire in 1980. A temporary building in the park, the Alexandra Pavilion, continues to be used for various events while plans go ahead for a £35 million 'People's Palace' due for completion in 1987 with sport, leisure and exhibition facilities. The attractive

Palm Court restored to its original appearance will be part of the new building.

Wood Green's new shopping centre was opened by the Queen in 1981; it includes department stores, shops, a market and restaurants, all in an air-conditioned environment. The *New River Sports Centre*, home of the Harringey Athletics Club, has an all-weather outdoor track and a 1000-seat stadium under construction.

Tottenham, 2 miles E of Wood Green, is a mixed industrial and residential area. The manor of Tottenham has Scottish antecedents and was once owned by Robert Bruce, king of the Scots. Edward I confiscated the manor from the Scottish Pretender and Sir William Compton replaced the old dwelling with the present mansion in 1514; it has since been altered many times. The local borough took over the building in 1891 and it is now the *Bruce Castle Museum*.

Bruce Castle Museum, Lordship Lane, N17. Tel. 01-808 8772. Open Tuesday to Friday 10.00-17.00, Saturday 10.00-12.30 and 13.30-17.00. Access: Underground, Seven Sisters.
    During the 19C the house was run as a school by Sir Rowland Hill, inventor of the adhesive postage stamp. As a result the museum has a large collection of postal memorabilia (1700-1840), including Victorian pillar-boxes, a postboy's riding boots and hat, and reports of mail robberies. The history of the Middlesex Regiment and changing exhibitions on local history make up the other sections of the museum.

Near the museum in Church Lane is the church of *All Hallows*, with a 14C tower; the adjoining vicarage, the Priory, dates from 1620. Several imposing Victorian buildings survive, including the former Tottenham Palace where Marie Lloyd sang (but now a bingo club).
    Tottenham Hotspurs Football Club, with its ground in White Hart Lane, was founded in 1882; current developments aim to preserve some of the original buildings (access: BR, White Hart Lane).
    The Cross in Tottenham's High Road is probably a medieval market cross rebuilt in 1600 and covered with Gothic stucco in the 19C.
    Stoke Newington, 2 miles S of Tottenham, now a rather shabby but improving residential area, preserves some of its ancient village atmosphere. The village predates the Saxon settlement in Stoke Newington Church Street and at Newington Green. Its most famous resident was Daniel Defoe who went to school at Newington Green and wrote 'Robinson Crusoe' while living at 95 Stoke Newington Church Street (blue plaque). His family was part of a Nonconformist settlement of the area, later followed by a Jewish community and more recently by immigrants from the Commonwealth. Defoe's tombstone from Bunhill Fields is preserved in the local library. Red-brick *St. Mary's Old Church*, also in Stoke Newington Church Street, dates from 1560, but there has been a church on this site for 1000 years. The 'new' church of St. Mary was designed by Sir George Gilbert Scott in 1858. Nearby Nonconformist *Abney Park Cemetery* was established in the wooded grounds of Abney House in 1840; the popular cemetery fell into decay and was taken over by Hackney Borough Council in 1974 for preservation. General William Booth and his wife Catherine, founders of the Salvation Army, and their son Bramwell Booth are buried here. Clissold Park has a small zoo.
    Stoke Newington Pumping Station in Green Lanes (skirting the W side of Clissold Park), a castle-like structure, is an interesting example of Victorian industrial architecture, designed in 1854-56 by Chadwell Mylne.

3 miles N of Edmonton, on the outer edge of Greater London and
with a country-town atmosphere, is **Enfield**. Its past as a royal
hunting-ground, Enfield Chase, survives in the open parkland at
Forty Hill, White Webbs and Trent Park. Elizabeth I spent some of
her childhood at Elsyinge Hall, which stood on Forty Hill, just N of
Forty Hall. *Forty Hall* was built for Sir Nicholas Raynton in 1629 and
it remains a fine example of Jacobean architecture, showing the
influence of Inigo Jones. It is now a local museum with several rooms
restored to their original splendour and reopened by the local Council
in 1966.

Forty Hall, Forty Hill, Enfield, Middlesex. Tel. 01-366 2244. Open Easter to
September, Tuesday to Friday 10.00-18.00, Saturday and Sunday 10.00-20.00;
October to Easter, Tuesday to Sunday 10.00-17.00. Cafeteria open Easter to
September. Car park. Access: BR, Enfield Town.

The drive leads past a duck-pond to the N entrance and an attractive porch
with carved turtle doves above. The entrance hall features fine plasterwork
from 1787; in the dining room is the original screen with a striking shell motif.
There are ornate fireplaces here and in the drawing room which has a plaster
ceiling with a bold strapwork design. In the Raynton Room the portrait of Sir
Nicholas Raynton may be by William Dobson. The plasterwork ceiling continues
in the attractive staircase hall. From the first landing there is a good view of a
200-year-old cedar of Lebanon in the grounds. The first floor rooms contain
furnishings and pictures of the 17 and 18C, local antiquities and maps. Forty
Hall has been extended and an exhibition gallery created in the outbuildings
where temporary exhibitions are held. The hammer-beamed banqueting hall
is available for private functions.
  To the N of the house is the home park with a lime-tree avenue. In the SW
corner of the grounds a pleasant rose garden is protected by high brick walls.
  In Forty Hill, the Goat pub has a striking exterior and comfortable bars.

Sir Nicholas Raynton, a Lord Mayor of London (d 1646) is commemorated in the parish church of *St. Andrew*. His massive marble
family monument dominates the N chapel of the 13C church, rebuilt
in 1824.
  Enfield used to be an important market town; a weekly market has
been held here since 1632 and now takes place on Saturdays in the
Market Place, near the church and the King's Head Hotel. Picturesque
Gentleman's Row to the W of the church, with 17 and 18C houses,
is now a conservation area. At No. 17, Clarendon Cottage, Charles
Lamb and his sister lived in 1827. The New River, a 20-mile system
of canals and aqueducts engineered by Sir Hugh Myddleton in 1613
to bring fresh water to the City of London, has been landscaped in
front of the gardens. Sir Hugh has given his name to Myddleton
House (1818), the mansion in Forty Hill, which is now the HQ of the
Lee [sic] Valley Regional Park (see below).
  Enfield Grammar School, in the Market Place, was established in
1555; John Keats was a pupil here. The compiler of Whitaker's
Almanac lived at White Lodge, a weather-boarded 18C house in
Silver Street, near the modern Civic Centre which has a sculpture of
the Enfield Beast of Enfield Chase outside.

In *Edmonton* to the S the Council has established a local arts centre
in a 16C building, *Salisbury House*, Bury Street (01-360 5306. Access:
BR, Lower Edmonton). Some original panelling remains. Charles
Lamb lived at Lamb's Cottage, Church Street, moving here from
Enfield (see above). He died in 1834 and is buried in the local
churchyard of All Saints. There is another arts centre at Millfield

House, Silver Street (01-803 6213. Access: BR, Silver Street).

At *Southgate* there are attractive houses by the Green including the Olde Cherry Tree Inn, and Southgate House, built in the 1720s and now known as *Arnos Grove*. It is decorated in the Adam style amd used as offices.

In *Palmers Green*, 17C *Broomfield House* is now a local museum used for temporary exhibitions. The entrance hall has a fine staircase, an 18C fireplace and murals attributed to Gerrard Lanscroon (early 18C). A fire in 1984 destroyed a large part of the building and the museum is closed indefinitely (further information from the London Borough of Enfield on 01-886 6555).

The poet Stevie Smith (1902-71) lived at Palmers Green, and used the area in some of her work.

NW of Enfield is *Trent Park*, a training college with attractive grounds, including a nature trail, open to the public (access: Underground, Cockfosters). The main building was refaced with bricks from William Kent's Devonshire House in Piccadilly, demolished in 1962. During the Second World War it was used as an interrogation centre and internment camp.

To the N is the remaining land of Enfield Chase and to the W are Hadley Wood and Hadley Common.

Lee Valley Regional Park. The Lee Valley Regional Park Authority was established in 1967 to develop the leisure potential of the River Lea [sic] along 23 miles from Ware (Herts) to London's East End once its useful commercial life had ended. The Lea was the ancient frontier between King Alfred's Wessex and the Danelaw, and later the boundary between Essex and Middlesex. During the Great Plague in 1664-65 the watermen of Ware brought fresh water supplies to the City down the river (see also Epping Forest, below). Today it is possible to follow the course of the Lea on foot past its many locks and reservoirs; by car the river-bank and individual leisure facilities are best approached from the A1010 to the W.

At the Greater London boundary to the N is *Waltham Abbey*, built by Harold II; he was buried here after his death at the Battle of Hastings in 1066. The abbey was the last to surrender to the authority of Henry VIII after the dissolution of the monasteries. The present church (open 10.00-15.00 in winter, 10.00-16.00 in summer, depending on services) includes the Nave begun by Harold, the Lady Chapel of 1316 and a West Tower of 1558. The massive columns of the nave are channelled with chevrons and spirals. Henry II extended the abbey to the E. The fine windows in the Victorian E end are by Burne-Jones. The raised chapel on the right has a fresco of the Last Judgment of c 1430 and a W window with tracery. The 16C tower has an impressive peal of 12 bells, the 'wild bells' of Tennyson's 'In Memoriam'. In the crypt there is a small exhibition of historical interest.

The Abbey Gardens contain remains of the monastic buildings; a stone marks the site of the high altar and Harold's tomb. Part of the moat also remains as does the ancient Harold's Bridge. There is a beautiful rose garden and a Country Park with 70 acres of water meadows. The *Epping Forest District Museum* at 39-41 Sun Street, Waltham Abbey, is open Mon, Fri to Sun 14.00-17.00, Tues 12.00-17.00 (free). It is housed in a timber-framed Tudor building with an exhibition of local history.

In Stubbins Hall Lane, Crooked Mile, half a mile from Waltham Abbey, Hayes
Hill and Holyfieldhall Farms are open to visitors. Farm animals, milking,
sheep-shearing and crafts demonstrations can be seen. There is a shop and
light refreshments at Hayes Hill Farm (more information on Nazeing 2291).

Across the Lea (1 mile W) is *Waltham Cross* which takes its name
from the Eleanor Cross (heavily restored), the last but one in the
series of crosses erected by Edward I in 1291 (see p 92). It stands on
a traffic island, with a modern shopping centre behind. Eleanor's
body rested at Waltham Abbey.
    Anthony Trollope lived at Waltham House in 1859-71. To the NW
is *Theobalds Park*, outside the Greater London boundary, where the
Temple Bar (see p 209) from the City was erected in 1888. Proposals
for its return are made from time to time.
    S of Waltham Cross is the King George Reservoir (sailing club).
Further S at *Picketts Lock* there is a large and well-equipped sports
and leisure centre.

Picketts Lock Centre, Picketts Lock Lane, Edmonton. Tel 01-803 4756. Access:
BR, Ponder's End. Open daily. Facilities include golf, squash, badminton,
roller-skating, bowls, and a swimming-pool; there are floodlit pitches for football
and hockey and tennis courts. Within the grounds is a camping and caravan
site. Day tickets and season permits to fish the River Lea may be obtained from
the Park Authority (call Lea Valley 717711)

Further S in *Leyton* (Lea Bridge Road) is the new *Lee Valley Ice
Centre* with facilities for skating, training, ice-hockey, and seating
for 1000 spectators. Skates can be hired (01-533 3151. Access:
Underground, Leytonstone). Also in Leyton is the *Eastway Sports
Centre* (Quarter Mile Lane; 01-519 0017) with badminton, basketball,
volleyball amd squash courts, as well as the Eastway Cycle Circuit.

The *Banbury Sailing Centre*, Greaves Pumping Station, North Circular Road,
E4 (01-531 1129) offers dinghy and board sailing on Banbury Reservoir.

Epping Forest. In 1878 Epping Forest, threatened by enclosure, was
saved for Londoners by an Act of Parliament initiated by the City of
London Corporation which has since managed the 6000 acres of
deciduous forest, spread over some 11 miles between the Lea and
Roding river valleys. Queen Victoria visited the forest on 6 May 1882
and declared it to be for 'the use and enjoyment of my people for all
time' from a specially constructed grandstand in the centre of the
forest at High Beach. An estimated half million Londoners came to
cheer her as she travelled by train to Chingford Station, and on by
open carriage.

Epping Forest originally covered a huge area of Essex. Archaeological evidence
shows Stone Age settlements; there are two Iron Age earthworks, Loughton
Camp (SW corner, at the junction of Green Ride and Clay Road at Sandpit
Plain, NW of Loughton) and Ambresbury Banks (by the B1393, S of Epping).
There are Roman remains in Wanstead Park and the site of a Roman tile kiln
near St. Margaret's Hospital. Later the forest became a Saxon stronghold,
although one Viking incursion up the River Lea penetrated as far as Hertford;
there have been Viking finds in the Walthamstow Marshes.
    The Normans introduced the Forest Law and the office of Verderer to
administer it; the office survives as an honorary appointment. The N part of the
forest became known as Waltham Forest as the importance of Waltham Abbey
grew, while Barking Abbey came to own most of Hainault Forest. During the
Tudor period Waltham Forest became a favourite royal hunting ground. Henry

VIII built the pavilion at Chingford which in 1581 Elizabeth I converted into the present Hunting Lodge. Deer were introduced at this time and Chingford Plain was cleared of trees. Elizabeth also visited Wanstead House (to the S), owned by Robert Dudlley, Earl of Leicester; the remains of the house can be seen in Wanstead Park. At the beginning of the 18C Dick Turpin robbed travellers through the forest. He is said to have hidden in a 'cave'—more of a hollow in fact—against the bank of Loughton Camp, now known as Turpin's Cave.

Epping Forest was an important source of timber and trees were 'lopped' to promote new growth; this pollarding did not stop until 1878 and some typical 'bushed' trees can still be seen. Oak, beech, lime, hornbeam, birch and holly grow freely. The fallow deer are confined to a sanctuary at Birch Hall but other wildlife includes badgers, foxes, weasels and squirrels. Cows also wander freely at certain times of the year—a privilege granted to farmers on forest land—drivers through Chingford and Woodford should look out for cattle on road verges in this area, particularly during autumn when grass in the forest is sparse.

During the 19C Epping Forest became a popular destination for Sunday outings from the City and East End. 'Retreats' were established to serve large numbers of meals for the day-trippers; the Turpin pub could serve up to 500 meals at a sitting and another retreat at High Beach served teas for up to 4000 children. Most then would have arrived by train but the tradition continues today; families arrive by car and picnic in the forest. Horse-riding is also popular.

Places of interest.

Queen Elizabeth Hunting Lodge, Epping Forest Museum, Rangers Road, Chingford (01-520 5822). Open Wednesday to Sunday 14.00-dusk (or -18.00) and Bank Holidays. Admission charge. Parking. Access: Underground, Chingford. This 16C timber-frame building has been carefully restored. The two upper storeys were originally open platforms with uninterrupted views of the forest and the progress of the deer hunt. The museum contains exhibitions on the history and natural history of Epping Forest.

The Royal Forest Steak House next to it occupies a neo-Tudor building; it serves light refreshments and full meals.

Beyond the Hunting Lodge is *Chingford Plain*, site of the Bank Holiday Chingford Fair. It is also a public golf course and the location of Gilwell Park, HQ of the Scout movement.

The *Epping Forest Conservation Centre*, High Beach, Loughton (01-508 7714), open Easter to end October, Wednesday to Sunday (winter weekends only) 10.00-12.30, 14.00-17.00 weekdays; 11.00-12.30, 14.00-17.00 (or -dusk) Sundays. Free. Access: Underground, Loughton. This is an educational centre offering adults' and children's study courses, guided walks through the forest, and displays, maps and publications in the centre itself.

Nearby is the pretty Victorian church of *High Beach*. Tennyson lived at High Beach House. Near Epping Copped Hall, a mansion with Tudor origins rebuilt in the 18C, has burnt down. Amberbury Banks and Loughton Camp, see above.

To the S the forest is broken up by residential development. Higham House, a mansion of 1768, now a school, overlooking the Higham Lake is at Woodford; Hollow Ponds, an attractive lake landscape, is by Whipps Cross; nearby is Eagle Pond, home of wild geese and other wildfowl (nearest Underground, Snaresbrook).

Wanstead Park opened to the public in 1881; there are three attractive lakes, the Ornamental Water, Heronry Pond and Perch

Pond. The remains of Wanstead House are in the grounds; it was designed and built in 1715 by Colen Campbell and set a new fashion in country houses with its severe Classical exterior contrasting with a sumptuous interior. Lord Mayors of London have added new trees to the forest at Wanstead Park.

S of Wanstead Park, off Aldersbrook Road, E12, is the *City of London Cemetery*, established by the Corporation in 1856 and still well maintained. It is the second largest cemetery in London, designed by William Haywood for posterity. Thousands of graves have been moved here from City churchyards; many feature impressive monuments.

Epping itself is to the N, outside the Greater London area; the new M25 motorway passes under Epping Forest where it crosses the A104.

Walthamstow, 2 miles SW of Woodford and on the edge of Epping Forest, was in the 18 and 19C a desirable suburb with many large houses. Its character changed as industrialisation spread to nearby areas and with the establishment of working-class housing in modest terraces. Today it boasts one of the longest street markets in the country, stretching half a mile along the High Street on Thursday, Friday and Saturday (access: Underground, Walthamstow), with nearly 500 stalls selling everything from jewellery, records, wholefoods and plants to live trout.

Walthamstow Village reflects the area as it was before the first suburban dwellers arrived. Approach via St. Mary's Road off Hoe Street. This leads to St. Mary's Church in Church Lane. Opposite is the 15C *Ancient House*. During the 19C this was divided into four shops but it is now reunited as a private dwelling, its timber frame somewhat askew. Further along are the *Squires Almshouses*, founded in 1795 'for the use of six decayed tradesmen's widows and no others', as the inscription outside says. *Sir George Monoux's Almshouses* are on the other side; both are still used. *St. Mary's Church* of 1108, which Pepys describes visiting, has its original brickwork encased in cement. Inside are two brasses and a striking monument to Lady Stanley (d 1630) surrounded by four of her daughters. The memorial to Lord and Lady Merry was sculpted by Nicholas Stone in 1633.

On the corner of Church Lane and Vestry Road a huge carved capital marks the entrance to the *Vestry House Museum*. The column once formed part of the facade of the Post Office in St. Martin's le Grand, demolished in 1913 and purchased by a local builder. Vestry House is a workhouse of 1730 which has also served as a police station (one cell remains outside and there is another within); it became a local museum in 1931.

Vestry House Museum, Vestry Road, E17. Tel. 01-527 5544. Open Monday to Friday 10.00-17.30, Saturday 10.00-17.00. Free.

Displays include local archaeological exhibits, a reconstructed Victorian parlour, costumes, local crafts, and exhibits of Victorian domestic life. Also on display is the Bremer Car, built in Walthamstow in 1895 and the earliest British car with an internal combustion engine. Panelling from Essex Hall, demolished in 1932, can be seen in the rear gallery.

One of Walthamstow's most illustrious residents was William Morris, born at Elm House in 1834. The family moved to Woodford Hall in 1847 but returned to *The Water House*, Walthamstow, in 1847. The house (c 1750) took its name from a moat in the grounds, now a park.

The Morris family lived here until 1856; the house was presented to the local Council in 1898 by a later occupant, the publisher Edward Lloyd who has given his name to the park. The house finally opened to the public in 1950 as the *William Morris Gallery*; as well as the Morris collection it includes the Brangwyn Gift. Frank Brangwyn, the artist, was a pupil of Morris and donated his collection in 1935.

William Morris Gallery, Lloyd Park, Forest Road, E17. Tel. 01-527 5544 ext. 4390. Open Tuesday to Saturday 10.00-13.00, 14.00- 17.00, first Sunday of each month 10.00-12.00, 14.00-17.00. Free. Access: Underground, Walthamstow Central. Limited parking.
  Ground floor displays show the development of Morris's career and the work of the Century Guild, including wallpapers, textiles, embroidery, rugs and carpets, furniture, stained glass and ceramics. Among the highlights are the helmet and sword designed for the Oxford Union murals, the Beauty and Beast tile panel designed by Burne-Jones, the Woodpecker tapestry and the Kelmscott Chaucer. In the upper gallery are some stunning Pre-Raphaelite paintings, including works by Rossetti and Burne-Jones.

Lloyd Park is a small park with the old moat of The Water House surviving as a pond. The Walthamstow Theatre in the park is used for light entertainment.

  In *Chingford*, to the N of Walthamstow, an obelisk was erected at Pole Hill in 1824 to mark the Greenwich Meridian. After the international agreement of 1884 the Meridian was realigned 19ft E of the pillar. *All Saints Church* was established in the 12C; it decayed and in the 19C was known as the Green Church—overgrown with ivy it became a popular subject for painters (see, for example, 'Home from Sea' by Arthur Hughes). The church was restored in 1929. The 'new' church of *St. Peter and St. Paul* was built next to Chingford Green in the mid 19C and houses the 12C marble font from the old church.

  Friday Hill House in Simmons Lane, the work of Lewis Vulliamy (1839), was built on the site of Chingford Manor.

Leyton and *Leytonstone*, S of Walthamstow, are mixed industrial and residential areas. *Etloe House* in Church Road, Leyton, dates to 1770 and has a striking Gothic facade; it was once the home of Cardinal Wiseman. The church of *St. Mary the Virgin* is 11C.

  Woodford, a prosperous and leafy suburb, traces its origins to Saxon times. It developed as a suburb with the arrival of the railway in the mid 19C. From 1924 to 1964 Sir Winston Churchill was Woodford's MP and his statue (by David McFall) was erected on Woodford Green (Woodford High Road) in 1959 by his constituents. Dr Barnardo opened a home for orphans at Manor Road, Woodford Bridge, in 1910. At Whipps Cross are the Hollow Ponds and at Snaresbrook Road is Eagle Pond, overlooked by Gilbert Scott's Royal Wanstead School (1843).

  Woodford's parish church, *St. Mary*, was completed in 1972 following the destruction by fire in 1969 of the old church. The 18C vicarage survives and is now the Crown Court.

  At *Wanstead* the Child family, of East India Company fame, are remembered in *St. Mary's*, the parish church. This was built by Thomas Hardwick in 1790; the church is dominated by an elaborate 20ft monument to Sir Joseah Child, portrayed in Roman armour.

  In *Ilford*, 3.5 miles SE of Woodford, the 17C mansion of *Valentines*, in Valentines Park, 1 mile N of Ilford Station (BR), survives as council offices, while the grounds have become a spacious park. Ilford is a

20C suburb devoid of much character. To the N was *Hainault Forest*
but only a fragment has survived.

The London Borough of Redbridge, which includes Woodford, Wanstead and
Ilford, takes its name from a red-brick bridge over the River Roding.

42   Newham, Barking and Dagenham, Romford, Hornchurch, Upminster

Newham. Beyond what is traditionally regarded as London's East
End (see Rte 25) are East Ham, West Ham and Stratford, all part of
the London Borough of Newham. The area is still dominated by the
docks and the industrialisation they encouraged, but it is now
undergoing a transformation which will give a much-needed
economic lift to a depressed part of London (see Docklands, p 294).
   Stratford in the N part of the borough has a modern shopping
centre, including a market, surrounded by a busy traffic system. Just
off the Great Eastern Road is the *Theatre Royal, Stratford East*, built
as a music-hall in 1884 and carefully preserved. As director, Joan
Littlewood put the theatre on the map in the 1950s and '60s with a
string of controversial productions; there is an attempt to maintain
this tradition today.
   The parish church of *St. John* in Stratford Broadway was built in
1834 in the Gothic Revival style; in the churchyard is a memorial to
18 Protestants burnt at the stake on Stratford Green in 1555. An
obelisk in the Broadway was erected in 1861 in memory of a local
banker, Samuel Guerney.
   Along Romford Road, just out of the centre of Stratford, is the
Passmore Edwards Museum, housed in a striking group of buildings
which include the public library and a college of technology, designed
by Gibson and Russell in 1898. At the time this was the only
purpose-built museum in Essex and it was intended to have comprehensive collections. It now extends to an 18C weather-boarded
annexe—a former hospital for the poor.

Passmore Edwards Museum, Romford Road, E15. Tel. 01-519 4269. Open
Monday to Friday 10.00-18.00, Saturday 10.00–17.00, Sunday 14.00-17.00. Free.
Access: Underground, Stratford.
   The attractive Rotunda Gallery houses the Victorian collection illustrating the
growth of Essex and local industry and crafts. The Natural History Gallery
includes a pond with local fish; other exhibits cover archaeology and geology.
Special exhibitions are held regularly and the museum has expanded to North
Woolwich Railway Station (see below).

Little remains of Stratford's ancient past except a few street names.
Stratford Langthorne Abbey was founded in 1135 and dissolved in
1538. It has given its name to Abbey Lane to the W of Stratford where
an early industrial area developed along the River Lea. The ornate
Abbey Mills Pumping Station, designed by Bazalgette and Cooper
in 1864, is a marvellous example of the Byzantine style applied to a
mundane purpose; the pumping station is now closed but can be
visited by appointment with the Thames Water Authority (01-534
6717). Charrington's has restored the *Clock Mill* of 1817 as offices in

the *Three Mills Conservation Area*, Three Mills Lane, Bromley by Bow. The derelict House Mills (1776) may be developed as a working museum.

In Grove Rd, Bow (E3) a blue plaque on the railway bridge marks the site where the first 'doodle bug' (V1) struck in 1944.

At the Widow's Son Inn, Devon's Rd, Bow, the collection of blackened hot cross buns grows each Good Friday when another one is presented by the Navy in recognition of a widow's son lost at sea some 200 years ago.

In *West Ham*, SW of Stratford, the parish church of *All Saints* was built in the 12C; the ragstone tower is 14C and inside there are Tudor and Stuart brasses and monuments. At *West Ham Park* there are Botanical Gardens. West Ham United's football ground is at Upton Park, Green Street (access: Underground, Upton Park).

East Ham, E of Stratford, has a Grade I listed church, *St. Mary Magdalen*, which has survived virtually unaltered since the 12C. The Norman aisleless church ends with a narrow apse; the tower was rebuilt in the 16C. Rubbings can be made from replicas of the original brasses in the church (01-470 4525). The large churchyard is now a nature reserve with its own Interpretive Centre (entrance in Norman Road; access: Underground, East Ham, then bus to Beckton).

At *North Woolwich Old Railway Station* on the Thames a new museum has been established in a listed building of 1847 in the Italianate style. Historical displays on the Great Eastern Railway are featured and include original steam engines.

North Woolwich Old Railway Station Museum, Pier Road, North Woolwich. Tel. 01-519 4296. Open Monday to Friday 10.00-17.00, Sunday 14.00-17.00. Free. Access: BR, North Woolwich.

From here there are good views of the Thames Barrier, the Woolwich Ferry and a pedestrian tunnel to Woolwich. The Thames Barrier Visitor Centre is on the S side and best approached from Greenwich (see p 318). Another fine view of the Thames Estuary and the Barrier is obtained from the top of Beckton's dry-ski slope, created from rubbish on reclaimed land and opened in 1985 (access: by car, A13 to Beckton; Underground, East Ham, then bus to Beckton).

Barking and **Dagenham** are important industrial centres with factories to the S on reclaimed marshland along the Thames, including the vast Ford works at Dagenham.

The land used to belong to Barking Abbey, founded in 666 by King Erkenwald who established his sister Ethelburga as abbess. By the 10C the Benedictine nunnery was the most important in the country and William the Conqueror made it his base while building started on the Tower of London. The abbey buildings were demolished after dissolution in 1539 but there are remnants in the grounds of 13C *St. Margaret's Church* (access: BR, Barking). Remains of walls have been excavated in the grounds; the Curfew or Fire Bell Gate of 1460 and the NE Gate can be seen. Some Norman masonry has also been used for the outer wall of the N aisle of the church itself. Captain James Cook, the circumnavigator, married Elizabeth Batts of Barking here in 1762 and is commemorated on a modern carved screen. The church also contains the marble tomb of William Pownsett (d 1553) by Nicholas Bellin of Modena. Elizabeth Fry (d 1845), the prison reformer, spent many summers in nearby Dagenham and is remembered on a

modern carved screen in the church. She is buried in the Quaker
Burial Ground in Barking, now a park.

Barking Power Station, once one of the largest in Europe, closed
in 1981.

Eastbury House in Ripple Road, Barking, is a good example of a
medium-sized manor house of the late 16C. It is owned by the
National Trust and used as the HQ of the Barking Arts Council. The
red-brick three-storey gabled house has black decoration and has its
origins in 1321.

There is a large Sunday market at Dagenham Dock.

Opposite the 13C church of *St. Peter and St. Paul* in Dagenham is
the Cross Keys pub (Church Elm Lane), of 15C origin and retaining
its Tudor exterior.

At *Dagenham*, 4m E of Barking, the manor house of *Valence* survives
as a local museum. The timberframe building dates mainly from the
late 17C and was partly moated. It became council offices in 1926
and a local history museum in 1974.

Open Monday to Friday 10.00-16.00, by appointment only (Tel. 01-592 2211).
Access: Underground, Becontree. In addition to the local history collection of
maps, archaeological finds and exhibits on the former ship-building industry at
Canning Town, the museum houses the important Fanshawe Collection of 48
family portraits by Lely, Dobson, Kneller and others.

Romford, 2 miles N of Dagenham, is proud of its status as an ancient
market town with a charter of 1247. The cattle market continued
until 1958 but Romford Market today is a mixture of antiques,
bric-a-brac, and stalls selling new goods. It is one of Britain's longest
markets (cf. Walthamstow), and is held on Wednesdays, Fridays and
Saturdays (nearest station BR Romford). The large estates in the area
house many resettled East Enders, who give this market a 'Cockney'
flavour.

Romford's historic past is well-disguised by its modern shopping centre and the
recently opened *Dolphin Leisure Centre* (1983) which features a leisure pool
with wave machine, bar, restaurant, and banqueting hall. Water for the pool is
heated by solar energy gathered by the aluminium-framed pyramidical roof;
the banqueting hall has a stage and seating for 400.

St. Edward's, the parish church, was rebuilt in 1850, but the 15C
Church House (once a coaching inn), next to it, survives.

Havering atte Bower, which gives its name to the London Borough
of Havering, is 4 miles NE of Romford. It once had a small medieval
royal palace, known as The Bower, which fell into decay in the 17C.
It was the official residence of Queens of England, including three
of Henry VIII's wives, and stood near the present Village Green.
Nearby is the present *Bower House*, built in 1729 and incorporating
the coat of arms from the ancient palace—it is used by the Ford Motor
Company. The house was designed by Henry Flitcroft; there are
murals by Sir John Thornhill in the stairwell.

On the Village Green the village stocks and whipping post (not
originals) set up in the 1700s can be seen.

Hornchurch, SE of Romford, is a 20C suburb with the modern
Queen Theatre. It has 12C origins; the parish church of *St. Andrew*
dates to that time but is now mainly 15C. It is the only church in
Britain with a bull's head and horns at the E end instead of a
cross—the town's seal, symbolising the early importance of its leather

industry. Elizabeth Fry's son Joseph is buried in the churchyard; he lived at Fairkytes, a 17C mansion.

At *Upminster*, to the SE, a fine smock-mill, built in 1803 and in use until 1934, survives in St. Mary's Lane. The Windmill has been restored and can be visited on application to the London Borough of Havering (Tel. 0708 46040 ext. 3169). Nearby is the 12C church of *St. Laurence*, rebuilt in the 18 and 19C. The *Clock House*, also in St. Mary's Lane, is the original stable block of New Place—a mansion now demolished—and is dated 1775. Nearby in Hall Lane the Council has converted a 15C tithe barn into a the *Upminster Tithe Barn Museum*, a local history museum run by the Upminster and Romford Historical Society. Open by arrangement and first weekend in month from April to Oct (040 24 47535).

Upminster is now a prosperous commuting suburb with pleasant houses and gardens, mostly dating to the inter-war period. 15C Upminster Hall is used as the club-house of Upminster Golf Club.

INDEX

Topographical names and subjects are indexed in Roman type; names of eminent people are in *italic* type. Names beginning with Saint (St.) are indexed under that heading.

Typeset by MCL Dataset Ltd, Ruislip, England using a Prefis Book Machine.
Printed in Great Britain by Butler & Tanner Ltd, Frome and London.

ATLAS

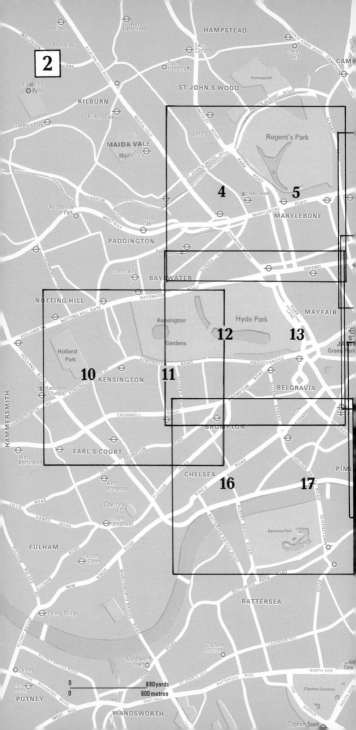

2

HAMPSTEAD

West
Hampstead

Kilburn

Willesden

Brondesbury

Swiss
Cottage

Chalk Farm Road

Primrose
Hill

CAMDEN

South
Hampstead

Brondesbury
Park

ST JOHN'S WOOD

Primrose Hill

KILBURN

Queen's Park

Kilburn Park

Kilburn High Road

MAIDA VALE

Maida Vale

Lords

Regent's Park

5

4

St John's Wood Road

Marylebone

Park Road

Baker Street

Albert Road

Westbourne
Park

HARROW ROAD

Royal
Oak

WESTWAY

MARYLEBONE ROAD

MARYLEBONE

PADDINGTON

Paddington

Queensway

BAYSWATER

Sussex Gardens

OXFORD

Oxford Street

MAYFAIR

NOTTING HILL

BAYSWATER ROAD

Notting Hill Gate

Kensington
Gardens

Hyde Park

PARK LANE

13

Holland
Park

12

KENSINGTON ROAD

KNIGHTSBRIDGE

Green Park

HOLLAND ROAD

10 KENSINGTON

Kensington
(Olympia)

11

Queen's Gate

BROMPTON ROAD

BELGRAVIA

HAMMERSMITH

CROMWELL ROAD

BROMPTON

Eaton Square

West
Kensington

EARL'S COURT

OLD BROMPTON ROAD

CHELSEA

16

King's Road

17

PIMLICO

Chelsea Bridge Road

Queenstown Road

West
Brompton

Chelsea
FC

Fulham
Broadway

FULHAM

Parson's
Green

Battersea Park

NEW KING'S ROAD

BATTERSEA PARK ROAD

Putney Bridge

WANDSWORTH BRIDGE ROAD

BATTERSEA

Clapham
Junction

LAVENDER HILL

Putney

WEST HILL

Wandsworth
Town

ST JOHN'S HILL

NORTH SIDE

Clapham
Com

East
Putney

UPPER RICHMOND ROAD

Clapham Common

PUTNEY

0 ____ 880 yards
0 ____ 800 metres

WANDSWORTH

Clapham South

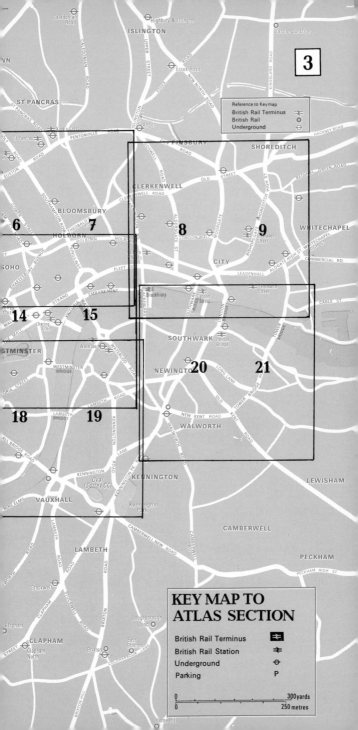

3

CALEDONIAN ROAD

Caledonian Road

Highbury & Islington

ISLINGTON

Dalston Junction

UPPER STREET

Essex Road

KINGSLAND ROAD

ST PANCRAS

CALEDONIAN ROAD

ST PANCRAS ROAD

St Pancras

King's Cross

Angel

PENTONVILLE ROAD

FINSBURY

SHOREDITCH

HACKNEY ROAD

EUSTON

EUSTON ROAD

CLERKENWELL

CLERKENWELL ROAD

OLD STREET

BETHNAL GREEN ROAD

6   **7**

BLOOMSBURY

HOLBORN

HOLBORN

8

GOSWELL ROAD

ALDERSGATE ST

LONDON WALL

MOORGATE

9

CITY ROAD

BISHOPSGATE

SHOREDITCH HIGH ST

Liverpool Street

WHITECHAPEL

SOHO

SHAFTESBURY AVENUE

KINGSWAY

FLEET STREET

CITY

LEADENHALL

ALDGATE HIGH ST

WHITECHAPEL

COMMERCIAL RD

SOUTHAMPTON ROW

STRAND

EMBANKMENT

VICTORIA

14   **15**

Charing Cross

Blackfriars

BLACKFRIARS

QUEEN VICTORIA ST

UPPER THAMES ST

Cannon Street

LONDON BRIDGE

Fenchurch Street

CABLE ST

WESTMINSTER

Waterloo

WATERLOO ROAD

SOUTHWARK

London Bridge

TOWER BRIDGE

20   **21**

WESTMINSTER BRIDGE

NEWINGTON

LAMBETH ROAD

LONG LANE

OLD KENT ROAD

TOWER BRIDGE ROAD

JOHN ... STREET

18   **19**

LAMBETH BRIDGE

NEW KENT ROAD

WALWORTH

WALWORTH ROAD

ALL ... BRIDGE ROAD

KENNINGTON

KENNINGTON ROAD

KENNINGTON LANE

Oval (Surrey CC)

KENNINGTON

Kennington Park

LEWISHAM

NINE ELMS

VAUXHALL

CAMBERWELL NEW ROAD

CAMBERWELL ROAD

CAMBERWELL

PECKHAM

LAMBETH

LAMBETH ROAD

WYVIL ROAD

STOCKWELL ROAD

BRIXTON ROAD

PECKHAM HIGH ST

Stockwell

CLAPHAM ROAD

Loughborough Junc.

CLAPHAM

Clapham North

BRIXTON

Brixton

East Brixton

COLDHARBOUR LANE

KEY MAP TO ATLAS SECTION

British Rail Terminus	≷
British Rail Station	≯
Underground	⊖
Parking	P

0 ——————— 300 yards
0 ——————— 250 metres

Herne Hill

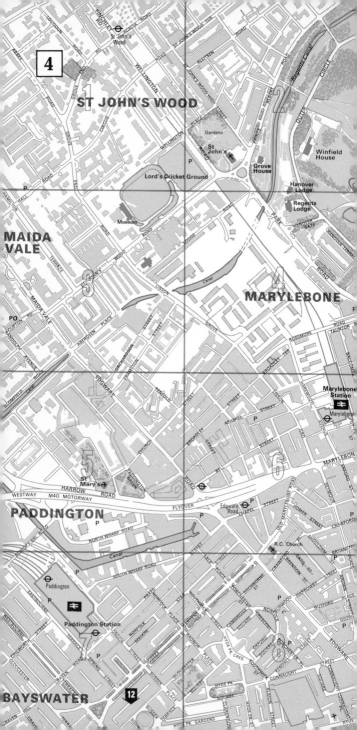

ST JOHN'S WOOD

St John's Wood

ACACIA ROAD

FINCHLEY ROAD

WELLINGTON ROAD

ST JOHN'S WOOD TERR.

ST JOHN'S WOOD HIGH STREET

ALLITSEN ROAD

ST JOHN'S WOOD ROAD

Regents Canal

OUTER CIRCLE

Gardens

St John's

Grove House

Winfield House

Hanover Lodge

Regents Lodge

HANOVER GATE

PRINCE ALBERT ROAD

Lord's Cricket Ground

P

MAIDA VALE

Museum

WELLINGTON ROAD

HAMILTON TERRACE

ST JOHN'S WOOD ROAD

LODGE ROAD

Canal

PARK

HANOVER GATE

HANOVER TERRACE

P

LISSON GROVE

MAIDA VALE

CLIFTON

RANDOLPH AVENUE

ABERDEEN PLACE

PO

MARYLEBONE

GROVE

ROSSMORE ROAD

TAUNTON ROAD

BALCOMBE

P

EDGWARE ROAD

PENFOLD STREET

BROADLEY STREET

ASHMILL STREET

LISSON STREET

RANDOLPH TER.

Marylebone Station

Marylebone

5

St Mary's

PADDINGTON GREEN

CHURCH STREET

BROADLEY

ENFORD STREET

HARCOURT

6

MARYLEBONE

PADDINGTON

WESTWAY M40 MOTORWAY

HARROW ROAD

FLYOVER

Edgware Road

CHAPEL STREET

P

R.C. Church

OLD MARYLEBONE ROAD

HOMER STREET

CRAWFORD

P

NORTH WHARF ROAD

Canal

SOUTH WHARF ROAD

STAR STREET

SOUTHWICK STREET

SALE STREET

CAMBRIDGE SQUARE

HERMITAGE

NORFOLK CRES.

HARROWBY

NUTFORD

BRYANSTON

GEORGE

EDGWARE

P

Paddington

BISHOPS BRIDGE ROAD

EASTBOURNE

WESTBOURNE TERRACE

Paddington Station

NORFOLK SQUARE

LONDON STREET

SUSSEX SQUARE

SOUTHWICK STREET

HYDE PK. CRES.

CAMBRIDGE

CONNAUGHT STREET

NORFOLK

BROWN STREET

P

8

CHILWORTH STREET

GLOUCESTER

CLEVELAND

RAVEN STREET

SPRING STREET

SUSSEX STREET

GLOUCESTER TER.

HYDE PARK SQUARE

ALBION

CONNAUGHT

BAYSWATER

12

HYDE PK. GARDENS

SUSSEX

HYDE PARK

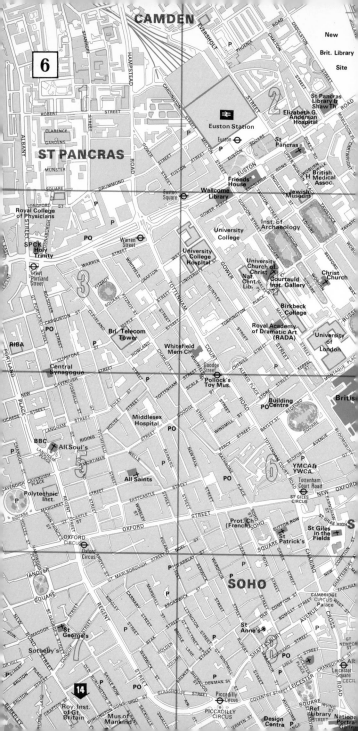

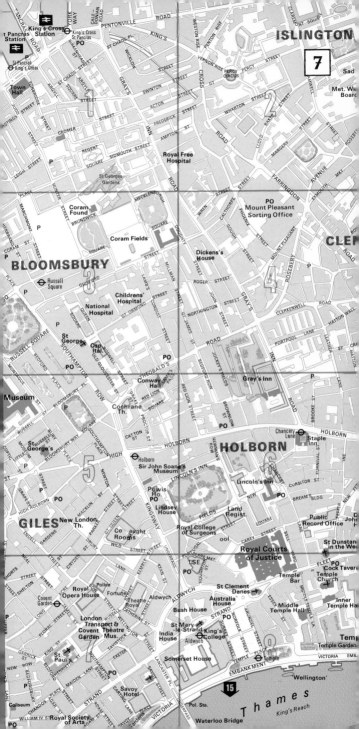

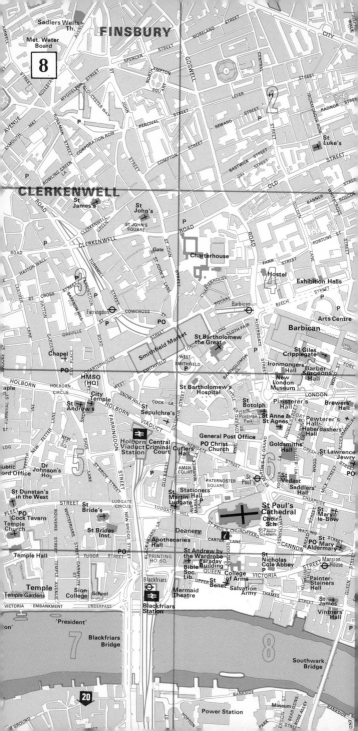

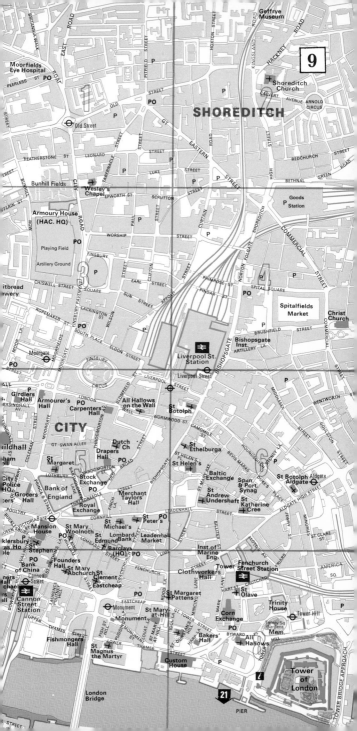

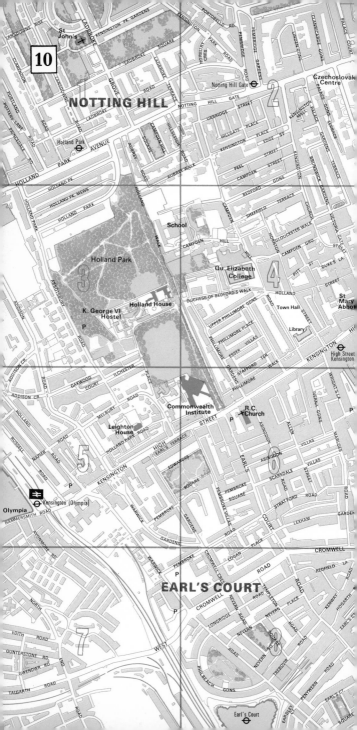

LANSDOWNE RISE
LADBROKE
KENSINGTON PK. GARDENS
PORTOBELLO RD
KENSINGTON
PARK
ROAD
PEMBRIDGE
CLARENDON CRES
PALACE COURT
St John's
CLARENDON RD
LANSDOWNE
GROVE
LADBROKE SQUARE
Czechoslovak Centre
PORTLAND RD
PRINCEDALE
POTTERY LANE
LADBROKE GROVE
LADBROKE
TERRACE
Notting Hill Gate
KENSINGTON MALL
PEMBRIDGE GDNS

NOTTING HILL

2

NOTTING HILL GATE
CHURCHILL
ST
UXBRIDGE
PALACE GARDENS TERRACE
KENSINGTON CHURCH STREET
BRUNSWICK GARDENS
VICTORIA GARDENS

Holland Park
HOLLAND
PARK
AVENUE
AUBREY RD
HILLGATE
PLACE
EDGE ST

HOLLAND
HOLLAND PK.
AUBREY WALK
CAMDEN HILL ROAD
PEEL STREET
CAMPDEN STREET
GDNS

HOLLAND PARK
HOLLAND PK. MEWS
CAMPDEN HILL
BEDFORD
SHEFFIELD
TERRACE
CHURCH
CAMPDEN GRO.
VICTORIA ROAD
DUKE'S LA.

School
HOLLAND
WALK
CAMPDEN
HILL
GLOUCESTER WALK

3 Holland Park
Qu. Elizabeth College
4

K. George VI Hostel
Holland House
DUCHESS OF BEDFORD'S WALK
HOLLAND
St Mary Abbot

ABBOTSBURY ROAD
ADDISON ROAD
UPPER PHILLIMORE GDNS
Town Hall
KENSINGTON STREET

PHILLIMORE PLACE
Library
High Street Kensington

ESSEX VILLAS
PHILLIMORE GARDENS
STAFFORD TER
KENSINGTON HIGH

OAKWOOD COURT
ILCHESTER
PLACE
PHILLIMORE WALK
WRIGHT'S LA.

ADDISON CR.
MELBURY ROAD
PHILLIMORE
VIENNA GDNS

Commonwealth Institute
R.C. Church
MARLOES

Leighton House
HOLLAND PARK ROAD
HIGH
EARL'S TERRACE
ABINGDON
SCARSDALE
ABINGDON
VILLAS

5 RUSSELL ROAD
NAPIER ROAD
KENSINGTON
STREET
EDWARDES
6 SCARSDALE ROAD
VILLAS

Olympia
Kensington (Olympia)
SQUARE
PEMBROKE SQUARE
PEMBROKE VILLAS
STRATFORD ROAD
LEXHAM

HAMMERSMITH ROAD
WARWICK GARDENS
PEMBROKE GARDENS
PEMBROKE COURT
GARDEN

WARWICK
PEMBROKE
CROMWELL

EARL'S COURT

LOGAN
REDFIELD LA.
CROMWELL ROAD
TEMPLETON PLACE
KENWAY
HOGARTH

7 NORTH
WEST
CROMWELL ROAD
LONGRIDGE ROAD
NEVERN ROAD
NEVERN PLACE
EARL'S
CT.

EDITH ROAD
NEVERN
SQUARE
NEVERN
TREVOIR

GUNTERSTONE RD
PHILBEACH
GARDENS
PENYWERN
EARL'S CT

GWENDWR RD
ROAD
Earl's Court
EARDLEY

TALGARTH ROAD

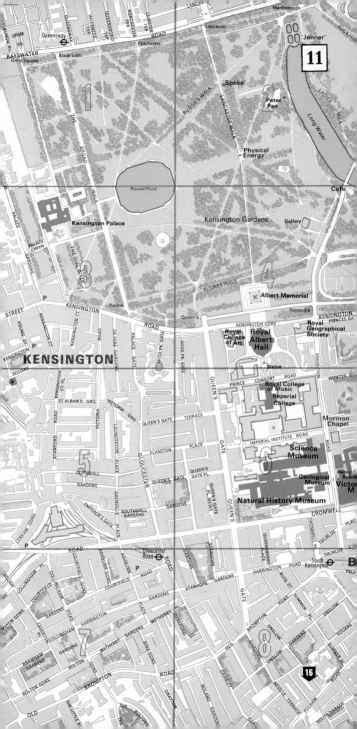

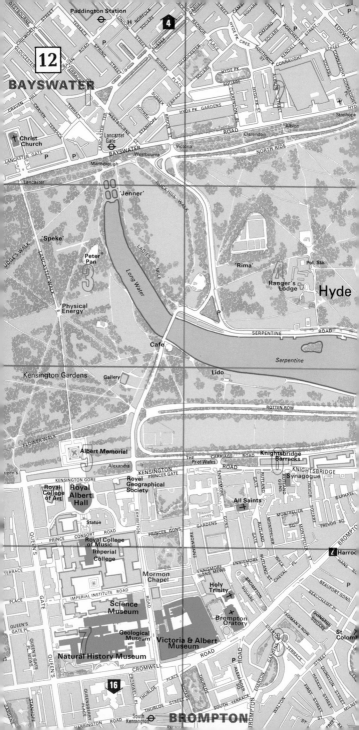

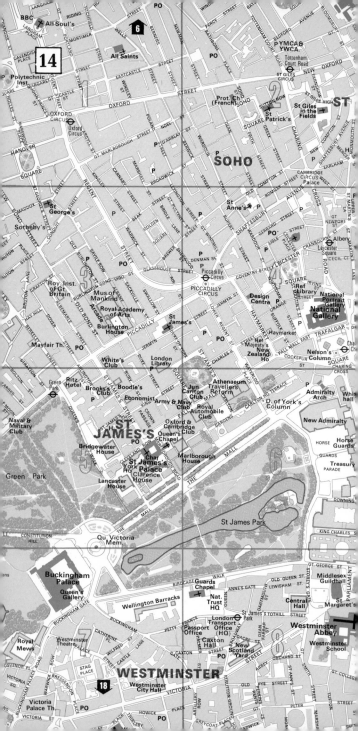

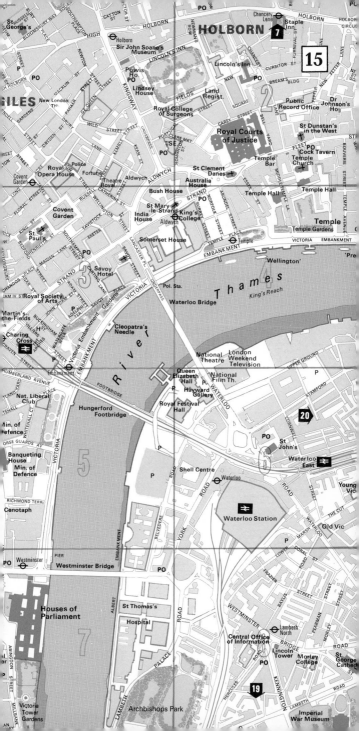

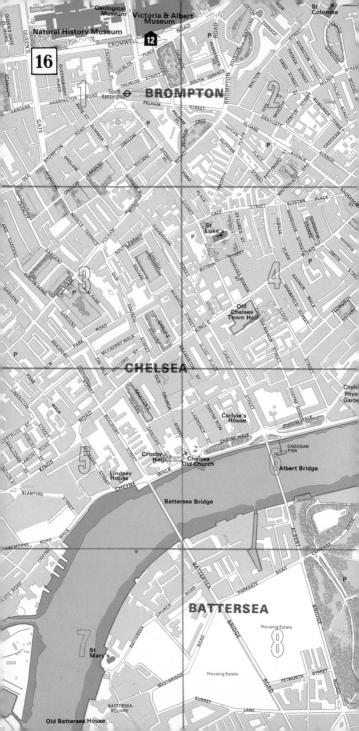

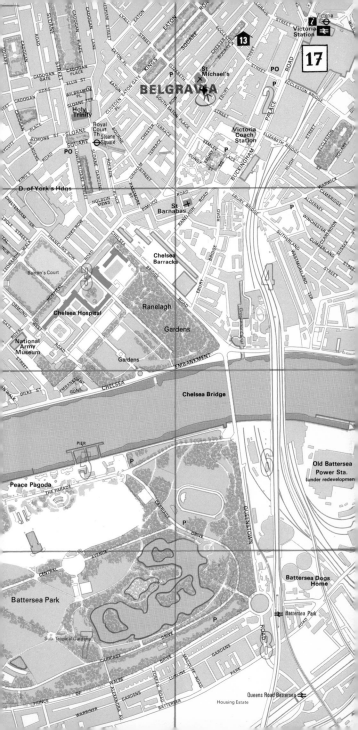

BELGRAVIA

St Michael's

Holy Trinity

Royal Court Th
Sloane
Square

CADOGAN

SLOANE

PO

D. of York's Hdqs

St Barnabas

Chelsea
Barracks

Burton's Court

Chelsea Hospital

Ranelagh

Gardens

National
Army
Museum

Gardens

EMBANKMENT

CHELSEA

Victoria
Station

PO

Victoria
Coach
Station

BUCKINGHAM PALACE ROAD

Chelsea Bridge

PIER

Peace Pagoda

THE PARADE

Battersea Park

CARRIAGE

DRIVE

CENTRAL

AVENUE

Sub Tropical Gardens

CARRIAGE

DRIVE

Old Battersea
Power Sta.
(under redevelopmen)

QUEENSTOWN

Battersea Dogs
Home

Battersea Park

QUEENSTOWN ROAD

PARK

Queens Road Battersea

Housing Estate

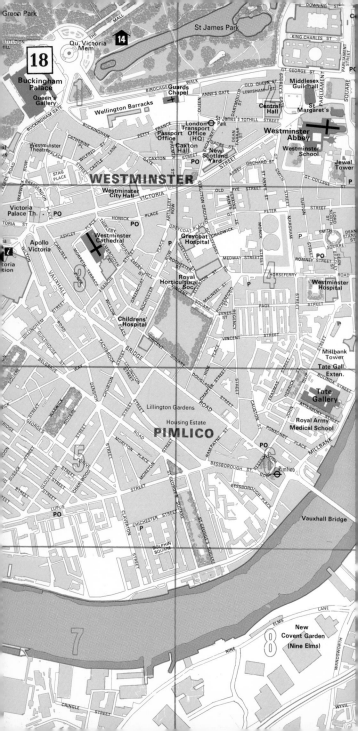

Green Park

St James Park

DOWNING ST

KING CHARLES ST

PARLIAMENT STREET

18

Qu. Victoria Mem

14

Buckingham Palace

Queen's Gallery

Guards Chapel

THE MALL

STATION HILL

BIRDCAGE WALK

ANNE'S GATE

OLD QUEEN ST

LEWISHAM ST

STOREY'S GATE

GT. GEORGE ST

Middlesex Guildhall

Central Hall

St Margaret's

PARLIAMENT SQUARE

Wellington Barracks

QUEEN

St James's Park

ST CHARTHOLIN

TOTHILL STREET

Westminster Abbey

Westminster School

BUCKINGHAM GATE

BUCKINGHAM

PALACE

CATHERINE PL

WILFRED ST

CASTLE

STAG PLACE

FRANCE ST

PETTY

London Transport Office (HQ)

Passport Office

Caxton Hall

New Scotland Yard

DEAN

ORCHARD ST

ST ANN'S

GT. COLLEGE ST

Jewel Tower

Westminster Theatre

Westminster Palace

ROW

BRESSENDEN

PLACE

WESTMINSTER

C. CAXTON

PO

PO

STREET

OLD PYE ST

ST ANN'S

PERKINS

TUFTON

Victoria Palace Th.

Westminster City Hall

VICTORIA

VICTORIA ST

Apollo Victoria

HOWICK PLACE

ASHLEY PLACE

CARLISLE PL

THIRLEBY RD

MORPETH TERRACE

Westminster Cathedral

FRANCIS ST

AMBROSDEN AVE

EMERY HILL ST

ROCHESTER ROW

GREYCOAT PLACE

ARTILLERY ROW

GREENCOAT PL

Greycoat Hospital

CHADWICK

MEDWAY STREET

MONCK

MARSHAM

PETER ST

ROMNEY STREET

SMITH SQUARE

DEAN BRADLEY ST

PO

Westminster Hospital

VAUXHALL

WILTON ROAD

WILLOW PLACE

TACHBROOK STREET

REGENCY STREET

Royal Horticultural Soc.

MAUNSEL ST

VINCENT

FYNES STREET

VINCENT STREET

PAGE STREET

HORSEFERRY ROAD

Victoria Station

Childrens' Hospital

GUILDHOUSE ST

BELGRAVE ROAD

DENBIGH STREET

CHARLWOOD STREET

CLARENDON STREET

VAUXHALL BRIDGE ROAD

SUTHERLAND ROW

CROWNDALE

DOUGLAS STREET

CHARLWOOD ST

Millbank Tower

Tate Gall. Exten.

Tate Gallery

Lillington Gardens Housing Estate

MORETON PLACE

MORETON STREET

PIMLICO

RAMPAYNE ST

CAUSTON ST

PONSONBY PLACE

ERASMUS ST

VINCENT SQUARE

ATTERBURY ST

Royal Army Medical School

MILLBANK

PO

GILLINGHAM

WARWICK SQUARE

ST GEORGE'S SQUARE

SUSSEX STREET

GLOUCESTER STREET

LUPUS STREET

PO

CHICHESTER STREET

CLAVERTON STREET

GEORGE'S

DOLPHIN SQUARE

ST GEORGE'S SQUARE

BESSBOROUGH ST

BESSBOROUGH PLACE

PO

Pimlico

Vauxhall Bridge

CRINGLE STREET

WANDSWORTH ROAD

NINE ELMS LANE

ELMS

New Covent Garden (Nine Elms)

WYVIL

1

2

3

4

5

6

7

8

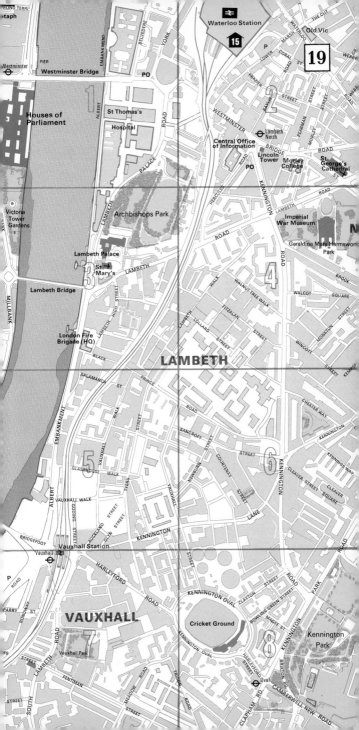

MOND TERR...
...staph

Westminster
⊖

Westminster Bridge

PO

Houses of Parliament

St Thomas's Hospital

Victoria Tower Gardens

Archbishops Park

Lambeth Palace

St Mary's

Lambeth Bridge

London Fire Brigade (HQ)

MILLBANK

EMBANKMENT

ALBERT EMBANKMENT

BELVEDERE

YORK ROAD

PIER

PALACE ROAD

LAMBETH PALACE ROAD

LAMBETH HIGH STREET

BLACK PRINCE ROAD

SALAMANCA ST

GLASSHOUSE WALK

VAUXHALL WALK

VAUXHALL STREET

TYERS STREET

GODING STREET

AUCKLAND STREET

GLYN STREET

BRIDGEFOOT

Vauxhall Station
Vauxhall ⊖

VAUXHALL

Vauxhall Park

P
PARRY Road

BONDWAY

SOUTH LAMBETH ROAD

FENTIMAN ROAD

MEADOW ROAD

Waterloo Station 🚉
P

Old Vic

THE CUT

WATERLOO ROAD

LOWER MARSH

CORAL STREET

FRAZIER STREET

BAYLIS ROAD

PEARMAN STREET

MORLEY STREET

WEBBE...

COSSER STREET

15

19

WESTMINSTER BRIDGE ROAD

Lambeth North ⊖

Central Office of Information

PO

Lincoln Tower

Morley College

St George's Cathedral

ST GEORGE'S ROAD

KENNINGTON ROAD

LAMBETH ROAD

HERCULES ROAD

Imperial War Museum

Geraldine Mary Harmsworth Park

N

BROOK DRIVE

WALCOT SQUARE

MONKTON STREET

WINCOTT STREET

LAMBETH

WALNUT TREE WALK

FITZALAN STREET

LAMBETH WALK

LOLLARD STREET

PRINCE

CHESTER WAY

KENNINGTON ROAD

KENNINGS WAY

CLEAVER STREET

CLEAVER SQUARE

SANCROFT STREET

COURTENAY STREET

NEWBURN STREET

VAUXHALL STREET

KENNINGTON LANE

KENNINGTON ROAD

KENNINGTON PARK ROAD

HARLEYFORD ROAD

HARLEYFORD STREET

KENNINGTON OVAL

CLAYTON STREET

BOWLING GREEN STREET

MAGEE ST

Cricket Ground

KENNINGTON OVAL

Oval ⊖

Kennington Park

BRIXTON ROAD

CAMBERWELL NEW ROAD

CLAPHAM RD

TRIGON ROAD

1   2   3   4   5   6   7   8

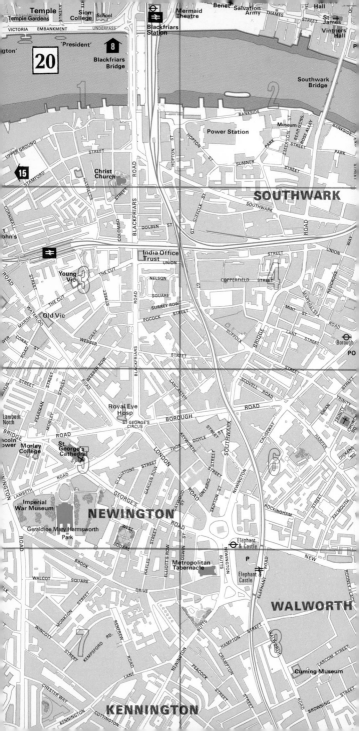

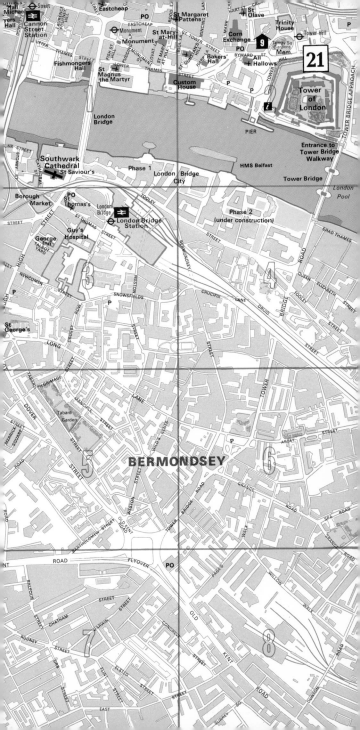

Hampstead Garden Suburb
Big Wood
Littleton Playing Fields
AYLMER

KINGSLEY WAY

MEADWAY

THE BISHOP'S AVENUE

Highgate GC.

Golders Green Cemetery

HOOP LANE

FINCHLEY ROAD

Garden of Remembrance

Hampstead Heath Extension

Hampstead GC.

Turners Wood

North Wood

Kenwood

HAMPSTEAD

GOLDERS GREEN

Golders Green

GOLDERS GREEN RD

NORTH END ROAD

HAMPSTEAD WAY

ROAD

North End

SPANIARDS ROAD

'The Spaniards'

Ken Wood

'Bull & Bush'

NORTH END WAY

Child's Hill

Golders Hill Park

Hampstead Heath

FINCHLEY

Pond

West Heath

WEST HEATH ROAD

Jack Straw's Castle

SPANIARDS

Vale of Health

East Heath

Parliamen

Hampstead Ponds

LANE

PLATTS

BRANCH HILL

WINDMILL HILL

Pond

EAST HEATH ROAD

OAK HILL WAY

HOLLY HILL

Qu Mary's Hosp.

WELL WALK

Fenton House

FROGNAL WAY

HAMPSTEAD HIGH ST

Old Hampstead

FORTUNE GREEN ROAD

CHURCH ROW

St John's

FLASK WALK

Hampstead

St John's

DOWNSHIRE HILL

KEATS GRO.

Keats Mem. House

Hampste Heath

FINCHLEY

FROGNAL LANE

University College School

FROGNAL

FITZJOHN'S AVENUE

FINCHLEY ROAD

POND STREET

FLEET

MILL LANE

WEST END LANE

ARKWRIGHT ROAD

Belsiz Par

West Hampstead

LYMINGTON

W. Hampstead, Midland

West End Lane

Finchley Road & Frognal

BELSIZE AVENUE

HAVERSTO

Belsize Park

West Hampstead

Finchley Road

COLLEGE CRES

South Hampstead

FINCHLEY RD

Swiss Cottage

Civic Centre

HAMPSTEAD & HIGHGATE

0 ————————— 1000 yds
0 ————————— 1000 m

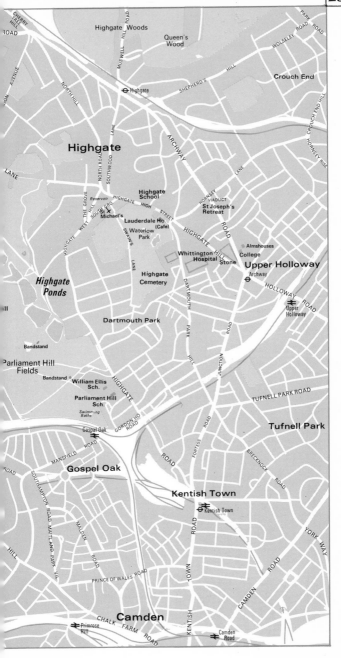

CHERRY
HILL
ROAD

Highgate Woods

Queen's
Wood

PARK ROAD

WOLSELEY ROAD

Crouch End

MUSWELL HILL ROAD

HILL

SHEPHERD'S

NORTH HILL

⊖ Highgate

CROUCH END HILL

HORNSEY RISE

ARCHWAY

LANE

SOUTHWOOD LANE

NORTH ROAD

Highgate

LANE

THE GROVE

Reservoir

Highgate
School

Highgate High Street

HORNSEY

VIADUCT

St Joseph's
Retreat

HIGHGATE WEST

HIGHGATE

SOUTH GRO

St
Michael's

Lauderdale Ho
(Cafe)

HIGHGATE

SWAINS

Waterlow
Park

ROAD

Almshouses
College

Whittington
Hospital

Hill
Stone

Upper Holloway

**Highgate
Ponds**

LANE

Highgate
Cemetery

DARTMOUTH

Archway
⊖

HOLLOWAY ROAD

Dartmouth Park

PARK

HILL

Upper
Holloway

Bandstand

JUNCTION

**Parliament Hill
Fields**

Bandstand

William Ellis
Sch.

HIGHGATE

Parliament Hill
Sch.

ROAD

TUFNELL PARK ROAD

Tufnell Park

Swimming
Baths

GORDON HO ROAD

BRECKNOCK

Gospel Oak

MANSFIELD
ROAD

ROAD

FORTESS ROAD

YORK WAY

Gospel Oak

ROAD

SOUTHAMPTON ROAD

MAITLAND PARK VIL.

Kentish Town

MALDEN

ROAD

Kentish Town

CAMDEN

ROAD

HILL

PRINCE OF WALES ROAD

KENTISH

TOWN

ROAD

Camden

CHALK FARM ROAD

Primrose
Hill

Camden
Road

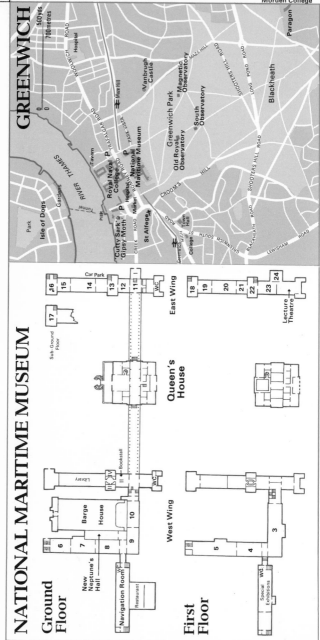

24

Morden College

GREENWICH

0   500yds
0   700metres

Isle of Dogs

Park

RIVER THAMES

Gardens

Tunnel

PIER

WOOLWICH ROAD

Hospital

TRAFALGAR ROAD

Tavern

P

Royal Naval
College

National
Maritime Museum

P

Market

Hospital

CHEEK

PARK VISTA

Maze Hill

Vanbrugh
Castle

MAZE HILL

Magnetic
Observatory

Greenwich Park

Old Royal
Observatory

South
Observatory

Blackheath

SHOOTERS HILL ROAD

LONG POND ROAD

Paragon

Blackheath

"Cutty Sark" &
"Gipsy Moth"

St Alfege

Greenwich

CROOM'S

ROAD

College

High St

Town Hall

GREENWICH SOUTH

SHOOTERS HILL ROAD

BLACKHEATH ROAD

LEWISHAM ROAD

HILL

ROAD

NATIONAL MARITIME MUSEUM

Ground
Floor

Car Park

16 15 14 13 12 11 11

17

Sub-Ground
Floor

WC

East Wing

18 19 20 21 22 23 24

Lecture
Theatre

Queen's
House

Library

Bookstall

WC

New Neptune's
Hall

6   7   8

Barge
House

9 10

Navigation Room

Restaurant

West Wing

First
Floor

5   4   3

Special
Exhibitions

WC

Blackheath

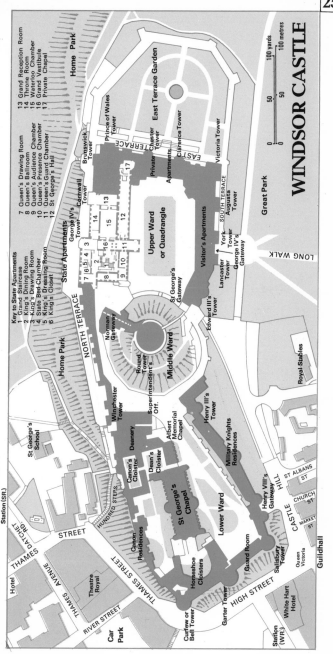

25

WINDSOR CASTLE

Key to State Apartments

1 Grand Staircase
2 King's Dining Room
3 King's Drawing Room
4 State Bed Chamber
5 King's Dressing Room
6 King's Closet
7 Queen's Drawing Room
8 Queen's Ballroom
9 Queen's Audience Chamber
10 Queen's Presence Chamber
11 Queen's Guard Chamber
12 St George's Hall
13 Grand Reception Room
14 Throne Room
15 Waterloo Chamber
16 Grand Vestibule
17 Private Chapel

Home Park

East Terrace Garden

Prince of Wales Tower

Chester Tower

Clarence Tower

Brunswick Tower

EAST TERRACE

Cornwall Tower

George IV's Tower

Private Apartments

Victoria Tower

State Apartments

Upper Ward or Quadrangle

Visitor's Apartments

SOUTH TERRACE

Augusta Tower

York Tower

George IV's Gateway

Lancaster Tower

Great Park

LONG WALK

NORTH TERRACE

Home Park

St George's Gateway

Edward III's Tower

Norman Gateway

Middle Ward

Round Tower

Superintendent's Off.

Winchester Tower

Deanery

Albert Memorial Chapel

Canon's Cloister

Dean's Cloister

Henry III's Tower

Military Knights Residences

St George's School

HUNDRED STEPS

St George's Chapel

Lower Ward

Royal Stables

Canon Residences

Horseshoe Cloisters

Guard Room

Henry VIII's Gateway

CASTLE HILL

ST ALBANS ST

CHURCH ST

MARKET ST

Salisbury Tower

Garter Tower

Curfew or Bell Tower

HIGH STREET

Queen Victoria

Guildhall

White Hart Hotel

Station (W.R.)

THAMES STREET

Theatre Royal

RIVER STREET

Car Park

THAMES AVENUE

DATCHET

THAMES

Hotel

STREET

Station (S.R.)

0   50   100 yards
0   50   100 metres

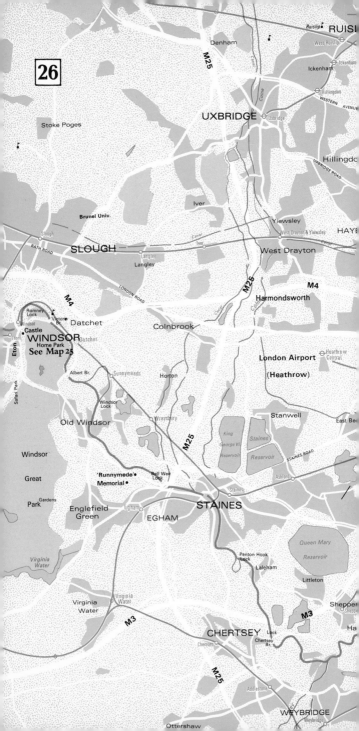

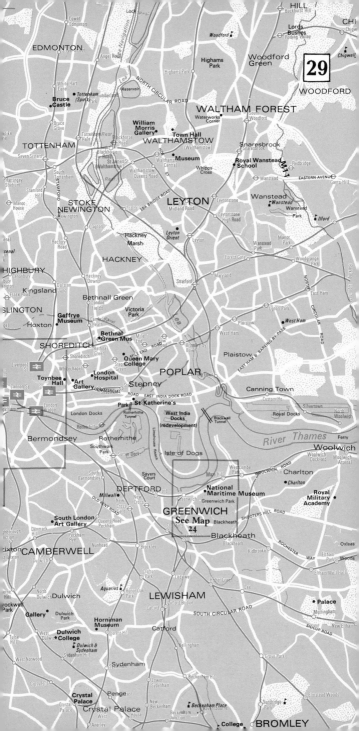

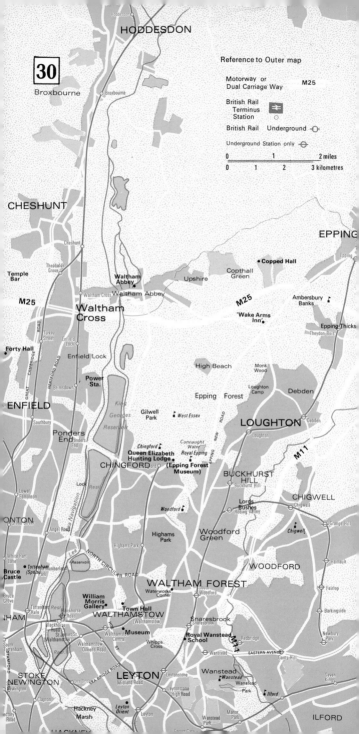

30
Broxbourne

HODDESDON

● Broxbourne

Reference to Outer map

Motorway or
Dual Carriage Way   M25

British Rail
Terminus
Station   ◯

British Rail   Underground ◯

Underground Station only ◯

0   1   2 miles
0   1   2   3 kilometres

CHESHUNT

EPPING

● Cheshunt

Epping

● Copped Hall

Temple
Bar

Theobalds
Grove

Copthall
Green

Upshire

Ambersbury
Banks

Waltham
Abbey

Waltham Abbey

M25

M25

'Wake Arms
Inn'●

Epping Thicks
Theydon Bois

Waltham Cross

Waltham
Cross

Forty Hall

Turkey
Street

GREAT CAMBRIDGE ROAD

HERTFORD ROAD

Enfield
Lock

Enfield Lock

Brimsdown

High Beach

Monk
Wood

Power
Sta.

ENFIELD

Southbury

King
Georges
Reservoir

Gilwell
Park

● West Essex

Epping Forest

Loughton
Camp

Debden

NEW ROAD

EPPING

LOUGHTON

Debden

Ponders
End

Ponders
End

Loughton

M11

Chingford

Connaught
Water
Royal Epping

Queen Elizabeth
Hunting Lodge

CHINGFORD

Chingford

(Epping Forest
Museum)

BUCKHURST
HILL

Buckhurst Hill

Lea Navigation

Lock

Reast

Woodford

Lords
Bushes
Roding Valley

CHIGWELL

Chigwell

Chigwell

Grange Hill

ONTON

Lower
Edmonton

Angel Road

Highams Park

Highams
Park

Woodford
Green

WOODFORD

Hainault

White Hart
Lane

Tottenham
(Spurs)

Reservoir

NORTH CIRCULAR ROAD

Fairlop

Bruce
Castle

Bruce
Grove

Cumberland

Park

Barkingside

WALTHAM FOREST

South
Woodford

Newbury
Park

JHAM

Tottenham
Hale

Blackhorse
Road

William
Morris
Gallery

Town Hall
(Walthamstow)

Waterworks
Corner

WOODFORD

St James St
Walthamstow

WALTHAMSTOW

Sharesbrook

Sharesbrook

M11

South
Tottenham

Blackhorse
Road

Walthamstow
Central

Museum

Walthamstow
Queens Road

Whipps
Cross

Royal Wanstead
School

Redbridge

Seven
Kings

Gants Hill

EASTERN AVENUE

Wanstead

STOKE
NEWINGTON

Newington

Clapton

LEA BRIDGE ROAD

LEYTON

Midland Road

Leytonstone

Wanstead
● Wanstead
Park

Wanstead

Ilford

ILFORD

Hackney
Marsh

Leyton
Orient

Leyton

Leytonstone
High Road

Manor
Park

actory
Road

Wanstead
Park

HACKNEY